EYEWITNESS *TRAVEL GUIDES*

AUSTRALIA

DK EYEWITNESS *TRAVEL GUIDES*

AUSTRALIA

DORLING KINDERSLEY

LONDON • NEW YORK • MUNICH

MELBOURNE • DELHI

www.dk.com

A DORLING KINDERSLEY BOOK

www.dk.com

Produced by Duncan Baird Publishers
London, England

MANAGING EDITOR Zoë Ross
MANAGING ART EDITORS Vanessa Marsh
(with Clare Sullivan and Virginia Walters)
EDITOR Rebecca Miles
COMMISSIONING DESIGNER Jill Mumford
DESIGNERS Dawn Davis-Cook, Lucy Parissi

CONSULTANT Helen Duffy
MAIN CONTRIBUTORS Louise Bostock Lang, Jan Bowen, Helen
Duffy, Paul Kloeden, Jacinta le Plaistrier, Sue Neales,
Ingrid Ohlssen, Tamara Thiessen.

PHOTOGRAPHERS
Max Alexander, Alan Keohane, Dave King,
Rob Reichenfeld, Peter Wilson.

ILLUSTRATORS
Richard Bonson, Jo Cameron, Stephen Conlin, Eugene Fleury,
Chris Forsey, Steve Gyapay, Toni Hargreaves, Chris Orr, Robbie
Polley, Kevin Robinson, Peter Ross, John Woodcock.

Reproduced by Colourscan (Singapore)
Printed and bound by South China Printing Co. Ltd., China

First published in Great Britain in 1998
by Dorling Kindersley Limited
80 Strand, London WC2R 0RL
Reprinted with revisions 1999, 2000, 2001, 2002 (twice)

Copyright 1998, 2002 © Dorling Kindersley Limited, London
A Penguin Company

**The information in this
DK Eyewitness Travel Guide is checked regularly**.
Every effort has been made to ensure that this book is as up-to-
date as possible at the time of going to press. Some details,
however, such as telephone numbers, opening hours, prices,
gallery hanging arrangements and travel information are liable to
change. The publishers cannot accept responsibility for any
consequences arising from the use of this book, nor for any
material on third party websites, and cannot guarantee that any
website address in this book will be a suitable source of travel
information. We value the views and suggestions of our readers
very highly. Please write to: Publisher, DK Eyewitness Travel
Guides, Dorling Kindersley, 80 Strand, London WC2R 0RL.

CONTENTS

Elephant in Sydney's Taronga Zoo

SYDNEY

Ben Boyd National Park on the south coast of New South Wales

Rippon Lea in Melbourne

How to Use this Guide

THIS GUIDE helps you to get the most from your visit to Australia. *Introducing Australia* maps the whole country and sets it in its historical and cultural context. The 17 regional chapters, including *Sydney*, describe important sights with maps, pictures and illustrations, as well as introductory features on subjects of regional interest. Suggestions on restaurants, accommodation, shopping and entertainment are in *Travellers' Needs*. The *Survival Guide* has tips on getting around the country. The cities of Sydney, Melbourne and Brisbane also have their own *Practical Information* sections.

SYDNEY

The centre of Sydney has been divided into four sightseeing areas. Each area has its own chapter which opens with a list of the sights described. All the sights are numbered and plotted on an *Area Map*. Information on each sight is easy to locate within the chapter as it follows the numerical order on the map.

Sights at a Glance lists the chapter's sights by category: Historic Streets and Buildings, Museums and Galleries, Parks and Gardens etc.

All pages relating to Sydney have red thumb tabs.

1 Area Map
Sights are numbered on a map. Sights in the city centre are also shown on the Sydney Street Finder (see pp140–47). Melbourne also has its own Street Finder (see pp404–411).

A locator map shows where you are in relation to other areas of the city centre.

2 Street-by-Street Map
This gives a bird's-eye view of the heart of each sightseeing area.

A suggested route for a walk covers the more interesting streets in the area.

Stars indicate sights that no visitor should miss.

3 Detailed Information on Each Sight
All the sights in Sydney are described individually. Useful addresses, telephone numbers, opening hours and other practical information are provided for each entry. The key to all the symbols used in the information block is shown on the back flap.

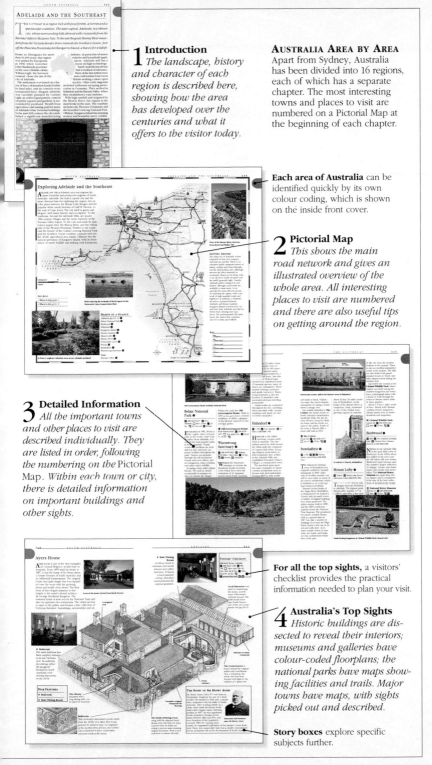

1 Introduction
The landscape, history and character of each region is described here, showing how the area has developed over the centuries and what it offers to the visitor today.

AUSTRALIA AREA BY AREA
Apart from Sydney, Australia has been divided into 16 regions, each of which has a separate chapter. The most interesting towns and places to visit are numbered on a Pictorial Map at the beginning of each chapter.

Each area of Australia can be identified quickly by its own colour coding, which is shown on the inside front cover.

2 Pictorial Map
This shows the main road network and gives an illustrated overview of the whole area. All interesting places to visit are numbered and there are also useful tips on getting around the region.

3 Detailed Information
All the important towns and other places to visit are described individually. They are listed in order, following the numbering on the Pictorial Map. Within each town or city, there is detailed information on important buildings and other sights.

For all the top sights, a visitors' checklist provides the practical information needed to plan your visit.

4 Australia's Top Sights
Historic buildings are dissected to reveal their interiors; museums and galleries have colour-coded floorplans; the national parks have maps showing facilities and trails. Major towns have maps, with sights picked out and described.

Story boxes explore specific subjects further.

Introducing Australia

Putting Australia on the Map

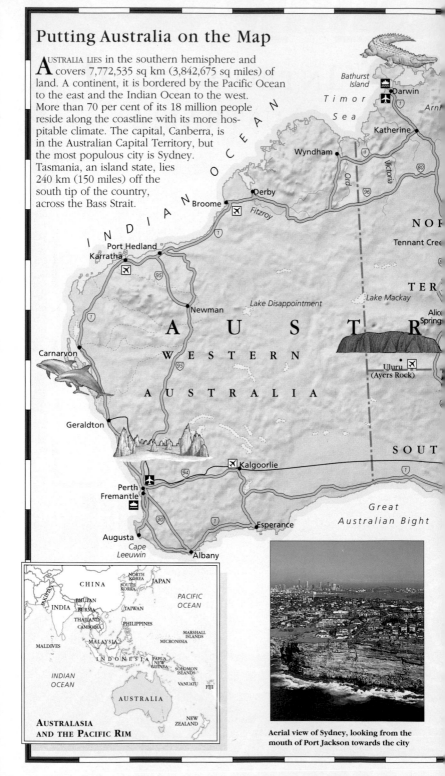

AUSTRALIA LIES in the southern hemisphere and covers 7,772,535 sq km (3,842,675 sq miles) of land. A continent, it is bordered by the Pacific Ocean to the east and the Indian Ocean to the west. More than 70 per cent of its 18 million people reside along the coastline with its more hospitable climate. The capital, Canberra, is in the Australian Capital Territory, but the most populous city is Sydney. Tasmania, an island state, lies 240 km (150 miles) off the south tip of the country, across the Bass Strait.

INDIAN OCEAN

Timor Sea

Bathurst Island

Darwin

Arn

Katherine

Wyndham

Ord

Victoria

Derby

Broome

Fitzroy

NO

Tennant Cree

Port Hedland

Karratha

Lake Disappointment

Lake Mackay

TER

Newman

A U S T R

Alice Spring

Carnarvon

W E S T E R N

Uluru (Ayers Rock)

A U S T R A L I A

Geraldton

SOUT

Kalgoorlie

Perth
Fremantle

Great Australian Bight

Augusta
Cape Leeuwin

Albany

Esperance

AUSTRALASIA AND THE PACIFIC RIM

PAKISTAN

CHINA

NORTH KOREA

SOUTH KOREA

JAPAN

INDIA

BHUTAN

BURMA

TAIWAN

PACIFIC OCEAN

THAILAND

CAMBODIA

PHILIPPINES

MALDIVES

MALAYSIA

MARSHALL ISLANDS

MICRONESIA

I N D O N E S I A

PAPUA NEW GUINEA

SOLOMON ISLANDS

INDIAN OCEAN

VANUATU

FIJI

AUSTRALIA

NEW ZEALAND

Aerial view of Sydney, looking from the mouth of Port Jackson towards the city

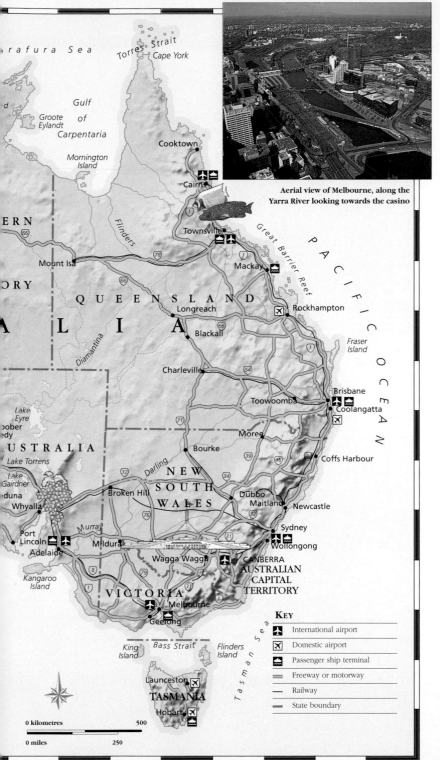

Arafura Sea

Torres *Strait*

Cape York

Gulf

Groote
Eylandt

of

Carpentaria

*Mornington
Island*

Cooktown

Cairns

**Aerial view of Melbourne, along the
Yarra River looking towards the casino**

ERN

Flinders

Townsville

Mackay

Great Barrier Reef

Mount Isa

ORY

Q U E E N S L A N D

Longreach

Blackall

Rockhampton

P   A   C   I   F   I   C

Diamantina

Charleville

*Fraser
Island*

Brisbane

Toowoomba

Coolangatta

Lake
Eyre
ober
dy

Lake Torrens

U S T R A L I A

Moree

Bourke

Darling

N E W

Coffs Harbour

O   C   E   A   N

*Lake
Gairdner*
duna

Whyalla

Broken Hill

S O U T H

W A L E S

Dubbo

Maitland

Newcastle

Port
Lincoln

Adelaide

Murray

Mildura

Sydney

Wollongong

*Kangaroo
Island*

Wagga Wagga

CANBERRA
**AUSTRALIAN
CAPITAL
TERRITORY**

V I C T O R I A

Melbourne

Geelong

*King
Island*

Bass Strait

*Flinders
Island*

T a s m a n   S e a

Launceston

TASMANIA

Hobart

KEY

✈	International airport
✕	Domestic airport
⚓	Passenger ship terminal
	Freeway or motorway
	Railway
	State boundary

0 kilometres   500

0 miles   250

A PORTRAIT OF AUSTRALIA

Australia is *the world's oldest continent, inhabited for more than 40,000 years by Aborigines. It was settled by the British just over 200 years ago, in 1788, and since then has transformed from a colonial outpost into a nation with a population of more than 18 million. For visitors, its ancient, worn landscape contrasts with the vitality and youthful energy of its inhabitants.*

Covering an area as large as the United States of America or the entire European continent, Australia's landscape is highly diverse, encompassing the dry Outback, the high plateaus of the Great Dividing Range, the lush woods of Tasmania, the rainforests and coral reefs of the tropical north and almost 18,000 km (11,000 miles) of coastline. The Great Dividing Range forms a spine down eastern Australia, from Queensland to Victoria, separating the fertile coastal strip from the dry and dusty interior.

Dominating the vegetation is the eucalypt, known as the "gum tree", of which there are some 500 varieties.

Aboriginal image of Namerredje

Australian trees shed their bark rather than their leaves, the native flowers have no smell and, with the exception of the wattle, bloom only briefly.

Australia has a unique collection of fauna. Most are marsupials, such as the emblematic kangaroo and koala. The platypus and echidna are among the few living representatives in the world of mammals that both lay eggs and suckle their young. The dingo, brought to Australia by the Aborigines, is considered the country's native dog.

Australia's antiquity is nowhere more evident than in the vast inland area known as the Outback.

Sydney Opera House, jutting into Sydney Harbour

◁ **Typical red soil and spinifex grass of Australia's Outback**

Ancient, eroded landscape of the Olgas, part of Uluru-Kata Tjuta National Park in the Northern Territory

Once a huge inland sea, its later aridity preserved the remains of the creatures that once inhabited the area. Some fossils found in Western Australia are 350 million years old – the oldest forms of life known on earth.

THE ABORIGINES

The indigenous inhabitants of Australia, the Aborigines, today constitute almost 1.6 per cent of the national population. Their situation is currently high on the nation's political agenda.

Aboriginal Australian

The early days of European colonialism proved disastrous for the Aborigines. Thousands were killed in hostilities or by unfamiliar diseases.

The kangaroo, a famous icon of Australia

During the 1850s, many Aborigines were confined to purpose-built reserves in a misguided attempt to overcome widespread poverty.

Since the 1950s there have been serious efforts to redress this lack of understanding. Conditions are improving, but even today, in almost every aspect of life, including health care, education and housing, Aborigines are worse off than other Australians. In 1992, a milestone occurred when the High Court overturned the doctrine of *terra nullius* – that Australia belonged to no one at the time of British settlement. The Native Title Act followed, which, in essence, states that where Aborigines could establish unbroken occupancy of an area, they could then claim that land as their own.

Almost all Australians support this reconciliation and are increasingly aware of the rich heritage of the Aborigines. The Aboriginal belief in the Dreamtime *(see pp26–7)* may never be completely assimilated into the Australian consciousness, but an understanding of ancestral beings is an invaluable guide to traditional lifestyles. Aboriginal painting began to be taken seriously by the international art scene in the 1970s and is now respected as one of the world's most ancient art forms. Aboriginal writers have also come to the forefront of Australian literature. Younger Aborigines are beginning to capitalize on this new awareness to promote equal rights and, with Aboriginal cultural centres being set up throughout the country, it is unlikely that Australia will dismiss its native heritage again.

SOCIETY

Given Australia's size and the fact that early settlements were far apart, Australian society is remarkably homogeneous. Its citizens are fundamentally prosperous and the way of life in the major cities and towns is much the same however many miles divide them. It takes a keen ear to identify regional accents.

However, there is some difference in lifestyle between city dwellers and the country people. Almost 90 per cent of the population lives in the fast-paced cities along the coast and has little more than a passing familiarity with the Outback. The major cities preserve pockets of colonial heritage, but the

A fortified wine maker takes a sample from a barrel of port in the Barossa Valley, South Australia

overall impression is modern, with new buildings reflecting the country's youth. In contrast, the rural communities tend to be slow-moving and conservative. For many years, Australia was said to have "ridden on the sheep's back", a reference to wool being the country's main money-earner. However, the wool industry is no longer dominant. Much of Australia's relatively sound economy is now achieved from natural coal and wheat, and as the largest diamond producer in the world. Newer industries such as tourism and wine making are also increasingly important. Australians are generally friendly and relaxed, with a self-deprecating sense of humour. On the whole, Australia has a society without hierarchies, an attitude generally held to stem from its convict beginnings.

Isolated Outback church in Silverton, New South Wales

Yet, contrary to widespread belief, very few Australians have true convict origins. Within only one generation of the arrival of the First Fleet in 1788, Australia had become a nation of immigrants. Originally hailing almost entirely from the British Isles, today one in three Australians comes from elsewhere. Australia's liberal postwar immigration policies led to an influx of survivors from war-torn Europe, most notably Greeks, Italians, Poles and Germans.

Indonesian satay stall at Parap Market in Darwin in the Northern Territory

The emphasis has shifted in recent years and today the majority of new immigrants hail from Southeast Asia. Although some racism does exist, this blend of nations has, on the whole, been a successful experiment and Australia is justifiably proud to have one of the most harmonious multicultural communities in the world.

POLITICS

Since 1901, Australia has been a federation, with its central government based in the purpose-built national capital, Canberra. Each state also has its own government. The nation inherited the central parliamentary system from England, and there is a two-party system consisting of the left (Labor) and the right (a coalition of Liberal and National parties). The prime minister is the head of federal government, while the heads of states are premiers. Australia is a self-governing member of the British Commonwealth and retains the English monarch as its titular head of state. At present, the national representative of the monarch is the governor general, but the nation is involved in an ongoing debate about its future as a republic. There is opposition from those who argue that the present system has led to one of the most stable societies in the world, while others believe that swearing allegiance to an English monarch has little meaning for the current population, many of whom are immigrants. A referendum in November 1999 saw the monarchy retained with 55 per cent of the votes. The debate continues.

The nation's character has always been shaped by its sparsely populated island location, far distant from its European roots and geographically closer to Southeast Asia. Today

View of the Parliamentary area and Lake Burley Griffin in Canberra

there is a growing realization that the country must look to the Pacific region for its future. Closer ties with Asia, such as business transactions with Indonesia and Japan, are being developed.

ART AND CULTURE

Blessed with a sunny climate and surrounded by the sea, outdoor leisure is high on the list of priorities for Australians – going to the beach is almost a national pastime. Australians are also mad about sport: football, cricket, rugby, tennis and golf are high on the national agenda.

Yet despite this reputation, Australians actually devote more of their time and money to artistic pursuits than they do to sporting ones, and as a result the national cultural scene is very vibrant. It is no accident that the Sydney Opera House is one of the country's most recognizable symbols. The nation is probably best known for its opera singers, among whom have been two of the all-time greats, Dame Nellie Melba and Dame Joan Sutherland. Opera Australia and the Australian Ballet, both in Sydney, are acknowledged for their high standards. Every state also has its own thriving theatre company and symphony orchestra. Major art galleries abound throughout the country, from the many excellent state galleries exhibiting international works to a multitude of small

Australian Rules football match in Melbourne

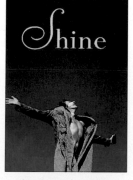
Young boogie boarder

Film poster of the Academy-Award winning *Shine*

private galleries exhibiting local and contemporary Australian and Aboriginal art.

The Australian film industry has also come into its own since the 1970s. The best-known Australian film is possibly *Crocodile Dundee* (1985), but lower budget productions such as *Shine* (1996) and *Muriel's Wedding* (1994) have an attractive, understated quality which regularly wins them international film awards.

This is not to say that Australia's cultural pursuits are entirely highbrow. Low-budget television soap operas such as *Neighbours* have become high-earning exports. Rock bands such as AC/DC also have an international following.

In almost all aspects, it seems, Australia lives up to its nickname of "the lucky country" and it is hard to meet an Australian who is not thoroughly convinced that this young and vast nation is now the best country on earth.

Australia's Landscape

GEOLOGICAL STABILITY has been largely responsible for creating the landscape of the earth's oldest, flattest and driest inhabited continent. Eighty million years ago, Australia's last major bout of geological activity pushed up the Great Dividing Range, but since then the continent has slept. Mountains have been eroded down, making it difficult for rain clouds to develop. Deserts have formed in once lush areas and today more than 70 per cent of the continent is arid. However, with some of the oldest rocks on earth, its landscapes are anything but uniform, and include rainforests, tropical beaches, glacial landforms, striking coastlines and flood plains.

Australia's drift *towards the equator has brought a northern monsoon climate, as in Kakadu National Park (see pp268–9).*

Cradle Mountain *(see p455) in southwest Tasmania was created by geological upheaval, glaciation and erosion. Here jagged mountain ranges, ravines and glacial lakes have formed a landscape that is quite unique in Australia.*

KATA TJUTA (THE OLGAS)
Geological remnants of an immense bed of sedimentary rock now almost covered by sand from erosion, Kata Tjuta's weathered domes may once have been a single dome many times the size of Uluru *(see pp278–81).*

Western Plateau

Central Lowlands

Great Dividing Range

There are three main geological regions in Australia: the coastal plain including the Great Dividing Range; the Central Lowlands; and the Western Plateau. The Great Dividing Range is a relatively new feature in geological terms. It contains Australia's highest mountains, deep rivers, spectacular gorges and volcanic landforms. The Central Lowlands subsided when the continental margins on either side rose up – a result of rifting caused by continental drift. The Western Plateau contains many of Australia's large deserts and is composed of some of the most ancient rocks in the world.

The area to the east of Queensland was flooded at the end of the last Ice Age, creating ideal conditions for a coral reef. The Great Barrier Reef (see pp204–9) now forms one of the world's most stunning sights.

The Nullarbor Plain (see p359) was created by the upthrust of an ancient sea floor. Today, sheer cliffs drop away from this desert landscape dotted with sinkholes and plunge into the sea below, creating one of Australia's most startling coastlines.

THE AUSTRALIAN CONTINENT

The Australian continent finally broke away from its last adjoining landmass, Antarctica, 40 million years ago and embarked on a long period of geographical isolation. During this time Australia's unique flora and fauna evolved and flourished *(see pp20–21)*. Aboriginal people lived undisturbed on this continent for at least 40,000 years, developing the land to their own needs, until the arrival of Europeans in 1770 *(see pp42–7)*.

Two hundred million years ago, the area of land that is now continental Australia was attached to the lower half of the earth's single landmass, Pangaea.

Between 200 and 65 million years ago, Pangaea separated to form two supercontinents, Gondwanaland in the south and Laurasia in the north.

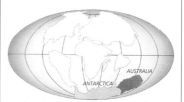

Fifty million years ago, Gondwanaland had broken up into the various southern continents with only Antarctica and Australia still attached.

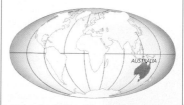

Today, the drifting of the continents continues and Australia is moving northwards towards the equator at the rate of 8 cm (3 ins) a year.

Flora and Fauna

FORTY MILLION YEARS of isolation from other major land masses have given Australia a collection of flora and fauna that is unique in the world. Low rainfall and poor soil has meant meagre food sources, and animals and plants have evolved some curious adaptations to help them cope. Surprisingly, these adverse conditions have also produced incredible biodiversity. Australia has more than 25,000 species of plants, and its rainforests are among the richest in the world in the number of species they support. Even its desert centre has 2,000 plant species and the world's greatest concentration of reptile species.

The platypus lives in an aquatic environment like a fish, suckles its young like a mammal, lays eggs and has the bill of a duck!

The lush rainforest is a haven for many endemic species of flora and fauna.

Epiphytes, ferns and vines abound around this rainforest creek.

At least 30 species of spinifex cover many of Australia's desert plains.

RAINFORESTS

The east coast rainforests are among the most ancient ecosystems on earth. At least 18,000 plant species exist here. Some trees are more than 2,500 years old, and many are direct descendants of species from Gondwana *(see p19).*

ARID REGIONS

The vast reaches of Australia's arid and semi-arid regions teem with life. Desert plants and animals have developed unique and specific behavioural and physical features to maximize their survival chances in such harsh conditions.

The tiny golden bower-bird of the rainforest builds spectacular bowers out of sticks as a platform for its mating displays. Some bowers reach well over 2 m (6.5 ft) in height.

The boab (baobab) tree sheds its leaves in the dry season to survive.

Spinifex grass, found across the desert, stores water and needs frequent exposure to fire to thrive.

The Wollemi pine was discovered in 1994 and caused a sensation. It belongs to a genus thought to have become extinct between 65 and 200 million years ago.

The thorny devil feeds only on ants and can consume more than 3,000 in one meal.

MAMMALS

Australian mammals are distinctive because the population is dominated by two groups that are rare or non-existent elsewhere. Monotremes, such as the platypus, are found only in Australia and New Guinea, and marsupials, represented by 180 species here, are scarce in other parts of the world. In contrast, placental mammals, highly successful on other continents, have been represented in Australia only by bats and rodents, and more recently by dingos. Mass extinctions of larger placentals occurred 20,000 years ago.

Red kangaroos are the most common of many species of this marsupial found in Australia.

The dingo was introduced into Australia by migrating humans c. 5,000 years ago.

Eucalypt trees provide food for possums and koalas.

Moist fern groundcover shelters a variety of small mammals and insects.

This coral garden is home to many molluscs, crustaceans and brightly coloured fish.

OPEN WOODLAND

The woodlands of the eastern seaboard, the southeast and southwest are known as the Australian bush. Eucalypt trees predominate in the hardy vegetation that has developed to survive fire, drought and poor-quality soil.

SEALIFE

Australia's oceans are poor in nutrients but rich in the diversity of life they support. Complex ecosystems create beautiful underwater scenery, while the shores and islands are home to nesting seabirds and giant sea mammals.

Koalas feed only on nutrient-poor eucalypt leaves, and have evolved low-energy lives to cope, such as sleeping for 20 hours a day.

Seagrass beds have high-saline conditions which attract many sea creatures. Shark Bay shelters the highest number of sea mammals in the world (see pp318–19).

Kookaburras are very efficient breeders: one of the young birds is kept on in the nest to look after the next batch of hatchlings, leaving both parents free to gather food.

The Australian sealion is one of two seal species unique to Australia. Its extended breeding cycle helps it contend with a poor food supply.

World Heritage Areas of Australia

THE WORLD HERITAGE CONVENTION was adopted by UNESCO in 1972 in order to protect areas of universal cultural and natural significance. Eleven sites in Australia are inscribed on the World Heritage List and include unusual landforms, ancient forests and areas of staggering biodiversity. Four of the locations (Kakadu National Park, Willandra Lakes, the Tasmanian wilderness and Uluṟu-Kata Tjuṯa National Park) are also listed for their Aboriginal cultural heritage.

Fossil sites *in Riversleigh (see p249) and Naracoorte chart Australia's important evolutionary stages.*

Kakadu National Park *is a landscape of wetlands and tropical splendour. Art sites document the interaction between Aborigines and the land (see pp268–9).*

NORTHERN TERRITORY

WESTERN AUSTRALIA

SOUTH AUSTRALIA

Australian Fossil Mammal Site at Naracoorte *(see p347)*

Shark Bay *is home to a vast colony of sea mammals. The bay's stromatolites (algae-covered rocks) are the oldest form of life known on earth (see pp318–19).*

Uluṟu-Kata Tjuṯa National Park *contains two major Aboriginal sites (see pp278–81). The world's largest monolith is an extraordinary geological phenomenon in the flat desert plains.*

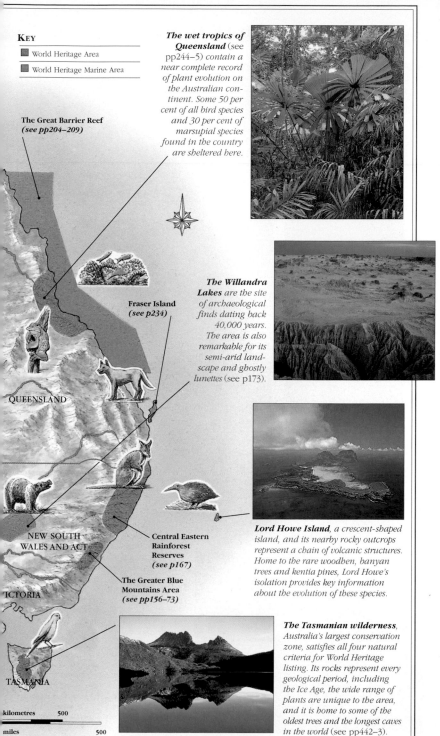

KEY

☐ World Heritage Area

☐ World Heritage Marine Area

The Great Barrier Reef
(see pp204–209)

The wet tropics of Queensland (see pp244–5) *contain a near complete record of plant evolution on the Australian continent. Some 50 per cent of all bird species and 30 per cent of marsupial species found in the country are sheltered here.*

Fraser Island
(see p234)

QUEENSLAND

The Willandra Lakes are the site of archaeological finds dating back 40,000 years. The area is also remarkable for its semi-arid landscape and ghostly lunettes (see p173).

NEW SOUTH
WALES AND ACT

Central Eastern
Rainforest
Reserves
(see p167)

The Greater Blue
Mountains Area
(see pp156–73)

VICTORIA

Lord Howe Island, a crescent-shaped island, and its nearby rocky outcrops represent a chain of volcanic structures. Home to the rare woodhen, banyan trees and kentia pines, Lord Howe's isolation provides key information about the evolution of these species.

TASMANIA

kilometres   500

miles   500

The Tasmanian wilderness, Australia's largest conservation zone, satisfies all four natural criteria for World Heritage listing. Its rocks represent every geological period, including the Ice Age, the wide range of plants are unique to the area, and it is home to some of the oldest trees and the longest caves in the world (see pp442–3).

The Australian Outback

Perenite goanna in the Outback

THE OUTBACK is the heart of Australia and one of the most ancient landscapes in the world. It is extremely dry – rain may not fall for several years. Dramatic red rocks, ochre plains and purple mountains are framed by brilliant blue skies. Development is sparse: "towns" are often no more than a few buildings and facilities are basic. There may be hundreds of miles between one petrol station and another. The Outback isn't easy to explore, but it can be a rewarding experience. Make sure you are well equipped *(see p550)*, or take an organized tour.

LOCATOR MAP

◼ *The Australian Outback*

Camels *were brought to Australia in the 1870s from the Middle East, as a means of desert transport. The Outback is now home to the only wild camels in the world. Camel safaris for tourists are available in many places.*

Saltbush, which gets its name from its ability to withstand saline conditions, is a typical form of vegetation.

OUTBACK LIFE

The enduring image of Australia's Outback is red dust, solitary one-storey shacks and desert views as far as the eye can see. Although small areas of the Outback have seen towns spring up over the past 100 years, and many interstate roads are now suitable for most vehicles, this image remains true to life across vast stretches of the interior landscape. Most of the Outback remains pioneering country far removed from the modern nation.

Camping *in the bush is one of the highlights of any trip into Australia's Outback, whether independently or with an organized tour. You will need a camping permit, a swag (canvas-covered bed roll), a mosquito net and a good camping stove to eat and sleep in relative comfort under the stars.*

The film industry has long been a fan of the Outback's vast open spaces and dramatic colours. Films such as the 1994 comedy The Adventures of Priscilla, Queen of the Desert *made spectacular use of the Red Centre's sparse and dusty landscape.*

Australian "hotels" in Outback areas often operate only as public houses, re-named hotels to counteract Australia's once strict licensing laws.

PIONEERS AND EXPLORERS

Many European explorers, such as Edward Eyre and John Stuart, ventured into the Outback during the 19th century. The most infamous expedition was Robert O'Hara Burke's from Victoria to the Gulf of Carpentaria *(see p49)*. Ironically, however, it was the rescue missions his inexperience incurred that truly opened up the interior of Australia from all corners of the nation.

Robert O'Hara Burke 1820–61

A solitary building set against vast areas of open desert landscape can be an evocative landmark in the Outback.

The Birdsville Races in Queensland are the biggest and best of the many horse races held in the Outback, where locals gather to bet and socialize.

Opal mining in towns such as Coober Pedy (see p360) is one source of the Outback's wealth. Tourists need a miner's permit, available from state tourist offices, to hunt for gems.

Aboriginal Culture

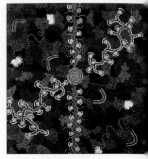

Men's Dreaming by Clifford Possum Tjapaltjarri

FAR FROM BEING one homogeneous race, at the time of European settlement in the 18th century the estimated 750,000 Aborigines in Australia had at least 300 different languages and a wide variety of lifestyles, depending on where they lived. The tribes of northern coastal areas, such as the Tiwis, had most contact with outsiders, especially from Indonesia, and their culture was quite different from the more isolated Pitjantjatjaras of Central Australia's deserts or the Koories from the southeast. However, there were features common to Aboriginal life and these have passed down the centuries to present-day traditions.

Ancient stone axe

Aboriginal artifacts and tools, decorated in traditional ornate patterns

TRADITIONAL ABORIGINAL LIFESTYLES

FOR THOUSANDS of years the Aborigines were a race of hunters leading a nomadic existence. They made lightweight, versatile tools such as the boomerang, and built temporary mud dwellings. The extent of their wanderings differed from region to region – people who lived in areas with a plentiful supply of food and water were relatively more static than those in areas where such essentials were scarce.

Through living in small groups in a vast land, Aboriginal society came to be broken up into numerous clans separated by different languages and customs. Even people with a common language would live apart in "core" family groups, consisting of a husband, wife, children and perhaps some close friends to share the responsibilities of daily life. Groups would come together

from time to time to conduct religious ceremonies, arrange marriages and settle inter-clan disputes. Trade was an important part of social life. Shell, ochre and wood were some of the goods exchanged along trade routes that criss-crossed the entire country.

The nomadic way of life largely ended when English settlers claimed vast tracts of land, but other aspects of traditional life have survived. In Aboriginal communities senior members are still held in great respect, and are responsible for maintaining laws and meting out punishments to those who break them or divulge secrets of ancient rituals. Such rituals are part of the Aboriginal belief system called "Dreamtime".

THE DREAMTIME

THE DREAMTIME (or Dreaming) is the English term for the Aboriginal system of laws and beliefs. Its basis is a rich mythology about the earth's creation. "Creation ancestors" such as giant serpents are believed to have risen up from the earth's core and roamed the world, creating valleys, rivers and mountains. Other progenitors caused the rain and sun, and created the people and wildlife. Sites where ancestral beings are thought to have emerged from the earth are sacred and are still used as the locations for ceremonies and rituals today.

The belief in the Dreamtime is, in essence, a religious ideology for all Aborigines, whatever their tribe, and forms the basis of Aboriginal life. Every Aborgine is

THE BOOMERANG

Contrary to popular belief, not all boomerangs will return to the thrower. Originally, "boomerang" simply meant "throwing stick". They were used for hunting, fighting, making fire, stoking the coals when cooking and in traditional games. A hunter did not normally require a throwing stick to return since its purpose was to injure its target sufficiently to enable capture. Over time, intricate shapes were developed that allowed sticks to swirl in a large arc and return to the thrower. The returning boomerang is limited to games, killing birds and directing animals into traps. Light and thin, with a deep curvature, the ends are twisted in opposite directions. The lower surface is flat and the upper surface convex.

Aboriginal boomerang

believed to have two souls – one mortal and one immortal, linked with their ancestral spirit (or totem). Each family clan is descended from the same ancestral being. These spirits provide protection: any misfortune is due to disgruntled forebears. Consequently some clan members have a responsibility for maintaining sacred sites. Anyone who fails in these duties is severely punished.

Each Dreamtime story relates to a particular landscape; as one landscape connects with another, these stories form a "track". These "tracks" are called Songlines and crisscross the Australian continent. Aborigines are able to connect with other tribes along these lines.

Aborigines being painted with white paint to ward off evil spirits

ABORIGINAL SONG AND DANCE

A BORIGINAL SONGS tell stories of Dreamtime ancestors and are intrinsically linked to the worship of spirits – the words of songs are often incomprehensible due to the secrecy of many ancestral stories. Simple instruments accompany the songs, including the didgeridoo, a 1-m (3-ft) long wind instrument with a deep sound.

Aborigines also use dance as a means of communicating with their ancestors. Aboriginal dance is experiencing a cultural renaissance, with new companies performing both traditional and new works.

ABORIGINAL ISSUES

A LTHOUGH FEW Aborigines now maintain a traditional nomadic lifestyle, the ceremonies, creation stories and art that make up their culture remain strong.

The right to own land has long been an issue for present-day Aborigines; they believe that they are responsible for caring for the land entrusted to them at birth. The Land Rights Act of 1976 has done much to improve these rights. The Act established Aboriginal Land Councils who negotiate between the government and Aborigines to claim land for its traditional owners (see pp54–5). Where Aboriginal rights have been established, that land cannot be altered in any way.

Decorating bark with natural ochre stains

In areas of large Aboriginal inhabitance the government has also agreed that white law can exist alongside black law, which allows for justice against Aboriginal offenders to be meted out according to tribal law. In many cases, this law is harsh and savage, but it allows for Aborigines to live by their own belief system.

The revival of Aboriginal art was at the forefront of seeing Aboriginal culture in a more positive light by Australians. Aboriginal artists such as Emily Kngwarreye combine traditional materials such as bark and ochre with acrylics and canvas, while telling Dreaming stories in a modern idiom (see pp26–7).

Many Aborigines have now moved away from their rural roots and live within the major cities, but they remain distinctly Aboriginal and generally choose to live within Aboriginal communities. Within designated Aboriginal lands (see pp254–5), many still follow bush medical practices and perform traditional rituals.

It cannot be denied that Aborigines are still disadvantaged in comparison with the rest of Australia, particularly in terms of housing, health and education. But the growing awareness of their culture and traditions is gradually leading to a more harmonious coexistence.

Aborigines performing a traditional dance at sunset

Aboriginal Art

Aboriginal rock art sign

As a nomadic people with little interest in decorating their temporary dwellings, Aborigines have long let loose their creativity on landscape features such as rocks and caves *(see pp43–4)*. Many art sites are thousands of years old, although they have often been re-painted over time to preserve the image. Rock art reflects daily Aboriginal life as well as religious beliefs. Some ancient sites contain representations of now extinct animals; others depict human figures with blue eyes, strange weapons and horses – evidently the arrival of Europeans. Aboriginal art is also seen in everyday objects – utensils and accessories such as belts and headbands.

Bark painting, *such as this image of a fish, has disappeared from southern areas, but still flourishes in Arnhem Land and on Melville and Bathurst islands.*

Cave rock was a popular "canvas" for traditional Aboriginal art, particularly when tribes took cover during the rainy season.

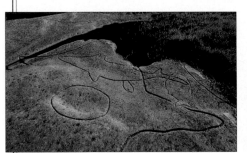

The outline style *of rock engraving was developed most fully in the Sydney-Hawkesbury area, due to vast areas of soft Hawkesbury sandstone. More than 4,000 figures have been recorded, often gigantic in size – one whale engraving is more than 20 m (65 ft) long. Groups of engravings can cover more than 1 ha (2.5 acres).*

Figures showing the human anatomy are often depicted in basic but exaggerated, stylized forms.

Darwin

Brisbane

Perth

Sydney

Adelaide

Melbourne

Hobart

MAJOR ABORIGINAL ART SITES

▨	Arnhem Land, Northern Territory
■	Central Desert
■	Uluru-Kata Tjuta National Park
■	Laura, Queensland
▨	Melville and Bathurst islands
▨	Sydney-Hawkesbury area

Quinkans *are stick-like figures found in far north Queensland's Laura region. They represent spirits that are thought to emerge suddenly from rock crevices and startle people, to remind them that misbehaviour will bring swift retribution.*

Burial poles *are an example of how important decoration is to Aborigines, even to commemmorate death. These brightly coloured Pukumani burial poles belong to the Tiwi people of Melville and Bathurst islands* (see p266).

Bush Plum Dreaming *(1991) by Clifford Possum Tjapaltjarri is a modern example of ancient Aboriginal techniques used by the Papunya tribe* (see p30).

The crocodile image personifies the force of nature, as well as symbolizing the relationship between humans and the natural environment. Both are common themes within Aboriginal art.

"X-ray art", *such as this figure at Nourlangie Rock in Kakadu National Park* (see pp268–9), *shows the internal and external anatomy of living subjects, including a range of animals.*

ARNHEM LAND ROCK ART

Arnhem Land is the 80,285-km (49,890-mile) Aboriginal territory which stretches from east of Darwin to the Gulf of Carpentaria *(see pp254–5)*. Magnificent rock art "galleries" in this region date from 16,000 BC *(see p43)* – some of the oldest Aboriginal art in the country.

Totemic art *at Uluru* (see pp278–81) *is thought to portray the beings in Aboriginal culture who are believed to have created the rock.*

Australian Artists and Writers

Frederick McCubbin

THE FIRST ARTISTS to paint Australia were Europeans who arrived in the *Endeavour (see pp46–7)*, but it was not until the prosperity generated by the 1850s gold rushes that art gained any public recognition. There had been colonial artists, of whom Conrad Martens (1801–78) was the best known, but in a country where survival was the most immediate problem, art was not a high priority. The first writings were also journals of early settlers; it was 100 years before Australia could claim the beginnings of a literary tradition, when Rolf Boldrewood (1826–1915) wrote *Robbery Under Arms* (1888), a heroic tale of the bush.

Sir Russell Drysdale

ARTISTS

THE SO-CALLED "Heidelberg School", named after an area around Melbourne, was the first distinctive Australian school of painting at the end of the 19th century. Its mainstays included Tom Roberts (1856–1931), Charles Conder (1868–1909), Frederick McCubbin (1855–1917) and Arthur Streeton (1867–1943). The group drew strongly on the *plein air* methods of the French Impressionists to capture the distinctive light and openness of the Australian landscape. Then in the early 1900s Hans Heysen captured the national imagination with his delicately coloured gum trees and his view of the Australian landscape. Sir Sidney Nolan (1917–92),

Kelly in Spring (1956), one of Sir Sidney Nolan's "Ned Kelly" series

best known for his "Ned Kelly" series of the 1940s based on the country's most notorious bushranger *(see p386)*, also produced landscape paintings which propelled Australian art on to the international scene for the first time.

The best known of the talented Boyd family, Arthur Boyd (born in 1920) is another great on the Australian art scene; his "Half-Caste Bride" series catapulted him into the art world in 1960.

Probably the greatest interpreter of Australia's Outback is Sir Russell Drysdale (1912–81), whose paintings depict the harshness of this landscape. Brett Whiteley (1939–92) is a more recent talent whose sensual work reflects his view of the world.

Winner of the Archibald Prize for portraiture, William Dobell (1899–1970) is often regarded as the figurehead of the Sydney Modernist movement. He achieved some level of notoriety when, in 1944, two fellow artists mounted a legal challenge to the granting of the Archibald for his portrait of Joshua Smith, claiming it was "not a portrait but a caricature". The action was unsuccessful but all Dobell's further work generated publicity for the wrong reasons.

Possibly the most popularly recognized Australian artist is Ken Done. Often dismissed for blatant commercialism, his brilliantly coloured work has achieved sales that most artists only dream of.

The most significant collection of Australian art can be seen at Canberra's National Gallery *(see pp194–5)*.

Toberua (1994) by Ken Done

THE ANTIPODEANS

FORMED IN MELBOURNE in 1959, the Antipodeans consisted of seven of Australia's best-known modern artists all born in the 1920s: Charles Blackman, Arthur Boyd, David Boyd, John Brack, Robert Dickerson, John Perceval and Clifton Pugh. The aim of the group was to support figurative painting rather than abstraction. The group denied that they were creating a national style and the name Antipodeans was adopted to avoid too narrow a focus on Australia, as the group aimed for international recognition at exhibitions in London. Ironically, it later came to apply to Australian art in general.

Portrait of Miles Franklin by Marie McNiven

WRITERS

MUCH OF Australian fiction is concerned with the difficulties Europeans experienced in a harsh land, or the relationship between white settlers and Aborigines. The themes can be traced back to an early Australian novelist, Henry Handel Richardson, the pseudonym of Ethel Robertson (1870–1946). Her trilogy, *The Fortunes of Richard Mahoney* (1929), was published to great acclaim, including a nomination for the Nobel Prize for Literature. Contemporary novelist David Malouf (born in 1934) continues to explore these issues in *Remembering Babylon* (1993), winner of the Prix Baudelaire, and *Conversations at Curlow Creek* (1996).

Film poster of *Schindler's List*, based on *Schindler's Ark*

Australia's most celebrated novelist is undoubtedly Patrick White (1912–90), who won the Nobel Prize in 1973 with *The Eye of the Storm*. White had made his mark in 1957 with *Voss*, the story of the explorer Ludwig Leichhardt, while his later novels include *A Fringe of Leaves* (1976) and *The Twyborn Affair* (1979).

Campaigner for women's suffrage, Louisa Lawson (1848–1920)·is credited with Australia's first feminist journal, *Dawn*, written between 1888 and 1905. At the same time, another feminist, Miles Franklin (1879–1954) defied traditional women's roles of the time by pursuing an independent life in Australia, England and the USA. Her life was documented in several autobiographies, beginning with *My Brilliant Career* (1901).

For descriptions of pre- and postwar Sydney life in the slums, the novels of Ruth Park (born in 1922), such as *Harp in the South* (1948) and *Fence around the Cuckoo* (1992), are unbeatable. Novelist Thomas Keneally (born in 1935) won the 1982 Booker Prize with *Schindler's Ark*, later made by Steven Spielberg into the acclaimed film *Schindler's List*.

Aboriginal writer Sally Morgan (born in 1951) has put indigenous Australian writing on the map with her 1988 autobiography *My Place*.

POETS

AUSTRALIA'S EARLY poets were mostly bush balladeers, articulating life in the bush and the tradition of the Australian struggle. "The Man from Snowy River" and "Clancy of the Overflow" by AB "Banjo" Paterson (1864–1941) are 19th-century classics still committed to

memory by every Australian schoolchild. Writing from the late 1800s until his death in 1922, Henry Lawson similarly wrote some enduring bush verse, but his poetry also had a more political edge. His first published poem in the *Bulletin* literary magazine in 1887 was the rallying "Song of the Republic".

Poets such as Judith Wright (born in 1945) and, in particular, Oodgeroo Noonuccal (1920–93), have sensitively and powerfully expressed the anguish of Aboriginal people in verse.

Henry Lawson

PLAYWRIGHTS

AUSTRALIA'S MOST prolific contemporary playwright is David Williamson, born in 1942. A satirist exploring middle-class life and values, Williamson has been an international success and several of his plays, such as *Dead White Males* (1995), have been performed both in London and New York.

Ray Lawler gained renown in 1955 with *Summer of the Seventeenth Doll*, which challenged the deep-rooted Australian concept of male friendship. The play has been adapted as an opera, with music by Australian composer Richard Meale.

Other notable contemporary playwrights are Nick Enright, Stephen Sewell and Louis Nowra.

The Wines of Australia

GRAPES HAVE BEEN GROWN and wine made in Australia virtually since European settlement in 1788 *(see pp46–7)*. Vines were first planted in Sydney soon after the arrival of the First Fleet. Pastoralists John and Elizabeth Macarthur became Australia's first commercial wine producers with a 90,000 l (20,000 gal) vintage in 1827 from their Sydney farm *(see p123)*. The Hunter Valley wine region was established in the 1830s by Scot

Ballandean Estate wine James Busby and by 1859 New South Wales, Victoria, South Australia, Tasmania, Western Australia and Queensland all had vineyards. Since the 1970s there has been an explosion in quality and quantity, rising from 53 million l (12 million gal) in 1960 to 500 million l (110 million gal) today. Australian wine is now sold worldwide.

LOCATOR MAP

■ *Major wine-producing regions of Australia*

Mount Hurtle winery *produces distinctive white table wines. It is located in one of South Australia's main wine regions, McLaren Vale (see pp330–31).*

Leeuwin Estate winery *in Margaret River, Western Australia (see pp306–7) is one of the nation's largest producers of top-quality table wines, including Chardonnay and Cabernet Sauvignon.*

• PERTH

ADELAIDE

0 kilometres   500
0 miles   500

KEY

■ Western Australia
□ Tasmania
□ South Australia
□ Queensland
□ Victoria
□ New South Wales and ACT

THE FATHER OF AUSTRALIAN WINE

James Busby

James Busby is often regarded as the father of the Australian wine industry. Scottish-born, he arrived in Sydney in 1824. During the voyage to Australia he wrote the country's first wine book, detailing his experiences of French vineyards. He established a property at Kirkton in the Hunter Valley, New South Wales, and returned to Europe in 1831, collecting 570 vine cuttings from France and Spain. These were cultivated at Kirkton and at the Sydney and Adelaide Botanic Gardens. In 1833, having founded Australia's first wine-producing region, he emigrated to New Zealand.

Ballandean Estate in Queensland is particularly renowned for its top-quality Semillon and Sauvignon Blanc, and cellar tours are available. The southwest of Queensland has a cool climate that supports a small but thriving wine industry.

GRAPE VARIETIES OF AUSTRALIA

Western Australia's most notable wines are Cabernet Sauvignon reds, Chardonnay, Semillon, Chenin Blanc and Verdelho whites. The Pinot Noir grape is of particular importance to **Tasmania**, benefiting from the cool climate. The Granite Belt in **Queensland** (an area with granite components in the soil) produces Cabernet Sauvignon, Shiraz, Pinot Noir and Merlot reds, Semillon, Chardonnay, Marsanne and Sauvignon Blanc whites. The most prominent varieties in **New South Wales** are Semillon and Chardonnay whites, Shiraz and Cabernet Sauvignon reds. **South Australia's** varied climate produces Grenache and Merlot reds and Riesling and Frontignac whites. **Victoria** is particularly known for its Marsanne.

BRISBANE

Darling River

Murray River

Brown Brothers *was established in 1889 by John Graham Brown and is now one of Victoria's premier wineries* (see pp370–71). *Its Cabernet Sauvignon is of world-class quality.*

SYDNEY

CANBERRA

MELBOURNE

HOBART

Pipers Brook in Tasmania was established in 1973 and produces fine Chardonnays.

Balmoral House *is part of the Rosemount Estate in the Upper Hunter Valley* (see pp154–5). *The house gives its name to the winery's excellent Balmoral Shiraz.*

Surfing and Beach Culture

Lifeguard and her surfboard

AUSTRALIA IS the quintessential home of beach culture, with the nation's beaches ranging from sweeping crescents with rolling waves to tiny, secluded coves. Almost all Australians live within a two-hour drive of the coast, and during the hot summers it is almost second nature to make for the water to cool off. The clichéd image of the sun-bronzed Australian is no longer the reality it once was, but popular beaches are still packed with tanned bodies basking on golden sands or frolicking in deep blue waves. Fines levied for inappropriate behaviour mean that the atmosphere is calm and safe at all times. Surfing has always been a national sport, with regular carnivals and competitions held on its coastline. There are also opportunities for beginners to try their hand at this daring sport.

Baked-brown bodies *and sun-bleached hair were once the epitome of beach culture.*

Surf carnivals *attract thousands of spectators, who thrill to races, "iron man" competitions, dummy rescues and spectacular lifeboat displays.*

SURFER IN ACTION

Riding the waves is a serious business. Wetsuit-clad "surfies" study the surfing reports in the media and think nothing of travelling vast distances to reach a beach where the best waves are running.

Crouching down into the wave's crest increases stability on the board.

WHERE TO SURF

The best surfing to be found in Australia is on the New South Wales coast *(see pp170–71)*, the southern Queensland coast, especially the aptly named Surfer's Paradise and the Sunshine Coast *(pp230–31)* and the southern coastline of Western Australia *(pp304–305)*. Tasmania also has some fine surfing beaches on its northwestern tip *(pp454–5)*. Despite superb north Queensland beaches, the Great Barrier Reef stops the waves well before they reach the mainland. In summer, deadly marine stingers (jellyfish) here make surf swimming impossible in many areas, unless there is a stinger-proof enclosure.

Surf lifesaving is an integral part of the Australian beach scene. Trained volunteer life-savers, easily recognized by their red and yellow swimming caps, ensure that swimmers stay within flag-defined safe areas and are ready to spring into action if someone is in trouble.

BEACH ACTIVITIES

Australian beaches are not only the preserve of surfers. Winter temperatures are mild in most coastal areas, so many beach activities are enjoyed all year. Weekends see thousands of pleasure boats, from small runabouts to luxury yachts, competing in races or just out for a picnic in some sheltered cove. The sails of windsurfers create swirls of colour on gusty days. Kite-flying has become an art form, with the Festival of the Winds a September highlight at Sydney's Bondi Beach *(see p36)*. Beach volleyball, once a knockabout game, is now an Olympic sport.

Festival of the Winds

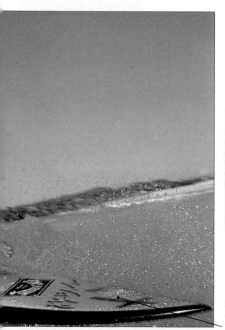

Takeaway snack food at the beach is an Australian tradition, since many sunlovers spend entire days by the ocean. Fish and chips, kebabs and burgers are on sale at beach cafés.

Surfboards, once made out of wood, are now built of light fibreglass, often in bright colours, improving speed and visibility.

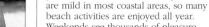

The Australian crawl revolutionized swimming throughout the world in the 1880s. For most Australians, swimming is an everyday sport, learned at a very early age.

SAFETY

Beaches are safe provided you follow a few guidelines:
• Always swim "between the flags".
• Don't swim alone.
• Note signs warning of strong currents, blue bottles or stingers.
• If you get into difficulty, do not wave but signal for help by raising one arm straight in the air.
• Use Factor 30+ sunscreen and wear a shirt and hat.

AUSTRALIA THROUGH THE YEAR

THE SEASONS IN AUSTRALIA are the exact opposite of those in the northern hemisphere. In the southern half of the country spring comes in September, summer is from December to February, autumn runs from March to May, while winter begins in June. In contrast, the tropical climate of the north

Reveller enjoying the Melbourne Festival

coast is more clearly divided into wet and dry seasons, the former between November and April. Australia's vast interior has a virtually unchanging desert climate – baking hot days and cool nights. The weather throughout Australia is reliable enough year-round to make outdoor events popular all over the country.

SPRING

WITH THE WARM weather, the profusion of spring flowers brings gardens and national parks to life. Food, art and music festivals abound in cities. Footballers finish their seasons, cricketers warm up for summer matches and the horse-racing fraternity gets ready to place its bets.

Australian Football League Grand Final in September

SEPTEMBER

Open Garden Scheme *(Sep–May)*, Victoria. The state's most magnificent private gardens open to the public *(see p366)*.
Mudgee Wine Festival *(1–21 Sep)*. Includes bush dances as well as wine *(see p169)*.
Festival of the Winds *(second Sun)*, Bondi Beach *(see p35)*. Multicultural kite-flying festival; music, dance.

Royal Melbourne Show *(last two weeks)*. Agricultural exhibitions, rides and displays.
Australian Contemporary Art Fair *(last week Sep–first week Oct)*, Sydney. Biennial event exhibiting the work of modern artists.
Australian Football League Grand Final *(last Sat in Sep)*, Melbourne *(see p389)*.
Australian Rugby League Grand Final *(last weekend)*, Sydney. National event.
Henley-on-Todd Regatta *(last weekend)*, Alice Springs. Races in bottomless boats along the dry Todd River.

OCTOBER

Melbourne Marathon *(first weekend)*. Fun-run through the centre of the city.
Lygon Street Festa *(first weekend)*, Melbourne. Flamboyant street carnival through the city's Italian district *(see p387)*.

Floriade, the October spring flower festival in Canberra

Floriade *(first three weeks)*, Canberra. Magnificent flower festival in Commonwealth Park *(see p187)*.
Tulip Festival *(first two weeks)*, Bowral. The Corbett Gardens are carpeted with flowers *(see p178)*.
Leura Garden Festival *(second to third weekends)*, Blue Mountains. Village fair and garden shows *(see p164)*.
Melbourne Writers' Festival *(middle two weeks)*. Readings and literary debates.

Henley-on-Todd Regatta at Alice Springs

Melbourne Festival *(last two weeks)*. The arts festival begins with a parade down Brunswick Street *(see p388)*.
Carnival of Flowers *(last week)*, Toowoomba. Popular floral festival including spectacular garden and flower displays *(see p232)*.
Rose and Rodeo Festival *(last weekend)*, Warwick. Australia's oldest rodeo attracts hundreds of visitors to watch expert riders from all over the world *(see p232)*.
Jacaranda Festival *(last Sat)*, Grafton. Australia's oldest flower festival features a Venetian Carnival and a Grand Float procession through the town *(see p170)*.

Santa Claus celebrating Christmas on Bondi Beach, Sydney

Race-goers dressed up for the Melbourne Cup in November

NOVEMBER

Rose Festival *(first two weeks)*, Benalla. Celebration of roses *(see p439)*.
Great Mountain Race of Victoria *(first Sat)*, Mansfield. Bush riders compete cross-country *(see p437)*.
Melbourne Cup *(first Tue)*. Australia's most popular horse race virtually halts the nation.
Maldon Folk Festival *(first weekend)*. Folk music concerts in this country town.

SUMMER

THE BEGINNING of the school holidays for Christmas marks the start of the summer in Australia and the festivities continue until

Australia Day on 26 January. Summer, too, brings a feast for sport lovers, with tennis, surfing events and a host of cricket matches. Arts and music lovers make the most of organized festivals.

DECEMBER

Carols by Candlelight *(24 Dec)*, Melbourne. Top musicians unite with locals to celebrate Christmas.
Christmas at Bondi Beach *(25 Dec)*. Holiday-makers hold parties on the famous beach *(see p122)*.
Sydney to Hobart Yacht Race *(26 Dec)*. Sydney Harbour teems with yachts setting off for Hobart *(see p448)*.
Cricket Test Match *(26 Dec)*, Melbourne.
New Year's Eve *(31 Dec)*, Sydney Harbour. Street parties and firework displays.

JANUARY

Hanging Rock Picnic Races *(1 Jan & 26 Jan)*. Premier country horse racing event *(see p427)*.
Australian Open *(last two weeks)*, Melbourne. Australia's popular Grand Slam tennis tournament.
Country Music Festival *(last two weeks)*, Tamworth. Australia's main country music festival, culminating in the Golden Guitar Awards *(see p169)*.
Midsumma Festival *(mid-Jan–mid-Feb)*, Melbourne. Melbourne's annual Gay and Lesbian festival includes street parades.

Opera in the Alps *(last Fri)*, Mount Buffalo. Music event in the Alps *(see p437)*.
Tunarama Festival *(last weekend)*, Port Lincoln. Tuna tossing competitions and fireworks *(see p358)*.
Australia Day Concert *(26 Jan)*, Sydney. Free evening concert commemorating the birth of the nation *(see p52)*.
Chinese New Year *(late Jan or early Feb)*, Sydney.
Cricket Test Match, Sydney.

Fireworks in Sydney for the Australia Day celebrations

FEBRUARY

Gay and Lesbian Mardi Gras Festival *(whole month)*, Sydney. Flamboyant street parades and events.
Festival of Perth *(mid-Feb–mid-Mar)*. Australia's oldest arts festival.
Leeuwin Estate Winery Music Concert *(mid-Feb)*, Margaret River. Concert attracting stars *(see p306)*.
Adelaide Festival *(mid-Feb–mid-Mar)*. Renowned biennial arts festival.

Australian Grand Prix, held in Melbourne in March

AUTUMN

AFTER THE humidity of the summer, autumn brings fresh mornings and cooler days that are tailor-made for outdoor pursuits such as bushwalking, cycling and fishing, as well as outdoor festivals. There are numerous sporting and cultural events to tempt the visitor. Many of the country's wineries open their doors during the harvest season and hold gourmet food and wine events. Lavish Easter parades take place in all the major cities and towns across the country. Anzac Day (25 April), observed annually since 1916, is a national holiday on which Australians commemorate their war dead.

Yarra Valley wine

MARCH

Australian Formula One Grand Prix *(first weekend)*, Melbourne. Top Formula One drivers compete, while the city celebrates with street parties *(see p395)*.
Yarra Valley Grape Grazing *(first weekend)*. Grape pressing, barrel races, good food and wine.
Begonia Festival *(first two weeks)*, Ballarat. Begonia displays in the Botanical Gardens *(see p425)*.
Moomba Festival *(second week)*, Melbourne. International aquatic events on the Yarra River *(see pp392–3)*, as well as cultural events throughout the city.

St Patrick's Day Parade *(17 Mar or Sun before)*, Sydney. Pubs serve green beer and a flamboyant parade travels from Hyde Park.

APRIL

Royal Easter Show *(week preceding Good Fri)* Sydney. Agricultural shows, funfair rides, local arts and crafts displays and team games.
International Surfing Competition *(Easter weekend)*, Bells Beach. Professional and amateur surfers arrive from all over the world to take part in this premier competition *(see p418)*.
Easter Fair *(Easter weekend)*, Maldon. An Easter parade and a colourful street carnival takes over this quaint country town *(see p422)*.

International Flower and Garden Show *(five days over Easter)*, Melbourne. Spectacular floral event held in the beautiful Exhibition Gardens *(see p387)*.
Melbourne International Comedy Festival *(first three weeks)*. Comedy acts from around the world perform in theatres, pubs and outdoors.
Bright Autumn Festival *(last week)*, Bright. Winery tours, art exhibitions and street parades are all part of this annual event *(see p437)*.
Anzac Day *(25 Apr)*. Australia's war dead and war veterans are honoured in remembrance services throughout the country.

MAY

Australian Celtic Festival *(first weekend)*, Glen Innes. Traditional Celtic events celebrate the town's British heritage *(see p168)*.
Kernewek Lowender Cornish Festival *(first weekend)*, Little Cornwall. A biennial celebration of the area's Cornish heritage which began with the copper discoveries of the 1860s *(see p355)*.
Torres Strait Cultural Festival *(last weekend)*, Thursday Island. Spiritual traditions of the Torres Strait Islanders celebrated through dance, song and art.

Anzac Day ceremony along Canberra's Anzac Parade

Racing in Alice Springs' Camel Cup

WINTER

WINTER IN THE EAST can be
cool enough to require
warm jackets, and it is often
icy in Victoria and Tasmania.
Many festivals highlight the
change of climate in celebration of freezing temperatures. Other events, such as
film festivals, are arts-based
and indoors. The warm
rather than sweltering climate
of the Outback in winter
offers the opportunity for
pleasurable outdoor events.

JUNE

**Three-day Equestrian
event** *(first weekend)*,
Gawler. Spectacular riding
skills are displayed at Australia's oldest equestrian event.
Sydney Film Festival *(two
weeks mid-Jun)*. The latest
blockbuster film releases are
combined with retrospectives
and showcases.
Melbourne Film Festival
(two weeks mid-Jun).
Australia's largest and most
popular film festival.

Aboriginal Dance Festival,
Cape York. Popular biennial,
alcohol-free celebration of
Aboriginal culture.
**Darling Harbour Jazz
Festival** *(mid-Jun – mid-Jul)*,
Sydney. Hugely popular
festival featuring bands.

JULY

Yulefest *(throughout Jul)*,
Blue Mountains. Hotels,
guesthouses and some
restaurants celebrate a mid-
winter "traditional Christmas"
with log fires and all the
usual yuletide trimmings.
Brass Monkey Festival,
(first weekend), Stanthorpe.
Inland Queensland turns the
freezing winter temperatures
into an opportunity for celebration *(see p232)*.
Alice Springs Show
(first weekend). Agricultural
and historical displays
combined with arts, crafts
and cookery demonstrations.
Cairns Show *(second
weekend)*. A cultural
celebration of historical and
contemporary life in the
Australian tropics *(see p246)*.

Camel Cup *(last weekend)*,
Alice Springs. Camel racing
on the dry Todd River.

Mount Isa Rodeo in August

AUGUST

Almond Blossom Festival
(first week), Mount Lofty. A
harvest festival and almond-
cracking competitions.
City to Surf Race *(second
Sun)*, Sydney A 14-km (9-
mile) fun run from the city
centre to Bondi Beach.
Shinju Matsuri Festival
(last weekend), Broome.
Oriental pearl festival.
Mount Isa Rodeo *(last
weekend)*. Australia's largest
rodeo event *(see p249)*.

Dragon Boat race, part of the Shinju Matsuri in Broome

The Climate of Australia

THIS VAST COUNTRY experiences a variable climate. Three-quarters of its land is desert or scrub and has low, unreliable rainfall. The huge, dry interior is hot year-round during the day but can be very cold at night. The southern half of Australia, including Tasmania, has warm summers and mild winters. Further north, seasonal variations lessen and the northern coast has just two seasons: the dry, and the wet, with its monsoon rains and occasional tropical cyclones.

NORTHERN QUEENSLAND

Average daily maximum temperature	30	32	29	26
Average daily minimum temperature	20	23	21	16
Average daily hours of sunshine	8 hrs	8 hrs	9 hrs	9 hrs
Average monthly rainfall	53 mm	422 mm	287 mm	41 mm
month	Jan	Apr	Jul	Oct

NORTH OF PERTH

°C				
	33	34	28	33
	26	22		22
			14	
	8 hrs	9 hrs	7 hrs	9 hrs
	160 mm	30 mm	5 mm	1 mm
month	Jan	Apr	Jul	Oct

DARWIN AND THE TOP END

°C				
	32	33	31	34
	25	24	19	25
	6 hrs	8 hrs	10 hrs	10 hrs
	386 mm	97 mm	0 mm	51 mm
month	Jan	Apr	Jul	Oct

THE RED CENTRE

°C				
	36	27	19	31
	21	12		14
			4	
	10 hrs	10 hrs	9 hrs	10 hrs
	43 mm	10 mm	8 mm	18 mm
month	Jan	Apr	Jul	Oct

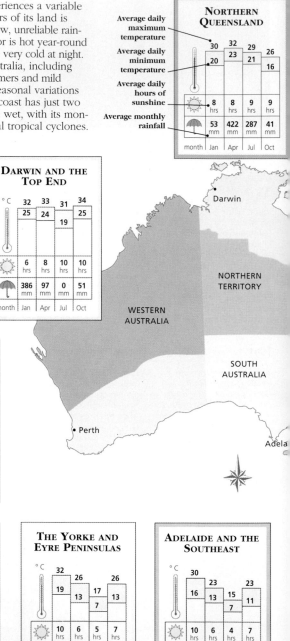

Darwin

NORTHERN TERRITORY

WESTERN AUSTRALIA

SOUTH AUSTRALIA

• Perth

Adela

PERTH AND THE SOUTHWEST

°C				
	29	24	17	21
	17	14	9	12
	10 hrs	7 hrs	5 hrs	8 hrs
	8 mm	43 mm	170 mm	56 mm
month	Jan	Apr	Jul	Oct

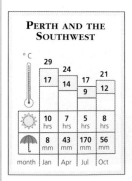

THE YORKE AND EYRE PENINSULAS

°C				
	32	26	17	26
	19	13	7	13
	10 hrs	6 hrs	5 hrs	7 hrs
	15 mm	18 mm	18 mm	23 mm
month	Jan	Apr	Jul	Oct

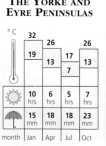

ADELAIDE AND THE SOUTHEAST

°C				
	30	23	15	23
	16	13	7	11
	10 hrs	6 hrs	4 hrs	7 hrs
	20 mm	46 mm	66 mm	43 mm
month	Jan	Apr	Jul	Oct

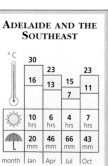

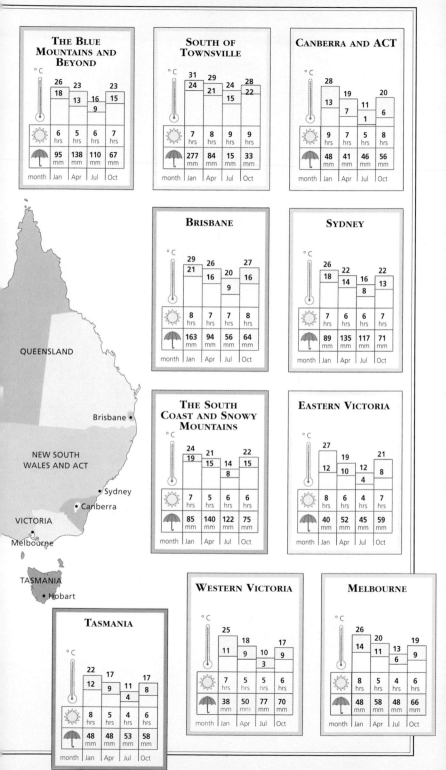

THE BLUE MOUNTAINS AND BEYOND

°C

26	23		23
18		16	15
	13	9	

6 hrs	5 hrs	6 hrs	7 hrs
95 mm	138 mm	110 mm	67 mm

| month | Jan | Apr | Jul | Oct |

SOUTH OF TOWNSVILLE

°C

31	29		28
24	21	24	22
		15	

7 hrs	8 hrs	9 hrs	9 hrs
277 mm	84 mm	15 mm	33 mm

| month | Jan | Apr | Jul | Oct |

CANBERRA AND ACT

°C

28	19		20
13	7	11	6
		1	

9 hrs	7 hrs	5 hrs	8 hrs
48 mm	48 mm	41 mm	56 mm

| month | Jan | Apr | Jul | Oct |

BRISBANE

°C

29	26		27
21	16	20	16
		9	

8 hrs	7 hrs	7 hrs	8 hrs
163 mm	94 mm	56 mm	64 mm

| month | Jan | Apr | Jul | Oct |

SYDNEY

°C

26	22		22
18	14	16	13
		8	

7 hrs	6 hrs	6 hrs	7 hrs
89 mm	135 mm	117 mm	71 mm

| month | Jan | Apr | Jul | Oct |

QUEENSLAND

Brisbane •

NEW SOUTH WALES AND ACT

• Sydney
• Canberra

VICTORIA
•
Melbourne

TASMANIA
• Hobart

THE SOUTH COAST AND SNOWY MOUNTAINS

°C

24	21		22
19	15	14	15
		8	

7 hrs	5 hrs	6 hrs	6 hrs
85 mm	140 mm	122 mm	75 mm

| month | Jan | Apr | Jul | Oct |

EASTERN VICTORIA

°C

27	19		21
12	10	12	8
		4	

8 hrs	6 hrs	4 hrs	7 hrs
40 mm	52 mm	45 mm	59 mm

| month | Jan | Apr | Jul | Oct |

TASMANIA

°C

22	17		17
12	9	11	8
		4	

8 hrs	5 hrs	4 hrs	6 hrs
48 mm	48 mm	53 mm	58 mm

| month | Jan | Apr | Jul | Oct |

WESTERN VICTORIA

°C

25	18		17
11	9	10	9
		3	

7 hrs	5 hrs	5 hrs	6 hrs
38 mm	50 mm	77 mm	70 mm

| month | Jan | Apr | Jul | Oct |

MELBOURNE

°C

26	20		19
14	11	13	9
		6	

8 hrs	5 hrs	4 hrs	6 hrs
48 mm	58 mm	48 mm	66 mm

| month | Jan | Apr | Jul | Oct |

THE HISTORY OF AUSTRALIA

USTRALIA *is a young nation in an ancient land. It is a nation of immigrants, past and present, forced and free. The first European settlers occupied a harsh country; they explored it, exploited its mineral wealth and farmed it. In so doing, they suffered at the hands of nature, as well as enduring depressions and wars. Out of all this, however, has emerged a modern and cosmopolitan society.*

The first rocks of the Australian landscape began to form some four-and-a-half billion years ago. Over time many older rocks were covered by more recent rocks, but in places such as the Pilbara region of Western Australia erosion has exposed a landscape 3,500 million years old *(see pp322–3)*. About 500 million years ago Australia, together with South America, South Africa, India and the Antarctic, formed a supercontinent known as Gondwanaland. This landmass moved through a series of different climatic zones; today's desert interior was once a shallow sea *(see pp18–19)*.

Australian coat of arms

THE FIRST IMMIGRANTS

Australia was first settled by Aboriginal people who arrived by sea from Asia more than 60,000 years ago. On landing, they quickly adapted to the climatic and geographical conditions. Nomadic hunters and gatherers, the Aborigines moved with the seasons and spread across the continent, reaching Tasmania 35,000 years ago. They had few material possessions beyond the tools and weapons required for hunting and obtaining food. The early tools, known today as core tools, were very simple chopping implements, roughly formed by grinding stone. By 8,000 BC Aborigines had developed the sophisticated returning boomerang *(see p26)* and possibly the world's first barbed spear. So-called flaked tools of varying styles were in use 5,000 years later, finely made out of grained stones such as flint to create sharp cutting edges.

Beneath the apparently simple way of life, Aboriginal society was complex. It was based on a network of mainly nomadic bands, comprising between 50 and 100 people, bound by kin relationships, who lived according to strictly applied laws and customs. These laws and beliefs, including the spiritual significance of the land, were upheld through a tradition of song, dance and art *(see pp26–9)*. With no centralized or formal system of government, individual groups were led by prominent, generally older men, who were held in great respect. Across the continent there were more than 200 languages spoken and approximately 800 dialects. In many respects, Aboriginal life

TIMELINE

60,000 BC	50,000 BC	40,000 BC	30,000 BC	20,000 BC	10,000 BC

43,000–38,000 BC Tools found in a grave pit beside Nepean River are among the oldest firmly dated signs of human occupation in Australia

35,000 BC Aborigines reach Tasmania

Diprotodon 20,000 BC

13,000 End of Ice Age

170–60,000 BC Aborigines thought to have reached Australia

42,000 BC Aboriginal engravings at Olary, South Australia

25,000 BC Woman is cremated at Lake Mungo – the world's oldest known cremation

20,000 BC Humans live in the Blue Mountains despite Ice Age. Remains of the largest marsupial, Diprotodon, date back to this period

◁ *Desmond, A New South Wales Chief (about 1825) by Augustus Earle*

was also very advanced: excavations at Lake Mungo provide fascinating evidence of ancient burial rituals, including what is believed to be the world's oldest cremation 25,000 years ago *(see p173).*

Woodcut of an "antipodean man" (1493)

THEORIES OF A SOUTHERN LAND

In Europe, the existence of a southern land was the subject of debate for centuries. As early as the 5th century BC, with the European discovery of Australia some 2,000 years away, the mathematician Pythagoras speculated on the presence of southern lands necessary to counterbalance those in the northern hemisphere. In about AD 150, the ancient geographer Ptolemy of Alexandria continued this speculation by drawing a map showing a landmass enclosing the Atlantic and Indian oceans. Some scholars went so far as to suggest that it was inhabited by "antipodes", a race of men whose feet faced backwards. Religious scholar St Augustine (AD 354–430) declared categorically that the southern hemisphere

contained no land; the contrary view was heretical. But not all men of religion agreed: the 1086 *Osma Beatus*, a series of maps illustrating the works of the monk Beatus, showed the hypothetical land as a populated region.

It was not until the 15th century, when Europe entered a golden age of exploration, that these theories were tested. Under the patronage of Prince Henry of Portugal (1394–1460), known as Henry the Navigator, Portuguese sailors crossed the equator for the first time in 1470. In 1488 they sailed around the southern tip of Africa, and by 1502 they claimed to have located a southern land while on a voyage to explore South America. The Italian navigator, Amerigo Vespucci, described it as Paradise, full of trees and colourful birds. The location of this land is not clear but it was definitely not Australia.

In 1519 another Portuguese expedition set off, under the command of Ferdinand Magellan, and was the first to circumnavigate the world. No drawings of the lands explored survive, but subsequent maps show Tierra del Fuego as the tip of a landmass south of the Americas. Between 1577 and 1580 the Englishman Sir Francis Drake also circumnavigated the world, but his maps indicate no such land. Meanwhile, maps prepared in Dieppe in France between 1540 and 1566 show a southern continent, Java la Grande, lying southeast of Indonesia.

THE DUTCH DISCOVERY

By the 17th century Portugal's power in Southeast Asia was beginning to wane, and Holland, with its control of the Dutch

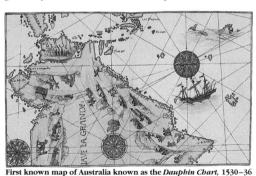

First known map of Australia known as the *Dauphin Chart,* 1530–36

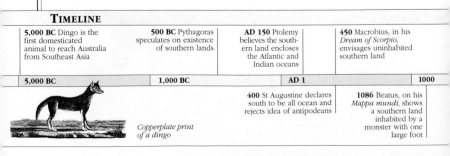

TIMELINE

5,000 BC Dingo is the first domesticated animal to reach Australia from Southeast Asia	500 BC Pythagoras speculates on existence of southern lands	AD 150 Ptolemy believes the southern land encloses the Atlantic and Indian oceans	450 Macrobius, in his *Dream of Scorpio,* envisages uninhabited southern land
5,000 BC	**1,000 BC**	**AD 1**	**1000**
		400 St Augustine declares south to be all ocean and rejects idea of antipodeans	1086 Beatus, on his *Mappa mundi,* shows a southern land inhabited by a monster with one large foot

Copperplate print of a dingo

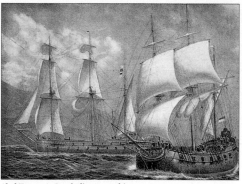

Abel Tasman's Dutch discovery ships

East Indies (Indonesia), was the new power and responsible for the eventual European discovery of Australia.

Willem Jansz, captain of the ship *Duyfken*, was in search of New Guinea, a land thought to be rich in gold, when he sailed along the Cape York Peninsula in 1606. He found the coast inhospitable and left the area quickly. In

1616 Dirk Hartog, commanding the *Eendracht*, was blown off course on his way to the East Indies. He landed on an island off Western Australia and nailed a pewter plate to a pole *(see p318)*.

Dutch navigator Abel Tasman charted large parts of Australia and New Zealand between 1642 and 1644, including Tasmania which he originally named Van Diemen's Land in honour of the Governor-General of the East Indies. The island eventually took Tasman's name in 1855.

The Dutch continued to explore the country for 150 years, but although their discoveries were of geographic interest they did not result in any economic benefit and they ceased exploring the land any further.

THE FIRST ENGLISHMAN

The first Englishman to land on Australian soil was the privateer and buccaneer William Dampier in 1688. Similarly unimpressed as his Dutch rivals with what he found, he nevertheless published a book of his journey, *New Voyage Round the World*, in 1697. Britain gave him command of the *Roebuck*, in which he explored the northwest Australian coast in great detail. His ship sank on the return voyage. The crew survived but Dampier was court martialled for the mistreatment of his subordinates.

THE FORGOTTEN SPANIARD

Bronze relief of Luis Vaez de Torres

In 1606, the same year that Willem Jansz first set foot on Australian soil, Luis Vaez de Torres, a Spanish Admiral, led an expedition in search of "Terra Australis". He sailed through the strait which now bears his name between Australia and New Guinea *(see p244)*. His discovery, however, was inexplicably ignored for 150 years. He sent news of his exploration to King Felipe III of Spain from the Philippines but died shortly after. Perhaps his early death meant that the news was not disseminated and the significance of his maps not realized.

Portrait of William Dampier

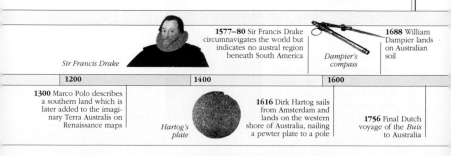

Sir Francis Drake

1577–80 Sir Francis Drake circumnavigates the world but indicates no austral region beneath South America

Dampier's compass

1688 William Dampier lands on Australian soil

1200	1400	1600

1300 Marco Polo describes a southern land which is later added to the imaginary Terra Australis on Renaissance maps

Hartog's plate

1616 Dirk Hartog sails from Amsterdam and lands on the western shore of Australia, nailing a pewter plate to a pole

1756 Final Dutch voyage of the *Buis* to Australia

The Colonization of Australia

Hat made from cabbage palm

B Y THE MID-18TH CENTURY England had taken over as the world's main maritime power. In 1768 Captain James Cook set off to find Australia in the *Endeavour* and in 1770 King George III formally claimed possession of the east coast, named New South Wales.

Overcrowding of jails and the loss of American colonies in the War of Independence led the English to establish a penal colony in the new land. The First Fleet, consisting of two men-of-war and nine transport ships, arrived in Sydney Cove in 1788. The initial settlement consisted of 750 convicts, approximately 210 marines and 40 women and children. Faced with great hardship, they survived in tents, eating local wildlife and rations from England.

Captain James Cook *(c.1800)*
The English navigator charted eastern Australia for the first time between 1770 and 1771.

Boat building at the Government dockyard

Aborigines depicted observing the new white settlement.

England Takes Possession
In 1770 the Union Jack was raised on the east coast of Australia, and England finally claimed possession of this new-found land.

Sir Joseph Banks
Aboard the Endeavour *with Captain Cook, botanist Joseph Banks was responsible for the proposal of Botany Bay as the first penal settlement.*

A VIEW OF SYDNEY COVE

This idyllic image, drawn by Edward Dayes and engraved by F Jukes in 1804, shows the Aboriginal peoples living peacefully within the infant colony alongside the flourishing maritime and agricultural industries. In reality, by the end of the 18th century they had been entirely ostracized from the life and prosperity of their native land. The first settlement was founded at Port Jackson, renamed Sydney Cove.

First Fleet Ship
This painting by Francis Holman (c.1787) shows three views of the Borrowdale, *one of the fleet's three commercial store ships.*

Scrimshaw
Engraving bone or shell was a skilful way to pass time during long months spent at sea.

Buildings looked impressive but were poorly built.

Convict housing

Governor Phillip's House, Sydney
This grand colonial mansion, flanked by landscaped gardens, was home to Australia's first government.

Barracks housing NSW Rum Corps

Prison Hulks
Old ships, unfit for naval service, were used as floating prisons to house convicts until the mid-19th century.

TIMELINE

1768 Captain James Cook sets out from England for Tahiti on his ship, the *Endeavour*

1775 English overcrowding of jails and prison hulks

Aborigine Bennelong

1788 Aborigine Bennelong is captured and held for five months, then taken to England to meet King George III

1770

1780

1790

1770 Cook discovers the east coast of Australia and takes possession for England

1779 Botanist Joseph Banks recommends Botany Bay for penal settlement

Merino sheep

1797 John Macarthur introduces merino sheep from the Cape of Good Hope (see p123)

EXPLORING THE COASTLINE

Once the survival of the first settlement was assured, both the government and the free settlers began to look beyond its confines. Faced with a vast, unknown continent and fuelled by desires for knowledge and wealth, they set out to explore the land. The 19th century was a period of exploration, discovery and settlement.

Between 1798 and 1799 the English midshipman Matthew Flinders and surgeon George Bass charted much of the Australian coastline south of Sydney. They also circumnavigated Tasmania, known at that time as Van Diemen's Land *(see p45)*. In 1801 Flinders was given command of the sloop *Investigator* and explored the entire Australian coastline, becoming the first man to successfully circumnavigate the whole continent.

John Batman and local Aboriginal chiefs

EXPLORING THE INTERIOR

Inland New South Wales was opened up for settlement in 1813, when George Blaxland, William Wentworth and William Lawson forged a successful route across the Blue Mountains *(see pp162–5)*. In 1824 explorers Hamilton Hume and William Hovell opened up the continent further when they travelled overland from New South Wales to Port Phillip Bay, the present site of Melbourne.

Between 1828 and 1830 Charles Sturt, a former secretary to the New South Wales Governor, led two expeditions along Australia's inland river systems. On his first journey he discovered the Darling River. His second expedition began in Sydney and followed the Murray River to the sea in South Australia. This arduous task left Sturt, like many such explorers before and after him, suffering from ill health for the rest of his life.

Sturt's party shown being attacked by Aborigines on their journey to the Murray River

NEW COLONIES

Individual colonies began to emerge across the continent throughout the 19th century. First settled in 1804, Tasmania became a separate colony in 1825; in 1829 Western Australia became a colony with the establishment of Perth. Originally a colony of free settlers, a labour shortage led to the westward transportation of convicts.

In 1835 a farmer, John Batman, signed a contract with local Aborigines to acquire 250,000 ha (600,000 acres) of land where Melbourne now stands *(see p373)*. His action resulted in a rush for land in the area. The settlement was recognized in 1837, and the separate colony of Victoria was proclaimed in 1851, at the start of its gold rush *(see pp50–51)*. Queensland became a separate colony in 1859.

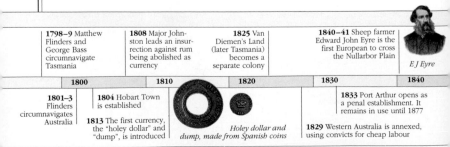

1798–9 Matthew Flinders and George Bass circumnavigate Tasmania	1808 Major Johnston leads an insurrection against rum being abolished as currency	1825 Van Diemen's Land (later Tasmania) becomes a separate colony	1840–41 Sheep farmer Edward John Eyre is the first European to cross the Nullarbor Plain *E J Eyre*

1800	1810	1820	1830	1840

1801–3 Flinders circumnavigates Australia	1804 Hobart Town is established 1813 The first currency, the "holey dollar" and "dump", is introduced	*Holey dollar and dump, made from Spanish coins*	1833 Port Arthur opens as a penal establishment. It remains in use until 1877 1829 Western Australia is annexed, using convicts for cheap labour

A typical colonial house in Hobart Town (now Hobart), Tasmania, during its early days in 1856

South Australia was established in 1836 as Australia's only convict-free colony. Based on a theory formulated by a group of English reformers, the colony was funded by land sales which paid for public works and the transportation of free labourers. It became a haven for religious dissenters, a tradition that still continues today.

CROSSING THE CONTINENT

Edward John Eyre, a sheep farmer who arrived from England in 1833, was the first European to cross the Nullarbor Plain from Adelaide to Western Australia in 1840.

In 1859 the South Australian government, anxious to build an overland telegraph from Adelaide to the north coast, offered a reward to the first person to cross the continent from south to north. An expedition of 20 to 40 men and camels left Melbourne in 1860 under the command of police officer Robert O'Hara Burke and surveyor William Wills. Burke, Wills and two other men travelled from their base camp at Cooper Creek to the tidal mangroves of the Flinders River which they mistook

THE RUM REBELLION

In 1808, the military, under the command of Major George Johnston and John Macarthur *(see p123)*, staged an insurrection known as the Rum Rebellion. At stake was the military's control of the profitable rum trade. Governor William Bligh (1754– 1817), target of a mutiny when captain of the *Bounty*, was arrested after he tried to stop rum being used as currency. The military held power for 23 months until government was restored by Governor Lachlan Macquarie.

William Bligh

for the ocean, before heading back south. They returned to the base camp only hours after the main party, who now believed them dead, had left. Burke and Wills died at the base camp from starvation and fatigue.

The crossing from south to north was finally completed by John McDouall Stuart in 1862. He returned to Adelaide sick with scurvy and almost blind.

The return of Burke and Wills to Cooper Creek in 1860

The 1850s Gold Rush

GOLD WAS DISCOVERED near Bathurst in New South Wales and at Ballarat and Bendigo in Victoria in 1851. Established towns were almost deserted as men from all over the country, together with immigrants from Europe and China, rushed to the gold fields. Some became extremely wealthy, while others returned empty-handed. By the 1880s, Australia was a prosperous country and cities were lined with ornate architecture, some of which was constructed by the last waves of convict labour. Despite gold found in Western Australia in the 1890s, however, the final decade of the 19th century was a period of depression, when wool prices fell, Victoria's land boom collapsed and the nation suffered a severe drought.

19th-century gold decoration

Edward Hargraves
In 1851 Hargraves made his name by discovering gold in Bathurst, New South Wales.

Panning dish

Lamp

Pick axe

Gold Mining Utensils
Mining for gold was initially an unskilled and laborious process that required only a few basic utensils. A panning dish to swill water, a pick axe to loosen rock and a miner's lamp were all that were needed to commence the search.

Eureka Stockade
In 1854 an insurrection took place just outside the town of Ballarat when miners rebelled against costly licences and burned them at a stockade (see p424).

DIGGING FOR GOLD

Edwin Stocqueler's painting *Australian Gold Diggings* (1855) shows the varying methods of gold mining and the hard work put in by thousands of diggers in their quest for wealth. As men and their families came from all over the world to make their fortune, regions rich in gold, in particular Victoria, thrived. Previous wastelands were turned into tent settlements and gradually grew into impressive new cities.

Might versus Right *(c.1861)*
ST Gill's painting depicts the riots on the Lambing Flag gold fields in New South Wales in 1861. Chinese immigrants, who came to Australia in search of gold, were met with violent racism by European settlers who felt their wealth and position were in jeopardy.

Tent villages covered the Victoria landscape in the 1850s.

Gold panning was the most popular extraction method.

Prosperity in Bendigo
The buildings of Williamson Street in Bendigo (see p422) display the prosperity that resulted from gold finds in Victoria.

Chinese Miners' Medal
Racism against the Chinese eventually subsided. This medal was given by the Chinese to the district of Braidwood, Victoria, in 1881.

Miners wore hats and heavyweight trousers to protect them from the sun.

The sluice was a trough which trapped gold in its bars as water was flushed through.

Gold Prospecting Camel Team
Just as the gold finds dried up in Victoria, gold was discovered in Western Australia in the 1890s. Prospectors crossed the continent to continue their search.

Souvenir handkerchief of the Australian Federation

FEDERAL BEGINNINGS

Following the economic depression at the end of the 19th century, Australia entered the 20th century on an optimistic note: the federation of its six colonies formed the Australian nation on 1 January 1901. Within the federation, there was one matter on which almost everyone agreed: Australia would remain "European" with strong ties to Britain. One of the first acts of the new parliament was to legislate the White Australia Policy. The Immigration Restriction Act required anyone wishing to emigrate to Australia to pass a dictation test in a European language. Unwanted immigrants were tested in obscure languages such as Gaelic. Between 1901 and 1910 there were nine different governments led by five different prime ministers. None of the three major political groups, the Protectionists, the Free Traders and the Labor Party, had sufficient support to govern in its own right. By 1910, however, voters were offered a clear choice between two parties, Labor and Liberal. The Labor Party won a landslide victory and since then the Australian government has come solely from one of these two parties.

A CALL FROM THE DARDANEL...

"Coo-...
Won't y...
come...

ENLIST NOW

Enlisting poster

WORLD WAR I

When Britain entered World War I in 1914, Australia followed to defend the "mother land". Most Australians supported the war, but they would not accept conscription or compulsory national service.

Australia paid a very high price for its allegiance, with 64 per cent of the 331,781 troops killed or wounded. Memorials to those who fought and died are found throughout the country, ranging from the simple to the impressive such as the Australian War Memorial in Canberra (see pp192–3). World War I was a defining moment in Australia's history. Anzac Day, rather than Australia Day, is felt by many to be the true national day. It commemorates the landing of the Australian and New Zealand Army Corps at Gallipoli in Turkey on the 25th April 1915, for their unsuccessful attempt to cross the Dardanelles and

LABOR STANDS FOR ALL WHO WORK!
VOTE LABOR

Labor government publicity poster

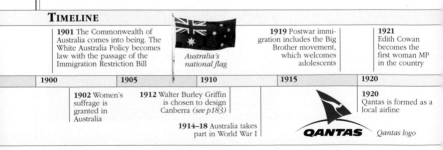

TIMELINE

1901 The Commonwealth of Australia comes into being. The White Australia Policy becomes law with the passage of the Immigration Restriction Bill		*Australia's national flag*		**1919** Postwar immigration includes the Big Brother movement, which welcomes adolescents	**1921** Edith Cowan becomes the first woman MP in the country
1900	**1905**		**1910**	**1915**	**1920**
	1902 Women's suffrage is granted in Australia	**1912** Walter Burley Griffin is chosen to design Canberra (see p183)	**1914–18** Australia takes part in World War I	*QANTAS*	**1920** Qantas is formed as a local airline *Qantas logo*

link up with the Russians. This was the first battle in which Australian soldiers fought as a national force and, although a failure, they gained a reputation for bravery and endurance. It is an event which many believe determined the Australian character and saw the real birth of the Australian nation.

BETWEEN THE WARS

During the 1920s, Australia, boosted by the arrival of some 300,000 immigrants, entered a period of major development. In 1920 Qantas (Queensland and Northern Territory Aerial Service Ltd) was formed, which was to become the national airline, and made its first international flight in 1934. Building of the Sydney Harbour Bridge began in 1923 *(see pp 76–7)*. Australia's population reached 6 million in 1925, but this new optimism was not to last.

In 1929 Australia, along with much of the world, went into economic decline. Wool and wheat prices, the country's major export earners, fell dramatically. By 1931, a third of the

Celebrating the opening of Sydney Harbour Bridge

country was unemployed. People slept in tents in city parks; swagmen (workers with their possessions on their backs) appeared as men left cities in search of work in the country.

Prices began to increase again by 1933 and manufacturing revived. From 1934 to 1937 the economy improved and unemployment fell. The following year, however, Australia again faced the prospect of war.

WORLD WAR II

Though World War II was initially a European war, Australians again fought in defence of freedom and the "mother land". However, when Japan entered the war, Australians felt for the first time that their national security was at risk. In 1942 Darwin, Broome and Townsville were bombed by the Japanese, the first act of war on Australian soil. The same year two Japanese midget submarines entered Sydney Harbour.

Britain asked for more Australian troops but for the first time they were refused: the men were needed in the

Swagmen during the Great Depression

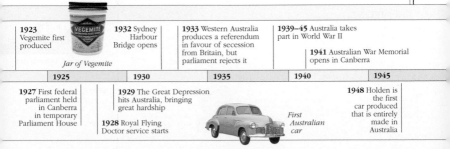

1923 Vegemite first produced	1932 Sydney Harbour Bridge opens	1933 Western Australia produces a referendum in favour of secession from Britain, but parliament rejects it	1939–45 Australia takes part in World War II
Jar of Vegemite			1941 Australian War Memorial opens in Canberra

1925	1930	1935	1940	1945

1927 First federal parliament held in Canberra in temporary Parliament House	1929 The Great Depression hits Australia, bringing great hardship		1948 Holden is the first car produced that is entirely made in Australia
	1928 Royal Flying Doctor service starts	*First Australian car*	

Pacific. This was a major shift in Australian foreign policy away from Britain and towards the USA. Australians fought alongside the Americans in the Pacific and nearly 250,000 US troops spent time in Australia during the war. This led, in 1951, to the signing of Australia's first defence treaty with a foreign country: the ANZUS treaty between Australia, New Zealand and the United States.

Again, war affected most Australian communities and towns. Nearly one million of Australia's seven million population went to fight: 34,000 were killed and 180,000 wounded.

Poster promoting travel and tourism in 1950s Australia

immigrants arrived in Australia in the 20 years following World War II, 800,000 of whom were not British. In 1956, the status of "permanent resident" allowed non-Europeans to claim citizenship. In 1958, the dictation entry test was abolished. Yet until 1966 non-Europeans had to have 15 years' residence before gaining citizenship, as opposed to five years for Europeans.

THE MENZIES ERA

From 1949 until 1966, Prime Minister Robert Menzies "reigned", winning eight consecutive elections. The increasing population and international demand for Australian raw materials during this time provided a high standard of living.

POSTWAR IMMIGRATION

The proximity of the fighting in World War II left Australia feeling vulnerable. The future defence of the country was seen to be dependent upon a strong economy and a larger population.

The postwar immigration programme welcomed not only British immigrants but also Europeans. Almost two million

British migrants arriving in Sydney in 1967 as part of the postwar wave of immigration

MABO AND BEYOND

In 1982, Edward Koiki (Eddie) Mabo, a Torres Strait Islander, took action against the Queensland government claiming that his people had ancestral land rights. After a ten-year battle, the High Court ruled that

Edward Koiki Mabo

Aborigines and Torres Strait Islanders may hold native title to land where there has been no loss of traditional connection. This ended the concept of *terra nullius* – that Australia belonged to no one when Europeans arrived there – and acknowledged that Aborigines held a valid title to their land. Subsequent legislation has provided a framework for assessing such claims.

TIMELINE

1955 Australian troops sent to Malaya

1966–72 Demonstrations against the Vietnam War

1958 Immigration dictation test abolished

1967 Referendum on Aborigines ends legal discrimination

1973 Sydney Opera House opens (see pp80–81)

Sydney Opera House

| 1955 | 1960 | 1965 | 1970 | 1975 |

1956 Melbourne hosts the Olympic Games

1965 Australian troops sent to Vietnam as part of their National Service

Neville Bonner

1971 Neville Bonner becomes Australia's first Aboriginal MP

1972 Edward Gough Whitlam elected as first Labor prime minister since 1949

1976 "Advance Australia Fa becomes national anthem

Anti-Vietnam demonstrations as US President Johnson arrives in Australia

In 1972, the Labor Party, under Edward Gough Whitlam, was elected on a platform of social reform. They abolished conscription, introduced free university education, lowered the voting age from 21 to 18 and gave some land rights to Aborigines. In 1974, an immigration policy without any racial discrimination was adopted. At the same time, however, inflation was increasing and there was talk of economic mismanagement.

Menzies understood his people's desire for peace and prosperity, and gave Australians conservatism and stability. He did, however, also involve them in three more wars, in Korea (1950), Malaya (1955) and Vietnam (1965). Vietnam was the first time Australia fought in a war in which Britain was not also engaged.

SOCIAL UNREST AND CHANGE

Opposition to conscription and the Vietnam War increased in the late 1960s and led to major demonstrations in the capital cities. At the same time there was concern for issues such as Aboriginal land rights and free education. In 1967, a constitutional referendum was passed by 90.8 per cent of the voters, ending the ban on Aboriginal inclusion in the national census. It also gave power to the federal government to legislate for Aborigines in all states, ending state discriminations.

RETURN TO CONSERVATISM

In 1975, the Liberal leader Malcolm Fraser won the election. Subsequent governments, both Liberal under Fraser (1975–83) and Labor under Bob Hawke and Paul Keating (1983–96), were more concerned with economic rather than social agendas.

Australia emulated most of the Western world with an economic boom in the 1980s, followed by recession in the 1990s. During this period Australia shifted its focus from Europe towards Asia and, by 1986, all legislative ties with Great Britain were broken.

The year 2000 saw Sydney host the Summer Olympic Games (*see p139*). The occasion was regarded as a positive start to the new millennium, as Australia looked to a new future, boosted by the stability of its past.

Prime Minister Whitlam hands over
Aboriginal land rights in 1975

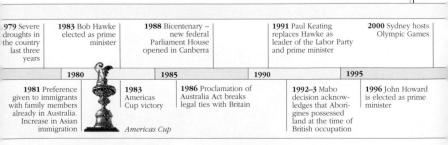

1979 Severe droughts in the country last three years

1983 Bob Hawke elected as prime minister

1988 Bicentenary – new federal Parliament House opened in Canberra

1991 Paul Keating replaces Hawke as leader of the Labor Party and prime minister

2000 Sydney hosts Olympic Games

1980	1985	1990	1995

1981 Preference given to immigrants with family members already in Australia. Increase in Asian immigration

1983 Americas Cup victory

Americas Cup

1986 Proclamation of Australia Act breaks legal ties with Britain

1992–3 Mabo decision acknowledges that Aborigines possessed land at the time of British occupation

1996 John Howard is elected as prime minister

SYDNEY

Central Sydney

THIS GUIDE DIVIDES the centre of Sydney into four distinct areas, and the majority of the city's main sights are contained in these districts. The Rocks and Circular Quay are the oldest part of inner Sydney. The City Centre is the central business district, and to its west lies Darling Harbour, which includes Sydney's well-known Chinatown. The Botanic Gardens and The Domain form a green oasis almost in the heart of the city. To the east are Kings Cross and Darlinghurst, hub of the café culture, and Paddington, an area that still retains its charming 19th-century character.

The Lord Nelson Hotel *is a traditional pub in The Rocks (see p467) which first opened its doors in 1834. Its own specially brewed beers are available on tap.*

KEY

	Major sight
	Other building
🚄	CityRail station
🚝	Monorail station
🚈	Sydney Light Rail station (SLR)
🚌	Bus terminus
🚍	Coach station
⛴	Ferry boarding point
🚢	JetCat/RiverCat boarding point
🚓	Police station
P	Parking
i	Tourist information
✚	Hospital with casualty unit
✝	Church
✡	Synagogue

Queen Victoria Building *is a Romanesque former produce market, built in the 1890s. It forms part of a fine group of Victorian buildings in the City Centre (see p86). Now a shopping mall, it retains many of its original features, including its ornate roof statues.*

◁ **Sydneysiders enjoying the sunshine in front of the distinctive Sydney Opera House**

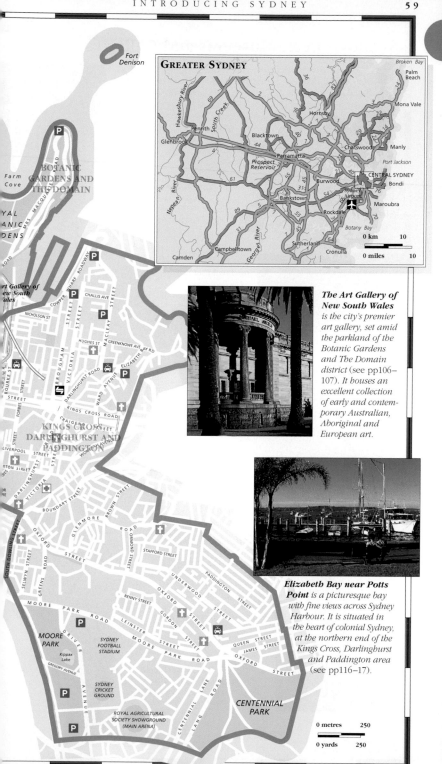

GREATER SYDNEY

Fort Denison

Broken Bay
Palm Beach
Mona Vale
Hornsby
Hawkesbury River
South Creek
Penrith
Blacktown
Glenbrock
Parramatta
Prospect Reservoir
Chatswood
Manly
Port Jackson
CENTRAL SYDNEY
Burwood
Bondi
Sydney Airport
Bankstown
Maroubra
Rockdale
Botany Bay
Sutherland
Cronulla
Campbelltown
Camden
Georges River
Nepean River

0 km 10
0 miles 10

BOTANIC GARDENS AND THE DOMAIN

Farm Cove

ROYAL BOTANIC GARDENS

Art Gallery of New South Wales

KINGS CROSS, DARLINGHURST AND PADDINGTON

MOORE PARK
Kippax Lake
SYDNEY FOOTBALL STADIUM
SYDNEY CRICKET GROUND
ROYAL AGRICULTURAL SOCIETY SHOWGROUND (MAIN ARENA)
CENTENNIAL PARK
STAFFORD STREET

0 metres 250
0 yards 250

The Art Gallery of New South Wales is the city's premier art gallery, set amid the parkland of the Botanic Gardens and The Domain district (see pp106–107). It houses an excellent collection of early and contemporary Australian, Aboriginal and European art.

Elizabeth Bay near Potts Point is a picturesque bay with fine views across Sydney Harbour. It is situated in the heart of colonial Sydney, at the northern end of the Kings Cross, Darlinghurst and Paddington area (see pp116–17).

Sydney's Best: Museums and Galleries

SYDNEY IS WELL ENDOWED with museums and galleries, and, following the current appreciation of social history, much emphasis is placed on the lifestyles of past and present Sydneysiders. Small museums are also a feature of the Sydney scene, with a number of historic houses recalling the colonial days. Most of the major collections are housed in architecturally significant buildings – the Classical façade of the Art Gallery of NSW makes it a city landmark, while the MCA or Museum of Contemporary Art has given new life to a 1950s Art Deco-style building at Circular Quay.

Bima figure, Powerhouse Museum

The Museum of Sydney includes The Edge of the Trees, *an interactive installation* (see p88).

THE ROCKS AND CIRCULAR QUAY

The Australian Centre for Craft and Design, set in the Customs House, shows Australian and international craft and design (see p79).

CITY CENTRE AND DARLING HARBOUR

The Museum of Contemporary Art has an excellent Aboriginal art section, with works such as Mud Crabs by Tony Dhanyula Nyoka, a Ramingining artist (see p74).

The National Maritime Museum is the home port for HMB Endeavour, a replica of the vessel that charted Australia's east coast in 1770, with Captain Cook in command (see pp96–7).

The Powerhouse Museum, set in a former power station, uses both traditional and interactive displays to explore Australian innovations in science and technology (see pp98–9).

0 metres   500

0 yards   500

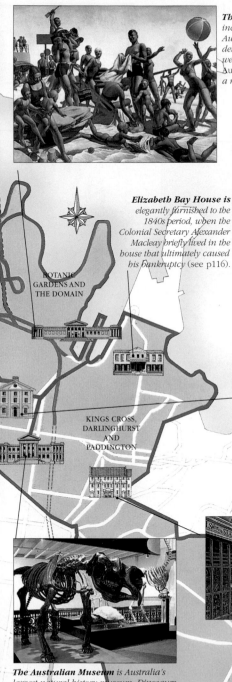

The Art Gallery of New South Wales *includes colonial watercolours in its Australian collection, which, to avoid deterioration, are only shown for a few weeks each year. Charles Meere's Australian Beach Pattern (1940) is a recent work (see pp106–109).*

Elizabeth Bay House is *elegantly furnished to the 1840s period, when the Colonial Secretary Alexander Macleay briefly lived in the house that ultimately caused his bankruptcy (see p116).*

BOTANIC GARDENS AND THE DOMAIN

KINGS CROSS, DARLINGHURST AND PADDINGTON

The Hyde Park Barracks were *originally built by convicts for their own incarceration. They were later home to poor female immigrants. Exhibits recall the daily life of these occupants (see p110).*

The Sydney Jewish Museum *documents the history of the city's Jewish community. Exhibits include reconstructed scenes, such as George Street in 1848, a Jewish business area (see p74).*

The Australian Museum *is Australia's largest natural history museum. Dinosaurs such as this large mammal or "megafauna" Diprotodon skeleton are a major attraction (see pp90–91).*

Sydney's Best: Architecture

For such a young city, Sydney possesses a great
diversity of architectural styles. They range from
the simplicity of Francis Greenway's Georgian buildings *(see p161)* to Jørn Utzon's Expressionist Sydney
Opera House *(see pp80–81)*. Practical colonial structures gave way to elaborate Victorian edifices such as
Sydney Town Hall. The same passion for detail is seen
in Paddington's terraces. Later, Federation warehouses
and bungalows introduced a uniquely Australian style.

*Colonial convict structures were
simple with shingled roofs, based
on the English homes of the first
settlers. Cadman's Cottage
is an example of this style
(see p74).*

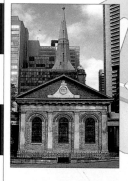

Contemporary
*architecture abounds in
Sydney, including
Governor Phillip Tower.
The Museum of Sydney is
at its base (see p88).*

Colonial Georgian *buildings
include St James Church (see
p111). Francis Greenway's
design was adapted to suit
the purposes of a church.*

***American
Revivalism*** *took
up the 1890s vogue
of arcades connec-
ting many differ-
ent streets. The
Queen Victoria
Building is a fine
example (see p86).*

THE ROCKS
AND
CIRCULAR
QUAY

Victorian
*architecture
abounds in the city.
Sydney Town Hall
includes a metal
ceiling, installed for
fear that the organ
would vibrate a plaster
one loose (see p89).*

CITY
CENTRE &
DARLING
HARBOUR

Contemporary Expressionism's *main
emphasis is roof design and the silhouette.
Innovations were made in sports stadiums
and museums, such as the National
Maritime Museum (see p96–7).*

Interwar Architecture
*encapsulates the spirit of Art Deco,
as seen in the Anzac Memorial in
Hyde Park (see p89).*

0 metres   500
0 yards   500

Modern Expressionism includes one of the world's greatest examples of 20th-century architecture. The construction of Jørn Utzon's Sydney Opera House began in 1959. Despite the architect's resignation in 1966, it was opened in 1973 (see pp80–81).

Australian Regency was popular during the 1830s. The best-designed villas were the work of John Verge. The beautiful Elizabeth Bay House is considered his masterpiece (see p116).

BOTANIC GARDENS AND THE DOMAIN

Early Colonial's first buildings, such as Hyde Park Barracks (see p110), were mainly built for the government.

KINGS CROSS, DARLINGHURST & PADDINGTON

Colonial military buildings were both functional and ornate. Victoria Barracks, designed by engineers, is a fine example of a Georgian military compound (see p120).

Victorian iron lace incorporated filigree of cast-iron in prefabricated patterns. Paddington's verandas are fine examples of this 1880s style (see pp118–19).

Colonial Grecian and Greek Revival were the most popular styles for public buildings designed during the 1820–50 period. The Darlinghurst Court House is a particularly fine example (see p117).

Sydney's Best: Parks and Reserves

Flannel flower

SYDNEY IS ALMOST completely surrounded by national parks and intact bushland. There are also a number of national parks and reserves within Greater Sydney itself. Here, the visitor can gain some idea of how the landscape looked before the arrival of European settlers. The city parks, too, are filled with plant and animal life. The more formal plantings of both native and exotic species are countered by the indigenous birds and animals that have adapted and made the urban environment their home. One of the highlights of a trip to Sydney is the huge variety of birds to be seen, from large birds of prey such as sea eagles and kites, to the shyer species such as wrens and tiny finches.

Garigal National Park *is made up of rainforest and moist gullies, which provide shelter for superb lyrebirds and sugar gliders.*

North Arm Walk is covered in spring with grevilleas and flannel flowers blooming profusely.

Lane Cove National Park *is an open eucalypt forest dotted with grass trees, as well as fine stands of blue gums and apple gums. The rosella, a type of parrot, is common in the area.*

Bicentennial Park *is situated at Homebush Bay (see p139). The park features a mangrove habitat and attracts many water birds, including pelicans.*

Hyde Park *is situated on the edge of the city centre (see p89). The park provides a peaceful respite from the hectic streets. The native iris is just one of the plants found in the lush gardens. The sacred ibis, a water bird, is often seen.*

Middle Head and Obelisk Bay are dotted with gun emplacements, tunnels and bunkers built in the 1870s to protect Sydney from invasion. The superb fairy wren lives here, and water dragons can at times be seen basking on rocks.

North Head is covered with coastal heathland, with banksias, tea trees and casuarinas dominating the cliff tops. On the leeward side, moist forest surrounds tiny, secluded harbour beaches.

Grotto Point's paths, winding through the bush to the lighthouse, are lined with bottlebrushes, grevilleas and flannel flowers.

Bradleys Head is a nesting place for the ringtail possum. Noisy flocks of rainbow lorikeets are also often in residence. The views across the harbour to Sydney are spectacular.

South Head contains unique plant species such as the sundew.

Nielsen Park is inhabited by the kookaburra, easily identified by its call, which sounds like laughter.

The Domain features palms and Moreton Bay figs. The Australian magpie, with its black and white plumage, is a frequent visitor (see p105).

Moore Park is filled with huge Moreton Bay figs which provide an urban habitat for the flying fox.

Centennial Park contains open expanses and groves of paperbark and eucalypt trees, bringing sulphur-crested cockatoos en masse. The brushtail possum is a shy creature that comes out at night (see p121).

0 kilometres   4

0 miles   2

Garden Island to Farm Cove

Waterlily in the Royal Botanic Gardens

SYDNEY'S VAST HARBOUR, also named Port Jackson after a Secretary in the British Admiralty who promptly changed his name, is a drowned river valley which was transformed over millions of years. Its intricate coastal geography of headlands and secluded bays can sometimes con-found even lifelong residents. This waterway was the lifeblood of the early colony, with the maritime industry a vital source of wealth and supply. The legacies of recessions and booms can be viewed along the shoreline: a representation of a nation where an estimated 70 per cent of the population cling to the coastal cities, especially in the east.

The city skyline *is a result of random development. The 1960s' destruction of architectural history was halted, and towers now stand amid Victorian buildings.*

Two harbour beacons, *known as "wedding cakes" because of their three tiers, are solar powered and equipped with a fail-safe back-up service. There are around 350 buoys and beacons now in operation.*

The barracks for the naval garrison date from 1888.

Garden Island marks a 1940s con-struction project with 12 ha (30 acres) reclaimed from the harbour.

Sailing on the harbour *is a pastime not exclusively reserved for the rich elite. Of the several hundred thousand pleasure boats registered, some are available for hire while others take out groups of inexperienced sailors.*

Mrs Macquaries Chair *is a carved rock seat by Mrs Macquaries Road (see p104). In the early days of the colony this was the site of a fruit and vegetable garden which was farmed until 1805.*

0 metres   250

0 yards   250

The Andrew (Boy) Charlton Pool *is a favourite bathing spot for inner-city residents, and is named after the 16-year old who won an Olympic gold medal in 1924. It was erected in 1963 on the Domain Baths' site, which had a grandstand for 1,700.*

Woolloomooloo Finger Wharf was a disembarkation point when most travellers arrived by sea.

LOCATOR MAP
See Street Finder, *map 2*

Harry's Café de Wheels, a snack van, has been a Sydney culinary institution for more than 50 years. Photographs of celebrity customers are pinned to the van, attesting to its fame.

The Royal Botanic Gardens display both flowering and non-flowering plants. Here the first trees were planted by the new European colonists; some of these trees survive today (see pp102–103).

Farm Cove has long been a mooring place for visiting naval vessels. The land opposite, now the Botanic Gardens, has been continuously cultivated for over 200 years.

Sydney Cove to Walsh Bay

Conservatorium of Music

IT IS ESTIMATED that over 70 km (43 miles) of harbour foreshore have been lost as a result of the massive land reclamation projects carried out since the 1840s. That the 13 islands existing when the First Fleet arrived in 1788 have now been reduced to just eight is a startling indication of rapid and profound geographical transformation.

Detail from railing at Circular Quay

Redevelopments around the Circular Quay and Walsh Bay area from the 1980s have opened up the waterfront for public use and enjoyment, acknowledging it as the city's greatest natural asset. Sydney's environmental and architectural aspirations recognize the need to integrate city and harbour.

1857 Man O'War Steps

The Sydney Opera House *was designed to take advantage of its spectacular setting. The roofs shine during the day and seem to glow at night. The building appears as a visionary landscape to the onlooker* (see pp80–81).

Government House, a Gothic Revival building, was home to the state's governors until 1996.

Harbour cruises *regularly depart from Circular Quay, taking visitors out and about both during the day and in the evening. They are an incomparable way to see the city and its waterways.*

The Sydney Harbour Bridge *was also known as the "Iron Lung" at the time of its construction. During the Great Depression it provided on-site work for approximately 1,400, while others worked in specialist workshops* (see p76–7).

| 0 metres | 250 |
| 0 yards | 250 |

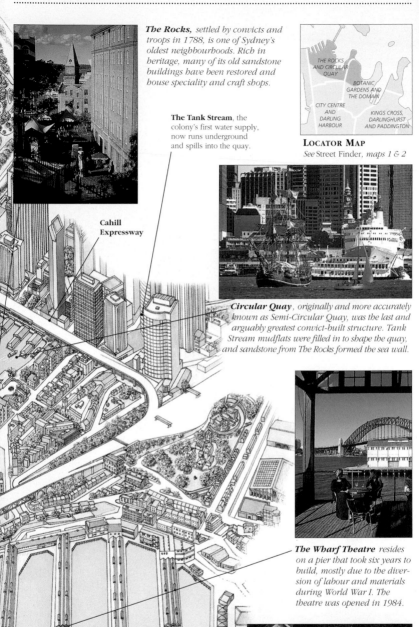

The Rocks, settled by convicts and troops in 1788, is one of Sydney's oldest neighbourhoods. Rich in heritage, many of its old sandstone buildings have been restored and house speciality and craft shops.

The Tank Stream, the colony's first water supply, now runs underground and spills into the quay.

LOCATOR MAP
See Street Finder, *maps 1 & 2*

Cahill Expressway

Circular Quay, originally and more accurately known as Semi-Circular Quay, was the last and arguably greatest convict-built structure. Tank Stream mudflats were filled in to shape the quay, and sandstone from The Rocks formed the sea wall.

The Wharf Theatre resides on a pier that took six years to build, mostly due to the diversion of labour and materials during World War I. The theatre was opened in 1984.

The wharves were completed in 1922.

The wharves' design included a rat-proof sea wall around the port. This was an urgent response to the 1900 bubonic plague outbreak, attributed to rats on the wharves.

Imports and exports to and from the city were stored in these wharves until 1977.

THE ROCKS AND CIRCULAR QUAY

CIRCULAR QUAY, once known as Semi-Circular Quay, is often referred to as the "birthplace of Australia". It was here, in January 1788, that the First Fleet landed its human freight of convicts, soldiers and officials, and the new British colony of New South Wales was declared. Sydney Cove became a rallying point whenever a ship arrived bringing much-needed supplies from "home". Crowds still gather here whenever there is a national or civic celebration. The Quay and The Rocks are focal points for New Year's Eve festivities. Circular Quay was the setting for huge crowds when, in 1994, Sydney was awarded the year 2000 Olympic Games. The Rocks area offers visitors a taste of Sydney's past, but it is a far cry from the time, less than 100 years ago, when most inhabitants lived in rat-infested slums, and gangs ruled its streets. Now scrubbed and polished, The Rocks forms part of the colourful promenade from the Sydney Harbour Bridge to the spectacular Sydney Opera House.

Sculpture on the AMP Building, Circular Quay

SIGHTS AT A GLANCE

Museums and Galleries
Justice and Police Museum ⓯
Museum of
    Contemporary Art ❷
National Trust Centre ⓫
The Rocks Toy Museum ❺
Sailors' Home ❹
Susannah Place ❶

Theatres and Concert Halls
*Sydney Opera House
    pp80–81* ⓱

Historic Streets and Buildings
Cadman's Cottage ❸
Campbell's Storehouses ❻
Customs House ⓮
Hero of Waterloo Hotel ❽
Macquarie Place ⓭
*Sydney Harbour Bridge
    pp76–7* ❼

Sydney Observatory ❿
Writers' Walk ⓰

Churches
Garrison Church ❾
St Philip's Church ⓬

GETTING THERE
Circular Quay is the best stop for ferries and trains. Sydney Explorer and bus routes 431, 432, 433 and 434 run regularly to The Rocks, while most buses through the city go to the Quay.

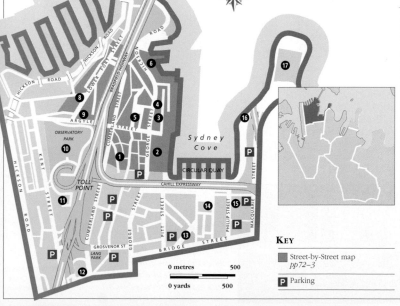

KEY

▨	Street-by-Street map *pp72–3*
P	Parking

◁ **The brilliant white walls of the Sailors' Home, home to the Sydney Visitor Centre in The Rocks**

Street-by-Street: The Rocks

Governor Arthur Phillip

NAMED FOR THE RUGGED CLIFFS that were once its dominant feature, this area has played a vital role in Sydney's development. In 1788, the First Fleeters under Governor Phillip's command erected makeshift buildings here, with the convicts' hard labour used to establish more permanent structures in the form of rough-hewn streets. The Argyle Cut, a road carved through solid rock using just hammer and chisel, took 18 years to build, beginning in 1843. By 1900, The Rocks was overrun with disease; the street now known as Suez Canal was once Sewer's Canal. Today, the area is still rich in colonial history and colour.

Hero of Waterloo
Lying beneath this historic pub is a tunnel originally used for smuggling **8**

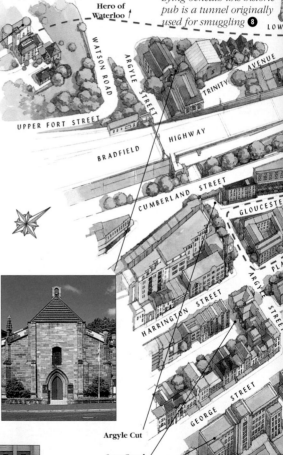

★ Sydney Observatory
The first European struc-ture on this prominent site was a windmill. The present museum holds some of the earliest astro-nomical instruments brought to Australia **10**

Garrison Church
Columns in this church are decorated with the insignia of British troops stationed here until 1870. Australia's first prime minister was educated next door **9**

Argyle Cut

Suez Canal

★ Museum of Contemporary Art
The stripped Classical façade belies the avant-garde nature of the Australian and inter-national art displayed in an ever-changing programme **2**

Walkway along Circular Quay West foreshore

The Rocks Market
is a hive of activity
every weekend,
offering an eclectic
range of craft items
and jewellery
utilizing Australian
icons from gum
leaves to koalas
(see p129).

LOCATOR MAP
See Street Finder, *map 1*

**The Rocks Toy
Museum**
*A collection of
more than
10,000 dolls and
toys is on show in
this restored
1850s coach
house* ❺

★ **Cadman's Cottage**
*John Cadman, government
coxswain, resided in what
was known as the Coxswain's
Barracks with his family. His wife
Elizabeth was also a significant
figure, believed to be the first
woman to vote in New South
Wales, a right she insisted on* ❸

0 metres	100
0 yards	100

KEY

- - - Suggested route

**The Overseas
Passenger Terminal**
is where some of the
world's luxury cruise
liners, including the
QEII, berth during
their stay in Sydney.

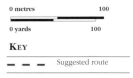

STAR SIGHTS

★ **Cadman's Cottage**

★ **Museum of
   Contemporary Art**

★ **Sydney Observatory**

Old-fashioned Australian goods at the corner shop, Susannah Place

Susannah Place **1**

58–64 Gloucester St, The Rocks. **Map**
1 B2. **(** *(02) 9241 1893.*
🚌 *Sydney Explorer, 431, 432, 433,
434.* **◯** *Jan: 10am–5pm daily;
Feb–Dec: 10am–5pm Sat & Sun.*
◉ *Good Fri, 25 Dec.* **🏷 📷**

THIS TERRACE of four brick
and sandstone houses dat-
ing back to 1844 has a rare
history of continuous domestic
occupancy from the 1840s
through to 1990. It is now a
museum examining the living
conditions of its former inhabitants. Rather than re-creating
a single period, the museum
retains the renovations carried out by different tenants.

Built for Edward and Mary
Riley, who arrived from Ireland
with their niece Susannah in
1838, these houses have basement kitchens and backyard
outhouses. Piped water and
sewerage were probably
added by the mid-1850s.

The terrace escaped the
wholesale demolitions that
occurred after the outbreak of
bubonic plague in 1900, as
well as later clearings of land
to make way for the Sydney
Harbour Bridge *(see pp 76–7)*
and the Cahill Expressway. In
the 1970s it was saved once
again when the Builders
Labourers' Federation imposed
a "green ban" on The Rocks,
temporarily halting all redevelopment work which was des-
tructive to cultural heritage.

Museum of Contemporary Art **2**

Circular Quay West, The Rocks.
Map 1 B2. **(** *(02) 9252 4033.*
🚌 *Sydney Explorer, 431, 432, 433
434.* **◯** *10am–6pm daily.* **◉** *25
Dec.* **♿** *book in advance.* **📷**

WHEN SYDNEY art collector
John Power died in 1943,
he left his entire collection
and a financial bequest to the
University of Sydney. In 1991
the collection, which by then
included works by Hockney,
Warhol, Lichtenstein and
Christo was transferred to this
1950s mock Art Deco building
at Circular Quay West. As well
as showing its permanent
collection, the museum hosts
exhibitions by local and
overseas artists. The MCA
Store sells distinctive gifts by
Australian designers.

Cadman's Cottage **3**

110 George St, The Rocks. **Map** 1 B2.
(*(02) 9247 5033.* **🚌** *431, 432,
433 434.* **◯** *9am–5pm daily.*
◉ *Good Fri, 25 Dec.*

THIS SIMPLE sandstone cottage
now serves as the infor-
mation centre and shop for
the Sydney Harbour National
Park. Built in 1816 as barracks
for the crews of the governor's
boats, it is Sydney's oldest
surviving dwelling.

The cottage is named after
John Cadman, a convict who
was transported in 1798 for
horse-stealing. By 1813, he was
coxswain of a timber boat and
later, coxswain of government
craft. He was granted a full
pardon and in 1827 he was
made boat superintendent and
moved to the four-room cottage that now bears his name.

Cadman married Elizabeth
Mortimer in 1830, another ex-
convict who was sentenced to
seven years' transportation for
the theft of one hairbrush.
They lived in the cottage until
1846. Cadman's Cottage was
built on the foreshore of
Sydney Harbour. Now, as
a result of successive land
reclamations, it is set well
back from the water's edge.

Mock Art Deco façade of the Museum of Contemporary Art

Sailors' Home ❹

106 George St, The Rocks. **Map** 1 B2.
((02) 9255 1788. **■** Sydney
Explorer, 431, 432, 433, 434.
○ 9am–6pm daily. **&**

B
UILT IN 1864 as lodgings
for visiting sailors, the
building now houses The
Sydney Visitors' Centre.
At the time it was built, the
Sailors' Home was a welcome
alternative to the many seedy
inns and brothels in the area,
saving sailors from the perils
of "crimping". "Crimps" would
tempt newly arrived men into
bars providing much sought-
after entertainment. While
drunk, the sailors would be
sold on to departing ships,
waking miles out at sea and
returning home in debt.
Sailors used the home until
1980. In 1994, it opened as a
tourist information and tour-
booking facility. On the third
floor, a re-creation of a 19th-
century sleeping cubicle gives
visitors an impression of the
spartan nature of the original
sailors' accommodation.

The Rocks Toy Museum ❺

2–6 Kendall Lane, The Rocks.
(9251 9793. **■** Sydney Explorer,
431, 432, 433, 434. **○**
10am–5:30pm daily. **▨**

T
HIS MUSEUM, in a restored
1850s coach house, is
home to a collection of more
than 10,000 toys, dating from
the 19th and 20th centuries. It
was assembled by local toy
aficionado Ken Hinds, who
continually adds new finds,
both modern and antique, to
the collection. Among the
delights on show over two
floors is a fine assembly of
model trains, including a
remarkably detailed Bing
train from the 1920s. On the
upper level is a display of
rare and unusual Australian
dolls, assembled by the Doll
Collectors Club of NSW. Here
there are some lovely porcelain dolls, as well as others
made of various materials,
including pressed papier
maché, celluloid, glazed
china, wood and cloth.

Terrace restaurants at Campbell's Storehouses on the waterfront

Campbell's Storehouses ❻

7–27 Circular Quay West, The Rocks.
Map 1 B2. **■** Sydney Explorer, 431,
432, 433, 434. **&**

R
OBERT CAMPBELL, a promi-
nent Scottish merchant in
the early days of Sydney,
purchased this land on
Sydney Cove in 1799. In 1802
he began constructing a
private wharf and storehouses
in which to house the tea,
sugar, spirits and cloth he
imported from India.
Campbell was the only
merchant operating in
Australia who managed to
infiltrate the monopoly held
by the British East India
Company. The first five
sandstone bays were built
between 1839 and 1844. A
further seven bays were built
between 1854 and 1861. The
full row of storehouses were
finally completed in 1890,
including a brick upper
storey. Part of the old sea
wall and 11 of the original
stores are still standing. The
pulleys that were used to
raise cargo from the wharf
can be seen near the top of
the preserved buildings.
The area fell into disrepair
during the first half of the
20th century. However, in the
1970s the Sydney Cove
Redevelopment Authority
finalized plans and began
renovating the site. Today the
bond stores contain a range
of fine restaurants catering to
all tastes, from contemporary
Australian to Chinese and
Italian. Their virtually
unimpeded views across
Circular Quay towards the
Sydney Opera House (see
pp80–81) and Sydney
Harbour Bridge (see pp 76–7)

make these outdoor eating
venues very popular with
local business people and
tourists alike.

Sydney Harbour Bridge ❼

See pp76–7.

The Hero of Waterloo Inn

Hero of Waterloo ❽

81 Lower Fort St, Millers Point. **Map**
1 A2. **(** (02) 9252 4553. **■** 431,
432, 433, 434. **○** 10am–11pm
Mon–Thu, 10am–11:30pm Fri–Sat,
10am–10pm Sun. **●** 25 Dec. **&**

T
HIS PICTURESQUE old inn is
especially welcoming in
the winter, when its log fires
are burning.
Built in 1844, this was a
favourite drinking place for
the nearby garrison's soldiers.
Some sea captains were said
to use the hotel to recruit.
Patrons who drank too much
were pushed into the cellars
via a trapdoor. Tunnels then
led to the wharves and on to
waiting ships.

Sydney Harbour Bridge ❼

COMPLETED IN 1932, the construction of the Sydney Harbour Bridge was an economic feat, given the depressed times, as well as an engineering triumph. Prior to this, the only links between the city centre on the south side of the harbour and the residential north side were by ferry or a circuitous 20-km (12-mile) road route which involved five bridge crossings. The single-span arch bridge, colloquially known as the "Coathanger",

Ceremonial scissors

took eight years to build, including the railway line. The bridge was manufactured in sections on the latter-day Luna Park site. Loans for the total cost of approximately 6.25 million old Australian pounds were eventually paid off in 1988.

The 1932 Opening
The ceremony was disrupted when zealous royalist Francis de Groot rode forward and cut the ribbon, in honour, he claimed, of King and Empire.

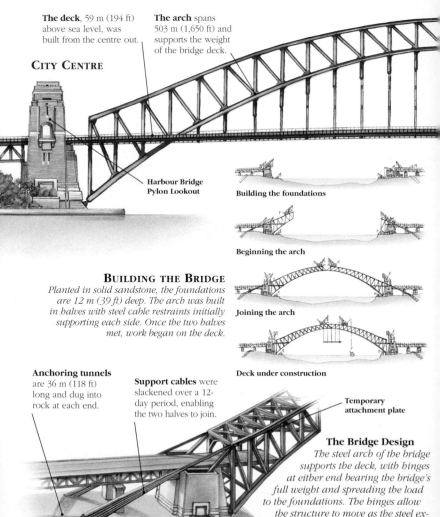

The deck, 59 m (194 ft) above sea level, was built from the centre out.

The arch spans 503 m (1,650 ft) and supports the weight of the bridge deck.

CITY CENTRE

Harbour Bridge
Pylon Lookout

Building the foundations

Beginning the arch

BUILDING THE BRIDGE
Planted in solid sandstone, the foundations are 12 m (39 ft) deep. The arch was built in halves with steel cable restraints initially supporting each side. Once the two halves met, work began on the deck.

Joining the arch

Deck under construction

Anchoring tunnels are 36 m (118 ft) long and dug into rock at each end.

Support cables were slackened over a 12-day period, enabling the two halves to join.

Temporary attachment plate

The Bridge Design
The steel arch of the bridge supports the deck, with hinges at either end bearing the bridge's full weight and spreading the load to the foundations. The hinges allow the structure to move as the steel expands and contracts in response to wind and extreme temperatures.

The Bridge in Curve *(1930) The bridge has inspired many artists. The huge structure towers over the nearby houses in this work by Grace Cossington Smith.*

VISITORS' CHECKLIST

Map 1 B1. (02) 9247 3408. All routes to The Rocks. Circular Quay. Circular Quay, Milsons Point. **Bridgeclimb** (02) 8247 7777. **Pylon Lookout** 10am–5pm daily. 25 Dec. **Films.**

Over 150,000 vehicles cross the bridge each day, about 15 times as as many as in 1932.

Bridge Workers *The bridge was built by 1,400 workers, 16 of whom were killed in accidents during construction.*

NORTH SHORE

Maintenance *Painting the bridge has become a metaphor for an endless task. Approximately 30,000 l (6,600 gal) of paint are required for each coat, enough to cover an area equivalent to 60 soccer pitches.*

The vertical hangers support the slanting crossbeams which, in turn, carry the deck.

FATHER OF THE BRIDGE

Chief engineer Dr John Bradfield shakes the hand of the driver of the first train to cross the bridge. Over a 20-year period, Bradfield supervised all aspects of the bridge's design and construction. At the opening ceremony, the highway linking the harbour's south side and northern suburbs was named in his honour.

Paying the Toll *The initial toll of sixpence helped pay off the construction loan. A toll is now used for maintenance and to pay for the 1992 Sydney Harbour Tunnel.*

A FLAGPOLE ON THE MUDFLATS

The modest flagpole on Loftus Street, near Customs House, flies a flag, the Union Jack, on the spot where Australia's first ceremonial flag-raising took place. On 26 January 1788, Captain Arthur Phillip hoisted the flag to declare the foundation of the colony. A toast to the king was drunk and a musket volley fired. On this date each year, the country marks Australia Day with a national holiday *(see p39)*. In 1788, the flagpole was on the edge of mudflats on Sydney Cove. Today, due to land reclamations, it is set back from the water's edge.

The Founding of Australia by Algernon Talmage

Garrison Church **9**

Cnr Argyle & Lower Fort sts, Millers Point. **Map** 1 A2. ☎ *(02) 9247 2664.* 🚌 *431, 433.* ⏰ *9am–6pm daily.* ♿

O FFICIALLY NAMED the Holy Trinity Church, this was dubbed the Garrison Church because it was the colony's first military church.

Henry Ginn designed the church and, in 1840, the foundation stone was laid. In 1855, it was enlarged to hold up to 600 people. Regimental plaques hanging along interior walls recall the church's military associations. A museum contains Australian military and historical items.

Other features to look out for are the brilliantly coloured east window and the carved red cedar pulpit.

East window, Garrison Church

Sydney Observatory **10**

Watson Rd, Observatory Hill, The Rocks. **Map** 1 A2. ☎ *(02) 9217 0485.* 🚌 *Sydney Explorer, 343, 431, stop 22.* ⏰ *10am–5pm daily.* **Night viewings** ⏰ *phone for opening times (bookings essential).* ● *25 Dec.* 📷 ♿ 🎫

I N 1982 this domed building, which had been a centre for astronomical observation and research for almost 125 years, became the city's astronomy museum. It has interactive

displays and games, along with night sky viewings; it is essential to book for these.

The building began life in the 1850s as a time-ball tower. At 1pm daily, the ball on top of the tower dropped to signal the correct time. At the same time, a cannon was fired at Fort Denison. This custom continues today *(see p104)*.

During the 1880s Sydney Observatory became known around the world when some of the first astronomical photographs of the southern sky were taken here. From 1890 to 1962 the observatory mapped some 750,000 stars as part of an international project that resulted in an atlas of the entire night sky.

National Trust Centre **11**

Observatory Hill, Watson Rd, The Rocks. **Map** 1 A3. ☎ *(02) 9258 0123.* 🚌 *Sydney Explorer, 343, 431, 432, 433, 434.* ⏰ *9am–5pm Mon–Fri.* **Gallery** ⏰ *11am–5pm Tue–Fri, noon–5pm Sat–Sun.* ● *some public hols.* ♿

T HE BUILDINGS that form the headquarters of the National Trust of Australia, date from 1815, when Governor Macquarie chose the site for a military hospital. Today they house tea rooms, a National Trust shop and the SH Ervin Gallery, containing

works by 19th- and 20th-century Australian artists such as Margaret Preston and Conrad Martens *(see p30)*.

St Philip's Church **12**

3 York St (enter from Jamison St). **Map** 1 A3. ☎ *(02) 9247 1071.* 🚌 *George St routes.* ⏰ *phone for opening times.* ● *26 Jan, 25 Apr.* 🎫

T HIS VICTORIAN GOTHIC church may seem overshadowed in its modern setting, yet when it was first built, the square tower was a local landmark.

Begun in 1848, St Philip's is by Edmund Blacket. In 1851 work was disrupted when its stonemasons left for the gold fields, but by 1856 the building was finally completed.

A peal of bells was donated in 1888 to mark Sydney's centenary and they still announce the services each Sunday.

Interior and pipe organ of St Philip's Church

Macquarie Place

Map 1 B3. 🚌 Circular Quay routes.

GOVERNOR MACQUARIE created this park in 1810 on what was once the vegetable garden of the first Government House. The sandstone obelisk, designed by Francis Greenway (see p161), was erected in 1818 to mark the starting point for all roads in the colony. The gas lamps recall the fact that this was also the site of the city's first street lamp in 1826.

Also in this area are the remains of the bow anchor and cannon from HMS Sirius, flagship of the First Fleet. The statue of Thomas Mort, a successful 19th-century industrialist, is today a marshalling place for the city's somewhat kamikaze bicycle couriers.

Customs House

Alfred St, Circular Quay. **Map** 1 B3. 🚇 (02) 9247 2285. 🚌 Circular Quay routes. ⬜ djamu shop 9:30am–5pm daily. ⬜ Objects Gallery and Store 10am–5pm daily. ⬤ 25 Dec, Good Fri. 📷 ♿ 🚻 🖥

COLONIAL ARCHITECT James Barnet designed this 1885 sandstone Classical Revival building on the same site as a previous Customs House. Its recalls the bygone days when trading ships berthed at Circular Quay. The building stands near the mouth of Tank Stream, the fledgling colony's freshwater supply. Among its many fine features are tall veranda columns made out of polished granite, a finely sculpted coat of arms and an elaborate clock face, added in 1897, which features a pair of tridents and dolphins.

Detail from Customs House

The Australian Centre for Craft and Design is found here, and its shop, The Object Store, sells contemporary glassware by Australian designers. There are also shops, cafés and a performance space. The City Exhibition Space explores Sydney's architecture and its plans for the future.

Montage of criminal "mug shots", Justice and Police Museum

Justice and Police Museum

8 Phillip St. **Map** 1 C3. 🚇 (02) 9252 1144. 🚌 Circular Quay routes. ⬜ 10am–5pm Sat & Sun. ⬤ Good Fri, 25 Dec. 📷 ♿

THE BUILDINGS housing this museum originally comprised the Water Police Court, designed by Edmund Blacket in 1856, the Water Police Station, designed by Alexander Dawson in 1858, and the Police Court, designed by James Barnet in 1885. Here the rough-and-tumble underworld of quayside crime, from the petty to the violent, was dealt swift and, at times, harsh justice. The museum exhibits illustrate that turbulent period, as they re-create legal and criminal history. Formalities of the late-Victorian legal proceedings can be easily imagined in the fully restored courtroom. Menacing implements from knuckledusters to bludgeons are displayed as the macabre relics of notorious crimes. Other interesting aspects of policing and the justice system are highlighted in special changing exhibitions.

The charge room, austere remand cell, prison uniforms, prison artifacts and slideshow evoke powerful images of the penal code of the time.

Writers' Walk

Circular Quay. **Map** 1 C2. 🚌 Circular Quay routes.

THIS SERIES of plaques is set in the pavement at regular intervals between East and West Circular Quay. It gives the visitor the chance to ponder the observations of famous Australian writers, both past and present, on their home country, as well as the musings of some noted literary visitors.

Each plaque is dedicated to a particular writer, consisting of a personal quotation and a brief biographical note. Australian writers in the series include the novelists Miles Franklin and Peter Carey, poets Oodgeroo Noonuccal and Judith Wright (see pp30–31), humorists Barry Humphries and Clive James, and the influential feminist writer Germaine Greer. Among the international writers included who visited Sydney are Mark Twain, Charles Darwin and Joseph Conrad.

Strolling along a section of the Writers' Walk at Circular Quay

Sydney Opera House ⑰

Advertising poster

No OTHER BUILDING ON EARTH looks like the Sydney Opera House. Popularly known as the "Opera House" long before the building was complete, it is, in fact, a complex of theatres and halls linked beneath its famous shells. Its birth was long and complicated. Many of the construction problems had not been faced before, resulting in an architectural adventure which lasted 14 years. An appeal fund was set up, eventually raising A$900,000, while the Opera House Lottery raised the balance of the A$102 million final cost. Today it is the city's most popular tourist attraction, as well as one of the world's busiest performing arts centres.

★ **Opera Theatre**
Mainly used for opera and ballet, this 1,547-seat theatre is big enough to stage grand operas such as Verdi's Aïda.

The Opera Theatre's ceiling and walls are painted black to focus attention on the stage.

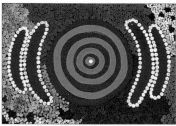

Detail of The Possum Dreaming *(1988)*
The mural in the Opera Theatre foyer is by Michael Tjakamarra Nelson, an artist from the central Australian desert.

Opera House Walkway
Extensive public walkways around the building offer the visitor views from many different vantage points.

Northern Foyers
The Reception Hall and the large northern foyers of the Opera Theatre and Concert Hall have spectacular views over the harbour and can be hired for conferences, lunches, parties and weddings.

STAR FEATURES

★ **Concert Hall**

★ **Opera Theatre**

★ **The Roofs**

★ Concert Hall
This is the largest hall, with seating for 2,690. It is used for symphony, choral, jazz, folk and pop concerts, chamber music, opera, dance and everything from body building to fashion parades.

The Monumental Steps
and forecourt are used for outdoor films and free entertainment.

Bennelong Restaurant
This is one of the finest restaurants in Sydney (see p500).

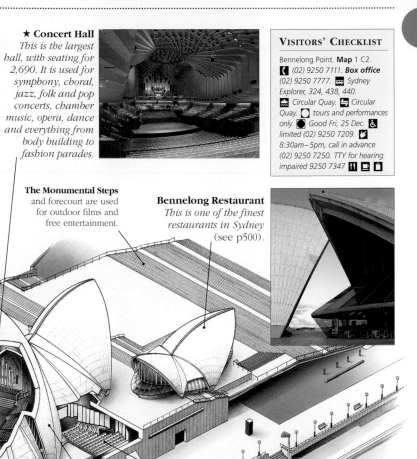

The Playhouse, seating almost 400, is ideal for intimate productions, while also able to present plays with larger casts.

★ The Roofs
Although apocryphal, the theory that Jørn Utzon's arched roof design came to him while peeling an orange is enchanting. The highest point is 67 m (221 ft) above sea level.

Curtain of the Moon *(1972)*
Designed by John Coburn, this and its fellow Curtain of the Sun *were originally used in the Drama and Opera theatres. Both have been removed for preservation.*

View from Harbourside Shopping Centre looking east towards the city

SIGHTS AT A GLANCE

Museums and Galleries
Australian Museum pp90–91 **10**
Motor World Museum and
 Gallery **16**
Museum of Sydney **7**
*National Maritime Museum
 pp96–7* **15**
Powerhouse Museum pp98–9 **18**

Markets
Paddy's Market **19**

Cathedrals and Synagogues
Great Synagogue **11**
St Andrew's Cathedral **13**
St Mary's Cathedral **8**

**Historic Streets and
Buildings**
AMP Tower p87 **5**
Chinatown **20**
Lands Department Building **6**
Martin Place **4**

Queen Victoria Building **1**
Strand Arcade **3**
Sydney Town Hall **12**

Parks and Gardens
Chinese Garden **17**
Hyde Park **9**

Entertainment
State Theatre **2**
Sydney Aquarium **14**

CITY CENTRE
AND DARLING HARBOUR

GEORGE STREET, Australia's first thoroughfare, was originally lined with mud and wattle huts, but following the gold rush shops and banks came to dominate the area. The city's first skyscraper, Culwulla Chambers, was completed in 1913. Hyde Park, on the edge of the city centre, was once a racecourse, attracting gambling taverns to Elizabeth Street. Today it provides a peaceful oasis,

Mosaic floor detail, St Mary's Cathedral

while the city's commercial centre is an area of department stores and arcades. The country's industrial age began in Darling Harbour in 1815 with the opening of a steam mill, but later the area became rundown. In the 1980s, it was the site of the largest urban redevelopment project ever carried out in Australia. Today, Darling Harbour contains many fine museums.

GETTING THERE

Town Hall, Wynyard, Martin Place, St James' and Museum railway stations all serve the city centre. There are numerous regular buses along Elizabeth and George streets. The Monorail stops are at City Centre, Park Plaza, World Square, Harbourside, Convention and Haymarket. Ferries run regularly to Darling Harbour wharf.

0 metres   500
0 yards   500

KEY

▭ Street-by-Street map pp84–5

▭ Street-by-Street map pp92–3

P Parking

🚉 Sydney Light Rail station (SLR)

🚊 Monorail station

Street-by-Street: City Centre

Sculpture outside
the MLC Centre

ALTHOUGH CLOSELY RIVALLED by Melbourne, Sydney is the business and commercial capital of Australia. Vibrant by day, at night the streets are far less busy when office workers and shoppers have gone home. The comparatively small city centre of this sprawling metropolis seems to be almost jammed into a few city blocks. Because Sydney grew in such a haphazard fashion, with many of today's streets following tracks from the harbour originally made by bullocks, there was no allowance for the expansion of the city into what has become a major international centre. A colourful night scene of cafés, restaurants and theatres is emerging, however, as more people return to the city centre to live.

★ Queen Victoria Building
Taking up an entire city block, this 1898 former produce market has been lovingly restored and is now a shopping mall ❶

State Theatre
A gem from the era when the movies reigned, this glittering and richly decorated 1929 cinema was once hailed as "the Empire's greatest theatre" ❷

To Sydney
Town Hall

The Queen Victoria Statue was found after a worldwide search in 1983 ended in a small Irish village. It had lain forgotten and neglected since being removed from the front of the Irish Parliament in 1947.

YORK STREET

GEORGE STREET

PITT STREET

PARK STREET

CASTLEREAGH

ELIZABE

MAR

STAR SIGHTS

★ AMP Tower
────────────────
★ Martin Place
────────────────
★ Queen Victoria
Building

0 metres	100
0 yards	100

KEY

– – –　Suggested route

Marble Bar was once a landmark bar in the 1893 Tattersalls hotel. It was carefully dismantled and re-erected in the Sydney Hilton in 1973.

Strand Arcade
A reminder of the late 19th century Victorian era when Sydney was famed as a city of elegant shopping arcades, this faithfully restored example is said to have been the finest of them all ❸

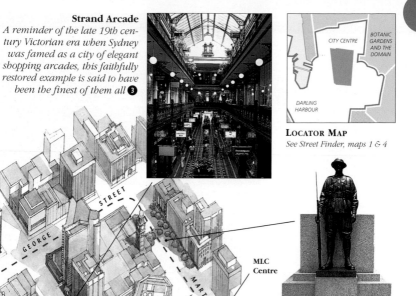

LOCATOR MAP
See Street Finder, maps 1 & 4

MLC
Centre

★ Martin Place
Martin Place's 1929 Art Deco Cenotaph is the site of annual Anzac Day war remembrance services ❹

**Theatre
Royal**

Skygarden is one of the city's newer arcades. It features elegant shops with designer labels and a popular food court on the top level.

Hyde Park's
northern end

★ AMP Tower
The tower tops the city skyline, giving a bird's eye view of the whole of Sydney. It rises 305 m (1,000 ft) above the ground and can be seen from as far away as the Blue Mountains ❺

Queen Victoria Building ❶

455 George St. **Map** 1 B5. 📞 *(02)
9264 9209.* 🚌 *George St routes.*
🕐 *9am–6pm Mon–Wed, 9am–9pm
Thu, 9am–6pm Fri & Sat, 11am–5pm
Sun; 11am–5pm public hols.* ♿ 🛍
See Shopping pp128–31.

F RENCH DESIGNER Pierre
Cardin called the Queen
Victoria Building "the most
beautiful shopping centre in
the world". Yet this ornate
Romanesque building, better
known as the QVB, began
life as the Sydney produce
market. Completed to the
design of City Architect
George McRae in 1898, the
dominant features are the
central copper dome and
the glass roof which
lets in a flood of
natural light.

The market
closed at the end
of World War I.
By the 1950s, the
building was
threatened with
demolition.

**Roof detail,
Queen Victoria Building**

Refurbished at a cost of over
A$75 million, the QVB re-
opened in 1986 as a shopping
gallery with more than 190
shops. A wishing well incorporates a stone from Blarney
Castle, a sculpture of Islay,
Queen Victoria's dog and a
statue of the queen herself.

Inside the QVB, suspended
from the ceiling, is the Royal
Clock. Designed in 1982 by
Neil Glasser, it features part
of Balmoral Castle above a
copy of the four dials of Big
Ben. Every hour, a fanfare is
played with a parade depicting scenes from the lives of
various English monarchs.

State Theatre ❷

49 Market St. **Map** 1 B5. 📞 *(02)
9373 6655.* **Tours** *(02) 9373 6660.*
🚌 *George St routes.* **Box office**
🕐 *9am–5:30pm Mon–Fri,
10am–2pm Sat.* ● *Good Friday, 25
Dec.* ♿ 🎫 *bookings necessary.*

W HEN IT OPENED in 1929,
this cinema was hailed
as the finest that local craftsmanship could achieve. The
State Theatre is one of the

Ornately decorated Gothic foyer of the State Theatre

best examples of ornate
period cinemas in Australia.
Its Baroque style is evident
in the foyer, with its high
ceiling, mosaic floor,
marble columns and
statues. The audito-
rium is lit by a
20,000-piece
chandelier. The
beautiful Wurlitzer
organ (under
repair) rises from
below stage before
performances. The
theatre is now one of the
city's special events venues.

Strand Arcade ❸

412–414 George St. **Map** 1 B5.
📞 *(02) 9232 4199.* 🚌 *George St
routes.* 🕐 *9am–5:30pm Mon–Wed
& Fri, 9am–8pm Thu, 9am–4pm Sat,
11am–4pm Sun.* ● *most public
hols.* ♿ *See Shopping pp128–31.*

V ICTORIAN SYDNEY was a city
of grand shopping arcades.
The Strand, joining George
and Pitt streets and designed

**Pitt Street entrance to the
majestic Strand Arcade**

by English architect John
Spencer, was the finest of all.
Opened in April 1892, it was
lit by natural light pouring
through the glass roof and the
chandeliers, each carrying 50
jets of gas as well as 50 lamps.

After a fire in 1976, the
building was restored to its
original splendour. Shopping,
followed by a visit to the Old
Sydney Coffee Shop near the
Pitt Street entrance, is a delight.

Martin Place ❹

Map 1 B4. 🚌 *George St & Elizabeth
St routes.*

T HIS PLAZA was opened in
1891 and made a traffic-
free precinct in 1971. It is
busiest at lunchtime as city
workers enjoy their sand-
wiches while watching free
entertainment in the amphitheatre near Castlereagh Street.

Every Anzac Day *(see p38)*
the focus moves to the Cenotaph at the George Street end.
Past and present service
personnel attend a dawn
service and wreath-laying
ceremony, followed by a
march past. The shrine, by
Bertram MacKennal, was
unveiled in 1929.

On the southern side of the
Cenotaph is the façade of the
Renaissance-style General Post
Office, considered to be the
finest building by James Bar-
net, colonial architect in 1866.

A stainless steel sculpture
of upended cubes, the Dobell
Memorial Sculpture, is a tribute
to Australian artist William
Dobell, created by Bert
Flugelman in 1979.

AMP Tower ❺

THE HIGHEST OBSERVATION DECK in the whole of the southern hemisphere, the AMP Tower (formerly the Sydney Tower) was conceived as part of the 1970s Centrepoint shopping centre, but was not completed until 1981. Approximately one million people visit the turret each year for the stunning 360° views of Sydney landmarks. Skytour, at the podium level, provides a multimedia journey around Australia in a series of virtual reality ports.

The 30-m (98-ft) spire completes the total 305 m (1,000 ft) of the tower's height.

The water tank holds 162,000 l (35,000 gal) and acts as an enormous stabilizer on very windy days.

Observation Level
Views from Level 4 stretch north to Pittwater, Botany Bay to the south, west to the Blue Mountains, and along the harbour out to the open sea.

Level 4: Observation

Level 3: Coffee shop

Level 2: Buffet restaurant

Level 1: A la carte restaurant

The turret's nine levels, with room to hold almost 1,000 people at a time, include two revolving restaurants, a coffee shop and the Observation Level.

The windows comprise three layers. The outer has a gold dust coating. The frame design prevents panes falling outwards.

The 56 cables weigh seven tonnes each. If laid end to end, they would reach from New Zealand to Sydney.

Construction of Turret
The eight turret levels were erected on the roof of the base building, then hoisted up the shaft using hydraulic jacks.

The shaft is designed to withstand wind speeds expected only once in 500 years, as well as unprecedented earthquakes.

The stairs are two separate, fireproofed emergency escape routes. Each year in September or October Sydney's fittest race up the 1,474 stairs.

Double-decker lifts can carry up to 2,000 people per hour. At full speed, a lift takes only 40 seconds to ascend the 76 floors to the Observation Level.

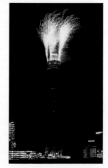

New Year's Eve
Every year, fireworks are set off on top of AMP Tower as part of the official public fireworks displays to mark the New Year.

Lands Department Building ⑥

23 Bridge St. **Map** 1 B3. 🚌 *325, George St routes.* ⬤ *only 2 weeks in the year, dates vary.* ♿

DESIGNED BY the colonial architect James Barnet, this three-storey Classical Revival sandstone edifice was built between 1877 and 1890. Pyrmont sandstone was used for the exterior, as it was for the GPO building.

All the decisions about the subdivision of much of rural eastern Australia were made in the offices within. Statues of explorers and legislators who "promoted settlement" fill 23 of the façade's 48 niches; the remainder are still empty. The luminaries include the explorers Hovell and Hume, Sir Thomas Mitchell, Blaxland, Lawson and Wentworth, Ludwig Leichhardt, Bass, Matthew Flinders and botanist Sir Joseph Banks.

The Lookout on Level 3 of the Museum of Sydney

Museum of Sydney ⑦

Cnr Phillip & Bridge sts. **Map** 1 B3. ☎ (02) 9251 5988. 🚌 *Circular Quay routes.* ⬤ *9:30am–5pm daily.* ⬤ *Good Fri, 25 Dec.* 🎫 ♿

SITUATED AT THE BASE of Governor Phillip Tower, the Museum of Sydney opened in 1995. The history of Sydney, from the 1788 arrival of the British colonists until the present, is recalled on the site of the first Government House. This was the home, office and seat of authority

Terrazzo mosaic floor in the crypt of St Mary's Cathedral

for the first nine governors of New South Wales from 1788 until 1846. The design assimilates the exhibition and the archaeological site within a modern office block.

Indigenous Peoples
A new gallery explores the culture, history, continuity and place of Sydney's original inhabitants. The collectors' chests hold items of daily use such as flint and ochre. In the square outside the complex, the *Edge of the Trees* sculptural installation symbolizes the first contact between the Aborigines and Europeans. Inscribed in the wood are signatures of First Fleeters and names of botanical species in both Aboriginal and Latin.

History of Sydney
Outside the museum, a paving pattern outlines the site of the first Government House. The original foundations, below street level, can be seen through a window. A segment of wall has now been reconstructed using the original sandstone.

The Colony display on Level 2 focuses on Sydney during the critical decade of the 1840s: convict transportation ended, the town officially became a city and then suffered economic depression. On Level 3, 20th century Sydney is explored against a panorama of images.

Display from Trade Exhibition on Level 2

St Mary's Cathedral ⑧

Cathedral St. **Map** 1 C5. ☎ (02) 9220 0400. 🚌 *Elizabeth St routes.* ⬤ *6:30am–6:30pm Mon–Fri, 8am–7:30pm Sat, 6:30am–7:30pm Sun.* ♿ *with advance notice.* 🎵 *noon Sun.*

ALTHOUGH CATHOLICS arrived with the First Fleet, the celebration of Mass was at first prohibited as it was feared priests would provoke civil strife among the colony's Irish Catholic population. It was not until 1820 that the first Catholic priests were officially appointed and services were permitted. In 1821, Governor Macquarie laid the foundation stone for St Mary's Chapel on the first land granted to the Catholic Church in Australia.

The initial section of this Gothic Revival-style cathedral was opened in 1882 and completed in 1928, but without the twin southern spires originally proposed by the architect William Wardell. By the entrance are statues of Australia's first cardinal, Moran, and Archbishop Kelly, who laid the stone for the final stage in 1913. They were sculpted by Bertram MacKennal, also responsible for the Martin Place Cenotaph *(see p85).* The crypt's terrazzo mosaic floor took 15 years to complete.

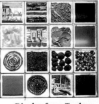

Hyde Park ❾

Map 1 B5. 🚌 *Elizabeth St routes.*

HYDE PARK was named after its London equivalent by Governor Macquarie in 1810. The fence around the park marked the outskirts of the township. Once an exercise field for garrison troops, it later incorporated a racecourse and a cricket pitch. Though much smaller today than the original park, it is still a quiet haven in the middle of the bustling city centre, with many notable features.

The 30-m (98-ft) high Art Deco Anzac Memorial commem-orates Australians who have died for their country. Opened in 1934 it now includes a military exhibition downstairs.

Sandringham Garden, filled with mauve wisteria, is a memorial to kings George V and George VI, opened by Queen Elizabeth II in 1954.

The bronze and granite Archibald Fountain commemorates the French and Australian World War I alliance. It was completed by François Sicard in 1932 and donated by JF Archibald, one of the founders of the popular *Bulletin* literary magazine.

The *Emden* Gun, on the corner of College and Liver-pool Streets, commemorates a World War I naval action. HMAS *Sydney* destroyed the German raider *Emden* off the Cocos Islands on 9 November 1914, and 180 crew members were taken prisoner.

Australian Museum ❿

See pp90–91.

Great Synagogue ⓫

187 Elizabeth St, entrance at 166 Castlereagh St. **Map** 1 B5.
📞 *(02) 9267 2477.* 🚌 *394, 396, 380, 382.* ⭕ *for services and tours only.* ♿ 📷 *noon Tue & Thu.*

THE LONGEST established Jewish Orthodox congre-gation in Australia, con-sisting of more than 900 families, assembles in this synagogue (consecrated in 1878). Although Jews had arrived with the First Fleet, worship did not commence until the 1820s. With its carved porch columns and wrought-iron gates, the synagogue is perhaps the finest work of Thomas Rowe, archi-tect of Sydney Hospital *(see p109)*. Among the interior features is a panelled ceiling, decorated with tiny gold leaf stars.

Candelabra in the Great Synagogue

Sydney Town Hall ⓬

483 George St. **Map** 4 E2. 📞 *(02) 9265 9333.* 🚌 *George St routes.*
⭕ *8:30am–6pm Mon–Fri.* ⬛ *public holidays.* ♿ 📷 *(02) 8223 3815.*

THE STEPS of Sydney Town Hall have been a favourite meeting place since it opened in 1869. Walled burial grounds originally covered the site.

Grand organ in Centennial Hall

It is a fine example of High Victorian architecture, even though the plans of the origi-nal architect, JH Wilson, were beyond the builders' capabil-ities. A succession of designers was then brought in. The vestibule, an elegant salon with stained glass and a crys-tal chandelier, is the work of Albert Bond. The clock tower was completed by the Brad-bridge brothers in 1884. From 1888–9, other architects design-ed Centennial Hall, with its imposing 19th-century organ with more than 8,500 pipes.

Some people believe this became Sydney's finest build-ing by accident, as each archi-tect strove to outdo the other. Today, it makes a good venue for concerts, dances and balls.

St Andrew's Cathedral ⓭

Sydney Square, cnr George & Bathurst sts. **Map** 4 E3. 📞 *(02) 9265 1661.*
🚌 *George St routes* ⭕ *contact the cathedral for opening times.*
♿ 📷

WHILE THE foundation stone for the country's oldest cathedral was laid in 1819, the building was not consecrated until 1868. The Gothic Revival design, by Edmund Blacket, was inspired by York Minster in England. Inside are memorials to Sydney pioneers, a 1539 Bible and beads made from olive seeds collected in the Holy Land.

The southern wall includes stones from London's St Paul's Cathedral, Westminster Abbey and the House of Lords.

Game in progress on the giant chessboard in Hyde Park

Australian Museum ⑩

Model head of
Tyrannosaurus rex

THE AUSTRALIAN MUSEUM, the nation's leading natural science museum, founded in 1827, was the first museum established and remains the premier showcase of Australian natural history. The main building, an impressive sandstone structure with a marble staircase, faces Hyde Park. Architect Mortimer Lewis was forced to resign his position when building costs began to far exceed the budget. Construction was completed in the 1860s by James Barnet. The collection provides a journey across Australia and the near Pacific, covering prehistory, biology, botany, environment and cultural heritage. Australian Aboriginal traditions are celebrated in a community access space also used for dance and other performances.

Museum Entrance
The façade features massive Corinthian square pillars or piers.

Rhodochrosite   Cuprite

Planet of Minerals
This section features a walk-through re-creation of an underground mine with a display of gems and minerals.

Mesolite with green apophyllite

Education Centre

Indigenous Australians
From the Dreaming to the struggle for self-determination and land rights, this exhibit tells the stories of Australia's first peoples.

Ground floor

Main entrance

STAR EXHIBITS

★ **More than Dinosaurs**

★ **Kids' Island**

★ **Search & Discover**

MUSEUM GUIDE

Aboriginal Australia is on the ground floor, as is the skeleton display. Mineral and rock exhibits are in two galleries on Level 1. Birds and Insects are found on Level 2, along with Human Evolution, Kids' Island, Biodiversity, Search and Discover and More than Dinosaurs.

The Skeletons Gallery, on the ground floor, provides a different perspective on natural history.

★ **Search & Discover**
*Sydneysiders bring bugs,
rocks and bones to this
area for identification.
The public can also access
CD-Roms for research.*

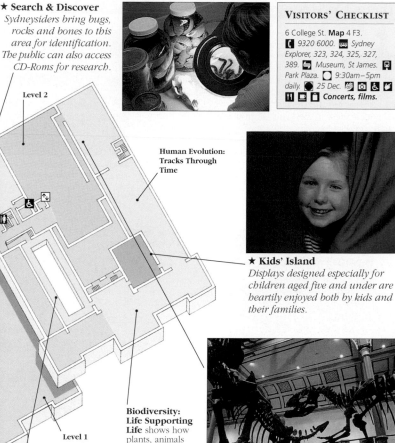

VISITORS' CHECKLIST

6 College St. **Map** 4 F3.
📞 9320 6000. 🚌 *Sydney
Explorer, 323, 324, 325, 327,
389.* 🚇 *Museum, St James.* 🅿
Park Plaza. ◐ *9:30am–5pm
daily.* ● *25 Dec.* 📷 🔲 🐕 💳
🍴 🔲 🎦 *Concerts, films.*

Level 2

**Human Evolution:
Tracks Through
Time**

★ **Kids' Island**
*Displays designed especially for
children aged five and under are
heartily enjoyed both by kids and
their families.*

Level 1

**Biodiversity:
Life Supporting
Life** shows how
plants, animals
and ecosystems
work together.

★ **More than Dinosaurs**
*Discover Australia's ancient megafauna in
this exhibition that features a time line
beginning 4,600 million years ago, and
includes some impressive dinosaur skeletons
looming alongside the giant prehistoric
relatives of Australia's marsupials.*

Birds and Insects
*Australia's most poisonous
spider, the male of the funnel-
web species, dwells exclusively
in the Greater Sydney region.*

KEY TO FLOORPLAN

☐	Australian Environments
☐	Kids' Island
☐	More than Dinosaurs
☐	Indigenous Australians
☐	Temporary exhibition space
☐	Non-exhibition space

"WELCOME STRANGER" GOLD NUGGET

In 1869, the largest gold nugget
ever found in Australia was
discovered in Victoria. It
weighed 71.06 kg (156 lb).
The museum holds a cast
of the original in a display
examining the impact of
the gold rush, when the
Australian population doubled
in ten years.

←—— 67.5 cm (26½ in) wide ——→

Street-by-Street: Darling Harbour

Carpentaria lightship, National Maritime Museum

DARLING HARBOUR was New South Wales' bicentennial gift to itself. This imaginative urban redevelopment, close to the heart of Sydney, covers a 54-ha (133-acre) site that was once a busy industrial centre and international shipping terminal catering for the developing local wool, grain, timber and coal trades. In 1984 the Darling Harbour Authority was formed to examine the area's commercial options. The resulting complex opened in 1988, complete with the National Maritime Museum and Sydney Aquarium, two of the city's tourist highlights. Free outdoor entertainment, appealing to children in particular, is a regular feature, and there are many shops, waterside cafés and restaurants, as well as several major hotels overlooking the bay.

Harbourside Complex offers restaurants and cafés with superb views over the water to the city skyline. There is also a wide range of speciality shops, selling unusual gifts and other items.

Walkway to Motor World Museum and Gallery (see p94)

DARLING DRIVE

WESTERN DISTRIBUTOR

WESTERN DISTRIBUTOR

The Convention and Exhibition Centre complex presents an alternating range of international and local trade shows displaying everything from home decorating suggestions to bridal wear.

The Tidal Cascades sunken fountain was designed by Robert Woodward, also responsible for the El Alamein Fountain (see p116). The double spiral of water and paths replicates the circular shape of the Convention Centre.

IMAX large-screen cinema

The Chinese Garden of Friendship is a haven of peace and tranquillity in the heart of Sydney. Its landscaping, with winding pathways, waterfalls, lakes and pavilions, offers an insight into the rich culture of China.

STAR SIGHTS

★ **Sydney Aquarium**

★ **National Maritime Museum**

LOCATOR MAP
See Street Finder, *maps 3 & 4*

Pyrmont Bridge opened in 1902 to service the busy harbour. It is the world's oldest swingspan bridge. and opens for vessels up to 14 m (46 ft) tall. The monorail track above the walkway also opens up for even taller boats.

Swingspan supports for Pyrmont Bridge are sunk 10 m (33 ft) below the harbour floor.

Star City

★ **National Maritime Museum**
The seafaring history of the nation, both before and after European settlement, is recorded in a range of compelling exhibits **15**

The *Vampire* destroyer (1959) is the largest in the vessel fleet moored outside the museum.

Wharf for harbour cruise departures

★ **Sydney Aquarium**
The aquatic life of Sydney Harbour, the open ocean and the Great Barrier Reef is displayed in massive tanks which can be seen from underwater walkways **14**

Cockle Bay Wharf, vibrant and colourful, is an exciting food and entertainment precinct.

0 metres	100
0 yards	100

KEY

— — — Suggested route

Sydney Aquarium ⓮

Aquarium Pier, Darling Harbour. **Map** 4 D2. *(02) 9262 2300. Sydney Explorer. Darling Harbour. Town Hall. Darling Park. 9:30am–10pm daily (last adm 9pm).*

SYDNEY AQUARIUM contains the country's most comprehensive collection of Australian aquatic species. More than 11,000 animals from approximately 650 species are held in a series of re-created marine environments.

For many visitors, the highlight is a walk "on the ocean floor", passing through two floating oceanaria with 145 m (480 ft) of acrylic underwater tunnels. These allow close observation of sharks, stingrays and schools of many types of fish. Fur and harbour seals may be viewed above and below water in a special seal sanctuary. Other exhibits include a Great Barrier Reef display, which documents the world's largest coral reef *(see pp204–209)*, and a Touch Pool, where visitors may touch marine invertebrates such as sea urchins and tubeworms, in an artificial rock pool.

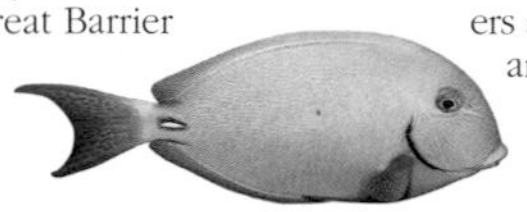

A tang fish in the Great Barrier Reef display

The aquarium ensures that none of the displays is harmful to the creatures, and many of the tanks provide practical information about marine environmental hazards.

National Maritime Museum ⓯

See pp96–7.

Motor World Museum and Gallery ⓰

320 Harris St, cnr Allen St, Pyrmont, inside Secure Parking building. **Map** 3 C3. *(02) 9552 3375. Convention Centre. 10am–5pm Fri–Sun. public hols.*

CELEBRATING A CENTURY of automotive history, the museum has more than 200 classic motor cars, commercial vehicles and motorcycles on display, along with stories of the world's great car designers and their successes and failures. Among the gleaming exhibits are an Edward VII Gardener's Serpollet steam car, the unique Delorean and a Model T BP tanker. In the midst of the exotic cars are everyday vehicles such as the Morris and Buick.

Anthony Quinn's 1959 Chevrolet, Motor World Museum and Gallery

Housed in a former 1890s woolstore, the museum also has Australia's largest international standard slot car track. Two eight-lane tracks run over 67 m (220 ft), with the "driver" racing against the clock.

Chinese Garden ⓱

Darling Harbour. **Map** 4 D3. *(02) 9281 6863. Haymarket. 9:30am daily. Closing times vary. about 60 percent.*

KNOWN AS the Garden of Friendship, the Chinese Garden was built in 1984. It is a tranquil refuge from the city streets. The garden's design was a gift to Sydney from its Chinese sister city of Guangdong. The Dragon Wall is in the lower section beside the lake. It has glazed carvings of two dragons, one representing Guangdong province and the other the state of New South Wales. In the centre of the wall, a carved pearl, symbolizing prosperity,

Structuralist design of the Sydney Aquarium and Pier

Twin Pavilion in the Chinese Garden, decorated with carved flowers

is lifted by the waves. The lake is covered with lotus and water lilies for much of the year and a rock monster guards against evil. On the other side of the lake is the Twin Pavilion. Waratahs (New South Wales' floral symbol) and flowering apricots are carved into its woodwork in Chinese style, and are also planted at its base.

A tea house, found at the top of the stairs in the Tea House Courtyard, serves traditional Chinese tea and cakes, as well as Western light refreshments.

Powerhouse Museum ⓲

See pp98–9.

Paddy's Market ⓳

Cnr Thomas & Hay sts, Haymarket. **Map** 4 D4. 🄲 *1300 361 589.*
🄟 *Haymarket.* ⭘ *10am–6pm Thu, 9am–4pm Fri–Sun & public holidays.* ⭘ *25 Apr, 25 Dec.* 🄳 *See also* **Shopping** *pp128–31.*

THE HAYMARKET DISTRICT, near Chinatown, is home to Paddy's Market, Sydney's oldest and best-known market.

It has been in this area, on a number of sites, since 1869 (with only one five-year absence). The origin of the name is uncertain, but is believed to have come from either the Chinese who originally supplied much of its produce, or the Irish who were among their main customers.

Once the shopping centre for the inner-city poor, Paddy's Market is now an integral part of the Market City Shopping Centre, which includes cut-price fashion outlet stores, an Asian food court and a cinema complex. Yet despite this transformation, the familiar clamour, smells and chaotic bargain-hunting atmosphere of the original marketplace remain. Every weekend the market is filled with up to 800 stalls selling everything from fresh produce to electrical products, homewares, leather goods, and pets, including rabbits, puppies and chickens.

Chinese food products in Chinatown

Chinatown ⓴

Dixon St Plaza, Sydney. **Map** 4 D4.
🄟 *Haymarket.*

ORIGINALLY concentrated around Dixon and Hay streets, Chinatown is now expanding to fill Sydney's Haymarket area, stretching as far west as Harris Street, south to Broadway and east to Castlereagh Street. It is close to the Sydney Entertainment Centre, where some of the world's best-known rock and pop stars perform in concert and many indoor sporting events are held (*see p134*).

For years, Chinatown was little more than a run-down district at the edge of the city's produce markets, where many Chinese immigrants worked at traditional businesses. Today, Dixon Street, its main thoroughfare, has been spruced up to equal many of the other popular Chinatowns around the world. There are authentic-looking street lanterns and archways, and a new wave of Asian immigrants fills the now up-market restaurants.

Chinatown is a distinctive area and now home to a new wave of Sydney's Asian population. There are excellent greengrocers, traditional herba-lists and butchers' shops with wind-dried ducks hanging in their windows. Asian jewellers, clothes shops and con-fectioners fill the arcades. There are also two Chinese-language cinema complexes, screening the increasingly popular new Chinese films.

Traditional archway entrance to Chinatown in Dixon Street

National Maritime Museum ⓯

1602 Willem Blaeu Celestial Globe

Bounded as it is by the sea, Australia's history is inextricably linked to maritime traditions. The museum displays material in a broad range of permanent and temporary thematic exhibits, many with inter-active elements. As well as artifacts relating to the enduring Aboriginal maritime cultures, the exhibits survey the history of European exploratory voyages in the Pacific, the arrival of convict ships, successive waves of migration, water sports and recreation, and naval life. Historic vessels on show at the wharf include a flimsy Vietnamese refugee boat, sailing, fishing and pearling boats, a navy patrol boat and a World War II commando raider.

Museum Façade
The billowing steel roof design by Philip Cox suggests both the surging sea and the sails of a ship.

Passengers
The model of the Orcades *reflects the grace of 1950s liners. This display also charts harrowing sea voyages made by migrants and refugees.*

Merana Eora Nora – First People traces the seafaring traditions of Aboriginal peoples and Torres Strait Islanders.

The Tasman Light was used in a Tasmanian lighthouse.

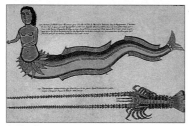

★ Navigators
This 1754 engraving of an East Indian sea creature is a European vision of the un-charted, exotic "great south".

The *Sirius* anchor is from a 1790 wreck off Norfolk Island.

Main entrance (sea level)

The Navy exhibit examines naval life in war and peace, as well as the history of colonial navies.

Linked by the Sea honours enduring links between the US and Australia. American traders stopped off in Aust-ralia on their way to China.

Key to Floorplan

- ☐ Navigators and Merana Eora Nora
- ☐ Passengers
- ☐ Commerce
- ☐ Watermarks
- ☐ Navy
- ☐ Linked by the Sea: USA Gallery
- ☐ Temporary exhibitions
- ☐ Non-exhibition space

Star Exhibits

- ★ **Navigators and Merana Eora Nora**
- ★ **Watermarks**
- ★ **Vampire**

Commerce
*This 1903 Painters'
and Dockers' Union
banner was carried by
waterfront workers in
marches. It shows the*
Niagara *entering the
dry dock at Cockatoo
Island (see p106).*

VISITORS' CHECKLIST

Darling Harbour. **Map** 3 C2.
9298 3777. *Sydney Explorer,
443, 888.* Pyrmont Bay.
Town Hall. Harbourside.
9:30am–5pm daily.
25 Dec.
Films, lectures.

Upper level

★ **Watermarks**
*This 1960s poster for Bondi
beach is part of the museum's*
Watermarks - adventure, sport and
play *exhibition. The displays,
including fully-rigged boats and
profiles of world champion scullers
and swimmers, celebrate Australia's
love affair with the water.*

**Nortel Networks
Gallery**

A replica of Captain
Cook's *Endeavour*
moors at this wharf
when in Sydney.

**Lightship
*Carpentaria***

**HMAS Onslow
(Oberon-class
submarine)**

Lighthouse
*Sailors were guided by
this 1874 lighthouse for
over a century. It was
rebuilt complete with
original kerosene lamp.*

★ **Vampire**
*The museum's largest vessel
is the 1959 Royal Australian
Navy destroyer, whose
insignia is shown here.
Tours of "The Bat" are
accompanied by simu-
lated battle action sounds.*

MUSEUM GUIDE
*The Leisure, Navy and Linked by the
Sea: USA Gallery exhibits are located
on the main entrance level (sea level).
The First Australians, Discovery,
Passengers and Commerce sections
are found on the first level. There is
access to the fleet from both levels.*

Powerhouse Museum ⑱

Woman's skirt, North Laos

THIS FORMER POWER STATION, completed in 1902 to provide power for Sydney's tramway system, was redesigned to cater for the needs of a modern, hands-on museum. Revamped, the Powerhouse opened in 1988. The early collection was held in the Garden Palace hosting the 1879 international exhibition of invention and industry from around the world. Few exhibits survived the devastating 1882 fire, and today's huge and ever-expanding holdings were gathered after this disaster. The buildings' monumental scale provides an ideal context for the epic sweep of ideas encompassed within: everything from the realm of space and technology to the decorative and domestic arts. The museum emphasizes Australian innovations and achievements celebrating both the extraordinary and the everyday.

Cyberworlds: Computers and Connections
This display explores the past, present and future of computers. Pictured here is a Japanese tin toy robot.

Soviet Organic Satellite Model
Replica spacecraft and a "habitation module", complete with kitchenette and sleeping area, detail the past and future of space exploration.

Level 3

Bayagul: Contemporary Indigenous Australian Communication
This handtufted rug, designed by Jimmy Pike, is displayed in an exhibit showcasing Aboriginal and Torres Strait Island cultures.

MUSEUM GUIDE

The museum is two buildings: the former powerhouse and the Neville Wran building. There are over 20 exhibitions on four levels, descending from Level 5, the restaurant level. The shop, entrance and main exhibits are on Level 4. Level 3 has thematic exhibits and a Design Gallery. Level 2 has experiments and displays on space, computers and transport.

KEY TO FLOORPLAN

▨	Level 5: Asian Gallery
▢	Level 4: Decorative Arts, Innovation & Temp. Exhibitions
▢	Level 3: Social History & Design
▢	Level 2: Science & Technology
▨	Non-exhibition space

Level 2

Egyptian Chair
The museum's collection of rare decorative arts includes Thomas Hope's Egyptian chair (c.1800), historic costumes and Wedgwood china.

VISITORS' CHECKLIST

500 Harris St, Ultimo. **Map** 4 D4.
9217 0111. 501.
Darling Harbour. Town Hall, Central. Haymarket.
10am–5pm daily. 25 Dec. W www.phm.gov.au

Level 5

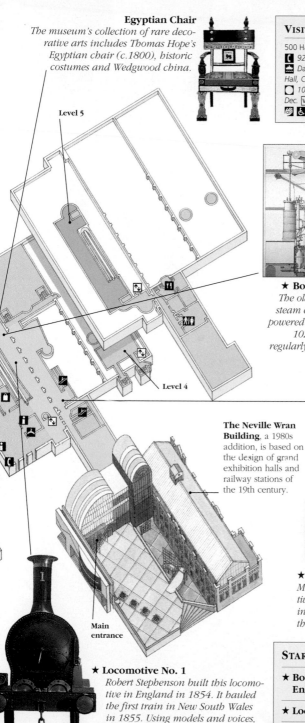

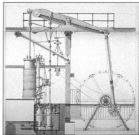

★ **Boulton & Watt Engine**
The oldest surviving rotative steam engine in the world, it powered a London brewery for 102 years from 1875. It is regularly put into operation in the museum.

Level 4

The Neville Wran Building, a 1980s addition, is based on the design of grand exhibition halls and railway stations of the 19th century.

★ **Interactive Displays**
More than 100 interactive units engage visitors in play while teaching them about science.

Main entrance

★ **Locomotive No. 1**
Robert Stephenson built this locomotive in England in 1854. It hauled the first train in New South Wales in 1855. Using models and voices, the display re-creates a 19th-century day trip for a group of Sydneysiders.

STAR EXHIBITS

★ **Boulton & Watt Engine**

★ **Locomotive No. 1**

★ **Interactive Displays**

BOTANIC GARDENS AND THE DOMAIN

Wooden angel, St James Church

THIS TRANQUIL PART of Sydney can seem a world away from the bustle of the city centre. It is rich in the remnants of Sydney's convict and colonial past: the site of the first farm and the boulevard-like Macquarie Street where the barracks, hospital, church and mint – bastions of civic power – are among the oldest surviving public buildings in Australia. This street continues to assert its dominance today as the location of the state government of New South Wales.

The Domain, an open, grassy space, was originally set aside by the colony's first governor for his private use. Today it is filled with joggers and touch footballers sidestepping picnickers and sunbathers. In January, during the Festival of Sydney, it hosts outdoor concerts. The Royal Botanic Gardens, which with The Domain was the site of Australia's first park, is a haven where visitors can stroll around and enjoy the extensive collection of native and exotic flora.

SIGHTS AT A GLANCE

Historic Streets and Buildings
Conservatorium of Music ❷
Hyde Park Barracks ⓫
Parliament House ❽
State Library of New South Wales ❼
Sydney Hospital ❾
Sydney Mint ❿

Museums and Galleries
Art Gallery of New South Wales pp106–109 ❺

Churches
St James Church ⓬

Islands
Fort Denison ❹

Monuments
Mrs Macquaries Chair ❸

Parks and Gardens
Royal Botanic Gardens pp102–103 ❶
The Domain ❻

GETTING THERE
Visit on foot, if possible. St James' and Martin Place train stations are close to most of the sights. The 311 bus from Circular Quay runs near the Art Gallery of NSW. The Sydney Explorer also stops at several sights.

0 metres	500
0 yards	500

KEY

▬ Royal Botanic Gardens pp102–103

🅿 Parking

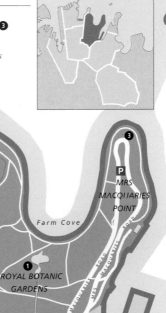

◁ **Succulents and cacti from the Succulent Garden in the Royal Botanic Gardens**

Royal Botanic Gardens ❶

THE ROYAL BOTANIC GARDENS, a 30-ha (75-acre) oasis in the heart of the city, occupy a superb position, wrapped around Farm Cove at the harbour's edge. Established in 1816 as a series of pathways through shrubbery, they are the oldest scientific institution in the country and house an outstanding collection of plants from Australia and overseas. A living museum, the gardens are also the site of the first farm in the fledgling colony. Fountains, statues and monuments are today scattered throughout. Plant specimens collected by Joseph Banks on Captain James Cook's epic voyage along the east coast of Australia in 1770 are displayed in the National Herbarium of New South Wales, an important centre for research on Australian plants.

Statue in the Botanic Gardens

LOCATOR MAP
See Street Finder, *maps 1 & 2*

Government House (1897)

★ **Palm Grove**
Begun in 1862, this cool summer haven is one of the world's finest outdoor collections of palms. There are about 180 species in the grove.

Conservatorium of Music *(see p104)*

★ **Herb Garden**
Herbs from around the world used for a wide variety of purposes – culinary, medicinal and aromatic – are on display here. A sensory fountain and a sundial modelled on the celestial sphere are also features.

★ **Sydney Tropical Centre**
Two glasshouses contain tropical ecosystems in miniature. Native vegetation is displayed in the Pyramid, while the Arc holds plants not found locally, commonly known as exotics.

| 0 metres | 200 |
| 0 yards | 200 |

Macquarie Wall
*In 1810, work began on
this 290-m (950-ft) long
wall intended to separate
the convict domain from
the town's "respectable
Class of Inhabitants".
Only a small section
remains standing today.*

Mrs Macquaries Chair,
where the governor's wife
liked to watch the har-
bour, is marked by a rock
ledge seat *(see p104).*

**Mrs Macquaries
Road**

VISITORS' CHECKLIST

Mrs Macquaries Rd. **Maps** 1 & 2.
9231 8111. **Guided tours**
9231 8125. Sydney Explorer,
438, 440, 441, 470, 888.
Circular Quay. Martin Place,
St James, Circular Quay. 7am–
8pm Nov–Mar, 7am–6:30pm Oct,
7am–6pm Apr & Sep, 7am–5:30pm
May & Aug, 7am–5pm Jun & Jul.
10:30am daily (excl.
public hols). **Tropical Centre**
10am–4pm daily.

The Fleet Steps
met those disem-
barking from ships
in Farm Cove.

Choragic Monument *(1870)*
*This replica of the eponymous statue
of Lysicrates in Athens was carved
in sandstone by Walter McGill.*

**Andrew (Boy)
Charlton Pool**
is a popular spot
for inner-city
swimming and
sunbathing.

★ Australia's First Farm
*Some oblong beds in the
Middle Garden follow the
direction of the first furrows
ploughed in the colony.*

**National Herbarium
of New South Wales**
*About one million dried plant
specimens document biological
diversity. Discovery and collection
of new plants aims to slow down
the extinction rate of entire species.*

ollemi
ine

STAR FEATURES

★ **Australia's First
Farm**

★ **Herb Garden**

★ **Palm Grove**

★ **Sydney Tropical
Centre**

Conservatorium of Music ❷

Macquarie St. **Map** 1 C3. ☎ (02) 9351 1222. 🚌 Sydney Explorer, Circular Quay routes. ☐ 9am–5pm Mon–Fri, 9am–4pm Sat, public areas only. Phone for details of concerts. ♿

W HEN IT WAS finished in 1821, this striking castellated Colonial Gothic building was meant to be the stables and servants' quarters for Government House, but construction of the latter was delayed for almost 25 years. That stables should be built in so grand a style, and at such great cost, brought forth cries of outrage and led to bitter arguments between the architect, Francis Greenway (see p161), and Governor Macquarie – and a decree that all future building plans be submitted to London.

Between 1908 and 1915 "Greenway's folly" underwent a dramatic transformation. A concert hall, roofed in grey slate, was built on the central courtyard and the building in its entirety was converted for the use of the new Sydney Conservatorium of Music.

Recently added facilities include a jazz bar and a rooftop area that has spectacular harbour views. With these features, the "Con" is a great tourist attraction at the same time as it continues its tradition as a training ground for Australia's future musicians.

Resting on the carved stone seat of Mrs Macquaries Chair

Mrs Macquaries Chair ❸

Mrs Macquaries Rd. **Map** 2 E2. 🚌 Sydney Explorer, 888. ♿ 📷

T HE SCENIC Mrs Macquaries Road winds alongside much of what is now the city's Royal Botanic Gardens, stretching from Farm Cove to Woolloomooloo Bay and back again. The road was built in 1816 at the instigation of Elizabeth Macquarie, wife of the Governor. In the same year, a stone bench, inscribed with details of the new road and its commissioner, was carved into the rock at the point where Mrs Macquarie would often stop to rest and admire the view on her daily stroll. Although today the outlook is much changed, it is just as arresting, taking in the broad sweep of the harbour with all its landmarks.

Rounding the cove to the west leads to Mrs Macquaries Point. These lawns are a popular picnic spot with Sydney-siders, particularly at sunset.

Fort Denison ❹

Sydney Harbour. **Map** 2 E1. ☎ (02) 9247 5033. ⛴ Circular Quay. ☐ Boat tours from Circular Quay at noon and 2pm daily, 10am Sat & Sun. ● 25 Dec. 📷 📷 visit is by guided tour only, bookings essential.

F IRST NAMED Rock Island, this prominent, rocky outcrop in Sydney Harbour was also dubbed "Pinchgut". This was probably because of the meagre rations given to convicts who were confined there as punishment. It had a grim

Fort Denison in 1907

history of incarceration in the early years of the colony.

In 1796, the convicted murderer Francis Morgan was hanged on the island in chains. His body was left to rot on the gallows for three years as a warning to the other convicts.

Between 1855 and 1857, the Martello tower (the only one in Australia), gun battery and barracks that now occupy the island were built as part of Sydney's defences. The site was renamed after the governor of the time. The gun, still fired at 1pm each day, helped mariners to set their ships' chronometers accurately.

Today the island is the perfect setting for watching the many harbour activities, such as the New Year fireworks displays (see p37). To explore Fort Denison, book one of the daily boat tours that leave from Circular Quay.

Art Gallery of New South Wales ❺

See pp106–107.

Conservatorium of Music at the edge of the Royal Botanic Gardens

The Domain ❻

Art Gallery Rd. **Map** 1 C4. 🚌 *Sydney Explorer, 888.* ♿

T HE MANY PEOPLE who swarm to the January concerts and other Festival of Sydney events in The Domain are part of a long-standing tradition. They come equipped with picnic baskets and blankets to enjoy the ongoing entertainment.

Once the governor's private park, this extensive space is now public and has long been a rallying point for crowds of Sydneysiders whenever emotive issues of public importance have arisen. These have included the attempt in 1916 to introduce military conscription and the sudden dismissal of the elected federal government by the then governor-general in 1975.

From the 1890s, part of The Domain was also used as the Sydney version of "Speakers' Corner". Today, you are more likely to see joggers or office workers playing touch football in their lunch hours, or simply enjoying the shade.

Harbour view from The Domain

State Library of New South Wales ❼

Macquarie St. **Map** 4 F1. 📞 *(02) 9273 1414.* 🚌 *Sydney Explorer, Elizabeth St routes.* ◯ *9am–9pm Mon–Fri, 11am–5pm Sat & Sun.* ● *most public hols.* ♿ 🎥 💻 📷

T HE STATE LIBRARY is housed in two separate buildings connected by a passageway and a glass bridge. The older building, the Mitchell Library wing (1906), is a majestic sandstone edifice facing the

Mosaic replica of the Tasman Map, State Library of New South Wales

Royal Botanic Gardens *(see pp102–103).* Huge stone columns supporting a vaulted ceiling frame the impressive vestibule. On the vestibule floor is a mosaic replica of an old map illustrating the two voyages made to Australia by Dutch navigator Abel Tasman in the 1640s *(see p45).* The two ships of the first voyage are shown off the south coast, the two from the second voyage are seen to the northwest. The original Tasman Map is held in the Mitchell Library as part of its collection of historic Australian paintings, books, documents and pictorial records.

The Mitchell wing's vast reading room, with its huge skylight and oak panelling, is just beyond the main vestibule. The newest section is an attractive contemporary structure that faces Macquarie Street *(see pp110–111).* This area now houses the State Reference Library, open to anyone who wishes to use it. Beyond the Mitchell wing is the Dixson Gallery, housing cultural and historical exhibitions which change regularly.

Outside the library, facing Macquarie Street, is a statue of the explorer Matthew Flinders, who first ventured into central Australia *(see pp48–9).* On the windowsill behind him is a statue of his travelling companion, his cat, Trim.

Parliament House ❽

Macquarie St. **Map** 4 F1. 📞 *(02) 9230 2111.* 🚌 *Sydney Explorer, Elizabeth St routes.* ◯ *when not in session: 9am–4:30pm Mon–Fri; in session 9am–7pm Mon–Fri.* ● *public hols.* ♿ 🎥

T HE CENTRAL SECTION of this building, which houses the State Parliament, is part of the original Sydney Hospital built from 1811–16 *(see p109).* It has been a seat of government since the 1820s when the newly appointed Legislative Council first held meetings here. The building was extended twice during the 19th century and again during the 1970s and 1980s. The current building contains the chambers for both houses of state parliament, as well as parliamentary offices.

Parliamentary memorabilia is on view in the Jubilee Room, as are displays showing Parliament House's development and the legislative history of the state. The corrugated iron building with a cast-iron façade tacked on at the southern end was a prefabricated kit from England. In

Malby's celestial globe, Parliament House

1856, this dismantled kit became the chamber for the new Legislative Council. Its packing cases were used to line the chamber; the rough timber can still be seen.

Art Gallery of New South Wales ❺

Established in 1874, the art gallery has occupied its present imposing building since 1897. Designed by the Colonial Architect WL Vernon, the gallery doubled in size following 1988 building extensions. Two equestrian bronzes – *The Offerings of Peace* and *The Offerings of War* – greet the visitor on entry. The gallery itself houses some of the finest works of art in Australia. It has sections devoted to Australian, Asian, European, photographic and contemporary and photographic works, along with a strong collection of prints and drawings. The Yiribana Gallery, the largest in the world to exclusively exhibit Aboriginal and Torres Strait Islander art and culture, was opened in 1994.

Cycladic figure (c.2,500 BC)

Sofala *(1947)*
Russell Drysdale's visions of Australia show "ghost" towns laid waste by devastating natural forces such as drought.

Sunbaker *(1937)*
Max Dupain's iconic, almost abstract, Australian photograph of hedonism and sun worship uses clean lines, strong light, and geometric form. Its power lies in its simplicity.

The Sculpture Terrace is a small outdoor area which has large-scale sculptures on display.

Madonna and Child with Infant St John the Baptist
This oil on wood (c.1541) is the work of Siena Mannerist artist Domenico Beccafumi.

Upper Level (closed)

Temporary exhibitions, often by much-acclaimed Australian artists, are held here throughout the year.

STAR EXHIBITS

★ **The Golden Fleece – Shearing at Newstead by Tom Roberts**

★ **Pukumani Grave Posts**

GALLERY GUIDE

The collection has five levels. The Upper Level is closed for renovation. The Ground Level has European and Australian works. Temporary exhibitions are held on Lower Level 1, 20th-century European prints are on Lower Level 2 and the Yiribana Aboriginal Gallery is on Lower Level 3.

Ground Level

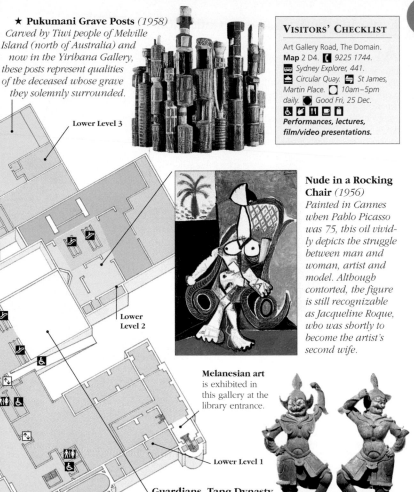

★ **Pukumani Grave Posts** *(1958)*
Carved by Tiwi people of Melville Island (north of Australia) and now in the Yiribana Gallery, these posts represent qualities of the deceased whose grave they solemnly surrounded.

Lower Level 3

Nude in a Rocking Chair *(1956)*
Painted in Cannes when Pablo Picasso was 75, this oil vividly depicts the struggle between man and woman, artist and model. Although contorted, the figure is still recognizable as Jacqueline Roque, who was shortly to become the artist's second wife.

Lower Level 2

Melanesian art
is exhibited in this gallery at the library entrance.

Lower Level 1

Guardians, Tang Dynasty
These 7th-century Chinese figures are part of a collection highlighting different traditions, periods and cultures from the many countries of Asia.

★ **The Golden Fleece** *(1894)*
Also known as Shearing at Newstead, *this work by Tom Roberts marks the coming of age of Australian Impressionist art.*

The sandstone entrance was added in 1909.

KEY TO FLOORPLAN

☐ Australian Art
☐ European Art
☐ Sculpture Terrace
☐ Photography
☐ Asian Art
☐ Prints, Drawings and Watercolours
☐ Contemporary Art
☐ Yiribana Gallery
☐ Temporary exhibition space
☐ Non-exhibition space

Exploring the Art Gallery's Collection

A LTHOUGH LOCAL WORKS had been collected since 1875, the gallery did not seriously begin seeking Australian and non-British art until the 1920s, and not until the 1940s did it begin acquiring Aboriginal and Torres Strait Islander paintings. These contrasting collections are now its greatest strength. The gallery also stages major temporary exhibitions regularly, with the annual Archibald, Wynne and Sulman prizes being among the most controversial and highly entertaining.

Study for Self Portrait, a Francis Bacon painting from 1976

Grace Cossington Smith's 1955 Interior with Wardrobe Mirror

AUSTRALIAN ART

A MONG THE most important colonial works is John Glover's *Natives on the Ouse River, Van Diemen's Land* (1838), an image of doomed Tasmanian Aborigines. The old wing also holds paintings from the Heidelberg school of Australian Impressionism *(see p30)*. Tom Roberts' *The Golden Fleece – Shearing at Newstead* (1894) hangs alongside fine works by Charles Conder, Frederick McCubbin and Arthur Streeton.

Australia was slow to take up Modernism. *Western Australian Gum Blossom* (1928)

is Margaret Preston at her most assertive during the 1920s. Sidney Nolan's works range from *Boy in Township* (1943) to *Burke* (c.1962), exploiting myths of early Australian history. There are also fine holdings of William Dobell, Russell Drysdale, Arthur Boyd, Grace Cossington Smith and Brett Whiteley *(see p30)*.

The Yiribana Gallery exhibits Aboriginal and Torres Strait Islander works. The ability of contemporary artists to apply traditional styles to new media forms while retaining "Aboriginality" is repeatedly demonstrated.

Significant early purchases were natural pigment paintings on bark and card, often containing a figurative motif of everyday life. The bark painting *Three Mimis Dancing* (1964) by Samuel Wagbara examines themes of ancestral spirits and the creation cycles. *Pukumani Grave Posts Melville Island* (1958) is a ceremonial work dealing with death. Emily Kame Kngwarreye honours the land from which she comes with very intricate dot paintings, created using new tools and technology.

EUROPEAN ART

T HE EUROPEAN collection ranges from medieval to modern. British art from the 19th and 20th centuries forms a large component, including artists such as Francis Bacon. Among the Old Masters are significant Italian works. Neo-Classical works are also held. *Chaucer at the Court of Edward III* (1845–51) by Ford Madox Brown is a fine Pre-Raphaelite work.

Henry Moore's Reclining Figure: Angles (1980)

The Impressionists and Post-Impressionists are represented by Pissarro and Monet. *Nude in a Rocking Chair* (1956) by Picasso, was bought in 1981. Among the sculptures is Henry Moore's *Reclining Figure: Angles* (1980).

PHOTOGRAPHY

A USTRALIAN photography from 1975 to the present day is represented in all its various forms. Recently, however, the emphasis has been on building up a body of 19th-century Australian work. Nearly 3,000 prints constitute this collection with pieces by Charles Kerry, Charles Bayliss and Harold Cazneaux, a major figure of early 20th-century Pictorialism.

Such international photographers as Muybridge, Robert Mapplethorpe and Man Ray are also represented here.

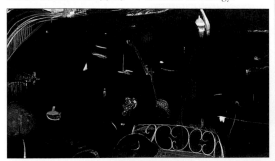

Brett Whiteley's vivid The Balcony (2) from 1975

ASIAN ART

THIS COLLECTION is one of the finest in Australia. Chinese art is represented from the pre-Shang dynasty (c.1600 –1027 BC) to the 20th century. The Ming porcelains, earthenware funerary pieces (*mingqi*) and the sculptures deserve close attention.

The Japanese collection has fine examples by major artists of the Edo period (1615–1867). The Southeast Asian and Indian art consists of lacquer, ceramics and sculptures.

PRINTS AND DRAWINGS

THIS COLLECTION represents the European tradition from the High Renaissance to the 19th and 20th centuries, with work by Rembrandt, Constable, William Blake, Edvard Munch and Egon Schiele. A strong bias towards Sydney artists of the past 100 years has resulted in an exceptional gathering of work by Thea Proctor, Norman and Lionel Lindsay and Lloyd Rees.

Egon Schiele's *Poster for the Vienna Secession* (1918)

CONTEMPORARY ART

THE CONTEMPORARY ART collection highlights the themes that have been central to art practice since the 1970s. Works by Australian artists such as Imants Tillers, Ken Unsworth and Susan Norrie are on display alongside pieces by international artists such as Cindy Sherman, Yves Klein and Philip Guston.

Il Porcellino, the bronze boar in front of Sydney Hospital

Sydney Hospital **9**

Macquarie St. **Map** 1 C4. **C** *(02) 9382 7111.* 🚌 *Sydney Explorer, Elizabeth St routes.* ◯ *daily.* 🎫 *for tours.* ♿ 📷 *book in advance.*

THIS IMPOSING collection of Victorian sandstone buildings stands on the site of what was once the central section of the original convict-built Sydney Hospital. It was known locally as the Rum Hospital because the builders were paid by being allowed to import rum for resale. Both the north and south wings of the Rum Hospital survive as Parliament House *(see p105)* and the Sydney Mint. The central wing was demolished in 1879 and the new hospital, which is still operational, was completed in 1894.

The Classical Revival building boasts a Baroque staircase and elegant stained-glass windows in its central hall. Florence Nightingale approved the design of the 1868 nurses' wing. In the inner courtyard, there is a brightly coloured Art Deco fountain (1907), somewhat out of place among the surrounding heavy stonework.

At the front of the hospital sits a bronze boar called *Il Porcellino*. It is a replica of a 17th-century fountain in Florence's Mercato Nuovo. Donated in 1968 by an Italian woman whose relatives had worked at the hospital, the statue is an enduring symbol of the friendship between Italy and Australia. Like his Florentine counterpart, *Il Porcellino* is supposed to bring good luck to all those who rub his snout. Coins tossed in the pool at his feet for luck and fortune are collected for the hospital.

Stained glass at Sydney Hospital

Sydney Mint **10**

Macquarie St. **Map** 1 C5. **C** *(02) 9692 8366.* 🚌 *Sydney Explorer, Elizabeth St routes.* ⬤ *to the general public.*

THE GOLD RUSHES of the mid-19th century transformed colonial Australia *(see pp50–51)*. The Sydney Mint opened in 1854 in the south wing of the Rum Hospital in order to turn recently discovered gold into bullion and currency. This was the first branch of the Royal Mint to be established outside London, but it was closed in 1927 as it was no longer competitive with the mints in Melbourne *(see p379)* and Perth *(see p297)*. The Georgian building then went into decline after it was converted into government offices.

The mint artifacts are now housed in the Powerhouse Museum *(see pp98–9)*. The Sydney Mint is under the auspices of the Historic Houses Trust of NSW and though the building is closed to the public there is a small historical display at the entrance.

Hyde Park Barracks ⓫

Queens Square, Macquarie St.
Map 1 C5. (02) 9223 8922.
St James, Martin Place.
9:30am–5pm daily. Good Fri,
25 Dec. level one only.
group tours.

Replica convict hammocks on the third floor of Hyde Park Barracks

Dᴇꜱᴄʀɪʙᴇᴅ ʙʏ Governor Macquarie as "spacious" and "well-aired", the beautifully proportioned barracks are the work of Francis Greenway and are considered his masterpiece *(see p161)*. They were completed in 1819 by convict labour and designed to house 600 convicts. Until that time convicts had been forced to find their own lodgings after their day's work. Subsequently, the building then housed, in turn, young Irish orphans and single female immigrants, before it later became courts and legal offices. Refurbished in 1990, the barracks reopened as a museum on the history of the site and its occupants.

The displays include a room reconstructed as convict quarters of the 1820s, as well as pictures, models and artifacts. Many of the objects recovered during archaeological digs at the site and now on display survived because they had been dragged away by rats to their nests; today the rodents are acknowledged as valuable agents of preservation.

The Greenway Gallery on the first floor holds varied exhibitions on history and culture. Elsewhere, the Barracks Café, which incorporates the original cell area, offers views of the courtyard, today cool and attractive but in the past the scene of brutal convict floggings.

Mᴀᴄǫᴜᴀʀɪᴇ Sᴛʀᴇᴇᴛ

Described in the 1860s as one of the gloomiest streets in Sydney, this could now claim to be the most elegant. Open to the harbour breezes and the greenery of The Domain, a stroll down this tree-lined street is a pleasant way to view the architectural heritage of Sydney.

This wing of the library was built in 1988 and connected to the old section by a glass walkway.

The Mitchell Library wing's portico (1906) has Ionic columns.

Parliament House was once the convict-built Rum Hospital's northern wing.

1. Sᴛᴀᴛᴇ Lɪʙʀᴀʀʏ ᴏꜰ NSW *(1906–41)*

2. Pᴀʀʟɪᴀᴍᴇɴᴛ Hᴏᴜꜱᴇ *(1811–*

The roof of the Sydney Mint has now been completely restored to replicate the original wooden shingles in casuarina (she-oak).

The Sydney Mint, like its twin, Parliament House, has an unusual double-colonnaded, two-storeyed veranda.

Hyde Park Barracks Café

4. Sʏᴅɴᴇʏ Mɪɴᴛ *(1816)*

St James Church ⑫

179 King St. **Map** 1 B5. ☎ (02) 9232 3022. 🚇 St James, Martin Place. ◻ 9am–5pm daily. ♿ in process.

THIS FINE Georgian building, constructed with convict-made bricks, was designed as a courthouse in 1819. The architect, Francis Greenway, was forced to convert it into a church in 1820, when plans to build a cathedral on George Street were abandoned.

Greenway designed a simple yet elegant church. Consecrated in 1824, it is the city's oldest church. Many additions have been carried out, including designs by John Verge in which the pulpit faced the high-rent pews, while convicts and the military sat directly behind the preacher where the service would have been inaudible. A Children's Chapel was added in 1930.

Prominent members of early 19th-century society, many of whom died violently, are commemorated with marble tablets. These tell the bloody stories of luckless explorers, the governor's wife dashed to her death from her carriage, and shipwreck victims.

Detail from the Children's Chapel mural in the St James Church crypt

---

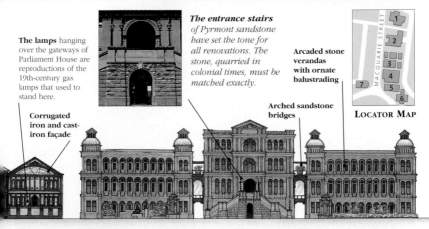

The lamps hanging over the gateways of Parliament House are reproductions of the 19th-century gas lamps that used to stand here.

Corrugated iron and cast-iron façade

The entrance stairs of Pyrmont sandstone have set the tone for all renovations. The stone, quarried in colonial times, must be matched exactly.

Arcaded stone verandas with ornate balustrading

Arched sandstone bridges

LOCATOR MAP

3. SYDNEY HOSPITAL (1868–94)

Georgian sandstone façade

Statue of Prince Albert

The Land Titles Office, a WL Vernon building from 1908, has a Classical form with some fine Tudor Gothic detailing.

The stained-glass windows in St James Church are mostly 20th century and represent the union formed by air, earth, fire and water.

Copper spire

. **HYDE PARK BARRACKS** (1817–19)   **6. LAND TITLES OFFICE** (1908–13)   **7. ST JAMES** (1820)

The front entrance to a lovingly restored Victorian terrace house in Paddington

SIGHTS AT A GLANCE

Historic Streets and Buildings
Darlinghurst Court House **7**
Elizabeth Bay House **3**
Five Ways **8**
Fox Studios **16**
Juniper Hall **10**
Old Gaol, Darlinghurst **6**
Paddington Street **14**
Paddington Town Hall **11**
Paddington Village **9**
Victoria Barracks **12**
Victoria Street **2**

Parks and Gardens
Beare Park **4**
Centennial Park **15**

Museums and Galleries
Sydney Jewish Museum **5**

Monuments
El Alamein Fountain **1**

Markets
Paddington Markets **13**

KINGS CROSS, DARLINGHURST AND PADDINGTON

SYDNEY'S KINGS CROSS and Darlinghurst districts are still remembered for their 1920s gangland associations. However, both areas are now cosmopolitan and densely populated parts of the city. Kings Cross has a thriving café society, in spite of the nearby red light district. Darlinghurst comes into its own every March, during the

**Façade detail,
Del Rio (see p115)**

flamboyant Gay and Lesbian Mardi Gras parade. The Victorian terraces of Paddington are still admired for their wrought-iron "lace" verandas. Paddington is also famed for its fine restaurants, galleries and antiques shops. On Saturdays, people flock to the Paddington Bazaar, spilling out into the pubs and cafés of the surrounding area.

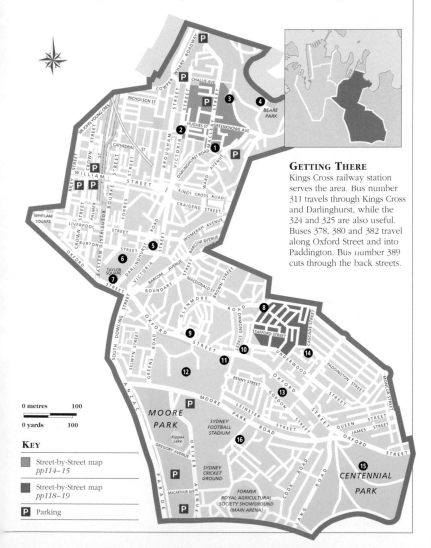

GETTING THERE

Kings Cross railway station serves the area. Bus number 311 travels through Kings Cross and Darlinghurst, while the 324 and 325 are also useful. Buses 378, 380 and 382 travel along Oxford Street and into Paddington. Bus number 389 cuts through the back streets.

KEY

Street-by-Street map
pp114–15

Street-by-Street map
pp118–19

P Parking

0 metres 100
0 yards 100

Street-by-Street: Potts Point

Beare Park fountain detail

THE SUBSTANTIAL VICTORIAN houses filling the streets of this old suburb are excellent examples of the 19th-century concern with architectural harmony. New building projects were designed to enhance rather than contradict the surrounding buildings and general streetscape. Monumental structures and fine details of moulded stuccoed parapets, cornices and friezes, even the spandrels in herringbone pattern, are all integral parts of a grand suburban plan. (This plan included an 1831 order that all houses cost at least £1,000.) Cool, dark verandas extend the street's green canopy of shade, leaving an impression of cold drinks enjoyed on summer days in fine Victorian style.

The McElhone Stairs were preceded by a wooden ladder that linked Woolloomooloo Hill, as Kings Cross was known, to the estate far below.

Horderns Stairs

These villas, from the Georgian and Victorian eras, can be broadly labelled as Classical Revival and are fronted by leafy gardens.

Kings Cross Station

★ **Victoria Street**
From 1972–4, residents of this historic street fought a sometimes violent battle against developers wanting to build high-rise towers, motels and blocks of flats ❷

Werrington, a mostly serious and streamlined building, also has flamboyant Art Deco detailing which is now hidden under brown paint.

STAR SIGHTS

★ **Elizabeth Bay House**

★ **Victoria Street**

Tusculum Villa was just one of a number of 1830s houses subject to "villa conditions". All had to face Government House, be of a high monetary value and be built within three years.

Challis Avenue is a fine and shady comple-ment to nearby Victoria Street. This Romanesque group of terrace houses has an unusual façade, with arches fronting deep verandas and a grand ground floor colonnade.

LOCATOR MAP
See Street Finder, *map 2*

Rockwall, a symmetrical and compact Regency villa, was built to the designs of the architect John Verge in 1830–37.

Del Rio is a finely detailed high-rise apartment block. It clearly exhibits the Spanish Mission in-fluence that filtered through from California in the first quarter of the 20th century.

Landmark Hotel

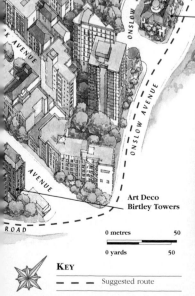

★ **Elizabeth Bay House**
A contemporary exclaimed over the beauty of the 1830s garden: "Trees from Rio, the West Indies, the East Indies, China . . . the bulbs from the Cape are splendid." ❸

The Arthur McElhone Reserve

Art Deco Birtley Towers

0 metres   50
0 yards   50

KEY
— — — Suggested route

Elizabeth Bay was part of the original land grant to Alexander Macleay. He created a botanist's paradise with ornamental ponds, quaint grottoes and prome-nades winding all the way down to the harbour.

El Alamein Fountain, commemorating the World War II battle

El Alamein Fountain ❶

Fitzroy Gardens, Macleay St, Potts Point. **Map** 2 E5. 🚌 *311.*

THIS DANDELION of a fountain in the heart of the Kings Cross district has a reputation for working so spasmodically that passers-by often murmur facetiously, "He loves me, he loves me not." Built in 1961, it commemorates the Australian army's role in the siege of Tobruk, Libya, and the battle of El Alamein in Egypt during World War II. At night, when it is brilliantly lit, the fountain looks surprisingly ethereal.

Victoria Street ❷

Potts Point. **Map** 5 B2. 🚌 *311, 324, 325.*

AT THE POTTS POINT end, this street of 19th-century terrace houses, interspersed with a few incongruous-looking high-rise blocks, is, by inner-city standards, almost a boulevard. The gracious street you see today was once at the centre of a bitterly fought conservation struggle, one which almost certainly cost the life of a prominent heritage campaigner.

In the early 1970s, many residents, backed by the "green bans" put in place by the Builders' Labourers Federation of New South Wales, fought to prevent demolition of old buildings for high-rise

development. Juanita Nielsen, heiress and publisher of a local newspaper, vigorously took up the conservation battle. On 4 July 1975, she disappeared without trace. An inquest into her disappearance returned an open verdict.

As a result of the actions of the union and residents, most of Victoria Street's superb old buildings still stand. Ironically, they are now occupied not by the low-income residents who fought to save them, but by the well-off professionals who eventually displaced them.

Juanita Nielsen

Elizabeth Bay House ❸

7 Onslow Ave, Elizabeth Bay. **Map** 2 F5. 📞 *(02) 9356 3022.* 🚌 *Sydney Explorer, 311.* 🕐 *10am–4:30pm Tue–Sun.* 🚫 *Good Fri, 25 Dec.* 📷

ELIZABETH BAY HOUSE contains the finest colonial interior on display in Australia. It is a potent expression of how the depression of the 1840s cut short the 1830s' prosperous optimism. Designed in Greek Revival style by John Verge, it was built for Colonial Secretary Alexander Macleay, from 1835–39. The oval saloon with its dome and cantilevered staircase is recognized as Verge's masterpiece. The exterior is less satisfactory, as the intended colonnade and portico were not finished owing to a crisis in Macleay's financial affairs. The present portico dates from

1893. The interior is furnished to reflect Macleay's occupancy from 1839–45, and is based on inventories drawn up in 1845 for the transfer of the house and contents to his son, William Sharp. He took the house in return for paying off his father's debts, leading to a rift that was never resolved.

Macleay's original 22-ha (55-acre) land grant was subdivided for flats and villas from the 1880s to 1927. In the 1940s, the house itself was divided into 15 flats. In 1942, the artist Donald Friend saw the ferry *Kuttabul* hit by a torpedo from a Japanese midget submarine from his flat's balcony.

The house was restored and opened as a museum in 1977. It is a property of the Historic Houses Trust of NSW.

The sweeping staircase under the oval dome, Elizabeth Bay House

Beare Park ❹

Ithaca Rd, Elizabeth Bay. **Map** 2 F5. 🚌 *311, 350.*

ORIGINALLY A PART of the Macleay Estate, Beare Park is now encircled by a jumble of apartment blocks. A refuge from hectic Kings Cross, it is one of only a few parks serving a populated area. Shaped like a natural amphitheatre, the park has glorious views of Elizabeth Bay.

The family home of JC Williamson, a famous theatrical entrepreneur who came to Australia from America in the 1870s, formerly stood at the eastern extremity of the park.

Star of David in the lobby of the Sydney Jewish Museum

Sydney Jewish Museum 5

148 Darlinghurst Rd, Darlinghurst. **Map** 5 B2. ☎ *(02) 9360 7999.* 🚌 *Sydney, Bondi & Bay Explorer, 311, 378.* ○ *10am–4pm Mon–Thu, 10am–2pm Fri, 11am–5pm Sun.* ● *Sat, Jewish hols.* ✋ ♿ ✋

SIXTEEN JEWISH convicts were on the First Fleet, and many more were to be transported before the end of the convict era. As with other convicts, most would endure and some would thrive, seizing all the opportunities the colony had to offer.

The Sydney Jewish Museum relates stories of Australian Jewry within the context of the Holocaust. The ground floor display explores present-day Jewish traditions and culture within Australia. Ascending the stairs to the mezzanine levels 1–6, the visitor passes through chronological and thematic exhibitions which unravel the tragic history of the Holocaust.

From Hitler's rise to power and *Kristallnacht,* through the evacuation of the ghettos and the Final Solution, to the ultimate liberation of the infamous death camps and Nuremberg Trials, the harrowing events are graphically documented. This horrific period is recalled using photographs and relics, some exhumed from mass graves, as well as audiovisual exhibits and oral testimonies.

Holocaust survivors act as guides on each level. Their presence, bearing witness to the recorded events, lends considerable power and moving authenticity to the exhibits throughout the museum.

Old Gaol, Darlinghurst 6

Cnr Burton & Forbes sts, Darlinghurst. **Map** 5 A2. ☎ *(02) 9339 8666.* 🚌 *378, 380, 382.* ○ *9am–5pm Mon–Fri.* ● *public hols.* ♿

ORIGINALLY KNOWN as the Woolloomooloo Stockade and later as Darlinghurst Gaol, this complex is now part of the Sydney Institute of Technology. It was constructed over a 20-year period from 1822.

Surrounded by walls almost 7 m (23 ft) high, the cell blocks radiate from a central roundhouse. The jail is built of stone quarried on the site by convicts which was then chiselled by them into blocks.

No fewer than 67 people were executed here between 1841 and 1908. Perhaps the most notorious hangman was Alexander "The Strangler" Green, after whom Green Park, outside the jail, is thought to have been named. Green lived near the park until public hostility forced him to live in relative safety inside the jail.

Some of Australia's most noted artists, including Frank Hodgkinson, Jon Molvig and William Dobell, trained or taught at the art school which was established here in 1921.

The former Governor's house, Old Gaol, Darlinghurst

Darlinghurst Court House 7

Forbes St, Darlinghurst. **Map** 5 A2. ☎ *(02) 9368 2947.* 🚌 *378, 380, 382.* ○ *Feb–Dec: 10am–4pm Mon–Fri & Sun.* ● *Jan, public hols.* ♿ ✋

ABUTTING THE GRIM old gaol, to which it is connected by underground passages, and facing tawdry Taylors Square, this unlikely gem of Greek Revival architecture was begun in 1835 by colonial architect Mortimer Lewis. He was only responsible for the central block of the main building with its six-columned Doric portico with Greek embellishments. The side wings were not added until the 1880s.

The Court House is still used by the state's Supreme Court, mainly for criminal cases, and these are open to the public.

Beare Park, a quiet inner-city park with harbour views

Street-by-Street: Paddington

PADDINGTON BEGAN TO FLOURISH in the 1840s, when the decision was made to build the Victoria Barracks. At the time much of it was "the most wild looking place . . . barren sand-hills with patches of scrub, hills and hollows galore." The area began to fill rapidly, as owner builders bought into the area and built rows of terrace houses, many very narrow because of the lack of building regulations. After the Depression, most of the district was threatened with demolition, but was saved and restored by the large influx of postwar migrants.

Victorian finial in Union Street

★ Five Ways
This shopping hub was established in the late 19th century on the busy Glenmore roadway trodden out by bullocks ❽

Duxford Street's terrace houses in toning pale shades constitute an ideal of town planning: the Victorians preferred houses in a row to have a pleasingly uniform aspect.

"Gingerbread" houses can be seen in Broughton and Union streets. With their steeply pitched gables and fretwork barge-boards, they are typical of the rustic Gothic Picturesque architectural style.

The London Tavern opened for business in 1875, making it the suburb's oldest pub. Like many of the pubs and delicatessens in this well-serviced suburb, it stands at the end of a row of terraces.

STAR SIGHTS
★ Five Ways
★ Paddington Street

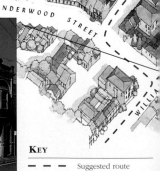

KEY	
– – –	Suggested route

The Sherman Gallery is housed in a strikingly modern building. It is designed to hold Australian and international contemporary sculpture and paintings. Suitable access gates and a special in-house crane enable the movement of large-scale artworks, including textiles.

LOCATOR MAP
See Street Finder, maps 5 & 6

Paddington's streets are a treasure trove of galleries, bars and restaurants. A wander through the area should prove an enjoyable experience.

Warwick, built in the 1860s, is a minor castle lying at the end of a row of humble terraces. Its turrets, battlements and assorted decorations, in a style somewhat fancifully described as "King Arthur", even adorn the garages at the rear.

Windsor Street's terrace houses are, in some cases, a mere 4.5 m (15 ft) wide.

Street-making in Paddington's early days was often an expensive and complicated business. A cascade of water was dammed to build Cascade Street.

★ **Paddington Street**
Under the established plane trees, some of Paddington's finest Victorian terraces exemplify the building boom of 1860–90. Over 30 years, 3,800 houses were built in the suburb ⑭

0 metres 50

0 yards 50

Balcony of the Royal Hotel

Five Ways ⑧

Cnr Glenmore Rd & Heeley St. **Map** 5 C3. 389.

At this picturesque junction, where three streets cross on Glenmore Road, a shopping hub developed by the tramline that ran from the city to Bondi Beach (see p122). On the five corners stand 19th- and early 20th-century shops, one now a restaurant.

Occupying another corner is the three-storey Royal Hotel, completed in 1888. This mixed Victorian and Classical Revival building, with its decorative cast-iron "lace" balcony offering harbour views, is typical of the hotel architecture of the time.

Paddington Village ⑨

Cnr Gipps & Shadforth sts. **Map** 5 C3. 378, 380, 382.

Paddington began its life as a working-class suburb of Sydney. The community mainly consisted of the carpenters, quarrymen and stonemasons who supervised the convict gangs that built the Victoria Barracks in the 1840s.

The 19th-century artisans and their families occupied a tight huddle of spartan houses crowded into the area's narrow streets. A few of these houses still remain. Like the barracks, these dwellings and surrounding shops and hotels were built of locally quarried stone.

The terraces of Paddington Village are now a popular address with young, up-and-coming Sydneysiders.

Juniper Hall ⑩

250 Oxford St. **Map** 5 C3. (02) 9258 0123. 378, 380, 382. special occasions only, phone first.

The emancipist gin distiller Robert Cooper built this superb example of colonial Georgian architecture for his third wife, Sarah. He named it after the main ingredient of the gin that made his fortune.

Completed in 1824, the two-storey home is the oldest dwelling still standing in Paddington. It is probably also the largest and most extravagant house ever built in the suburb. It had to be: Cooper already had 14 children when he declared that Sarah would have the finest house in Sydney. Once resident in the new house, he subsequently fathered 14 more.

Juniper Hall was saved from demolition in the mid-1980s and has been restored in fine style. Now under the auspices of the National Trust, the building is used as private office space.

Paddington Town Hall ⑪

Cnr Oxford St & Oatley Rd. **Map** 5 C3. 378, 380, 382. 10am–4pm Mon–Fri. public hols.

Paddington town hall was completed in 1891. A design competition was won by local architect JE Kemp. The Classical Revival building still dominates the area.

No longer a centre of local government, the building now houses a cinema, library, radio station, commercial offices and a large ballroom.

Paddington Town Hall

Victoria Barracks ⑫

Oxford St. **Map** 5 B3. (02) 9339 3330. 378, 380, 382. **Museum** 10am–1pm Thu; 10am–3pm Sun. Sun. 25 Dec. **Parade & tour:** 10am Thu.

Victoria barracks are the largest and best-preserved group of late Georgian architecture in Australia, covering almost 12 ha (30 acres). They

The colonial Georgian façade of the superbly restored Juniper Hall

are widely considered to be one of the best examples of a military barracks in the world.

Designed by the colonial engineer Lieutenant Colonel George Barney, the barracks were built between 1841 and 1848 using local sandstone quarried by convict labour. Originally intended to house 800 men, they have been in continuous use ever since and still operate as a centre of military administration.

The main block is 225 m (740 ft) long and has symmetrical two-storey wings with cast-iron verandas flanking a central archway. The perimeter walls have foundations 10 m (40 ft) deep in places. A former gaol block now houses a museum tracing New South Wales' military heritage.

The archway at the Oxford Street entrance to Victoria Barracks

Paddington Markets ⑬

395 Oxford St. **Map** 6 D4. 📞 *(02) 9331 2923.* 🚌 *378, 380, 382.* 🕐 *10am–4pm Sat.* ⬤ *25 Dec.* ♿ See *Shopping p129.*

THIS MARKET, which began in 1973, takes place every Saturday, come rain or shine, in the grounds of Paddington Village Uniting Church. It is probably the most colourful market in Sydney – a place to meet and be seen as much as to shop. Stallholders come from all over the world and young designers, hoping to launch their careers, display their wares. Other offerings are jewellery, pottery and other arts and crafts, as well as new and second-hand clothing.

Whatever you are looking for, from organic bananas to a full Oriental massage, you are likely to find it here.

The lush green expanse of Centennial Park

Paddington Street ⑭

Map 6 D3. 🚌 *378, 380, 382.*

WITH ITS HUGE plane trees shading the road and fine terrace houses on each side, Paddington Street is one of the oldest and loveliest of the suburb's streets.

Paddington grew rapidly as a commuter suburb in the late 19th century and most of the terraces were built for renting to Sydney's artisans. They were decorated with iron lace, Grecian-style friezes, worked parapets and cornices, pilasters and scrolls.

By the 1900s, the terraces became unfashionable and people moved out to newly emerging "garden suburbs". In the 1960s, however, their architectural appeal came to be appreciated again and the area was reborn.

Paddington Street now has a chic atmosphere where small art galleries operate out of quaint and grand shopfronts.

Paddington Street terrace house

Centennial Park ⑮

Map 6 E5. 📞 *(02) 9339 6699.* 🚌 *Clovelly, Coogee, Maroubra, Bronte, Randwick, City, Bondi Beach & Bondi Junction routes.* 🕐 *Mar– Apr & Sep–Oct: 6am– 6pm daily; May–Aug: 6:30am–5:30pm daily; Nov–Feb: 6am–8pm daily.* 🚻 *upon request.*

ONCE A SIMPLE common, the 220-ha (550-acre) Centennial Park was dedicated "to the enjoyment of the people of New South Wales forever" on 26 January 1888, the centenary of the foundation of the colony. On 1 January 1901, 100,000 people gathered here to witness the Commonwealth of Australia come into being, when the first Australian federal ministry was sworn in by the first governor-general *(see p52).*

The park boasts landscaped lawns, rose gardens, ornamental ponds and swamps that are home to many species of waterbirds. Bikes and in-line skates can be hired nearby and there is a café serving breakfast, lunch and snacks.

Fox Studios ⑯

Lang Rd, Moore Park. 📞 *9383 4000.* **Map** 5 C5. 🚌 *339, 355.* 🕐 *Many retail shops open 10am–10pm.* 🌐 *www.foxstudios.com.au*

THESE WORKING FILM STUDIOS offer a collection of restaurants, cafés and bars, as well as plenty of shops – clothes, music, homewares and books. There are also 16 cinema screens, a weekend market, and three well-designed playgrounds for children.

Further Afield

BEYOND SYDNEY'S INNER CITY, numerous places vie for the visitor's attention. Around the harbour shores are picturesque suburbs, secluded beaches and historic sights. To the north is the beautiful landscape of Ku-ring-gai Chase National Park. Manly is the city's northern playground, while Bondi is its eastern counterpart. Further west at Parramatta there are sites that recall and evoke the first days of European settlement.

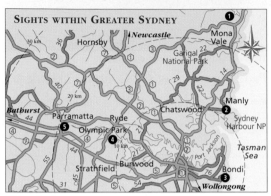

SIGHTS WITHIN GREATER SYDNEY

10 km = 6 miles

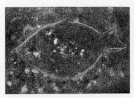

Aboriginal rock art in Ku-ring-gai Chase National Park

SIGHTS AT A GLANCE

Bondi Beach ❸
Ku-ring-gai Chase
  National Park ❶
Manly ❷
Parramatta ❺
Sydney Olympic Park ❹

KEY

▢	Central Sydney
▢	Greater Sydney
③	Metroad (city) route
▬	Highway
▬	Major road

Ku-ring-gai Chase National Park ❶

McCarrs Creek Rd, Church Point.
🏠 1 Park St, Mona Vale (02) 9472
8949. 🕐 10am–4pm Thu–Sun.

KU-RING-GAI CHASE National Park lies on Sydney's northernmost outskirts, 30 km (19 miles) from the city, and covers 15,000 ha (37,000 acres). It is bounded to the north by Broken Bay, at the mouth of the Hawkesbury River, with its eroded valleys formed during the last Ice Age. Sparkling waterways and golden beaches are set against the backdrop of the national park. Picnicking, bushwalking, surfing, boating and windsurfing are popular pastimes with visitors.

The Hawkesbury River curls around an ancient sandstone landscape rich in Aboriginal rock art. The national park has literally hundreds of Aboriginal art sites, the most common being rock engravings thought to be 2,000 years old. They include whales up to 8 m (26 ft) long, sharks, wallabies and echidnas, as well as ancestral spirits.

Manly ❷

🚉 Manly. **Oceanworld** West
Esplanade. 📞 (02) 9949 2644.
🕐 10am–5:30pm daily. ⬤ 25 Dec.
📷 ♿ 🚻

IF ASKED TO SUGGEST a single excursion outside the city, most Sydneysiders would nominate the 11-km (7-mile) ferry ride from Circular Quay to Manly. This narrow stretch of land lying between the harbour and the ocean was named by Governor Phillip, even before the township of

Brass band playing on The Corso, Manly's esplanade

Sydney got its name, for the impressive bearing of the Aboriginal men.

To the right of the rejuvenated Manly wharf is the lively fun fair that occupies the adjacent pier and, on the left, the tranquil harbourside beach known as Manly Cove. **Oceanworld** is at the far end of Manly Cove, where visitors can see sharks, giant stingrays and other species in an underwater viewing tunnel. You can also dive with the sharks here if you are brave enough.

The Corso is a lively pedestrian thoroughfare of souvenir shops and fast food outlets. It leads to Manly's ocean beach, popular with sunbathers, with its promenade lined by towering Norfolk pines.

Bondi Beach ❸

🚌 380, 382, 389, 321.

THIS LONG crescent of golden sand has long been a mecca for the sun and surf set *(see pp136–7)*. Surfers visit from far and wide in search of the perfect wave, and inline skaters hone their skills on the promenade.

Crescent-shaped Bondi Beach, Sydney's most famous beach, looking towards North Bondi

But the beach life that once defined many Australians has declined in recent times, partly due to an awareness of the dangers of sun exposure.

People now seek out Bondi for its trendy seafront cafés and cosmopolitan milieu as much as for the beach. The pavilion, built in 1928 as changing rooms, is now a busy venue for festivals, plays, films and arts and crafts displays.

Sydney Olympic Park ❹

Homebush Bay. 🚉 *Olympic Park.*
📞 *(02) 9714 7888.*

THE MAJOR SITE for the 2000 Games was at Sydney Olympic Park at Homebush Bay, 14 km (8.5 miles) west of the city *(see p139)*. This 760-ha (1,900-acre) waterfront site was the venue for 14 sports, including the football final, gymnastics and pentathlon.

At 52 m (170 ft) from ground level to its translucent roof, Stadium Australia was the centrepiece of the games, and with seating for 110,000 spectators had the largest capacity of any modern Olympiad. The Sydney International Aquatic Centre, with seating for 17,500, was the venue for swimming and other indoor water sports. The Sydney Showground Exhibition Halls, with their 15,000 seats, hosted the gymnastics and handball finals.

Parramatta ❺

📮 *Parramatta.* 🚉 *Parramatta.*
ℹ️ *346a Church St (02) 9630 3703.*

THE FERTILE SOIL of this Sydney suburb resulted in its foundation as Australia's first rural settlement, celebrating its first wheat crop in 1789. The area is now an excellent place to visit to gain an insight into the city's early European history.

Elizabeth Farm, dating from 1793, is the oldest surviving home in Australia. Once the home of John Macarthur, it was also the first farm to breed merino sheep, so vital to the country's economy *(see p47)*. With its period furnishings from 1820–50, the house is now a museum evoking the first inhabitants' life and times.

Old Government House in Parramatta Park is the oldest intact public building in Australia, built in 1799. The Doric porch, added in 1816, has been attributed to Francis Greenway *(see p161)*. A collection of early 19th-century furniture is housed inside the National Trust building.

Sydney's early history can also be witnessed at **St John's Cemetery**, where many of the settlers who arrived on the First Fleet *(see p46)* are buried.

🏛 **Elizabeth Farm**
70 Alice St, Rosehill. 📞 *(02) 9635 9488.* ⬜ *10am–5pm daily.* ⬤ *Good Fri, 25 Dec.* ♿ 📷
🏛 **Old Government House**
Parramatta Park (entry by Macquarie St). 📞 *(02) 9635 8149.* ⬜ *daily.* ⬤ *Good Fri, 18–26 Dec.* ♿ 📷
⛪ **St John's Cemetery**
O'Connell St. 📞 *(02) 9635 5904.* ♿

Drawing room in Old Government House in Parramatta

GETTING AROUND SYDNEY

I N GENERAL, the best way to see Sydney's many sights and attractions is on foot, coupled with use of the public transport system. Buses and trains will take visitors to within easy walking distance of anywhere in the inner city. They also serve the suburbs and outlying

Sydney taxi company sign

areas. Passenger ferries provide a fast and scenic means of travel between the city and the many harbourside suburbs. Of the many composite and multiride tickets available, most visitors will find it best to invest in one that includes all three modes of public transport.

DRIVING IN SYDNEY

D RIVING IS NOT the ideal way to get around Sydney: the city road network is confusing, traffic is congested and parking can be expensive. If using a car, it is best to avoid the peak hours (about 7:30–9:30am and 5–7:30pm).

Overseas visitors can use their usual driving licences to drive in Sydney, but must have proof that they are simply visiting and keep the licence with them when driving.

Parking in Sydney is strictly regulated, with fines for any infringements. Vehicles are often towed away if parked illegally. Contact the **Sydney Traffic Control Centre** if this happens. There are many car parks in and around the city. Also look for blue and white "P" signs or metered parking zones, many of which apply seven days a week, but it varies from council to council.

TAXIS

T AXIS ARE plentiful in the city: there are many taxi ranks and taxis are often found outside the large city hotels.

Meters indicate the fare plus any extras, such as booking fees and waiting time. It is customary to round the fare up to the next dollar.

Sydney has a fleet of taxis that cater to disabled passengers, including those in wheelchairs. Book these with any major taxi company.

Cycling in Centennial Park

SYDNEY BY BICYCLE

W HILE CYCLING is permitted on all city and suburban roads, visitors are advised to stay within designated cycling tracks or areas with light motor traffic. Centennial Park is a popular cycling spot. Helmets are compulsory by law. Those who wish to take advantage of Sydney's undulating terrain can seek advice from **Bicycle New South Wales**. Bicycles are permitted on CityRail trains *(see p126)* but you may have to pay an extra fare.

TRAMS

I N 1997, Sydney reintroduced trams to its transport system, after an absence of 36 years. A fleet of seven trams journey

around the downtown area, from Central Station *(see p126)* to Lilyfield via Pyrmont, taking in a large proportion of the area's sights *(see pp72–3)*. Tickets can be purchased at Central Station.

COMPOSITE TICKETS

S YDNEY'S TRANSPORT is good value, particularly with one of the composite tickets available from **State Transit Information and Ticket Kiosks** or railway stations.

TravelTen tickets, as the name suggests, entitle you to make ten bus journeys. TravelPasses allow unlimited seven-day travel on Sydney's buses, trains and ferries within stipulated zones. The SydneyPass allows three, five or seven days' travel in any seven-day period on buses and ferries.

A BusTripper allows one day's unlimited travel on all buses. DayPasses allow one day's unlimited travel on both buses and ferries.

USEFUL INFORMATION

Bicycle New South Wales
Lvl 2, 209 Castlereagh St. **Map** 4 E3.
(*(02) 9283 5200.*

Sydney Traffic Control Centre
(13 27 01. *(24-hour service.)*

State Transit Information and Ticket Kiosks
Sydney Airport
In arrivals halls at international and domestic terminals.
(13 15 00.
Circular Quay
Cnr Loftus and Alfred sts. **Map** 1 B3.
(*(02) 9224 3553.*

Transport Infoline
(13 15 00.

For Hire light ——

Taxi licence number

Taxi company name

Driver's photo licence

Travelling by Bus

STATE TRANSIT'S SYDNEY BUSES provide a punctual service that links up conveniently with the city's rail and ferry systems. As well as covering city and suburban areas, there are two Airport Express services and two excellent sightseeing buses – the Sydney Explorer and the Bondi Explorer. The **Transport Infoline** can advise you on routes, fares and journey times for all Sydney buses. Armed with the map on the inside back cover of this book and a composite ticket, you can avoid the difficulties and expense of city parking.

Automatic stamping machine for validating composite tickets

USING SYDNEY BUSES

ROUTE NUMBERS and journey destinations are displayed on the front, back and left side of all State Transit buses. An "X" in front of the number means that it is an express bus. Only single-journey tickets can be purchased on board regular buses. Single fares are bought from the driver. Try to have coins ready as drivers are not always able to change large notes. You will be given a ticket valid for that journey only – if you change buses you will have to pay again.

If using a TravelTen ticket or TravelPass, you must insert it in the automatic stamping machine as you board. Make sure that the arrow is facing towards you and pointing downwards. If sharing a TravelTen ticket, insert it into the machine once for each person travelling.

Front seats must be given up to elderly or disabled passengers. Eating, drinking, smoking and playing music are prohibited on buses. To signal that you wish to alight, press one of the stop buttons – they are mounted on the vertical handrails on each seat – well before the bus reaches your stop. The doors are electronic and can only be opened by the bus drivers.

BUS STOPS

BUS STOPS are indicated by yellow and black signs displaying a profile of a bus. Below this symbol, the numbers of all buses along the route are clearly listed.

Timetables are usually found at main bus stops. Public holidays follow the Sunday timetable. While bus stop timetables are kept as up-to-date as possible, it is best to carry a current timetable with you. They are available from State Transit Information and Ticket Kiosks, as well as some tourist information facilities.

Express bus

SIGHTSEEING BY BUS

TWO SYDNEY bus services, the red Sydney Explorer and the blue Bondi Explorer, offer flexible sightseeing with commentaries. The Sydney Explorer covers a 26-km (16-mile) circuit and stops at 22 of the city's most popular attractions. The Bondi Explorer travels through a number of Sydney's eastern suburbs, taking in much of the area's coastal scenery.

The red buses run daily every 17 minutes, the blue every 30 minutes. The great advantage of these services is that you can explore at will, getting on and off the buses as often as you wish in the course of a day. The best way to make the most of your journey is to choose the sights you most want to see and plan a basic itinerary. Be sure to note the various opening times of museums, art galleries and shops; the bus drivers can often advise you about these. Explorer bus stops are clearly marked by the colours of the bus (red or blue).

Tickets for both Explorer buses can be bought when boarding and are available from State Transit Information and Ticket Kiosks.

A typical Sydney bus used for standard services

The Bondi Explorer bus

The Sydney Explorer bus

Travelling by Train and Monorail

CityRail logo

As well as providing the key transport link between the city and suburbs, Sydney's railway network also serves a large part of the central business district. CityRail's double-decker trains operate on seven major lines. The City Circle loop, which runs mostly underground, is the main line through the city centre, stopping at Central, Town Hall, Wynyard, Circular Quay, St James and Museum. All suburban lines connect with the City Circle at Central and Town Hall stations.

Pedestrian concourse outside Central Railway Station

FINDING YOUR WAY AROUND CITYRAIL

Part of state rail, Sydney's CityRail system is mainly used by commuters. It is the most efficient and economical way to travel to and from the suburbs such as Parramatta *(see p122)*. The system is easy to follow and **CityRail Information** will offer all details of services and timetables.

Trains run from 4:30am to midnight. Be vigilant when using trains at night: stand in the "Nightsafe" areas and only use carriages near the train guard, marked by a blue light.

USING THE CITYRAIL ROUTE MAP

The five cityrail lines are colour-coded and route maps are displayed at all CityRail stations and inside train carriages. Simply trace the line from where you are to your destination, noting if and where you need to change and make connections. All five of the cityrail lines travel through the Central and Town Hall railway stations in central Sydney.

Note that the distances shown on the CityRail map are not to the correct scale.

COUNTRY AND INTERURBAN TRAINS

State rail has **Countrylink Travel Centres** throughout the city, which provide information about all its rail and coach services and also take ticket bookings. The NSW Discovery Pass, valid for one month, allows unlimited travel in New South Wales.

Inter-urban trains run to a variety of areas, including the Blue Mountains *(see pp162–5)*, Wollongong *(see p178)* and Newcastle *(see p161)*.

Monorail leaving the city centre, backed by Sydney Tower

SIGHTSEEING BY MONORAIL

More novel than practical, Sydney's Monorail runs along a scenic loop through central Sydney, Chinatown and Darling Harbour. Although it only covers a short distance, the Monorail can be a convenient way to travel from the city centre to Darling Harbour.

It runs from 7am–midnight, Mondays to Saturdays, and 8am–9pm on Sundays. Trains run every 5 minutes and the full circuit takes approximately 12 minutes. Ticket machines are found at each station. They accept most Australian notes and coins and give change.

A Monorail Day Pass allows unlimited rides for an entire day. It can be bought at any Monorail information booth.

USEFUL ADDRESSES

CityRail Information
Central Railway Station
Map 4 E5.
[(02) 131500.
Circular Quay Railway Station
Map 1 B3. **[** (02) 9224 3553.

Countrylink Travel Centres
Central Railway Station
Sydney Terminal. **Map** 4 E5.
[(02) 132232.
Circular Quay Railway Station
Map 1 B3.
[(02) 9224 3400.
Town Hall Railway Station
Map 4 E3.
[(02) 9379 3600.

Metro Light Rail & Monorail
[(02) 8584 5288.

THE SYDNEY LIGHT RAIL

The SLR is Sydney's most recent transport development and is designed to link Central Railway Station with Glebe and Lilyfield, via Darling Harbour. These efficient and environmentally friendly trains offer a quicker and quieter means of travelling around parts of the city. Tickets are available on board from the conductor.

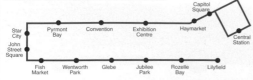

Travelling by Ferry and Water Taxi

For more than a century, harbour ferries have been a picturesque, as well as a practical, feature of the Sydney scene. Today, they are as popular as ever. Travelling by ferry is both a pleasure and an efficient way to journey between Sydney's various harbour suburbs. Sightseeing cruises are operated by various private companies as well as by State Transit *(see p124)*. Water taxis can be a convenient and fast alternative means of travel, although they are more expensive.

A water taxi on Sydney Harbour

Harbour ferries coming and going at Circular Quay Ferry Terminal

USING SYDNEY'S FERRIES

There is a steady procession of State Transit Sydney Ferries traversing the harbour between 6am and 10pm daily. They service most of Sydney Harbour and several stops along the Parramatta River.

Staff at the **Sydney Ferries Information Office**, open 7am–7pm daily, will answer passenger queries and provide ferry timetables.

All ferry journeys start at the Circular Quay Ferry Terminal. Electronic destination boards at the entrance to each wharf indicate the wharf from which your ferry will leave, and also give departure times and all stops made en route. Tickets and TravelPasses can be bought from the **Sydney Ferries Information Office**. You can also buy your ticket from the machines that are located on each wharf. On some ferries, tickets can be purchased on board.

Manly's ferry terminal is serviced both by ferries and the speedy JetCats. Tickets and information can be obtained from the ticket windows in the centre of the terminal. No food or drink is permitted on JetCat or Supercat ferries.

SIGHTSEEING BY FERRY

State Transit has a variety of well-priced cruises which take in the history and sights of Sydney Harbour. They are a cheap alternative to the commercial harbour cruises. There are morning, afternoon and evening tours, all with a commentary throughout. The day cruises show aspects of the city that are rarely seen, while the evening cruises offer spectacular views of the sun setting over the city's landmarks at sunset. Food and drink are available on board, but passengers may bring their own.

The **Australian Travel Specialists** has information on all river and harbour cruises from Circular Quay and Darling Harbour.

WATER TAXIS

Small, fast taxi boats are available for hire to carry passengers around the harbour. You can flag them down like normal road cabs if you spot one cruising for a fare. Circular Quay near the Overseas Passenger Terminal is the best place to look.

Water taxis will pick up and drop off passengers at any navigable pier. However, this novel way of getting around the harbour is certainly not cheap. Rates vary, with some drivers charging for the boat (about $40) and a fee per person ($7–8).

USEFUL INFORMATION

Australian Travel Specialists
Wharves 2 & 6,
Circular Quay.
Map 1 B3.
℡ (02) 9555 2700.

Sydney Ferries Lost Property
Wharf 3,
Circular Quay.
Map 1 B3.
℡ (02) 9207 3170.

Water Taxi Companies
Harbour Taxi Boats
℡ (02) 9555 8888.
Taxis Afloat
℡ (02) 9955 3322.

Electronic destination board for all ferries leaving Circular Quay

SHOPPING IN SYDNEY

FOR MOST TRAVELLERS, shopping can be as much of a voyage of discovery as sightseeing. The variety of shops in Sydney is wide and the quality of goods is high. The city has many elegant arcades, shopping galleries

Gowings menswear store logo

and popular weekly and monthly markets. The range of merchandise available is vast and local talent is promoted. Nor does the most interesting shopping stop at the city centre; there are several "satellite" alternatives.

The Tin Shed, a junk shop cum café in Balmain

SHOPPING HOURS

MOST SHOPS are open from 9am to 5:30pm during the week, and from 9am to 4pm on Saturdays. Many shops in the city stay open until 9pm on Thursdays. Some main shops are open late every evening and most of these also open on Sundays.

HOW TO PAY

MAJOR CREDIT CARDS are accepted at many shops, but there may be a minimum purchase requirement. You will need identification, such as a valid passport, when using

traveller's cheques. Shops will generally exchange goods or refund your money if you are not satisfied with the product, provided it is accompanied by some proof of purchase. There is a Goods and Services Tax (GST) which is usually included in the price.

SALES

MANY SHOPS CONDUCT sales all year round. The big department stores of **David Jones** and **Grace Bros** have two clearance sales a year. The post-Christmas sales start on 26 December and last into January. The other major sale time is during July, after the end of the financial year.

TAX-FREE SALES

DUTY-FREE SHOPS are found in the centre of the city as well as at Sydney Airport. Some shops also have branches in the larger suburbs.

Overseas visitors can save around 30 per cent on goods such as perfume, jewellery, cameras and alcohol at shops that offer duty-free shopping. You must show your passport and onward ticket when you collect your purchases.

Most duty-free merchandise must be kept in its sealed bag until you leave the country. Cameras and video cameras are exceptions to this rule. Some duty-free shops in the city will also deliver your purchases to the airport, where you can pick them up prior to your departure.

Chifley Tower, with the Chifley Plaza shopping arcade at its base

ARCADES AND MALLS

ARCADES and shopping malls in Sydney range from the ornately Victorian to modern marble and glass. The Queen Victoria Building *(see p86)* is Sydney's most palatial shopping space. Four levels contain more than 200 shops.

The elegant Strand Arcade *(see p86)* was originally built in 1892. Jewellery, lingerie, high fashion, antiques and fine cafés are its stock in trade.

Pitt Street Mall is home to several shopping centres. **Skygarden** is the place for homeware, designer fashions and art galleries of distinction. A food gallery offers everything from *antipasto* to Thai takeaway. The **Mid City Centre** is home to the HMV music store and shops selling clothes, accessories and gifts. **Centrepoint**

Interior design shop on William Street in Paddington

has more than 140 speciality shops that stock everything from avant-garde jewellery to leather goods.

Both the **MLC Centre** and nearby **Chifley Plaza** cater to the prestige shopper. Gucci, Cartier and Tiffany & Co are just some of the shops found in these arcades.

Harbourside Shopping Centre has dozens of shops and waterfront restaurants. Goods include fine arts, jewellery and Australiana.

BEST OF THE DEPARTMENT STORES

THE SPRING and Mother's Day floral displays in the **David Jones** Elizabeth Street store are legendary, as is the luxurious perfumery and cosmetics hall on the ground floor. The building has seven floors of quality merchandise, including women's clothing, lingerie, toys and stationery. The Market Street store specializes in menswear, furniture, fabrics and china. The food hall is famous for its range of gourmet food and fine wines.

Grace Bros is a good venue for cosmetics, hats, Australian fashion, lingerie or hosiery.

Gowings, which has been in continuous operation since 1868, is a Sydney institution. This unpretentious family-owned menswear store also sells such merchandise as sunglasses, watches and Swiss army knives. Genuine Australiana, such as kangaroo leather wallets and plaited leather belts, is also for sale.

Part of the spring floral display in David Jones department store

Canopy over the harbourside Rocks Market

MARKETS

SCOURING MARKETS for the cheap, the cheerful and the unusual has become a popular pastime in Sydney.

Balmain Market, held each Saturday, includes a food hall selling Japanese, Thai and Indian dishes. The **Bondi Beach Market** on Sundays is known for its trendy second-hand clothing: expect to see the occasional pop star and stars of Australian TV among the browsers. The market is also noted for its cactus plants, glassware and tourist art.

The **Rocks Market**, held all weekend under a canopy, has around 140 stalls. Posters, lace, stained glass and leather are among the goods. You can watch a sculptor making art out of stone or have your portrait sketched in charcoal.

Sydney Fish Market is the ideal place to buy fresh seafood. You can choose from more than 100 species, both live and prepared. The market also has sushi bars and fish cafés. The Sydney Seafood School operates above the market, offering lessons in preparing and serving seafood.

The **Tarpeian Market** on Sundays displays arts and crafts in a spectacular setting next to the Opera House. It is an eclectic mix, from English porcelain thimbles to ornate wooden smoking pipes, prints of Sydney, jewellery and healing crystals. If you are lucky, you can catch performance artists, who are often happy to pose for photographs.

Two other good markets are Paddy's Market (*see p95*) and Paddington Markets (*see p121*).

Paddy's Market (see p95) and Paddington Markets (see p121).

DIRECTORY

ARCADES AND MALLS

Centrepoint
Cnr Pitt, Market & Castlereagh sts. **Map** 1 B5.
📞 (02) 9231 1000.

Chifley Plaza
2 Chifley Square.
Map 1 B4.
📞 (02) 9221 4500.

Harbourside Shopping Centre
Darling Harbour.
Map 3 C2.
📞 (02) 9281 3999.

Mid City Centre
197 Pitt Street Mall.
Map 1 B5.
📞 (02) 9221 2422.

MLC Centre
19–29 Martin Place.
Map 1 B5.
📞 (02) 9224 8333.

Skygarden
77 Castlereagh St.
Map 1 B5.
📞 (02) 9231 1811.

DEPARTMENT STORES

David Jones
Cnr Elizabeth & Castlereagh sts.
Map 1 B5.
📞 (02) 9266 5544.

Gowings
319 George St.
Map 1 B5.
📞 (02) 9262 1281.

Grace Bros
436 George St. **Map** 1 B5.
📞 (02) 9238 9111.

MARKETS

Balmain Market
Cnr Darling St and Curtis Rd, Balmain. **Map** 3 A4.

Bondi Beach Market
Bondi Beach Public School, Campbell Parade, North Bondi.

Sydney Fish Market
Cnr Pyrmont Bridge Rd & Bank St, Blackwattle Bay.
Map 3 B2.

Tarpeian Market
Western Boardwalk, Sydney Opera House. **Map** 1 C2.

The Rocks Market
George St, The Rocks. **Map** 1 B5.

Specialist Shopping in Sydney

SMART CASUAL is a term often heard in Sydney, applied to both dress and occasion. Clothes shops do not neglect the formal dresser, however, and stylish Australian labels vie with the international designer names on offer. Sydney also offers an extensive range of gift and souvenir ideas, from unset opals and jewellery to handmade crafts and Aboriginal art. Museum shops often have specially commissioned items on sale which are a unique reminder of your visit.

Australian designer fashion show

AUSTRALIANA

AUSTRALIANA has become more than just souvenirs: it is now an art form in itself. **Australian Craftworks** sells souvenirs that double as art, including woodwork, pottery and leather goods.

Done Art and Design has distinctive prints by Ken and Judy Done *(see p30)*. At **Weiss Art** you will find minimalist designs on clothes, umbrellas, and cups. **Makers Mark** is a showcase for wood, glass and silver artisans. Victoria Walk in the Queen Victoria Building *(see p86)* is dominated by Australiana shops.

The Australian Museum *(see pp90–91)* shop sells unusual gift items such as bark paintings, Australian animal puppets, puzzles and games.

MEN'S CLOTHES

UP-MARKET MEN'S labels, including Bally, Zegna and Gant, are available from **Stewart's Gentlemen's Outfitters**. **Leona Edmiston**'s clothes are in demand by rock stars and models.

Skin Deep has retro gear for men – suits from the 1940s and 1950s, old silk ties and tie pins. **Aussie Boys**, popular with the gay crowd, stocks trendy gym gear and the very latest in party wear.

WOMEN'S CLOTHES

SMART DAYWEAR and casual clothes are the province of **Country Road**, which has shops throughout Sydney. **Carla Zampatti** is an Australian designer whose speciality is chic day and evening wear.

The **Sportsgirl** stores are great for bright accessories and up-to-the-minute fashions.

Collette Dinnigan uses Italian and French lace, silk and tulle to produce exquisite lingerie. **Lisa Ho** is another designer who caters for the style-conscious woman.

Chanel shop in Castlereagh Street, Sydney's "designer row"

AUSTRALIAN FASHION

AUSTRALIAN "outback fashion", from elastic-sided riding boots and Akubra hats to Driza-bone oilskin coats, are found at **RM Williams**. Beach and surf wear labels can be found at **Hot Tuna**. The **Mambo Friendship Store** carries Mambo label surf wear and accessories. The **Great Australian Jumper Company** has classic knitwear made from Australian wool.

BOOKS AND MUSIC

THE LARGER book chains, such as **Dymocks**, have a range of guide books and maps on Sydney. For more eclectic browsing, there is **Abbey's Bookshop** and **Ariel**. The State Library of NSW *(see p105)* bookshop has a good choice of Australian books.

Many specialist music shops can be found in the city. **Red Eye Records** sells collectables and alternative music. **Good Groove Records** has vinyl 45s and CD reissues. **Central Station Records and Tapes** has mainstream music. **Birdland** stocks blues, jazz, soul and avant-garde.

JEWELLERY

SYDNEY OFFERS a variety of gems and jewellery. **Flame Opals** sells gems from all the major Australian opal fields. At **The Rocks Opal Mine** there is a mine shaft elevator for simulated opal mining as well as gems on sale. The **Gemstone Boutique** sells an extensive range of opals, coral, pearls, jade and gold.

Long-established jewellers include **Fairfax & Roberts**.

Trendy surf gear shop, Hot Tuna, in Paddington

World-class pearls are found in the seas off the northwestern coast of Australia and examples can be found at **Paspaley Pearls**.

Victoria Spring Designs sells costume jewellery with filigree and glass beading worked into its pendants, rings, earrings and Gothic crosses. **Glitz Bijouterie** has affordable silver and gold necklaces in up-to-the minute styles.

ABORIGINAL ART

TRADITIONAL PAINTINGS, fabric, jewellery, boomerangs, carvings and cards can be bought at the **Aboriginal and Tribal Art Centre**. At **New Guinea Arts** you will find tribal artifacts from Aboriginal Australia, Papua New Guinea and Oceania.

Souvenir boomerangs

The **Coo-ee Aboriginal Art Gallery** boasts a selection of limited edition prints, fabrics, books and Aboriginal music. The **Hogarth Galleries Aboriginal Art Centre** holds work by Papunya Tula and Balgo artists and works from respected painters such as Kathleen Petyarre and Rosella Namok.

DIRECTORY

AUSTRALIANA

Australian Craftworks
127 George St, The Rocks.
Map 1 B2.
📞 (02) 9247 7156.
One of two branches.

Done Art and Design
123 George St,
The Rocks. **Map** 1 B2.
📞 (02) 9251 6099.
One of several branches.

Makers Mark
72 Castlereagh St. **Map** 1 B5. 📞 (02) 9231 6800.

Weiss Art
85 George St,
The Rocks. **Map** 1 B2.
📞 (02) 9241 3819.
Harbourside Festival Shopping Centre, Darling Harbour. **Map** 3 C2.
📞 (02) 9281 4614.

MEN'S CLOTHES

Aussie Boys
102 Oxford St,
Darlinghurst. **Map** 5 A2.
📞 (02) 9360 7011.

Marcs
Mid City Centre, Pitt St.
Map 1 B5.
📞 (02) 9221 4583.

Stewart's Gentlemen's Outfitters
Rydge's Sheraton Wentworth Hotel, 61 Phillip St. **Map** 1 B4.
📞 (02) 9221 2203.

Skin Deep
141 Elizabeth St.
Map 1 B5.
📞 (02) 9264 1239.

WOMEN'S CLOTHES

Carla Zampatti
143 Elizabeth St.
Map 1 B5.
📞 (02) 9264 3257.

Collette Dinnigan
39 William St,
Paddington. **Map** 6 D3.
📞 (02) 9360 6691.

Country Road
142 Pitt St.
Map 1 B5.
📞 (02) 9394 1818.
One of several branches.

Lisa Ho
2a–6a Queen St,
Woollahra. **Map** 6 E4.
📞 (02) 9360 2345.

Sportsgirl
Skygarden. **Map** 1 B5.
📞 (02) 9223 8255.
One of several branches.

AUSTRALIAN FASHION

Bondi Surf Co
72–76 Campbell Parade,
Bondi Beach.
📞 (02) 9130 3271.

Great Australian Jumper Company
Chifley Plaza. **Map** 1 B4.
📞 (02) 9231 3511.
One of three branches.

Mambo Friendship Store
17 Oxford St,
Paddington.
Map 5 B3.
📞 (02) 9331 8034.

RM Williams
389 George St.
Map 1 B5.
📞 (02) 9262 2228.
One of three branches.

BOOKS AND MUSIC

Abbey's Bookshop
131 York St.
Map 1 A5.
📞 (02) 9264 3111.

Ariel
42 Oxford St,
Paddington.
Map 5 B3.
📞 (02) 9332 4581.

Dymocks
424 George St.
Map 1 B5.
📞 (02) 9235 0155.
One of many branches.

Birdland
3 Barrack St
Map 1 A4.
📞 (02) 9299 8527.

Central Station Records and Tapes
46 Oxford St,
Darlinghurst.
Map 4 F4.
📞 (02) 9361 5222.

Good Groove Records
336 Crown St, Surry Hills.
📞 (02) 9331 2942.

Red Eye Records
66 King St.
Map 1 B5.
📞 (02) 9299 4233.

JEWELLERY

Flame Opals
119 George Street,
The Rocks.
Map 1 B2.
📞 (02) 9247 3446.

Gemstone Boutique
388 George St.
Map 1 B5.
📞 (02) 9223 2140.

Rocks Opal Mine
Clocktower Square,
35 Harrington St,
The Rocks. **Map** 1 B2.
📞 (02) 9247 4974.

Fairfax & Roberts
44 Martin Place.
Map 1 B4.
📞 (02) 9232 8511.
One of two branches.

Glitz Bijouterie
Imperial Arcade. **Map** 1 B5.
📞 (02) 9231 1383.

Paspaley Pearls
142 King St. **Map** 1 A4.
📞 (02) 9232 7633.

Victoria Spring Designs
110 Oxford St,
Paddington. **Map** 6 D3.
📞 (02) 9331 7862.

ABORIGINAL ART

Aboriginal and Tribal Art Centre
117 George St, The Rocks.
Map 1 B2.
📞 (02) 9247 9625.
One of several branches.

Coo-ee Aboriginal Art Gallery
98 Oxford St, Paddington.
Map 5 B3.
📞 (02) 9332 1544.

Hogarth Galleries Aboriginal Art Centre
7 Walker Lane, off Brown St, Paddington. **Map** 5 C3.
📞 (02) 9360 6839.
One of two branches.

New Guinea Arts
8th Flr, Dymocks Building,
428 George St. **Map** 1 B5.
📞 (02) 9232 4737.
One of two branches.

ENTERTAINMENT IN SYDNEY

SYDNEY HAS the standard of entertainment and nightlife you would expect from a cosmopolitan city. Everything from opera and ballet at Sydney Opera House to Shakespeare by the sea at the Balmoral Beach amphitheatre is on offer. Venues such as the Capitol, Her Majesty's Theatre and the Theatre Royal play host to the latest musicals, while Sydney's many smaller theatres are home to interesting fringe theatre,

A Wharf Theatre production poster

modern dance and rock and pop concerts. Pub rock thrives in the inner city and beyond; and there are many nightspots for jazz, dance and alternative music. Movie buffs are well catered for with film festivals, art-house films and foreign titles, as well as the latest Hollywood blockbusters. One of the features of harbourside living is the free outdoor entertainment, very popular with children.

Signs outside the Dendy repertory cinema in Martin Place *(see p86)*

INFORMATION

FOR DETAILS of events in the city, you should check the daily newspapers first. They carry cinema, and often arts and theatre advertisements daily. The most comprehensive listings appear in the *Sydney Morning Herald's* "Metro" guide every Friday. The *Daily Telegraph* has a gig guide on Thursdays, with opportunities to win free tickets to special events. *The Australian's* main arts pages appear on Fridays and all the papers review new films in weekend editions.

The **NSW Information Line**'s tourist information kiosks and most of the major hotels have useful free guides such as *What's on in Sydney*, published quarterly, and the weekly *Where Magazine*.

Music fans are well served by the free weekly guides *On the Street*, *Drum Media* and *3D World*, with youth culture information, interviews and tour guides. They are found at video and music shops, pubs and clubs. *3D World* has dance club information.

Many venues have leaflets about forthcoming attractions, while the major centres have information telephone lines.

BUYING TICKETS

SOME OF THE popular operas, shows, plays and ballets in Sydney are sold out months in advance. While it is better to book ahead, many theatres do set aside tickets to be sold at the door on the night.

You can buy tickets from the box office or by telephone. Some orchestral performances do not admit children under seven, so check with the box office before buying. If you make a phone booking using a credit card, the tickets can be mailed to you. Alternatively, tickets can be collected from the box office half an hour before the show. The major agencies will take overseas bookings.

A busker at Circular Quay

If you are desperate to see a sold-out rock concert, there may be touts selling tickets

outside, but often at hugely inflated prices. If all else fails, hotel concierges have a reputation for being able to secure hard-to-get tickets.

BOOKING AGENCIES

SYDNEY HAS TWO main ticket agencies: **Ticketek** and **Ticketmaster 7**. They represent all major entertainment and sporting events.

Ticketek has more than 50 outlets throughout the state, open from 9am to 5pm weekdays, and Saturdays from noon to 4pm. Telephone bookings can be made from 8:30am–9pm, Monday to Saturday, and 10am–7pm Sundays. Overseas bookings can be faxed. The Ticketmaster office is open Monday to Friday, from 9am–6pm. Other offices are open 10am–9pm and can be found at all the Greater Union

The annual Gay and Lesbian Mardi Gras Festival's Dog Show *(see p37)*

cinemas, the State Theatre, Theatre Royal, Capitol Theatre and Footbridge Theatre. First-call also has a 24-hour telephone service.

Agencies accept traveller's cheques, bank cheques, cash, VISA, MasterCard (Access) and American Express. However, some agencies do not accept Diners Club. A booking fee applies, with a postage and handling charge also added if tickets are mailed out. There are generally no refunds (unless a show is cancelled) or exchanges available.

If one agency has sold out its allocation for a show, it is worth checking to see if the other agency still has tickets.

The Spanish firedancers *Els Comediants* at the Sydney Festival

Halftix booth selling cut-price tickets in Martin Place

DISCOUNT TICKETS

WHEN A SHOW isn't sold out, **Halftix** offers half-price tickets (plus a small booking fee) for the theatre, concerts, opera and ballet on the day of the performance only (except for matinées and Sunday performances, tickets to which can be bought the day before). Bus tour, theatre restaurant, boat cruise, art gallery and film tickets are also available at half price. Pay by cash or credit card. There is no limit on the number of tickets you can buy.

You can ring Halftix from 11am for recorded information on discounts available, and the office is open from noon until 5:30pm, Monday to Saturday. Arrive early to avoid queues during the Sydney Festival. Halftix is also a Ticketek agency for advance sales.

Tuesday is budget-price day at most cinemas. Some independent cinemas have special prices during the week. The Sydney Symphony Orchestra (*see p134*) offers a special Student Rush price to

students when tickets are available. These can only be bought on the day of the performance. A student card must be shown.

CHOOSING SEATS

IF BOOKING IN PERSON at either the venue or the agency, you will be able to look at a seating plan. Be aware that in the State Theatre, row A is the back row. In Sydney, there is little difference in price between stalls and dress circle.

If booking by telephone with Ticketek, you will only be able to get a rough idea of where your seats are. The computer will select the "best" tickets available.

DISABLED VISITORS

MANY OLDER VENUES were not designed with the disabled visitor in mind, but this has been redressed in most newer buildings. It is best to phone the box office beforehand to request special

Publicity shot of the Australian Chamber Orchestra (*see p134*)

requirements. Ask about the best street entrance. The Sydney Town Hall has wheelchair access at its Druitt Street entrance. The Sydney Opera House has disabled parking, wheelchair access and a loop system in the Concert Hall for the hearing impaired. A brochure, *Services for the Disabled*, is also available.

DIRECTORY

USEFUL NUMBERS

Darling Harbour Information Line
📠 1902 260 568.

NSW Information Line
☎ 13 20 77.

People with Disabilities NSW
☎ (02) 9319 6622.

Sydney Opera House Information Desk
☎ (02) 9250 7111.

Disabled Information
☎ (02) 9250 7185.

Sydney Symphony Orchestra
☎ (02) 9334 4600.

TICKET AGENCIES

Ticketmaster 7
☎ 1300 136 166.
🌐 www.ticketmaster7.com

Halftix
201 Sussex St, Darling Park
Map 1 A5.
☎ (02) 9286 3310.
🌐 www.halftix.com.au

Ticketek
☎ (02) 9266 4800.
FAX (02) 9267 4460.
🌐 www.ticketek.com.au

Entertainment Venues in Sydney

SYDNEY'S THEATRES are notable for their atmosphere and stimulating mix of productions. Comedy is also finding a strong niche as a mainstream performance art. Australian films have a fine international reputation and there are many annual film festivals. Classical music buffs cannot possibly visit Sydney without seeing a performance in the Sydney Opera House. Sydney also draws the biggest names in contemporary music.

Sydney Dance Company poster

FILM

THE CITY'S main cinema strip is on George Street, near the Town Hall *(see p89)*. **Village Hoyts** and **Greater Union** show all the latest blockbusters. The **Dendy** cinemas show the latest arthouse films – the Martin Place Dendy has a bar, bistro and a shop. Other repertory venues are **Cinema Paris** and **Chauvel**. The **Movie Room** has science fiction, cult and 3-D films. Most cinemas offer half-price tickets on Tuesdays.

Sydney Film Festival poster

The annual **Sydney Film Festival** *(see p39)* includes documentaries, retrospectives and new films from all over the globe.

THEATRE

MUSICALS are staged at the **Theatre Royal**, the State Theatre *(see p86)*, the **Capitol** and Star City's **Lyric Theatre**.

Smaller venues include the **Seymour Theatre Centre**, the **Ensemble** and the **Footbridge Theatre**. The **Stables Theatre** specializes in new Australian playwrights.

The Sydney Theatre Company (STC) is the city's best and performs at **The Wharf**.

Open-air summer events include performances by **Shakespeare by the Sea** at Balmoral Beach and the popular **Sydney Fringe Festival** which features new plays by up-and-coming playwrights *(see p31)*.

COMEDY

SYDNEY'S BEST comedy venue is the **Comedy Store**. There are comics, sketches or revues Tuesday to Saturday. Monday night has comedy at both the **Bridge Hotel** and in the Fringe Bar in the **Unicorn Hotel**.

OPERA AND CLASSICAL MUSIC

THE AUSTRALIAN OPERA (AO) was formed in 1956 and its two seasons at the Opera House are January to March and June to October.

Sydney's main provider of orchestral music and recitals is the **Sydney Symphony Orchestra** (SSO). Concerts are held in the Sydney Opera House Concert Hall or the Sydney Town Hall *(see p89)*. The Conservatorium of Music *(see p104)* performs symphony, wind and chamber concerts and jazz big bands. Concerts of the Australian Chamber Orchestra are held at the Sydney Opera House *(see pp80–81)* throughout the year.

The Sydney Philharmonia Choirs, the city's finest, also perform at the Opera House. The newest major classical venue is the City Recital Hall, which regularly plays host to a variety of local and international stars.

Sydney Opera House

DANCE

THERE IS AN eclectic variety of dance to be found in the city. The Australian Ballet performs at the Opera House March–April and November–December. The repertoire spans classic to modern.

Sydney Dance Company is the city's leading modern dance group and perform at their studio at The Wharf. The **Aboriginal Islander Dance Theatre** is also contemporary with a traditional flavour. Its performances are at the Seymour Theatre Centre.

ROCK, JAZZ AND BLUES

ROCK'S BIGGEST names perform at the **Sydney Entertainment Centre**, the Sydney Cricket Ground and Sydney Superdrome. Venues such as the **Orient Hotel** and Selina's at **Coogee Bay Hotel** also draw crowds.

For jazz music, try **The Basement**, a long-standing venue. The blues are played at the **Rose of Australia** and the **Cat & Fiddle Hotel**.

NIGHTCLUBS

NIGHTSPOTS OFFERING a range of dance music style include the larger clubs, such as **Home**, **Gas** and **Tank**. Clubs into house and hip hop are **Q**, **Soho Lounge Bar**, **The Slip Inn**, **Goodbar** and **Club 77**.

Gay clubs include the **Beresford**, **D.C.M** and **Oxford** hotels and the **Midnight Shift**.

DIRECTORY

FILM

Cinema Paris
Fox Studios
(02) 9332 1633.

Chauvel
Paddington Town Hall,
Cnr Oatley Rd & Oxford St
(02) 9361 5398.

Dendy Cinema
Martin Place
MLC Centre, 19 Martin Pl.
Map 1 B4.
(02) 9233 8166.
Opera Quays
2 East Circular Quay.
(02) 9247 3800.
Newtown
261–263 King St,
Newtown.
(02) 9550 5699.

Greater Union
525 George St.
Map 4 E3.
(02) 9267 8666.

Movie Room
112 Darlinghurst Rd,
Darlinghurst.
Map 5 B2.
(02) 9360 7853.

**Sydney Film
Festival**
(02) 9660 3844.

**Village Hoyts
Centre**
505 George St.
Map 4 E3.
(02) 9273 7431.

THEATRE

Capitol Theatre
13 Campbell St, Haymarket.
Map 4 E4.
(02) 9320 5000.

**Ensemble
Theatre**
78 McDougall St, Kirribilli.
(02) 9929 0644.

**Footbridge
Theatre**
University of Sydney,
Parramatta Rd, Glebe.
Map 3 A5.
(02) 9266 4800.

**Seymour Theatre
Centre**
Cnr Cleveland St
& City Rd,
Chippendale.
(02) 9351 7940.

**Shakespeare by
the Sea**
(02) 9557 1651.

Stables Theatre
10 Nimrod St,
Kings Cross.
Map 5 B1.
(02) 9250 7799.

**Sydney Fringe
Festival**
(02) 8308 1017.

Theatre Royal
MLC Centre,
King St.
Map 1 B5.
(02) 13 61 66.

Wharf Theatre
Pier 4, Hickson Rd,
Millers Point.
Map 1 A1.
(02) 9250 1777.

COMEDY

Comedy Store
Fox Studios, Moore Park
Rd, Moore Park.
(02) 9357 1419.

Bridge Hotel
135 Victoria Rd,
Glebe.
(02) 9810 1260.

Unicorn Hotel
106 Oxford St,
Paddington.
Map 5 B3.
(02) 9360 3554.

OPERA AND
CLASSICAL MUSIC

**Opera
Australia**
(02) 9319 1088.

**Sydney
Philharmonia
Choirs**
(02) 9251 3115.

**Sydney Symphony
Orchestra**
(02) 9334 4600.

DANCE

**Aboriginal
Islander Dance
Theatre**
(02) 9252 0199.

**Sydney Dance
Company**
(02) 9221 4811.

ROCK, JAZZ
AND BLUES

The Basement
29 Reiby Place.
Map 1 B3.
(02) 9251 2797.

**Cat & Fiddle
Hotel**
456 Darling St,
Balmain.
(02) 9810 7931.

**Coogee Bay
Hotel**
Cnr Coogee Bay Rd and
Arden St,
Coogee.
(02) 9665 0000.

**Eastern Creek
Raceway**
Brabham Drive,
Eastern Creek.
(02) 9672 1000.

Orient Hotel
89 George St,
The Rocks. **Map** 1 B2.
(02) 9247 2979.

**Rose of
Australia**
1 Swanson St,
Erskenville.
(02) 9565 1441.

**State
Theatre**
49 Market St.
Map 1 B5.
(02) 9373 6655.

**Sydney
Entertainment
Centre**
Harbour St,
Haymarket.
Map 4 D4.
(02) 9320 4200.
1 900 957 333

NIGHTCLUBS

D.C.M
33 Oxford St,
Darlinghurst.
Map 4 F4.
(02) 9267 7380.

Beresford Hotel
354 Bourke St,
Darlinghurst.
Map 5 A3.
(02) 9331 1045.

Cave
Star City, Pirrama Rd,
Pyrmont.
(02) 9566 4753.

Club 77
77 William St,
East Sydney.
(02) 9361 4981.

Gas
477 Pitt St, Haymarket.
(02) 9211 3088.

Goodbar
11a Oxford St,
Paddington.
Map 5 B3.
(02) 9360 6759.

Home
Cockle Bay Wharf,
Darling Harbour.
(02) 9266 0600.

Midnight Shift
85 Oxford St,
Darlinghurst.
Map 5 A2.
(02) 9360 4319.

Oxford Hotel
134 Oxford St,
Darlinghurst. **Map** 5 A2.
(02) 9331 3467.

Q
Level 2, 44 Oxford St,
Darlinghurst.
Map 4 F4.
(02) 9360 1375.

Slip Inn
111 Sussex St.
(02) 9299 1700.

Soho Lounge Bar
171 Victoria St,
Potts Point.
(02) 9358 4221.

Tank
232 George St.
(02) 9240 3094.

Sydney's Beaches

BEING A CITY built around the water, it is no wonder that many of Sydney's recreational activities involve the sand, sea and sun. There are many harbour and surf beaches in Sydney, most of them accessible by bus (see p125). Even if you're not a swimmer, the beaches offer a chance to get away from it all for a day or weekend and enjoy the fresh air and relaxed way of life.

Scuba diving at Gordons Bay

SWIMMING

YOU CAN SWIM at either harbour or ocean beaches. Harbour beaches are generally smaller and sheltered. Popular harbour beaches include Camp Cove, Shark Bay and Balmoral Beach.

At the ocean beaches, surf lifesavers in their red and yellow caps are on duty. Surf lifesaving carnivals are held throughout the summer. Call **Surf Life Saving NSW** for a calendar. Well-patrolled, safer surf beaches include Bondi, Manly and Coogee.

The beaches can become polluted, especially after heavy rainfall. The **Beach Watch Info Line** provides updated information on beaches and bays.

SURFING

SURFING is more a way of life than a leisure activity for some Sydneysiders. If you're a beginner, try Bondi, Bronte, Palm Beach or Collaroy.

Two of the best surf beaches are Maroubra and Narrabeen. Bear in mind that local surfers know one another well and do not take kindly to "intruders" who drop in on their

waves. If you'd like to learn, local surf shops should be able to help. To hire a surfboard, try the **Bondi Surf Company**.

If you'd like to catch some of the action but stay dry, there are many vantage points on the walk from Bondi Beach (see p122) to Tamarama.

WINDSURFING AND SAILING

THERE ARE LOCATIONS around Sydney suitable for every level of windsurfer. Boards can be hired from **Balmoral Windsurfing, Sailing & Kayaking School & Hire**.

Good spots include Palm Beach, Narrabeen Lakes, La Perouse, Brighton-Le-Sands and Kurnell Point (for beginner and intermediate boarders) and Long Reef Beach, Palm Beach and Collaroy (for more experienced boarders).

One of the best ways to see the harbour is while sailing. A sailing boat, including skipper, can be hired for the afternoon from the **Australian Sailing Academy**. To learn how to sail, the **Sirsi Newport Marina** has two-day courses and also hires out sailing boats and motor cruisers to experienced sailors.

SCUBA DIVING

THE GREAT BARRIER REEF it may not be, but there are some excellent dive spots around Sydney, especially in winter when the water is clear, if a little cold. Favoured spots are Shelly Beach, Gordons Bay and Camp Cove.

Pro Dive Coogee offers a complete range of courses, escorted dives, introductory dives for beginners, and hire equipment. **Dive Centre Manly** also runs courses, hires equipment and conducts boat dives seven days a week.

DIRECTORY

Australian Sailing Academy
The Spit, Mosman.
((02) 9960 3077.

Balmoral Windsurfing, Sailing & Kayaking School & Hire
2 The Esplanade, Balmoral Beach.
((02) 9960 5344.

Beach Watch Info Line
((1) 800 036 677.

Bondi Surf Co.
Shop 2, 72–76 Campbell Parade, Bondi Beach.
((02) 9365 0870.

Dive Centre Manly
10 Belgrave St, Manly.
((02) 9977 4355.

Pro Dive Coogee
27 Alfreda St, Coogee.
((02) 9665 6333.

Sirsi Newport Marina
122 Crescent Rd, Newport.
((02) 9979 6213.

Surf Life Saving NSW
((02) 9984 7188.

Rock baths and surf lifesaving club at Coogee Beach

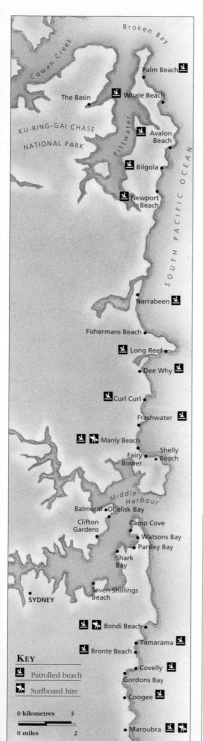

TOP 30 BEACHES

THESE BEACHES have been selected for their safe swimming, water sports, facilities available or their picturesque setting.

	Swimming Pool	Surfing	Windsurfing	Fishing	Scuba Diving	Picnic/Barbecue	Restaurant/Café
Avalon	●	■	●	■		■	
Balmoral	●		●	■	●	●	●
The Basin	●					■	
Bilgola							
Bondi Beach	●	■		■	●	■	●
Bronte	●	■		■		■	●
Camp Cove					●		
Clifton Gardens	●		●		■	■	
Clovelly				■	●		
Coogee	●		●		●	■	●
Curl Curl	●	■		■			
Dee Why	●	■		■	●	■	●
Fairy Bower					●		
Fishermans Beach		■	●	■			
Freshwater	●	■		■			
Gordons Bay				■	●		
Long Reef		■	●	■			
Manly Beach	●	■				●	■	●
Maroubra		■		■	●	■	●
Narrabeen	●	■		■			
Newport Beach	●	■	●	■		■	
Obelisk Bay							
Palm Beach	●	■	●	■			
Parsley Bay						■	
Seven Shillings Beach	●						
Shark Bay	●					■	●
Shelly Beach					●	■	●
Tamarama		■		■	●	■	●
Watsons Bay	●				●		●
Whale Beach	●	■	●	■		■	●

FISHING IN SYDNEY

Surprisingly for a thriving city port, there is a wide variety of fish to be caught in the waters around Sydney. From the rocks and head-lands of the northern beaches, such as Palm Beach and Bilgola, tuna, whiting and blenny abound. The Narrabeen Lakes offer estuary fishing, with a population of flathead and bream. The sheltered Middle Harbour has many angling spots and is home to more bream and mulloway.

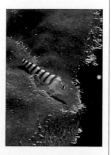

Triplefin blenny

SPORTING SYDNEY

THROUGHOUT AUSTRALIA sport is a way of life and Sydney is no exception. On any day you'll see locals on golf courses at dawn, running on the streets keeping fit, or having a quick set of tennis after work. At weekends, during summer and winter, there is no end to the variety of sports you can watch. Thousands gather at the Sydney Football Stadium and Sydney Cricket Ground every weekend while, for those who cannot make it, sport reigns supreme on weekend television.

CRICKET

DURING THE SUMMER months Test cricket and one-day internationals are played at the Sydney Cricket Ground (SCG). Tickets for weekday sessions of the Tests can often be bought at the gate, although it is advisable to book well in advance (through **Ticketek**) for weekend sessions of Test matches and for all the one-day international matches.

RUGBY LEAGUE AND RUGBY UNION

THE POPULARITY of rugby league knows no bounds in Sydney. This is what people are referring to when they talk about "the footie". There are three major competition levels: local, State of Origin – which matches Queensland against New South Wales – and Tests. The "local" competition fields teams from all over Sydney as well as Newcastle, Canberra, Brisbane, Perth, the Gold Coast and Far North Queensland.

These matches are held all over Sydney, although the Sydney Football Stadium (SFS) is by far the biggest venue. Tickets for State of Origin and

Australia versus the All Blacks, SFS

Test matches often sell out as soon as they go on sale. Call Ticketek to check availability.

Rugby union is the second most popular football code. Again, matches at Test level sell out very quickly. For some premium trans-Tasman rivalry, catch a Test match between Australia's "Wallabies" and the New Zealand "All Blacks" at the Sydney Football Stadium. Phone Ticketek for details.

GOLF AND TENNIS

GOLF ENTHUSIASTS need not do without their round of golf. There are many courses throughout Sydney where visitors are welcome at all times. These include **Moore Park**,

St Michael's and Warringah golf courses. It is sensible to phone beforehand for a booking, especially at weekends.

Tennis is another favoured sport. Courts available for hire can be found all over Sydney. Many centres also have floodlit courts available for night time. Try **Cooper Park** or **Parkland Sports** Centre.

Playing golf at Moore Park, one of Sydney's public courses

AUSTRALIAN RULES FOOTBALL

ALTHOUGH NOT as popular as in Melbourne, "Aussie Rules" has a strong following in Sydney. The local team, the Sydney Swans, plays its home games at the Sydney Cricket Ground during the season. Check a local paper for details.

Rivalry between the Sydney supporters and their Melbourne counterparts is always strong. Busloads of diehard fans from the south arrive to cheer on their teams. Tickets can usually be bought at the ground on the day of the game.

BASKETBALL

BASKETBALL HAS grown in popularity as both a spectator and recreational sport in recent years. Sydney has male and female teams competing in the National Basketball League. The games, held at the Sydney Superdome at

One-day cricket match between Australia and the West Indies, SCG

Aerial view of the Sydney Football Stadium at Moore Park

Homebush, have much of the pizzazz, colour and excitement of American basketball. Tickets can be purchased from either Ticketek or at the box office at the Superdome.

CYCLING AND INLINE SKATING

SYDNEY BOASTS excellent, safe locations for the whole family to go cycling. One of the most frequented is Centennial Park *(see p127)*. You can hire bicycles and safety helmets from **Centennial Park Cycles**.

Another popular pastime in summer is inline skating. **Bondi Boards & Blades**, near Centennial Park, hires inline skates, helmets and protective gear by the hour. If you're tempted to skate from there to Bondi Beach, remember there are several hills on the way back. **Action Inline** at Manly also hires out skates and gear.

For those who like to keep both feet firmly on the ground, you can watch skateboarders and inline skaters practising their moves at the ramps at Bondi Beach *(see p137)*.

Inline skaters enjoying a summer evening on the city's streets

HORSE RIDING

FOR A LEISURELY RIDE, head to Centennial Park or contact the **Centennial Parklands Equestrian Centre**. They will give you details of the four riding schools that operate in the park. **Samarai Park Riding School** conducts trail rides through Ku-ring-gai Chase National Park *(see pp154-5)*.

Further afield, you can enjoy the magnificent scenery of the Blue Mountains *(see pp160-61)* on horseback. The **Megalong Valley Heritage Farm** has trail rides lasting from one hour to an overnight ride. All levels of experience are catered for.

Horse riding in one of the parks surrounding the city centre

ADVENTURE SPORTS

YOU CAN PARTICIPATE in guided bushwalking, mountain biking, canyoning, potholing, rock climbing and abseiling expeditions in the nearby Blue Mountains National Park. The **Blue Mountains Adventure Company** runs one-day or multi-day courses and trips for all standards of adventurer.

In the centre of Sydney, the **City Crag Climbing Centre** has indoor classes and walls on which you can practise.

SYDNEY STREET FINDER

THE PAGE GRID superimposed on the *Area by Area* map below shows which parts of Sydney are covered in this *Street Finder*. Map references given for all sights, hotels, restaurants, shopping and entertainment venues described in this guide refer to the maps in this section. All the major sights are clearly marked so they are easy to locate. The key, set out below, indicates the scale of the maps and shows what other features are marked on them, including railway stations, bus terminals, ferry boarding points, emergency services, post offices and tourist information centres. Map references are also given for hotels *(see pp466–8)* and restaurants *(see pp498–9)*.

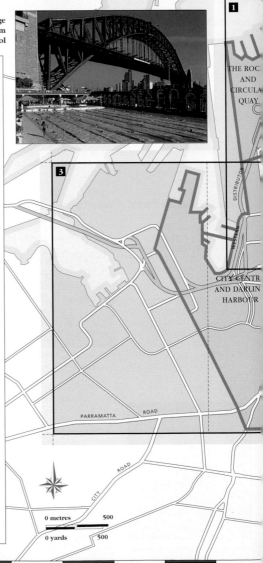

Sydney Harbour Bridge *(see pp76–7)* viewed from **North Sydney Olympic Pool**

KEY TO STREET FINDER

▦	Major sight
▦	Place of interest
▦	Other building
⬟	CityRail station
⬟	Monorail station
⬟	Sydney Light Rail station SLR
▦	Bus terminus
⬟	Coach station
⬟	Ferry boarding point
⬟	RiverCat/JetCat boarding point
⬟	Taxi rank
P	Parking
ℹ	Tourist information
✚	Hospital with casualty unit
⬟	Police station
✝	Church
✡	Synagogue
☪	Mosque
⊠	Post office
⛳	Golf course
▦	Freeway
═	Railway line
―	Monorail
‑ ‑	Ferry route
←	One-way street
▦	Pedestrianized street

0 metres	250
0 yards	250

THE ROCKS
AND
CIRCULAR
QUAY

CITY CENTRE
AND DARLING
HARBOUR

PARRAMATTA ROAD

CITY ROAD

0 metres	500
0 yards	500

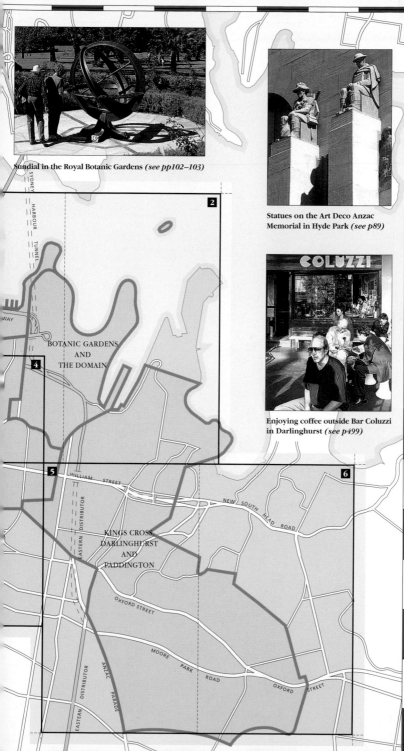

Sundial in the Royal Botanic Gardens *(see pp102–103)*

Statues on the Art Deco Anzac
Memorial in Hyde Park *(see p89)*

Enjoying coffee outside Bar Coluzzi
in Darlinghurst *(see p499)*

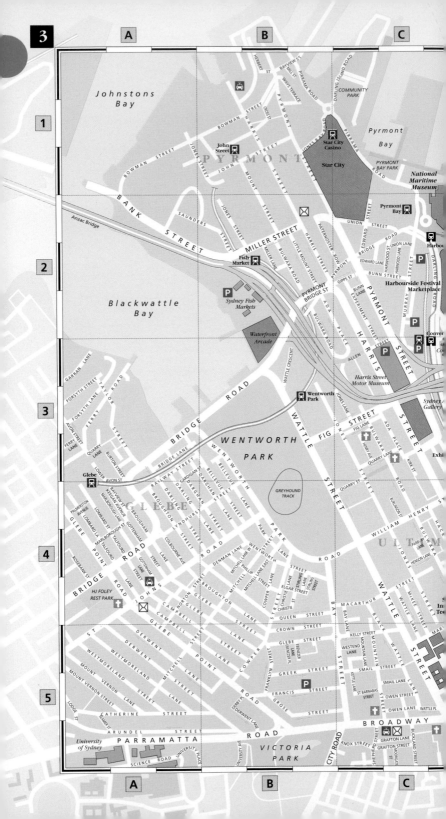

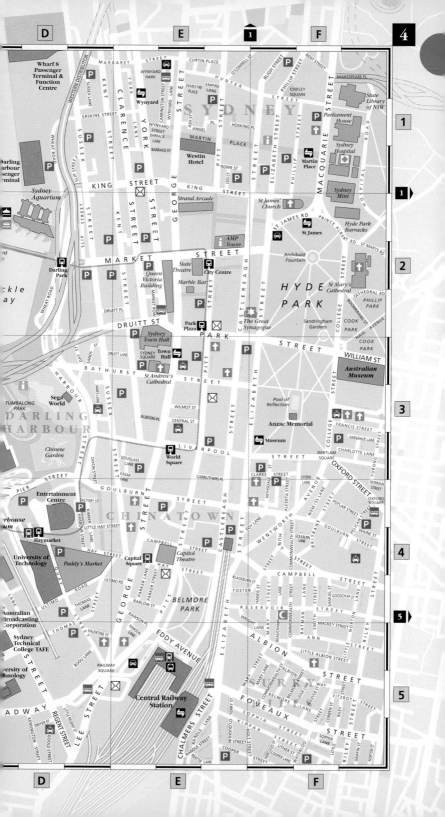

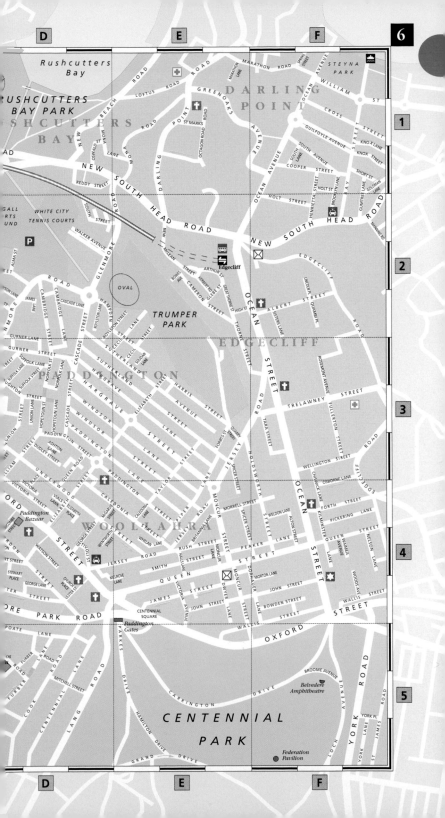

NEW SOUTH WALES AND ACT

New South Wales and ACT at a Glance

THIS SOUTHEASTERN CORNER of the continent, around Sydney Cove, was the site of the first European settlement in the 18th century and today it is the most densely populated and varied region in Australia, and home to its largest city, Sydney *(see pp56–147)*, as well as Canberra, the nation's capital. It also contains the country's highest mountain, Mount Kosciuszko. In the east there are farmlands and vineyards, the Blue Mountains and the ski resorts of the Snowy Mountains. To the west is a desert landscape. The coastline is tropically warm in the north, cooler in the south.

LOCATOR MAP

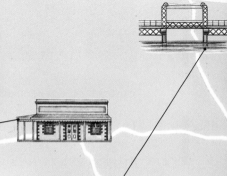

Broken Hill *is one of the few 19th-century mining towns in Australia that continues to survive on its mineral resources (see p173). It is also the location of the Royal Flying Doctor Service headquarters, and tours detailing the history of the service are popular with visitors.*

THE BLUE MOUNTAINS AND BEYOND
(see pp156–73)

Bourke's *major attraction is its remote location. Irrigated by the Darling River, the town is also a successful agricultural centre (see p173). A lift-up span bridge crosses the river.*

Mount Kosciuszko, *in Kosciuszko National Park, is Australia's highest mountain. Panoramic views of the Snowy Mountains can be found at the Mount Kosciuszko Lookout, accessible via a walking trail or a chairlift (see pp152–3).*

◁ **The Breadknife rock formation in the Warrumbungle National Park north of Dubbo, New South Wales**

Tenterfield's School of Arts *building has a proud history as the site of Sir Henry Parkes' Federation speech in 1889, which was followed, 12 years later, by the founding of the Commonwealth of Australia* (see p52). *A museum in the town details the event.*

Tamworth *is the heart of Australian country music. The Golden Guitar Hall, fronted by a model guitar, holds concerts* (see p169).

The Three Sisters *rock formation is the most famous sight within the Blue Mountains National Park. At night it is floodlit for a spectacular view* (see pp162–5).

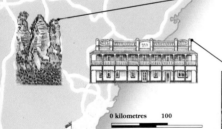

| 0 kilometres | 100 |
| 0 miles | 100 |

Windsor *is one of the best preserved 19th-century towns in the state. The Macquarie Arms Hotel is considered to be the oldest operational hotel in Australia* (see p160).

**ANBERRA
ND ACT**
(pp182–99)

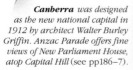

**THE SOUTH
COAST AND
SNOWY
MOUNTAINS**
(see pp174–81)

Canberra *was designed as the new national capital in 1912 by architect Walter Burley Griffin. Anzac Parade offers fine views of New Parliament House, atop Capital Hill* (see pp186–7).

The Snowy Mountains

THE SNOWY MOUNTAINS stretch 500 km (310 miles) from Canberra to Victoria. Formed more than 250 million years ago, they include Australia's highest mountain, Mount Kosciuszko, and the country's only glacial lakes. In summer, wildflowers carpet the meadows; in winter, snow gums bend beneath the cold winds. The Snowy Mountains are preserved within the Kosciuszko National Park and are also home to two of Australia's largest ski resorts, Thredbo and Perisher. The Snowy Mountains Scheme dammed four rivers to supply power to much of inland eastern Australia (see p175).

KEY

▬	Major road
═	Minor road
•••	Walking trail
🎿	Ski trail
△	Camp site
ℹ	Tourist information
❊	Viewpoint

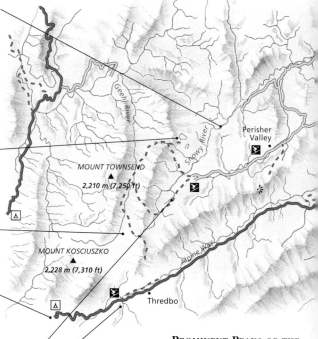

The Snowy River rises below Mount Kosciuszko and is now dammed and diverted to provide hydroelectricity for Melbourne and Sydney as part of the Snowy Mountains Scheme.

Blue Lake is a spectacular glacial lake, one of only a few in the country, which lies in an ice-carved basin 28 m (90 ft) deep.

Seaman's Hut, built in honour of a skier who perished here in 1928, has saved many lives during fierce blizzards.

The Alpine Way offers a spectacular drive through the mountains, best taken in spring or summer, via the Thredbo River Valley.

Geehi River

Snowy River

Perisher Valley

MOUNT TOWNSEND
▲
2,210 m (7,250 ft)

MOUNT KOSCIUSZKO
▲
2,228 m (7,310 ft)

Alpine Way

Thredbo

Dead Horse Gap is a striking pass that gives access to both the beautiful wilderness to the west and The Pilot and Coberras to the south. It was named after a group of "brumbies" (wild horses) that tragically perished in a snowdrift here during the 19th century.

PROMINENT PEAKS OF THE SNOWY MOUNTAINS

Mount Kosciuszko is Australia's highest mountain, and may be approached by gentle walks across alpine meadows from Thredbo or from Charlottes Pass. Mount Townsend is only slightly lower but, with a more pronounced summit, is often mistaken for its higher and more famous neighbour.

Charlottes Pass marks the start of the summit walk to Mount Kosciuszko. It was named after Charlotte Adams who, in 1881, was the first European woman to climb the peak.

0 kilometres 5

0 miles 5

Downhill and cross-country skiing *and snow-boarding are popular in the Snowy Mountains between June and September.*

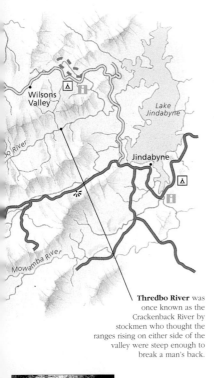

Thredbo River was once known as the Crackenback River by stockmen who thought the ranges rising on either side of the valley were steep enough to break a man's back.

The Yarrangobilly Caves, *about 130 km (80 miles) north of Thredbo, are a system of 70 limestone caves formed 750,000 years ago. They contain magnificent white columns, cascading frozen waterfalls and delicate underground pools.*

NATURE IN THE SNOWY MOUNTAINS

The Snowy Mountains are often harsh, windswept and barren, yet myriad flowers, trees and wildlife have evolved to survive all seasons. Almost all species here are unique to the alpine regions of Australia.

The Flora

Silver snow daisies, *with their white petals and yellow centres, are the most spectacular of all the alpine flowers en masse.*

Mountain plum pine *is a natural bonsai tree, which grows slowly and at an angle. The pygmy possum feeds on its berries.*

Sphagnum moss *surrounds the springs, bogs and creeks in the highest regions.*

Snow gums, *with their distinctive bark, can survive at higher altitudes than most trees.*

The Fauna

Corroboree frogs *live only in the fragile sphagnum moss bogs of the region.*

Mountain pygmy possums *live under the snow, high up in the mountains.*

Brown and rainbow trout, *both introduced species, thrive in the cool mountain streams.*

Wines of New South Wales and ACT

Hunter Valley Chardonnay

NEW SOUTH WALES and ACT were the cradle of Australian wines. A small consignment of vines was on board the First Fleet when it landed at Sydney Cove in January 1788 *(see pp46–7)*, and this early hope was fulfilled in the steady development of a successful wine industry. The state is now the home of many fine wineries with an international reputation. New South Wales is currently in the vanguard of wine industry expansion, planting new vineyards and developing established districts to meet steadily rising domestic and export demand.

LOCATOR MAP

New South Wales wine regions

Sand Hills Vineyard *in the Lachlan Valley near Forbes produces both traditional and modern wines. Shiraz reds along with classic dry whites such as Chardonnay are particularly good.*

Cooraminta Estate *is one of the Hilltops region wineries which benefits from rich alluvial soil and regular rainfall.*

De Bortoli *is a family-owned winery in the Riverina district. Its speciality wines, such as Dry Botrytis Semillon, are matched by its consistently reasonable prices.*

Charles Sturt University Winery *is a major innovator of winemaking techniques and viticultural science. Traditional wines are made using high-tech equipment.*

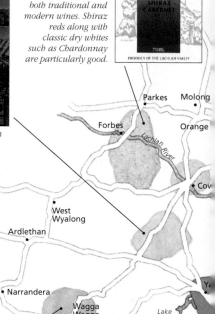

Parkes　Molong

Forbes　Orange

Lachlan River

Cov

West Wyalong

Ardlethan

Griffith

Narrandera

Wagga Wagga

Lake Burrinjuck

Gundagai　CANBERRA

Tumut

Tumbarumba

Albury　Kiandra

Murray River

Lake Eucumbene

Coo

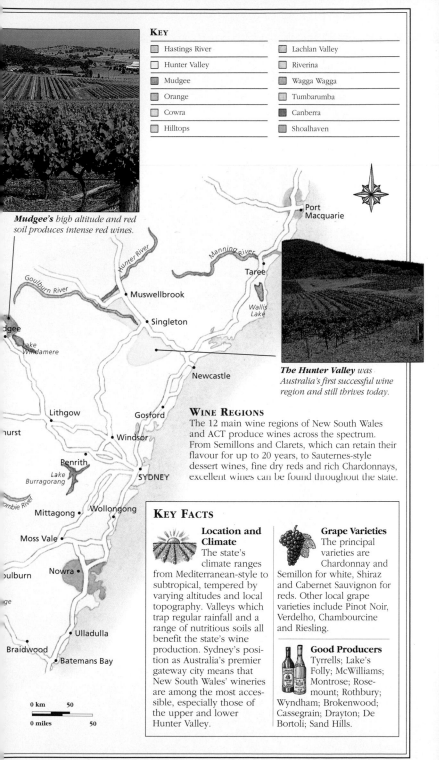

KEY

▨ Hastings River	▨ Lachlan Valley
▢ Hunter Valley	▢ Riverina
▨ Mudgee	▨ Wagga Wagga
▢ Orange	▢ Tumbarumba
▢ Cowra	▨ Canberra
▢ Hilltops	▢ Shoalhaven

Mudgee's high altitude and red soil produces intense red wines.

The Hunter Valley *was Australia's first successful wine region and still thrives today.*

WINE REGIONS

The 12 main wine regions of New South Wales and ACT produce wines across the spectrum. From Semillons and Clarets, which can retain their flavour for up to 20 years, to Sauternes-style dessert wines, fine dry reds and rich Chardonnays, excellent wines can be found throughout the state.

KEY FACTS

Location and Climate

The state's climate ranges from Mediterranean-style to subtropical, tempered by varying altitudes and local topography. Valleys which trap regular rainfall and a range of nutritious soils all benefit the state's wine production. Sydney's position as Australia's premier gateway city means that New South Wales' wineries are among the most accessible, especially those of the upper and lower Hunter Valley.

Grape Varieties

The principal varieties are Chardonnay and Semillon for white, Shiraz and Cabernet Sauvignon for reds. Other local grape varieties include Pinot Noir, Verdelho, Chambourcine and Riesling.

Good Producers

Tyrrells; Lake's Folly; McWilliams; Montrose; Rosemount; Rothbury; Wyndham; Brokenwood; Cassegrain; Drayton; De Bortoli; Sand Hills.

0 km   50

0 miles   50

THE BLUE MOUNTAINS AND BEYOND

Think of northern *New South Wales and vibrant colours spring to mind. There are the dark blues of the Blue Mountains; the blue-green seas of the north coast; the verdant green of the rainforests near the Queensland border; and the gold of the wheat fields. Finally, there are the reds and yellows of the desert in the far west.*

Ever since English explorer Captain James Cook claimed the eastern half of Australia as British territory in 1770 and named it New South Wales, Sydney and its surroundings have been at the forefront of Australian life.

On the outskirts of Sydney, at Windsor and Richmond, early convict settlements flourished into prosperous farming regions along the fertile Hawkesbury River. The barrier of the Blue Mountains was finally penetrated in 1812, marking the first spread of sheep and cattle squatters north, west and south onto the rich plains beyond. In the middle of the 19th century came the gold rush around Bathurst and Mudgee and up into the New England Tablelands, which led to the spread of roads and railways.

Following improved communications in the late 19th and early 20th centuries, northern New South Wales now contains more towns, a denser rural population and a more settled coastline than anywhere else in the country. Fortunately, all this development has not robbed the region of its natural beauty or assets. From the grand and daunting wilderness of the Blue Mountains to the blue waters and surf of Byron Bay, the easternmost point in Australia, the region remains easy to explore and a delight to the senses. It is most easily divided into three parts: the coastline and mild hinterland, including the famous Hunter Valley vineyards; the hills, plateaus and flats of the New England Tablelands and Western Plains with their rivers, national parks and thriving farming areas; and the remote, dusty Outback, west of the vast Great Dividing Range.

The combination of urban civilization, with all the amenities and attractions it offers, and the beautiful surrounding landscape, make this region a favourite holiday location with locals and tourists all year round.

Cape Byron lighthouse on Australia's most easterly point

◁ **The Three Sisters rock formation in the Blue Mountains National Park, seen from Echo Point**

Exploring the Blue Mountains and Beyond

DISTANCES CAN BE LONG in northern New South Wales so the extent of any exploration will depend on the time available. Within easy reach of Sydney are historic gold rush towns such as Windsor, the cool mountain retreats of the Blue Mountains, the old gold towns between Bathurst and Mudgee, and the gentle, green hills of the Hunter Valley and its vineyards. The north coast and its hinterland are best explored as part of a touring holiday between Sydney and the Queensland capital, Brisbane, or as a short break to the beaches and fishing areas around Port Macquarie, Taree and Coffs Harbour.

KEY

The Blue Mountains and Beyond

West of the Divide pp172–3

Impressive Three Sisters rocks in the Blue Mountains National Park

SIGHTS AT A GLANCE

Armidale ❼
Barrington Tops WHA ❻
Blue Mountains National Park
pp162–5 ❶
Gibraltar Range National Park ❽
Gosford ❸
Inverell ❿
Mudgee ⓬
Newcastle ❹
Tamworth ⓫
Tenterfield ❾
Windsor ❷

Tour
Hunter Valley ❺

West of the Divide
See pp172–3
Bourke ⓯
Broken Hill ⓰
Dubbo ⓭
Lightning Ridge ⓮
Wagga Wagga ⓲
Willandra National Park ⓱

YETMA

TAMWORTH

MERRIWA

GULGONG

GOULBURN RIVER
NATIONAL PARK

⓬ MUDGEE

WOLLEMI
NATIONAL
PARK

PARKES

FORBES

BATHURST

LITHGOW

WINDSOR

COWRA

Lake
Burragorang

BLUE MOUNTAINS
NATIONAL PARK

Canberra

Brisbane

⑨ **TENTERFIELD**

44 **CASINO**

BYRON BAY

Clarence River

15

8 38

EREIL

GLEN INNES

GIBRALTAR RANGE NATIONAL PARK

GRAFTON

78

COFFS HARBOUR

⑦ **ARMIDALE**

Macleay River

WERRIKIMBE NATIONAL PARK

34

PORT MACQUARIE

⑥ **ARRINGTON OPS WORLD RITAGE AREA**

TAREE

LETON

per River

SSNOCK

5

④ **NEWCASTLE**

GOSFORD

Cape Byron, Byron Bay; mainland Australia's easternmost point

GETTING AROUND

An extensive rail and bus network up the north coast and to major towns such as Coffs Harbour, Byron Bay and Armidale makes this region very accessible. However, a car is still the best way to see the natural highlights of the area. Highways are good, although rarely dual carriageway, with the exception of the coastal Princes Hwy. Other routes are the New England Hwy to the Northern Tablelands, the Newell Hwy to Moree and the Great Western Hwy through the Blue Mountains to Bathurst.

SEE ALSO

• **Where to Stay** pp468–9

• **Where to Eat** pp501–502

0 kilometres   50

0 miles   50

KEY

🚃 Highway

▬ Major road

▨ Scenic route

〰 River

❃ Viewpoint

Extensive green vineyards of the Hunter Valley

Blue Mountains National Park ❶

See pp162–5.

Windsor ❷

🏃 *1,850.* ☒ 🚃 🚌 🚆 ⓘ *7*
Thompson Square (02) 4577 2310.

WINDSOR was named by Governor Macquarie and this well-preserved colonial settlement is one of the five "Macquarie towns". Established on the banks of the Hawkesbury River in 1794, the town provided farmers with both fertile land and the convenience of river transport for their produce.

In the centre of town, St Matthew's Church, designed by Francis Greenway, is a fine example of Georgian colonial architecture and is considered to be his most successful work. Other buildings of interest include the Macquarie Arms, which claims to be Australia's oldest hotel, and the **Hawkesbury Museum**, set in a Georgian residence. The museum chronicles Windsor's early colonial history.

🏛 **Hawkesbury Museum**
7 Thompson Square. 📞 *(02) 4577 2310.* ⭕ *daily.* ● *Good Fri, 25 Dec.* ♿

St Matthew's Church in Windsor, designed by Francis Greenway

ENVIRONS: One of the other five "Macquarie towns" is Richmond, which lies 6 km (3.5 miles) west of Windsor. This attractive settlement was established five years earlier, in 1789. The farmstead of Mountainview, built in 1804, is one of the oldest surviving homes in the country.

Gosford ❸

🏃 *38,000.* 🚃 🚌 🚆 ⛴ ⓘ *200 Mann St, (02) 4385 4430.*

GOSFORD is the principal town of the popular holiday region known as the Central Coast, and provides a good base for touring the surrounding area. The rural settlements that once dotted this coastline have now evolved into one continuous beachside suburb, stretching as far south as Ku-ring-gai Chase National Park *(see p122)*. Gosford itself sits on the calm northern shore of Brisbane Waters, an excellent spot for sailing and other recreational activities. The Effalong Markets in the town centre are well worth a look. The nearby coastal beaches are renowned for their great surf, clear lagoons and long stretches of sand. The beaches here are so numerous that it is still possible to find a deserted spot in any season except high summer.

Old Sydney Town, 12 km (7.5 miles) west of Gosford, is

Preserved 18th-century Custom House at Old Sydney Town near Gosford

a faithful reproduction of the original first settlement *(see pp46–7)*. Inhabitants, dressed in 18th-century fashions, go about the daily business of colonial life. Next door, the **Australian Reptile Park** is home to many types of reptiles, including crocodiles, massive goannas, snakes and other species.

🐢 Old Sydney Town
Old Pacific Hwy, Somersby.
📞 *(02) 4340 1104.* ⏰ *10am–4pm daily.* ● *25 Dec.* 📷 ♿ *limited.*
🦎 Australian Reptile Park
Old Pacific Hwy, Somersby. 📞 *(02) 4340 1022.* ⏰ *9am–5pm daily.*
● *25 Dec.* 📷 ♿

ENVIRONS: There are several national parks within a short distance of Gosford. Worth a visit is the Bulgandry Aboriginal site in Brisbane Waters National Park. This features a rock gallery with engravings of human and animal figures dating back thousands of years.

Newcastle ❹

🏠 *138,000.* ✈ 🚃 🚌 🚍 ℹ *363 Hunter St (02) 4974 2999.*

ONE VISITOR to Newcastle, Australia's second-oldest city, remarked in the 1880s: "To my mind the whole town appeared to have woke up in fright at our arrival and to have no definite ideas of a rendezvous whereat to rally." The chaos to which he referred was largely the result of the city's reliance on coal mining and vast steel works. Building progressed only as profits rose and town planning was left largely to accident.

Today this chaos only adds to Newcastle's charm. The city curls loosely around a splendid harbour and its main streets rise randomly up the surrounding hills. Industry is still the mainstay, but this does not detract from the city's quaint beauty. The main thoroughfare of Hunter Street has many buildings of diverse architectural styles. The Courthouse follows a style known as Late Free Classical; the

Italianate post office in Newcastle

Court Chambers are High Victorian; the post office was modelled on Palladio's Basilica in Venice and the town's cathedral, Christ Church, is an elaborate and impressive example of Victorian Gothic.

The modern **Newcastle Region Art Gallery** houses works by some of the country's most prominent 19th- and 20th-century artists, including the Newcastle-born William Dobell, Arthur Boyd and Brett Whiteley *(see pp30–31)*.

Queens Wharf is the main attraction of the harbour foreshore. It was redeveloped during the 1980s as part of a bicentennial project. There are splendid views from its promenade areas and outdoor

cafés *(see pp501–502)*. On the southern side of the harbour, Nobbys Lighthouse sits at the end of a long causeway; the vista back over old Newcastle makes the brief walk worthwhile.

Further on lies **Fort Stratchley**, built originally to repel the coal-seeking Russians in the 1880s. Despite constant surveillance, the fort did not open fire until the 1940s, when the Japanese shelled Newcastle during World War II. Good surfing beaches lie on either side of the harbour's entrance.

🏛 Newcastle Region Art Gallery
Cnr Darby & Laman sts. 📞 *(02) 4974 5100.* ⏰ *Tue–Sun.* ● *25 Dec, Good Fri.* ♿
🐢 Fort Stratchley
Nobbys Rd. 📞 *(02) 4929 2257.* ⏰ *10am–4pm Tue–Sun.* **Military Tunnels** ⏰ *noon–4pm Sat & Sun.* ● *Good Fri, 25 Dec.* 📷 ♿

ENVIRONS: Four times the size of Sydney Harbour *(see pp70–99)*, Lake Macquarie lies 20 km (12 miles) south of Newcastle. The lake's vast size facilitates nearly every kind of water sport imaginable. On the western shore, at Wangi Wangi, is Dobell House, once home to the renowned local artist, William Dobell.

FRANCIS GREENWAY, CONVICT ARCHITECT

Until recently, Australian $10 notes bore the portrait of the early colonial architect Francis Greenway. This was the only currency in the world to pay tribute to a convicted forger. Greenway was transported from England to Sydney in 1814 to serve a 14-year sentence for his crime. Under the patronage of Governor Lachlan Macquarie, who appointed him Civil Architect in 1816, Greenway designed more than 40 buildings, of which 11 still survive today. He received a full King's Pardon in 1819, but soon fell out of favour because he charged exorbitant fees for his architectural designs while still on a government salary. Greenway eventually died in poverty in 1837.

Francis Greenway (1777–1837)

Blue Mountains National Park ●

Kookaburra

THE LANDSCAPE of the Blue Mountains was more than 250 million years in the making as sediments built up then were eroded, revealing sheer cliff faces and canyons. Home to Aboriginal communities for an estimated 14,000 years, the rugged terrain proved, at first, a formidable barrier to white settlers *(see p164)*, but since the 1870s it has been a popular holiday resort. The mountains get their name from the release of oil from the eucalyptus trees which causes a blue haze. Excellent drives and walking trails allow for easy exploration of the region.

The Cathedral of Fern is an area of green foliage set amid streams, resembling tropical rainforest.

Mount Wilson
A basalt cap, the result of a now extinct volcano, provides the rich soil for the gardens of this attractive summer retreat.

The Zig Zag Railway is a steam train line between Sydney and Lithgow.

FLORA AND FAUNA IN THE BLUE MOUNTAINS

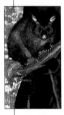

Possum

Many flora and fauna species which are unique to Australia can be easily seen in the Blue Mountains. For example, the superb lyrebird is a fan-tailed bird found in the forests, distinguishable by its high-pitched cry. The sassafras (*Doryphora sassafras*) tree is one of the species of the warm temperate rainforest and produces tiny white flowers. The shy brushtail possum seeks shelter in the woodlands by day and forages at night.

MUDGEE

Lithgow

Bells Line of Road

Bell

Hartley

Mount Victoria

Blackheath

Jenolan Caves Road

Hampton

JENOLAN STATE FOREST

Jenolan Caves
Nine spectacular limestone caves are open to the public; stalactites and stalagmites can be seen in beautiful and striking formations.

Katoomba is the largest town in the vicinity of the national park and has a full range of accommodation for tourists.

THE BLUE MOUNTAINS AND BEYOND

Mount Tomah Botanic Garden
*Cool-climate species from around the
world are grown here, including
rhododendrons from the Himalayas.*

Wentworth Falls
*This waterfall is evidence of
a massive slip in the escarpment. Pockets of rainforest
thrive along its edges.*

0 kilometres   5

0 miles   5

Leura
*Elegant old residences such
as the Leura Mansion are
features of this pretty village.*

KEY

▬	Major road
═	Minor road
🚶	Walking trail start-point
i	Tourist information
▬	Railway
△	Camp site
⛱	Picnic area
☀	Viewpoint

Three Sisters
*Erosion has formed this spectacular rock formation.
Aboriginal legend has it that the rock is in fact three sisters,
imprisoned by their father to protect them from a bunyip.*

Exploring the Blue Mountains

THE BLUE MOUNTAINS, reaching 1,100 m (3,600 ft) above sea level at their highest point, at first made the early colonists virtual prisoners of the Sydney Cove area. Many settlers were convinced that plains suitable for grazing and crops would be found beyond the mountains, but attempts to reach the imagined pastures repeatedly failed. In 1813, however, three farmers, Gregory Blaxland, William Lawson and William Charles Wentworth, set out on a well-planned mission, following the ridge between the Grose and Cox rivers, and emerged successfully on the western side of the mountains. The construction of roads and a railway made the mountains an increasingly attractive destination, and resorts and country homes were soon established. In 1959, the Blue Mountains National Park was gazetted, ensuring the preservation of the large tracts of remaining wilderness.

🏛 Norman Lindsay Gallery and Museum
14 Norman Lindsay Crescent, Faulconbridge. 【 *(02) 4751 1067.* 🔲 *daily.* ⬤ *25 Dec.* 🎟 ⬤
Norman Lindsay, one of Australia's most recognized artists, inspired considerable controversy during his lifetime with his sumptuous nudes and risqué novels. Born in 1879, he bought his mountain retreat in 1913 and set about producing an enormous body of work, much of which reflects his rejection of the moral and sexual restraints of his era.

His beautifully preserved home is now a gallery for his many paintings, cartoons, mythological garden sculptures and children's books. There is a whole room devoted to *The Magic Pudding*, a perennial favourite with children and adults alike. There is also a re-creation of the interior of his original studio, and a peaceful garden set amid the mountain bushland.

Leura
ℹ *Echo Point, Katoomba.* 【 *1300 653 408.* ⬤ *first Sunday of the month.*
This small town on the Great Western Highway, with its European gardens and Art Deco architecture, recalls the elegance of life in the 1920s. Its secluded, tree-lined main street is a magnet for fine art galleries, cafés, shops and up-market restaurants.

Six km (3.5 miles) from Leura, Everglades House is an Art Deco fantasy of curves, balconies and rose-pink walls. The Everglades gardens are considered classic examples of cool-climate design from the 1930s. They include a shaded alpine garden, a grotto pool, rhododendron stands, an arboretum and peacocks roaming around the grounds.

Some other gardens in the area are opened to the public during the Leura Garden Festival each October *(see p36)*.

Visitors can get an overview of the surrounding landscape by taking the Cliff Drive to Katoomba. The lookout at Sublime Point, at the end of Sublime Point Road, also provides startling views across the Jamison Valley.

Scenic Skyway ride over the Blue Mountains from Katoomba

Katoomba
ℹ *Echo Point, Katoomba.* 【 *1300 653 408.*
Katoomba is the bustling tourism centre of the Blue Mountains and a good base from which to explore the mountains. However, it still manages to retain a veneer of its gracious former self, when it first attracted wealthy Sydneysiders in need of mountain air during the 1870s. The Paragon Café, with its dark-wood panelling and mirrored walls, is a reminder of these glory days, as are the imposing guesthouses with their fresh air and beautiful views across the Jamison Valley.

Within a few minutes' drive of the town are the region's most popular attractions. Echo Point is home to a large information centre and lookout, with views across to the imposing bulk of Mount Solitary and the most famous of icons, the Three Sisters *(see pp162–3)*. A short walk leads down to this striking rock formation, while further on the Giant Staircase – steps hewn out of the rock face – curls around its eastern side.

Picturesque tree-lined Main Street in Leura

Beyond the Staircase is the Leura Forest, a peaceful retreat and a superb example of the warm temperate rainforest flora and fauna.

On the western side of town, the Scenic Skyway departs every ten minutes for a rope-way ride 205 m (670 ft) above the valley floor. Alternatively, the Scenic Railway offers a nerve-wracking plummet down a mountain gorge. Reputed to be the steepest rail track in the world, it was originally built in the 1880s to transport miners down to the valley's rich coal deposits.

Blackheath
ℹ *Govetts Leap Rd.* **📞** *(02) 4787 8877.*

Blackheath is a small village that offers a quieter prospect than many of the busy mountain towns further east. The excellent standard of restaurants and accommodation available in the town often induces visitors to stay one or two nights here, rather than make the return to Sydney the same day. But the real draw of this area is the chance to explore the mist-enshrouded rifts and ravines of the beautiful Grose Valley.

The best place to start is the Heritage Centre, 3 km (2 miles) from Blackheath along Govetts Leap Road. Displays document the geological, Aboriginal and European histories of the region and local flora and fauna, while park officers are available to offer advice on the best walks in the area. Govetts Leap, with its heady views across Grose Valley, provides a point of orientation and is the starting place for a number of tracks. A clifftop track leads off in a southerly direction past Bridal Falls, the highest waterfalls in the Blue Mountains, and through stretches of exposed mountain heathland.

A steep and arduous 8-hour return trek into the valley leads to Blue Gum Forest, so called because of the smoky blue trunks of the eucalypt species that dominate this pretty woodland. The Grand Canyon is a destination only for the fit – this 5-hour walk,

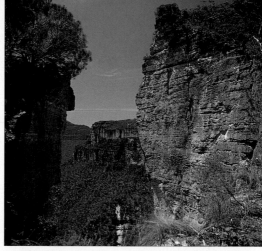

Eroded gorge in Grose Valley, near the town of Blackheath

through deep gorges and sandstone canyons, sheds some light on the geological mysteries of the mountains.

🏕 Jenolan Caves
Jenolan Caves Rd. **📞** *(02) 6359 3311.* **◯** *daily.* **📷** **♿** *to small section of Orient Cave.*

The Jenolan Caves lie southwest of the mountain range. The Great Western Highway passes the grand old hotels of Mount Victoria before a south turn is taken at Hartley, the centre of the first grazing region established by Blaxland, Lawson and Wentworth from 1815 onwards. The southern stretch of the road, cutting across the escarpment of Kanimbla Valley, is one of the most scenic in the mountains.

Limestone formations in the Jenolan Caves

The Jenolan Caves were first discovered in 1838 and are remarkable for their complexity and accessibility. More than 300 subterranean chambers were formed in a limestone belt that was deposited more than 300 million years ago. The nine caves that are open to the public are replete with a variety of delicately wrought limestone formations, pools and rivers, including the ominously named Styx River.

🌸 Mount Tomah Botanic Gardens
Bells Line of Road. **📞** *(02) 4567 2154.* **◯** *daily.* **●** *25 Dec.* **📷** **♿**

Mount Tomah lies along the Bells Line of Road, a quiet but increasingly popular route with tourists to the area.

Tomah takes its name from the Aboriginal word for "fern". The Botanic Gardens were set up as an annex to Sydney's Royal Botanic Gardens *(see pp102–103)* in order to house species that would not survive the coastal conditions. Of special interest are the southern hemisphere plants which developed in isolation once Australia broke away from Gondwanaland into a separate continent *(see p19)*.

The overall layout of the gardens is a feat of engineering and imagination, and the views north and south across Grose Valley are breathtaking.

A Tour of the Hunter Valley [5]

Lakes Folly [3]
Max Lake started this vineyard in the 1960s, successfully growing Cabernet Sauvignon grapes in the Hunter Valley for the first time since the 1900s.

THE FIRST COMMERCIAL VINEYARDS in Australia were established on the fertile flats of the Hunter River in the 1830s. Originally a specialist area for fortified wines, the Hunter Valley is now one of Australia's premier table wine districts, producing high-quality reds and whites. February and March are harvest months, when the vineyards are at their busiest. With 70 wineries, most open daily to visitors, and a range of restaurants and accommodation *(see pp466–523)*, the Hunter Valley is a popular tourist destination.

Rothbury Estate [4]
Cask Hall was the vision of wine writer Len Evans. The vineyard's wines are now world famous, as are its music concerts.

Tyrrells' Vineyards [5]
The Tyrrell family has been making wine here since 1858. An outdoor tasting area gives views over the vineyards.

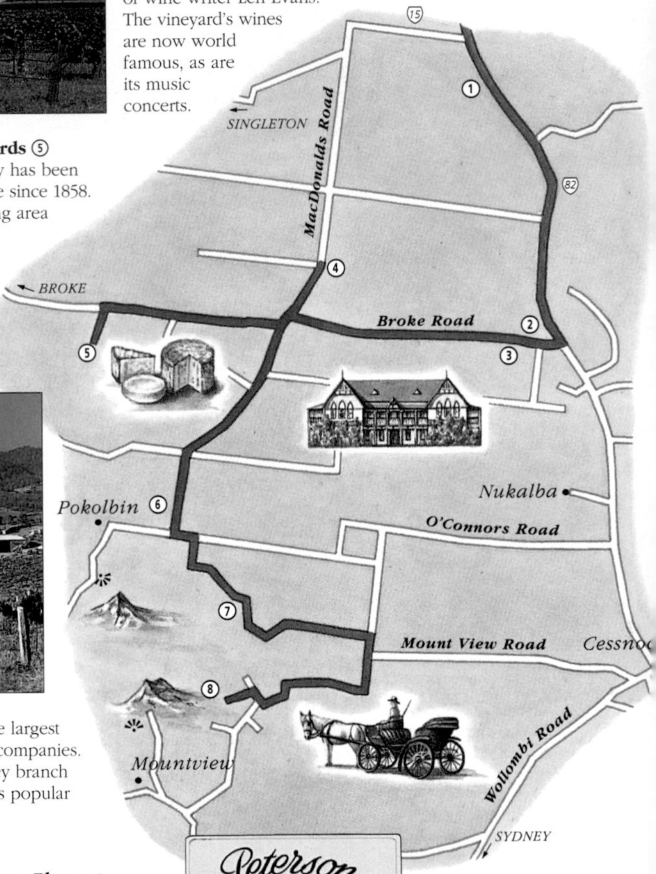
15
SINGLETON
MacDonalds Road
82
BROKE
Broke Road
Nukalba
Pokolbin
O'Connors Road
Mount View Road
Cessnoc
Mountview
Wollombi Road
SYDNEY

Lindemans [6]
This is one of the largest Australian wine companies. The Hunter Valley branch is the home of its popular "Ben Ean" wine.

McWilliams Mount Pleasant Winery [7]
This winery was run for many years by the legendary winemaker Phil Ryan, and is home to the Mount Pleasant Elizabeth Semillon, one of Australia's best quality white wines.

Petersons
HUNTER VALLEY
Chardonnay
Vintage 1986
750ML PRODUCT OF AUSTRALIA 12.5%ALC/VOL

Petersons Winery [8]
This small family winery is known for its unique experimentation with champagne-style wine production in the Hunter Valley.

Rothbury ①
An early morning champagne breakfast and hot-air balloon flight over the Hunter Valley from this town is a luxurious way to start a day touring the wineries.

The Hunter Valley Wine Society ②
This group organizes wine tastings from many local vineyards and offers excellent advice for the novice. Shiraz and Semillon are the two most recognizable Hunter Valley styles.

0 kilometres   5

0 miles   5

KEY

▬▬ Tour route

══ Other roads

☆ Viewpoint

TIPS FOR DRIVERS

Tour length: 60 km (37 miles). While there are no limits on the numbers of wineries that can be visited, three or four in one day will give time to taste and discuss the wines leisurely. Don't forget Australia's strict drink-driving laws (see p549).
Starting point: Cessnock is the gateway to the Hunter Valley and is home to its major visitors' centre.
Stopping-off points: Apart from the picnic areas and restaurants at the wineries, Pokolbin has plenty of cafés, a general store and a bush picnic area. The Mount Bright lookout gives a panoramic view over the region.

Panoramic mountain view from Barrington Tops

Barrington Tops World Heritage Area ❻

🏞 Gloucester. 🛈 27 Denison St, Gloucester (02) 6558 1408. ⏱ daily.

F LANKING THE NORTH of the Hunter Valley is the mountain range known as the Barringtons. One of the highest points in Australia, its high country, the "Barrington Tops", reaches 1,550 m (5,080 ft), and light snow is common in winter. The rugged mountains, cool-climate rainforest, gorges, cliffs and waterfalls make Barrington Tops a paradise for hikers, campers, birdwatchers and climbers. Its 280,000 ha (690,000 acres) of forest, with 1,000-year-old trees, are protected by the Barrington Tops National Park. The rainforest was declared a World Heritage Area in 1986 and a Wilderness Area in 1996 as part of the Central Eastern Rainforest Reserves (*see pp22–3*).

Barrington Tops has been a favourite weekend escape for Sydneysiders for more than 100 years. Tourist operators organize environmentally friendly 4WD trips into the heart of the wild forests, with camping along the Allyn River, hiking trails at Telegherry and Jerusalem Creek and swimming in the rock pool at Lady's Well.

Barrington Tops is best reached through Dungog or from Gloucester.

Armidale ❼

🏘 22,000. ✈ 🚉 🏢 🚌 🛈 82 Marsh St (02) 6772 4655. ⏱ daily.

L YING IN THE heart of the New England Tablelands, Armidale is a sophisticated university city surrounded by some of the state's most magnificent national parks. The university gives the city a high-brow atmosphere, and concerts, plays, films and lectures fill its many theatres, pubs and university halls.

Some 35 buildings in Armidale are classified by the National Trust, testament to the land booms of the 19th century, including the town hall, courthouse and St Peter's Anglican Cathedral. The **New England Regional Art Museum** holds the A\$20 million Howard Hinton and Chandler Coventry collections, with many works by Australian artists, including Tom Roberts and Norman Lindsay (*see p30*). To the east of Armidale is the 90-ha (220-acre) **Oxley Wild Rivers National Park**, containing the 220-m (720-ft) high Wollomombi Gorge, one of the highest waterfalls in Australia.

Spinning wheel from the Armidale Folk Museum

🏛 **New England Regional Art Museum**
Kentucky St. 📞 (02) 6772 5255. ⏱ 10:30am–5pm daily. ● 1 Jan, Good Fri, 25 Dec. 🅿 ♿
♣ **Oxley Wild Rivers National Park**
Waterfall Way. 📞 (02) 6776 4260. ⏱ daily. ♿ limited.

Wilderness stream in Gibraltar Range National Park

Gibraltar Range National Park ⑧

Gwydir Hwy. ☎ (02) 6732 5133.
◯ daily. 🏛️ ♿

SITUATED 70 km (43 miles) east of Glen Innes, Gibraltar Range National Park is known for its giant rocky tors towering 1,200 m (4,000 ft) above sea level, surrounded by heath and swamp land. The area is at its most beautiful in the summer, when wildflowers such as waratahs and Christmas bells come into bloom. The park also has good walking trails and camping facilities.

Gibraltar Range National Park is linked to Washpool National Park by a 100-km (60-mile) World Heritage walk. Washpool remains a wilderness park, accessible only to experienced walkers.

Glen Innes and its surrounding villages of Glencoe, Ben Lomond and Shannon Vale are known as Australia's "Celtic Country". Settled by Scottish, Welsh, Irish and Cornish immigrants in 1852, the area's heritage is celebrated by the annual Australian Celtic Festival *(see p38)*. The town's Standing Stones are a traditional monument to all Celtic settlers.

Sapphire mining remains a major industry. Public digging, known as "fossicking", for sapphires, topaz, garnet and beryl is still possible near the mining villages of Emmaville and Torrington. Glen Innes hosts a gem and mineral fair in September each year.

Tenterfield ⑨

🏘️ 33,000. ✈️ 🚌 🚍 ℹ️ 157 Rouse St (02) 6736 1082.

THE RURAL TOWN of Tenterfield, to the north of the New England Tablelands, occupies a special place in Australian history. Often described as the "Birthplace of Our Nation", it was at the town's School of Arts building on 24 October 1889 that local politician and towering figure of 19th-century Australian politics, Sir Henry Parkes, made his historic

Plaque celebrating Henry Parkes' speech

"One Nation" speech. The address explained his vision of all the colonies in Australia uniting to form one country. Parkes' Tenterfield address led to a popular movement of support, resulting in Australian Federation on 1 January 1901 *(see p52)*. The School of Arts was the first building to be acquired by the New South Wales National Trust because of its political and historic importance.

Other historic buildings in this small town include the Victorian mansion Stannum House, the bluestone saddlers' shop (made famous in the song "Tenterfield Saddler"), and the restored courthouse with its glass ceiling.

Also not to be missed are Bald Rock and Boonoo Boonoo, about 40 km (25 miles) north of Tenterfield. Bald Rock is the second biggest monolith in Australia after Uluru *(see pp278–81)*. It offers fine views of volcanic ranges to the east, Girraween National Park in Queensland to the north and Mount McKenzie to the south. Boonoo Boonoo Falls cascade 210 m (690 ft) into the gorge below, ideal for swimming.

To the east of Tenterfield in the Boonoo State Forest is the **Woollool Woolloolni Aboriginal Place**, a sacred site of the local Gidabal people which is open to the public.

🔷 Woollool Woolloolni Aboriginal Place

Via 157 Rouse St, Tenterfield. ☎ (02) 6736 1082. ◯ daily. ● Good Fri, 25 Dec. 🏛️ for tour. ♿ limited.

Tenterfield's School of Arts building

Inverell ⑩

🏃 10,000. ✈ 🚌 🚍 ℹ *Water Towers Complex, Campbell St (02) 6728 8161.*

INVERELL IS KNOWN as "Sapphire City" because the majority of the world's sapphires are mined in the area. Many of the buildings in the main street were built during the 1880s mining boom and are well preserved. The **Inverell Pioneer Village** features buildings gathered from around the district and relocated to create this tourist theme town.

Just south of Inverell lies the mighty Copeton Dam. Whitewater rafting below the dam on the wild Gwydir River is an exhilarating experience.

🏛 **Inverell Pioneer Village**
Tingha Rd, Inverell. 📞 *(02) 6722 1717.* ⏰ *10am–5pm Tue–Sun.* ⬤ *Good Fri, 25 Dec.* 🎫 ♿

Tamworth ⑪

🏃 35,000. ✈ 🚌 🚍 🚍 ℹ *cnr Murray & Peel sts (02) 6755 4300.*

TAMWORTH IS A thriving rural city, located at the centre of fertile agricultural plains. Yet despite its 150-year history, fine old buildings and claim to fame as the first Australian city with electric street lighting, it remains best known as Australia's country music capital.

Every January, thousands of country music fans and performers flock here for the ten-day Country Music Festival, which includes country music, blue grass, busking, bush ballads, harmonica

playing and the Golden Guitar Awards *(see p37)*. Reflecting the city's main interest there is the Tamworth Information Centre built in the shape of a horizontal guitar, the Country Music Gallery of Stars, where Australia's country music greats are immortalized in wax, the Roll of Renown dedicated to musicians who have made a major contribution to the industry and the Country Music Hands of Fame cornerstone.

Tamworth's other source of fame is as the equestrian centre of Australia. The Quarter Horse Association and Appaloosa Association are based here and rodeos and show-jumping events are part of its busy equestrian calendar.

Mudgee ⑫

🏃 7,500. 🚌 🚍 *Lithgow.* ℹ *84 Market St (02) 6372 1020.*

MUDGEE IS A magnificent old rural town with gardens and grand buildings, many of which are protected by the National Trust.

Situated on the banks of the Cudgegong River, the town was first settled by William Lawson, who discovered its good grazing country in 1821. The settlement was surveyed and planned in 1824 by Robert Hoddle. The design was so successful that he copied Mudgee's grid layout 14 years later for the city of Melbourne *(see pp374–5)*. Historic buildings not to be missed include the Regent Theatre on Church Street, the many churches, banks and civic buildings on Market Street, the railway station and the restored

Sheep grazing under a tree in the Mudgee region

West End Hotel that now houses the excellent Colonial Inn Museum.

Mudgee is also famous for its surrounding wineries and the Mudgee Wine Festival held each September *(see p36)*. From the surrounding countryside come local gourmet foods such as yabbies, trout, lamb, peaches and asparagus.

ENVIRONS: During the 1850s and 1860s, gold was discovered to the south of Mudgee, bringing thousands of hopeful prospectors to the region *(see pp50–51)*. The villages of Hill End, Hargraves, Windeyer and Sofala once had populations of more than 20,000 each, but became ghost towns once the boom was over. Hill End is the most famous of these and is now classed as a Living Historic Site with almost all of its buildings dating back to the 1870s. The creeks of Windeyer continued to yield alluvial gold until the 1930s. Panning for gold in the river is a popular tourist activity.

One of Australia's most famous writers, Henry Lawson, hailed from the region *(see p31)*, and Gulgong, a quaint gold rush village famous for being depicted on the original A$10 note, contains the **Henry Lawson Centre**. A collection of records, manuscripts, documents and other Lawson memorabilia is housed here.

🏛 **Henry Lawson Centre**
147 Mayne St, Gulgong. 📞 *(02) 6374 2049.* ⏰ *daily.* ⬤ *Good Fri, 25 Dec.* 🎫

Tamworth Information Centre, fronted by a huge golden guitar

Northern New South Wales Coastline

The northern New South Wales coastline is known for its mix of natural beauty, mild climate and good resorts. Australia's most easterly mainland point, Byron Bay, is an attractive, up-market resort which is enhanced by its unspoiled landscape and outstanding beaches. Elsewhere, clean and isolated beaches directly abut rainforest, with some national parks and reserves holding World Heritage status *(see pp22–3)*. Sugar cane and bananas are commonly grown in the region.

***Coffs Harbour** is one of the most popular tourist destinations in New South Wales. Surrounded by excellent beaches, there is also an attractive man-made harbour and a range of top quality tourist facilities.*

Red Cliff Beach 4

🌊 🏄 ⛑ 🚻 ⛺

Adjacent to the beautiful Yuraygir National Park, Red Cliff is one of several sandy, isolated beaches in the immediate vicinity.

Moonee Beach 5

🌊 🏄 ⛑ 🚻 ⛺

A creek meandering through bush country to the ocean offers perfect opportunities for safe swimming, picnics and camping.

Urunga 6

🌊 🏄 ⛵ ⛑ 🚻

Two rivers, the Bellingen and the Kalang, reach the ocean in this picturesque beach resort. Its safe waters make it a particularly popular holiday site for families.

Arakoon 9

🌊 🏄 ⛑

This picturesque headland is part of a state recreation area. Nearby is Trial Bay Gaol, a progressive 19th-century prison that re-opened during World War I to house prisoners of war from various countries.

Third Headland Beach 7

🌊 🏄 ⛑ 🚻 ⛺

Like its neighbour Hungry Head Beach, 5 km (3 miles) north, Third Headland is a popular surfing beach with strong waves hitting the headland cliffs.

***Grafton** is a quaint 19th-century rural town, with elegant streets and riverside walks. The town is best known for its abundance of jacaranda trees, whose striking purple blooms are celebrated in a festival each October* (see p37).

★ Crowdy Bay 12

🌊 🏄 ⛵ ⛑ 🚻

Part of a national park, Crowdy Bay's lagoons, forests and swamps are abundant with native wildlife here. Coarse-fishing is a popular activity from the sea's edge.

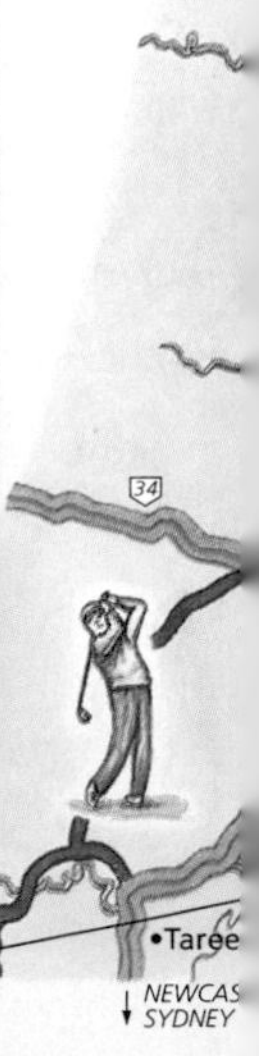

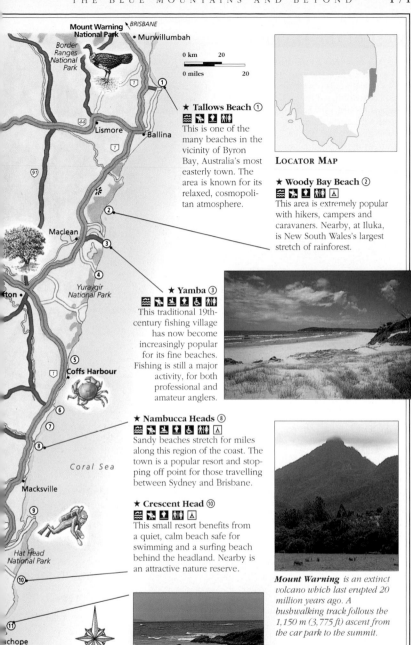

Mount Warning National Park
Brisbane
• Murwillumbah

Border Ranges National Park

0 km 20

0 miles 20

Lismore

• Ballina

Maclean

Yuraygir National Park

—ton •

Coffs Harbour

Coral Sea

Macksville

Hat Head National Park

—chope

★ Tallows Beach ①

This is one of the many beaches in the vicinity of Byron Bay, Australia's most easterly town. The area is known for its relaxed, cosmopolitan atmosphere.

★ Woody Bay Beach ②

This area is extremely popular with hikers, campers and caravaners. Nearby, at Iluka, is New South Wales's largest stretch of rainforest.

★ Yamba ③

This traditional 19th-century fishing village has now become increasingly popular for its fine beaches. Fishing is still a major activity, for both professional and amateur anglers.

★ Nambucca Heads ⑧

Sandy beaches stretch for miles along this region of the coast. The town is a popular resort and stopping off point for those travelling between Sydney and Brisbane.

★ Crescent Head ⑩

This small resort benefits from a quiet, calm beach safe for swimming and a surfing beach behind the headland. Nearby is an attractive nature reserve.

Mount Warning is an extinct volcano which last erupted 20 million years ago. A bushwalking track follows the 1,150 m (3,775 ft) ascent from the car park to the summit.

KEY

▦	Highway
▬	Major road
▭	Minor road
⌒	River
☼	Viewpoint

★ Port Macquarie ⑪

Established as a penal settlement in 1821, the port only became successful in the 1970s. Its fine climate makes it a popular resort.

West of the Divide

IN STARK CONTRAST to the lush green of the Blue
Mountains and the blue waters of the New South
Wales coastline, the western region of the state is arche-
typal of Australia's Outback. This dusty, dry landscape,
parched by the sun, is an understandably remote area,
dotted with a few mining towns and national parks.
Dubbo and Wagga Wagga are the main frontier towns,
but anything beyond is commonly referred to as "Back
o' Bourke" and ventured into by only the most determined of tourists. Even the most adventurous
should avoid the area in high summer.

LOCATOR MAP

◼ *West of the Divide*

▢ *The Blue Mountains*
   pp156–71

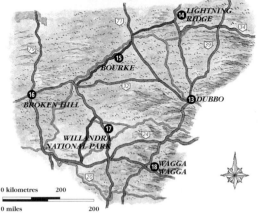

SIGHTS AT A GLANCE

Bourke **15**
Broken Hill **16**
Dubbo **13**
Lightning Ridge **14**
Wagga Wagga **18**
Willandra National Park **17**

KEY

━━ Highway

━━ Major road

〜 River

0 kilometres   200

0 miles   200

Dubbo **13**

🏛 *28,000.* ✈ 🚌 🚍 🚆
ℹ *cnr Newell Hwy & Macquarie St
(02) 6884 1422.*

DUBBO IS LOCATED at the
geographical heart of
the state and is the regional
capital of western New South
Wales. The area was first noted
for its rich agricultural potential in 1817 by explorer John
Oxley, sited as it is on the
banks of the Macquarie River.
The city has since grown into
a rural centre producing $45
million worth of food and
agricultural goods annually.

Dubbo also has a strong
colonial history and period
architecture. Among the more
interesting buildings are the
1876 Dubbo Museum, with its
ornate ceilings and cedar staircase, the 1890 Italianate courthouse and the 1884 Macquarie
Chambers, with their Tuscan
columns and terracotta tiles.

At the **Old Dubbo Gaol**,
visitors can hear the tragic
story of Jacky Underwood, an
Aborigine hung for his part in
the Breelong massacre of
1900, when eleven white
settlers were killed. Dubbo
magistrate Rolf Boldrewood
drew on the characters of the
gaol's inmates to write the
classic novel *Robbery Under
Arms (see p30).*

The most popular sight in
Dubbo is the **Western Plains
Zoo**, 5 km (3 miles) from the

Rhinoceros in Western Plains Zoo

town. The zoo's emphasis is
on breeding endangered species and visitors can see more
than 800 exotic and 1,000
native animals living freely.

🏛 **Old Dubbo Gaol**
Macquarie St. 🕐 *(02) 6882 8122.*
◯ *daily.* ● *Good Fri, Dec 25.* ✎
✘ **Western Plains Zoo**
Obley Rd. 🕐 *(02) 6882 5888.*
◯ *daily.* ✎ ♿

Lightning Ridge **14**

🏛 *1,500.* ✈ 🚌 ℹ *Morilla St
(02) 6829 1466.*

LIGHTNING RIDGE is a small
mining village and home
of the treasured black opal –
a rare dark opal shot with red,
blue and green. Gem enthusiasts from around the world
come to try their luck on the
opal fields. The town is also
famous for its hearty welcome
to visitors, unusual within
mining communities, and its
mine tours, plethora of opal
shops and hot bore spas.

Bourke ⑮

🏠 3,400. ✕ 🚌 🚐 ℹ️ 24 Anson St (02) 6872 2280.

SITUATED ON the Darling River, part of Australia's longest river system, Bourke is a colourful town that was once the centre of the world's wool industry. It still produces 55,000 bales per year.

Bourke's heyday is evident in the colonial buildings and the old weir, wharf, lock and lift-up span bridge which recall the days of the paddle-steamer trade to Victoria *(see p421)*. The town's cemetery tells something of Bourke's history: Afghan camel drivers who brought the animal to Australia from the Middle East in the 19th century are buried next to a number of bush-rangers and farm pioneers.

Broken Hill ⑯

🏠 23,500. ✕ 🚊 🚌 🚐 ℹ️ cnr Blende and Bromide sts (08) 8087 6077.

THE UNOFFICIAL centre of Outback New South Wales, Broken Hill is a mining city perched on the edge of the deserts of inland Australia. The town was established in 1883, when vast deposits of zinc, lead and silver were discovered in a 7-km (4-mile) long "Line of Lode" by the then-fledgling company, Broken Hill Pty Ltd. Broken Hill has since grown into a major town and BHP has become Australia's biggest corporation.

Broken Hill's now declining mining industry is still evident; slag heaps are piled up, there

MUNGO WORLD HERITAGE AREA

Lake Mungo is an area of great archaeological significance. For 40,000 years, it was a 15-m (50-ft) deep lake, around which Aborigines lived. The lake then dried up, leaving its eastern rim as a wind-blown sand ridge known as the Walls of China. Its age was determined in the 1960s when winds uncovered an Aboriginal skeleton known as Mungo Man. Lake Mungo has been protected as part of the Willandra Lakes World Heritage Area since 1981 *(see pp22–3)*.

Walls of China sand ridges

are more pubs per head than any other city in the state and streets are named after metals.

Surprisingly, Broken Hill also has more than 20 art galleries featuring desert artists. The city is also the base of the Royal Flying Doctor Service *(see p249)* and School of the Air.

To the northwest of Broken Hill is **Silverton**, once a thriving silver mining community and now a ghost town. It is popular as a location for films such as *Mad Max* and *Priscilla, Queen of the Desert*.

Willandra National Park ⑰

ℹ️ Hilston Mossgiel Rd (02) 6967 8159. ⬜ daily. ⚫ in wet weather. 🏞️ ♿ to homestead.

LESS THAN 20,000 years ago, Willandra Creek was a major river system and tributary of the Lachlan River, providing wetlands of at least 1,000 sq km (400 sq miles).

Now the Willandra Lakes are dry and Willandra Creek is little more than a small stream.

A glimpse of the area's past is found in Willandra National Park. Wetlands emerge each year after the spring rain, providing sanctuary for a range of waterbirds and emus.

Wagga Wagga ⑱

🏠 58,000. ✕ 🚊 🚌 ℹ️ Tarcutta St (02) 6926 9621.

NAMED BY ITS original inhabitants, the Widadjuri people, as "a place of many crows", Wagga Wagga has grown into a large, modern city serving the surrounding farming community. It has won many accolades for its wines and the abundance of gardens has earned it the title of "Garden City of the South".

The large Botanic Gardens and the Wagga Historical Museum are well worth a visit. The Widadjuri track is a popular walk along the Murrumbidgee River banks.

ENVIRONS: The gentle town of **Gundagai**, nestling beneath Mount Parnassus on the banks of the Murrumbidgee River, has been immortalized in the popular bush ballad "Along the Road to Gundagai". More tragic is Gundagai's place in history as the site of Australia's greatest natural disaster when catastrophic floods swept away the original town in 1852, drowning 83 inhabitants.

Historic pub in the ghost town of Silverton, near Broken Hill

THE SOUTH COAST AND SNOWY MOUNTAINS

A LTHOUGH THE BUSIEST HIGHWAY IN AUSTRALIA *runs through southern New South Wales, the area remains one of the most beautiful in the country. Its landscape includes the Snowy Mountains, the surf beaches of the far south, the historic Southern Highland villages and the farming towns of the Murray and Murrumbidgee plains.*

Ever since European settlers crossed the Blue Mountains in 1812 *(see p164)*, the southern plains of New South Wales around Goulburn, Yass and Albury have been prime agricultural land. Yet the wilderness of the Snowy Mountains to the east and the steep escarpment which runs the length of the beautiful South and Sapphire coasts, from Wollongong to the Victoria border, has never been completely tamed. Today, the splendour of southern New South Wales is protected by a number of large national parks.

The great Snowy Mountains offer alpine scenery at its best. In summer the wild flower-scattered meadows, deep gorges and cascading mountain creeks seem to stretch endlessly into the distance; in winter the jagged snow-capped peaks and twisted snow gums turn this summer walking paradise into a playground for keen downhill and cross-country skiers.

The area also has a long and colourful cultural heritage: Aboriginal tribes, gold diggers and mountain cattlemen have all left their mark here. During the 1950s and 1960s, the region became the birthplace of multicultural Australia, as thousands of European immigrants came to work on the Snowy Mountains Scheme, an engineering feat which diverted the flow of several rivers to provide hydroelectricity and irrigation for southeastern Australia.

But southern New South Wales is more than just landscapes; civilization is never far away. There are excellent restaurants and hotels along the coast, Wollongong is an industrial city and the gracious towns of the Southern Highlands offer historic attractions.

Snowy Mountains landscape in autumn

◁ **Red rocks and blue waters of the Sapphire Coast at Merimbula Wharf**

Exploring the South Coast and Snowy Mountains

THE GREAT DIVIDING RANGE, which runs from the Blue Mountains *(see pp162–5)* down to the Snowy Mountains and into Victoria, divides the region into three areas. There is the coastal strip, a zone of beautiful beaches, which starts at Wollongong and runs south for 500 km (310 miles) to Eden, hemmed in by the rising mountain range to its west. On the range lie the Southern Highlands, Mount Kosciuszko and the Snowy Mountains. West of the range are the farming plains of the Murrumbidgee River.

Waterfall in the beautiful Morton-Budawang National Park

Golden inlet at Ben Boyd National Park, on the southern tip of New South Wales

GETTING AROUND

A car is essential to do full justice to this region, with the Hume Hwy providing excellent access to the Southern Highlands and the western farming towns. Wollongong and the southern beaches are linked from Sydney to the Victoria border by the coastal Princes Hwy. From Canberra, the Monaro Hwy is the best route to the Snowy Mountains. From Bega to the east or Gundagai and Tumut in the west, take the Snowy Mountains Hwy. A train service between Sydney and Canberra stops at the Southern Highlands and Hume Hwy towns, while the coastal resorts are serviced by buses from both Sydney and Melbourne.

SEE ALSO

Dubb

CANBERRA

QUEANBEYAN

KOSCIUSZKO NATIONAL PARK

Tantangara Reservoir

KIANDRA

Lake Eucumbene

Lake Jindabyne

6 COOMA AND THE SNOWY MOUNTAINS

JINDABYNE

THREDBO VILLAGE

Murrumbidgee River

Snowy River

Bombala River

BOMBALA

0 kilometres   25

0 miles   25

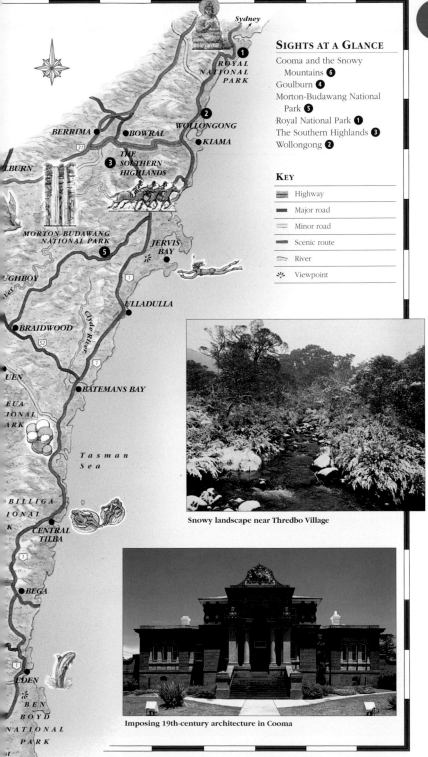

Sydney

1
ROYAL
NATIONAL
PARK

2
WOLLONGONG

BERRIMA ● ● BOWRAL ● KIAMA

3
THE
SOUTHERN
HIGHLANDS

LBURN

MORTON-BUDAWANG
NATIONAL PARK

5

JERVIS
BAY

UGHBOY
er

● BRAIDWOOD
52

UEN

EUA
IONAL
ARK

● ULLADULLA

Clyde River

● BATEMANS BAY

Tasman
Sea

BILLIGA-
IONAL
K

● CENTRAL
TILBA

● BEGA

EDEN

BEN
BOYD
NATIONAL
PARK

SIGHTS AT A GLANCE

Cooma and the Snowy
  Mountains **6**
Goulburn **4**
Morton-Budawang National
  Park **5**
Royal National Park **1**
The Southern Highlands **3**
Wollongong **2**

KEY

▬	Highway
▬	Major road
▬	Minor road
▬	Scenic route
〜	River
※	Viewpoint

Snowy landscape near Thredbo Village

Imposing 19th-century architecture in Cooma

Royal National Park ❶

🚇 *Loftus, then tram to Audley (Sun only).* 🚇 *Sutherland.* 🚌 *Sutherland.* ⛴ *Bundeena.* ℹ️ *Farnell Ave, Audley (02) 9542 0648.* 🌐

DESIGNATED a national park in 1879, the "Royal" is the oldest national park in Australia and the oldest in the world after Yellowstone in the USA. It covers 16,000 ha (37,000 acres) of spectacular landscape.

To the east, waves from the Pacific Ocean have undercut the sandstone and produced coastal cliffs, interspersed with creeks, waterfalls, lagoons and beaches. Sea eagles and terns nest in caves at the Curracurrang Rocks, where there is also a quiet swimming hole. Heath vegetation on the plateau merges with woodlands on the upper slopes and rainforest in the gorges. The park is ideal for bushwalking, swimming and bird-watching.

Wollongong ❷

🏛 *184,000.* 🚇 🚌 🚌
ℹ️ *93 Crown St (02) 4227 5545.*

THE THIRD LARGEST city in the state, Wollongong is situated on a coastline of beautiful surf beaches. Mount Kembla and Mount Keira provide a backdrop to the city.

Originally a coal and steel industrial city – the BHP steel mill at Port Kembla is still a major employer – Wollongong is fast building a reputation as a leisure centre. Northbeach is the most famous of its 17 surf beaches. Flagstaff Point, with its lighthouse, boat harbour, beach views and seafood restaurants, is popular with visitors. The city also boasts Australia's largest regional art gallery, with an outstanding collection of 20th-century paintings and sculptures. The Nan Tien Temple, the largest Buddhist temple in the southern hemisphere, was built for the large Chinese community of greater Sydney.

Figure in Nan Tien Temple

The Southern Highlands ❸

🚇 *Bowral, Moss Vale, Mittagong, Bundanoon.* ℹ️ *62–70 Main St, Mittagong (02) 4871 2888.*

QUAINT VILLAGES, country guesthouses, pioneering homesteads and beautiful gardens are scattered across the lush landscape of the Southern Highlands. The region has been a summer retreat for wealthy Sydneysiders for almost 100 years. Villages such as Bowral, Moss Vale, Berrima and Bundanoon are also ideal places in the winter for pottering around antiques shops, dining on hearty soups, sitting by open fires and taking bush walks and country drives.

The region's gardens are renowned for their blaze of colours in the spring and autumn. The Corbett Gardens at Bowral are a showpiece during its October Tulip Festival (*see p36*).

Bowral is also home to the **Bradman Museum**, where a fascinating collection of photos and cricketing memorabilia commemorates the town's famous son, cricketer Sir Donald Bradman. Bradman is said to have first showed signs of greatness as a child, hitting a golf ball against a water tank stand with a wicket-wide strip of wood.

Visiting the village of Berrima is like stepping back in time. The settlement, now home to an abundance of antiques and craft shops, is one of the most unspoilt examples of a small Australian town of the 1830s.

Popular walks in the area include Mount Gibraltar, Carrington Falls, the magnificent Fitzroy Falls at the northern tip of Morton-Budawang National Park and the majestic Kangaroo Valley. The five Wombeyan Caves, west of the

Fishing boats moored along Wollongong Harbour

Impressive peak of Pigeon House in Morton-Budawang National Park

town of Mittagong, form an imposing underground limestone cathedral with delicate formations, pillars and spires.

🏛 Bradman Museum
St Jude St, Bowral. **[** (02) 4862 1247. **◯** 10am–5pm daily. ⊘ &

Sandstone house in Goulburn

Goulburn ❹

🏘 22,000. 🚆 🚍 🚌 **ℹ** 201 Sloane St (02) 4823 4492.

GOULBURN is at the heart of the Southern Tablelands, with its rich pastoral heritage. Proclaimed in 1863, the town's 19th-century buildings, such as the courthouse, post office and railway station, are testament to the continuing prosperity of the district.

The Big Merino, a giant, hollow concrete sheep, marks Goulburn as the "fine wool capital of the world".

ENVIRONS: The town of **Yass** is known for its fine wool and cool-climate wines. Worth a visit is the historic Cooma Cottage, now owned by the National Trust. It was once the home of Australian explorer Hamilton Hume, between 1839 and 1873.

Morton-Budawang National Park ❺

🚆 Bundanoon. 🚌 Fitzroy Falls. **ℹ** Fitzroy Falls (02) 4887 7270.

MORTON-BUDAWANG National Park stretches for 200 km (125 miles) from Batemans Bay to Nowra. Fitzroy Falls are at the northern end of the park. At Bundanoon, magnificent sandstone country can be explored along walking tracks.

To the south, views of the coastline and Budawang wilderness can be found at Little Forest Plateau and the top of Pigeon House Mountain.

Cooma and the Snowy Mountains ❻

🏘 8,000. ✈ 🚆 🚌 **ℹ** 119 Sharp St (02) 6450 1742.

COLOURFUL COOMA has a rich history as a cattle, engineering and ski town. During the construction of the Snowy Mountains Scheme (see p175),

Cooma was also the weekend base for the thousands of immigrants working up in the mountains during the week. Stories surviving from this era include tales of frontier-like shootouts in the main street, interracial romances and bush mountain feats. However, Cooma is now a sleepy rural town that acts as the gateway to the Snowy Mountains and the southern ski slopes.

The modern resort town of Jindabyne on Lake Jindabyne is home to the Kosciuszko National Park information centre, a myriad of ski shops and lodges, and plenty of nightlife. The two major ski resorts are Thredbo Village along the Alpine Way and the twin resort of Perisher Blue, linked by the ski tube train to Lake Crackenback and the Blue Cow ski fields. Take the chairlift from Thredbo in summer to walk to the summit of Australia's highest mountain, Mount Kosciuszko (see p152), or simply to stroll among the wildflowers and snow gums in the alpine meadows. Another recommended walk is to Blue Lake and the Cascades from Dead Horse Gap. Lake Eucumbene and the Thredbo and Eucumbene rivers offer excellent fly-fishing.

ENVIRONS: The ghost settlement of **Kiandra** has a marked historic walking trail detailing the gold rush era in the town (see pp50–51). Nearby is the gentle ski resort of Mount Selwyn and the spectacular Yarrangobilly Caves with their underground walks set among limestone stalactites and stalagmites, and hot thermal pools.

Resort town of Jindabyne in the Snowy Mountains

The South Coast

F ROM NOWRA to the border with Victoria, the south coast of New South Wales is a magical mix of white sand beaches, rocky coves and coastal bush covered with spotted gums and wattles, and alive with a variety of birds. The coastline is rich in Aboriginal sites, fishing villages and unspoilt beach settlements. The 400 km (250 miles) of coast are divided into three distinct areas – the Shoalhaven Coast to the north, the Eurobodalla ("Land of Many Waters") Coast in the centre and the Sapphire Coast in the far south.

Whale Museum harpoon gun

Ulladulla *is a small fishing village flanked by the dovecote-shaped peak of Pigeon House Mountain in the Morton-Budawang National Park. A bushwalk offers breathtaking coastal views.*

Central Tilba *is a delightful historic farming village, backed by the 800-m (2,600-ft) Mount Dromedary. The town itself is famous for its weatherboard cottages and shops, now housing some of the region's finest cafés and arts and crafts shops, and its cheese and wine. The cheese factory and wineries are all open to visitors.*

★ **Horseshoe Bay Beach, Bermagui** ⑦
Writer Zane Grey brought fame to this tiny game fishing town with his tales of marlin fishing.

★ **Merimbula Beach** ⑩
The tourist centre of the Sapphire Coast is famous for its oysters, deep-sea fishing and surrounding white sandy beach.

★ **Eden** ⑪
Set on the deep Twofold Bay, this was once a whaling station. It is now the centre of whale-watching on the south coast during spring. It is also a major tuna fishing town and centre for the local timber industry.

Nowra *is the town centre of the beautiful Shoalhaven Coast, near the mouth of the Shoalhaven River. The name means "black cockatoo" in the local Aboriginal language. Nearby are the resorts of Culburra and Shoalhaven Heads, adjacent to Seven Mile Beach National Park.*

0 kilometres   25

0 miles   25

Moruya

Bodal

Cent
Til

Bega

ORBOST

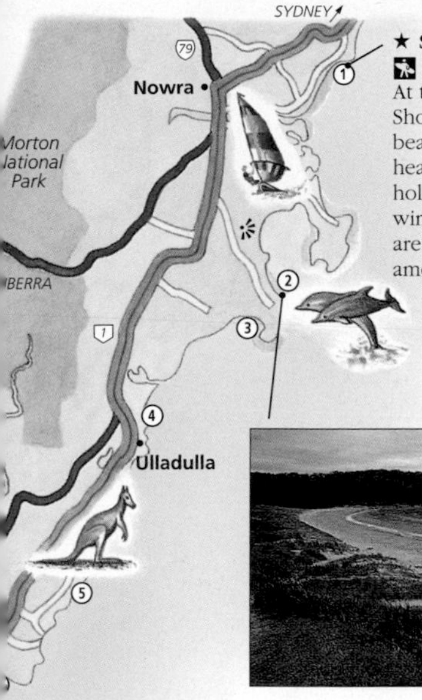

★ Shoalhaven Heads 1

🏄 🌊 ⛱ 🚻 ⛺

At the mouth of the Shoalhaven River, this beach resort is at the heart of a popular holiday area. Sailing and windsurfing on the river are popular activities among the locals.

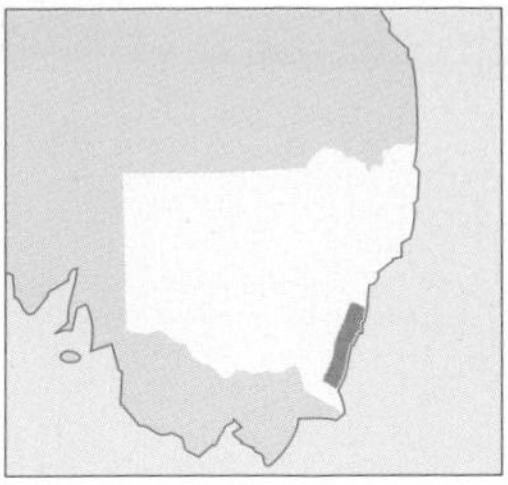

Locator Map

★ Jervis Bay 2

🌊 ⛱ 🚻 ⛺

This is one of the most beautiful natural harbours in Australia, famous for its naval bases, national park, tiny settlements of Husskinson and Vincentia, and some of the whitest beaches and crystal clear waters in the world.

Wreck Bay 3

🌊 ⛱

This area, within Jervis Bay National Park, abounds with Aboriginal history. The cultural centre offers walkabout tours of local bushlife and archaeology. Nearby Cave Beach is one of the region's most popular for its secluded location.

Lake Conjola 4

🌊 🚻 ⛺

This lake, 10 km (6 miles) north of Ulladulla, is one of many lakes in the region popular with canoeists. Camp sites are also available.

Batemans Bay 6

🏄 🌊 ⛱ 🚻 ⛺

The Clyde River enters the sea here, marking the start of the Eurobodalla coastline with its rivers, lakes and chain of heavenly quiet beaches popular with Canberrans.

Mimosa Rocks 8

⛱ ⛺

This coastal park, just off the south coast road, offers exceptional bushwalking opportunities and idyllic beaches. Secluded camp sites, with minimum facilities, are popular with families and anglers.

Tathra Beach 9

🏄 🌊 ⛱ 🚻 ⛺

This tiny fishing village and holiday haven includes a maritime museum, housed in a 150-year-old wharf building.

Ben Boyd National Park 12

🌊 ⛱ ⛺

Camping, bushwalks and fine beaches are all features of this park. Temperate rainforests begin to take over the landscape in the surrounding region. The ascent to Mount Imlay offers panoramic views of the coast.

★ Pebbly Beach 5

🏄 🌊 ⛱

Set within Murramarang National Park, this beach is famous for its tame kangaroos which sometimes venture into the water at dusk and dawn, and have been seen to "body surf".

Key

- Highway
- Major road
- Minor road
- River
- Viewpoint

CANBERRA AND AUSTRALIAN CAPITAL TERRITORY

*L*OCATED WITHIN NEW SOUTH WALES, *some 300 km (185 miles) southwest of Sydney, Canberra is Australia's capital and its political heartland. The city was planned in 1908 as the new seat of federal parliament to end rivalry between Sydney and Melbourne. The surrounding Australian Capital Territory features bush and mountain terrain.*

Canberra was once little more than a sheep station on the edge of the Molonglo River. American architect Walter Burley Griffin won an international competition to design the city. He envisaged a spacious, low-level, modern city, with its major buildings centred on the focal point of Lake Burley Griffin. Canberra (its name is based on an Aboriginal word meaning "meeting place") is a city of contradictions. It consists of more than just politics, diplomacy and monuments. Lacking the traffic and skyscrapers of Australia's other main cities, it has a serenity and country charm suited to strolling around the lake, bush driving and picnicking.

Canberra is the national capital and the centre of political and administrative power in Australia, yet it is also a rural city, ringed by gum trees, with the occasional kangaroo seen hopping down its suburban streets. The city holds the majority of the nation's political, literary and artistic treasures, and contains important national institutions such as the High Court of Australia, the Australian National University and the Australian War Memorial, but it has a population of fewer than 500,000. These contradictions are the essence of the city's attraction. Canberra's hidden delights include Manuka's elegant cafés *(see pp503–5)*, excellent local wines and sophisticated restaurants. Special events include the annual spring flower festival, Floriade, which turns the north shore of the lake into a blaze of colour, and the spectacular hot-air ballooning festival in April.

Outside the city lie the region's natural attractions. Tidbinbilla Nature Reserve is home to wild kangaroos, wallabies, emus, koalas and platypuses. The Murrumbidgee River is excellent for canoeing, and the wild Namadgi National Park has bush camping, Aboriginal art sites, alpine snow gums and mountain creeks for trout fishing.

Hot-air ballooning festival over Lake Burley Griffin, near the National Library of Australia

◁ **The imposing flag-topped Parliament House in Canberra**

Exploring Canberra and ACT

Central Canberra lies around Lake Burley Griffin, framed by the city's four hills – Black Mountain and Mount Ainslie to the north and Capital Hill and Red Hill to the south. Most of Canberra's main sights are accessible from the lake. Scattered throughout the northern suburbs are other places of interest such as the Australian Institute of Sport. To the south lies the wilderness and wildlife of Namadgi National Park.

View of Canberra from Mount Ainslie

Sights at a Glance

Historic Streets and Buildings
Australian War Memorial
  pp192–3 **8**
Telstra Tower **10**
Civic Square **7**
Cockington Green **13**
Government House **3**
Mount Stromlo Observatory **15**
Royal Australian Mint **2**
Yarralumla **5**

Parks and Gardens
Australian National Botanic
  Gardens **9**
Namadgi National Park p199 **19**
Red Hill **1**

Modern Architecture
Parliament House pp190–91 **4**

Museums and Galleries
Australian Institute of Sport **12**
Canberra Space Centre **17**
National Gallery pp194–5 **6**
National Museum of Australia **14**

Aquariums and Nature Reserves
National Aquarium and
  Wildlife Park **11**
Tidbinbilla Nature Reserve **18**

Rivers
Murrumbidgee River **16**

0 kilometres   1

0 miles   1

See Also

GETTING AROUND

Many of the sights around Lake Burley Griffin are within walking distance of each other. The Canberra Explorer red bus also travels between attractions. The city centre's layout can make driving difficult, but to explore the bush suburbs a car is essential as there is no suburban train system. Most of the sights in ACT are within half an hour's drive of the city.

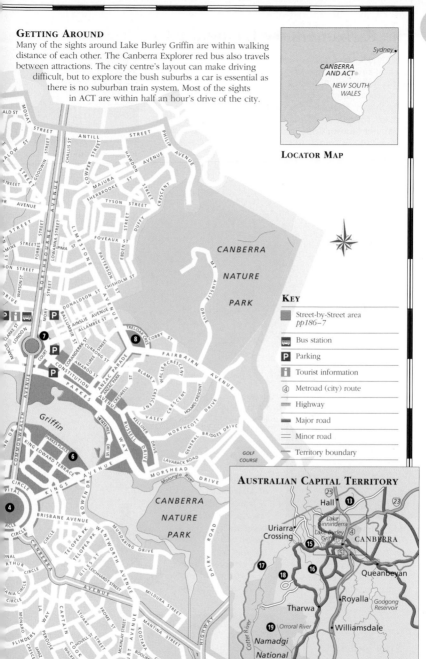

LOCATOR MAP

KEY

	Street-by-Street area *pp186–7*
	Bus station
P	Parking
i	Tourist information
4	Metroad (city) route
	Highway
	Major road
	Minor road
	Territory boundary

AUSTRALIAN CAPITAL TERRITORY

0 kilometres 20

0 miles 20

The Parliamentary Triangle

CANBERRA'S MAJOR MONUMENTS, national buildings and key attractions are all situated around Lake Burley Griffin within the Parliamentary Triangle. Designed to be the focal point of Canberra's national activities by the architect Walter Burley Griffin *(see p189)*, the Parliamentary Triangle has Capital Hill at its apex, topped by Parliament House. Commonwealth Avenue and Kings Avenue fan out from Capital Hill, cross the lake and end at Parkes Way. Running at a right angle from the base of the triangle is Anzac Parade, which leads to the Australian War Memorial *(see pp192–3)* and completes the basic symmetry of Burley Griffin's plan.

★ **Parliament House**
Completed in 1988, this is one of the world's most impressive parliamentary buildings ❹

Capital Hill

Old Parliament House
This was the first parliamentary building in the new capital. Built in 1927, it remained as the centre of Australian politics until 1988. It is now open to the public.

Questacon is an action-packed science and technology centre with hundreds of hands-on displays.

Kings Avenue

★ **National Gallery of Australia**
This impressive art gallery contains an excellent collection of Australian colonial and Aboriginal art, as well as many significant European works ❻

The High Court of Australia is the highest court of justice in the country.

STAR SIGHTS

★ **Australian War Memorial**

★ **National Gallery of Australia**

★ **Parliament House**

Blundell's Cottage
Built in 1858, this is a fine example of an early colonial cottage typical of remote farming life of the time.

Lake Burley Griffin
This artificial lake was created by damming the Molonglo River in 1963. The water feature was central to Walter Burley Griffin's elegant design for Canberra.

CANBERRA

LOCATOR MAP

The National Library is the country's largest and includes Captain Cook's original journals.

Commonwealth Avenue

The Captain Cook Memorial Jet in the middle of Lake Burley Griffin spurts water to a height of 137 m (450 ft).

Commonwealth Park is ablaze with colour during September and October when it is home to the city's annual spring flower festival, Floriade *(see p36)*.

Parkes Way

St John the Baptist Church and Schoolhouse were built in 1844 and are two of Canberra's oldest buildings.

★ **Australian War Memorial**
The nation's tribute to its 102,000 war dead is also a remarkable museum ❽

Anzac Parade
Nine memorials line the boulevard, commemorating Australia's war efforts in the 20th century.

The Australian-American Memorial was given to Australia by the United States as a thank you for the Pacific alliance during World War II *(see pp53–4)*.

| 0 metres | | 500 |
| 0 yards | | 500 |

Exploring the Parliamentary Triangle

CANBERRA, with its still lake and impressive national monuments and institutions, can at first glance appear cold and somewhat forbidding to visitors. But venture inside the various buildings dotted around Lake Burley Griffin within the Parliamentary Triangle, and a treasure trove of architecture, art, history and politics will be revealed. The lake itself, surrounded by gardens, cycle paths and outdoor sculptures and memorials, is a picturesque location for relaxing picnics and leisurely strolls. Exploring the entire Parliamentary Triangle can take one or two days. It is, however, more easily tackled by dividing it into two parts, taking in first the north and then the south of the lake.

Old Parliament House
King George Terrace, Parkes. (02) 6270 8222. daily. 25 Dec.

Built in 1927 as the first parliamentary building in the new national capital, Old Parliament House was the centre of Australian politics for more than 60 years. It was replaced by the new Parliament House in 1988 (see pp190–91).

This building has witnessed many historic moments: Australia's declaration of war in 1939; news of the bombing of Australia's northern shores by the Japanese in 1942; the disappearance and presumed drowning of Prime Minister Harold Holt in 1967 and the dismissal of the Whitlam government by Sir John Kerr in 1975 (see pp54–5).

Kings Hall, the old House of Representatives and Senate chambers can all be explored. Visitors can also examine the hidden peephole with its precision lens set in the wall of

the prime minister's office, discovered during renovations in 1990. An excellent sound and light show, "Order, Order", relives the building's greatest moments.

The National Portrait Gallery is also located here, as are the rose gardens.

Blundell's Cottage

Blundell's Cottage
Wendouree Drive, Parkes. (02) 6273 2667. 11am–4pm daily. 25 Dec.

This small sandstone farmhouse was built in 1858 by the Campbell family, owners of a large farming property at

Duntroon Station, for their head ploughman. It was later occupied by bullock driver George Blundell, his wife, Flora, and their eight children.

This excellent example of a colonial cottage also conveys all the remoteness of early farming life. Blundell's Cottage once looked out over sheep paddocks, but these were flooded by Lake Burley Griffin (see pp186–7).

National Capital Exhibition
Commonwealth Park. (02) 6257 1068. daily. 25 Dec.

The rotunda housing the National Capital Exhibition, on the north side of Lake Burley Griffin at Regatta Point, is recommended as a starting point for any tour of Canberra. Inside are models, videos and old photographs showing the history and growth of Canberra as the federal capital of Australia. These provide an excellent orientation of the city's major features before any further tour is undertaken.

From the windows of the rotunda is a clear view of Lake Burley Griffin, the Parliamentary Triangle and the Captain Cook Memorial Jet and Globe. The jet fountain and bronze, copper and enamel globe on the edge of the lake were added to the city's special features in 1970, as a bicentennial commemoration of the claiming of the east coast of Australia by

Neo-Classical façade of Old Parliament House and its impressive forecourt

British navy officer Captain James Cook in 1770 *(see p46)*. The elegant fountain lifts a column of water 147 m (480 ft) out of the lake from 10am until noon and from 2pm until 4pm daily, provided the weather is not too windy.

National Library of Australia

Parkes Place, Parkes. *(02) 6262 1111.* 9am–5pm Mon–Sat, 1:30–5pm Sun. Good Fri, 25 Dec.

The five-storey National Library of Australia, considered to be an icon of 1960s architecture, is the repository of Australia's literary and documentary heritage. Containing more than 5 million books, as well as copies of every newspaper and magazine published in Australia, thousands of cine-films, tapes, manuscripts, prints, maps and old photographs, it is the nation's largest library and leading research and reference centre. There are also historic items on display such as Captain Cook's original journal from his *Endeavour* voyages. Selected old cine-films from the library's archives are regularly shown.

Leonard French stained glass

The building, designed by Sydney architect Walter Bunning and completed in 1972, includes some notable works of art. Foremost are the modern stained-glass windows by Australian architect and artist Leonard French, made of Belgian chunk glass and depicting the planets. There are also the Australian life tapestries by French artist Mathieu Mategot.

Questacon – The National Science and Technology Centre

Cnr King Edward Terrace & Parkes Place, Parkes. *(02) 6270 2800.* daily. 25 Dec.

With 200 hands-on exhibits in six different galleries arranged around the 27-m (90-ft) high cylindrical centre of the building, science need never be dull again. A must for anyone visiting Canberra, Questacon clearly demonstrates that

science can be fascinating, intriguing, fun and an everyday part of life.

Visitors can freeze their shadow to a wall, play a harp with no strings, experience an earthquake and feel bolts of lightning. You can also enjoy giant slides and a roller coaster simulator, and there are also regular science demonstrations and special lectures during the week.

High Court of Australia

Parkes Place, Parkes. *(02) 6270 6811.* 9:45am–4:30pm Mon–Fri. Sat–Sun, public hols.

British and Australian legal traditions are embodied in this imposing lakeside structure, opened in 1980 by Queen Elizabeth II. The High Court is centred on a glass public hall, designed to instil respect for the justice system. Two six-panel murals by artist Jan Sensberg look at the Australian constitution, the role of the Federation and the significance of the High Court. There are also three courtrooms, and rooms for the Chief Justice and six High Court judges. Sittings are open to the public.

On one side of the steps at the entrance is a sculpture of a waterfall constructed out of speckled granite. This feature

is intended to convey how the decisions of this legal institution trickle down to all Australian citizens.

Jan Sensberg mural in the High Court

St John the Baptist Church and Schoolhouse Museum

Constitution Ave, Reid. *(02) 6249 6839.* 10am–noon Wed, 2–4pm Sat, Sun. Good Fri, 25 Dec.

Built in 1844 of local bluestone and sandstone, the Anglican church of St John the Baptist and its adjoining schoolhouse are Canberra's oldest surviving buildings. They served the pioneer farming families of the region. Memorials on the walls of the church commemorate many early settlers, including statesmen, scientists and scholars.

Within the schoolhouse is a museum containing various 19th-century memorabilia.

WALTER BURLEY GRIFFIN

In 1911, the Australian government, then located in Melbourne, decided on Canberra as the best site for a new national capital. An international competition for a city plan was launched, and the first prize was awarded to a 35-year-old American landscape architect, Walter Burley Griffin. Influenced by the design of Versailles, his plan was for a garden city, with lakes, avenues and terraces rising to the focal point of Parliament House atop Capital Hill. On 12 March 1913, a

Walter Burley Griffin

foundation stone was laid by Prime Minister Andrew Fisher, but bureaucratic arguments and then World War I intervened. By 1921, little of Canberra had begun to be constructed, and Burley Griffin was dismissed from his design post. He stayed in Australia until 1935, when, reduced to municipal designs, he left for India. He died there in 1937, although his original vision lives on in the ever-expanding city of Canberra.

Red Hill ❶

Via Mugga Way, Red Hill.

ONE OF THE HIGHLIGHTS of a visit to Canberra is a drive to the top of Red Hill, which offers excellent views over Lake Burley Griffin,

Panoramic view of Canberra from Red Hill

Parliament House, Manuka and the embassy suburb of Yarralumla *(see p192)*. Behind Red Hill stretch the southern suburbs of Canberra, with the beautiful green of the Brindabella Ranges to the west.

An alternative view of Canberra, offering a better understanding of Walter Burley Griffin's carefully planned city design, can be seen from the top of Mount Ainslie, on the north side of the lake behind the Australian War Memorial *(see pp192–3)*.

Royal Australian Mint ❷

Denison St, Deakin. 📞 *(02) 6202 6819.* 🚌 *30, 31.* ⏱ *9am–4pm Mon–Fri; 10am–4pm Sat–Sun, public hols.* ⏹ *Good Fri, 25 Dec.* ♿ 📷

THE ROYAL AUSTRALIAN MINT produces 600 million coins per year – 2 million coins per day. It has made more than 8 billion decimal coins since it opened in 1965. Visitors can watch coins being made out of silver, gold and alloy blanks, see designers at work and visit the on-site museum to learn about the history of coinage in Australia. They can also mint their own A$1 coin.

Parliament House ❹

PARLIAMENT HOUSE is the centre of government and democracy in Australia. Opened in 1988, the A$1.1 billion building on Capital Hill is the fourth home of the national parliament since 1901, when Australia first became a federation *(see p52)*. The architecture of the building, with the open planning of its 4,700 rooms, reflects Australia's commitment to democratic government.

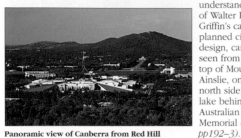

The steel flagpole reaches a height of 81 m (256 ft) and weighs 220 tonnes.

Members' Hall

House of Representatives Chamber
This chamber accommodates the 148 elected members of the House of Representatives.

★ **The Great Hall**
This hall is used for state functions. The 20-m (65-ft) tapestry is based on an Arthur Boyd painting.

The coin shop sells many Australian commemorative coins and medals. These include the silver and gold "bird series" collectors' coins of A\$5 and A\$10 (not part of everyday currency), which depict native Australian birds.

Government House ❸

Dunrossil Drive, Yarralumla. ☎ (02) 6283 3533. ☐ various dates – phone ahead to check. 📷 ✓

GOVERNMENT HOUSE has been the official residence of the Governor General, the representative of the monarch in Australia, since 1927. The

Elegant façade and front grounds of Government House

house was once part of a large sheep station called Yarralumla, which was settled in 1828, and is now where heads of state and the Royal Family stay when visiting Australia.

The house is closed to the public, except on special open days; however, a lookout point on Lady Denman Drive offers good views of the residence and the large gardens.

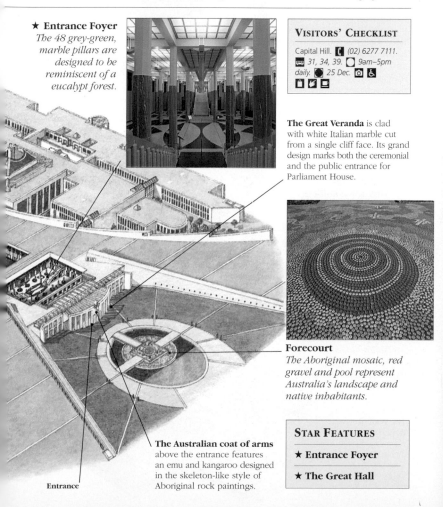

★ **Entrance Foyer**
The 48 grey-green, marble pillars are designed to be reminiscent of a eucalypt forest.

VISITORS' CHECKLIST

Capital Hill. ☎ (02) 6277 7111.
🚌 31, 34, 39. ☐ 9am–5pm daily. ● 25 Dec. 📷 ♿
🚻 ✓ ■

The Great Veranda is clad with white Italian marble cut from a single cliff face. Its grand design marks both the ceremonial and the public entrance for Parliament House.

Forecourt
The Aboriginal mosaic, red gravel and pool represent Australia's landscape and native inhabitants.

Entrance

The Australian coat of arms above the entrance features an emu and kangaroo designed in the skeleton-like style of Aboriginal rock paintings.

STAR FEATURES

★ **Entrance Foyer**

★ **The Great Hall**

Yarralumla [5]

Yarralumla. ☎ *(02) 6205 0044.* 🚌 *901, 31.* *for embassy open days.* ♿ *variable.*

THE SUBURB OF Yarralumla, on the edge of Capital Hill, is home to more than 80 of Australia's foreign embassies and diplomatic residences. A drive through the tree-lined streets gives a fascinating view of the architecture and cultures of each country represented, as embodied in their embassies and grand ambassadorial residences.

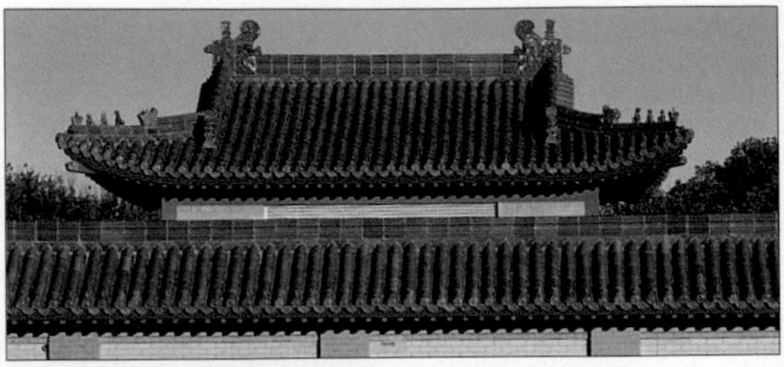

The traditional style of the Chinese Embassy in Yarralumla

Distinctive buildings include the vast Chinese Embassy at No. 15 Coronation Drive, with its red columns, dragon statues and pagoda-shaped roofs. On Moonah Place, the Indian Embassy has pools, a shallow moat and a white temple building in the Mogul architectural style, with a gold spire on

Australian War Memorial [8]

THE AUSTRALIAN WAR MEMORIAL was built to commemorate all Australians who have died while serving their country. The Roll of Honour and the symbolic Tomb of the Unknown Australian Soldier serve as a reminder of the horror and sadness of war. Other galleries in the memorial document the history of all the wars in which Australia has participated.

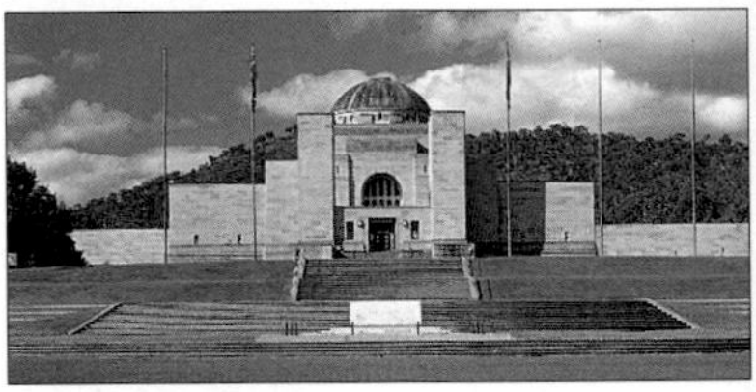

Façade of the Australian War Memorial

STAR FEATURES

★ **Roll of Honour**

★ **Tomb of the Unknown Soldier**

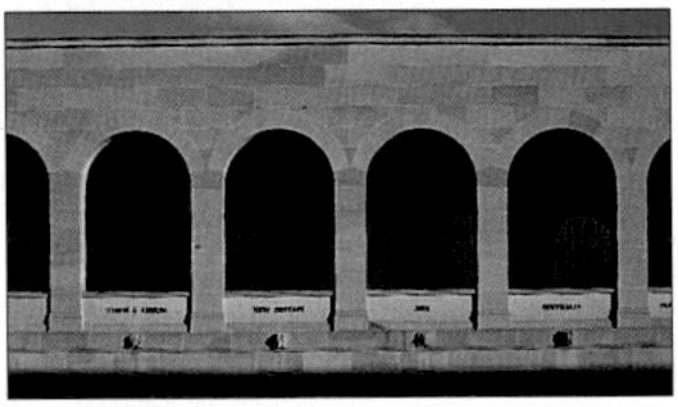

★ Roll of Honour
Names of all the 102,600 Australians killed in action are written on bronze panels in the cloisters.

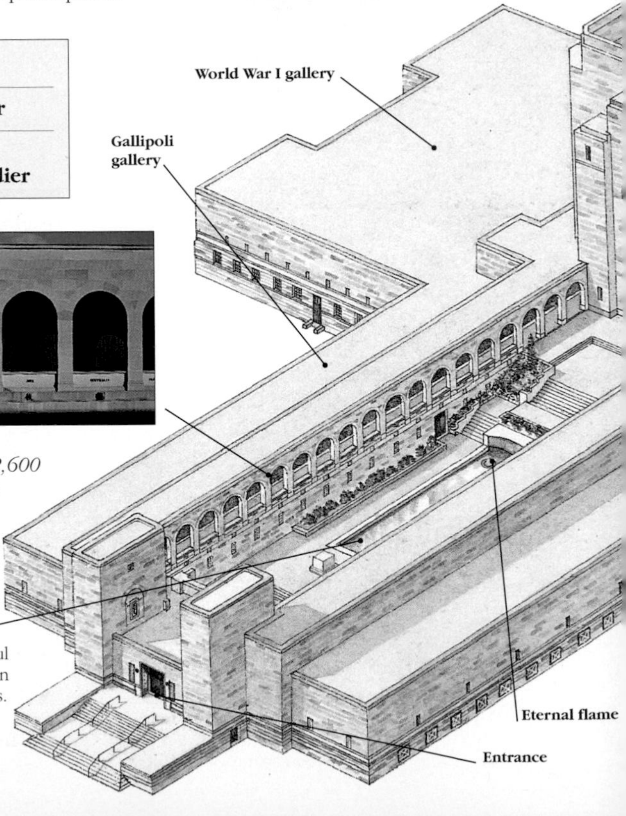
World War I gallery
Gallipoli gallery
Eternal flame
Entrance

The Pool of Reflection is a peaceful place where families can mourn their loved ones. Rosemary planted by the pool symbolizes remembrance.

top. The High Commission of Papua New Guinea on Forster Crescent is built as a Spirit House, with carved totem poles outside; the Mexican Embassy on Perth Avenue boasts a massive replica of the Aztec Sun Stone.

Just across Adelaide Avenue is The Lodge, the official residence of the Australian prime minister and his family.

National Gallery of Australia **6**

See pp194–5.

Civic Square **7**

Civic Centre. 🚌 *many routes.*

THE COMMERCIAL HEART of Canberra is the Civic Centre, on the north side of Lake Burley Griffin close to the northwest corner of the Parliamentary Triangle *(see pp186–7)*. It is the centre of many administrative, legal and local government functions in Canberra, as well as having the highest concentration of offices and private

Ethos Statue, Civic Square

sector businesses. It is also the city's main shopping area.

The central Civic Square, as envisaged by Walter Burley Griffin in his original city plan, is a common meeting place and relaxing area. It is dominated by the graceful bronze statue of Ethos, by Australian sculptor Tom Bass, located at the entrance of the ACT Legislative Assembly. In the adjacent Petrie Plaza is a traditional carousel, a much-loved landmark among the citizens of Canberra.

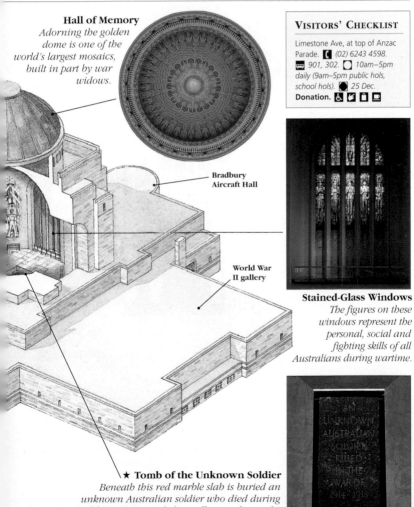

Hall of Memory
Adorning the golden dome is one of the world's largest mosaics, built in part by war widows.

Bradbury Aircraft Hall

World War II gallery

VISITORS' CHECKLIST

Limestone Ave, at top of Anzac Parade. 📞 *(02) 6243 4598.*
🚌 *901, 302.* 🕐 *10am–5pm daily (9am–5pm public hols, school hols).* ⬤ *25 Dec.*
Donation. ♿ ▢ ▢ ▢

Stained-Glass Windows
The figures on these windows represent the personal, social and fighting skills of all Australians during wartime.

★ Tomb of the Unknown Soldier
Beneath this red marble slab is buried an unknown Australian soldier who died during World War I. He symbolizes all Australians who have been killed while serving their country.

National Gallery of Australia ❻

AUSTRALIAN SOCIETY is diverse, multicultural and vibrant, and the 100,000 works of art owned by the National Gallery of Australia reflect the spirit of the country. The National Gallery opened in 1982, and the core of its collection consists of Australian art, from European settlement to present day, by some of its most famous artists, such as Tom Roberts, Arthur Boyd, Sidney Nolan and Margaret Preston *(see p30)*. The oldest art in Australia is that of its indigenous inhabitants *(see pp28–9)*, and the Aboriginal art collection offers fine examples of both ancient and contemporary works. The gallery's Asian and international collections are also growing. Modern sculptures are on display in the gardens.

Upper level

Entrance level

★ In a Corner on the MacIntyre *(1895)*
Tom Roberts' depiction of this country's bushland is painted in the fractured light style of the Australian School of Impressionists.

Native Fuchsia *(1925)*
This painting is typical of the hand-coloured wood-block techniques of artist Margaret Preston, best known for depicting Australian flowers.

The Mountain **by Aristide Maillol**

SCULPTURE GARDEN

The National Gallery makes the most of its picturesque, lakeside gardens as the site for an impressive collection of sculptures, from classical, such as Aristide Maillol's *The Mountain*, to modern. Two of the best known and loved contemporary sculptures in the garden are *Cones* by Bert Flugelman and *The Pear*s by George Baldessin.

GALLERY GUIDE

The National Gallery is easily visited within two hours, although an excellent one-hour tour of the highlights is offered twice daily. On the entrance level is the Aboriginal art collection, which is not to be missed, and the international collections. Also highly recommended, on the upper level, is the extensive Australian art collection. A new extension is home to a range of touring "blockbuster" art exhibitions which visit from around the world.

Prince Shotoku Praying to Buddha *(c. 1300)*
This statue from the Kamakura period depicts the two-year-old prince who, in the 6th century AD, went on to become a founding father of the Japanese state.

VISITORS' CHECKLIST

Parkes Place. *(02) 6240 6502.*
(02) 6240 6501. 34.
10am–5pm daily. 25
Dec. *(special exhibitions).*

Blue Poles *(1952)*
One of the gallery's most famous works, by US artist Jackson Pollock, was bought for a controversial $1.2 million in 1973 and outraged conservative Australians, who maintained that it looked like it had been painted by a child or a drunk.

★ The Aboriginal Memorial *(1988)*
These log poles by the Ramingining people honour all Aborigines who have died during white settlement.

Lower level

KEY TO FLOORPLAN

- Temporary exhibition space
- International art
- Aboriginal art
- Art of Africa & the Americas
- Modern European & American art
- Australian art
- Non-exhibition space

STAR EXHIBITS

★ **The Aboriginal Memorial by Ramingining Artists**

★ **In a Corner on the MacIntyre by Tom Roberts**

Main entrance

Rock Garden section of the Australian National Botanic Gardens

Australian National Botanic Gardens ❾

Clunies Ross Rd, Acton. ☎ (02) 6250 9540. ◯ Jan–Feb: 9am–8pm daily, Mar–Dec: 9am–5pm daily. ● 25 Dec. ♿ ✇

O N THE SLOPES of Black Mountain, the Australian National Botanic Gardens hold the finest scientific collection of native plants in the country. Approximately 90,000 plants of more than 5,000 species are featured in its displays.

The Rainforest Gully, one of the most popular attractions, features the plants from the rainforests of eastern Australia. One fifth of the nation's eucalypt species are found on the Eucalypt Lawn, which is also ideal for picnics. The Aboriginal Trail is a self-guided walk that details how Aborigines have utilized plants over thousands of years.

Telstra Tower ❿

Black Mountain Drive, Acton. ☎ (02) 6248 1911. ▦ 904. ◯ 9am–10pm daily. ✇ ♿

K NOWN AFFECTIONATELY by locals as "the giant syringe", the Telstra Tower soars 195 m (640 ft) above the summit of Black Mountain. The tower houses state-of-the-art communications equipment, such as television transmitters, radio pagers and cellular phone bases. The tower also features an exhibition on the history of telecommunications in Australia, from its first telegraph wire in Victoria in 1854 and on into the 21st century.

There are three viewing platforms at different levels of the tower offering spectacular 360° views of Canberra and the surrounding countryside both by day and by night. In 1989, Telstra Tower was made a member of the World Federation of Great Towers, an organization that also includes such venerable buildings as the Empire State Building in New York and England's Blackpool Tower.

National Zoo and Aquarium ⓫

Lady Denman Drive, Scrivener Dam. ☎ (02) 6287 1211. ◯ 9am–5:30pm daily. ● 25 Dec. ✇ ♿ ✇ by arrangement.

A WONDERFUL COLLECTION of Australia's fish, from native freshwater river fish to brilliantly coloured cold sea, tropical and coral species are on display in the National Zoo and Aquarium. There are about 20 aquariums on show, including a number of smaller tanks containing freshwater and marine animals. The Aquarium also organizes scuba dives among the coral. The dives are for beginners and last between 20 and 30 minutes.

The 7-ha (17-acre) landscaped grounds of the adjacent **Zoo** have excellent displays of numerous native animals including koalas, wombats, dingoes, fairy penguins, Tasmanian devils, emus and kangaroos. As well as the native residents of the zoo there are many favourites, including big cats, primates and African antelopes.

Australian Institute of Sport ⓬

Leverrier Crescent, Bruce. ☎ (02) 6214 1010. ▦ 80. ◯ **Tours** 10:20am, 11:30am & 2:30pm Mon–Fri, 10am, 11:30am, 1pm & 2:30pm Sat, Sun & public hols. ● 25 Dec. ✇ ♿ ✇ obligatory.

A USTRALIAN OLYMPIC medallists are often on hand to show visitors around the world-class Australian Institute of Sport (AIS), the centre of Australia's sports efforts. Here you can see where the athletes sleep, train and eat, see how your fitness levels compare and test your sports skills. There is also an exhibition of interactive sports displays.

Cockington Green ⓭

11 Gold Creek Rd, Nicholls. ☎ (02) 6230 2273. ▦ 51, 52. ◯ 9:30am–4:30pm daily. ● 25–26 Dec. ✇ ♿

C OCKINGTON GREEN is a whimsical, meticulously crafted miniature British village, set in beautifully landscaped gardens. You can stroll through the gardens and see waist-high replicas of a Scottish castle, a Kentish oast house, a typical English pub, a Sussex thatched cottage and even Stonehenge. There are even scenes of cricket and football matches with hand-crafted clay figures, animals and birds bringing the scenes to life. An Intercity 125 train travels through the "countryside", stopping en route. Another section features a range of miniature Australian and international buildings. There is also a challenging, traditional hedge maze and a fragrant heritage rose walk.

Turtle in the National Aquarium

The *Harvest of Endurance* scroll, depicting the 1861 Lambing Flat Riots, in the National Museum of Australia

National Museum of Australia ⓮

Acton Peninsula. ☎ *(02) 6208 5000.*
🚌 *34.* 🕐 *9am–5pm daily.* ● *25 Dec.* ♿ *by arrangement.* 📷 *(special exhibitions).* 🌐 *www.nma.gov.au*

Established by an Act of Parliament in 1980, the National Museum of Australia moved to its permanent home on the Acton Peninsula in early 2001. It shares its location with the Australian Institute of Aboriginal and Torres Strait Islander Studies. The innovative, purpose-built facility quickly became an architectural landmark. Its unique design was inspired by the idea of a jigsaw puzzle.

Before beginning a tour of the museum, visitors can experience an audiovisual introduction to the museum in the Circa, a novel rotating cinema. A huge, three-dimensional map of Australia is visible from three floors. Using digital animation and interactive media stations, it helps to place the displays in their geographical context.

The permanent exhibitions explore the people, events and issues that have shaped and influenced the country. The museum's aim is to be a focus for sharing stories and promoting debate, and interactive displays involve visitors by inviting their contributions. Many rare objects from the museum's collection are also on display.

The **First Australians** gallery is the largest permanent exhibition and relates the stories and experiences of Aboriginal and Torres Strait Islander people. It not only illuminates their history but also deals frankly with contemporary social issues. Displays include a monumental public sand sculpture, used in burial ceremonies in northeast Arnhem land, and a Torres Island outrigger canoe.

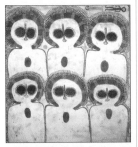

***Untitled* by Charlie Alyungurra, in the First Australians gallery**

Nation: Symbols of Australia uses more than 700 props and artifacts to look at the way symbols help to define a sense of national identity. Exhibits such as the kangaroo, as well as official symbols, such as the flag and Anzac Day. The **Horizons** gallery reviews the ways in which immigration has shaped the country. Since 1788 more than 10 million people have arrived in Australia as immigrants, and this gallery uses individual stories, as well as objects from the museum's collection, to look at the remarkable diversity of the Australian experience.

One of the more moving exhibitions is **Eternity**, in which the personal stories of 50 Australians are brought to life. The intention of this unique display is to explore history through emotion. "Your Story", an interactive exhibit, allows visitors to record their own stories, which then become part of the collection.

The museum also acknowledges the significance of the land in Australia's identity. In **Tangled Destinies**, the relationship between people and the environment is examined.

The landscaping of the museum is also notable and includes the striking Garden of Australian Dreams, which incorporates many symbols of Australian culture. The Backyard Café spills out into the innovative garden.

In addition, the museum hosts a range of temporary exhibitions. There are also children's galleries and performance spaces, as well as a television broadcast studio.

The Mermaid Coffin by Gaynor Peaty, in Eternity

Further Afield in the ACT

MORE THAN 70 PER CENT of the Australian Capital Territory is bushland. A one-day tour along Tourist Drive 5 provides an opportunity to see native animals in the wild, swim in the majestic Murrumbidgee River, visit a deep-space tracking station, and relax in the lovely gardens of the historic Lanyon Homestead.

Distinctive silver dome of Mount Stromlo Observatory

Mount Stromlo Observatory **⑮**

Via Cotter Rd. **☏** *(02) 6125 0232.* **◯** *9:30am–4:30pm daily.* **●** *25 Dec.* 🖼 ♿ ✇

MOUNT STROMLO Observatory has been a central part of Canberra's astronomical world since 1942. However, the science centre only opened up its fascinating exhibits to the general public in 1997.

Set in the Mount Stromlo pine forest just outside the city, this elevated area has clear views of the night skies. Tours are available of the high-powered telescope, astronomers talk about their work and interactive displays explain the stellar formations of the southern hemisphere.

Murrumbidgee River **⑯**

🛈 *Canberra Visitors' Centre, 330 Northbourne Ave (02) 6207 2425.*

THE MURRUMBIDGEE river meets the Cotter River at Casuarina Sands, a beautiful place to fish and canoe. Nearby is Cotter Dam, good for picnics, swimming and camping.

Situated on the bank of the Murrumbidgee River south of Canberra is **Lanyon Home-stead**, a restored 1850s' home

attached to a sheep station. The house is complemented by peaceful gardens.

On the same property is the Sidney Nolan Gallery, which features the Ned Kelly series of paintings *(see p30)*. Nolan considered Lanyon a good place for his paintings to rest.

⌂ Lanyon Homestead

Tharwa Drive, Tharwa. **☏** *(02) 6237 5136.* **◯** *10am–4pm Tue–Sun.* **●** *Good Fri, 24 & 25 Dec.* 🖼 ♿

Canberra Space Centre **⑰**

Via Paddys River Rd (Tourist Drive 5). **☏** *(02) 6201 7880.* **◯** *9am–5pm daily.* ♿ ✇ *by arrangement.*

CANBERRA SPACE CENTRE at the Canberra Deep Space Communication Complex is managed by the Common-wealth Scientific and Industrial Research Organization (CSIRO)

Tracking dish at Canberra Space Centre, known as an "antenna"

and the American NASA organization. It is one of only three such deep-space tracking centres in the world linked to the NASA control centre in California.The centre has six satellite dishes, the largest of which measures 70 m (230 ft) in diameter and weighs a hefty 3,000 tonnes.

Visitors to the Space Centre can see a piece of moon rock 3.8 billion years old, examine a real astronaut's space suit, learn about the role of the complex during the Apollo moon landings and see recent photographs sent back from Mars, Saturn and Jupiter.

Emu at Tidbinbilla Nature Reserve

Tidbinbilla Nature Reserve **⑱**

Via Paddys River Rd (Tourist Drive 5). **☏** *(02) 6205 1233.* **◯** *9am–6pm daily.* **●** *25 Dec.* 🖼 ♿ *limited.* ✇

THE TRANQUIL Tidbinbilla Nature Reserve, with its 5,450 ha (13,450 acres) of forests, grasslands, streams and mountains, is a paradise for wildlife lovers. Kangaroos and their joeys bask in the sun, emus strut on the grassy flats, platypuses swim in the creeks, koalas thrive on the eucalypt branches and bower birds and superb lyrebirds can be seen in the tall forests.

The reserve is set at the end of a quiet valley. Visitors hike up to Gibraltar Rock or take a night stroll with a ranger to see sugar gliders and possums. The Birrigai Time Trail is a 3-km (2-mile) walk through different periods of history. The visitors' centre features Aboriginal artifacts and pioneer relics.

Namadgi National Park ⑲

NAMADGI NATIONAL PARK covers almost half of the Australian Capital Territory. It is a beautiful, harsh landscape of snow, mountains, river valleys and Aboriginal rock art. Only 35 km (22 miles) south of Canberra, Namadgi is remote and solitary. Many days could be spent exploring the park, but even a day's walking will reward you with breathtaking views of the country.

Corin Dam stores high-quality water from the Cotter River, sourced in the Bimberi Wilderness.

0 km   2
0 miles   2

THARWA

Bendora Dam

Paddys River

Tidbinbilla Road

Naas Road

Cotter River

Corin Road

Smokers Trail

ORRORAL VALLEY

Apollo Road

Booromba Rocks

BILLY RANGE

Rendezvous Creek

Visitors' Centre
Trail maps of the park and information on ranger-guided walks are available here.

Nursery Swamp

Bogong Creek

BOOTH RANGE

Naas River

Boboyan Pine Forest

Old Boboyan Road

Naas Creek

Boboyan Road

Orroral Bush Camp Site
Camping out in this wild, bush setting amid the wildlife is an experience not to be missed.

COOMA   Grassy Creek

Mount Clear
is one of only two camping grounds in the park.

KEY

—	Major road
=	Minor road
- -	Walking trail
～	River
ℹ️	Tourist information
🏞️	Picnic area
⬛	Camp site
⚹	Viewpoint

Yankee Hat
Ancient Aboriginal rock art thought to date back thousands of years has been discovered in this area.

QUEENSLAND

Queensland at a Glance

AUSTRALIA'S second-largest state encompasses some 1,727,000 sq km (667,000 sq miles) and is the country's most popular tourist destination, after Sydney, due to its tropical climate. Brisbane, the state capital, is a modern city, with skyscrapers looking out over the Brisbane River. The southern coastline is a haven for surfers and is the region that most typifies the nation's beach culture. Further north is the Great Barrier Reef, one of the natural wonders of the world. Inland, cattle stations and copper mines generate Queensland's wealth. The Far North remains remote and unspoiled, with rainforests and savannah land abundant with native wildlife.

Cairns *is Queensland's most northerly city and is a popular boarding point for touring the Great Barrier Reef. The city's hub is its esplanade, lined with cafés (see p246).*

NORTHERN AND OUTBACK QUEENSLAND
(see pp240–49)

Mount Isa *is Australia's largest inland city and revolves almost entirely around its copper, zinc and lead mining industries (see p249).*

0 kilometres   150

0 miles   150

Longreach *is in the heart of Queensland's Outback, and its most popular sight is the Stockman's Hall of Fame, documenting Australia's Outback history. Longreach is also the site of Qantas' original hangar (see p249).*

◁ **Fairy basslets among the coral in the Great Barrier Reef**

Ravenswood is now a ghost town, but its lovingly restored Victorian buildings evoke the atmosphere of its heyday during the 1860s when it was at the centre of Queensland's gold rush (see p238).

The Great Barrier Reef is the largest coral reef in the world. Hundreds of islands scatter the coastline, but only a few are developed for tourists, who come here to dive among the coral and tropical fish (see pp204–209).

Maryborough is known for its Queenslander houses, their wide verandas shading residents from the tropical sun (see p233).

Brisbane, the state capital, is a highly modern yet relaxing city. Skyscrapers blend with older edifices, such as the impressive City Hall (see pp210–25).

SOUTH OF
TOWNSVILLE
(see pp226–39)

Surfers Paradise is the main city of the Gold Coast region and more than lives up to its name. Chic hotels, pulsating nightclubs, high fashion stores and beach poseurs can all be found here (see p231).

The Great Barrier Reef

CORAL REEFS are among the oldest and most primitive forms of life, dating back at least 500 million years. Today, the Great Barrier Reef is the largest reef system in the world, covering 2,000 km (1,250 miles) from Bundaberg to the tip of Cape York and an area of approximately 350,000 sq km (135,000 sq miles). Between the outer edges of the reef and the mainland there are more than 2,000 islands and almost 3,000 separate reefs, of differing types. On islands with a fringing reef coral can be viewed at close hand, although the best coral is on the outer reef, about 50 km (30 miles) from the mainland.

Saddled butterflyfish

LOCATOR MAP

The channel of water between the inner reef and Queensland's mainland is often as deep as 60 m (200 ft) and can vary in width between 30 km (20 miles) and 60 km (40 miles).

Coral is formed by tiny marine animals called polyps. These organisms have an external "skeleton" of limestone. Polyps reproduce by dividing their cells and so becoming polyp colonies.

Fringing reefs *surround islands or develop off the mainland coast as it slopes away into the sea.*

TYPICAL SECTION OF THE REEF

In this typical section of the Great Barrier Reef, a deep channel of water runs close to the mainland. In shallower water further out are a variety of reef features including coral cays, platform reefs and lagoons. Further out still, where the edge of the continental shelf drops off steeply, is a system of ribbon reefs.

Platform reef

Coral cays are sand islands, formed when reef skeletons and other debris such as shells are exposed to the air and gradually ground down by wave movement into fine sand.

Platform reefs *form in shallow water, growing outwards in a circle or oval rather than upwards in a wall.*

Queensland's tropical rainforest is moist and dense, thriving on the region's heavy, monsoon-like rains and rich soil.

Tidal flats consist of either dead or dying coral, since coral cannot survive exposure to air for an extended period of time.

Coral on the outer reef is built up in "walls" on ancient limestone bases. The coral survives down to a depth of about 30 m (100 ft), where enough sunlight penetrates the water and the temperature is above 17.5° C (65° F).

Ribbon reefs are narrow strips that occur only in the north along the edge of the continental shelf. Exactly why they form here remains a mystery to marine biologists.

How the Reef was Formed

The growth of coral reefs is dependent on sea level, as coral cannot grow above the water line or below 30 m (100 ft). As sea level rises, old coral turns to limestone, on top of which new coral can build, eventually forming barrier reefs. The Great Barrier Reef consists of thousands of separate reefs and is comparatively young, most of it having formed since the sea level rose after the end of the last Ice Age. An outer reef system corresponds with Queensland's continental shelf. Reef systems nearer the mainland correspond with submerged hills.

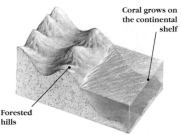

Coral grows on the continental shelf

Forested hills

1 Approximately 18,000 years ago, during the last Ice Age, waters were low, exposing a range of forested hills. Coral grew in the shallow waters of the continental shelf.

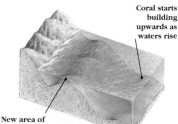

Coral starts building upwards as waters rise

New area of coral growth

2 Approximately 9,000 years ago, following the last Ice Age, the water level rose to submerge the hills. Coral began to grow in new places.

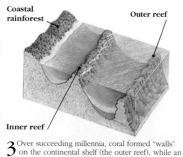

Coastal rainforest

Outer reef

Inner reef

3 Over succeeding millennia, coral formed "walls" on the continental shelf (the outer reef), while an array of fringing and platform reefs, coral cays and lagoons formed around the former hills (the inner reef).

Life on the Great Barrier Reef

MORE THAN 2,000 species of fish and innumerable species of hard and soft coral are found in the waters of the Great Barrier Reef. The diversity of life forms is extraordinary, such as echinoderms (including sea urchins), crustaceans and sponges. There is also an array of invertebrates, such as the graceful sea slug, some 12 species of sea grasses and 500 types of algae. The reef islands and coral cays support a wonderfully colourful variety of tropical birdlife. This environment is protected by the Great Barrier Reef Marine Park Authority, established by an Act of Parliament in 1975.

Blue-faced angelfish

Diving amid the dazzling colours and formations of soft coral.

Hard coral is formed from the outer skeleton of polyps *(see p204)*. The most common species is staghorn coral.

Soft coral has no outer skeleton and resembles the fronds of a plant, rippling in the waves.

***Wobbegongs** are members of the shark family. They sleep during the day under rocks and caves, camouflaged by their skin tones.*

Manta rays are huge fish, measuring up to 6 m (20 ft) across. Despite their size, they are gentle creatures that are happy to be touched by divers.

Potato cod are known for their friendly demeanour and are often happy to swim alongside divers.

Great white sharks are occasional visitors to the reef, although they usually live in the open ocean and swim in schools.

Giant clams, which are large bivalves, are sadly a gourmet delicacy. Australian clams are now protected by law to save them from extinction.

The sea bed of the Barrier Reef is 60 m (195 ft) deep at its lowest point.

***Coral groupers** inhabit the reef waters and grow up to 15 kg (33 lbs). They are recognizable by their deep red skin.*

THE FRAGILE REEF

Ecotourism is the only tourism that is encouraged on the Great Barrier Reef. The important thing to remember on the Barrier Reef is to look but not touch. Coral is easily broken; avoid standing on it and be aware that the taking of coral is strictly forbidden and carefully monitored. Camping on the reef's islands requires a permit from the Great Barrier Reef Marine Park Authority.

Beaked coralfish *are abundant and some of the most attractive fish of the Barrier Reef. They often swim in pairs, in shallow waters and around coral heads.*

Gobies feed on sand, ingesting the organic matter. They are found near the shoreline.

Blenny

Butterflyfish

THE REEF AS A MARINE HABITAT

Hard corals are the building blocks of the reef. Together with soft corals, they form the "forest" within which the fish and other sea creatures dwell.

Schultz pipefish

Goatfish

Clown anemonefish have an immunity to the stinging tentacles of sea anemones, among which they reside.

Moray eels grow to 2 m (6 ft) in length but are gentle enough to be hand-fed by divers.

Batfish *swim in large groups and colonize areas of the reef for long periods before moving on elsewhere. They mainly feed on algae and sea jellies.*

The crown of thorns starfish feeds mainly on staghorn coral. In the 1960s a sudden growth in the numbers of this starfish led to worries that it would soon destroy the whole reef. However, many now believe that such a population explosion is a natural and common phenomenon. It contributes to reef life by destroying old coral and allowing new coral to generate.

BIRDS OF THE GREAT BARRIER REEF

Gulls, gannets, frigate birds, shearwaters and terns all make use of the rich environment of the islands of the Great Barrier Reef to breed and rear their young, largely safe from mainland predators such as cats and foxes. The number of sea birds nesting on some of the coral cays (see p204) is astounding – for example, on the tiny area of Michaelmas Cay, 42 km (26 miles) northeast of Cairns, there are more than 30,000 birds, including herons and boobies.

Red-footed booby

Activities on the Great Barrier Reef

F EWER THAN 20 of the Great Barrier Reef's 2,000 islands cater for tourists (see map and table below). Accommodation on the islands ranges from luxury resorts to basic camp sites. To make the most of the coral, take a tourist boat trip to the outer reef; most operators provide glass-bottomed boats or semi-submersibles to view the coral. The best way of seeing the reef, however, is by diving or snorkelling. There are numerous day trips from the mainland to the reef and between the islands.

Ornate butterfly fish

Reef walking *involves walking over dead stretches of the reef at low tide. Wear strong shoes and be very careful to avoid standing on living coral under the water.*

Snorkelling *is one of the most popular activities in the Barrier Reef, offering the chance to see beautiful tropical fish at close range.*

THE MAIN ISLANDS

Tropical fish are largely harmless – the majority will let you swim close, but may nip your fingers if you attempt to touch them.

DIVING ON THE GREAT BARRIER REEF

The Great Barrier Reef is one of the most popular, as well as one of the more reasonably priced, places to dive in the world. The best places to find dive schools are Townsville or Cairns, although many schools exist along the coast. Some boat trips also offer hand-held dives for complete beginners; some offer night dives.

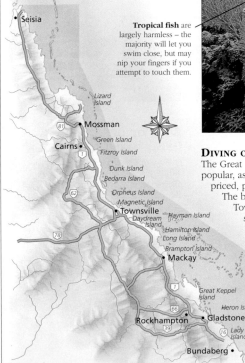

Map labels:
Seisia
Lizard Island
Mossman
Cairns
Green Island
Fitzroy Island
Dunk Island
Bedarra Island
Orpheus Island
Magnetic Island
Townsville
Daydream Island
Hayman Island
Hamilton Island
Long Island
Brampton Island
Mackay
Great Keppel Island
Heron Island
Rockhampton
Gladstone
Lady Elliot Island
Bundaberg

KEY

=== Highway

0 km   150
0 miles   150

Heron Island is one of the few coral cay resorts and is known for its excellent diving. From October to March, turtle-spotting is a popular activity as they make their way up the beach to lay their eggs. Bird-watching is also popular as the island's pisonia trees are home to thousands of birds, including terns. Guided nature walks around the cay are available.

Gorgonian fan coral grows in thickets in the deep waters of the Barrier Reef and is recognizable by its orange-yellow colour.

Scuba is an acronym for Self-contained Underwater Breathing Apparatus.

GETTING TO THE TOURIST ISLANDS

Bedarra Island 🚢 *from Dunk Island.* **Brampton Island** ✈ 🚢 *from Mackay.* **Daydream Island** 🚢 *from Shute Harbour.* **Dunk Island** 🚢 *from Mission Beach.* **Fitzroy Island** 🚢 *from Cairns.* **Great Keppel Island** ✈ *from Rockhampton.* **Green Island** 🚢 *from Cairns.* **Hamilton Island** ✈ *from all state capitals & Cairns.* 🚢 *from Shute Harbour.* **Hayman Island** ✈ 🚢 *from Hamilton Island.* **Heron Island** ✈ *from Gladstone.* **Lady Elliot Island** ✈ *from Bundaberg, Gladstone, Hervey Bay.* **Lizard Island** ✈ *from Cairns.* **Long Island** 🚢 *from Shute Harbour.* **Magnetic Island** ✈ 🚢 *from Townsville.* **Orpheus Island** ✈ *from Cairns & Townsville.*

Hamilton Island is a popular resort island featuring a wide range of activities, including parasailing, skydiving, golf, tennis and children's entertainments.

The Low Isles, 25 km (15 miles) offshore from Port Douglas, are a perfect example of the reef's day-trip opportunities. This glass-bottomed boat offers sunbathing areas, snorkelling, views of reef life and lunch, before returning to the mainland.

ACTIVITIES ON THE TOURIST ISLANDS

These islands are easily accessible and offer a range of activities.

	DIVING	SNORKELLING	FISHING	DAY TRIPS	BUSHWALKING	WATERSPORTS	CAMPING
Bedarra Island					●		
Brampton Island		■		■	●	■	
Daydream Island		■		■		■	
Dunk Island *(see p247)*					●		
Fitzroy Island	●			■	●	■	
Gt Keppel Island		■	●	■	●	■	
Green Island *(see p245)*		●					
Hamilton Island	●	■		■	●	■	
Hayman Island		■		■	●	■	
Heron Island		●					
Lady Elliot Island					■		
Lizard Island	●	■		●	●		
Long Island				■	●	■	
Magnetic Island *(see p239)*		●					
Orpheus Island	●	■					●

BRISBANE

BRISBANE IS THE CAPITAL *of Queensland and, with a population of nearly 1.5 million, ranks third in size in Australia after Sydney and Melbourne. Situated on the Brisbane River and surrounded by misty blue hills, the city is known for its scenic beauty, balmy climate and friendly atmosphere. Its tropical vegetation is a great attraction, particularly the bougainvillea, poinciana and fragrant frangipani.*

In 1823, the Governor of New South Wales, Sir Thomas Brisbane, decided that some of the more intractable convicts in the Sydney penal settlement needed more secure incarceration. The explorer John Oxley was dispatched to investigate Moreton Bay, noted by Captain Cook on his journey up the east coast 50 years earlier. Oxley landed at Redcliffe and thought he had stumbled across a tropical paradise. He was soon disappointed, however, as the reality failed to live up to expectations – water was short, the local Aborigines were decidedly hostile when they realized their land was being purloined and the convicts proved less than willing labourers. It was therefore decided to move the colony inland up the Brisbane River.

Free settlers began arriving in 1837, although they were not permitted to move closer than 80 km (50 miles) to the famously harsh penal settlement. This set a pattern of decentralization which is still evident today: Brisbane consists of several distinct communities as well as the central area. The city's growth was rapid and, in 1859, when Queensland became a self-governing colony, Brisbane was duly named as the state capital.

As Queensland's natural resources, including coal, silver, lead and zinc, were developed, so its major city flourished. Brisbane's status as a truly modern city, however, is relatively recent, beginning with a mining boom in the 1960s. Hosting the Commonwealth Games in 1982 and the 1988 Expo' were also milestones, bringing thousands of visitors to the city. Today, Brisbane is a cosmopolitan place boasting some superb restaurants, streetside cafés and a lively arts scene. Yet amid all the high-rises and modernity, pockets of traditional wooden cottages with verandas can still be found, and the relaxed manner of the locals tempers the urban bustle.

Sheep in the Australian Woolshed animal park in Brisbane

◁ An old paddlesteamer on the Brisbane River, set against the city's modern skyline

Exploring Central Brisbane

B RISBANE'S CITY CENTRE fits neatly in a U-shaped
loop of the Brisbane River, so one of the best ways
to get acquainted with the city is by ferry. The city
centre can also be easily explored on foot. The streets
follow a grid and are named after British royalty:
queens and princesses run north–south, kings and
princes run east–west. Brisbane's suburbs also have
their own distinct feel: to the east is chic Kangaroo
Point; just west of the centre is trendy Paddington;
while to the northwest Fortitude Valley has a multicultural population and wonderful restaurants.

Cenotaph in Anzac Square

Mount Coot-tha Botanic Gardens

KEY

▨	Street-by-Street area *pp214–15*
🚌	Bus terminus
P	Parking
ℹ	Tourist information
◯	Metroad (city) route
▬	Highway
▬	Major road
—	Minor road

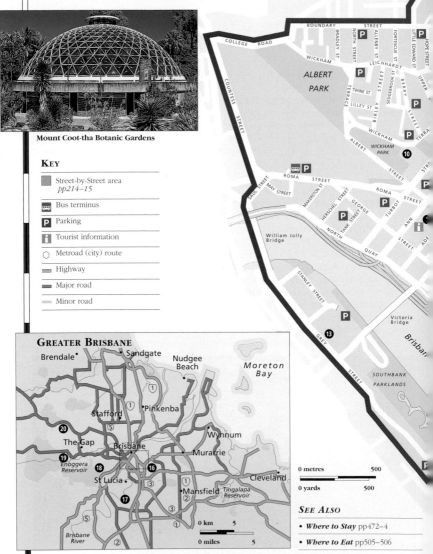

GREATER BRISBANE

Brendale ·   · Sandgate   Nudgee Beach   *Moreton Bay*

Stafford   ·Pinkenba

20   The Gap   Wynnum

19   *Enoggera Reservoir*   18   Brisbane   16   ·Muarrie

St Lucia ·   Cleveland

17   ·Mansfield   *Tingalapa Reservoir*

Brisbane River

0 km   5
0 miles   5

0 metres   500
0 yards   500

SEE ALSO

- **Where to Stay** pp472–4
- **Where to Eat** pp505–506

LOCATOR MAP

SIGHTS AT A GLANCE

Historic Streets and Buildings

Anzac Square **9**

Fortitude Valley and Chinatown **12**

City Hall **7**

Commissariat Store Museum **3**

Customs House **8**

General Post Office **1**

Newstead House **16**

Old Government House **6**

Old Windmill **10**

Parliament House **4**

Churches and Cathedrals

St John's Anglican Cathedral **11**

St Stephen's Cathedral **2**

Parks and Gardens

Botanic Gardens **5**

Brisbane Botanic Gardens **18**

Brisbane Forest Park **19**

Lone Pine Koala Sanctuary **17**

South Bank Precinct **14**

Museums and Galleries

Australian Woolshed **20**

Queensland Cultural Centre pp220–21 **13**

Queensland Maritime Museum **15**

GETTING AROUND

Tours of the city centre are readily available and public transport is cheap and efficient. City centre bus stops are colour-coded for easy route identification and the City Circle bus No. 333 does a clockwise loop around the main city area. The best place for boarding the city's ferries is Riverside Centre.

Street-by-Street: Central Brisbane

CENTRAL BRISBANE is a blend of glass and
steel high-rises co-existing with graceful
19th-century constructions. The latter fortunately managed to survive the frenzy of demol-
ishing old buildings that took place throughout
the country during the 1970s. Queen Street,
now a pedestrian mall, is the hub of the city.
Reflecting the city's beginnings as a port, most
of the historic buildings are found near the
river. Near the city's first Botanical Gardens, which border Alice Street, many
old pubs have been renovated to cater
for a largely business-lunch clientele.

**Central Brisbane's modern skyline, looming
over the Brisbane River**

St Stephen's Cathedral
*One of the landmarks of
Brisbane's city centre is
this Gothic-style cathedral.
Particularly notable are
its white twin spires* **2**

Elizabeth Arcade
is filled with New
Age, alternative
and bohemian-
style bookstores
and retail shops.

Sciencentre
*This science
museum was once
a printing office;
"printing devil"
gargoyles
remain on
the parapet.*

★ Commissariat Store Museum
*The original façade of these former 19th-
century granary stores has been preserved,
although the interior is now a museum
detailing Queensland's history* **3**

The former Coal Board building was erected in the mid-1880s and is an example of the elaborate warehouses that once dominated the city.

Smellie & Co. was a 19th-century hardware merchant housed in this attractive building. Note the Baroque doorway on the eastern side.

Queensland Club
This charming old building has housed the private, men-only Queensland Club since 1884. Panelled wood walls and elegant columns were intended to emulate British gentlemen's clubs.

LOCATOR MAP

KEY

 — — Suggested route

STAR SIGHTS

★ **Commissariat Store Museum**

★ **Parliament House**

STREET

ALICE STREET

ALICE STREET

The Mansions
The Mansions are a row of 1890s three-storey, red brick terrace houses. The arches of lighter coloured sandstone create a distinctive design. Stone cats sit atop the parapets at each end of the building.

| 0 metres | 100 |
| 0 yards | 100 |

★ **Parliament House**
This stained-glass window depicting Queen Victoria is one of the many beautiful features of this late 19th-century building. Unlike many early parliamentary buildings in Australia, it is still used for its original purpose ❹

South façade of the restored colonial Commissariat Store Museum

General Post Office **❶**

261 Queen St. **📞** 13 13 18.
🚆 Brisbane Central. **🚌** 333.
⛴ Eagle St Pier. **🕐** 7am–6pm
Mon–Fri. **♿**

B UILT BETWEEN 1871 and
1879, this attractive Neo-
Classical building was erected
to house the city's first official
postal service. It replaced the
barracks for female convicts
which had previously occupied
the site. The building continues to operate as central
Brisbane's main post office.

Post Office Square, oppo-
site the General Post Office,
is a pleasant place to relax,
while looking out over the
landscaped greenery and
fountains of Anzac Square.

St Stephen's Cathedral **❷**

249 Elizabeth St. **📞** (07) 3224 3111.
🚆 Brisbane Central. **🚌** 333. **⛴**
Eagle St Pier. **🕐** 8am–6pm Mon–Fri,
7am–6pm Sat–Sun. **♿ 📷**

E ARLY SETTLERS provided
the funds for this lovely
English Gothic-style Catholic
cathedral, designed by noted
colonial architect Benjamin
Backhouse and completed in
1874. The main façade features
restored twin spires on each
side of the elaborate stained-
glass windows.

Next door is St Stephen's
Church, the oldest church in
Brisbane. It was designed by
AW Pugin, an English archi-
tect who also worked on Lon-
don's Houses of Parliament.

Commissariat Store Museum **❸**

115 William St. **📞** (07) 3221 4198.
🚆 South Brisbane. **🚌** 333.
⛴ North Quay. **🕐** 10am–4pm
Tues–Sun. **●** Good Fri, Easter Sun,
25 Dec, 26 Dec. **📷 ♿**

T HE Commissariat Stores,
constructed by convict
labour in 1829, is the only
surviving building from
Brisbane's penal colony days
open to the public. Having
been restored in 2000, it is
now open to visitors and
houses the Royal Historical
Society of Queensland.

Parliament House **❹**

Cnr George and Alice sts. **📞** (07)
3406 7637. **🚆** Brisbane Central.
🚌 1a, 1b, 5, 5b, 5c, 7, 7a, 333. **⛴**
Gardens Point. **🕐** 9:30am–4:15pm
Mon–Fri, 10am–2pm Sun. **●** public
hols. **♿ 📷** obligatory.

Q UEENSLAND'S Parliament
House was designed in
French Renaissance style by
architect Charles Tiffin,
who won an architectural
competition. Begun in 1865, it
was completed in 1868. Tiffin
added features more suited to
Queensland's tropical climate,
such as shady colonnades,
shutters and an arched roof
which is made from Mount
Isa copper (see p249). Other
notable features are the cedar
staircases and the intricate
gold leaf detailing on the
Council Chamber ceilings.

The building is still used
for its original purpose and
the public is permitted into
the chambers when parliament
is not in progress. Unlike other
state parliaments, consisting
of an Upper and Lower House,
Queensland has only one
parliamentary body.

Parliament House is also
notable as being the first legislative building in the British
Empire to be lit by electricity.

**Interior of the Assembly Chamber
in Parliament House**

Botanic Gardens **❺**

Alice St. **📞** (07) 3403 8888.
🚆 Brisbane Central. **🚌** 333.
⛴ Edward St. **🕐** 24 hours.
♿ 📷

B RISBANE'S FIRST Botanic
Gardens on the Brisbane
River are the second oldest
botanic gardens in Australia.
Their peaceful location is a

Mangrove boardwalk in the Botanic Gardens

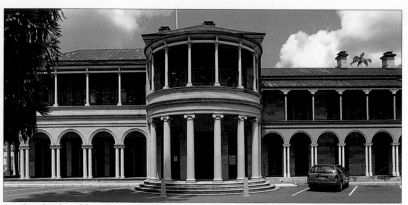

Arcade and arches of the north façade of Old Government House

welcome haven from the city's usual bustle and high-rise buildings.

In its earliest incarnation, the area was used as a vegetable garden by convicts. It was laid out in its present form in 1855 by the colonial botanist Walter Hill, who was also the first director of the gardens. An avenue of bunya pines dates back to the 1850s, while an avenue of weeping figs was planted in the 1870s.

Hundreds of water birds, such as herons and plovers, are attracted to the lakes dotted throughout the gardens' 18 ha (44 acres). Brisbane River's renowned mangroves are now a protected species and can be admired from a specially built boardwalk.

Old Government House **6**

Queensland University of Technology Campus, Gardens Point, George St. **(07) 3229 1788.** Brisbane Central. 333. Gardens Point. 9am– 4:30pm Mon–Fri. public hols. ground floor only.

HOME TO THE National Trust of Queensland since 1973, the state's first Government House was designed by colonial architect Charles Tiffin and completed in 1862. The graceful sandstone building served not only as the state governor's residence, but also as the administrative base and social centre of the state of Queensland until 1910.

Following its vice-regal term of office, the building was occupied by the fledgling University of Queensland (now situated in the suburb of St Lucia). Of particular architectural note are the Norman-style arches and arcades on the ground floor.

City Hall **7**

King George Square. **(07) 3403 4048.** Brisbane Central. 333, Adelaide St routes. Eagle St Pier. 8:30am–5pm Mon–Fri. public hols. **Clocktower** 8:30am–3:30pm Mon–Fri, 10:30am–1:30pm Sat. public hols. **Gallery** 10am–5pm daily.

COMPLETED IN 1930, the Neo-Classical City Hall is home to Brisbane City Council, the largest council in Australia.

Brisbane's early settlement is depicted by a beautiful sculpted tympanum above the main entrance. In the King George Square foyer, some particularly fine examples of traditional craftsmanship are evident in the floor mosaics, ornate ceilings and woodwork carved from Queensland timbers. City Hall's 92-m (300-ft) Italian Renaissance-style tower gives a panoramic view of the city from a platform at its top. A display of both contemporary and Aboriginal art and ceramics is housed in the City Hall Art Gallery.

The attractive King George Square, facing City Hall, continues to resist the encroachment of high-rise office blocks and has several interesting statues, including *Form del Mito* by Arnaldo Pomodoro. The work's geometric forms and polished surfaces, for which this Italian sculptor is noted, reflect the changing face of the city from morning through to night. The bronze *Petrie Tableau*, by Tasmanian sculptor Stephen Walker, was designed for Australia's bicentenary. It commemorates the pioneer families of Brisbane and depicts one of Queensland's earliest explorers, Andrew Petrie, being bid farewell by his family as he departs on an inland expedition.

Façade of City Hall, with its Italian Renaissance clocktower

Customs House

399 Queen St. *(07) 3365 8999.*
Brisbane Central. 333.
Riverside. 10am–10pm Tue–Sat,
10am–5pm Sun & Mon. *public
hols.*

Restored by the University
of Queensland in 1994,
Customs House, with its
landmark copper dome and
stately Corinthian columns, is
now open to the public. Commissioned in 1886, this is one
of Brisbane's oldest buildings,
predating both City Hall *(see
p217)* and the Treasury. Early
renovations removed the hall
and staircase, but these have
now been carefully recon-
structed from the original
plans. Today, the building is
used for numerous civic
functions, and houses an art
gallery and a restaurant.

Anzac Square ❾

Ann & Adelaide sts. *Brisbane
Central.* 333. *Waterfront
Place, Eagle St Pier.*

All Australian cities commemorate those who
have given their life for their
country. Brisbane's war
memorial is centred on Anzac
Square, an attractive park
planted with, among other
flora, rare boab (baobab) trees.
The Eternal Flame burns in a
Greek Revival cenotaph at the
Ann Street entrance to the
park. Beneath the cenotaph
is the Shrine of Memories,
containing various tributes
and wall plaques to those
who gave their lives in war.

Distinctive view of Old Windmill

Old Windmill ❿

Wickham Terrace. *Brisbane
Central.* 333. *to public.*

Built in 1828, the Old Windmill is one of two buildings
still standing in Brisbane
from convict days, the old
Commissariat Stores being the
other survivor *(see p216)*.
Originally the colony's first
industrial building, it proved
unworkable without the availability of trained operators,
so it was equipped with
treadmills to punish recalcitrant
convicts. It later served as a
time signal, with a gun fired
and a ball dropped each day
at exactly 1pm.

The picturesque mill was
also chosen as the first television image in Australia in the
1920s. The windmill is not
open to the public, but it
makes a striking photograph.

St John's Anglican Cathedral ⓫

373 Ann St. *(07) 3835 2231.*
Brisbane Central. 333.
Riverside Centre. 7am–5pm
daily (restricted access Sat).

Designed along French
Gothic lines in 1901, St
John's Anglican Cathedral is
regarded as one of the most
splendid churches in the
southern hemisphere. The
interior is of Helidon sandstone.
The cathedral is still to be
finished after a century of work.

Over the years, kneeling
cushions have been donated to
St John's by the parishes of
Queensland, each designed
with a theme appropriate to
the state. It was also here, in
1859, that Queensland was
made a separate colony (it had
been part of New South Wales).

The Deanery is the former
residence of the first governor
of Queensland.

**Nave and altar of St John's
Anglican Cathedral**

Fortitude Valley and Chinatown ⓬

Brunswick & Ann sts, Fortitude Valley.
Brunswick St. 333.

The ship *Fortitude* sailed
from England and up the
Brisbane River in 1859 with
250 settlers on board, and
the name stuck to the valley
where they disembarked.
For a time the area was the
trading centre of the city and
some impressive buildings
were erected during the 1880s

Greek cenotaph in Anzac Square

Entrance to the Pedestrian Hall in Chinatown, Fortitude Valley

and 1890s. It then degenerated into one of Brisbane's seedier areas.

In the 1980s, the city council began to revive the district. It is now the bohemian centre of Brisbane, with some of the city's best restaurants *(see pp505–6)*. McWhirter's Emporium, an Art Deco landmark, is home to a popular indoor clothes market. On Saturday mornings, there is also a busy outdoor market in Brunswick Street. The area should be avoided at night.

Also within the valley is Brisbane's Chinatown, a bustling area of Asian restaurants, super-markets, cinemas and martial arts centres. The lions at the entrance to the area were turned around when a *feng shui* expert considered their original position to be bad for business.

Queensland Cultural Centre ⓭

See pp220–21.

South Bank Precinct ⓮

Brisbane River foreshore, South Bank. 🚋 South Bank. 🚌 12, Adelaide St & George St routes. ⛴ South Bank 1, 2, 3. 🅰 **Visitors' Centre** 📞 (07) 3867 2051. 🕐 9am–6pm Sat–Thu, 9am–10pm Fri.

THE SOUTH BANK of the Brisbane River was the site of Expo '88 and has now been redeveloped into a 16 ha (40 acres) centre of culture, entertainment and recreation. The area known as the parklands includes the Queensland Performing Arts Centre, the State Library, the Queensland Museum, Queensland Art Gallery, the Conservatorium, Opera Queensland, two colleges and an exhibition centre. The South Bank area abounds with restaurants, cafés, weekend market stalls and street entertainers. Classical music and pop concerts are also regularly held here. There is even a man-made lagoon with a

Butterfly at South Bank Parklands

"real" sandy beach, complete with suntanned lifesavers.

South Bank's Imax Theatre has a giant screen and shows 2D and 3D films made specifically for the large screen.

One of the most recent additions includes a 450-m (1,500-ft) pedestrian and cycle bridge, linking the southern end of the area with the city's Botanic Gardens.

Queensland Maritime Museum ⓯

Cnr Sidon & Stanley sts. 📞 (07) 3844 5361. 🚋 South Bank. 🚌 174, 175, 203, 204. ⛴ River Plaza, South Bank 3. 🕐 9:30am–4:30pm daily. ⬤ Good Fri, 25 Apr am, 25 Dec. 🈺 🅰 🅿

QUEENSLAND Maritime Museum lists among its exhibits shipbuilders' models, reconstructed cabins from early coastal steamers and relics from early shipwrecks in the area. In the dry dock, as part of the National Estate, sits HMAS *Diamantina*, a frigate that served during World War II.

A coal-fired tug, *Forceful*, is maintained in running order and cruises with passengers to Moreton Bay two seasons a year. Also on display is the pearling lugger *Penguin* and the bow of a Japanese pleasure boat, a *yakatabume*, donated to Brisbane by Japan after Expo '88.

HMAS *Diamantina* at the Queensland Maritime Museum

Queensland Cultural Centre ⑬

THE QUEENSLAND CULTURAL CENTRE is the hub of Brisbane's arts scene. It incorporates the Queensland Art Gallery, a museum, performing arts centre and library. The Gallery is the most renowned of these, first established in 1895 and part of the cultural centre since 1982. It has a fine collection of Australian art, including works by Sidney Nolan and Margaret Preston, together with Aboriginal art. The international collection includes 15th-century European art and Asian art from the 12th century. Also noteworthy is the collection of contemporary Asian art, established in 1993.

Under the Jacaranda
R. Godfrey Rivers' work is part of a collection of Australian art.

Level 4

★ **Bushfire** (*1944*)
Russell Drysdale is known for his depiction of harsh Outback life, such as this farmhouse destroyed by a natural disaster.

Level 3

★ **La Belle Hollandaise** (*1905*)
One of Picasso's transitional works between his blue and rose periods, this was painted during a visit to the Netherlands. The gallery paid a then world record price of £55,000 in 1959 for the work of a living artist.

Bathers (*1906*)
One of Australia's most highly regarded artists, Rupert Bunny achieved international fame with his paintings of Victorian life. Here the luxurious bathing scene is matched by the sumptuous scale and composition.

Level 2

STAR PAINTINGS

★ **Bushfire**

★ **La Belle Hollandaise**

KEY

- Contemporary, indigenous and Asian art
- Australian art, pre-1970s
- European art
- Decorative art
- Works on paper
- Non-exhibition space
- Water mall
- Sculpture courtyard

VISITORS' CHECKLIST

Cnr Melbourne & Grey sts, South
Bank. ☐ South Brisbane.
☐ 174, 175, 203, 204. ☐
South Bank. **Queensland Art
Gallery** ☐ (07) 3840 7333.
☐ 10am–5pm daily. ☐ Good
Fri, Anzac Day (until midday), 25
Dec. ☐ ☐ ☐ 11am, 1pm,
2pm, Mon–Fri; 11am, 2pm, 3pm
Sat–Sun. ☐

QUEENSLAND ART GALLERY GUIDE

*The collection is housed over three levels. Contem-
porary, indigenous and Asian art are found on
Levels 2 and 4. Decorative art is displayed on
Level 2. European art also begins on this level
and moves up to Level 3. Level 3 also
contains Australian art after 1970.*

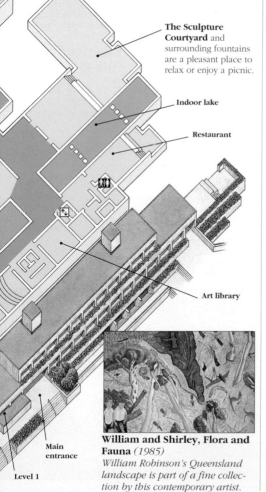

**The Sculpture
Courtyard** and
surrounding fountains
are a pleasant place to
relax or enjoy a picnic.

Indoor lake

Restaurant

Art library

**Main
entrance**

Level 1

**William and Shirley, Flora and
Fauna** *(1985)*
*William Robinson's Queensland
landscape is part of a fine collection by this contemporary artist.*

🏛 Queensland Museum
☐ (07) 3840 7555. ☐ 9:30am–
5pm daily. ☐ public hols, 25 Dec.
This imaginative natural
history museum is filled with
full-scale models, both prehistoric and current. A large-
scale model of Queensland's
unique dinosaur, the *Mutta-
burrasaurus*, stands in the
foyer. There are also displays
on local megafauna and
endangered species such as
the central Australian bilby.

**Performers of the acclaimed
Queensland Ballet company**

🎭 Queensland Performing
Arts Centre
☐ 13 62 46. ☐ performance
times only.
Queensland's Performing Arts
Centre comprises a main concert hall and three theatres.
Internationally acclaimed
opera, classical music and
theatrical productions are
staged at the centre, ranging
from fringe productions to
large-scale Broadway musicals.
The highly respected Queensland Ballet is also based here.

🏛 State Library
☐ (07) 3840 7666. ☐ daily. ☐
The State Library houses
collections from around the
world. Its extensive resources
cover all interests and most of
its services are free. You can
explore the Internet (bookings
essential), watch a classic
film, explore Queensland's
past or trace your own family
history. There are free films
every Sunday and a free tour
of the library every Tuesday.

Newstead House ⓰

Newstead Park, Breakfast Creek Rd,
Newstead. 📞 (07) 3216 1846.
🚊 Bowen Hills. 🚌 300, 306, 322.
🕐 10am–4pm Mon–Fri, 2–5pm
Sun. ⬤ Sat, Good Fri, 25 Apr,
25–26 Dec. 📷 ♿ limited. 📷

BUILT IN 1846 for Patrick
Leslie, one of the first
European settlers in the Darling Downs region, Newstead
House is the oldest surviving
home in Brisbane. Overlooking the river, this charming
building was sold in 1847 to
government resident and magistrate, Captain John Wickham.
It then became an unofficial
government house until the
real Government House was
completed in 1862 *(see p217)*.

The centre of the new
colony's social life, Newstead
House was the scene of lavish
parties. A huge fig tree, under
which elegant carriages once
waited, still graces the drive.
Restored by the Newstead
House Trust from 1976, the
house has been refurnished
with Victorian antiques.

Music box in Newstead House

Lone Pine Koala Sanctuary ⓱

Jesmond Rd, Fig Tree Pocket. 📞 (07)
3378 1366. 🚌 445. 🚢 North Quay.
🕐 8am–5pm daily. ⬤ morning of
25 April. 📷 ♿

THE OLDEST koala sanctuary
in Australia, opened in
1927, is now one of Brisbane's
most popular tourist attractions.
Lone Pine has more than 100
koalas, as well as kangaroos,
emus, possums, dingoes,
wombats, reptiles and many
Australian birds, including
various species of parrot.
Lone Pine insists that it is more
than just a zoo, a claim that is
supported by its nationally
respected koala breeding
programme. For a small fee,
visitors can have their photograph taken holding a koala.

A pleasant and scenic way
to get to Lone Pine Sanctuary
is by ferry. There are daily
departures at 10am from
Victoria Bridge.

Brisbane Botanic Gardens ⓲

Mt Coot-tha Rd, Toowong.
📞 (07) 3403 2533. 🚌 333.
🕐 Sep–Mar: 8am–5:30pm daily;
Apr–Aug: 8am–5pm daily.

BRISBANE BOTANIC GARDENS, in
the foothills of Mount
Coot-tha Forest Park 8 km (5
miles) from the city centre,
were founded in 1976 and
feature more than 20,000
specimens, representing 5,000
species, of exotic herbs,
shrubs and trees laid out in
themed beds. Highlights
include eucalypt groves, a
Japanese Garden, a Tropical
Display Dome, which includes
lotus lilies and vanilla orchids,
a Lagoon and Bamboo Grove
and a large collection of
Australian native plants. Many
arid and tropical plants,
usually seen in greenhouses,
thrive in the outdoor setting.
Also in the Gardens complex,
the Sir Thomas Brisbane
Planetarium is the largest of
Australia's planetariums.

Mount Coot-tha Forest Park
offers both spectacular views
and attractive picnic areas.
The Aboriginal name means
"mountain of dark native
honey", a reference to the
tiny bees found in the area.
On a clear day, from the
summit lookout you can see
Brisbane, snugly encircled by
the river, Moreton and Stradbroke islands, the Glasshouse
Mountains (so named by
Captain Cook because they
reminded him of the glass
furnaces in his native
Yorkshire) and the Lamington
Plateau backing onto the Gold
Coast *(see pp230–31)*. The
park also contains some
excellent, easygoing walking
trails through the woodland,
including Aboriginal trails
which detail traditional uses
of native plants.

Brisbane Forest Park ⓳

🚌 385. ℹ️ The Gap (07) 3300
4855. 🕐 8:30am–4:30pm Mon–Fri,
9am–4:30pm Sat, Sun & public hols.
⬤ 25 Dec.

BRISBANE FOREST PARK, within
the D'Aguilar Mountain
Range, stretches for more
than 50 km (30 miles) northwest of Brisbane city centre.
Covering more than 28,500
ha (70,250 acres) of natural
bushland and eucalypt forests,
the park offers driving routes
with breathtaking views over
the surrounding countryside.
The most scenic driving route
is along Mount Nebo Road,

Koala at Lone Pine Koala Sanctuary

Lush landscape of the Brisbane Botanic Gardens backed by one of the city's modern skyscrapers

which winds its way through the lush mountains.

Another scenic drive extends from Samford up to the charming mountain village of Mount Glorious and down the other side. It is worth stopping from time to time to hear the distinctive calls of bellbirds and whipbirds.

Six km (3.5 miles) past Mount Glorious is the Wivenhoe Outlook, with spectacular views down to Lake Wivenhoe, an artificial lake created to prevent the Brisbane River from flooding the city. One km (0.6 miles) north of Mount Glorious is the entrance to Maiala Recreation Area, where there are picnic areas, some wheelchair accessible, and several walking trails of varying lengths, from short walks to longer, half-day treks. These pass through the rainforest, which abounds with animal life. Other excellent half-day walks are at Manorina and at Jolly's Lookout, the oldest formal lookout in the park, which has a good picnic area. Also in the park is the Westridge Outlook, a boardwalk with sweeping views, which is totally wheelchair-accessible.

The engrossing **Walkabout Creek Wildlife Centre** at the park's headquarters is a re-created large freshwater environment. Water dragons, pythons, water rats, catfish and tiny rainbow fish flourish within these natural surroundings. Visitors also have the chance to see the extraordinary lungfish, a unique species which is equipped with both gills and lungs. The on-site restaurant looks out over the beautiful bush landscape.

About 4 km (2 miles) from the park headquarters is Bellbird Grove, which includes an outdoor Aboriginal collection of bark huts. It has a picnic area and swing ropes for children to enjoy. There are also play areas at Ironbark Gully and Lomandra, as well as a Ropes Adventure Course, which consists of high and low ropes and accompanying problem-solving sections.

➤ Walkabout Creek Wildife Centre

60 Mt Nebo Rd, The Gap.
☎ (07) 3300 4855.
🕐 9am–4:30pm daily. ⬤ 25 Dec.
♿ 🅿

Australian Woolshed ⑳

148 Samford Rd, Ferny Hills. ☎ (07) 3872 1100. 🚉 Ferny Grove.
🕐 7:30am–4pm daily. ⬤ 25 Dec. 🅿 ram show. ♿ 🍴

THE AUSTRALIAN WOOLSHED offers an instant insight into Australian country life. Ram shows are held daily, with trained rams of various breeds going through their paces, along with commentary explaining the way different breeds are used in Australian farming. There are also performances of didgeridoo music. In a recreated outback, working sheep dogs gather sheep for demonstrations of shearing and, later, wool-spinning.

Koalas, kangaroos and other native animals roam free in the grounds. Visitors have the opportunity to hand-feed kangaroos and wallabies, or have a digital picture taken while holding a koala.

The Woolshed Restaurant is a good place to stop for lunch and, on selected dates, visitors can participate in bush dinner dances.

Traditional sheep shearing at the Australian Woolshed

BRISBANE PRACTICAL INFORMATION

B RISBANE IS A SAFE, clean and welcoming city. Despite its relatively new status as a tourist destination, most of the city's facilities are well established and services are of a high standard. Top central hotels can be expensive, but there is plenty of good-quality medium and budget accommodation in and around the city *(see pp472–4)*. There are restaurants and cafés in all price ranges

Myer Centre precinct sign

which take advantage of the city's access to tropical produce and seafood *(see pp505–506)*. Public transport is comprehensive and cheap, and a Rover ticket allows unlimited, value-for-money travel on all modes of transport. Taxis are plentiful and operate on metered fares. Tourist information centres, identifiable by the international "I" symbol, are situated throughout the city.

SHOPPING

T HE HEART OF Brisbane's Central Business District shopping area is the pedestrianized Queen Street Mall *(see pp212–13)*. The mall now showcases two state-of-the-art entertainment venues, four open-air restaurants, much public art and seasonally rotated landscape design. The large **Myer Centre** is at its core and contains department stores and more than 200 individual shops. There is also a dining court and food hall offering a variety of international fast food. Both are crowded with office workers at lunchtime. On the fifth floor there is an indoor roller coaster, popular with both children and adults.

Restored interior of the 19th-century Brisbane Arcade

Gaming wheel at the Conrad International Treasury Casino

Other shopping arcades, all in or near the Queen Street Mall, are **Broadway on the Mall**, Brisbane Arcade and Rose Arcade. The Wintergarden has fashion and jewellery. Inner suburbs, such as Paddington and Milton, have a range of interesting arts and crafts galleries and bookshops.

Australian opals are tax free to international visitors and are available from a few specialist stores such as **Quilpie Opals**. Aboriginal art and artifacts can be found in **Aboriginal Creations**. Eagle Street is a popular weekend market site and is the best place to go for good-value local arts and crafts.

Brisbane's shopping hours are 9am to 5:30pm, Monday to Thursday, and until 9pm on Friday. Most shops are open 9am to 5pm on Saturday and 10:30am to 4pm on Sunday.

ENTERTAINMENT

T HE SOUTH BANK precinct is the main entertainment centre in the city: the **Queensland Performing Arts Centre** produces both concerts and drama *(see p221)*. South Bank Parklands has a range of street performers, bands, shows and an outdoor cinema. Jazz can be enjoyed at various clubs, and discos are a feature in the Riverside area or Caxton Street in Petrie Terrace. For those who want to try their hand at blackjack and other gambling pursuits, the **Conrad Brisbane Treasury** Casino is at the Brisbane River end of Queen Street Mall.

Details of all the current entertainment events in the city can be found in free listings magazines such as *This Week in Brisbane, Hello Brisbane* and *Time Off*.

CityCat ferry cruising the Brisbane River

Tickets for the majority of Brisbane's events can be obtained from **Ticketek**.

GETTING AROUND

BRISBANE IS a compact city which is easy to explore on foot. Maps are available from most hotels and information centres. There are excellent self-guided heritage trails and riverside pathways on both sides of the river. A mangrove walkway meanders along the Botanic Gardens riverbank (*see p217*).

Public transport in Brisbane includes buses, commuter trains and ferries. CityCat ferries service some of the most popular locations including South Bank, Eagle Street, Riverside, Dockside, New Farm and Kangaroo

CityCat ferry sign

City Sights logo

Point. The two main points of departure are in Eagle Street, but there are various stopping-off points along the river. Tour boats supply a commentary and lunch or dinner.

The most economical way to travel on all Brisbane's public transport if you are making several journeys is with a Rover ticket, available from the **Administration Centre** or at most newsagents. This can offer unlimited travel for a day, or at off-peak times.

Another flexible and economical way to see the city is on a **City Sights Bus Tour**, which runs a regular shuttle service around all Brisbane's main sights and attractions. There is a standard fare and you can get on and off whenever you choose. To get back on a Bus, simply hail one from one of the City Sights' clearly signposted stops and show your ticket.

Brisbane's Citybus service travels around the centre of the city. The Cityxpress buses service the suburbs. All buses stop at the Queen Street Bus Station near the Myer Centre.

Commercially operated tour companies also offer coach tours of the city's highlights, as well as to the surrounding areas, including Stradbroke Island, Moreton Bay and Surfers Paradise (*see pp230–31*) and the mountainous hinterland (*see pp232–3*).

City Sights Bus taking in the sights of central Brisbane

(see p217). (see pp230–31) (see pp232–3).

DIRECTORY

SHOPPING

Aboriginal Creations
199 Elizabeth St.
((07) 3224 5730.

Broadway on the Mall
Queen Street Mall.
((07) 3229 5233.

Myer Centre
Queen Street Mall.
((07) 3223 6900.

Quilpie Opals
68 Queen Street.
((07) 3221 7369.

ENTERTAINMENT

Queensland Performing Arts Centre
Cnr Grey & Melbourne sts, South Bank. ((1 800) 777 699.

Conrad Brisbane Treasury
21 Queen St. ((07) 3306 8888.

Ticketek
((07) 3223 0444.

PUBLIC TRANSPORT

Administration Centre
69 Ann Street.
((07) 3403 8888. (24 hrs)

City Sights Bus Tour
Myer Bus Tunnel (under Myer Centre). ((07) 3407 2330.

Transinfo
(for public transport information)
(13 12 30.

TOURIST INFORMATION CENTRES

Brisbane Marketing
((07) 3006 6200.

Queen Street Mall
((07) 3006 6290.

All types of public transport run until midnight, and taxis are plentiful in the centre of the city at night. Driving is also not generally a problem, although parking spaces can be hard to find. There are numerous, well-maintained bike tracks around the city for keen cyclists.

SOUTH OF TOWNSVILLE

SOUTHERN QUEENSLAND *is renowned for two distinct features: its fine coastal surfing beaches and, inland, some of the richest farming land in Australia. The area is the centre of the country's beef and sugar industries, and the Burdekin River Delta supports a fertile "salad basin" yielding tomatoes, beans and other small crops. Ports such as Mackay and Gladstone service some rich inland mines.*

Recognizing the land's potential, pastoralists followed hard on the heels of the explorers who opened up this region in the 1840s. Sugar production had begun by 1869 in the Bundaberg area and by the 1880s it was a flourishing industry, leading to a shameful period in the country's history. As Europeans were considered inherently unsuited to work in the tropics, growers seized on South Sea Islanders for cheap labour. Called Kanakas, the labourers were paid a pittance, housed in substandard accommodation and given the most physically demanding jobs. Some Kanakas were kidnapped from their homeland (a practice called "blackbirding"), but this was outlawed in 1868 and government inspectors were placed on all Kanakas ships to check that their emigration was voluntary. It was not until Federation in 1901 that the use of island labour stopped but by then some 60,000 Kanakas had been brought to Queensland.

In tandem with this agricultural boom, southern Queensland thrived in the latter half of the 19th century when gold was found in the region. Towns such as Charters Towers and Ravenswood have preserved much of their 19th-century architecture as reminders of the glory days of the gold rush. Although much of the gold has been extracted, the region is still rich in coal and has the world's largest sapphire fields. Amid this mineral landscape, there are also some beautiful national parks.

Today, the area is perhaps best known for its coastal features. Surfers from all over the world flock to the aptly named resort of Surfers Paradise, and the white sand beaches of the Gold Coast are crowded throughout the summer months. The region is also the gateway to the southern tip of the Great Barrier Reef and visitors come to Magnetic Island to snorkel and admire the coral.

Beach fishing as dawn breaks in Surfers Paradise

◁ Sandstone Bluff near the entrance of Violet Gorge in the ruggedly beautiful Carnarvon National Park

Exploring South of Townsville

WITH EASY ACCESS from Brisbane *(see pp210–25)*, the southern coastline of Queensland is one of the most popular holiday locations in Australia, with its sunny climate, sandy beaches and good surf. Behind the fertile coastal plains are many of the 1850s gold rush "boom towns", now notable for the insight they provide into that unique era. The Capricorn Hinterland, inland from Rockhampton, has the fascinating gem fields around Emerald and the dramatic sandstone escarpments of the Carnarvon and Blackdown Tableland national parks. To the north of the region is the busy city of Townsville, a major gateway to the many islands of the Great Barrier Reef *(see pp204–209)*.

Well-preserved 19th-century Railway Hotel in Ravenswood

SIGHTS AT A GLANCE

Ayr **13**
Blackdown Tableland
   National Park **10**
*Carnarvon National
   Park p237* **11**
Charters Towers **15**
Darling Downs **2**
Eungella National Park **12**
Fraser Island p234 **6**
Gladstone **8**
Hervey Bay **5**
Lamington National Park **1**
Maryborough **4**
Mon Repos Environmental
   Park **7**
Ravenswood **14**
Rockhampton **9**
Sunshine Coast Hinterland **3**
Townsville and Magnetic
   Island **16**

SEE ALSO

- *Where to Stay* pp474–5
- *Where to Eat* p507

KEY

≡≡≡ Highway

▬▬ Major road

▬▬ Scenic route

〜 River

⁂ Viewpoint

0 kilometres   100

0 miles   100

(Map labels:) TOWNSVILLE AND MAGNETIC ISLAND • AYR • RAVENSWOOD • CHARTERS TOWERS • COLLINSVILLE • EUNGELLA NATIONAL PARK • Mount Isa • Cape River • Burdekin River • CLERMONT • EMERALD • Longreach • CARNARVON NATIONAL PARK

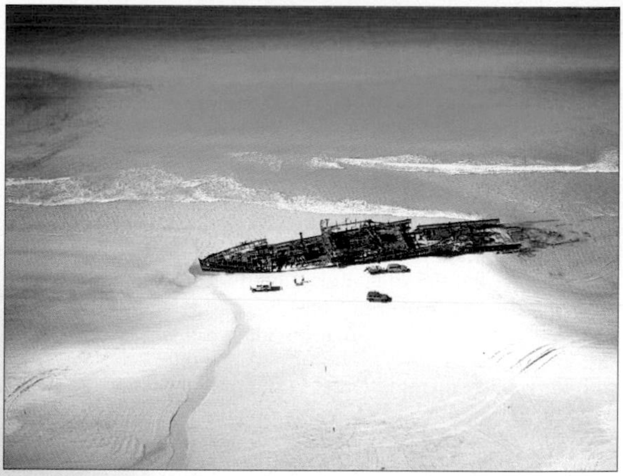

Shipwreck of the *Maheno*, lying on the coast of Fraser Island

GETTING AROUND

The major cities of Townsville, Rockhampton and Gladstone are accessible by air, as are some of the smaller regional centres. There are frequent coach services along the Bruce Hwy and the main inland roads. The Brisbane-Cairns railway runs alongside the Bruce Hwy with stops at all the major centres (the trip from Brisbane to Townsville takes about 25 hours). However, the best way to see the area is by car. Some companies may insist on 4WD in remote areas.

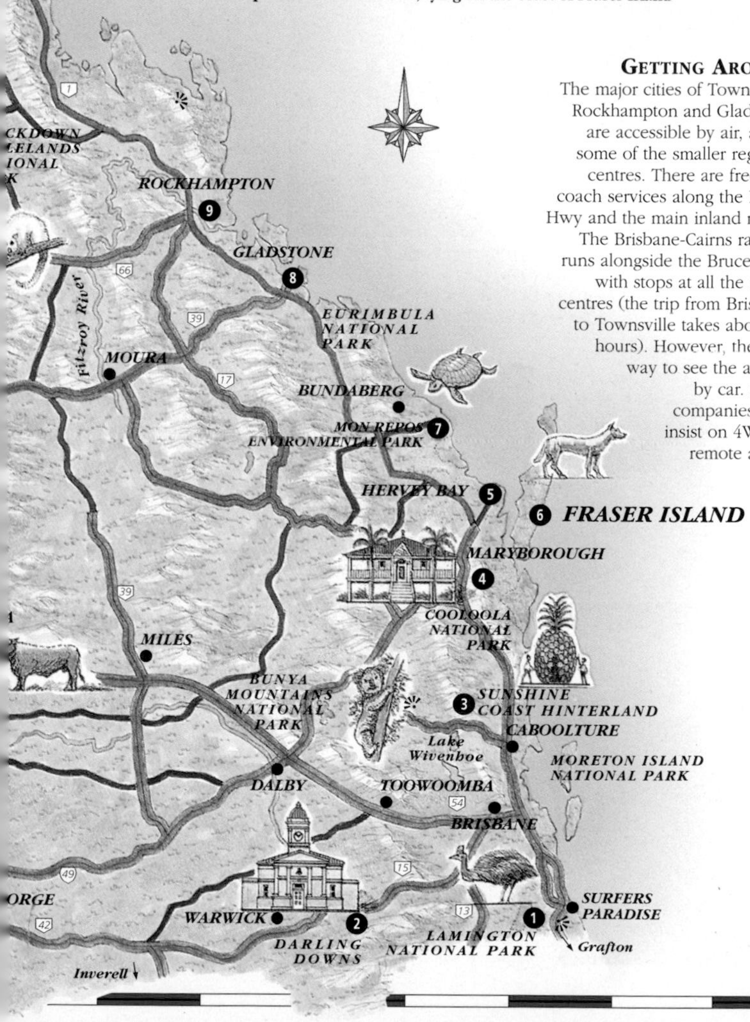
MACKAY
Coral Sea
ROCKHAMPTON
9
GLADSTONE
8
EURIMBULA NATIONAL PARK
Fitzroy River
MOURA
BUNDABERG
MON REPOS ENVIRONMENTAL PARK
7
HERVEY BAY
5
6 FRASER ISLAND
MARYBOROUGH
4
COOLOOLA NATIONAL PARK
MILES
BUNYA MOUNTAINS NATIONAL PARK
3 SUNSHINE COAST HINTERLAND
CABOOLTURE
Lake Wivenhoe
MORETON ISLAND NATIONAL PARK
DALBY
TOOWOOMBA
BRISBANE
SURFERS PARADISE
WARWICK
2
DARLING DOWNS
1
LAMINGTON NATIONAL PARK
Grafton
Inverell
ORGE
1
66
39
17
54
15
13
49
42

Southern Queensland Coastline

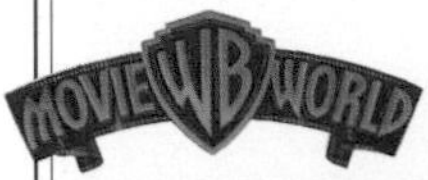

Movie World entrance sign on the Gold Coast

An hour's drive either north or south of Brisbane, the southern Queensland coast is Australia's most popular beach playground. The famous Gold Coast extends 75 km (45 miles) south of Brisbane and is a flashy strip of holiday apartments, luxury hotels, shopping malls, nightclubs, a casino and, above all, 42 km (25 miles) of golden sandy beaches. To the north, the Sunshine Coast is more restrained and elegant. Inland, the Great Dividing Range provides a cool alternative to the hot coastal climate, with flourishing arts and crafts communities, superb bushwalking and wonderful panoramas.

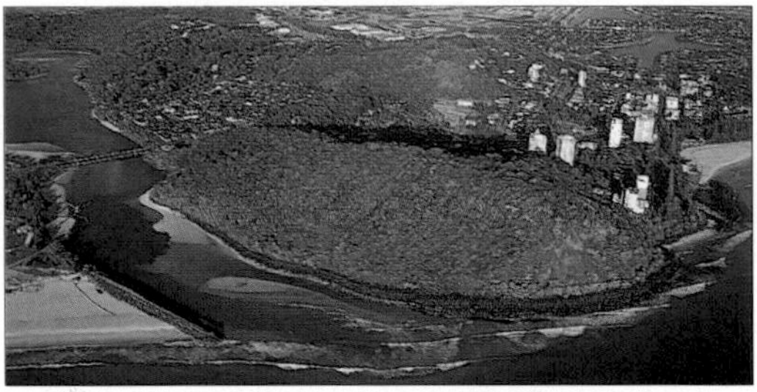

Burleigh Heads National Park *is a tiny park which preserves the dense eucalypt forests that once covered the entire region. The nutritious volcanic soil stemming from Mount Warning, 30 km (20 miles) southwest of the park, allows the rainforest to thrive.*

Coomera *is the site of three theme parks on the Gold Coast. Sea World has dolphin, sea lion and penguin displays; Warner Bros. Movie World features stunt shows and tours of replica film sets; Dreamworld is a family fairground park with wildlife attractions that include Bengal tigers.*

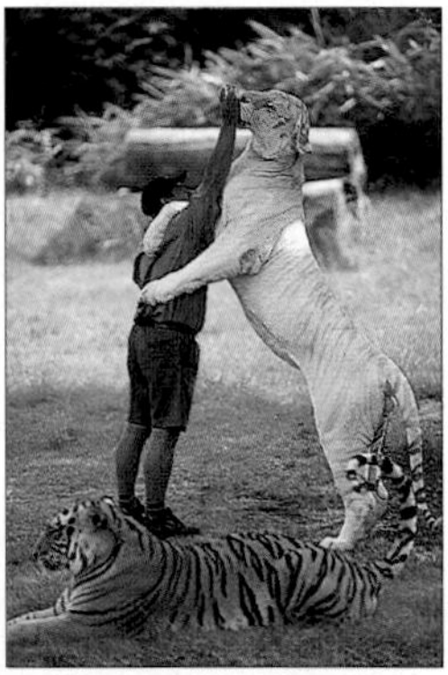

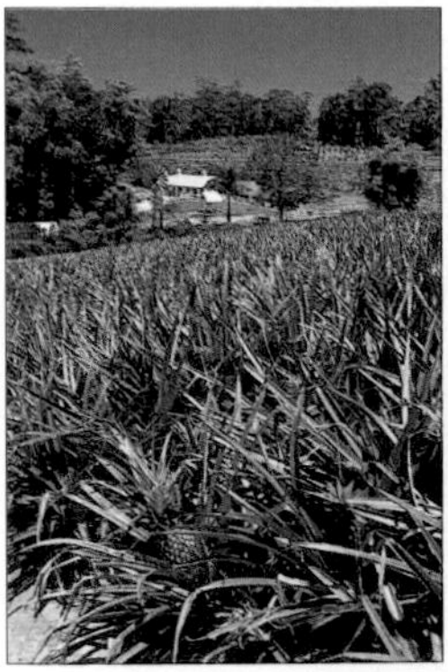

The Sunshine Plantation *is a vast pineapple plantation. Pineapples are one of Queensland's major crops. Trips around the plantation are available on a cane train. The entrance is marked by a giant fibreglass model of a pineapple.*

Tewantin ②

🛟

This well-known town is in the heart of the Sunshine Coast area, with spectacular sunsets and beautiful beaches. It is also the ferry access point to Cooloola National Park.

MARYBOROUGH

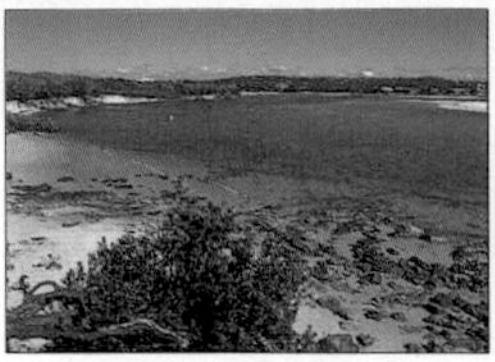

Maroochydore Beach ⑤

🏄 🏊 🤿 🛟 ♿ 🚻

An ocean beach and the Maroochy river front make the main commercial centre of the Sunshine Coast a popular holiday destination, with good hotels and restaurants.

Mooloolaba Wharf ⑥

🏄 🏊 🤿 🛟 ♿

The wharf at Mooloolaba is a popular tourist development. Underwater World, said to be the largest oceanarium in the southern hemisphere, contains crocodiles and barramundi.

Bulcock Beach, Caloundra ⑦

🏊 🤿 🛟 ♿ 🚻

The central location of sandy Bulcock Beach means it is often crowded with tourists and families. Nearby Golden Beach and Shelly Beach are also beautiful but quieter.

Moreton Bay ⑧

🏊 🤿 🛟 ♿ 🚻

This is the access point to some 370 offshore islands, the most popular being Moreton, Bribie and South Stradbroke. Fishing, bird-watching and boating are the main activities.

Coolangatta ⑫

🏄 🏊 🤿 🛟 ♿ 🚻

On the Queensland-New South Wales border, Coolangatta has some of the best surfing waters in the area but relatively uncrowded beaches. Surfing tuition and boards for hire are available here.

★ Cooloola National Park ①

Attractive lakes and sclerophyll woodland abound in this area. A 60-km (35-mile) 4WD to Rainbow Beach passes the Teewah Coloured Sands, produced by natural chemicals.

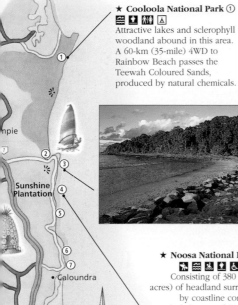

LOCATOR MAP

★ Noosa Heads, Main Beach ③

Extraordinary natural beauty, a north-facing beach and an extensive river system have combined to make Noosa a fashionable holiday resort.

★ Noosa National Park ④

Consisting of 380 ha (940 acres) of headland surrounded by coastline containing secluded coves, this national park is inhabited with koalas.

★ Sanctuary Cove ⑨

Situated on Hope Island, the glamorous resort of Sanctuary Cove is aimed particularly at golfers and includes two luxury golf courses.

★ South Stradbroke Island Beach ⑩

This unspoiled sand island offers peaceful but relatively basic accommodation. Catching crabs and bird-watching are popular activities.

```
0 kilometres      20

0 miles              20
```

★ Surfers Paradise Beach ⑪

This is the focal point of the Gold Coast with block after block of high-rise developments and a range of entertainment options for visitors.

Sunshine Plantation

• Gympie

• Caloundra

• Caboolture

• Redcliffe

BRISBANE

Moreton Island

North Stradbroke Island

Coomera

Burleigh Heads National Park •

BYRON BAY ↓

KEY

▬	Highway
▬	Major road
—	Minor road
〜	River
☀	Viewpoint

Lamington National Park ❶

🚌 Canungra. ℹ️ Park Ranger Office (07) 5544 0634. 🕐 Mon–Fri.

Lamington national park, set within the McPherson Mountain Range, is one of Queensland's most popular parks. Declared in 1915, it contains 200 sq km (80 sq miles) of thick wooded country, with more than 160 km (100 miles) of walking tracks through subtropical rain-forests of hoop pine and red cedars. The latter were fortunate to be saved from 1890s timber merchants because of their remote location. The highest ridges in the park reach more than 900 m (3,000 ft) and are lined with Antarctic beeches – the most northerly in Australia. Some 150 species of birds, such as the Albert lyrebird, make bird-watching a popular pastime.

Nearby Macrozamia National Park has macrozamia palms (cycads) – one of the oldest forms of vegetation still growing in the world.

Darling Downs ❷

🚌 Toowoomba. 🚆 Toowoomba. ℹ️ Toowoomba (07) 4639 3797.

Only 90 minutes' drive from Brisbane, stretching west of the Great Dividing Range, is the fertile country of the Darling Downs. The first area to be settled after Brisbane, the region encompasses some of the most productive agricultural land in Australia, as well as one of the most historic areas in Queensland.

Toowoomba is the main centre of the Downs and is also one of Queensland's biggest cities. Early settlers transformed this one-time swamp into the present "Garden City", famous for its jacarandas and Carnival of Flowers (see p37).

About 45 km (28 miles) northwest of Toowoomba along the Warrego Hwy is the

Warwick's well-known cheese

Jondaryan Woolshed. Built in 1849 to handle 200,000 sheep in one season, it has now been restored as a working memorial to the early pioneers of the district.

South of Toowoomba is Warwick, the oldest town in Queensland after Brisbane and known for its cheese, its roses and its 19th-century sandstone buildings. It also claims one of the oldest rodeos in Australia, dating from 1857 when £50 (a year's pay) was wagered on the outcome of the riding contest. Today the rodeo follows the Rose and Rodeo Festival in October and offers prize money of more than A$70,000 (see p37).

About 60 km (40 miles) south of Warwick and 915 m (3,000 ft) above sea level, Stanthorpe actively celebrates its freezing winter temperatures

with the Brass Monkey Festival in July (see p39). The town is at the heart of the Granite Belt, one of Queensland's few wine regions (see p33).

Queen Mary Falls National Park is a 78-ha (193-acre) rainforest park with picnic areas and a 40-m (130-ft) waterfall.

🏛 **Jondaryan Woolshed**
Evanslea Rd, Jondaryan. 📞 (07) 4692 2229. 🕐 9am–4pm daily. ⬤ Good Fri, 25 Dec. 🅿️ ♿

Sunshine Coast Hinterland ❸

🚌 Nambour. 🚌 Maroochydore. ℹ️ Cnr 6th Ave & Melrose Pde, Maroochydore (07) 5479 1566.

To the west of the Sunshine Coast is the Blackall Mountain Range. Lined with small, pretty villages, the area has become a centre for artists and artisans, with numerous guesthouses and some fine

Waterfall in Queen Mary Falls National Park, Darling Downs

The Glasshouse Mountains, a Queensland landmark on the hinterland of the Sunshine Coast

restaurants. The most attractive centres are Montville and Maleny. The drive from Maleny to Mapleton is one of the most scenic in the region, with views across to Moreton Island, encompassing pineapple and sugar cane fields.

Consisting of ten volcanic cones, the Glasshouse Mountains were formed 20 million years ago. They were named by Captain Cook in 1770 because they reminded him of the glass furnaces in his native Yorkshire.

Maryborough ❹

🏠 25,000. ✈ 🚉 🚌 🛈 BP South Tourist Complex, Bruce Hwy (07) 4121 4111.

SITUATED ON the banks of the Mary River, Maryborough has a strong link with Australia's early history. Founded in 1843, the town provided housing for Kanakas' labour (see p227) and was the only port apart from Sydney where free settlers could enter. This resulted in a thriving town – the buildings reflecting the wealth of its citizens.

Many of these buildings survive, earning Maryborough the title of "Heritage City". A great many of the town's private residences also date from the 19th century, ranging from simple workers' cottages to beautiful old "Queenslanders". These houses are distinctive to the state, set high off the ground to catch the cool air currents and with graceful verandas on all sides.

Hervey Bay ❺

🏠 44,000. ✈ 🚌 🚢 🛈 401 The Esplanade, Scarness, Hervey Bay (07) 4124 4050.

AS RECENTLY AS the 1970s Hervey Bay was simply a string of five fishing villages. However, the safe beaches and mild climate have quickly turned it into a metropolis of 30,000 people and one of the fastest growing holiday centres in Australia.

Hervey Bay is also one of the best places for whale-watching. Humpback whales migrate more than 11,000 km (7,000 miles) every year from the Antarctic to northern Australian waters to mate and calve. On their return, between August and October, they rest at Hervey Bay to give the calves time to develop a protective layer of blubber before they begin their final run to

Bundaberg rum

Antarctica. Since whaling was stopped in the 1960s, numbers have quadrupled from 300 to approximately 1,200.

ENVIRONS: The sugar city of central Queensland, Bundaberg is 62 km (38 miles) north of Hervey Bay. It is the home of Bundaberg ("Bundy") rum, the biggest selling spirit label in Australia.

Bundaberg is an attractive town with many 19th-century buildings. The city's favourite son, Bert Hinkler (1892–1933), was the first man to fly solo from England to Australia in 1928. His original "Ibis" aircraft is displayed in the **Bundaberg and District Historical Museum**.

🏛 Bundaberg and District Historical Museum
Young St, Botanic Gardens. 📞 (07) 4152 0101. ◯ 10am–4pm daily. ⬤ Good Fri, 25 Apr, 25 Dec. ♿ 📷

Classic Queenslander-style house in Maryborough

Fraser Island 6

SITUATED OFF THE Queensland coast near Maryborough *(see p233)*, Fraser Island World Heritage area is the largest sand island in the world. Measuring 123 km (76 miles) in length and 25 km (16 miles) across, the island is a mix of hills and valleys, rainforest and clear lakes. Ferries to the island operate from Urangan, River Heads and Inskip Point. There is a range of resorts and numerous camp sites on the island. Vehicle and camping permits are required.

VISITORS' CHECKLIST

🚶 Fraser Coast–South Burnett Regional Tourism, (07) 4122 3444
🚢 from Urangan, River Heads & Inskip Point. ♿ 🏠 🚻 🍴 🅿

Sandy Cape has treacherous waters; its lighthouse has saved many ships from potential danger.

Lake Allom, fringed by melaleuca trees and sedges, is surrounded by a towering rainforest. Freshwater turtles can be seen in the lake.

Indian Head was named by Captain James Cook *(see pp46–7)* as a result of "a number of the natives" he saw assembled here on arrival.

HERVEY BAY

Watumba

The Cathedrals
These striking, deep red sand formations stretch 18km (11 miles) along the beach.

Lake McKenzie
The beautiful clear waters here are surrounded by white sands and blackbutt trees.

Central Station was once the hub of the island's logging industry and is a starting point for beautiful walks.

PACIFIC OCEAN

Kingfisher Bay

Lake Birabeen   Eurong

Lake Boomanjin

Seventy-Five Mile Beach is notable as the site of the *Maheno*, the only visible shipwreck on the island.

Eli Creek is large and spectacular, pouring gallons of water each hour into the surf.

```
0 km       5
0 miles    5
```

KEY

━━━ 4WD road
- - - Walking trail
🚶 Tourist information
🏞 Picnic area
🅰 Camp site
🚢 Ferrypoint
☀ Viewpoint

Hook Point

JAMES AND ELIZABETH FRASER

In 1836, survivors from the shipwreck *Stirling Castle*, including Captain James Fraser and his wife Elizabeth, landed on Fraser Island and were captured by Aborigines. Captain Fraser perished, but Elizabeth was rescued and returned to England. She was eventually committed to an insane asylum. The story inspired Patrick White's novel *A Fringe of Leaves (see p31)*.

Survivor Elizabeth Fraser

Loggerhead turtle laying eggs on Mon Repos Beach

Mon Repos Conservation Park 7

🚗 from Bundaberg. 📞 (07) 4159 1652. ⏰ daily. 📷 ♿ 📹 obligatory Nov–Mar.

Mon repos beach, 15 km (9 miles) from Bundaberg (see p233), is one of the most significant and accessible turtle rookeries on the Australian mainland. Egglaying of loggerhead and other turtles takes place from November to February. By January, the first young turtles begin to hatch and make their way down the sandy beach to the ocean.

There is an information centre within the environmental park which has videos and other information about these fascinating reptiles. Supervised public viewing ensures that the turtles are not unduly disturbed by curious tourists.

Just behind Mon Repos Beach is an old stone wall built by Kanakas and now preserved as a memorial to these South Sea Island inhabitants (see p227).

Gladstone 8

🏘 28,000. ✈ 🚌 🚕 🚌
ℹ Gladstone Marina, Bryan Jordan Drive (07) 4972 9922.

Gladstone is a town dominated by industry. The harbour struggles valiantly to retain its natural beauty, surrounded as it is by huge grain silos, gigantic fuel tanks and mountains of coal. The world's largest alumina refinery is located here, processing bauxite mined in Weipa on the west coast of Cape York Peninsula. Five per cent of the nation's wealth and 20 per cent of Queensland's wealth is generated by Gladstone's industries. Gladstone's port, handling more than 35 million tonnes of cargo a year, is one of the busiest in Australia.

There are, however, more attractive sights in and around the town. The town's main street has an eclectic variety of buildings, including the Grand Hotel, rebuilt to its 1897 form after fire destroyed the original in 1993. Gladstone's Botanic Gardens were first opened in 1988 as a bicentennial project and consist entirely of native Australian plants. South of Gladstone are the tiny coastal villages of Agnes Waters and the quaintly named "1770" in honour of Captain Cook's brief landing here during his journey up the coast (see p46). About 20 km (12 miles) out of town lies the popular holiday location of Boyne Island.

Gladstone is also the access point for Heron Island, considered by many to be one of the most desirable of all the Great Barrier Reef islands, with its wonderful coral and diving opportunities. Other islands in the southern half of the reef can also be accessed from Gladstone by boat or helicopter (see pp208–9).

Pretty coastal village of Agnes Waters, near Gladstone

Rockhampton 9

66,000. Customs House, 208 Quay St (07) 4922 5339.

ROCKHAMPTON IS situated 40 km (25 miles) inland, on the banks of the Fitzroy River. Often referred to as the "beef capital" of Australia, the town is also the administrative and commercial heart of central Queensland. A spire marks the fact that, geographically, the Tropic of Capricorn runs through the town.

Rockhampton was founded in 1854 and contains many restored 19th-century buildings. Quay Street flanks the tree-lined river and has been classified in its entirety by the National Trust. Particularly outstanding is the sandstone Customs House, with its semi-circular portico. The beautiful **Botanic Gardens** were established in 1869, and have a fine collection of tropical plants. There is also on-site accommodation.

Built on an ancient tribal meeting ground, the **Aboriginal Dreamtime Cultural Centre** is owned and operated by local Aborigines. Imaginative displays give an insight into their life and culture.

Botanic Gardens
Spencer St. *(07) 4922 1654.*
daily.

Aboriginal Dreamtime Cultural Centre
Bruce Hwy. *(07) 4936 1655.*
10am–3:30pm Mon–Fri.
public hols.

Sandstone cliff looking out over Blackdown Tableland National Park

ENVIRONS: The heritage township of Mount Morgan is 38 km (25 miles) southwest of Rockhampton. A 2 sq km (0.5 sq mile) open-cut mine of first gold, then copper, operated here for 100 years and was one of the most important features of Queensland's economy until the minerals ran out in 1981.

Plaque at base of the Tropic of Capricorn spire

Some 25 km (15 miles) north of Rockhampton is Mount Etna National Park, containing spectacular limestone caves, discovered in the 1880s. These are open to the public via Olsen's Capricorn Caverns and Camoo Caves. A major feature of the caves is "cave coral" – stone-encrusted tree roots that have forced their way through the rock. The endangered ghost bat, Australia's only carnivorous bat, nests in these caves.

The stunning sandy beaches of Yeppoon and Emu Park are only 40 km (25 miles) northeast of the city. Rockhampton is also the access point for Great Keppel Island *(see pp208–9)*.

Blackdown Tableland National Park 10

Off Capricorn Hwy, via Dingo. **Park Ranger** *(07) 4986 1964.*

BETWEEN Rockhampton and Emerald, along a 20-km (12-mile) untarmacked detour off the Capricorn Highway, is Blackdown Tableland National Park. A dramatic sandstone plateau which rises 600 m (2,000 ft) above the flat surrounding countryside, the Tableland offers spectacular views, escarpments, open forest and tumbling waterfalls. Wildlife includes gliders, brushtail possums, rock wallabies and the occasional dingo.

Emerald is a coal mining centre and the hub of the central highland region, 75 km (45 miles) west of the park; the town provides a railhead for the surrounding agricultural areas. Its ornate 1890 railway station is one of the few survivors of a series of fires between 1936 and 1969 that destroyed much of the town's heritage. Near Lake Maraboon is a headstone marking the mass grave of 19 European settlers killed in 1861 by local Aborigines. At the junction of the Nagoa and Comet rivers is a tree carved with the initials of explorer Ludwig Leichhardt during his 1844 expedition to Port Essington *(see p241)*.

More in tune with its name, Emerald is also the access point for the largest sapphire fields in the world. The lifestyle of the gem diggers is fascinating: many of them live in tin shacks and extract gems by hand, using "rigs" built from old car parts, so that the area looks like a vast junk yard.

Façade of Customs House on Quay Street, Rockhampton

Carnarvon National Park ⓫

THE MAIN ACCESS to Carnarvon National Park lies 250 km (155 miles) south of Emerald, while the park itself covers some 298,000 ha (730,000 acres). There are several sections of the park, but the stunning Carnarvon Gorge is the most accessible area to visitors. A 32-km (20-mile) canyon carved by the waters of Carnarvon Creek, the gorge consists of white cliffs, crags and pillars of stone harbouring plants and animals which have survived through centuries of evolution. The area is also rich in Aboriginal culture, and three art sites are open to the public. Comfortable cabin accommodation is available or there are various camp sites, provided you have an advance booking and a camping permit (see p465).

Upper Aljon Falls are in a cavern and only see the sun for a few moments each day.

The Amphitheatre's sheer walls were carved into the rock by water.

Carnarvon Gorge
The gorge is filled with lush eucalypt forests, sandstone cliffs and streams.

Kooramilya Creek

• Big Bend

Parrabooya

Kongaboola Creek

Kamooloo Creek

Amooloongie Creek

CASUARINA GROVE

Wagoovon Creek

Boolimba Bluff has spectacular sunrise views of the park.

HELLHOLE GORGE

Koolaroo Creek

Carnarvon Creek

VIOLET GORGE

ℹ️ 🅰

WARRUMBAH BLUFF

Warrumbah Creek

Mickey Creek

Cathedral Cave is a massive rock shelter, more than 30 m (100 ft) high. It is one of the major Aboriginal art sites in the park.

| 0 kilometres | 1 |
| 0 miles | 1 |

The Art Gallery
This important Aboriginal art site features stencil art of boomerangs, stone tomahawks and shell pendants. The stencils were painted with ochre and water.

Moss Garden
This lush greenery of ferns, creepers, hornworts and liverworts is sustained by seepage from the spring waters down the rock walls.

Irrigating sugar cane fields in Mackay, near Eungella National Park

Eungella National Park ⑫

🚉 Mackay. 🚌 Mackay. ℹ️ Mackay (07) 4952 2677. **Park Ranger** ℂ (07) 4958 4552.

EUNGELLA NATIONAL PARK is the main wilderness area on the central Queensland coast and encompasses some 50,000 ha (125,000 acres) of the rugged Clarke Ranges. Volcanic rock covered with rainforest and subtropical flora is cut by steep gorges, crystal clear pools and impressive waterfalls tumbling down the mountainside.

Finch Hatton Gorge is the main destination for tourists, where indigenous wildlife includes gliders, ring-tailed possums, bandicoots and pademelons (a kind of wallaby). Broken River is one of the few places in Australia where platypuses can often be spotted at dusk.

The main access point for Eungella is the prosperous sugar town of **Mackay**. Somewhat low-key from a tourist point of view, Mackay boasts a balmy climate by way of the surrounding mountains trapping the warm coastal air even in winter. Thirty beautiful white sand beaches are lined with casuarinas. All around the town

sugar cane can be seen blowing in the wind in the many sugar cane fields.

The town centre of Mackay also has a number of historic buildings worth visiting, including the Commonwealth Bank and Customs House, both classified by the National Trust. The second-largest coal-loader in the world is at Hay Point, where trains more than 2 km (1 mile) long haul coal from the western mines for shipping overseas.

Ayr ⑬

🏛️ 8,600. 🚉 🚌 ℹ️ Plantation Park, Bruce Hwy (07) 4783 5988.

THE BUSY TOWN of Ayr, at the heart of the Burdekin River Delta, is the major sugar cane-growing area in Australia.

Within the town itself is the modern Burdekin Cultural Complex, which includes a 530-seat theatre, a library and an art gallery. Among its art collection are the renowned "Living Lagoon" sculptures crafted by the contemporary Australian sculptor Stephen Walker. The Ayr Nature Display consists of an impressive rock wall made from 2,600 pieces of North Queensland rock, intricate pictures made from preserved insects and a display of Australian

"Living Lagoon" sculpture, Burdekin Complex, Ayr

reptiles, shells, fossils and Aboriginal artifacts. The Mount Kelly Orchid Gardens feature a modern laboratory where visitors can watch orchids being cloned and propagated.

ENVIRONS: Approximately 55 km (35 miles) north of Ayr is Alligator Creek, the access point for Bowling Green Bay National Park. Here geckos and chirping cicadas live alongside each other in this lush landscape. Within the park are idyllic, isolated rock pools, perfect for swimming, and plunging waterfalls.

Victorian stove in Ravenswood's Courthouse Museum

Ravenswood ⑭

🏛️ 300. ℹ️ Courthouse Museum, McCrossin St (07) 4770 2047.

RAVENSWOOD's heyday was during the gold rush of the 1860s *(see pp50–51)*. The town then disintegrated into a ghost town with only echoes of its former glory, but it has slowly flickered back to life following the opening of a new mine in 1994. A tour of the new mine is available with advance notice.

Many of the town's original 19th-century structures are still standing, although many are in a state of disrepair. Four different heritage walks take in buildings such as St Patrick's Church, a miner's cottage and the post office, which doubles up as the town's general store. The Courthouse Museum contains a visual history of the region.

Ornate 19th-century façade of City Hall in Charters Towers

Charters Towers ⑮

🏃 10,000. 🚉 🚌 🚏 ℹ 74
Mosman St (07) 4752 0314.

CHARTERS TOWERS was once the second-largest town in Queensland with a population of 30,000, following the 1871 discovery of gold in the area by a 10-year-old Aboriginal boy. Gold is still mined in the area, as well as copper, lead and zinc.

The old Charters Towers Stock Exchange is a historic gem set amid a group of other splendid 19th-century buildings in the city centre. This international centre of finance was the only such exchange in Australia outside a capital city and was built during the gold-mining days.

Charters Towers fell into decline when the gold ran out in the 1920s. Its economy now depends on the beef industry and its status as the educational centre for Queensland's Outback and Papua New Guinea – school students make up one-fifth of the population.

Townsville and Magnetic Island ⑯

🏃 140,000. ✈ 🚉 🚌 🚏 ⛴
ℹ *Flinders Mall (07) 4721 3660.*

TOWNSVILLE is the second-largest city in Queensland and a major port for the beef, sugar and mining industries. Boasting, on average, 300 sunny days a year, the beach-front is a source of local pride.

The city was founded in the 1860s by Robert Towns, who began the practice of "black-birding" – kidnapping Kanakas from their homeland and bringing them to Australia as cheap labour *(see p227)*.

Among the city's tourist attractions is **Reef HQ**, a "living coral reef aquarium" and the **Museum of Tropical Queensland**, which displays artifacts from the *Pandora*. Townsville is also an access point for the Barrier Reef and a major diving centre, largely because of the nearby wreck of the steamship *Yongala*, which sank in 1911.

Situated 8 km (5 miles) off-shore and officially a suburb of Townsville, Magnetic Island has 2,500 inhabitants and is the only reef island with a significant permanent population. It was named by Captain Cook, who erroneously believed that magnetic fields generated by the huge granite boulders he could see were causing problems with his compass. Today, almost half of the island's terrain is designated as a national park.

⚓ Reef HQ
Flinders St East. 📞 *(07) 4750 0800.*
⭘ *daily.* ⬤ *25 Dec.* 🏷 ♿
🏛 Musuem of Tropical Qld
Flinders St East. 📞 *(07) 4726 0606*
⭘ *daily.* ⬤ *25 Dec, Good Fri.* 🏷

Idyllic blue waters of Rocky Bay on Magnetic Island

NORTHERN AND OUTBACK QUEENSLAND

EUROPEAN EXPLORERS *who made epic journeys into the previously impenetrable area of Northern and Outback Queensland in the 1800s found a land rich in minerals and agricultural potential. They also discovered places of extreme natural beauty, such as the Great Barrier Reef and other unique regions now preserved as national parks.*

Northern Queensland was first visited by Europeans when Captain Cook was forced to berth his damaged ship, the *Endeavour*, on the coast. The area remained a mystery for almost another 100 years, however, until other intrepid Europeans ventured north. These expeditions were perilous and explorers were faced with harsh conditions and hostile Aboriginal tribes. In 1844, Ludwig Leichhardt and his group set out from Brisbane to Port Essington, but most of the men were wounded or killed by Aborigines. In 1848, Edmund Kennedy led an expedition from Cairns to the top of Cape York. All but two of this party perished, including Kennedy, who was speared by Aborigines.

In the late 19th century, Northern Queensland found sudden prosperity when gold was discovered in the region. The population rose and towns grew up to service the mines, but by the beginning of the 20th century much of the gold had dried up. These once thriving "cities" are now little more than one-street towns, lined with 19th-century architecture as a reminder of their glory days. Today, much of the area's wealth stems from its booming tourist trade. Luxury resorts line the stunning coastline, and tourists flock to experience the spectacular natural wonders of the Great Barrier Reef.

Queensland's Outback region has a strong link with Australia's national heritage. The Tree of Knowledge at Barcaldine marks the meeting place of the first Australian Labor Party during the great shearer's strike of 1891. The town of Winton is where "Banjo" Paterson *(see p31)* wrote Australia's national song "Waltzing Matilda" in 1895. Today, the vast Outback area is known for agriculture and for gold, silver and iron ore mining.

A rodeo rider and clown perform in Laura near Lakefield National Park in Northern Queensland

◁ **The beautiful coral cay of Green Island on the Great Barrier Reef**

Exploring Northern Queensland

THE AREA NORTH OF TOWNSVILLE leading up to Cairns is Australia's sugar-producing country, the cane fields backed by the Great Dividing Range. Northern Queensland is sparsely populated: Cairns is the only city, while Port Douglas and Mossman are small towns. The only other villages of note in the region are Daintree and Cooktown. Cape York Peninsula is one of the last untouched wildernesses in the world, covering 200,000 sq km (77,220 sq miles) – roughly the same size as Great Britain. The landscape varies according to the time of year: in the wet season (November–March) the rivers are swollen and the country is green; during the dry winter the riverbeds are waterless and the countryside is bare and arid.

Lush rainforest in Daintree National Park, near Cairns

Pier Marketplace and Marlin Marina in Cairns

1 TORRES STRAIT ISLANDS

SEISIA

JARDINE RIVER NATIONAL PARK

Dulhunty River

MAPOON

WEIPA

CAPE YORK PENINSULA

ARCHER BEND NATIONAL PARK

Edward River

Coleman River

Crosbie Creek

Gulf of Carpentaria

MITCHELL AND ALICE RIVERS NATIONAL PARK

Palmer River

DUNBAR

STAATEN RIVER NATIONAL PARK

Mount Isa

GETTING AROUND

Cairns is well served by public transport, with regular air, train and coach connections from southern Queensland and other states. It also benefits from an international airport. North of Port Douglas and the Outback region require a car unless you take an organized tour. The 326-km (202-mile) coast road from Cairns to Cooktown requires a 4WD vehicle after Cape Tribulation, although most car rental companies will insist on a 4WD all the way. During the wet season, Cape York is generally impassable.

Dunk Island seen from the Queensland coast

KEY

■	*Northern Queensland*
■	*Queensland's Outback* pp248–9

SIGHTS AT A GLANCE

Atherton Tableland **8**
Babinda and the Boulders **10**
Bellenden Ker National Park **9**
Cairns p246 **7**
Cooktown **3**
Daintree National Park **4**
Dunk Island **11**
Green Island **6**
Hinchinbrook Island **12**
Lakefield National Park **2**
Port Douglas **5**
Torres Strait Islands **1**

Queensland's Outback
See pp248–9
Burketown **14**
Longreach **16**
Mount Isa **15**
Normanton & Gulf
   Savannah **13**

SEE ALSO

• *Where to Stay* pp475–6

• *Where to Eat* pp507–509

KEY

▬	Highway
▬	Major road
▬	Minor road
▬	Scenic route
⌒	River
☲	Viewpoint

0 kilometres   100

0 miles   100

T STEWART
KEFIELD
TIONAL
RK

3 COOKTOWN

Normanby River

Coral Sea

4 DAINTREE NATIONAL PARK

5 PORT DOUGLAS

● MOSSMAN

6 GREEN ISLAND

7 CAIRNS

9

ATHERTON TABLELAND

8

ll River

BELLENDEN KER NATIONAL PARK

10 BABINDA AND THE BOULDERS

● RAVENSHOE

11 DUNK ISLAND

12 HINCHINBROOK ISLAND

● INGHAM

Burdekin River

Charters
Towers

Townsville ▸

Lakefield National Park ❶

🚗 Cooktown. 🚌 Cooktown (07) 4069 5446. **Park Office** Lakefield (07) 4069 5777. ⏰ Mon–Fri.

COVERING approximately 540,000 ha (1,300,000 acres), Lakefield National Park is the second-largest national park in Queensland. It encompasses a wide variety of landscapes, including river forests, plains and coastal flats. The centre of the park abounds with birds such as brolgas and egrets. Camping is the only accommodation option and a permit must be obtained from the park ranger. The park is largely inaccessible during the wet season between December and April when the rivers flood the plains.

The nearby town of **Laura**, at the base of the Cape York Peninsula, is a typical Australian Outback town, with a newly sealed road flanked by a pub, a general store and a few houses. During the late 19th century, Laura was the rail terminus for the Palmer River gold fields and some 20,000 people passed through here each year. Today, it is almost forgotten, but the discovery in 1959 of Aboriginal art sites of great antiquity is reviving interest in the area. One of the most notable sites is the "giant horse gallery", which contains huge horse paintings thought to record the first sightings of European explorers.

River forest in Lakefield National Park

Thursday Island, in the Torres Strait island group

Torres Strait Islands ❷

✈ from Cairns. 🚢 from Cairns. 🛈 Cairns (07) 4051 3588.

THE TORRES STRAIT divides the northern coastline of Australia from Papua New Guinea and is dotted with numerous islands. Approximately 17 of these islands are inhabited and have been governed by Queensland since 1879.

Thursday Island is the "capital" island and was once the centre of the local pearling industry. Many Japanese pearlers who lost their lives in this occupation are buried in the island's cemetery. In 1891, Green Hill Fort was built to prevent invasion by the Russians. Murray Island was the birthplace of Eddie Mabo, who, in 1992, won his claim to traditional land in the Australian High Court and changed Aboriginal–European relations (see p54).

Cooktown ❸

🏠 2,000. ✈ 🚗 🚌 🛈 Charlotte St (07) 4069 5446.

WHEN THE Endeavour was damaged by a coral reef in 1770, Captain Cook and his crew spent six weeks in this area while repairs to the ship were made (see pp46–7).

Chinese gravestone in Cooktown

Cooktown's proud boast, therefore, is that it was the site of the first white settlement in Australia.

Like most towns in the area, Cooktown originally serviced the gold fields and its present-day population of less than 2,000 is a far cry from the 30,000 inhabitants who once sustained its 100 pubs and a reputedly equal number of brothels. However, many of its historic buildings survive, including the Westpac Bank with its stone columns supporting an iron-lace veranda. The **James Cook Museum**, which houses the old anchor from the Endeavour, started life in the 1880s as a convent. In the cemetery of the town, a memorial, two crematoriums and numerous gravestones are testimony to the difficulties faced by the many Chinese who came to the gold fields in the 1850s (see p51).

Between Cooktown and Bloomfield, Black Mountain National Park is named after the geological formation of huge black granite boulders. The boulders were formed around 260 million years ago below the earth's surface and were gradually exposed as surrounding land surfaces eroded away.

🏛 **James Cook Museum**
Cnr Helen & Furneaux sts.
📞 (07) 4069 5386. ⏰ 9:30am–4pm daily. 📷 ♿

Daintree National Park 4

🚌 *from Port Douglas.* ℹ *Port Douglas (07) 4099 5599.* **Park Office** *Mossman (07) 4098 2188.* 🕐 *Mon–Fri.*

DAINTREE NATIONAL PARK, north of Port Douglas, covers more than 76,000 ha (188,000 acres). The Cape Tribulation section of the park is a place of great beauty, and one of the few places where the rainforest meets the sea. Captain Cook named Cape Tribulation in rueful acknowledgment of the difficulties he was experiencing navigating the Great Barrier Reef. Today, it is a popular spot with backpackers.

The largest section of the park lies inland from Cape Tribulation. It is a mostly inaccessible, mountainous area, but 5 km (3 miles) from Mossman lies the Mossman Gorge, known for its easy and accessible 2.7-km (1-mile) track through the rainforest.

Tropical Myall Beach in Daintree National Park

Port Douglas 5

👥 *3,500.* 🚌 🚍 ℹ *23 Macrossan St (07) 4099 5599.*

SITUATED 75 km (47 miles) from Cairns, Port Douglas was once a tiny fishing village. Today it is a tourist centre, but it has managed to preserve some of its village atmosphere.

Typical of Australian country thoroughfares, Macrossan Street is extremely wide, harking back to the days when a turning-circle was needed for bullock-led drays. Many 19th-century buildings still line the street, such as the Courthouse Hotel, and the modern shopping centres have been designed to blend with the town's original architecture.

The original port was set up during the gold rush of the 1850s, but it was superseded by Cairns as the main port of the area. A disastrous cyclone in 1911 also forced people to move elsewhere, leaving the population at less than 500. The construction of the luxurious Sheraton Mirage Resort in the early 1980s, however, heralded the beginning of a new boom, and now a range of accommodation and restaurants is on offer *(see p476)*.

Port Douglas is also the main departure point for Quicksilver, a major Great Barrier Reef tour operator *(see p209)*.

Green Island 6

🚆 *Cairns.* 🚌 *Cairns.* ⛴ *from Cairns.* ℹ *(07) 4051 3588.*

GREEN ISLAND is one of the few inhabited coral cays of the Great Barrier Reef *(see pp208–9)*. Despite its small size (a walk around the entire island will take no more than 15 minutes), it is home to an exclusive five-star resort which opened in 1994.

Green Island's proximity to the mainland tourist areas and the consequent marine traffic and pollution means that the coral is not as spectacular as around islands further afield. But its accessibility by ferry from Cairns makes the island very popular.

Also on Green Island is the Marineland Melanesia complex, where there are crocodile enclosures and an aquarium of sea creatures.

Green Island, a coral cay at the heart of the Great Barrier Reef

Cairns ❼

Boomerang from Kuranda craft market

CAIRNS IS the main centre of Northern Queensland. Despite its beachfront esplanade, it has a city atmosphere and instead of sandy beaches there are mud-flats, abundant with native bird-life. Its main attraction is as a base for exploring the Great Barrier Reef *(see pp204–9)*, the Daintree Rainforest *(p245)* and the Atherton Tableland *(p247)*. However, Cairns itself does have several places of interest to visit.

VISITORS' CHECKLIST

🏙 130,000. ✈ 6 km (3.5 miles) N of the city. 🚉 Cairns railway station, Bunda St. 🚌 Lake St Terminus, Lake St; (interstate); Trinity Wharf, Wharf St. ⚓ Marlin Marina, Pier Point Rd. 🛈 51 The Esplanade (07) 4051 3588. 🎭 The Reef Festival (Oct); Cairns Show (Jul).

🚢 Trinity Wharf

Wharf St.
Trinity Wharf is the departure point for most cruises to the Great Barrier Reef. Some 19th-century façades nearby offer a glimpse of the city's early life.

Cairns is known as the game-fishing centre of Austra-lia and, from August to Decem-ber, tourists crowd Marlin Jetty to see big-game anglers return with their catch.

Adjacent Pier Marketplace is the tourist hub of the city. Sunday markets, selling local crafts, are a Cairns institution.

🌿 Flecker Botanic Gardens

Collins Ave, Edge Hill. 📞 (07) 4044 3398. ⭘ daily. ♿
Dating from 1886, the Flecker Botanic Gardens are known for their collection of

Tropical orchid in the Flecker Botanic Gardens

more than 100 species of palm trees, but they also house many other tropical plants.

The gardens also include an area of Queensland rainforest, complete with native birdlife. The gardens' Centenary Lakes were constructed in 1976 to commemorate the city's first 100 years.

🏛 Cairns Museum

City Place, cnr Lake & Shield sts.
📞 (07) 4051 5582. ⭘ 10am–3pm Mon–Sat. ⬤ Good Fri, 25 Apr, 25 Dec. 📷
Housed in the 1907 School of Arts building, this museum is a fine example of the city's early architecture. Among the exhibits are the contents of an old Chinese joss house.

ENVIRONS: On the eastern edge of the Atherton Table-lands is the tiny village of **Kuranda**. A hippie hang-out in the 1960s, it has since developed into an arts and crafts centre with markets held here four times a week. Nearby, at Smithfield, is the Tjapukai Cultural Centre, home to the renowned Aboriginal Tjapukai Dance Theatre.

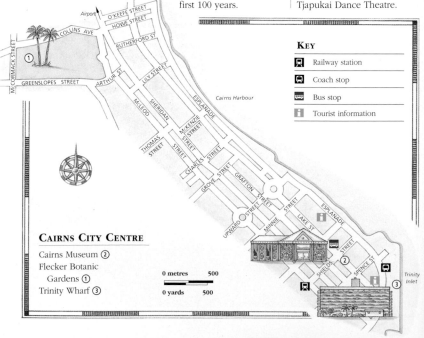

CAIRNS CITY CENTRE

Cairns Museum ②
Flecker Botanic Gardens ①
Trinity Wharf ③

0 metres   500
0 yards   500

KEY

🚉 Railway station

🚍 Coach stop

🚌 Bus stop

🛈 Tourist information

Airport O'KEEFE STREET
HOWE STREET
COLLINS AVE
RUTHERFORD ST
McCORMACK STREET
GREENSLOPES STREET
ARTHUR ST
LILY STREET
McLEOD STREET
SHERIDAN STREET
THOMAS STREET
MCKENZIE STREET
CHARLES STREET
ESPLANADE
Cairns Harbour
GROVE STREET
GRAFTON STREET
UPWARD STREET
MINNIE STREET
LAKE ST
ESPLANADE
SHIELDS ST
SPENCE ST
Trinity Inlet

Mount Hypipamee Crater's green lake, Atherton Tableland

Atherton Tableland **8**

🚗 *Atherton.* ℹ️ *Cnr Silo & Herberten rds, Atherton (07) 4091 4222.* ⏰ *9am–5pm daily.* ● *1 Jan, Good Fri, Easter Sun, 25 Dec, 26 Dec.*

RISING SHARPLY from the coastal plains of Cairns, the northern landscape levels out into the lush Atherton Tableland. At their highest point, the tablelands are 900 m (3,000 ft) above sea level. The cool temperature, heavy rainfall and rich volcanic soil make this one of the richest farming areas in Queensland. For many decades, tobacco was the main crop, but, with the worldwide decline in smoking, farmers have diversified into peanuts, macadamia nuts and avocados.

The town of **Yungaburra**, with its many historic buildings, is listed by the National Trust. Nearby is the famed "curtain fig tree". Strangler figs attach themselves to a host tree and eventually kill the original tree. In this case, the aerial roots, growing down from the tree tops, form a 15-m (50-ft) screen. Also near Yungaburra is the eerie, green crater lake at Mt Hypipamee. Stretching 60 m (200 ft) in diameter, its granite sides rule out a volcanic origin, and its formation remains a mystery.

Millaa Millaa contains the most spectacular waterfalls of the region. A circuit drive takes in the Zillie and Ellinjaa falls, while not far away are the picturesque Mungalli Falls.

Atherton is the main town of the region, named after its first European settlers, John and Kate Atherton, who established a cattle station here in the mid-19th century. The wealthy agricultural centre of Mareeba now stands on the site of this former ranch.

Bellenden Ker National Park **9**

🚗 *Innisfail.* 🚌 *Innisfail.* ℹ️ *1 Edith St, Innisfail (07) 4061 7422.*

BELLENDEN KER National Park contains the state's two highest mountains. Bartle Frere, reaching 1,611 m (5,285 ft) and Bellenden Ker, rising to 1,591 m (5,220 ft), are often swathed in cloud. Cassowaries (large flightless birds, under threat of extinction) can often be spotted on the mountains.

Much of the park is wilderness, although tracks do exist. A popular area to visit is Josephine Falls to the south of the park, about 8 km (5 miles) from the Bruce Highway.

Babinda and the Boulders **10**

🚶 *1,300.* 🚗 🚌 ℹ️ *Cnr Munro St & Bruce Hwy, Babinda (07) 4067 1008.*

THE RURAL TOWN of Babinda is a quaint survivor of old-world Queensland, lined with veranda-fronted houses and wooden pubs.

The Babinda Boulders, 7 km (4 miles) inland, are water-worn rock shapes and a popular photographic subject.

Dunk Island **11**

🚗 *Tully.* 🚌 *Mission Beach.* 🚢 *Mission Beach.* ℹ️ *Mission Beach (07) 4068 7099.*

DUNK ISLAND is one of the best known of the Barrier Reef islands *(see p209)*. The rugged terrain is covered with a variety of vegetation. Day trips from the mainland are popular, offering snorkelling, diving and windsurfing.

Dunk Island is perhaps best known as the setting for EJ Banfield's 1906 book, *Confessions of a Beachcomber*. Today it is also known for its resident artists' colony and as a convenient stepping stone to exclusive Bedarra Island, 30 minutes away by launch.

Hinchinbrook Island **12**

🚗 *Ingham.* 🚌 *Cardwell.* 🚢 *Lucinda, Cardwell.* ℹ️ *Ingham (07) 4776 5211.*

HINCHINBROOK is the largest island national park in Australia, covering 635 sq km (245 sq miles). Dense rainforest, much of which remains unexplored, makes the island popular with bushwalkers. Hinchinbrook's highest point, Mount Bowen, rises 1,142 m (3,745 ft) above sea level and is often capped with cloud. The native wildlife includes wallabies, dugongs and the magnificent blue Ulysses butterfly. The island is separated from the mainland town of Cardwell by a narrow, mangrove-fringed channel.

Water-worn boulders near the town of Babinda

Queensland's Outback

I N STARK CONTRAST to the lush green of the eastern
rainforests, the northwest of Queensland is made up
of dry plains, mining areas and Aboriginal settlements.
The vast distances and high temperatures often dissuade
tourists from venturing into this harsh landscape; yet
those willing to make the effort
will be rewarded with unique
wildlife and an insight
into Australia's harsh
Outback life.

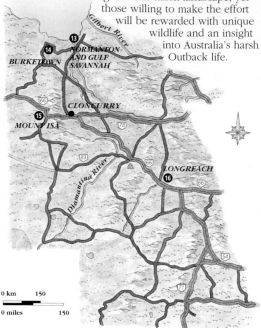

LOCATOR MAP

    Queensland's Outback

    Northern Queensland
    pp240–47

SIGHTS AT A GLANCE

Burketown ⑭
Longreach ⑯
Mount Isa ⑮
Normanton and
   Gulf Savannah ⑬

KEY

▬▬▬	Highway
▬▬	Major road
▬▬▬	Minor road
▬▬▬	River

0 km   150

0 miles   150

Normanton and Gulf Savannah ⑬

🚌 Normanton. ℹ Normanton (07)
4745 5177.

N ORMANTON, situated 70 km
(45 miles) inland on the
Norman River, is the largest
town in the region. It began
life as a port, handling copper
from Cloncurry and then gold
from Croydon. The famous
Gulflander train still commutes
once a week between Nor-
manton and Croydon.

En route from Normanton
to the Gulf of Carpentaria,
savannah grasses give way to
glistening salt pans, barren of
all vegetation. Once the rains
come in November, however,
this area becomes a wetland
and a breeding ground for
millions of birds, including
jabirus, brolgas, herons and
cranes, as well as crocodiles,
prawns and barramundi.
Karumba, at the mouth of the
Norman River, is the access
point for the Gulf of Carpentaria and the headquarters of
a multi-million-dollar prawn
and fishing industry. It remains
something of an untamed
frontier town, especially when
the prawn trawlers are in.

Covering approximately
350,000 sq km (135,000 sq
miles), the most northwest-
erly region of Queensland is
the Gulf Savannah. Largely
flat and covered in savannah
grasses, abundant with bird
and animal life, this is the
remotest landscape in Australia. The economic base of
the area is fishing and cattle.
Prawn trawlers go out to the
Gulf of Carpentaria for
months at a time and cattle
stations cover areas of more
than 1,000 sq km (400 sq
miles). Given the distances,
local pastoralists are more
likely to travel via light
aircraft than on horseback.

Gum trees and termite mounds on the grassland of Gulf Savannah

Mount Isa, dominated by Australia's largest mine

Burketown ⑭

🏛 160. ✕ 🛈 19 Musgrave St (07) 4745 5177.

IN THE LATE 1950s, Burketown found fleeting fame as the setting for Neville Shute's famous novel about life in a small Outback town, *A Town Like Alice*. Situated 30 km (18 miles) from the Gulf of Carpentaria, on the Albert River, Burketown was once a major port servicing the hinterland. The old wharf can still be seen, although today the town is little more than a forgotten outpost. The inhabitants of Burketown are aware of their isolation – the shire clerk once contacted the Department of Foreign Affairs, asking for his town to be included in its foreign aid programme.

About 150 km (90 miles) west of Burketown is Hell's Gate, an area so named at the beginning of the 20th century because it was the last outpost where the state's police guaranteed protection.

Mount Isa ⑮

🏛 25,000. ✕ 🚉 🚌
🛈 19 Marian St (07) 4749 1555.

MOUNT ISA is the only major city in far western Queensland. Its existence is entirely based around the world's largest silver and lead mine, which dominates the town both visually and psychologically. Ore was first discovered at Mount Isa in 1923 by a prospector called John Miles and the first mine

was set up in the 1930s. In those early days, "the Isa" was a shanty town, and Tent House, now owned by the National Trust, is an example of the half-house-half-tents that were home to most early settlers. Also in town is the **Riversleigh Interpretive Centre**, which gives an insight into some of the world's most important fossil fields *(see pp22–3)*.

One of the most popular events in town is the Mount Isa Rodeo in August *(see p39)*. With prize money totalling more than A$100,000, riders come from all over the world to perform spectacular displays of horsemanship.

🏛 **Riversleigh Interpretive Centre**
19 Marian St. 📞 *(07) 4749 1555.*
⭘ *daily.* ● *Good Fri, 25 Dec.* 📷 ♿

ENVIRONS: Cloncurry, 120 km (75 miles) east of Mount Isa, was the departure point for the Queensland and Northern Territory Aerial Service's (QANTAS) first flight in 1921. Now Australia's national airline, Qantas is also the oldest airline in the English-speaking world.

Longreach ⑯

🏛 4,500. ✕ 🚉 🚌 🛈 Qantas Park, Eagle St (07) 4658 3555.

SITUATED IN the centre of Queensland, Longreach is the main town of the central west of the state.

From 1922 to 1934, Longreach was the operating base of Qantas and there is a Founders Museum at Longreach Airport. Opened in 1988, the **Stockman's Hall of Fame** is a fascinating tribute to Outback men and women. Aboriginal artifacts, as well as documented tales of the early European explorers who opened up the Outback to white settlers are included in the impressive displays.

There are daily flights or a 17-hour coach ride from Brisbane to Longreach. Other access points are Rockhampton and Townsville.

🏛 **Stockman's Hall of Fame**
Landsborough Hwy. 📞 *(07) 4658 2166.* ⭘ *daily.* ● *25 Dec.* 📷 ♿

THE ROYAL FLYING DOCTOR SERVICE

The Royal Flying Doctor Service was founded by John Flynn, a Presbyterian pastor who was sent as a missionary to the Australian Outback in 1912. The young cleric was disturbed to see that many of his flock died due to the lack of basic medical care and he founded the Australian Inland Mission together with Hudson Fysh (the founder of Qantas),

A Royal Flying Doctor plane flying over Australia's Outback

self-made millionaire Hugh Victor McKay, Alfred Traeger (the inventor of the pedal wireless) and Dr Kenyon St Vincent Welch. Today, the Royal Flying Doctor Service deals with some 130,000 patients a year, and most Outback properties have an airstrip on which the Flying Doctor can land. Emergency medical help is rarely more than two hours away and advice is available over a special radio channel.

THE NORTHERN TERRITORY

The Northern Territory at a Glance

THAT MOST FAMOUS of Australian icons, the red monolith of Uluru (Ayers Rock) lies within the Northern Territory, but it is just one of the area's stunning natural features, which also include the tropical splendour of Kakadu National Park. The main centres are Darwin in the lush north and Alice Springs in the arid Red Centre. Much of the Outback land is Aboriginal-owned, enabling their ancient culture to flourish. The Northern Territory has yet to achieve full statehood owing to its low population and relatively small economy, but it has been self-governing since 1978.

Melville and Bathurst islands (see p266) *lie 80 km (50 miles) off the north coast. The islands are inhabited by Tiwi Aborigines, who have preserved a culture distinct from the mainland which includes unique characteristics such as these burial poles.*

```
0 kilometres      150
0 miles           150
```

Darwin (see pp262–5) *is the Northern Territory's capital city with an immigrant population of more than 50 nationalities (see pp256–7). The colonial Government House is one of the few 19th-century survivors in what is now a very modern city.*

THE RED CENTRE
(see pp270–281)

Kakadu National Park (see pp268–9) *is an ancient landscape of tropical rainforest and majestic rock formations. Covering 1.7 million ha (4.3 million acres), it is the largest national park in Australia. The Jim Jim Falls are the most impressive in the park, and the Aboriginal rock art sites are among the most important in the country.*

Uluru-Kata Tjuta National Park (see pp278–81) *is dominated by the huge sandstone rock rising up out of the flat, arid desert. Nearby are the Olgas, a series of 36 mysterious rock domes.*

◁ **Desert oaks (**Allocasuarina**) in the heart of the Northern Territory**

Elsey Homestead, *110 km (70 miles) south-east of Katherine (see pp266–7), was the setting for Jeannie Gunn's novel* We of the Never Never, *depicting 19th-century Outback life.*

DARWIN AND THE TOP END
(see pp258–269)

Devil's Marbles (see p277) *are a remarkable collection of granite boulders in the heart of the flat, sandy desert. Caused by millions of years of erosion, their huge shapes provide shade for many desert plants and birds.*

Alice Springs (see pp274–5) *lies at the heart of Australia. Its Old Telegraph Station Historical Reserve was the site of the area's first settlement in 1871.*

Chambers Pillar Historical Reserve (see p276) *is a strange, 50-m (165-ft) sandstone column which served as a landmark for explorers of the area in the 19th century.*

Aboriginal Lands

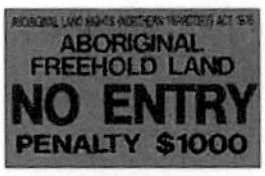

Sign for Aboriginal site

ABORIGINAL PEOPLE are thought to have lived in the Northern Territory for between 20,000 and 50,000 years. The comparatively short 200 years of European settlement have damaged their ancient culture immensely, but in the Northern Territory more traditional Aboriginal communities have survived intact than in other states – mainly due to their greater numbers and determination to preserve their identity. Nearly one-third of the Northern Territory's people are Aboriginal and they own almost 50 per cent of the land via arrangements with the federal government *(see p55)*. For Aborigines, the concept of land ownership is tied to a belief system that instructs them to care for their ancestral land.

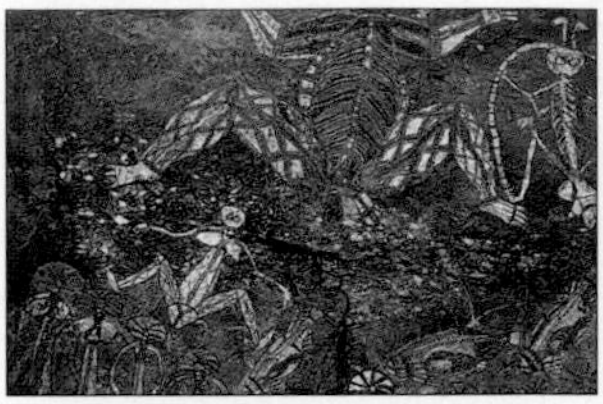

This X-ray image *(see p29) of the dreaming spirit Namarrgon at Nourlangie Rock is centuries old, but was continually repainted until the 1900s.*

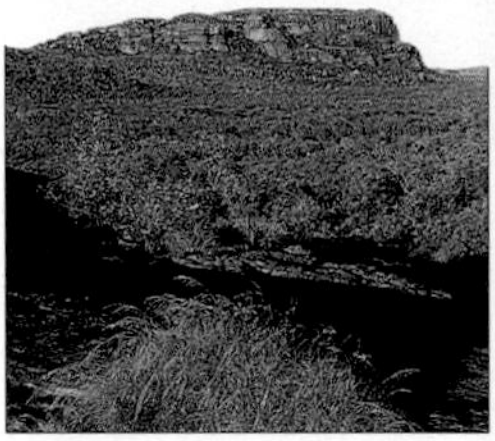

Nourlangie Rock *in Kakadu National Park is significant to Aborigines as home of the Lightning Dreaming* (see pp268–9).

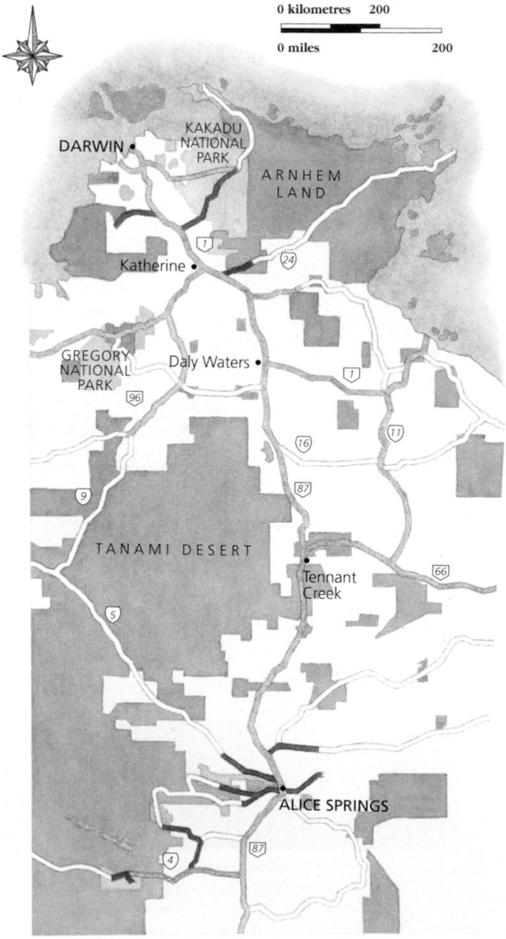

KEY

- Aboriginal land
- National park
- Highway
- Major road
- Unsurfaced road

ACCESS AND PERMITS

Northern Land Council
(08) 8920 5100.
For access to all Aboriginal land in the Top End, including Arnhem Land.

Northern Territory Parks and Wildlife Commission
(08) 8999 4814 or (08) 8999 4795. For permits to Gurig National Park.

Tiwi Land Council
(08) 8981 4898.
For access to Melville and Bathurst islands.

Central Land Council
(08) 8951 6320.
For access to all Central Australian Aboriginal lands.

ABORIGINAL TOURISM

Most visitors who come to the Northern Territory are keen to learn more about the region's unique Aboriginal culture. There are now many Aboriginal organizations which take tourists into Aboriginal areas that would otherwise be inaccessible, and explain the Aboriginal view of the land. Excursions available include boat trips in Kakadu National Park *(see pp268–9)* with a Guluyambi guide; bush camping with the Manyalluluk community near Katherine; or a safari camp in Arnhem Land with Umorrduk Safaris. Also well worth visiting are the information and cultural centres, such as those in Kakadu and Uluru-Kata Tjuta national parks, where native owners share their creation stories and culture, adding another layer to visitors' appreciation of these special places.

Ubirr Rock *in Kakadu National Park is one of the finest Aboriginal rock art sites in the Northern Territory. Many paintings in Ubirr's gallery depict the area's wildlife in an x-ray style (see p29), such as this barramundi. They date from 20,000 years ago to the present day.*

Visitors climbing to the lookout at Ubirr Rock

Uluru *(see pp278–81) has many sites sacred to the Anangu people around its base. Almost all of these are closed to the public, but it is possible to walk around the area and learn the associated stories.*

Bush Tucker Dreaming, *painted in 1991 by Gladys Napanangka of the Papunya community of the Central Western Desert, records the Dreaming or creation stories passed down to the artist through hundreds of generations (see pp26–7).*

ABORIGINAL CULTURE AND LAW

Every Aboriginal tribe lives according to a set of laws linking the people with their land and their ancestors. These laws have been handed down through generations and are embedded in Aboriginal creation stories. The stories, which tell how the first spirits and ancestors shaped and named the land, also form a belief system which directs all aspects of Aboriginal life. All Aborigines are born into two groups: their family clan and a "Dreaming" totem group such as the crocodile – determined by place and time of birth. These decide their links with the land and place in the community and the creation stories they inherit.

Aborigines in body make-up for a traditional tribal dance

Multicultural Northern Territory

Thai dish

T HE NORTHERN TERRITORY, with its proximity to Indonesia and the Pacific Islands, has long served as Australia's "front door" to immigrants. Around 500 years ago, Portuguese and Dutch ships charted the waters of the northern coast and from the 1700s traders from the Indonesian archipelago visited the northern shores. From 1874, when Chinese gold prospectors arrived in Darwin, the tropical north has appealed to Southeast Asians and, being closer to Indonesia than to Sydney or Melbourne, the city markets itself as Australia's gateway to Asia. There are now more than 50 ethnic groups living in Darwin, including Greeks and Italians who arrived in the early 20th century, and East Timorese, Indonesians, Thais and Filipinos, together with the town's original mix of Aborigines and those of Anglo-Celtic stock.

Harry Chan, *elected in 1966, was the first Lord Mayor of Darwin of Chinese descent.*

Mindil Beach market *is one of several Asian-style food markets in the Darwin area. More than 60 food stalls serve Thai, Indonesian, Indian, Chinese, Sri Lankan, Malaysian and Greek cuisine* (see p264).

All Darwin children are taught Bahasa, a major Indonesian language, in recognition of Indonesia's proximity to the city.

THE CHINESE IN THE TOP END

In 1879, a small carved figure dating from the Ming dynasty (1368–1644) was found in the roots of a tree on a Darwin beach, causing much speculation that a Chinese fleet may have visited this coast in the 15th century. If so, it was the start of an association between China and the Top End which endures today. Chinese came here in search of gold in the 1870s. By 1885, there were 3,500 Chinese in the Top End, and 40 years later Darwin had become a Chinese-run shanty town

Chinese man using buffalo to haul wood in early 19th-century Darwin

with Chinese families managing its market gardens and general stores. Today, many of the area's leading families are of Chinese origin; Darwin has had two Lord Mayors of Chinese descent, and fifth generation Chinese are spread throughout the city's businesses.

Aboriginal people are believed to have arrived in the Northern Territory 20,000 to 50,000 years ago, overland from Asia when the sea level was much lower. Here, young male initiates from an Arnhem Land tribe are carried to a ceremony to be "made men".

With a quarter of its present population born overseas and another quarter Aboriginal, Darwin's racial mix is best seen in the faces of its children.

THE CHILDREN OF DARWIN

The faces of Darwin's children show an incredible ethnic diversity, something many believe will be typical of all Australia in 50 years time. The Northern Territory, and especially Darwin, is renowned for a relaxed, multicultural society and a racial tolerance and identity rarely found in other Australian cities.

Darwin's children, whatever their ethnic origin, are united by their casual Australian clothes and relaxed attitude.

The Filipino community in Darwin preserves its traditions, as seen by these two girls in national costume at the Festival of Darwin.

Paspaley Pearls is Darwin's wealthiest local company. Founded by Greek settlers, it owns pearl farms across northern Australia.

The East Timorese community of Darwin perform traditional dancing at a city arts festival. Most of the East Timorese have arrived in the city since 1975, in the wake of Indonesia's invasion of East Timor.

DARWIN AND THE TOP END

THE TROPICAL TIP *of the Northern Territory is a lush, ancient landscape. For thousands of years it has been home to large numbers of Aborigines and contains the greatest and oldest collection of rock art in the world. Its capital, Darwin, is small and colourful. The World Heritage-listed Kakadu National Park has a raw beauty combined with the fascinating creation stories of its Aboriginal tribes.*

The Port of Darwin was first named in 1839, when British captain John Lort Stokes, commander of HMS *Beagle*, sailed into an azure harbour fringed by palm trees, sandy beaches and mangroves, and named it after his friend Charles Darwin. Although the biologist would not publish his theory of evolution in the *Origin of the Species* for another 20 years, it proved to be a wonderfully apt name for this tropical region, teeming with unique and ancient species of birds, plants, reptiles and mammals. The Aboriginal tribes that have lived for many thousands of years in the northern area known as the Top End are recognized by anthropologists as one of world's oldest races.

Darwin itself is a city that has fought hard to survive. From 1864, when the first settlement was established at Port Darwin, it has endured isolation, bombing attacks by the Japanese in World War II *(see p262)* and devastation by the force of Cyclone Tracy in 1974 *(see p264)*. Despite having been twice rebuilt, it has grown into a multicultural modern city, with a relaxed atmosphere, great beauty and a distinctly Asian feel.

Beyond Darwin is a region of Aboriginal communities and ancient art sites, wide rivers and crocodiles, lotus-lily wetlands and deep gorges. For visitors, Kakadu National Park superbly blends sights of great scenic beauty with a cultural and spiritual insight into the complex Aboriginal culture. Also to be enjoyed are the plunging waterfalls and giant termite mounds of Litchfield National Park, the deep red-rock gorge of Nitmiluk (Katherine Gorge) National Park, and expeditions into the closed Aboriginal communities of Arnhem Land and Melville and Bathurst islands.

An Aboriginal child gathering water lilies in the lush and tropical Top End

◁ **Katherine Gorge cutting an awesome scar across the landscape**

Exploring Darwin and the Top End

THE AUSTRALIAN TOP END is a seductive, tropical region on the remote tip of the massive dry Northern Territory. On the turquoise coast there are palm trees; inland are winding rivers, grassy wetlands, gorge pools and ochre escarpments. The Territory's capital, Darwin, has many attractions and is a good base for day trips to areas such as Berry Springs and Melville and Bathurst islands. The climate is hot, but the dry season has low humidity, making it the best time to visit. The wet season, however, compensates for its humidity and tropical downpours with the spectacle of thundering rivers and waterfalls and lush vegetation.

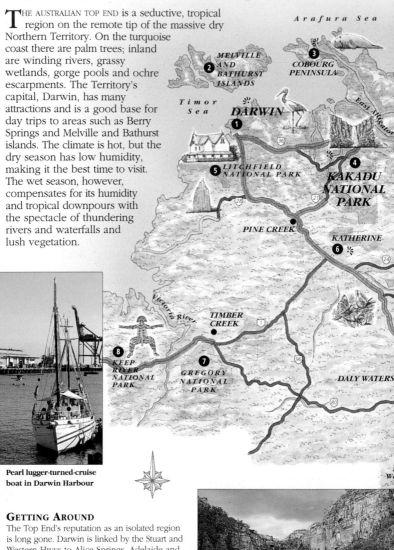

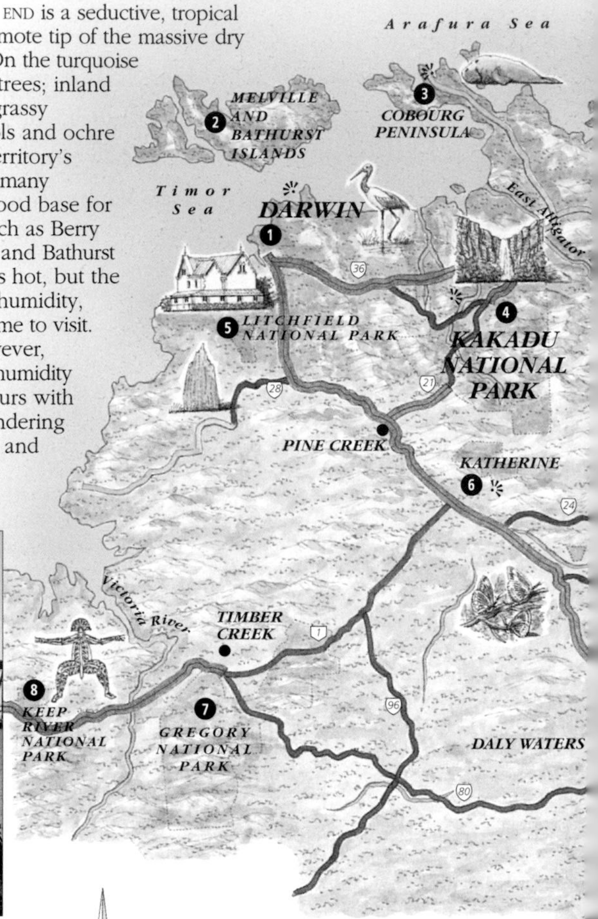
Arafura Sea
MELVILLE AND BATHURST ISLANDS
COBOURG PENINSULA
Timor Sea
DARWIN
East Alligator
LITCHFIELD NATIONAL PARK
KAKADU NATIONAL PARK
PINE CREEK
KATHERINE
Victoria River
TIMBER CREEK
KEEP RIVER NATIONAL PARK
GREGORY NATIONAL PARK
DALY WATERS
36
21
28
24
1
96
80

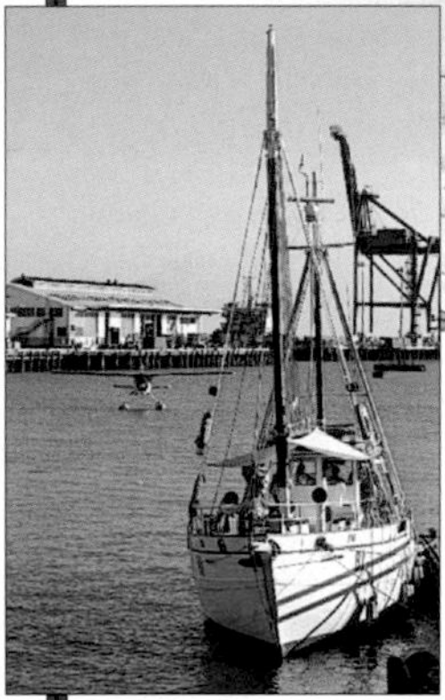

Pearl lugger-turned-cruise boat in Darwin Harbour

GETTING AROUND

The Top End's reputation as an isolated region is long gone. Darwin is linked by the Stuart and Western Hwys to Alice Springs, Adelaide and Melbourne in the south, and along interstate Hwys to Mount Isa, Cairns and Brisbane in the east. The centre of Darwin can be explored on foot or using the open trolley Tour Tub which stops at all the main attractions in an hourly circuit. The Top End's major attractions, such as Kakadu National Park and Katherine Gorge, can be visited without driving on a dirt road. Bus connections to the main towns are regular, but a car is vital to make the most of the scenery. Distances are not great for Australia; Kakadu is 210 km (130 miles) from Darwin and Katherine 300 km (186 miles) away on the Stuart Hwy.

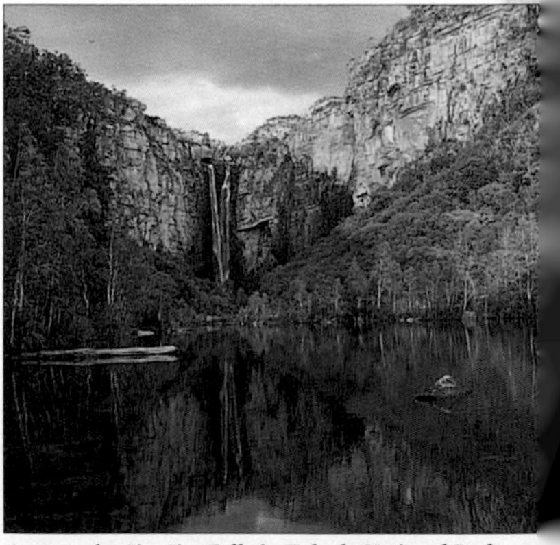

Spectacular Jim Jim Falls in Kakadu National Park

Unusual sandstone formations of the Lost City, Litchfield National Park

SEE ALSO

- **Where to Stay** pp476–7

- **Where to Eat** pp509–10

SIGHTS AT A GLANCE

Cobourg Peninsula ❸
Darwin pp262–5 ❶
Gregory National Park ❼
*Kakadu National Park
   pp268–9* ❹
Katherine ❻
Keep River National Park ❽
Litchfield National Park ❺
Melville and Bathurst Islands ❷

KEY

▬	Highway
▬	Major road
▭	Minor road
▬	Scenic route
～	River
※	Viewpoint

0 kilometres   100

0 miles   100

Darwin ●

FOLLOWING EUROPEAN SETTLEMENT in 1864, for the first century of its life Darwin was an outpost of the British Empire, with vast cattle farms being established around it. In its short, colourful history it has experienced the gold rush of the 1890s, life as an Allied frontline during World War II and almost total destruction in 1974 by the fearful winds of Cyclone Tracy *(see p264)*. Darwin has now emerged as a modern but relaxed town where more than 50 ethnic groups of Asian-born Australians mingle with Aborigines, Europeans, particularly Greeks, and Chinese from earlier periods of immigration.

Old pearl diver's helmet

Shady palm trees in Bicentennial Park, seen from The Esplanade

♿ Old Darwin Town Hall
Smith St. &
The limestone ruin of the Old Darwin Town Hall lies at the bottom of Smith Street. The original council chambers, built in 1883, were damaged by a terrible cyclone in 1897. The building subsequently became a bank, and then a museum, before being destroyed by Cyclone Tracy in 1974. Curved brick paving built against the remaining wall symbolizes the fury of the cyclone's winds.

♿ Brown's Mart
Smith St. ((08) 8981 5522. &
Directly opposite the town hall ruins is Brown's Mart, built in 1885 during the gold boom. It was once a mining exchange and is now home to performing arts groups.

♿ Old Police Station and Courthouse
Cnr Smith St & The Esplanade.
((08) 8999 7103. &
The 1884 limestone Old Police Station and Courthouse have both been restored after being damaged by Cyclone Tracy and are now administration offices.
Across the road is Survivors' Lookout, which overlooks the harbour. Here photographs

and written accounts tell of Darwin's wartime ordeal as an Allied frontline. Thousands of US and Australian troops were based in the Top End, which endured 65 bombing raids by Japanese forces *(see p53)*.

♿ Lyons Cottage
74 The Esplanade. ((08) 8981 1750. ☐ 10am–4:30pm daily.
● Easter, 25 Dec. ◪
The old stone building known as Lyons Cottage was built in 1925. It is maintained in a 1920s style and contains an exhibition of photographs detailing life in the Top End during that era.

⬛ Smith Street Mall
Bennett & Knuckey sts. &
The heart of Darwin's shopping area is Smith Street Mall, with its glass air-conditioned plazas shaded by tall tropical trees. Always full of buskers, tour operators offering trips, locals and visitors, the mall is a favourite meeting place. Noteworthy buildings include the 1890 Victoria Hotel, a popular landmark and one of the few old structures in the town to survive Cyclone Tracy.

♣ Bicentennial Park
The Esplanade. &
This lush, green park, with its pleasant shady walks and panoramic lookouts, is home to many World War II memorials. One commemorates the attack by Japanese bombers which flew over Darwin Harbour on 19 February 1942, sinking 21 of the 46 US and Australian naval vessels in port and killing 243 people. It was the closest Australia came to war on its own soil.

Front entrance of Parliament House

♿ Parliament House
State Square. ((08) 8946 1425.
☐ Mon–Sat. ● public hols. &
Dominating the edge of Darwin's sea cliffs is the new Parliament House, which was opened in 1994. With architecture that appears to borrow from both Middle Eastern and Russian styles, this imposing building is home to the territory's 33 parliamentarians, who administer just 180,000 people. It has a granite and timber interior which is filled with Aboriginal art. Visitors may also get a glimpse of the parliamentarian chambers and use the library – the largest in the territory, with an excellent local reference section.

Darwin's Old Police Station and Courthouse

⚜ Government House

The Esplanade. **☎** *(08) 8999 7103.* ♿

On a small plateau above the harbour, Government House is Darwin's oldest surviving building, built in 1879. Wooden gables have been added to the stone hall with a canvas roof. It is now home to the Administrator of the Northern Territory, the representative of the Queen and Commonwealth of Australia in the territory.

⚜ Admiralty House

Cnr Knuckey St & The Esplanade.

Across the road from Lyons Cottage is Admiralty House, once the headquarters of the Australian navy and one of the oldest surviving buildings in Darwin. It was built in the 1930s by the territory's principal architect, Beni Carr Glynn Burnett, in an elevated tropical style using louvres, open eaves and three-quarter-high walls to aid ventilation.

⚜ Stokes Hill Wharf

McMinn St. ♿

The long, wooden Stokes Hill Wharf, stretching out into Darwin Harbour, was once the town's main port area. Now a centre for tourist and local life, it has restaurants, bars and shops. Sea planes and boats leave on tours from the wharf.

At the wharf entrance is the excellent Indo-Pacific Marine exhibit, which has re-created local coral reef ecosystems, with bright tropical fish in its tanks. In the same building, the Australian Pearling Exhibition describes the history and science of local pearl farming.

A restaurant at the end of Stokes Hill Wharf overlooking the harbour

DARWIN CITY CENTRE

Admiralty House ③
Bicentennial Park ①
Brown's Mart ⑦
Government House ⑨
Lyons Cottage ②
Old Darwin Town Hall ⑥
Old Police Station and
   Courthouse ⑧
Parliament House ⑤
Smith Street Mall ④
Stokes Hill Wharf ⑩

0 metres 250
0 yards 250

Darwin Harbour

KEY

🚌 Bus station

🅿 Parking

ℹ Tourist information

Greater Darwin

Decorated emu egg

MANY OF Darwin's best attractions are not in the city centre but located a short drive away. The Tour Tub, an open-sided trolley bus that picks up from major hotels, does an hourly circuit of tourist attractions, allowing visitors to hop on and off at will for a daily charge. Outside Darwin, alongside the mango farms and beef cattle stations, there are some fine bush and wetland areas which provide excellent opportunities for swimming, fishing and exploring.

Feeding the friendly fish at Aquascene in Doctor's Gully

➤ Aquascene

Doctor's Gully, cnr of Daly St & The Esplanade. 【 (08) 8981 7837. ◯ daily, with the tide. ● 25 Dec. ♿
Ever since the 1950s, the fish of Darwin Harbour have been coming in on the tides for a feed of stale bread in Doctor's Gully. At Aquascene, visitors can feed and play with hundreds of scats, catfish, mullet and milkfish. Feeding times vary from day to day.

Ethnic food stall at Mindil Beach Sunset Markets

◻ Mindil Beach Sunset Markets

Mindil Beach. 【 (08) 8981 3454. ◯ Apr–Oct: Thu, Sun; Jun–Sep: Sun. ♿
Thursday nights during the dry season are when Darwinians flock to Mindil Beach at dusk to enjoy more than 60 outdoor food stalls serving a host of ethnic cuisines while watching the sun set over Darwin Harbour.

♣ Botanic Gardens

Gardens Rd, Stuart Park. 【 (08) 8981 1958. ◯ daily. ♿ limited.
Just north of town, the 42-ha (100-acre) Botanic Gardens, established in the 1870s, boast more than 1,500 thriving tropical species, including a unique display of 400 palm varieties, and wetland mangroves.

⚔ East Point Military Museum and Fannie Bay Gaol

East Point Rd, East Point. 【 (08) 8981 9702. ◯ 9:30am–5pm daily. ● Good Fri, 25 Dec. 📷 ♿
Wallabies graze at dusk in this attractive harbourside reserve which contains an artificial lake, ideal for swimming, and the East Point Military Museum. Nearby Fannie Bay Gaol is now an interesting museum.

🏛 Australian Aviation Heritage Centre

557 Stuart Hwy, Winnellie. 【 (08) 8947 2145. ◯ daily. ● Good Fri, 25 Dec. 📷 ♿
Along the Stuart Highway at Winnellie, 6 km (4 miles) from the city centre, Darwin's Aviation Centre displays a variety of historic and wartime aircraft. Its exhibits are dominated by a B-52 bomber, one of only four in the world on display outside the US.

🦎 Territory Wildlife Park and Berry Springs

Cox Peninsula Rd, Berry Springs. 【 (08) 8988 7200. ◯ daily. ● 25 Dec. 📷 ♿
Only 70 km (45 miles) from Darwin is the town of Berry Springs and the Territory Wildlife Park with its hundreds of unique indigenous species, in natural surroundings. Nearby, Berry Springs Nature Reserve has a series of deep pools, fringed with vegetation, that make for great swimming.

🦆 Howard Springs Nature Park

Howard Springs Rd. 【 (08) 8983 1001. ◯ daily. ♿ limited.
This nature park, 25 km (16 miles) from Darwin, has clear, freshwater spring-fed pools, filled with barramundi and turtles. These offer safe bathing and are an ideal place for a cool swim and a barbecue after a hot day exploring.

CYCLONE TRACY

Cyclone Tracy's devastation

Late Christmas Eve, 1974, a weather warning was issued that Cyclone Tracy, gathering force off the coast, had turned landward and was heading for Darwin. Torrential rain pelted down and winds reached a record 280 km/h (175 mph) before the measuring machine broke. On Christmas morning, 66 people were dead, thousands injured and 95 per cent of the buildings flattened. More than 30,000 residents were airlifted south in the biggest evacuation in Australia's history. The city ruins were bulldozed and Darwin has been rebuilt, stronger and safer than before.

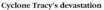

Museum and Art Gallery of the Northern Territory

THE MUSEUM AND ART GALLERY of the Northern Territory has exhibitions on regional Aboriginal art and culture, maritime exploration, visual arts and natural history.

The museum's collection of Aboriginal art is considered to be the best in the world and has some particularly fine carvings and bark paintings, along with explanations of Aboriginal culture. Other displays include a chilling exhibition on Cyclone Tracy and models that explain the evolution of some of the Top End's unique and curious wildlife, including the popular 5-m (16-ft) stuffed crocodile named "Sweetheart".

VISITORS' CHECKLIST

Conacher St. **C** (08) 8999 8201.
4, 5. 9am–5pm Mon–Fri,
10am–5pm Sat & Sun. some
public hols.

KEY

- Aboriginal Art Gallery
- Natural Sciences Gallery
- Cyclone Tracy Gallery
- Visual Art Gallery
- Craft Gallery
- Maritime Galleries
- Temporary exhibitions
- Non-exhibition space

★ **Aboriginal Art Gallery**
In this gallery, exhibits describe both the anthropology and creation stories of local Aboriginal groups as an introduction to the artworks on display that portray their lives and culture.

Upper floor

Ground floor

Entrance

Aboriginal Burial Poles
These ancient ceremonial burial poles, on display in the museum gardens, are unique to the Tiwi culture of the Melville and Bathurst Islands (see p266).

Façade of the Museum and Art Gallery
Located 4 km (2.5 miles) north of Darwin's centre, the museum's stylish low-level building is in a tropical beachside setting overlooking Fannie Bay.

STAR FEATURE

★ **Aboriginal Art Gallery**

Tiwi islander making handicrafts from local fibres, Bathurst Island

Melville and Bathurst Islands ❷

⊠ 🛈 *Tiwi Tours (08) 8924 1115.*

JUST 80 km (50 miles) north of Darwin lie the Tiwi Islands, the collective name given to the small island of Bathurst and its larger neighbour, Melville. The latter is the second-largest island off the Australian coast after Tasmania and is rich in history and Aboriginal culture. The islands' inhabitants, the Tiwi people, had little contact with mainland Aborigines until the 20th century.

With beautiful waters, sandy beaches and lush forest, the islands are a tropical paradise, but, because of their ownership by the Tiwi, can only be visited on guided tours from Darwin. Running May to October, day trips offer a glimpse of the unique blend of Aboriginal, Indonesian and Tiwi traditions. On the islands, tourists can visit Aboriginal art centres, Tiwi batik printworks and a *pukumani* burial site with painted wood burial poles.

Cobourg Peninsula ❸

🛈 *Darwin (08) 8936 2499.*

THE COBOURG PENINSULA is one of the most remote parts of Australia. It is only accessible by vehicle during the dry season and with an access permit *(see p254),*

travelling through the closed Aboriginal Arnhem Land to reach the wild coastal beaches of Gurig National Park. The number of vehicles allowed to enter the region each week is restricted and a weekly permit fee is charged by the Coburg Peninsula Sanctuary and Marine Park Board.

Gurig is a large park, with sandy beaches and the calm waters of Port Essington. Two attempts by the British to settle this area in the early 19th century were abandoned, due to inhospitable Aborigines and malaria epidemics. The ruins of Victoria Settlement can be reached by boat from Smith Point. Luxury accommodation is available at Seven Spirit Bay Wilderness Lodge *(see p476),* which is reached by plane from Darwin.

Kakadu National Park ❹

See pp268–9.

Litchfield National Park ❺

🚌 *Batchelor.* 🛈 *National Parks and Wildlife Commission for Northern Territory (08) 8976 0282.*

THE SPECTACULAR Litchfield National Park, only 140 km (85 miles) south of Darwin, is very popular with Darwinians. There are waterfalls, gorges and deep, crocodile-free pools for swimming at Florence Falls, Wangi and Buley Rockhole.

Giant magnetic termite mound in Litchfield National Park

The park has some amazing giant magnetic termite mounds. They are so-called because they point north in an effort by the termites to control temperature by having only the mound's thinnest part exposed to the sun. Also popular are the sandstone block formations further south, known as the "Lost City" due to their resemblance to ancient ruins.

Katherine ❻

🏛 *11,000.* ⊠ 🚆 🛈 *Cnr Stuart Hwy & Lindsay St (08) 8972 2650.*

THE TOWN OF Katherine, situated on the banks of the Katherine River, 300 km (185 miles) south of Darwin, is both a thriving regional centre and a major Top End tourist destination. Home for thousands of years to the Jawoyn Aborigines, Katherine River has long been a rich source of food for the Aboriginal people. The river was first crossed by white explorers in 1844, and the area was not settled by Europeans until 1878, with the completion of the Overland Telegraph and the arrival of the first cattle pastoralist, Alfred Giles. Giles built his homestead, Springvale, on the banks of the Katherine River. Today it is the Territory's oldest building and a camp site.

Only 30 km (20 miles) from town lies the famous **Nitmiluk (Katherine Gorge) National Park**. Its string of 13 separate gorges along 50 km (30 miles) of the Katherine River has been carved out by torrential summer rains cutting through cliffs of red sandstone which are 1,650 million years old. The result is a place of deep pools, silence and grandeur.

The best way to explore the park is by boat or canoe. Canoe trips are self-guided, with nine navigable gorges and overnight camping possible. There are also boat trips operated by the Jawoyn people, who own the park and run it in conjunction with the Northern Territory's Parks and Wildlife Commission. Each gorge can be explored in a separate boat, interspersed with swimming holes and

Upper waterfall and pools of Edith Falls, Nitmiluk (Katherine Gorge) National Park near Katherine

short walks. There are also 100 km (60 miles) of marked trails in the park, ranging from the spectacular but easy lookout walk to the five-day 72-km (45-mile) hike to lovely Edith Falls, which can also be reached by car from the Stuart Highway.

ENVIRONS: Just south of Katherine are the Cutta Cutta caves, limestone rock formations 15 m (50 ft) under the earth's surface and formed five million years ago. They are home to both the rare orange horseshoe bat and the brown tree snake.

Further southeast, 110 km (70 miles) from Katherine, lies the small town of Mataranka. This is "Never Never" country, celebrated by female pioneer Jeannie Gunn in her 1908 novel, *We of the Never Never,* about life at nearby Elsey Station at the turn of the century. The area is named Never Never country because those who live here and love it, find

Limestone Gorge, Gregory National Park

they can never, never leave it. About 8 km (5 miles) east of Mataranka is Elsey National Park. Visitors can swim in the hot waters of the Mataranka Thermal Pool which flow from Rainbow Springs to this idyllic spot surrounded by rainforest. The nearby **Mataranka Homestead** resort is an authentic replica of Jeannie Gunn's Elsey Station homestead, which was made for the 1981 film version of her novel.

Mataranka Homestead
(08) 8975 4544. daily.

Gregory National Park 7

Timber Creek. Timber Creek (08) 8975 0888. 7am–4pm Mon–Fri.

THIS MASSIVE, wild national park lies in the heart of cattle country, 200 km (125 miles) southwest of Katherine. Broken into two sections, its eastern part contains a 50-km (31-mile) section of the Victoria River gorge. In the north of the larger western section of the park are some crocodile-infested areas of the Victoria River. Here exciting boat trips combine close-up

views of the crocodiles. In the west of the park, the stunning Limestone Gorge has dolomite blocks, huge cliffs and good fishing opportunities.

Walking trail by a sandstone escarpment, Keep River National Park

Keep River National Park 8

Victoria Hwy (08) 9167 8827. Apr–Sep: daily; Oct–Mar: Mon–Fri.

LOCATED ONLY 3 km (2 miles) from the Western Australian border, Keep River National Park includes the dramatic Keep River gorge and some of Australia's most ancient rock art sites. The park, once the location of an ancient Aboriginal settlement, today has some superb walking trails for all levels of trekkers.

Kakadu National Park 4

Aboriginal calendar at the Bowali Visitors' Centre

THE vast 20,000 sq km (8,000 sq miles) of Kakadu National Park, with its stunning diversity of stony plateaux, red escarpment cliffs, waterfalls, billabongs, long twisting rivers, flood plains and coastal flats, is one of Australia's most extraordinary places. A UNESCO World Heritage Area *(see pp22–3)*, Kakadu encompasses both scenic wonders and huge galleries of Aboriginal rock art. The park is Aboriginal land leased back to the government *(see p55)* and is managed jointly. The entire catchment area of the South Alligator River lies within the park, and is home to thousands of plant and animal species. Some areas in Kakadu are not accessible during the wet season.

Yellow Water
A cruise on the wetlands of Yellow Water shows Kakadu in all its glory. Lotus lilies, crocodiles, kookaburras, magpie geese, jabirus and other bird species can be seen.

FLORA AND FAUNA IN KAKADU NATIONAL PARK

More than one-third of all bird species recorded in Australia live in Kakadu National Park; as do more than 60 mammal species, 75 reptile species, 1,200 plant species and at least 10,000 insect species. Approximately 10 per cent of the birds are estimated to be unique to Kakadu. Magpie geese are especially abundant; at times there are three million in the park, 60 per cent of the world's population.

The stately jabiru, seen near shallow water in the dry season

Gunlom Waterhole
The southern and drier end of Kakadu is less visited, but holds some magical places such as the Gunlom waterhole, home to the rainbow serpent, Borlung, in Aboriginal legend.

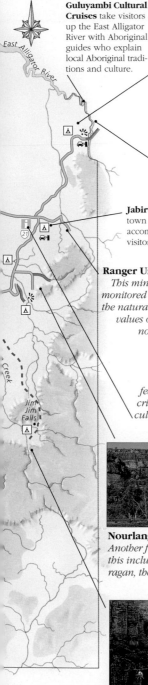

Guluyambi Cultural Cruises take visitors up the East Alligator River with Aboriginal guides who explain local Aboriginal traditions and culture.

Ubirr Rock
This rock has many Aboriginal rock art galleries, some with paintings more than 20,000 years old (see p29).

Oenpelli is a small Aboriginal town just outside Kakadu. Some Aboriginal day tours take visitors to this usually prohibited area.

Jabiru is a small town that provides accommodation for visitors to the park.

Ranger Uranium Mine
This mine is rigorously monitored to ensure that the natural and cultural values of the park are not endangered.

Bowali Visitors' Centre
This award-winning centre features excellent displays describing the animals, Aboriginal culture and geology of Kakadu.

Nourlangie Rock
Another fine Aboriginal rock art site, this includes paintings of Namaragan, the Lightning Man (see p254).

KEY

━━	Highway
━━	Major road
- -	4WD only
—	National park boundary
🚗	Petrol station
⛺	Camp site
ℹ	Tourist information
☀	View Point

Twin Falls
This spectacular waterfall (accessible by 4WD) is visible only after the wet season, when it thunders over a high plateau into deep rock pools.

0 kilometres   20

0 miles   20

THE RED CENTRE

THE RED CENTRE *stretches roughly from Tennant Creek to the South Australian border, and is made up almost entirely of huge desert areas. The region occupies the centre of the Australian continent, with its main town, Alice Springs, at the country's geographical heart. Its signature colour is red: red sand, soil, rocks and mountains are all pitched against a typically blue sky.*

The Red Centre contains some of the finest natural scenery in the world, much of it dating back about 800 million years. At that time, central Australia was covered by an inland sea; here sediments were laid down which form the basis of some of the region's best-known topographical features today. These include the huge monolith Uluṟu (formerly Ayers Rock), the domes of Kata Tjuṯa (also known as the Olgas), the giant boulders of the Devil's Marbles and the majestic MacDonnell Ranges. Between these sights are vast open spaces where remnants of tropical plant species grow beside desert-hardy stock. Verdant plants fed by occasional rains flourish next to animal skeletons.

Aboriginal people have lived in the region for more than 30,000 years, and their ancient tradition of rock painting is one of many tribal rituals still practised. By comparison, the history of white settlement here is recent. Explorers first arrived in the area during the 1860s. Alice Springs, founded in 1888, was a tiny settlement until improved communications after World War II led to the town's growth. It is now a modern, bustling town with much to offer. Tennant Creek, the only other sizeable settlement in the area, lies on the main Stuart Highway that bisects the Red Centre.

Much of the Territory has now been returned to its Aboriginal owners *(see pp254–5)*, and today many Aborigines are actively involved in tourism. Access to Aboriginal lands is restricted but visiting them is a rewarding encounter to add to the unforgettable experience of the Red Centre.

Trekking through the desert landscape on a camel safari near Alice Springs

◁ **The monolith Uluṟu, sacred to the Aborigines, set against a brilliant blue sky**

Exploring the Red Centre

THE RED CENTRE'S biggest draw is its stunning array of natural features. Alice Springs is the main city, with other towns at Yulara (Ayers Rock Resort) and Tennant Creek. The best time to travel is from April to October, thus avoiding the intense summer heat. The MacDonnell Ranges run like a huge spine on either side of Alice Springs; elsewhere the land is largely flat, formed by millions of years of erosion, and covered by spinifex grasslands. The region's gorges have been carved out by rivers, many of which flow only once or twice a year, soaking the surrounding desert plains.

●KALKARINGI

96

9

T A N A M I   D E S E R T

Lander River

5

Lake Macdonald

5

Visually striking Olga Gorge in Uluṟu-Kata Tjuṯa National Park

KEY

▨	Highway
▬	Major road
▦	Minor road
▤	Scenic route
～	River
✹	Viewpoint

MACDONNELL RANGES **4**

Lake Neale

7 KINGS CANYON

HENBURY METEORI CONSERVATION RESE

ULURU-KATA TJUTA NATIONAL PARK

Lake Amadeus

4

8

ERLDU

SIGHTS AT A GLANCE

Colourful mural painted on a shopping centre in Alice Springs

0 kilometres   100

0 miles   100

↑ *Darwin*

❻ **TENNANT CREEK**

87

66

❺
**DEVIL'S
MARBLES
CONSERVATION
RESERVE**

14

Bundey River

12

Marshall River

❶ **ALICE SPRINGS**

**CHAMBERS PILLAR
HISTORICAL RESERVE**

GETTING AROUND

There is a wide range of transport options available in central
Australia. Domestic airports serve Alice Springs and Yulara.
Overland, coaches connect the region with all the state capital
cities, and the famous Ghan railway *(see p275)* operates
between Alice Springs and Adelaide. The most popular way
to explore the region, however, is by car, and there are many
car rental companies in the area. Standard vehicles are adequate
for most journeys, but 4WD is advisable for off-road travel.
Alternatively, many guided tours are also available. The
Stuart Hwy is the main road running through the area,
linking Port Augusta in South Australia with
Darwin in the north. Alice Springs itself has
taxis, bike hire and a town bus service, but the
relatively short distances within the city also
make walking popular.

**Desert wildflowers in Simpsons
Gap, near Alice Springs**

Alice Springs ➊

ALICE SPRINGS is named after the Alice Spring permanent waterhole, near which a staging post for the overland telegraph line was built in the 1870s. The waterhole was named after Alice Todd, wife of the line's construction manager. The town developed nearby in the 1880s, but with no rail link until 1929 and no surfaced road link until the 1940s, it grew slowly. The huge increase in tourism since the 1970s, however, has brought rapid growth and Alice Springs is now a lively city with around 400,000 visitors a year, many of whom use it as a base from which to tour the surrounding spectacular natural sights.

Exploring Alice Springs

Although many of its sights are spread around the city, Alice Springs is small enough to tour on foot. Its compact centre, just five streets across running from Wills Terrace in the north to Stuart Terrace in the south, contains many of the town's hotels and restaurants, as well as the pedestrianized Todd Mall. The city's eastern side is bordered by Todd River, dry and sandy most of the time and scene of the celebrated Henley-on-Todd Regatta *(see p36)*.

🏕 Anzac Hill
West Terrace. &

At the northern end of Alice Springs, Anzac Hill overlooks the city and affords fine views of the MacDonnell Ranges *(see p276)*. Named after the 1934 Anzac memorial at the site, the hill is a perfect vantage point for visitors to familiarize themselves with the city's layout, as well as for viewing the area at sunrise or sunset, when it is bathed in a beautiful light.

🏛 Museum of Central Australia
Alice Springs Cultural Precinct, Larapinta Dr. ((08) 8951 5335. ○ daily. ● Good Fri, 25 Dec. 🎫 &

This museum, situated in the Cultural Precinct, concentrates on local natural history with displays of fossils, flora and fauna, meteorite pieces and minerals. It also has a fine collection of Aboriginal art and artifacts.

Meteorite fragment in the Museum of Central Australia

🏚 Adelaide House
Todd Mall. ((08) 8952 1856. ○ Mon–Sat. ● Good Fri. 🎫 &

Adelaide House, Alice Springs' first hospital, opened in 1926. It was designed by John Flynn, founder of the Royal Flying Doctor Service *(see p249)*, and is preserved as a museum dedicated to his memory.

🏚 Old Courthouse
Cnr Parsons & Hartley sts. ((08) 8952 9006. ○ 10am–5pm daily. ● mid-Dec–1 Feb **Donation.** &

Built in 1928 by Emil Martin, who was also responsible for The Residency, the Old Courthouse was in use until 1980,

when new law courts were opened nearby. The building has recently been restored and now features exhibitions devoted to the achievements of Australia's pioneer women.

Stuart Town Gaol

🏚 Stuart Town Gaol
Parsons St. ((08) 8952 4516. ○ Mon–Sat. ● mid Dec–1 Feb, public hols. 🎫 &

The oldest surviving building in central Alice Springs is the Stuart Town Gaol, which operated as a jail between 1909 and 1938 when a new prison was built on Stuart Terrace. The gaol is now open to the public.

🏚 The Residency
29 Parsons St. ((08) 8951 5688. ○ daily. ● mid Dec–1 Feb, Good Fri, 25 Dec. **Donation.** &

The Residency, built in 1927 for the regional administrator of Central Australia, was the home of Alice Springs' senior public servant until 1973. After restoration, it was opened to the public in 1996 and now houses a local history display.

🏛 Panorama Guth
65 Hartley St. ((08) 8952 2013. ○ Feb–mid Dec: daily. ● mid Dec–1 Feb. 🎫

Panorama Guth is a fantastic 360-degree painting of the Red Centre's main attractions, by Dutch-born artist Hendrik Guth who has lived in the town for more than 30 years. Also on display is an interesting exhibition of Aboriginal artifacts.

🏚 Alice Springs Telegraph Station Historical Precinct
Off Stuart Hwy. ((08) 8952 3993. ○ daily. ● 25 Dec. 🎫 &

This, the site of the first settlement in Alice Springs, features the original buildings and

View over central Alice Springs from the top of Anzac Hill

equipment of the telegraph station built in 1871. A small museum describes the task of setting up the station. Evening fireside slide shows are available from June to August.

Alice Springs Desert Park

Larapinta Drive. ☎ *(08) 8951 8788.* ○ *7:30am–6pm daily.* ● *25 Dec.* 💳 ♿

An excellent introduction to the area, this park lies on the western edge of the city and features three artificial habitat types: desert river, sand country and woodlands. Visitors may see many of the birds and animals of Central Australia here at close range.

Old Ghan Train Museum

MacDonnell Siding. ☎ *(08) 8955 5047.* ○ *daily.* ● *Good Fri, 25 Dec.* 💳 🍴 ☕ ♿

South of the city centre, this museum has an extensive collection of Ghan memorabilia. The Ghan train first ran from Adelaide to Alice Springs in 1929. It was named after the Afghans who once ran camel trains along the same route.

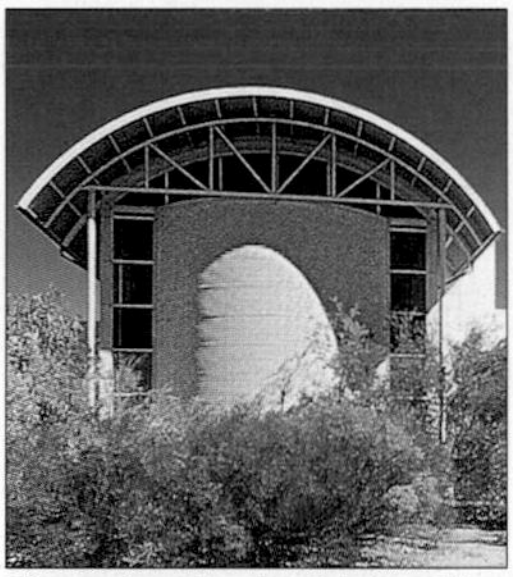

The modern façade of the Strehlow Research Centre in Alice Springs

Strehlow Research Centre

Alice Springs Cultural Precinct, Larapinta Drive. ☎ *(08) 8951 1111.* ○ *10am–5pm daily.* ● *1 Jan, Good Fri, 25 Dec.* 💳 ♿

Dedicated to the work of Professor Ted Strehlow (1908–78) among Aborigines in this area, this centre has the best collection of rare Aboriginal artifacts in Australia. Strehlow, born at Hermannsburg Mission west of Alice Springs, returned to this area after graduating from Adelaide University in 1931 to study the Aranda people. Realizing that their traditional ways were threatened, elders asked him to record secret rituals and keep their sacred objects. Many of these cannot be exhibited due to tribal taboo, but the centre has a fine display of other Aboriginal items.

Visitors' Checklist

👥 *27,000.* ✈ *14 km (8.5 miles) S of town.* 🚉 *George Crescent.* [i] *Gregory Terrace (08) 8952 5800.* 📅 *Henley-on-Todd Regatta (Oct); Camel Cup (Jul).*

Château Hornsby Winery

Petricks Rd. ☎ *(08) 8955 5133.* ○ *10am–5pm daily.* ● *Jan–Feb.* 💳 *for wine tasting.* ♿

Central Australia's only winery was opened 15 km (10 miles) south of Alice Springs in 1974. Five grape varieties are grown here with the aid of bore-water irrigation. Popular with locals, the winery has tastings, barbecues, a restaurant and live jazz on Sunday afternoons.

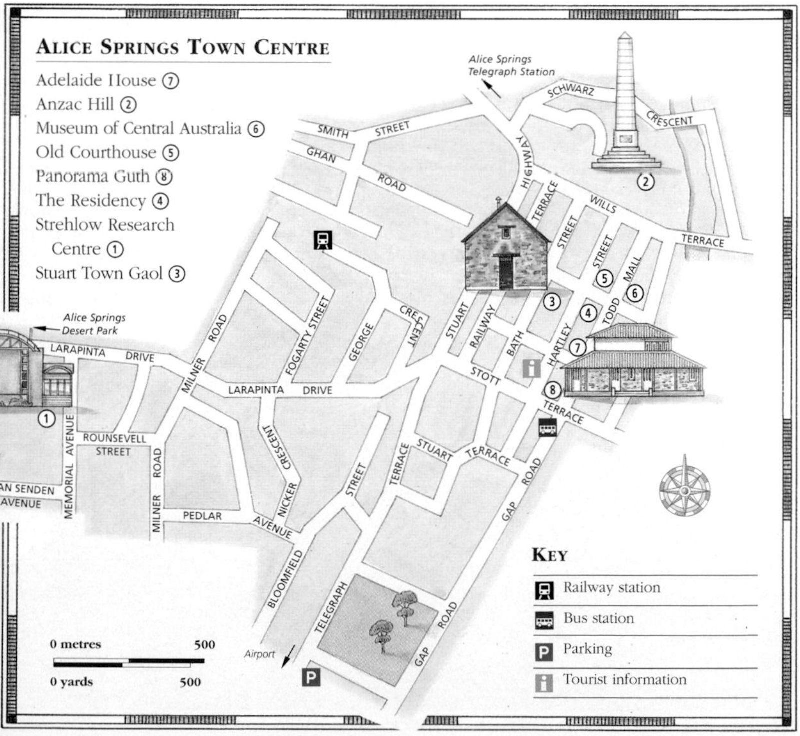
ALICE SPRINGS TOWN CENTRE
Adelaide House 7
Anzac Hill 2
Museum of Central Australia 6
Old Courthouse 5
Panorama Guth 8
The Residency 4
Strehlow Research Centre 1
Stuart Town Gaol 3
Alice Springs Telegraph Station
Alice Springs Desert Park
Airport
SCHWARZ CRESCENT
SMITH STREET
GHAN ROAD
HIGHWAY
WILLS TERRACE
LARAPINTA DRIVE
MILNER ROAD
FOGARTY STREET
GEORGE CRESCENT
STUART TERRACE
RAILWAY
BATH STREET
HARTLEY STREET
TODD MALL
STOTT TERRACE
ROUNSEVELL STREET
VAN SENDEN AVENUE
MEMORIAL AVENUE
PEDLAR AVENUE
NICKER CRESCENT
BLOOMFIELD STREET
TELEGRAPH TERRACE
GAP ROAD
0 metres 500
0 yards 500
KEY
Railway station
Bus station
Parking
Tourist information

Chambers Pillar Historical Reserve ❷

📞 (08) 8951 8211. 🚂 Alice Springs.
🚌 Alice Springs. ✔

CHAMBERS PILLAR, a 50-m (165-ft) high sandstone obelisk, was used by explorers as an important navigational landmark during early colonial exploration. The pillar is made of mixed red and yellow sandstone deposited more than 350 million years ago. Many of the explorers, such as John Ross who visited the area in 1870, carved their names and inscriptions into the rock.

Located 160 km (110 miles) south of Alice Springs, with the final section of the journey accessible only by 4WD vehicles, the pillar is also a sacred Aboriginal site.

Henbury Meteorites Conservation Reserve ❸

📞 (08) 8951 8211. 🚂 Alice Springs.
🚌 Alice Springs. ✔

THIS CLUSTER of 12 craters, located 147 km (90 miles) southwest of Alice Springs, was formed by a meteorite which crashed to earth several thousand years ago. It is believed that local Aborigines witnessed the event, as one of the Aboriginal names for the area suggests a fiery rock falling to earth. The largest crater in the group is 180 m (590 ft) across and is 6 m (20 ft) deep. Signs on a trail around the craters mark all their significant features.

Lush Palm Valley in Finke Gorge National Park, MacDonnell Ranges

MacDonnell Ranges ❹

🚂 Alice Springs. 🚌 Alice Springs.
ℹ Alice Springs (08) 8952 5800.
Simpsons Gap ◯ daily. ⚒
Standley Chasm ◯ daily. 🖼 ⚒

THE MACDONNELL RANGES are the eroded remnants of an ancient mountain chain which was once as monumental as the Himalayas. Still impressive and filled with striking scenery, the East and West MacDonnells contain gorges, waterholes and walking tracks. Running east and west of Alice Springs and easily accessible, they are popular with day-trippers. Visitors will notice the ranges' thrust-up layers of rock, evidence of geological movements more than 300 million years ago. Culturally, they contain many areas sacred to the Aranda people. In the West MacDonnells, 7 km

(4 miles) from Alice Springs, is John Flynn's Memorial Grave, which honours Presbyterian minister, Rev John Flynn, who founded the Royal Flying Doctor Service (see p249).

A further 10 km (6 miles) from town, **Simpsons Gap** is the first of a series of attractive gorges in the MacDonnells. A pretty spot, it is home to some rare local plant species. Nearby is **Standley Chasm**, a narrow, deep gorge whose sheer rock-faces glow a glorious red, particularly under the midday sun.

The large 18-m (60-ft) deep permanent waterhole within Ellery Gorge at Ellery Creek Big Hole is a good swimming spot. Serpentine Gorge, 20 km (12 miles) further west, is another narrow gorge created by an ancient river. A walking track leading to a lookout gives a fine view of its winding path.

Pushed up out of Ormiston Creek, the 300-m (985-ft) high walls of Ormiston Gorge are an awesome sight. The gorge consists of two layers of quartzite, literally doubled over each other, thus making it twice the height of others in the region.

Along Larapinta Drive is the small Aboriginal settlement of Hermannsburg, site of an 1870s Lutheran Mission which pre-dates Alice Springs. Famous as the home of the popular Aboriginal painter Albert Namatjira (1902–59), most of the town is contained within the **Hermannsburg Historic Precinct**, which includes a museum devoted to the mission and an art gallery.

Twenty km (12 miles) south of here lies the popular **Finke Gorge National Park**, home to Palm Valley, an unusual tropical oasis in

Sacred site of Corroboree Rock in the East MacDonnell Ranges near Alice Springs

the dry heart of the country with a host of rare and ancient palm species.

On the other side of Alice Springs, the East MacDonnell Ranges boast some beautiful sites accessible via the Ross Highway. Close to town is Emily Gap, one of the most significant Aranda sites in Australia. Further east, Corroboree Rock, a strangely shaped outcrop, has a crevice once used to store sacred Aranda objects. Trephina Gorge is the most spectacular of the East MacDonnell sights, featuring quartzite cliffs, red river gums and a number of scenic walks.

�📷 Hermannsburg Historic Precinct
Larapinta Drive. 📞 (08) 8956 7402. ○ daily. ⬤ 25 Dec. 🏵 🔂
♣ Finke Gorge National Park
🚃 Alice Springs. 🚌 Alice Springs. 🛈 Alice Springs (08) 8952 5800.

Mining building at Battery Hill, Tennant Creek

Tennant Creek ➏

🏚 3,500. ✖ 🚌 🛈 Battery Hill Regional Centre, Peko Rd (08) 8962 3388.

TENNANT CREEK was chosen as the site of a telegraph station on the Overland Telegraph Line in the late 1800s. The town grew after gold was discovered in the area in 1932. The **Tennant Creek Stamp Battery** is now a working museum, crushing ore to extract the gold.

Tennant Creek today is the second-largest town in the Red Centre. Nearly 500 km (310 miles) north of Alice Springs, it is also a major stopover along the Stuart Highway, between Darwin and South Australia. Other local attractions include the recreational Mary Ann Dam, 5 km (3 miles) out of town and ideal for boating and swimming. The remote **Telegraph Station**, 12 km (8 miles) north of the town, built in 1874, is now a museum.

�📷 Tennant Creek Stamp Battery
Battery Hill Regional Centre, Peko Rd.
📞 (08) 8962 3388. ○ daily. ⬤ Good Fri, 25 Dec. 🏵 🔂 🔂
�📷 Telegraph Station
🛈 Battery Hill Regional Centre, Peko Rd (08) 8962 3388. 🔂

Kings Canyon ➐

🚌 Alice Springs. 🚌 Alice Springs, Yulara. 🛈 Alice Springs (08) 8952 5800.

THE SPECTACULAR sandstone gorge of Kings Canyon, set within Watarrka National Park, has walls more than 100 m (330 ft) high that have been formed by millions of years of erosion. They contain the fossilized tracks of ancient marine creatures, and even ripplemarks of an ancient sea are visible. Several walking tracks take visitors around the rim of the gorge where there are some stunning views of the valley below. Watarrka National Park has many waterholes and areas of lush vegetation that contain more than 600 plant species. The park also provides a habitat for more than 100 bird species and 60 species of reptiles.

Spherical boulders of the Devil's Marbles

Devil's Marbles Conservation Reserve ➎

📞 (08) 8962 3388. 🚌 Tennant Creek. 🚍 from Tennant Creek Tourist Information. 🔂 🔂

APPROXIMATELY 104 km (65 miles) south of Tennant Creek, the Devil's Marbles Conservation Reserve comprises a collection of huge, spherical, red granite boulders, scattered across a shallow valley in the Davenport Ranges. The result of geological activity occurring 1,700 million years ago, the boulders were created when molten lava was compressed to create huge domes just below the earth's surface. Subsequent erosion of the overlying rock exposed the marbles. They are particularly beautiful at sunset.

Rich vegetation deep in the sandstone gorge of Kings Canyon

Uluṟu-Kata Tjuṯa National Park ⑧

THE MOST INSTANTLY recognizable of all Australian symbols is the huge, red monolith of Uluṟu (Ayers Rock). Rising high above the flat

Thorny devil desert landscape, Uluṟu is one of the world's natural wonders, along with the 36 rock domes of Kata Tjuṯa (The Olgas) and their deep valleys and gorges. Both sights are in Uluṟu-Kata Tjuṯa National Park, 463 km (288 miles) southwest of Alice Springs, which was established in 1958 and was named as a World Heritage site in 1987 *(see pp22–3)*. The whole area is sacred to Aboriginal people and, in 1985, the park was handed back to its indigenous owners and its sights reassumed their traditional names. As Aboriginal land, it is leased back to the Australian government and jointly managed with the local Aṉangu people. Within the park is an excellent cultural centre which details the Aboriginal lives and traditions of the area. Yulara, 12 km (7 miles) from Uluṟu, is the park's growing tourist resort *(see p281)*.

The Maruku Gallery
This Aboriginal-owned gallery sells traditional and modern Aboriginal crafts.

Kata Tjuṯa's domes rise in the distance behind Uluṟu.

Kata Tjuṯa (The Olgas)
This magnificent view of Kata Tjuṯa's domes is from the sunset viewing area. The site has drinking water and interpretive panels giving information on local flora and fauna.

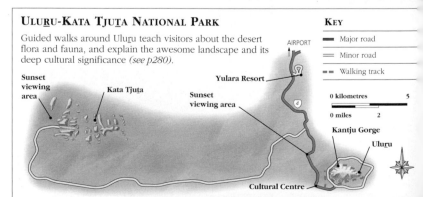

ULUṞU-KATA TJUṮA NATIONAL PARK

Guided walks around Uluṟu teach visitors about the desert flora and fauna, and explain the awesome landscape and its deep cultural significance *(see p280)*.

KEY
━━ Major road
══ Minor road
╍╍ Walking track

0 kilometres 5
0 miles 2

AIRPORT

Sunset viewing area
Kata Tjuṯa
Sunset viewing area
Yulara Resort
Kantju Gorge
Uluṟu
Cultural Centre

Olga Gorge
This scenic gorge runs between two of Kata Tjuta's huge domes. A walking track leads to a cliff face at the end where there is a rock pool and a trickling stream.

VISITORS' CHECKLIST

Hwy 4. ☒ Connellan Airport, 5 km (3 miles) N of Yulara/Ayers Rock Resort. ℹ Cultural Centre (08) 8956 3138. ◯ daily (times vary seasonally). 📷 ∅ in Cultural Centre. ♿ 📷 🏠 🖥

Uluru is famous for its colour changes, which range from deep red at sunrise and sunset to shiny black after rain.

Hare Wallaby
This mammal is significant to the Anangu people, who call it Mala. According to tradition, Mala people lived at Uluru and created many of the rock formations that are seen today.

DEHYDRATION IN THE DESERT

Uluru-Kata Tjuta National Park is in the heart of Australia's vast desert region. It can experience summer daytime temperatures of more than 45°C (113°F). To avoid dehydration and heat exhaustion all visitors are advised to wear hats, long-sleeved shirts with collars and sunscreen, and to avoid any strenuous activity between 10am and 4pm. Most importantly, each person should drink one litre of water per hour while walking in hot weather.

Vegetation is sparse on this desert plain except for a few areas of greenery found in sheltered spots where rainwater collects.

Mala Walk
This free, ranger-guided walk leads visitors to places created and used by the ancestral Mala people. It ends at Kantju Gorge, sacred to the Anangu, which contains a waterhole beneath a waterfall.

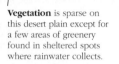

Exploring Uluṟu-Kata Tjuṯa National Park

Entrance sign to Uluṟu-Kata Tjuṯa National Park

I T IS IMPOSSIBLE to arrive at Uluṟu-Kata Tjuṯa National Park and not be filled with awe. The sheer size of the world's largest monolith, Uluṟu, rising from the flat desert plain, is a moving and impressive sight. Just as magical are the rounded humps of Kata Tjuṯa not far distant. All the rocks change colour from oranges and reds to purple during the day. Getting around the park, understanding some of its deep Aboriginal significance and learning about its geology, flora and fauna should not be rushed. There is much more to this fascinating area than can be seen or experienced in one day, and a two- or three-day stay is recommended.

Tourists enjoying the Mala walk around part of the base of Uluṟu

Blue-tongued lizard basking in the sun

🐾 Uluṟu (Ayers Rock)

Uluṟu, 3.6 km (2.25 miles) long and 2.4 km (1.5 miles) wide, stands 348 m (1,142 ft) above the plains. It is made from a single piece of sandstone which extends 5 km (3 miles) beneath the desert surface. Besides its immense Aboriginal cultural significance, Uluṟu is an outstanding natural phenomenon, best observed by watching its changing colours at dusk and taking a guided walk at the rock's base.

There are a number of walking trails around Uluṟu. The three-hour, 9.5-km (6-mile) guided walk around the base gives the greatest sense of its size and majesty. Sacred sights en route are fenced off, and entering is an offence. The Mala (hare wallaby) walk takes in several caves, some with rock art. The Liru (snake) walk starts at the cultural centre, with Aboriginal tour guides explaining how they use bush materials in their daily lives. The Kuniya (python) walk visits the Mutijulu waterhole on the southern side of Uluṟu where local Aṉangu people tell creation stories and display art describing various

legends. Details of all walks can be found at the Uluṟu-Kata Tjuṯa Cultural Centre.

🐾 Kata Tjuṯa (The Olgas)

Kata Tjuṯa, meaning "many heads", is a collection of massive rounded rock domes, 42 km (25 miles) to the west of Uluṟu. Beyond lies a vast, remote desert; permits from the Central Land Council (*see*

p254), 4WDs and full travel survival kits are needed in this inhospitable land.

Kata Tjuṯa is not one large rock; it is a system of gorges and valleys that you can walk around, making it a haunting, quiet and spiritual place. To the Aṉangu people, it is of equal significance to Uluṟu, but fewer stories about it can be told as they are restricted to initiated tribal men. The tallest rock, Mount Olga, is 546 m (1,790 ft) high, nearly 200 m (660 ft) higher than Uluṟu. There are two recommended walking trails. The Valley of the Winds walk takes about three hours and wanders through several deep gorges. This walk is partially closed when the temperature exceeds 36°C (97°F).

CLIMBING ULUṞU

The climbing of Uluṟu by the chain-rope path that has been in place since the 1960s is a contentious issue. Physically, it is a steep, 1.6-km (1-mile) climb in harsh conditions, and several tourists die each year from heart attacks or falls. Culturally, the route to the top follows the sacred path taken by the ancestral Mala (hare wallaby) men for important ceremonies. The Aṉangu ask that visitors respect their wishes and do not climb the rock. Despite increasing numbers of visitors to Uluṟu, fewer people climb each year.

If you do decide to climb, the ascent takes about two hours. Climbing the rock is banned for the remainder of the day if the temperature at any point of the climb reaches 36°C (97°F). A dawn climb is most popular.

Sign warning tourists of the dangers of climbing Uluṟu

THE ANANGU OF ULURU

Archaeological evidence suggests that Aboriginal people have lived at Uluru for at least 22,000 years and that both Uluru and Kata Tjuta have long been places of enormous ceremonial and cultural significance to a number of Aboriginal tribes.

The traditional owners of Uluru and Kata Tjuta are the Anangu people. They believe that both sites were formed during the creation period by ancestral spirits who also gave them the laws and rules of society that they live by today. The Anangu believe they are direct descendants of these ancestral beings and that, as such, they are responsible for the protection and management of these lands.

The Anangu Aborigines performing a traditional dance

The Olga Gorge (Walpa Gorge) walk leads up the pretty Olga Gorge to its dead-end cliff face and a rock pool. Walkers here may spot the small brown spinifex bird or the thorny devil spiked lizard.

🏛 Uluru-Kata Tjuta Cultural Centre
📞 (08) 8956 3138.
🕐 daily. 🈂 ♿

Near to the base of Uluru is an award-winning cultural centre, with multilingual displays, videos and exhibitions. It is an excellent introduction to the park and well worth visiting before exploring the rock and its surrounding area. The Nintiringkupai display focuses on the history and management of Uluru-Kata Tjuta National Park and includes up-to-date brochures and information on walking trails, sights and tours. The Tjukurpa display, with its art, sounds and videos, is a good introduction to the complex system of Anangu beliefs and laws. Attached to the cultural centre is the Aboriginal-owned Maruku Arts and Craft shop, where artists are at work and dancers and

musicians give performances for the tourists. The traditional art, on bark and canvas, tells the story of Uluru Tjukurpa legends.

Ayers Rock Resort
Yulara Drive. 🛈 (08) 8957 7377.
Yulara is an environmentally friendly, modern tourist village well equipped to cater for the 500,000 annual visitors. Nestling between the desert

dunes 20 km (12 miles) north of Uluru and just outside the national park boundary, it serves as a comfortable, green and relaxing base for exploring Uluru and Kata Tjuta. The resort offers all standards of accommodation, from five-star luxury to backpacker accommodation and camping grounds, and is the only option for those who want to stay in the immediate vicinity (see pp478–9).

The visitors' centre at Yulara has information about the park and its geology, flora and fauna. It also sells souvenirs and helps to arrange tours with the licensed operators in the park. Every day at 7:30am there is a free, early morning guided walk through the wonderful native garden of the Sails in the Desert Hotel (see p479). Each evening at the Amphitheatre there is an hour-long concert of Aboriginal music featuring a variety of indigenous instruments, including the didgeridoo. A Night Sky Show is also available, and this describes both the Anangu and ancient Greek stories of the stars.

Yulara also has a shopping centre, which includes a post office, bank and supermarket, and many different restaurants and outdoor eating options (see p511). Other tourist facilities include a childcare centre catering for children up to the age of eight.

Aerial view of Yulara Resort, with Uluru in the distance

WESTERN AUSTRALIA

Western Australia at a Glance

THE HUGE STATE OF Western Australia encompasses a land mass of more than 2,500,000 sq km (1,000,000 sq miles). In recent years, the state's popularity as a tourist destination has increased, with large numbers of visitors drawn to its many areas of extreme natural beauty. The landscape ranges from giant karri forests, imposing mountains and meadows of wild flowers to vast expanses of untamed wilderness with ancient gorges and rock formations. The coastline has an abundance of beaches, ideal for surfing, and some stunning offshore reefs. In the east, great deserts stretch to the state border. The capital, Perth, is home to 80 per cent of the state's population but there are many historic towns scattered around the southwest, such as the gold field settlements of Kalgoorlie and Coolgardie.

Shark Bay World Heritage and Marine Park *is Australia's westernmost point. Visitors flock to this protected area to watch the dolphins swim in the waters close to the shore (see pp318–19).*

Perth *is Australia's most isolated yet most modern state capital. Gleaming skyscrapers, an easy-going atmosphere and coastal setting make it a popular destination (see pp294–9).*

Fremantle's *heyday as a major port was at the end of the 19th century. Many of its historic buildings remain. Today the town is renowned for its crafts markets (see pp302–303).*

◁ **Perth city skyline at night**

Karijini National Park is in the Pilbara region and is a spectacular landscape of gorges, pools and waterfalls. The area is particularly popular with experienced hikers; guided tours are also available for more novice bush-walkers (see p321).

Purnululu (Bungle Bungle) National Park is one of Australia's most famous natural sights, with its multi-coloured rock domes. Access is limited, but helicopter flights offer views of the area (see p323).

NORTH OF PERTH
(see pp312–23)

Wave Rock is 15 m (50 ft) high, 110 m (360 ft) long and is so named because its formation resembles a breaking wave. The illusion is further enhanced by years' worth of water stains running down its face (see p310).

PERTH AND THE SOUTHWEST
(see pp290–311)

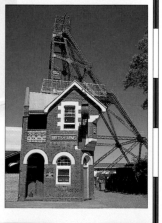

Kalgoorlie made its name in the 1890s when gold was discovered in the region. Much of its 19th-century architecture has been preserved (see p310).

0 km   100

0 miles   100

Wild Flowers of Western Australia

W ESTERN AUSTRALIA is truly the nation's wild flower state. In the spring, from August to November, more than 11,000 species of flowers burst into brilliantly coloured blooms, carpeting deserts, plains, farmland and forests with blazing reds, yellows, pinks and blues.

A staggering 75 per cent of these flowers are unique to the state, giving it one of the world's richest floras. It is home to such remarkable plants as the kangaroo paw, the cowslip orchid and the carnivorous Albany pitcher plant, as well as giant jarrah and karri forests.

The elegant kangaroo paw looks exactly like its name suggests. The state's floral emblem, it has many different species and mostly grows in coastal heath and dry woodland areas.

WHEN AND WHERE TO SEE THE WILD FLOWERS

Bushwalking or driving among the flower carpets of Western Australia is an experience not to be missed. Most of the wild flowers bloom in spring, but exactly when depends on their location in this vast state. The wild flower season begins in the northern Pilbara in July and culminates in the magnificent flowering around the Stirling Ranges and the south coast in late October and November.

The Albany pitcher plant grows near coastal estuaries around Albany in the southwest. One of the world's largest carnivorous plants, it traps and devours insects in its sticky hairs.

The magnificent royale hakea is one of many hakea species in Western Australia. It is found on the coast near Esperance and in Fitzgerald River National Park.

Much of Western Australia is arid, dusty outback country where the only vegetation is dry bush shrubs and, after rainfall, wild flowers.

Many wild flowers possess an incredible ability to withstand even the driest, hottest ground.

Red flowering gum trees in the Stirling Ranges burst into bright red flowers every November, attracting honey bees.

The cowslip orchid is a bright yellow orchid with red streaks and five main petals. It can usually be found in October, in the dramatic Stirling Ranges region.

Leschenaultia biloba is a brilliant blue bell-shaped flower found in jarrah forests near Collie, or in drier bush and plain country where it flowers in carpets of blue.

The boab (baobab) tree is specimen related to the African baobab. Growing in the rocky plains of the Kimberley (see pp322–3), it holds a great deal of water in its swollen trunk and can grow many metres in circumference.

The bright daisy flowers of the everlastings come in a host of creams, pinks, yellows, oranges and reds.

GIANTS OF THE WESTERN AUSTRALIAN FOREST

It is not only the native flowers that are special to Western Australia. So too are the trees – especially the towering jarrah and karri eucalypts of the southern forests. A major hardwood timber industry, harvesting the jarrah and karri, remains in the state's south-west near Manjimup and Pemberton *(see p307)*. Today, however, thousands of trees are preserved in national parks such as Shannon and Walpole-Nornalup which has a walkway high in the trees for visitors.

Giant karri trees grow to a height of 85 m (280 ft). They live for up to 300 years, reaching their maximum height after 100 years.

EVERLASTING FLOWERS

Native to Australia, everlastings carpet vast areas in many parts of Western Australia. Especially prolific in the southeast, they can also be seen from the roadside in the north, stretching as far as the eye can see.

Everlastings are so called because the petals stay attached to the flower even after it has died.

The scarlet banksia (see p442), is one of 41 banksia species found in Western Australia. It is named after Sir Joseph Banks, the botanist who first noted this unusual tree and its flower in 1770.

Sturt's desert pea is actually South Australia's floral emblem but is also prolific in the dry inland areas of Western Australia. Its bright flowers spring up after rain in the deserts, sometimes after lying dormant for years.

The Kimberley

Dingo cave painting

ONE OF THE LAST truly remote regions in Australia, the Kimberley in north-western Australia covers 421,000 sq km (165,000 sq miles), yet has a population of less than 25,000. Geologically it is one of the oldest regions on earth. Its rocks formed up to 2,000 million years ago, with little landscape disturbance since. Aboriginal people have lived here for thousands of years but this unique land has been a tourist attraction only since the 1980s.

KEY

━━ Highway

━━ Major road

═══ Unsealed road

—— National park boundary

THE BUNGLE BUNGLES

The tiger-striped beehive mountains that comprise the Bungle Bungle range were only discovered by tourists in the 1980s. These great geological and scenic wonders are now protected in Purnululu National Park *(see p323)*. The large, weathered sandstone domes are most easily viewed by air from Kununurra or Halls Creek, but visitors who make the effort to explore this 4WD-only park will also encounter some stunning narrow gorges and clear pools.

The black and orange moulded domes of the Bungle Bungles

Windjana Gorge National Park is one of the three stunning Devonian Reef national parks *(see p323)*.

The Great Northern Highway is a sealed road that runs from the Northern Territory border to Broome and Perth beyond.

0 kilometres   100

0 miles   100

Cape Leveque

Charnley River

Isdell River

King Sound

Windjana Gorge National Park

Gibb River Road

Derby

Meda River

Tunnel Creek National Park

GREAT SANDY DESERT

Fitzroy River

Geikie Gorge National Park

Broome

Fitzroy Crossing

Cable Beach at Broome attracts many visitors with its vast white beaches and gentle surf. Tourism in the Kimberley is still in its infancy, but some 50,000 tourists now enjoy Broome's tropical atmosphere each year.

The Cockburn Ranges have deep inaccessible caves and sandstone cliffs separating the summit from the surrounding plains. The ranges tower above the crocodile-infested Pentecost River on the Gibb River Road. As with many sites in the region, they hold great Aboriginal significance.

Gibb River Road is a rough highway which is used by locals and adventurous travellers.

Emma Gorge is one of hundreds of deep, cool waterholes hidden across the Kimberley. Located near El Questro Station, it was made by waterfalls cascading off the red sandstone plateau into gorges and valleys below.

THE ABORIGINES OF THE KIMBERLEY

Legend suggests that the first Aborigines arrived on the continent, near Broome, 200,000 years ago *(see p43)*. While this view has yet to be validated by scientific evidence, the fact that many of the "songlines" *(see p27)* marked by landmarks and ceremonial sites all end or start around the Kimberley certainly suggests that the area has seen a very long period of human habitation.

Two-thirds of the region's population remains Aboriginal, and Aboriginal culture here is one of the most traditional in Australia. Local Aboriginal communities equip their children with a strong identity to help them cope with the demands of living in a mixed-race society.

Aboriginal art in the Kimberley differs from most other parts of Australia. Dot art does not predominate; instead there are the outstanding Wandjina figures of the central Kimberley, and the object paintings of the Purnululu community based near the Bungle Bungles.

The mysterious Wandjina figures can be seen throughout the Kimberley region.

Aboriginal rock art in the Kimberley has now been dated back 125,000 years, 80,000 years earlier than previously thought.

PERTH AND THE SOUTHWEST

ESTERN AUSTRALIA'S PRETTY CAPITAL, Perth, is the most isolated city in the world, closer to Southeast Asia than it is to any other Australian city. The state's stunning southern region takes in magnificent forests and diverse coastal scenery. To the east, the vast Nullarbor Plain covers more than 250,000 sq km (100,000 sq miles), and rolling wheat fields lead to the arid interior and the gold fields.

Aborigines have lived in the southern region of Western Australia for at least 30,000 years. However, within 20 years of the settlement of the state's first European colony, in 1829, most Aboriginal groups had been either forcibly ejected from the region, imprisoned or stricken by European diseases.

Europeans visited the southern part of the state as early as 1696, but it was not until 1826 that British colonist Captain James Stirling arrived in the Swan River area, declaring the Swan River Colony, later Perth, in 1829. Convicts arrived in 1850 and helped to build public buildings and the colony's infrastructure, until transportation to Western Australia ceased in 1868.

In the 1890s, gold strikes in Coolgardie and Kalgoorlie led to a wave of prosperity in the region. Many ornate late Victorian-style buildings were erected, many of which are still standing.

The beginning of the 20th century saw huge changes: a telegraph cable was laid connecting Perth with South Africa and London, and, in 1917, the railway arrived to join Kalgoorlie with the eastern states. In the 1920s, immigrants and returning World War I servicemen were drafted to the area to clear and develop land under the Group Settlement Scheme. Much of the land, however, was intractable and many people abandoned it.

Today, Perth and the Southwest are fast becoming popular international tourist destinations. Blessed with superb beaches and a glorious climate, the region has everything to offer visitors from climbing the tallest fire-lookout tree in the country to whale-watching along the coast. World-class wineries abound in the Margaret River region and, in springtime, vast tracts of the south are covered with wild flowers.

Dramatic beauty of the Stirling Ranges rising from the plains in the southwest of the state

◁ **The glittering night skyline of Western Australia's vibrant state capital, Perth**

Exploring Perth and the Southwest

THE CITY OF PERTH lies on the Swan River, just 10 km (6 miles) from where it flows into the Indian Ocean. The coastal plain on which it stands is bordered to the north and west by the Darling Range, beyond which lie the region's wheat fields. To the south is a diverse landscape: forests with some of the tallest trees on earth, mountains that dramatically change colour during the course of each day and a spectacular coastline. Inland are the gold fields that kept the colony alive in the 1890s; beyond lies the Nullarbor Plain, bordering the raging Southern Ocean.

Beach and raging surf in Leeuwin Naturaliste National Park, near the mouth of the Margaret River

GETTING AROUND

Perth's public transport is fast and reliable, and travel within the city centre is free. Westrail, Greyhound and Skywest (the state's airline) offer rail, coach and air services to many of the region's towns. Distances are not overwhelming, so travelling by car allows visits to the many national parks in the area. The arterial routes are fast roads often used by gigantic road trains. However, there are many tourist routes which lead to places of interest and great natural beauty. Some national parks have unsealed roads, and a few are accessible only by 4WD.

SIGHTS AT A GLANCE

SEE ALSO

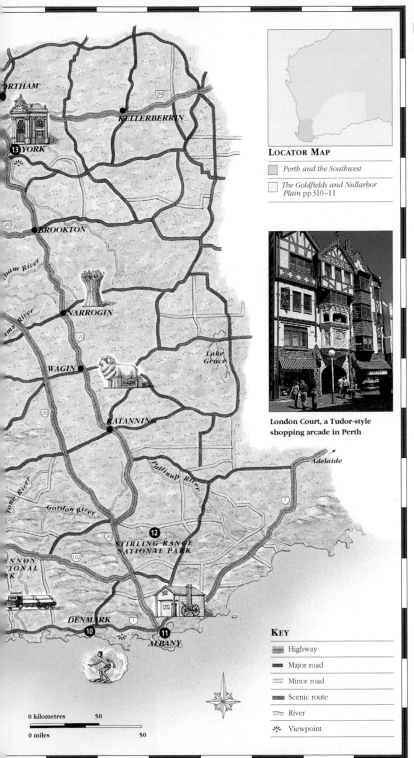

LOCATOR MAP

Perth and the Southwest

The Goldfields and Nullarbor Plain pp 310–11

London Court, a Tudor-style shopping arcade in Perth

KEY

Highway

Major road

Minor road

Scenic route

River

Viewpoint

0 kilometres 50

0 miles 50

Street-by-Street: Perth ❶

Fire Brigade badge

THE HISTORY OF PERTH has been one of building and rebuilding. The makeshift houses of the first settlers were soon replaced with more permanent buildings, many erected by convicts in the latter half of the 19th century. The gold rush of the 1890s and the mining boom of the 1960s and 1970s brought waves of prosperity, encouraging the citizens to replace their older buildings with more prestigious symbols of the state's wealth. As a result, much of the early city has gone, but a few traces remain, hidden between skyscrapers or in the city's public parks.

Supreme Court Gardens

★ St George's Anglican Cathedral
This Victorian Gothic Revival-style cathedral, built in the late 19th century, has a fine rose window (see p296).

Government House
Hidden behind walls and trees, the original residence of the state governor was built by convicts between 1859 and 1864. The building's patterned brickwork is typical of the period.

STAR SIGHTS

★ Perth Mint

★ St George's Anglican Cathedral

The Deanery
Built in 1859, the Deanery was originally the residence of the Dean of St George's. It now houses the Cathedral administration.

Old Fire Station
Built at the turn of the century, the Old Fire Station was, for about 80 years, home to Perth's Fire Brigade. It is now a museum (see p297).

St Mary's Roman Catholic Cathedral
Built by the Benedictines in 1844, St Mary's was modified in 1929. Opposite the cathedral is the beautiful Convent of Mercy.

| 0 metres | 100 |
| 0 yards | 100 |

KEY

— — — Suggested route

Perth Concert Hall

★ Perth Mint
Perth Mint is Australia's oldest working mint. Built in 1899 to utilize the finds of the gold rush, it is now open to the public for tours and gold pouring demonstrations (see p297).

Central Perth

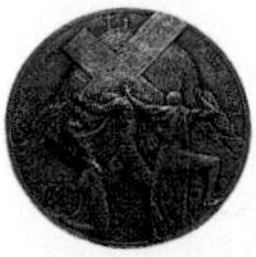
Bronze plaque in St George's Cathedral

PERTH IS A RELATIVELY SMALL and quiet city compared with those on the east coast. Its main commercial and shopping areas can be easily explored on foot. The city's atmosphere is brisk but not hurried, and traffic is by no means congested. Redevelopment projects in the 1970s brought skyscrapers and more roads, but they also made space for city parks and courtyards lined with cafés and shady trees. The city centre is bordered to the south and east by a wide stretch of the Swan River known as Perth Water, and to the north lies Northbridge, Perth's restaurant and entertainment centre.

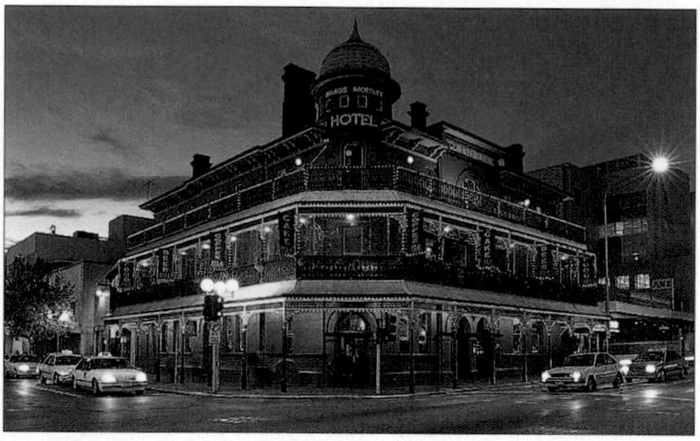

The elaborately decorated Brass Monkey Hotel on William Street

Exploring Central Perth

St Georges Terrace is Perth's main commercial street. At its western end stands Parliament House, and in front of this is Barracks Archway. Further east, the Cloisters, built in 1850 as a school, boast some fine decorative brickwork. Nearby is the Old Perth Boys' School, a tiny one-storey building that was Perth's first school for boys.

Perth's shopping centre lies between William and Barrack streets. It is a maze of arcades, plazas and elevated walkways. The main areas are Hay Street Mall and Murray Street Mall. On the corner of William Street and St Georges Terrace lies the Town Hall (1870), close to the site where Perth was founded.

Beyond the railway tracks is Northbridge, the focus of much of Perth's nightlife. James Street is lined with many restaurants, cafés and food halls offering a variety of ethnic cuisines. Also on this street, the ornate Brass Monkey Hotel is a perfect example of the colonial architecture of the gold rush period.

Barracks Archway

Cnr St Georges Terrace & Elder St.

Barracks Archway is all that remains of the 1863 barracks that once housed the soldiers who were brought in to police the convict population.

Perth Cultural Centre

James St. *(08) 9492 6600.* *10am–5pm daily.* *25 Dec, 1 Jan, Good Fri, 25 Apr.*

To the north of the city centre is the Perth Cultural Centre, a pedestrianized complex on a number of different levels, with various garden areas. The centre is home to the Art Gallery of Western Australia, which contains a collection of modern Aboriginal and Australian art, and some European and Asian pieces. It also has space for temporary exhibitions, such as travelling shows from major world collections. The cultural centre also houses the Perth Institute of Contemporary Art (PICA).

Western Australian Museum

Francis St. *(08) 9427 2700.* *9:30am–5pm daily.* *25 Apr, Good Fri, 25 Dec, 26 Dec, 1 Jan.* *limited.*

In the same area as the Perth Cultural Centre stands the Western Australian Museum complex. Among its buildings are the Old Perth Gaol (1856), with exhibitions on life in the original Swan River colony, and Roe Street Cottage (1863), one of the colony's first homes restored on this site in 1991. The museum's jewel is its exhibition entitled "Patterns of Life in a Vast Land", which covers the history, lifestyle and culture of Western Australian Aborigines and the work of archaeologists in the state.

St George's Anglican Cathedral

Cnr Pier St & St Georges Terrace (enter from Cathedral Ave).

(08) 9325 5766. *daily.*

St George's Cathedral, consecrated in 1888, was only the second permanent Anglican place of worship in Perth. Between 1841 and 1845 Perth's first Anglican church was built, in Classical Revival style, on the site of the existing cathedral, but in 1875 it was decided that the community required a more prestigious place of worship. The old church was demolished as soon as the new St George's was built, but some artifacts from the old building remain, including some of the jarrah pews and the carved eagle lectern. This Gothic Revival building was built in redbrick and limestone, largely from

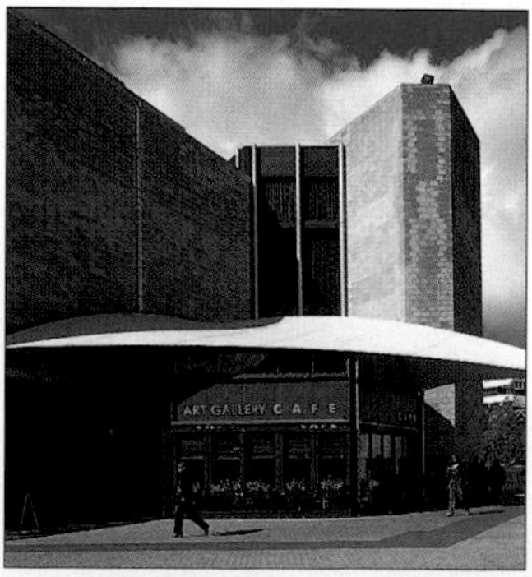

Perth Cultural Centre plaza

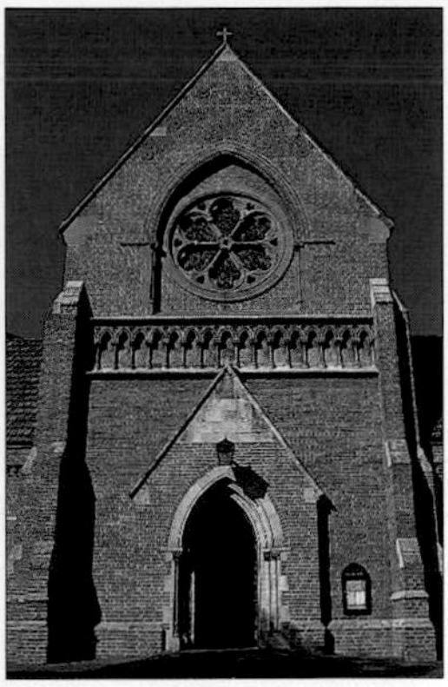

Western façade of St George's Cathedral showing rose window

local sources. Some of its more notable features include the intricate English alabaster *reredos* at the base of the east window, the modernistic medallions cast for the Stations of the Cross and some original 19th-century Russian icons.

Perth Mint

310 Hay St. ☎ *(08) 9421 7277.* 🕐 *9am–4pm daily.* ● *Good Fri, 25 April, 25 Dec, 1 Jan.* 🎫 ♿

Perth Mint was opened in 1899, under British control, to refine the gold found in the gold fields of Western Australia at that time and turn it into British sovereigns and half-sovereigns. Although it no longer produces coins for general circulation nor refines gold on the premises, the mint still produces proof coins and specialist pure precious metal coins. This production makes it Australia's oldest operating mint.

The graceful mint building contains a museum with coin and precious metal exhibits and displays on gold mining and refining in Western Australia. Every hour a "Gold Pour" takes place in the Melting House that has been in operation for 100 years. This shows visitors how a 200-ounce gold bar is made from pure molten gold. The museum also has a gift shop selling gold and silver jewellery and other souvenirs.

Old Fire Station

Cnr Murray & Irwin sts. ☎ *(08) 9323 9468.* 🕐 *Mon–Fri.* ● *public hols.* ♿

Perth's City Fire Brigade moved from this, its original home, to a much larger site at the eastern end of Hay Street in 1979.

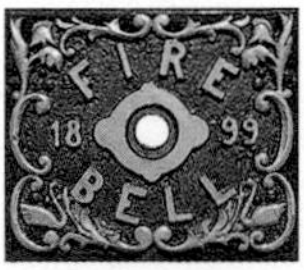
FIRE
18 99
BELL

Perth Fire Station's original fire bell

The Old Fire Station is now home to a fascinating museum charting the history of the fire service in Perth and other parts of Western Australia, and a fire safety centre. Educational exhibits here include some well-preserved old fire appliances and reconstructions showing the original use of various rooms in the station.

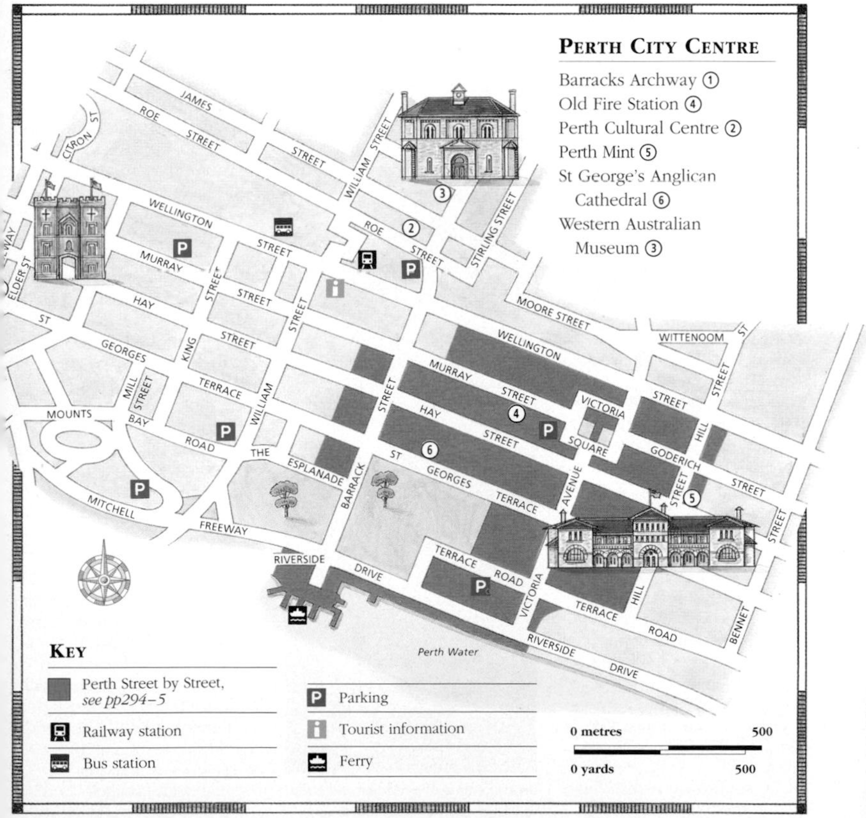
PERTH CITY CENTRE
Barracks Archway ①
Old Fire Station ④
Perth Cultural Centre ②
Perth Mint ⑤
St George's Anglican Cathedral ⑥
Western Australian Museum ③
JAMES STREET
ROE STREET
CITRON ST
WILLIAM STREET
WELLINGTON STREET
MURRAY STREET
HAY STREET
ST GEORGES TERRACE
KING STREET
MILL STREET
MOUNTS BAY ROAD
MITCHELL FREEWAY
THE ESPLANADE
BARRACK STREET
RIVERSIDE DRIVE
STIRLING STREET
MOORE STREET
WITTENOOM ST
VICTORIA SQUARE
VICTORIA AVENUE
GODERICH STREET
HILL STREET
TERRACE ROAD
BENNET STREET
ELDER ST
Perth Water
KEY
Perth Street by Street, see pp294–5
Railway station
Bus station
Parking
Tourist information
Ferry
0 metres 500
0 yards 500

Exploring Greater Perth

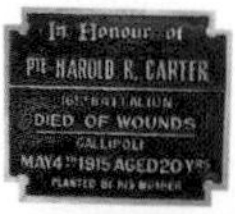

Kings Park memorial

BEYOND THE CITY CENTRE, Greater Perth covers the Darling Range in the northeast to the Indian Ocean in the west. It has several large parks, including Kings Park, overlooking the river. On the coast, beaches stretch from Hillarys Boat Harbour in the north to Fremantle in the south *(see pp302–303)*. Perth's suburbs are accessible by train, local bus or car.

Sights at a Glance

Hills Forest 3
Kings Park 1
Museum of Childhood 7
Perth Zoo 5
Sunset Coast 2
Underwater World 6
Whiteman Park 4

Key

- Central Perth
- Greater Perth
- Highway
- Major road
- Minor road

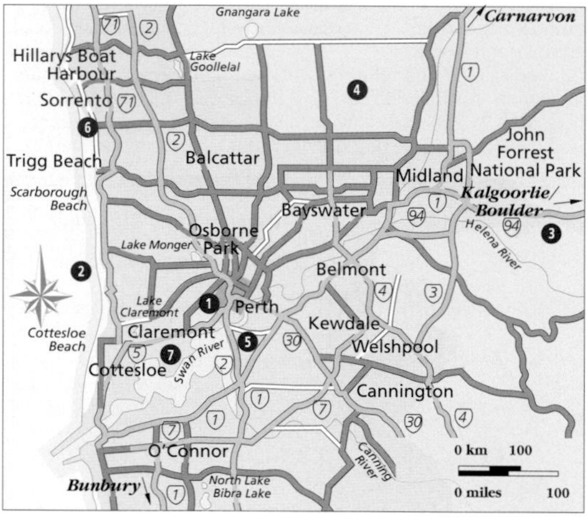

Kings Park

Fraser Ave, West Perth. ☎ (08) 9480 3600. 🕒 daily. ♿

Established at the end of the 19th century, Kings Park is 400 ha (1,000 acres) of both wild and cultivated parkland. Situated on Mount Eliza, it offers fine views of the city and the Swan River. Most of the park is bushland, which can be seen from the top of the DNA Lookout Tower, the park's highest point. There are many walking trails and barbecue areas.

A landscaped area on the eastern side includes the Botanic Gardens and a series of artificial pools and waterfalls. The War Memorial on Anzac Bluff is dedicated to the Western Australians who died in the two world wars.

The Minmara Gun Gun and Pioneer Women's Memorial are monuments to the women who helped build the Swan River Colony and, later, the state.

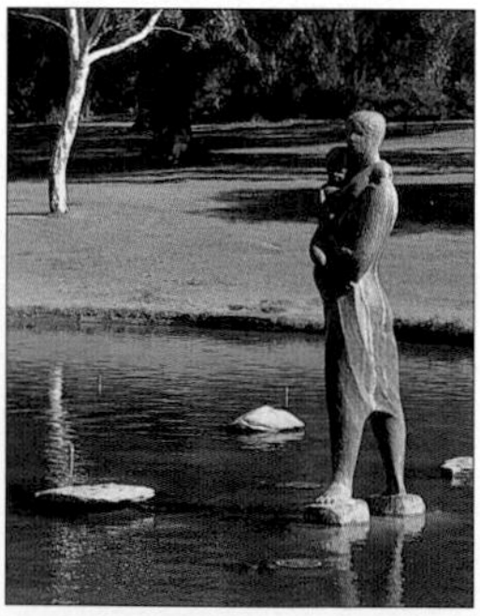

Bronze statue of a mother and child in Kings Park Botanic Gardens

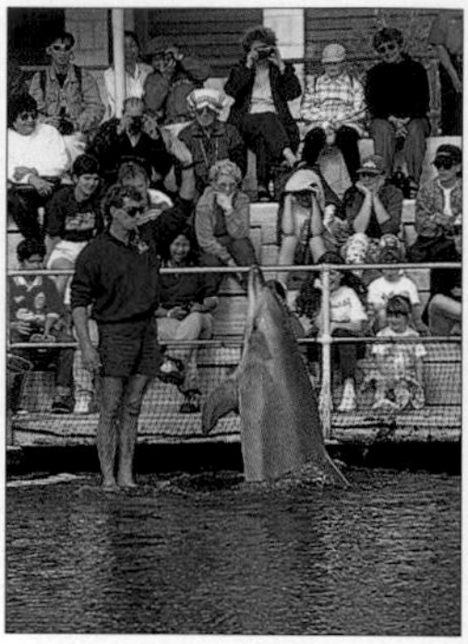

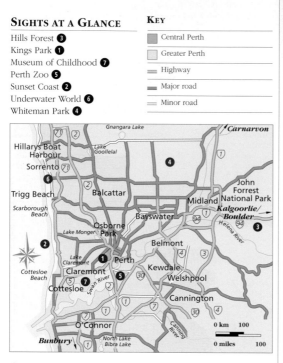

Dolphin performing for crowds at Underwater World, north of Perth

Aquarium of Western Australia

Hillarys Boat Harbour, Southside Drive, Sorrento. ☎ (08) 9447 7500. 🕒 9am–5pm daily. ⛔ 25 Dec. 📋 ♿

At Hillarys Boat Harbour, to the north of Perth's Sunset Coast, this is a magnificent aquarium complex. A transparent submerged tunnel allows visitors to observe native sea creatures, including sharks and stingrays. There is a Touch Pool, where rays and sharks can be stroked. The denizens of the outside seal pool never fail to delight visitors of all ages.

Museum of Childhood

Edith Cowan University, Claremont Campus, Bay Rd, Claremont. ☎ (08) 9442 1373. 🕒 10am–4pm Mon–Fri. ⛔ public hols. 📋 ♿

In the suburb of Claremont, this engaging museum is dedicated to the history of childhood in Australia. Its comprehensive collection exhibits toys and games, and details schooling and home life.

Sunset Coast

Via West Coast Hwy.

Perth's Sunset Coast is lined with 30 km (20 miles) of white sandy beaches, many of them virtually deserted during the week. There are beaches to suit all tastes. Cottesloe Beach, at the southern end, is fringed with grassland and trees, and offers safe swimming and good services, making it popular with families, as is Sorrento Beach in the north.

Scarborough Beach is very popular with surfers, but it is for experienced swimmers only as strong currents can make it dangerous on windy days. Trigg Beach just above Scarborough is also a good surfing spot. Just north of Cottesloe, Swanbourne Beach is a naturist beach.

Many of the city's beaches have no shade whatsoever and Perth residents are constantly reminded that the sun's rays, unshielded due to the hole in the ozone layer, can burn within minutes. Beach-goers are strongly advised to take sunscreen, a hat, T-shirt and sun umbrella.

Students admiring a magnificent tiger in Perth Zoo

Surfing on Cottesloe Beach

🦘 Perth Zoo

20 Labouchere Rd. 📞 *(08) 9367 7988.* 🕐 *9am–5pm daily.* 🅿️ ♿

In South Perth, a ferry-ride away from the city centre, lies Perth Zoo. Dedicated to conservation, it has all the features of an international-standard zoo, here delightfully set amid pretty gardens. Attractions include a very interesting Nocturnal House, a wildlife park and an African savannah exhibit.

🍃 Hills Forest

Via Great Western Hwy.

Only 30 minutes' drive from Central Perth, Hills Forest lies in the Darling Range and offers a wide range of bush-related activities. Conserved since 1919 as the catchment area for the Mundaring Reservoir, which provided water for the southern gold fields in the 19th century *(see p51)*, Hills Forest is now managed as a conservation and recreation area. It is well served with barbecue and picnic areas and camp sites. At Mundaring Weir landscaped gardens are a lovely backdrop for picnics. On the northern edge of the forest is John Forrest National Park, Western Australia's first national park. It consists of dense woodland and heathland with trails leading to beautiful pools and waterfalls, including the charming Hovea Falls.

🍃 Whiteman Park

Lord St, Whiteman. 📞 *(08) 9249 2446.* 🕐 *daily.* 🅿️ 🚻 ♿

Northeast of the city centre lies popular Whiteman Park. Visitors can tour the park on a 1920s tram or by train. A craft village displays local craftsmanship and there is also a motor museum with a collection of vehicles from the last 100 years. As well as an emu and kangaroo enclosure, there is also a museum displaying farm machinery and a café offering refreshments.

A horse-drawn wagon taking visitors on a tour of Whiteman Park

Rottnest Island ❷

Less than 20 km (12 miles) west of Fremantle lies the idyllic island of Rottnest. Settled by Europeans in 1831, it was used as an Aboriginal prison between 1838 and 1902. In 1917, in recognition of its scenic beauty and rich bird life, the island became a protected area and today it is a popular tourist destination. Rottnest's oldest settlement, Thomson Bay, dates from the 1840s. The island's other settlements, all built in the 20th century, are found at Longreach Bay, Geordie Bay and Kingstown. Rottnest's rugged coastline comprises beaches, coves and reefs – ideal for many water-based activities – salt lakes and several visible shipwrecks. Private cars are not allowed on the island, so the only way to get around is by bicycle or bus, or on foot.

Aerial View of Rottnest
Rottnest is 12 km (7.5 miles) long, 4.5 km (3 miles) wide, and is governed by strict conservation regulations.

City of York Bay was named after Rottnest's most tragic shipwreck. In 1899, a sea captain mistook a lighthouse flare for a pilot's signal and headed towards the rocks.

Rottnest Lighthouse
The lighthouse on Wadjemup Hill was built in 1895. Wadjemup is the Aboriginal name for the island.

Rocky Bay
Overlooked by the sandy Lady Edeline beach, this popular, picturesque bay also contains the wreck of the barque Mira Flores *which sank in 1886.*

Strickland Bay
was named after Sir Gerald Strickland, governor of Rottnest from 1909 to 1912, and is a prime surfing spot.

0 metres	1000
0 yards	1000

Cape Vlamingh Lookout
Named after Dutch explorer Willem de Vlamingh, Rottnest's most famous early European visitor, this lookout stands at the furthest tip of the island, 10.5 km (6.5 miles) from Thomson Bay. The view is spectacular.

KEY

═══	Minor road
– –	Paths and trails
🔺	Camp site
🏕	Picnic area
✈	Aerodrome
⛴	Ferry
ℹ	Tourist information
✵	Viewpoint

The Rottnest Hotel
With its turrets and crenellations, this was built in 1864 as the state governor's summer residence. Known locally as the Quokka Arms, it is now a hotel.

Little Parakeet Bay is popular with snorkellers. The bay is also an excellent spot to see the rock parrots after which it is named.

The Basin is the most popular beach on Rottnest Island, particularly with families camping with children, as it is easily accessible on foot from Thomson Bay.

The Rottnest Museum is housed in the old granary, which dates from 1857. Exhibits cover the island's geology, its many shipwrecks, flora and fauna, and memorabilia of the early settlers and convicts.

Thomson Bay Settlement

Geordie/ Longreach Settlement

Lake Baghdad

Herschell Lake

PERTH

Serpentine Lake

Government House Lake

• Kingstown

Mabel Cove

Henrietta Rocks are a hazardous place for shipping. No less than three ships have been wrecked in the waters off this point.

THE QUOKKA

When de Vlamingh first visited Rottnest in 1696, he noted animals somewhat bigger than a cat, with dark fur. Thinking they were a species of rat, he called the island the "rats' nest". In fact the animals were a type of wallaby, called quokkas by the Aborigines. Although there is a small mainland population in Western Australia, this is the best place to see these timid creatures in areas of undergrowth. On Rottnest such habitat is scarce, and they are often visible at dusk. Quokkas are wild and should not be fed.

Oliver Hill
At this lookout stand two 9.2-inch (23.5-cm) guns, brought here for coastal defence purposes in 1937, but obsolete since the end of World War II. A railway to the hill has been renovated recently by volunteers.

Fremantle ❸

FREMANTLE IS ONE OF Western Australia's most historic cities. A wealth of 19th-century buildings remains, including superb examples from the gold rush period. Founded on the Indian Ocean in 1829, at the mouth of the Swan River, Fremantle was intended to be a port for the new colony, but was only used as such when an artificial harbour was dredged at the end of the 19th century. The town still has thriving harbours and, in 1987, it hosted the America's Cup. Many sites were renovated for the event, and street cafés and restaurants sprang up.

Anchor from the Maritime Museum

Busy fruit and vegetable stall in the Fremantle Markets

Twelve-sided Round House

🚔 The Round House
10 Arthur Head Rd. ◯ *daily.* ♿
Built in 1830, the Round House is Fremantle's oldest building. It was the town's first gaol and, in 1844, site of the colony's first hanging. Inside its stark limestone walls, cells overlook a small courtyard. Beneath the gaol is a tunnel, dug in 1837, which allowed whalers to transfer their cargo easily from the jetty to the High Street.

To the left of the site, where the port's first courthouse once stood, there are clear views across Bathers Bay to Rottnest Island *(see pp300–301).*

⚓ St John the Evangelist Anglican Church
Cnr Adelaide & Queen sts. ◖ *(08) 93 35 2213.* ◯ *daily.* ♿
This charming church, completed in 1882, replaced a smaller church on the same site. Its Pioneer Window tells the story of a pioneer family across seven generations, from its departure from England in the 18th century, to a new life in a Western Australian farming community. The window next to it came from the old church. St John's ceiling and altars are made out of local jarrah wood.

🏛 Fremantle Markets
Cnr South Terrace & Henderson St. ◖ *(08) 9335 2515.* ◯ *Fri–Sun, public hols.* ● *Good Fri, 25 Dec.* ♿
In 1897, a competition was announced to design a suitable building to act as Fremantle's market hall. The winning design was built in 1892 and still stands today. It underwent renovation in 1975, and since then has again been used as a market at weekends. Visitors can browse around more than 170 stalls offering a wide variety of wares, from fresh vegetables to opals.

🏛 Western Australian Maritime Museum
Cnr Cliff St & Marine Terrace. ◖ *(08) 9431 8444.* ◯ *daily.* ● *Good Fri, 25 Dec.* **Donation.** ♿
This museum's most prized possession is a reconstruction of part of the hull of the Dutch East Indiaman *Batavia* from timbers discovered at the site of its wreck off the Abrolhos Islands in 1628 *(see p316).* The exhibit tells the story of the shipwreck and mutiny of the vessel and gives an insight into life on board. The museum has also reconstructed a stone arch from blocks found in the coral near the wreck, apparently cut in Holland and meant to be erected in Jakarta, Indonesia, the ship's original destination.

The museum's curators research, locate and explore the many shipwrecks in this part of the Indian Ocean. On display are beautiful and sometimes valuable salvaged items.

Another exhibit tells the story of the HMS *Success*, which brought Captain James Stirling to survey the Swan River area in the late 1820s.

THE AMERICA'S CUP BONANZA

The America's Cup yachting race has been run every four years since 1851. Not until 1983, however, did a country other than the United States win this coveted trophy. This was the year that *Australia II* carried it home. In 1987, the Americans were the challengers, and the races were run in *Australia II*'s home waters, off Fremantle. Investment poured into the town, refurbishing the docks, cafés, bars and hotels for the occasion.

The Americans regained the trophy, but Fremantle remains forever changed by being, for once, under the world's gaze.

The 1983 winner, *Australia II*

🏛 Fremantle Museum and Arts Centre

Cnr Ord & Finnerty sts. ☎ (08) 9430 7966. ○ daily. ● Good Fri, 25 Dec, 26 Dec, 1 Jan. **Donation.** *♿ limited.*

Surprisingly, this beautiful Gothic Revival mansion with its shady gardens was first conceived as an asylum for the insane. The main wing was built between 1861 and 1865, and now houses the Fremantle Museum. It was extended between 1880 and 1902, and the newer section contains the Fremantle Arts Centre.

The building, used variously as an asylum, the wartime headquarters for US forces, and the home of the Western Australian Maritime Museum, was slated for demolition in 1967. But, principally through the efforts of Fremantle's mayor, it was rescued and renovated.

The Fremantle Museum is dedicated to the study of the daily lives of the people who came to Western Australia in the 19th century in search of a new life. Its exhibits describe how they lived, the obstacles they overcame and the lives and families they left behind.

The Fremantle Arts Centre showcases local contemporary artists and many of the works are for sale. It also stages open-air concerts and sponsors various arts and crafts–related events in the grounds.

VR
1855

Fremantle Prison's striking façade

Visitors' Checklist

👥 25,000. 🚆 Elder Place. 🚌 Elder Place. ℹ Town Hall, Kings Square (08) 9431 7878. 🎉 Festival Fremantle (Nov).

🏛 Fremantle Prison

The Terrace, off Hampton Rd. ☎ (08) 9430 7177. ○ daily. ● Good Fri, 25 Dec. 📷 ♿ limited.

In the 1850s, when the first group of convicts arrived in the Swan River Colony, the need arose for a large-scale prison. Fremantle Prison, an imposing building with a sturdy gatehouse and cold, forbidding limestone cell blocks, was built by those first convicts in 1855. It was not closed until 1991. Today, visitors tour the complex, visiting cells (some have murals painted by inmates), punishment cells, the chapel and the chilling gallows room, last used in 1964. Candlelight tours are available.

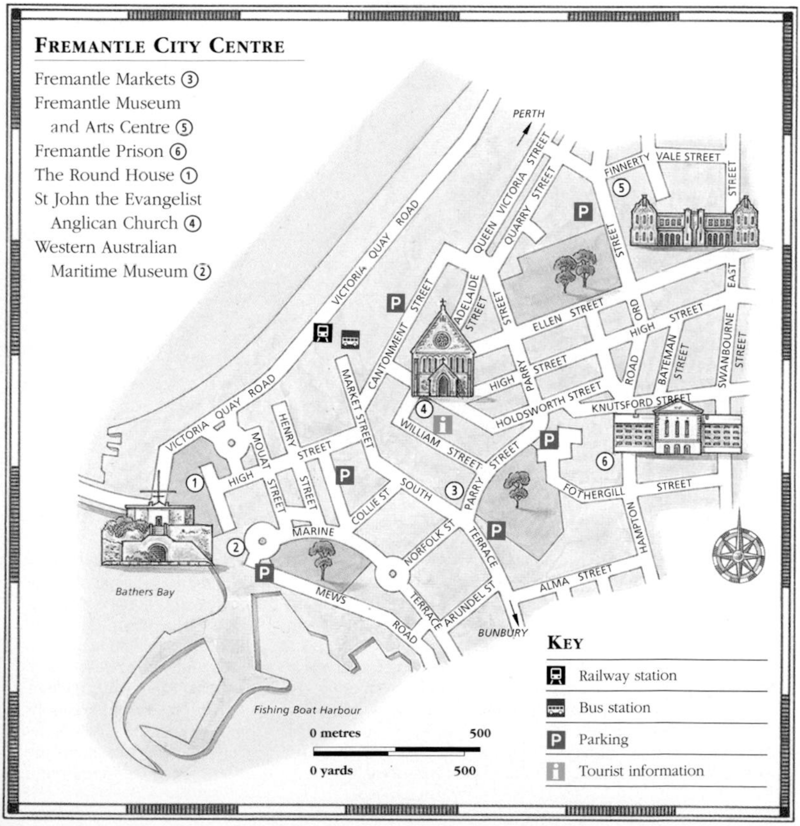
FREMANTLE CITY CENTRE
Fremantle Markets ③
Fremantle Museum and Arts Centre ⑤
Fremantle Prison ⑥
The Round House ①
St John the Evangelist Anglican Church ④
Western Australian Maritime Museum ②
PERTH
VICTORIA STREET
QUEEN VICTORIA STREET
QUARRY STREET
FINNERTY
VALE STREET
STREET
EAST STREET
VICTORIA QUAY ROAD
CANTONMENT STREET
ADELAIDE STREET
ELLEN STREET
ORD STREET
HIGH STREET
BATEMAN STREET
SWANBOURNE STREET
MARKET STREET
PARRY STREET
HOLDSWORTH STREET
KNUTSFORD STREET
WILLIAM STREET
HENRY STREET
MOUAT STREET
SOUTH STREET
COLLIE ST
FOTHERGILL STREET
HAMPTON ROAD
MARINE
MEWS ROAD
NORFOLK ST
TERRACE
ARUNDEL ST
ALMA STREET
BUNBURY
Bathers Bay
Fishing Boat Harbour
0 metres 500
0 yards 500
KEY
Railway station
Bus station
Parking
Tourist information

The Southern Coastline

Western Australia's southwest corner has diverse coastal scenery. Two oceans meet here, the Indian and the Southern, resulting in discernible climate changes: the southern coastline is often windy and cooler than the western coast, and the oceans are much less gentle. Lined by national parks, the coast incorporates limestone, reefs, granite formations, beautiful sand dunes and crags topped by low vegetation. There are also world-class surfing spots in the region.

★ Flinders Bay, Augusta ⑤

🌊 🏊 ⛑ 🚻 ⛺

Augusta was founded in 1830 and is the third oldest settlement in the state. Only 5 km (3 miles) from Cape Leeuwin, the southwestern tip of the continent, today it is a popular holiday resort. The beautiful Flinders Bay is particularly favoured by windsurfers.

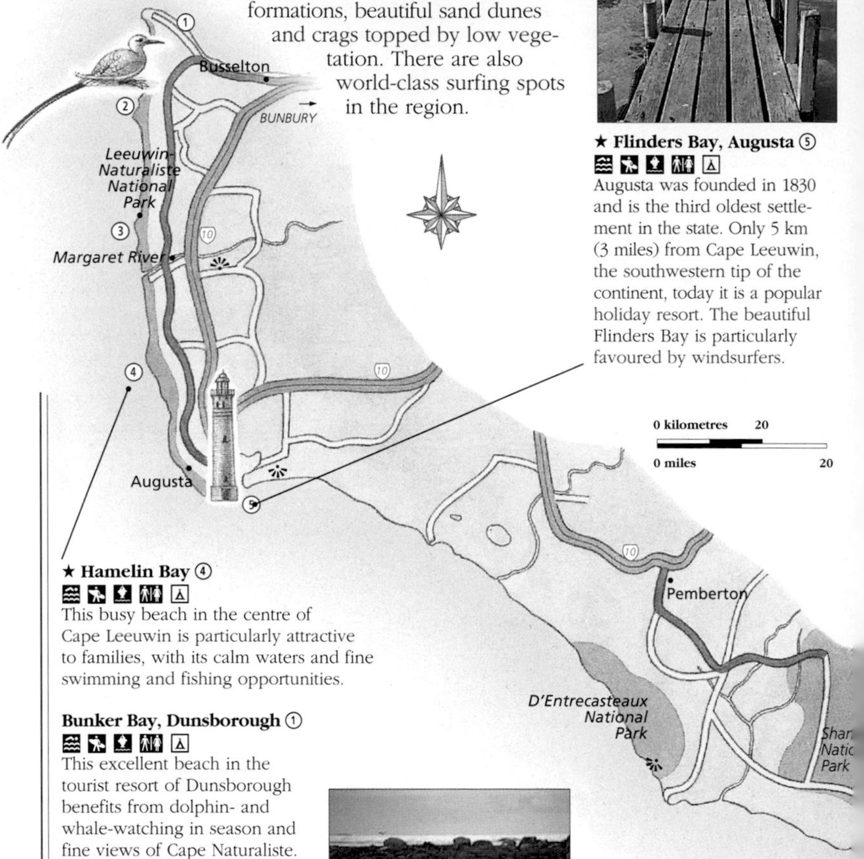
Busselton
BUNBURY
Leeuwin-Naturaliste National Park
Margaret River
Augusta
10
Pemberton
D'Entrecasteaux National Park
0 kilometres 20
0 miles 20

★ Hamelin Bay ④

🌊 🏊 ⛑ 🚻 ⛺

This busy beach in the centre of Cape Leeuwin is particularly attractive to families, with its calm waters and fine swimming and fishing opportunities.

Bunker Bay, Dunsborough ①

🌊 🏊 ⛑ 🚻 ⛺

This excellent beach in the tourist resort of Dunsborough benefits from dolphin- and whale-watching in season and fine views of Cape Naturaliste.

Smiths Beach, Yallingup ②

🌊 🏊 ⛑ 🚻 ⛺

This popular honeymoon spot (Yallingup is Aborigine for "place of lovers") is also a haven for surfers. Nearby is the spectacular Yallingup Cave.

Boodjidup Beach, Margaret River ③

🌊 🏊 ⛑ 🚻 ⛺

The coastline in this holiday town consists of long beaches, sheltered bays and cliff faces looking out on to the surf.

Peaceful Bay ⑦

🌊 🏊 ⛑ 🚻 ⛺

Keen anglers and sailors can often be spotted within this aptly named inlet, which is also a popular picnic spot. Nearby Walpole is the gateway to Walpole-Nornalup National Park, with its impressive karri and eucalypt trees.

Middleton Beach, Albany ⑩

🌊 🏊 ⛑ 🚻 ⛺

The waters of Middleton Beach are regularly filled with windsurfers and boogeyboarders (surfing the waves on a short body board). A short drive around the point is Torndirrup National Park, with a multitude of natural coastal formations, including offshore islands and some excellent locations for whale-watching in season.

Lake Cave, near Margaret River, is just one of an estimated 200 underground caves along the Leeuwin-Naturaliste Ridge that runs from Busselton to Augusta. It is one of the few caves open to the public and is a fairyland of limestone formations, reflected in dark underground waters.

LOCATOR MAP

D'Entrecasteaux National Park, 40 km (25 miles) southwest of Pemberton, is a wild and rugged park with spectacular coastal cliffs, pristine beaches and excellent coastal fishing. Much of the park, including some isolated beach camp sites, is only accessible by 4WD. Inland, heathland is home to a range of animal and plant habitats.

Leeuwin-Naturaliste National Park *is a 15,500-ha (40,000-acre) protected area of scenic coastline, caves, heathlands and woodlands. Its rugged limestone coast with long beaches and sheltered bays faces the Indian Ocean. It has long been popular as a holiday destination and has excellent opportunities for swimming, surfing and fishing.*

★ Ocean Beach, Denmark ⑧

Denmark is a well-known and popular haunt for surfers from many countries. Ocean Beach, in particular, is the setting for international surfing competitions *(see pp34–5).*

★ Wilson Inlet ⑨

From Denmark's main street it is a relatively short walk through well-kept woodland to Wilson Inlet where there are some spectacular and varied coastal views.

↑ ESPERANCE

Walpole ⑦

Walpole Nornalup National Park ⑥ ⑦

William Bay National Park ⑧

Southern Ocean

West Cape Howe National Park

Albany ⑩

Torndirrup National Park

★ Conspicuous Beach ⑥

Impressive cliffs face on to the beautiful white sands of Conspicuous Beach. It is also the access point for the Valley of the Giants, with its massive red tingle trees.

KEY

▬	Highway
▬	Major road
▬	Minor road
⌒	River
⁂	Viewpoint

Wide first-floor veranda and ornate ironwork of the Rose Hotel, Bunbury

Bunbury ❹

🏠 28,000. 🚊 🚌 🚢 🅿 🛈 *Old Railway Station, Carmody Place (08) 9721 7922.*

T HE CITY OF Bunbury lies about 180 km (110 miles) south of Perth at the southern end of the Leschenhault Inlet. The state's second-largest city, it is the capital of the south-west region. Since the 19th century it has grown into a thriving port and a centre for local industry. It is also a popular holiday destination, with many water sports available.

Historic buildings in Bunbury include the Rose Hotel, built in 1865, with its first-floor veranda and intricate ironwork detail *(see p479)*. The Roman Catholic St Patrick's Cathedral contains the beautiful Pat Usher Memorial Window, in memory of Bunbury's mayor from 1972 to 1983. St Boniface (Anglican) Cathedral also contains some pretty stained glass. Nearby are the Bunbury Art Galleries, housed in the former Sisters of Mercy convent built in the 1880s. Today they are the centre for community arts events.

On the beachfront stands the **Dolphin Discovery Centre**, which has fascinating audio-visual exhibits. Wild dolphins regularly appear off the coast here, and visitors come to see them and swim with them.

The **King Cottage Museum**, is run by the Bunbury Historical Society. It exhibits local artifacts dating from the 1880s to the 1920s and a wealth of photographs documenting the area's history.

🐬 Dolphin Discovery Centre
Koombana Drive. 📞 *(08) 9791 3088.* ⬜ *daily.* ⬤ *25 Dec.* 📷 ♿
🏛 King Cottage Museum
77 Forrest Ave. 📞 *(08) 9721 7546.* ⬜ *phone for opening times.* 📷 ♿

Busselton ❺

🏠 14,200. ✈ 🚌 🛈 *38 Peel Terrace (08) 9752 1288.*

S TANDING ON the shores of Geographe Bay, Busselton boasts more than 30 km (19 miles) of beaches and a vast array of water-based activities, including scuba-diving, fishing and whale-watching. Busselton Jetty, 2 km (1 mile) long and once the longest in Australia, is a reminder of the town's beginnings as a timber port.

Some of Busselton's oldest surviving buildings are located at the Old Courthouse site,

Entrance to Busselton's original courthouse building

now used as an arts complex. Here, the jail cells, police offices, courthouse and bond store all date from 1856. Local crafts are sold in the old jail cells, and other outbuildings act as studio space for artists.

The 1871 *Ballarat*, the first steam locomotive used in the state, stands in Victoria Park.

ENVIRONS: About 10 km (6 miles) north of Busselton is **Wonnerup House**, a lovingly restored house built by pioneer George Layman in 1859 and now owned by the National Trust. Three other buildings share the site, the earliest being the first house Layman erected in the 1830s. Both buildings stand in pretty grounds within farmland and are furnished with Layman family memorabilia and artifacts. In 1874, Layman's son built a school and, in 1885, a teacher's house close by. These buildings also have period exhibits inside.

About 20 km (12 miles) north of Busselton is the beautiful Ludlow Tuart Forest National Park, probably the largest area of tuart trees left in the world.

🏚 Wonnerup House
Layman Rd. 📞 *(08) 9752 2039.* ⬜ *daily.* ⬤ *Good Fri, 25 Dec.* 📷 ♿

Margaret River ❻

🏠 6,000. ✈ 🚌 🛈 *Bussell Hwy (08) 9757 2911.*

T HE ATTRACTIVE TOWN of Margaret River, close to the Indian Ocean, was first settled by Europeans in the 1850s. The town became the centre of an agricultural and timber region, but in the past few decades has gained fame for its wineries *(see pp32–3)*, and for its splendid surfing beaches.

Within the town is the **Old Settlement**, a privately owned outdoor museum detailing the lives of those who worked on the Group Settlement Scheme in the 1920s *(see p53)*. The museum buildings include a group house, a blacksmith's shop and a schoolhouse.

Set in 12 ha (30 acres) of bush on the outskirts of town, the **Eagles Heritage Raptor Wildlife Centre** has a huge collection of birds of prey and gives eagle-flying displays.

🏛 Old Settlement
Bussell Hwy at Rotary Bridge.
📞 (08) 9757 9335. ⬭ daily
⬤ 24–26 Dec. 🅰 🏠

🦅 Eagles Heritage Raptor Wildlife Centre
Lot 303 Boodjidup Rd. 📞 (08) 9757 2960. ⬭ daily. ⬤ 25 Dec. 🅰 ♿

ENVIRONS: Eight km (5 miles) north of Margaret River stands the region's first homestead, Ellensbrook, built by pioneer Alfred Bussell in the 1850s. The stone cottage is close to a forest trail which leads to the pretty Meekadarribee Falls.

Visiting Margaret River's out-lying wineries is very popular. Many, from Vasse-Felix, the oldest, to the large Leeuwin Estates Winery and a host of family-run properties, offer tastings and cellar-door sales.

Ellensbrook Pioneer Homestead, near the town of Margaret River

Bridgetown 🟤

🏃 3,000. 🚉 ℹ️ 154 Hampton St (08) 9761 1740.

NESTLED AMID rolling hills on the banks of Blackwood River, Bridgetown began as a single one-room homestead in the 1850s. It was built by settler John Blechynden and can still be seen standing next to the second home he built, Bridgedale House. Both are National Trust properties.

The town's tourist centre is home to its municipal history museum and the unusual Brierly Jigsaw Gallery, which has hundreds of puzzles from all over the world.

Hilltop view of picturesque Bridgetown

Sutton's Lookout, off Philips Street, offers panoramic views of the town and surrounding countryside. The Blackwood River and local jarrah and marri forests afford opportunities for walks and drives, and several river-based activities, including canoeing and marron fishing.

Manjimup 🟤

🏃 5,000. 🚉 ℹ️ cnr Rose & Edwards sts (08) 9771 1831.

IF YOU ARE TRAVELLING south from Perth, Manjimup acts as the gateway to the great karri forests for which the southwest is so famous. The town was settled in the late 1850s, and has been associated with the timber industry ever since. The tourist office is within the **Manjimup Timber Park**, with its Timber Museum, Historical Hamlet and Bunnings Age of Steam Museum. A sculpture of a woodsman at the entrance commemorates the region's timber industry pioneers.

🏛 Manjimup Timber Park
Cnr Rose & Edwards sts.
📞 (08) 9771 1831
⬭ daily. ⬤
25 Dec. ♿

ENVIRONS: About 25 km (16 miles) west of Manjimup on Graphite Road lies Glenoran Pool, a pretty swim-ming hole on the Donnelly River. The adjacent One-

Sculpture of a woodsman at Manjimup Timber Park

Tree Bridge is the site where early settlers felled a huge karri and used it to carry a bridge across the river. Nearby are the Four Aces, four giant karri trees in a straight line, thought to be up to 300 years old.

Pemberton 🟤

🏃 1,200. 🚉 ℹ️ Brockman St (08) 9776 1133.

AT THE HEART of karri country, Pemberton has the look and feel of an old timber town. The Pemberton Tramway, ori-ginally built to bring the trees to mills in town, now takes visitors through the forests. The **Karri Forest Discovery Centre** provides information on the ecology of the karri forest.

🏛 Karri Forest Discovery Centre
Brockman St. 📞 (08) 9776 1133.
⬭ daily. ⬤ 25 Dec. **Donations.** ♿

ENVIRONS: Southeast of the town lies Gloucester National Park, home to the famous giant karri, the Gloucester Tree. At 61 m (200 ft), it is one of the highest fire look-out trees in the world with fantastic views at the top. Southwest of Pemberton is Warren National Park with its beautiful cascades, swimming holes and fishing spots. Beedelup National Park, to the northwest of Pemberton, offers some delightful walks.

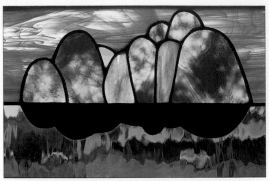
Example of Andy Ducker's stained glass in Denmark

Denmark **10**

🚶 *3,500.* 🅿️ ℹ️ *Strickland St (08) 9848 1265.*

Lying on Western Australia's southern coastline, Denmark was founded as a timber company settlement in 1895, but by the 1920s it was a fully fledged town. The town now attracts a host of visitors, many of whom come seeking the good surf of the Southern Ocean. There is also a large population of artists and artisans, and the atmosphere is distinctly bohemian.

Denmark's oldest building is St Leonard's Anglican Church, built by volunteers in 1899. Its Scandinavian-style pitched roof and interior detail are reminders of the Norwegian timber workers in the town at that time.

Nearby is Mandala Studio, one of Denmark's many craft galleries, where visitors can admire and buy stained-glass items made by local artist Andy Ducker and watch him at work.

Berridge Park, on the banks of the Denmark River, is often the scene for summertime open-air concerts.

Environs: Denmark has many beautiful beaches. A popular surfing spot is Ocean Beach; more sheltered locations for swimmers include Cosy Corner and Peaceful Bay. The coastline and Wilsons Inlet are popular with boaters and anglers.

Albany **11**

🚶 *29,000.* ✈️ 🅿️ 🚌 ℹ️ *Old Railway Station, Proudlove Parade (08) 9841 1088.*

Albany was first visited by Captain Vancouver in 1791, but it was not until 1826 that the British settled here. Until Fremantle harbour was constructed *(see pp302–303)*, Albany acted as the colony's main port and the harbour is still the commercial heart of the city. Whale migrations bring them close to the city's shores, which made it a base for whalers until the whaling moratorium of 1979.

The town includes many old buildings. **St John the Evangelist Anglican Church**, built in 1848, was the first Anglican church consecrated in Western Australia and is the epitome of an English country church. Inside, the Lady Chapel contains a piece of an arch from St Paul's Cathedral in London. Much of the stained glass was brought from England at the beginning of the 19th century.

Ship's wheel in Jaycee's Whaleworld

A number of old buildings stand near the western end of Stirling Terrace. The Residency Museum, originally part of the convict hiring depot built in the 1850s, details the history of the town and its surrounding area. The convict hiring depot itself and the Old Gaol now house the collection of the Albany Historical Society.

In Duke Street is Patrick Taylor Cottage, built before 1836 of wattle and daub, and the oldest building in Albany.

On Albany's foreshore is an impressive, fully-fitted replica of the brig *Amity*, which brought the first settlers here from Sydney in 1826.

🛕 St John the Evangelist Anglican Church
York St. 📞 *(08) 9841 5015.* 🔲 *daily.* ♿

Environs: The world's largest whaling museum is **Jaycee's Whaleworld**. Tour guides take visitors around the remains of the Cheyne Beach whaling station and explain the process of extracting whale oil. From July to October, incredible breaching displays of migrating whales can sometimes be seen offshore.

🏛 Jaycee's Whaleworld
Frenchman Bay Rd. 📞 *(08) 9844 4021.* 🔲 *daily.* ● *25 Dec.* 📷 🖥 ♿

Replica of the brig *Amity*

Stirling Range National Park **12**

🅿️ *Albany.* ℹ️ *Albany (08) 9841 1088.* **Park Ranger & information** 📞 *(08) 9827 9230.*

Overlooking the rolling farmland to the north of Albany is the Stirling Range National Park. The mountain peaks, noted for their colour changes from purple to red to blue, rise to more than 1,000 m (3,300 ft) above sea level and stretch for more than 65 km (40 miles). The highest peak is Bluff Knoll, which reaches 1,073 m (3,520 ft). Because of its sudden rise from the

View of Stirling Range National Park from Chester Pass Road

surrounding plains, the park has an unpredictable climate which encourages a wide range of unique flora and fauna, including ten species of mountain bell. No less than 60 species of flowering plants are endemic to the park. They are best seen from October to December, when they are likely to be in flower. The park offers visitors a number of graded and signposted walks in the mountains (all are steep) and there are several picturesque barbecue and picnic areas.

York ⓭

🚶 3,000. 🚐 ℹ 81 Avon Terrace (08) 9641 1301. 🎪 Festival of Motoring (Jul).

THE TOWN OF YORK was founded in 1831, in the new colony's drive to establish its self-sufficiency via agriculture. Now registered as a historic town, it retains many mid–19th-century buildings, the majority of which are on Avon Terrace, the main street. The cells of York's Old Gaol, in use from 1865 until 1981, provide a chilling insight into the treatment of 19th-century offenders. Other historic buildings include Settler's House (1860s), now a hotel and restaurant *(see p513)*, and Castle Hotel, built in stages between 1850 and 1932, with its unusual timber verandas.

Nearby stands the **York Motor Museum**, with one of the largest collections of veteran cars and vehicles in Australia. These include the 1886 Benz (the world's first car), the very rare 1946 Holden Sedan Prototype and the extraordinary Bisiluro II Italcorsa racing car.

Also of note is the York Residency Museum, housed in the former home of York magistrate Walkinshaw Cowan, father-in-law to Edith Cowan, the state's first female Member of Parliament *(see p52)*. This extensive collection of artifacts and photographs is justly said to be the finest small museum in the state.

York's 1892 flour mill has now been converted into the Jah-Roc Mill Gallery, which exhibits and sells furniture made from jarra wood and other arts and crafts.

🏛 York Motor Museum
116 Avon Terrace. 📞 (08) 9641 1288. ◯ daily. ⬤ 25 Dec. 🖼 ♿

Northam ⓮

🚶 7,000. 🚐 🚐 ℹ 2 Grey St (08) 9622 2100.

AT THE HEART of the Avon Valley and the state's wheat belt, Northam is Western Australia's largest inland town. Settled as an agricultural centre early in the colony's history, the town became a gateway to the gold fields of Kalgoorlie-Boulder for prospectors in the 1890s *(see p310)*. It retains a number of historic buildings, including the Old Girls' School (1877), now the town's Art Centre, and the beautiful St John's Church (1890). The town's jewel is Morby Cottage, built in 1836 and a fine example of the architectural style adopted by the early colonists.

Spanning the Avon River is the longest pedestrian suspension bridge in the country, offering views of the river and its population of white swans.

Original 1925 Rolls Royce in the York Motor Museum

The Gold Fields and Nullarbor Plain

W ESTERN AUSTRALIA'S southeast is a sparsely populated, flat region of extreme aridity and little fresh water. Vast stretches of its red, dusty landscape are inhabited by small Aboriginal communities and mining companies. The gold rush around Kalgoorlie in the 1890s ensured the state's success, but many places waned and ghost towns now litter the plains. Traversing the Nullarbor Plain, the Eyre Highway runs from Norseman to South Australia, 730 km (455 miles) away, and beyond. To the south is the windswept coast of the Great Australian Bight.

KEY

◻ The Gold Fields and Nullarbor Plain

◻ Perth and the Southwest pp290–309

SIGHTS AT A GLANCE

Esperance ⑱
Kalgoorlie-Boulder ⑯
Norseman ⑰
Nullarbor Plain ⑲
Wave Rock ⑮

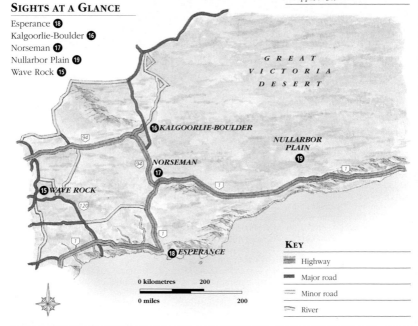

G R E A T
V I C T O R I A
D E S E R T

⑯ KALGOORLIE-BOULDER

NULLARBOR PLAIN
⑲

NORSEMAN
⑰

⑮ WAVE ROCK

⑱ ESPERANCE

0 kilometres   200

0 miles   200

KEY

▨ Highway

▬ Major road

⋯ Minor road

〜 River

Wave Rock, in the shape of a perfect wave about to break

Wave Rock ⑮

🏠 Hyden. **Visitors' Centre** 📞 (08) 9880 5182. ⏰ 9am–6pm daily. 📷 ♿ 🅿 by arrangement.

I N WESTERN AUSTRALIA'S wheat belt, 5 km (3 miles) east of the small settlement of Hyden, stands one of the state's most surprising rock formations. A great granite wave has been created from a huge outcrop by thousands of years of chemical erosion, and reaction with rainwater has given it red and grey stripes. Other rock formations nearby include the Breakers and Hippo's Yawn. Facing Wave Rock, Lace Place is the unusual location for the largest collection of lacework in the southern hemisphere.

About 20 km (12 miles) northeast of Hyden lies Mulka's Cave, where several Aboriginal rock paintings can be seen.

Kalgoorlie-Boulder ⑯

🏚 30,000. ✈ 🚋 🏠 🚌 ℹ 250 Hannan St (08) 9021 1966.

K ALGOORLIE and the nearby town of Boulder, with which it was amalgamated in 1989, constantly remind visitors of their gold-fever past. Gold was first discovered here by Irishman Paddy Hannan in 1893, and, within weeks, the area was besieged with prospectors. Gold fields in other areas soon dwindled, but this field has yielded rich pickings to this day, bolstered by nickel finds in the 1960s. Today, gold is mined in the world's largest open-cut mine and more than 150,000 visitors a year come to see historic Kalgoorlie.

A variety of heritage trails and tours are available, and details are at the tourist office. The **WA Museum Kalgoorlie–Boulder** has an impressive collection of gold nuggets and jewellery, as well as natural history displays and a history of the gold rush. At the Mining Hall of Fame, visitors can go down a shaft and see gold pours and panning demonstrations.

The ornate buildings hastily erected during the boom years are best seen on Hannan Street, in the York and Exchange hotels, classic examples of gold rush architecture, and Kalgoorlie Town Hall.

Around Kalgoorlie-Boulder there are many ghost towns, such as Ora Banda and Broad Arrow, deserted by prospectors early this century in their search for new mines.

Bronze statue of Paddy Hannan

🏛 **WA Museum Kalgoorlie–Boulder**
17 Hannan St. 📞 *(08) 9021 8533.*
⭕ *daily.* ⬤ *Good Fri, 25 Dec.*
Donation. ♿

Baxters Cliff, east of Esperance, on the shores of the Southern Ocean

Norseman ⑰

🏘 *11,000.* 🚌 ℹ *68 Roberts St (08) 9039 1071.*

AT THE START of the Eyre Highway, Norseman is the gateway to the Nullarbor Plain and the eastern states beyond. Like Kalgoorlie-Boulder, the town stands on a gold field, discovered when a horse pawed the ground, uncovering gold deposits. In gratitude, miners named the town after the horse, and its statue was erected in the main street. Many visitors try fossicking, or learn more about the history of gold mining in the area at the **Norseman Historical and Geological Museum** housed in the old School of Mines. Nearby, Beacon Hill offers a panoramic view of the town and surrounding countryside.

🏛 **Norseman Historical and Geological Museum**
Battery Rd. 📞 *(08) 9039 1593.*
⭕ *Mon–Sat.* ⬤ *Good Fri, Easter Mon, 25 Apr, 25 Dec.* 🈺

Esperance ⑱

🏘 *10,000.* ✈ 🚌 ℹ *Museum Village, Demster St (08) 9071 2330.*

ALTHOUGH THIS AREA was visited by Europeans as far back as 1627, it was not until 1863 that British colonists arrived here to establish a settlement. Fronting the Southern Ocean, this part of the coast is said to have some of the most beautiful beaches in Australia. Offshore is the Recherche Archipelago, with its 100 islands, one of which, Woody Island, is a wildlife sanctuary and can be visited.

In Esperance itself, Museum Village includes the town's art gallery and several historic buildings, and Esperance Municipal Museum contains a fine array of local artifacts.

Nullarbor Plain ⑲

🚌 *Kalgoorlie.* 🚌 *Norseman.*
ℹ *Norseman (08) 9039 1071.*

THE NULLARBOR PLAIN stretches across the southeast of the state and into South Australia (*see p359*). "Nullarbor" derives from the Latin meaning "no trees", and this is indeed a vast treeless plain. Only one road, the Eyre Highway, leads across the plain – one of the great Australian road journeys.

A few tiny settlements consisting only of roadhouses lie along the Eyre Hwy. Cockle-biddy, lying 438 km (270 miles) east of Norseman, has one of the world's longest caves and, at Eucla, 10 km (6 miles) from the state border, a telegraph station's remains can be seen. Nearby Eucla National Park has some fine views of the coastal cliffs.

York Hotel in Hannan Street, Kalgoorlie (*see p479*)

NORTH OF PERTH AND THE KIMBERLEY

WESTERN AUSTRALIA *covers one-third of Australia, and visitors to the area north of Perth start to get a feel for just how big the state really is. The region has many treasures: Ningaloo Reef and the Pinnacles rock formations; the gorges of the Kimberley; and a host of national parks, including the amazing Bungle Bungles.*

The first people to set foot on the Australian land mass, the Aborigines, did so some 60,000 years ago in the north of Western Australia. This area is rich in Aboriginal petroglyphs, and some are thought to be more than 20,000 years old. The north of Western Australia was also the site of the first European landing in 1616 *(see p45)*. In 1688, English explorer William Dampier charted the area around the Dampier Peninsula and, on a later voyage, discovered Shark Bay and the area around Broome.

In the 1840s, the Benedictines set up a mission in New Norcia and, by the 1860s, settlements had sprung up along the coast, most significantly at Cossack, where a pearling industry attracted immigrants from Japan, China and Indonesia. In the 1880s, pastoralists set up cattle and sheep stations in a swathe from Derby to Wyndham. Gold was struck in 1885 at Halls Creek, and the northern part of the state was finally on the map. In the 1960s, mining came to prominence again with the discovery of such minerals as iron ore, nickel and oil, particularly in the Pilbara region.

Today, the region is fast becoming a popular tourist destination, particularly with those visitors interested in ecotourism *(see p528)*. Its climate varies from Mediterranean-style just north of Perth to the tropical wet and dry pattern of the far north. Wildlife includes endangered species such as the dugongs of Shark Bay. Even isolated spots, such as the Kimberley and the resorts of Coral Bay and Broome, are receiving more visitors every year.

Visitors enjoying close contact with the dolphins of Monkey Mia in Shark Bay World Heritage and Marine Park

◁ **The strange silica- and lichen-covered domes of the Bungle Bungles in Purnululu National Park**

Exploring North of Perth

THE NORTH OF Western Australia is a vast area of diverse landscapes and stunning scenery. North of Perth lies Nambung National Park, home to the bizarre Pinnacles Desert. Kalbarri National Park is a region of scenic gorges on the Murchison River. The Indian Ocean coastline offers uninhabited islands, coral reefs, breathtaking cliffs and sandy beaches, none more spectacular than in Shark Bay World Heritage and Marine Park. At the tip of the region is the Pilbara, the state's mining area and home to the fascinating national parks of Karijini and Millstream-Chichester.

St Francis Xavier Cathedral, Geraldton

The Pinnacles in Nambung National Park at dusk

SIGHTS AT A GLANCE

NINGALOO
REEF
MARINE
PARK
9 EXMOUTH
8

Lake
MacLeod

CARNARVON **7**   Gascoyne River

6

SHARK BAY
WORLD
HERITAGE
AND MARINE
PARK

KALBARRI
NATIONAL
PARK **5**

HOUTMAN
ABROLHOS
ISLANDS
4

GERALDTON **3**

MUL

NAMB
NATIO
PAR
2

0 kilometres   100

0 miles   100

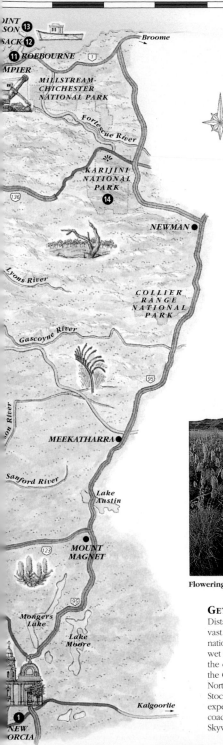

POINT SON 13
SACK 12
11 ROEBOURNE
MPIER

MILLSTREAM-CHICHESTER NATIONAL PARK

Broome

Fortescue River

KARIJINI NATIONAL PARK 14

NEWMAN

Lyons River

COLLIER RANGE NATIONAL PARK

Gascoyne River

MEEKATHARRA

Sanford River

Lake Austin

MOUNT MAGNET

Mongers Lake

Lake Moore

Kalgoorlie

NEW ORCIA

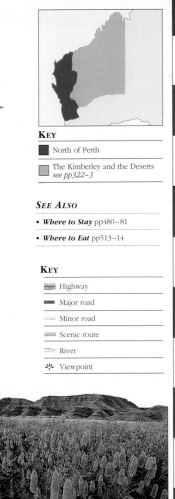

KEY

North of Perth

The Kimberley and the Deserts
see pp322–3

SEE ALSO

- *Where to Stay* pp480–81

- *Where to Eat* pp513–14

KEY

═══ Highway

━━ Major road

---- Minor road

═══ Scenic route

═══ River

🌄 Viewpoint

Flowering mulla mullas in Karijini National Park

GETTING AROUND

Distances in the north of Western Australia are vast. A 4WD vehicle is desirable if visiting any national parks by road and essential during the wet season. The North West Coastal Hwy skirts the coast as far as Port Hedland, where it joins the Great Northern Hwy, heading towards the Northern Territory. Gunbarrel Hwy and Canning Stock Route across the Gibson Desert are only for experienced travellers. Greyhound has regular coach services between major towns, and Skywest and Ansett also fly to Perth *(see pp544–5).*

New Norcia ❶

🏛 70. 🚗 ℹ *New Norcia Museum and Art Gallery (08) 9654 8056.*

ONE OF Western Australia's most important heritage sites is New Norcia, 130 km (80 miles) northeast of Perth. A mission was established here by Spanish Benedictine monks in 1846, and it is still home to a small monastic community who own and run the historic buildings. There are daily tours of the monastery and visitors can stay at the attached guesthouse, also run by the monks.

The town, known for its Spanish colonial architecture, has a pretty cathedral, built in 1860, at its centre. Also of note are two elegant colleges built early in the 20th century: St Gertrude's Residence for Girls and St Ildephonsus' Residence for Boys. The **New Norcia Museum and Art Gallery** has some fine art treasures and artifacts tracing the town's history.

🏛 New Norcia Museum and Art Gallery

Great Northern Hwy. 📞 *(08) 9654 8056.* 🕐 *daily.* ● *25 Dec.* 📷 ♿ *ground floor only.*

Minarets adorning St Ildephonsus' Residence for Boys, New Norcia

Nambung National Park ❷

ℹ *CALM office at Cervantes (08) 9652 7043.* 🕐 *Mon–Fri.*

THIS UNUSUAL national park is composed of beach and sand dunes, with the dunes extending inland from the coast. It is best seen in spring when wildflowers bloom and the heat is not too oppressive. The park is famous for The Pinnacles, a region of curious

The extraordinary Pinnacles, Nambung National Park

limestone pillars, the tallest of which stand 4 m (13 ft) high. Visitors can take either a 3-km (2-mile) driving trail or a shorter walking trail which leads to lookouts with stunning views of the Pinnacles and the coastline.

Most of the park animals are nocturnal, but some, including kangaroos, emus and many reptiles, may be seen in the cool of dawn or dusk.

Geraldton ❸

🏛 26,000. ✈ 🚌 🚆 ℹ *cnr Chapman Rd & Bayly St (08) 9921 3999.*

THE CITY OF Geraldton lies on Champion Bay, about 425 km (265 miles) north of Perth. It is known as "Sun City" because of its average eight hours of sunshine per day. The pleasant climate brings hordes of sun-seekers from all over Australia who take advantage of fine swimming and surfing beaches. It can also be very windy at times, a further enticement to windsurfers, for whom Geraldton (particularly Mahomets Beach) is a world centre.

The history of European settlement in the area extends back to the mutiny of the Dutch ship *Batavia*, after it was wrecked on the nearby Houtman Abrolhos in 1628. Two crew members were marooned here

Geraldton's Point Moore Lighthouse

as a punishment. In 1721, the Dutch ship *Zuytdorp* was wrecked, and it is thought that survivors settled here for a brief period. Champion Bay was first mapped in 1849 and a lead mine was established shortly afterwards. Geraldton grew up as a lead shipping point, and today is a port city with a large rock-lobster fleet.

The city retains many of its early historic buildings. The **Museum of Geraldton** includes Geraldton Maritime Museum, which contains relics of the area's early shipwrecks. The Old Railway Building has exhibits on local history, wildlife and geology. Geraldton has two fine cathedrals: the modern Cathedral of the Holy Cross, with its beautiful stained glass, and St Francis Xavier Cathedral, built from 1916 to 1938, in Byzantine style. Point Moore Lighthouse, with its distinctive red and white stripes, was shipped here from Britain and has been in continuous operation since 1878. The 1870 **Lighthouse Keeper's Cottage**, the town's first lighthouse, now houses Geraldton's Historical Society. Also in town, the **Geraldton Art Gallery** is one of the best galleries in the state, exhibiting the work of local artists and pieces from private and public collections.

A number of lookouts such as Separation Point Lookout and Mount Tarcoola Lookout give panoramic views of the city and ocean.

🏛 **Museum of Geraldton**
Battavia Coast Marina. 📞 *(08) 9921 5080.* ⬭ *daily.* ⬤ *Good Fri, 25 & 26 Dec.* **Donation.** ♿
🏚 **Lighthouse Keeper's Cottage**
355 Chapman Rd. 📞 *(08) 9921 8505.* ⬭ *Thu.* ⬤ *25 Dec.*
🏛 **Geraldton Art Gallery**
24 Chapman Rd. 📞 *(08) 9921 6811.* ⬭ *daily.* ⬤ *Good Fri, 25 Dec– 1 Jan.* ♿

Houtman Abrolhos ❹

🚉 *Geraldton.* 🚢 *from Geraldton.* ℹ *Geraldton (08) 9921 3999.*

Aᴮᴼᵁᵀ 60 km (37 miles) off Geraldton lie more than 100 coral islands called the Houtman Abrolhos. The world's southernmost coral island formation, it contains some unique coral species. While it is not possible to stay on the islands, tours enable visitors to fly over them or to fish and dive among the coral.

Kalbarri National Park ❺

🚉 *Kalbarri.* ℹ *Kalbarri (08) 9937 1104.* ⬭ *sunrise–sunset daily.*

Tʜᴇ ᴍᴀɢɴɪꜰɪᴄᴇɴᴛ landscape of Kalbarri National Park includes stunning coastal scenery and beautiful inland gorges lining the Murchison River. The park has a number of coastal and river walking trails which lead to breathtaking views and fascinating rock formations. The trails vary in length, from brief two-hour strolls to four-day hikes. Highlights of the park include Hawks Head, a picnic area with views of the gorge; Nature's Window, where a rock formation frames a view of the river; and Ross Graham Lookout, where visitors can bathe in the river pools. By the ocean, Pot Alley provides awesome views of the rugged coastal cliffs and Rainbow Valley is made up of layers of multi-coloured rocks.

The access town for the park, Kalbarri, is situated on the coast and provides good tourist facilities and a base for tours into the park. The park's roads are accessible to most vehicles, but are unsuitable for caravans or trailers. The best time to visit is from July to October, when the weather is dry and the temperatures are not prohibitive. In summer, they can soar to 40°C (104°F).

Shark Bay World Heritage and Marine Park ❻

See pp 318–19.

Fine arts and crafts centre in Carnarvon

Carnarvon ❼

👥 *7,000.* ✈ 🚌 🚐 ℹ *11 Robinson St (08) 9941 1146.*

Tʜᴇ ᴛᴏᴡɴ of Carnarvon, standing at the mouth of the Gascoyne River, acts as the commercial and administrative centre for the surrounding Gascoyne region, the gateway to Western Australia's north. Tropical fruit plantations, including bananas, melons and mangoes, line the river for 16 km (10 miles), some offering tours and selling produce.

In Carnarvon itself, One Mile Jetty on Babbage Island is a popular place for fishing, and Jubilee Hall, built in 1887, houses a fine arts and crafts centre. Carnarvon is also home to a busy prawn and scallop processing industry.

Eɴᴠɪʀᴏɴꜱ: About 70 km (43 miles) north of Carnarvon lie the Blowholes, a spectacular coastal rock formation where air and spray is forced through holes in the rocks in violent spurts up to 20 m (66 ft) high.

Stunning gorge views from Hawks Head Lookout, Kalbarri National Park

Shark Bay World Heritage and Marine Park ❻

Historical jetty sign, Monkey Mia

SHARK BAY MARINE PARK was designated a World Heritage Area in 1991 (see pp22–3). The park is home to many endangered species of both plants and animals, and various unusual natural processes have, over the millennia, given rise to some astounding natural features and spectacular coastal scenery. Because this is a World Heritage Area, visitors are asked to abide by conservation rules, particularly when fishing. The only way to travel around the park is by car, and large areas are only accessible by 4WD.

BERNIER ISLAND

DORRE ISLAND

François Peron National Park
At the tip of Peron Peninsula, this national park, now accessible by 4WD, was a vast sheep station until 1990.

Cape Inscription is the place where Dutchman Dirk Hartog became the first known European to set foot in Australia in 1616 (see p45).

DIRK HARTOG ISLAND

Denham Sound

FRANÇOIS PERON NATIONAL PARK

Peron Homestead
Originally the centre of the Peron sheep station, the homestead offers an insight into pastoral life. The station also has two artesian bores which carry hot water (44°C, 111°F) to tubs at the surface in which visitors may bathe.

Denham was originally settled as a pearling community, but is now mainly a fishing and tourist centre.

Useless Loop

Steep Point faces the Indian Ocean and is the westernmost point of mainland Australia. From here it is possible to see the Zuytdorp Cliffs.

Useless Loop Road

Eagle Bluff
The top of this bluff offers fine panoramic views across Freycinet Reach, with a chance of seeing the eagles that nest on the offshore islands and marine creatures in the clear ocean waters.

The Zuytdorp Cliffs are named after the Dutch ship *Zuytdorp*, wrecked in these waters in 1721.

VISITORS' CHECKLIST

Off Northwest Coastal Hwy. 🛈
71 Knight Terrace, Denham (08)
9948 1253; Dolphin Information
Centre, Monkey Mia (08) 9948
1366. 🚌 from Perth. ♿ to
Monkey Mia. 🅿 🖊 🍴 ▯

Monkey Mia
*Visitors flock to this small beach to meet
the friendly wild dolphins that come to
shore to be fed almost every morning.
Also available are boat trips that go in
search of dugongs, turtles and dolphins.*

Shell Beach
*This 60-km (40-mile)
beach is unique in
being comprised of
tiny cockle shells,
piled on top of each
other to a depth of
some 10 m (33 ft).*

Hamelin Pool Stromatolites
*These columns, formed by cyanobac-
teria, the earliest life on earth, tell scientists much about how life developed.*

KEY

━━	Highway
━━	Major road
━━	Minor road
═══	Unsurfaced road
- - -	4WD only
▢	Marine park
—	National park border
Ⓐ	Camp site
🛈	Tourist information
☀	Viewpoint

EXMOUTH
Gascoyne River
arvon
Northwest Coastal Highway
Wooramel Seagrass Bank
hark Bay
Wooramel River
FAURE ISLAND
HAMELIN POOL MARINE NATURE RESERVE
Hamelin Pool
Denham-Hamelin Road
Henri Freycinet Harbour
Useless Loop Road
GERALDTON

0 kilometres 20
0 miles 20

Ningaloo Reef Marine Park ❽

🅿 *Exmouth.* ℹ *Milyering Visitors' Centre, Yardie Creek Rd, Cape Range National Park (08) 9949 2808.*
⭕ *daily.* ⬤ *Good Fri, 25 Dec.*

THIS MARINE PARK runs for 260 km (162 miles) along the west coast of Exmouth Peninsula and around the tip into Exmouth Gulf. The Ningaloo Reef is the largest fringing barrier reef in the state and offers many of the attractions of the east coast's Great Barrier Reef *(see pp204– 9)*. In many places, it lies very close to the shore, and its turquoise waters are popular with snorkellers. Apart from numerous types of coral and brightly coloured fish, the marine park also protects a number of species. Several beaches at the northern end of the park are used by sea turtles as mating and breeding areas. Further offshore, it is possible to see the gentle whale shark from late March to May. Capable of growing to up to 18 m (60 ft), this is the largest fish in the world.

The best areas for snorkelling are Turquoise Bay or the still waters of Coral Bay. A number of companies offer organized scuba diving outings. Visitors can camp on the park's coastline at several sites managed by the Department of Conservation and Land Management (CALM). Fishing is another popular pursuit here, but catches are very strictly controlled.

Yardie Creek Gorge in Cape Range National Park, near Exmouth

Exmouth ❾

🏃 *3,100.* ✈ 🚌 ℹ *Murat Rd (08) 9949 1176.*

SITUATED ON the eastern side of the Exmouth Peninsula, this small town was originally built in 1967 to service the local airforce base. A military presence is still very much in evidence, but today the town is more important as a tourist destination, used as a base for exploring the Ningaloo Reef Marine Park and the Cape Range National Park. Giant turtles and whale sharks can frequently be seen from the nearby coastline.

Slightly outside of town, at Vlaming Head, lies the wreck of the SS *Mildura*, a cattle transporter which sank in 1907 and is still visible from the shore. Nearby stands the Vlaming Lighthouse, on a high bluff offering striking, panoramic views across the entire peninsula.

ENVIRONS: Cape Range National Park contains a low mountain range with spectacular gorges and rocky outcrops. This area was originally under water and it is possible to discern the fossils of ancient coral in the limestone. Local wildlife includes kangaroos, emus and large lizards. There are two main wilderness walks, but visitors should not attempt these in summer as temperatures can reach as high as 50°C (120°F).

Yardie Creek is on the western side of the park, only 1 km (0.5 miles) from the ocean. A short walk along gorge cliffs leads visitors into the spectacular canyon, where it is possible to catch sight of rock wallabies on the far canyon wall. A cruise through the gorges is also available.

Dampier ❿

🏃 *1,100.* ✈ 🚌 ℹ *4548 Karratha Rd, Karratha (08) 9144 4600.*

DAMPIER stands on King Bay on the Burrup Peninsula, facing the 40 or so islands of the Dampier Archipelago. It was established and still acts as a service centre and port for mining areas inland; natural gas from the nearby Northwest Shelf Project is processed here for domestic and export markets. The town also has the largest desalination plant in Australia. This can be viewed from the Dampier Solar Evaporated Salt Mine Lookout. Dampier is also a popular base for offshore and beach anglers. Every August, game-fishing enthusiasts converge on the town for the Dampier Classic and Game Fishing Classic.

The Burrup Peninsula is one of the most renowned ancient Aboriginal art sites in Australia, created by the Yapurrara Aborigines.

ENVIRONS: The Dampier Archipelago, within 45 km (28 miles) of the town, offers a range of activities from game

White sands of Turquoise Bay in Ningaloo Reef Marine Park

Honeymoon Cove, one of the most popular beaches in Point Samson

fishing to whale-watching. Sport fishing here is particularly good, with reef and game species such as tuna, trevally and queenfish on offer.

Almost half of the islands are nature reserves and are home to rare species, including the Pilbara olive python and the king brown snake. Access to the islands is by boat only.

Simple façade of the Holy Trinity Church in Roebourne

Roebourne ⓫

🏠 *1,400.* 🚌 🛈 *Queen St (08) 9182 1060.*

ABOUT 14 KM (9 miles) inland, Roebourne, established in 1866, is the oldest town in the Pilbara. The town retains several late 19th-century stone buildings, including the Old Gaol which now houses the tourist office and a craft gallery and the Holy Trinity Church (1894). Roebourne also marks the start of the 52-km (32-mile) Emma Withnell Heritage Trail, which takes a scenic route from here to Cossack and Point Samson. Trail guides are available at the tourist office.

ENVIRONS: Some 150 km (93 miles) inland lies the 200,000-ha (500,000-acre) **Millstream-Chichester National Park** with its lush freshwater pools and rich animal and plant life.

Cossack Historical Town ⓬

🚌 🛈 *Queen St, Roebourne (08) 9182 1060.*

IN 1863, the town of Tien Tsin Harbour was established and quickly became the home of a burgeoning pearling industry that attracted people from as far away as Japan and China. The settlement was renamed Cossack in 1872 after a visit by Governor Weld aboard HMS *Cossack*. However, the town's moment soon passed. The pearling industry moved on to Broome *(see p322)* and by 1910 Cossack's harbour had silted up. In the late 1970s, restoration work of this ghost town began and today, under the management of the Shire of Roebourne, it has become a curiosity that continues to fascinate many visitors.

Old courthouse in Cossack Historical Town

Point Samson ⓭

🏠 *200.* 🛈 *Queen St, Roebourne (08) 9182 1060.*

THIS SMALL settlement was founded in 1910 to take on the port duties formerly performed by Cossack. Today, there is a modest fishing industry and two harbours. The town's best beaches are found at Honeymoon Cove and Samson Reef, where visitors can snorkel among the coral or search for rock oysters at low tide.

Karijini National Park ⓮

🛈 *Tom Price (08) 9188 1112.* ⭕ *daily (weather permitting).*

SET IN THE Hamersley Range, in the heart of the Pilbara region, Karijini National Park covers some 600,000 ha (1,500,000 acres). It is the second-largest national park in the state after Purnululu National Park *(see p323)*.

The park has three types of landscape: rolling hills and ridges covered in eucalypt forests; arid, low-lying shrubland; and, in the north, spectacular gorges. The best times to visit the park are in winter, when the days are temperate, and in spring, when carpets of wildflowers are in spectacular bloom.

The Kimberley and the Deserts

AUSTRALIA'S LAST FRONTIER, the Kimberley is a vast, remote upland region of dry, red landscape. Deep rivers cut through mountain ranges, and parts of the coastline have the highest tidal range in the southern hemisphere. Seasonal climatic extremes add to the area's sense of isolation as the harsh heat of the dry season and the torrential rains of the wet hamper access to the hostile terrain. April to September is the best time to visit, offering views of the country's best natural sights such as the Wolfe Creek Meteorite Crater and the Bungle Bungles. To the south lie the huge, inhospitable Great Sandy and Gibson deserts.

Pearler's diving helmet, Broome

LOCATOR MAP

■	*The Kimberley and the Deserts*
■	*North of Perth pp312–21*

Map labels:
WYNDHAM **19**
PURNULULU (BUNGLE BUNGLE) NATIONAL PARK
DERBY **16**
18
BROOME **15**
HALLS CREEK **17**
GREAT SANDY DESERT
Lake Mackay
GIBSON DESERT
Lake Carnegie
WARBURTON ROAD
GREAT VICTORIA DESERT

0 kilometres 200
0 miles 200

Broome **15**

🏠 13,000. ✈ 🚌 🚍 ℹ cnr Bagot St & Broome Hwy (08) 9192 2222.

BROOME, first settled by Europeans in the 1860s, soon became Western Australia's most profitable pearling region. Pearl divers from Asia swelled the town in the 1880s and helped give it the multi-cultural flavour that remains today. The tourist industry has now superseded pearling, but the town's past can still be seen in several original stores, as well as the Chinese and Japanese cemeteries that contain the graves of hundreds of pearl divers.

Just outside town is the popular Cable Beach. On Cable Beach Road, **Broome Crocodile Park** has more than 1,000 of these voracious near-relatives of the dinosaurs.

🐊 **Broome Crocodile Park**
Cable Beach Rd. **(** (08) 9192 1489. ○ daily. 🈺 ♿

Camel trekking along the famous Cable Beach near Broome

KEY

▬	Highway
▬	Major road
▬	Minor road
∿	River

A freshwater crocodile basking in the sun, Windjana Gorge, near Derby

Derby ⑯

🏠 5,000. ✈ 🚌 🛈 2 Clarendon St (08) 9191 1426.

DERBY IS THE GATEWAY to a region of stunning gorges. Points of interest in the town include the 1920s Wharfingers House, Old Derby Gaol, and the Botanical Gardens.

South of town is the 1,000-year old Prison Boab (baobab) tree, 14 m (45 ft) in circumference. At the end of the 19th century, it was used to house prisoners overnight before their final journey to Derby Gaol.

ENVIRONS: Derby stands at the western end of the Gibb River Road, which leads towards the three national parks collectively known as the **Devonian Reef National Parks**. These parks – Windjana Gorge, Tunnel Creek and Geikie Gorge – contain some of the most spectacular gorge scenery in Australia.

❀ Devonian Reef National Parks
🚌 to Derby. 🛈 Derby (08) 9191 1426. ◷ Mon–Sat. ● public hols.

Halls Creek ⑰

🏠 1,400. 🚌 🛈 Community Resource Centre, Great Northern Hwy (08) 9168 6262.

HALLS CREEK was the site of Western Australia's first gold rush in 1885, and today is a centre for mineral mining. Close to the original town site is a vertical wall of quartz rock, known as China Wall. About

130 km (80 miles) to the south is the world's second-largest meteorite crater, in **Wolfe Creek Crater National Park**.

❀ Wolfe Creek Crater National Park
🚌 Halls Creek. 🛈 Halls Creek (08) 9168 6262. ◷ Apr–Sep: daily. ● wet weather (roads impassable).

Purnululu (Bungle Bungle) National Park ⑱

🚌 Kununurra, Halls Creek. 🛈 Kununurra (08) 9168 1177. ◷ Apr–Nov: daily. 🅿 📷

COVERING SOME 320,000 ha (790,000 acres) of the most isolated landscape in Western Australia, Purnululu National Park was declared in 1987. It is home to the local Kija and

The intriguing domes of the Bungle Bungles, Purnululu National Park

Jaru people, who co-operate with national park authorities to develop cultural tourism.

The most famous part of the park is the Bungle Bungle Range, consisting of unique beehive-shaped domes of rock encased in a skin of silica and cyanobacterium.

Wyndham ⑲

🏠 900. ✈ 🚌 🛈 6 Great Northern Hwy (08) 9161 1281.

THE PORT OF Wyndham lies at the northern tip of the Great Northern Highway, on Cambridge Gulf. The town was established in 1888, partly to service the Halls Creek gold rush and partly as a centre for the local pastoral industry. It also provided supplies, which were carried by Afghan camel-trains, for cattle stations in the northern Kimberley. The town's Afghan cemetery is a reminder of those hardy traders who were essential to the survival of pioneer home-steads in the interior.

The part of the town known as Old Wyndham Port was the original town site and still contains a number of 19th-century buildings, including the old post office, the old courthouse and Anthon's Landing, where the first jetty was erected. The Port Museum displays a vivid photographic history of the port.

The area around Wyndham has a large crocodile popula-tion. Freshwater and saltwater crocodiles can be seen at **Wyndham Crocodile Park** or occasionally in the wild at Blood Drain Crocodile Look-out and Crocodile Hole. To complete the picture, a 4-m (13-ft) high concrete saltwater crocodile greets visitors at the entrance to the town. Salt-water crocodiles have a taste for people, so caution should be exercised near the water.

About 25 km (15 miles) from Wyndham, Aboriginal petro-glyphs can be seen at the pic-nic spot of Moochalabra Dam.

✗ Wyndham Crocodile Farm
Barylettes Rd. ☎ (08) 9161 1124. ◷ daily. ● 25 Dec. 🅿 ♿

SOUTH AUSTRALIA

South Australia at a Glance

SOUTH AUSTRALIA contains a wide range of landscapes. A striking coastline of sandy beaches and steep cliffs gives way to lush valleys, mountains and rolling plains of wheat and barley. Further inland, the terrain changes starkly as the climate becomes hotter and drier. The Far North encompasses huge areas and includes the Flinders Ranges and Coober Pedy, the opal-mining town with troglodyte homes. Most of the state's population lives in the capital, Adelaide, and the wine-making towns of the Clare and Barossa valleys.

THE YORKE AND EYRE PENINSULAS AND THE FAR NORTH
(see pp350–61)

Coober Pedy's golf course is one of the few features above ground in this strange Outback mining town. Many of the town's houses are built underground to escape the area's harsh, dusty climate (see p360).

Port Augusta (see p357) *is a major road and rail hub that also serves as the gateway to the Far North of the state. It retains several early homesteads among its modern buildings.*

Kangaroo Island (see p346) *is an unspoilt haven for abundant native wildlife. At Kirkpatrick Point in the southwest lie the Remarkable Rocks, sculpted by the wind, rain and sea.*

0 kilometres 100

0 miles   100

◁ **Profile of the rich red soil in a Coonawarra winery in South Australia**

Quorn (see p361) *was an important railway town at the end of the 19th century and has many reminders of its pioneerng days. Today it marks the start of the Pichi Richi Railway, a restored track running vintage trains and locomotives for tourists.*

The Flinders Ranges (see p361) *stretch from north of St Vincent's Gulf far into the Outback. They include some of South Australia's most rugged scenery and offer fine bushwalking.*

The Barossa wine region *encompasses the Barossa Valley and Eden Valley. Both are lush areas of rolling hills and home to dozens of famous wineries dating from the 19th century (see pp348–9).*

Adelaide (see pp336–41) *is an elegant state capital with many well-preserved colonial buildings. Its cosmopolitan atmosphere is enhanced by a lively restaurant, arts and entertainment scene.*

ADELAIDE
AND THE
SOUTHEAST
(see pp332–49)

Mount Gambier (see p346) *lies on the slopes of an extinct volcano of the same name. One of the volcano's crater lakes, Blue Lake, shows its intense hue in the summer months.*

Birds of South Australia

THE VAST, VARIED habitats of South Australia are home to some 380 bird species. Gulls, sea eagles and penguins live along the coast, while waders, ducks and cormorants are found in the internal wetlands. Rosellas and other parrots are common in Adelaide's parkland. The mallee scrub, which once covered much of the state, is home to the mallee fowl and an array of honeyeaters. The Flinders Ranges and the Far North are the domain of birds of prey such as the peregrine falcon and the wedge-tailed eagle. Although much land has been cleared for farming, many habitats are protected within the state's national parks.

South Australian budgerigar

Little penguins *are the smallest penguins found in Australia. The only species to breed on the mainland, they feed on fish and squid skilfully caught underwater.*

THE FLINDERS RANGES AND OUTBACK HABITAT

The rugged mountains and deep gorges of the Flinders Ranges support a wide variety of bird species. Most spectacular are the birds of prey. Wedge-tailed eagles' nests can be found in large gum trees or on rock ledges, and the eagles are commonly seen feeding on dead animals in the arid Outback regions.

MALLEE SCRUB HABITAT

Much of this low-level scrubland has been cleared for agriculture. Remaining areas such as Billiat National Park near Loxton provide an important habitat for several elusive species. Golden whistlers, red and brush wattlebirds and white-eared honeyeaters can be seen here by patient bird-watchers. The best seasons to visit are late winter, spring and early summer.

Wedge-tailed eagles*, with their huge wingspan of up to 2.3 m (7 ft 6 in), typically perch on dead trees and telephone poles.*

Mallee fowls*, a wary species, stand 60 cm (24 in) tall and move quietly. They lay their eggs in a ground nest made of decomposing leaves and twigs.*

Peregrine falcons *do not build nests but lay their eggs on bare ledges or in tree hollows. Magnificent in flight, they descend on their prey at great speed with wings half or fully closed.*

Western whipbirds *are scarce and extremely secretive, keeping to the undergrowth. They run and fly swiftly, and are usually first noted by their harsh, grating call.*

THE EMU

Emus are huge flightless birds unique to Australia. Second only to the ostrich in height, they stand 1.5–1.9 m (5–6 ft 3 in) tall. They have long powerful legs and can run at speeds of up to 50 km/h (30 mph) over short distances. The females have a distinctive voice like a thudding drum. They lay their eggs on the ground on a thin layer of grass and leaves. The male incubates them for seven weeks, then broods and accompanies the young for up to 18 months. Common all over Australia, emus are found mainly in open, pastoral areas. Moving alone or in flocks, they are highly mobile and have a large home range.

Alert gaze of the Australian emu

Soft, grey-black plumage of the emu

WETLAND HABITAT

Wetlands such as Coorong National Park *(see p343)* are vital feeding and breeding grounds for a wide range of water birds. They provide essential refuge in times of drought for many endangered birds. Migratory birds, such as sharp-tailed sandpipers from Siberia, use these areas to feed and rest before continuing on their annual journeys.

Brolgas *stand up to 1.3 m (4 ft 3 in) tall with a wingspan of up to 2.3 m (7 ft 6 in). They are renowned for their impressive dancing displays, leaping, bowing and flapping.*

Freckled ducks *are similar to primitive waterfowl, with swan-like characteristics. Dark, with no obvious markings, they are hard to spot. This is one of the world's rarest ducks.*

WOODLAND HABITAT

Habitats in woodland areas such as the Belair National Park near Adelaide support many species such as honeyeaters, rosellas and kookaburras. There is usually an abundance of food in such places and good opportunities to nest and roost. Despite increased human settlement in these areas, the birdlife is still rich. Dawn and dusk are the best times for seeing birds.

Adelaide rosellas *are commonly found in the Mount Lofty Ranges and the parklands of Adelaide. Their plumage is in brilliant shades of red, orange and blue.*

Laughing kookaburras *are the world's largest kingfishers. They are renowned for their loud, manic laughing call, often begun by one bird and quickly taken up by others.*

Wines of South Australia

SOUTH AUSTRALIA makes more than half of Australia's wines, including some of its finest. From its numerous vineyards comes a dazzling diversity of wines, ranging from ports made more than a century ago to Australia's most famous wines, Penfolds Grange and Jacob's Creek. The latter is the first Australian wine to become an internationally known label. Virtually all wineries welcome tourists for tastings.

Seven Hills Winery is in the heart of the Clare Valley, one of South Australia's prime wine-producing regions.

Tim Knappstein, an award-winning Clare Valley winery, produces Riesling that is European in style.

Bridgewater Mill winery is renowned in the area for an excellent restaurant. Daily tastings of its own brands are offered at the cellar door.

WINE REGIONS

South Australia has eight designated wine regions, the most famous being the Barossa Valley *(see pp348–9)* which has been producing wine for 150 years. The Clare Valley is noted for its Rieslings, Cabernet Sauvignon and Shiraz. Coonawarra is Australia's best red wine region, thanks to its red soil on a bed of soft limestone. McLaren Vale, the Murray Valley, the Adelaide Plains, the Riverland, the Limestone Coast, and the Adelaide Hills are the other major districts.

Kadina •   Clare •

• Gaw

ADELAIDE •

Cape Jervis •

Cabernet Sauvignon grapes are very successful in the state, with a ripe, fruity flavour.

The Adelaide Hills are known for their excellent Pinot Noir, Chardonnay and Riesling grapes.

Wolf Blass' Barossa Black Label has a rich, oaky flavour, and is just one of this world-renowned vintner's individual wines. Blass has earned more than 2,000 international medals for his wine.

KEY

☐ Clare Valley	☐ McLaren Vale & Langhorne Creek
☐ Padthaway	☐ Adelaide Hills
☐ Mount Benson	☐ Barossa Valley
☐ Coonawarra & the Southeast	
☐ Murray Valley	

NTRODUCING SOUTH AUSTRALIA

KEY FACTS

Location and Climate

The climate of Australia's central state ranges from Mediterranean-style in the Murray Valley to the cool Adelaide Hills and districts in the southeast. Vintage begins in high summer, when grapes are often picked and crushed at night to preserve the maximum flavour.

Grape Varieties

South Australian vintners draw on a range of grape varieties, including Shiraz, Cabernet Sauvignon, Grenache, Merlot and Pinot Noir reds; Chardonnay, Riesling, Semillon, Sauvignon Blanc and Frontignac whites.

Good Producers

Penfolds, Bethany, Grant Burge, St Hallett, Henschke, Seppelt, Mountadam, Hardy, Seaview, Orlando, Wolf Blass, Yalumba, Grosset, Jim Barry, Pauletts, Taylors, Wynns, Mildara, Chapel Hill, d'Arenberg, Peter Lehmann, Renmano, Tim Knappstein, Bridgewater Mill, Seven Hills. (This list represents only a sampling of the state's quality producers.)

Barrel maturation at the Berri Renmano winery in the Murray Valley is one of the traditional techniques still used in the production of top-quality table wines.

Thomas Hardy & Sons, in the Padthaway region, was established in 1853. The Rhine Riesling Beerenauslese is considered its finest wine.

Wynns Winery at Coonawarra is known for fine Cabernet Sauvignon and other reds. The winery itself is equally distinctive, with its triple gable architecture shown on the wine labels.

Yalumba Vineyard, founded in 1849, is one of the oldest in the Coonawarra region. Coonawarra is regarded as the best table wine region in Australia. The climate is similar to that of Bordeaux in France.

Olary Creek

nda Creek

Murray River

Waikerie • Renmark

lem Bend

•Keith

Kingston •

Reedy Creek

Mount Gambier

0 km   50

0 miles   50

ADELAIDE AND THE SOUTHEAST

THE SOUTHEAST *is a region rich with pine forests, wineries and a spectacular coastline. The state capital, Adelaide, is a vibrant city, whose surrounding hills abound with vineyards from the Barossa Valley to McLaren Vale. To the east the great Murray River meanders from the Victoria border down towards the Southern Ocean. Just off the Fleurieu Peninsula lies Kangaroo Island, a haven for wildlife.*

Home to Aborigines for more than 10,000 years, this region was settled by Europeans in 1836 when Governor John Hindmarsh proclaimed the area a British colony. William Light, the Surveyor General, chose the site of the city of Adelaide.

The settlement was based on a theory of free colonization funded solely by land sales, and no convicts were transported here. Elegant Adelaide was carefully planned by Colonel Light: its ordered grid pattern, centred on pretty squares and gardens, is surrounded by parkland. Wealth from agriculture and mining paid for many of Adelaide's fine Victorian buildings. In the mid-20th century the city established a significant manufacturing industry, in particular of motor vehicles and household appliances. Adelaide still has a focus on high technology.

South Australia has always had a tradition of tolerance. Many of the first settlers were non-conformists from Great Britain seeking a more open society. Other early migrants included Lutherans escaping persecution in Germany. They settled in Hahndorf and the Barossa Valley, where they established a wine industry.

With high rainfall and irrigated by the Murray River, the region is the most fertile in the state. The coastline includes the Fleurieu Peninsula and the beautiful Coorong National Park. Offshore, Kangaroo Island has stunning scenery and bountiful native wildlife.

Port and sherry casks at a winery in the Barossa Valley

◻ The tall twin spires of the neo-Gothic St Peter's Cathedral in Adelaide

Exploring Adelaide and the Southeast

ADELAIDE AND THE SOUTHEAST area encompass the most bountiful and productive regions of South Australia. Adelaide, the state's capital city and the most obvious base for exploring the region, lies on a flat plain between the Mount Lofty Ranges and the popular white sandy beaches of Gulf St Vincent, to the east of Cape Jervis. The city itself is green and elegant, with many historic sites to explore. To the northeast, beyond the Adelaide Hills, are quaint 19th-century villages and the many wineries of the Barossa Valley region. To the east and south lie Australia's largest river, the Murray River, and the rolling hills of the Fleurieu Peninsula. Further to the southeast the beauty of the coastal Coorong National Park and the Southern Ocean coastline contrasts with the flat, agricultural area inland. Offshore lies the natural splendour of Kangaroo Island, with its abundance of native wildlife and striking rock formations.

0 kilometres 50

0 miles 50

SEE ALSO

Birds enjoying the wetlands of Bool Lagoon in the Naracoorte Caves Conservation Park

St Peter's Anglican Cathedral, seen across Adelaide parkland

SIGHTS AT A GLANCE

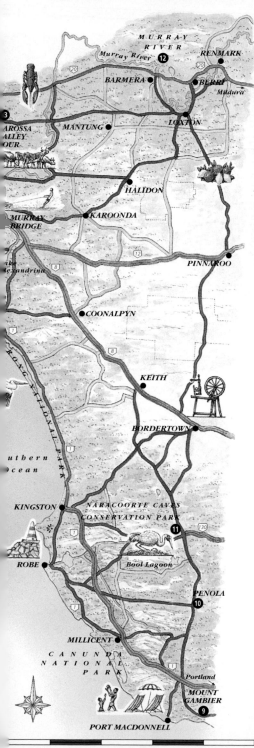

View of the Murray River, between Swan Reach and Walker Flat

GETTING AROUND

The inner city of Adelaide is best explored on foot; it is compact, well laid out and flat. There is an extensive public transport system of trains, coaches and buses through-out the metropolitan area, although services are often restricted at weekends. However, for those with a car, the city's roads are good and the traffic generally light. Outside Adelaide, public transport is very limited, although coach tours are available to most areas. A car provides the most efficient means of exploring the region, with a net-work of high-standard roads and highways. In addition, a domestic air service operates between Adelaide and Mount Gambier. Kangaroo Island is serviced by air from Adelaide and also by ferry from Cape Jervis. The predom-inantly flat landscape also makes this a popular area for cyclists and walkers.

KEY

▄▄▄	Highway
▅▅▅	Major road
┈┈┈	Minor road
▄▄▄	Scenic route
～～	River
✷	Viewpoint

Street-by-Street: Adelaide ❶

ADELAIDE'S CULTURAL CENTRE lies between the grand, tree-lined North Terrace and the River Torrens. Along North Terrace is a succession of imposing 19th-century public buildings, including the state library, museum and art gallery and two university campuses. To the west, on the bank of the river, is the Festival Centre. This multi-purpose complex of theatres, including an outdoor amphitheatre, is home to the renowned biennial Adelaide Festival *(see p37)*. To the east, also by the river, lie the botanic and zoological gardens.

Museum figure

River Torrens
Visitors can hire paddleboats to travel along this gentle river and see Adelaide from water level.

The Migration and Settlement Museum tells the stories of the thousands of people from more than 100 nations who left everything behind to start a new life in South Australia.

Festival Centre
Completed in 1977, this arts complex enjoys a picturesque riverside setting and is a popular place for a picnic.

Parliament House
Ten marble Corinthian columns grace the façade of Parliament House, which was completed in 1939, more than 50 years after construction first began.

★ **Botanic Gardens**
Begun in 1855, these peaceful gardens cover an area of 20 ha (50 acres). They include artificial lakes and the beautiful Bicentennial Conservatory in which a tropical rainforest environment has been re-created.

VISITORS' CHECKLIST

🏠 1.7 million. ✈ West Beach, 10 km (6 miles) W of city. 🚉 North Terrace (interstate); Richmond Rd, Keswick. 🚌 Central Bus Station, Franklin St. ⛴ Glenelg Jetty, Glenelg Beach. ℹ 18 King William St (08) 8303 2033. 🎭 Adelaide Festival of Arts; Womadelaide (both Feb, alternate years).

Art Gallery of South Australia
Contemporary works, such as Christopher Healey's Drinking Fountains, *feature here alongside period painting and sculpture.*

0 metres	100
0 yards	100

KEY

– – – Suggested route

STAR SIGHTS

★ **Botanic Gardens**

★ **South Australian Museum**

The South Australian Police Museum is housed in the old mounted police barracks, built in 1851. It has exhibitions on the history of law and order in the state.

★ **South Australian Museum**
Chiefly a natural history museum, the South Australian Museum has an excellent reputation for its fine Aboriginal collection, including this painting on bark, Assembling the Totem, *by a Melville Island artist (see p266).*

Exploring Adelaide

South Australian Museum boomerangs

ADELAIDE, a city of great charm with an unhurried way of life, is easily explored on foot. Well planned on a grid pattern, it is bordered by wide terraces and parkland. Within the city are a number of garden squares and gracious stone buildings. However, while Adelaide values its past, it is very much a modern city. The balmy climate and excellent local food and wine have given rise to an abundance of streetside restaurants and cafés. With its acclaimed arts-based Adelaide Festival *(see p37)*, the city also prides itself on being the artistic capital of Australia.

Detail of the ornate front parapet of Edmund Wright House

🚌 Victoria Square
Flinders & Angas sts.

Victoria Square lies at the geographic heart of the city. In its centre stands a fountain designed by sculptor John Dowie in 1968. Its theme is the three rivers from which Adelaide draws its water: the Torrens, the Murray and the Onkaparinga. Government buildings were erected around much of the square during colonial days and many of these buildings still stand as reminders of a bygone age.

On the north side of Victoria Square stands the General Post Office, an impressive building with an ornate main hall and a clock tower. Opened in 1872, it was hailed by English novelist Anthony Trollope as the "grandest edifice in the town".

On the corner of Wakefield Street, to the east of Victoria Square, stands St Francis Xavier Catholic Cathedral. The original cathedral, dedicated in 1858, was a simpler building and plans for expansion were hampered by the lack of rich Catholics in the state. The cathedral was only completed in 1996, when the spire was finally added.

To the south of the square is Adelaide's legal centre and the Magistrates Court. The Supreme Court, built in the 1860s, has a Palladian façade.

🚌 Adelaide Town Hall
128 King William St. 📞 (08) 8203 7203. 🕐 Mon–Fri. ● public hols. ♿

When Adelaide Town Hall, designed in Italianate style by Edmund Wright, was built in 1866, it became the most significant structure on King William Street. It was not long before it took over as the city's premier venue for concerts and civic receptions and is still used as such today. Notable features of the building include its grand staircase and highly ornate and decorative ceiling

🚌 Edmund Wright House
59 King William St. 📞 (08) 8226 8555. 🕐 Mon–Fri. ● public hols. ♿

Edmund Wright House, originally built for the Bank of South Australia in 1878, was set to be demolished in 1971. However, a general outcry led to its public purchase and restoration. The building was renamed after its main architect, Edmund Wright. The skill and workmanship displayed in the finely proportioned and detailed façade is also evident in the beautiful interior. Today the building is home to the History Trust of South Australia

Further along King William Street, at the corner of North Terrace, stands one of Adelaide's finest statues, the South African War Memorial. It shows a "spirited horse and his stalwart rider" and stands in memory of those who lost their lives in the Boer War.

Apples on display in Adelaide's Central Market

🛒 Central Market
Gouger St. 📞 (08) 8203 7494. 🕐 Tue, Thu–Sat. ● public hols. ♿

Just west of Victoria Square, between Gouger and Grote streets, Adelaide Central Market has provided a profusion of tastes and aromas in the city for more than 125 years. The changing ethnic pattern of Adelaide society is reflected in the diversity of produce available today. Asian shops now sit beside older European-style butchers and delicatessens, and part of the area has become Adelaide's own little Chinatown. Around the market are dozens of restaurants and cafés where local food is adapted to various international cuisines.

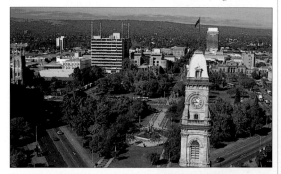

View overlooking Victoria Square in the centre of Adelaide

🏛 Tandanya

253 Grenfell St. ☎ *(08) 8224 3200.*
○ *daily.* ● *Good Fri, 25 Dec, 1 Jan.*
🎫 ☕ 🛍 ♿

Tandanya, the Aboriginal name for the Adelaide area, is an excellent Aboriginal cultural institute featuring indigenous art galleries, workshops and performance areas. It also has a café and a gift shop selling Aboriginal crafts.

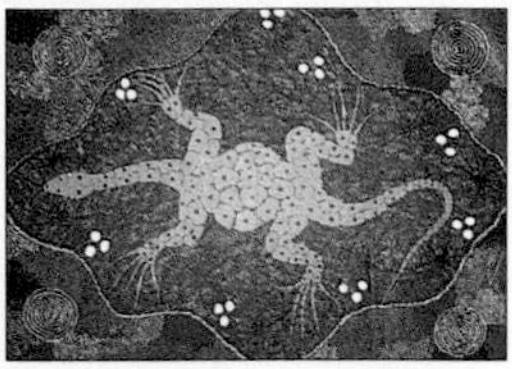

***Goanna Dreaming '96*, by Michael Tommy Jabanardi, in Tandanya**

🏛 Migration and Settlement Museum

82 Kintore Ave. ☎ *(08) 8207 7580.*
○ *daily.* ● *Good Fri, 25 Dec.* ♿

The Migration and Settlement Museum is located behind the State Library in what was once Adelaide's Destitute Asylum. It reflects the cultural diversity of South Australian society by telling the stories of people from many parts of the world who came here to start a new life. Exhibits, including re-creations of early settlers' houses, explain the immigrants' reasons for leaving their homeland, their hopes for a new life, their difficult journeys and what they then found on arrival in the new colony.

🏛 South Australian Museum

North Terrace. ☎ *(08) 8207 7500.*
○ *daily.* ● *Good Fri, 25 Dec.* ♿

Beyond its entrance, framed on either side by huge whale skeletons, the South Australian Museum has a number of interesting collections including an Egyptian room and many natural history exhibits. Its most important collection, however, is its extensive and internationally acclaimed collection of Aboriginal artifacts which boasts more than 37,000 individual items and 50,000 photographs, as well as many sound and video recordings.

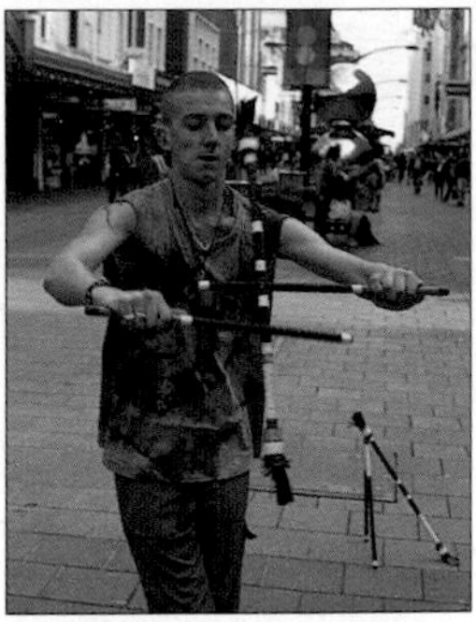

A street performer in Rundle Mall, Adelaide's main shopping precinct

🛍 Rundle Mall

Adelaide Arcade. ☎ *(08) 8223 5522.*
○ *daily.* ● *public hols.*

Adelaide's main shopping area is centred on Rundle Mall, with its mixture of department stores, boutiques and small shops. Several arcades run off the mall, including Adelaide Arcade. Built in the 1880s, it has Italianate elevations at both ends and a central dome. The interior was modernized in the 1960s, but has since been fully restored to its former glory.

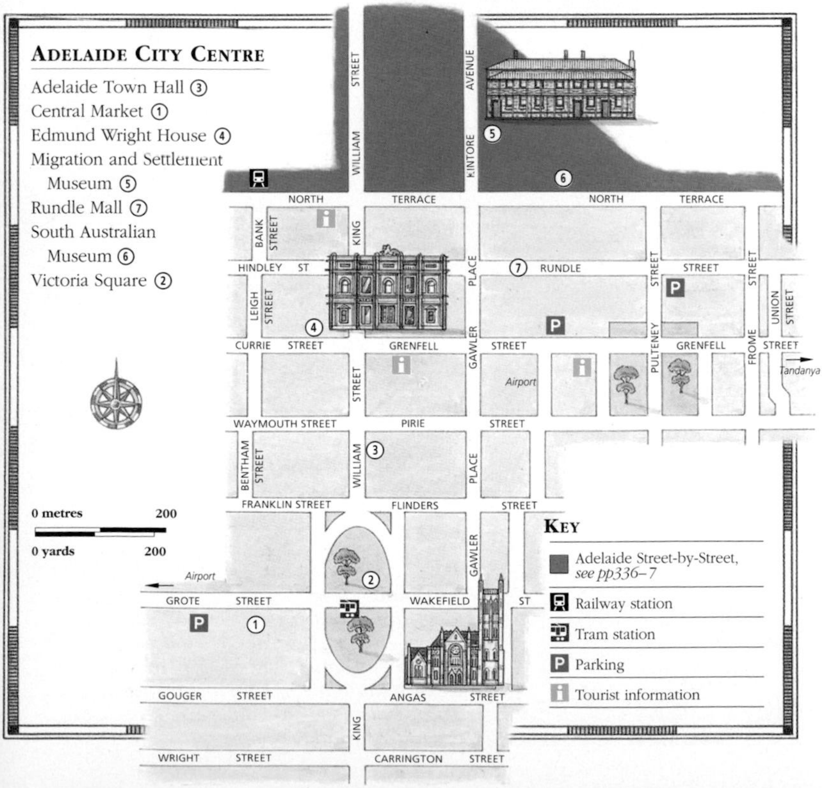
ADELAIDE CITY CENTRE
Adelaide Town Hall ③
Central Market ①
Edmund Wright House ④
Migration and Settlement Museum ⑤
Rundle Mall ⑦
South Australian Museum ⑥
Victoria Square ②
0 metres 200
0 yards 200
NORTH TERRACE
HINDLEY ST
RUNDLE STREET
CURRIE STREET
GRENFELL STREET
WAYMOUTH STREET
PIRIE STREET
FRANKLIN STREET
FLINDERS STREET
GROTE STREET
WAKEFIELD ST
GOUGER STREET
ANGAS STREET
WRIGHT STREET
CARRINGTON STREET
WILLIAM STREET
KINTORE AVENUE
BANK STREET
KING
LEIGH STREET
BENTHAM STREET
GAWLER PLACE
PULTENEY STREET
FROME STREET
UNION STREET
KING WILLIAM
Airport
Tandanya
KEY
Adelaide Street-by-Street, see pp336–7
Railway station
Tram station
Parking
Tourist information

Ayers House

AYERS HOUSE is one of the best examples of colonial Regency architecture in Australia. From 1855 until his death in 1897, it was the home of Sir Henry Ayers, a former Premier of South Australia and an influential businessman. The original house was quite simple but was expanded over the years with the growing status and wealth of its owner. The final form of this elegant mansion is due largely to the noted colonial architect Sir George Strickland Kingston. The restored house is now run by the National Trust and also incorporates two restaurants. The oldest section is open to the public and houses a fine collection of Victorian furniture, furnishings, memorabilia and art.

Front of the house viewed from North Terrace

Corrugated roof

★ **Bedroom**
The main bedroom has been carefully restored to its late-Victorian style. Its authentic furnishings reflect the prosperity brought by South Australia's rich mining discoveries in the 1870s.

STAR FEATURES
★ Bedroom
★ State Dining Room

The Library, furnished with a long dining table, can be hired for functions.

Ballroom
This intricately decorated cornice dates from the 1870s. It is likely that it was painted by Charles Gow, an employee of the Scottish firm of Lyon and Cottier, who is believed to have undertaken extensive work at the house.

★ State Dining Room
Sir Henry loved to entertain, and lavish dinners were often held here. It boasts a hand-painted ceiling, stencilled woodwork and the original gasoliers.

Local bluestone was used in constructing the house, as with many 19th-century Adelaide houses. The north façade faces onto North Terrace, one of the city's main streets *(see pp336–7)*.

Entrance to main restaurant

The Conservatory is based around the original stables and coachhouse. Now a restaurant, the whole area has been flooded with light by the addition of a glass roof.

Front entrance

Veranda's original chequered tile flooring

The family drawing room, along with the adjacent family dining room, has had test strips removed from its walls and ceiling to uncover some stunning original decoration. Work is now underway to restore this fully.

THE STORY OF SIR HENRY AYERS

Sir Henry Ayers (1821–97) was born in Hampshire, England, the son of a dock worker. He married in 1840 and, a month later, emigrated with his bride to South Australia. After working briefly as a clerk, Ayers made his fortune in the state's new copper mines. Entering politics in 1857, he was appointed South Australia's Premier seven times between 1863 and 1873, and was President of the Legislative Council, 1881–93. Among many causes, he supported exploration of the interior (Ayers Rock, now Uluru, was named after him), but is chiefly remembered for his prominent role in the development of South Australia.

Statesman and businessman, Sir Henry Ayers

The Southeast Coastline

THE COASTLINE south of Adelaide is rich and varied with beautiful beaches, magnificent coastal scenery and abundant birdlife. The southern coastline of the Fleurieu Peninsula is largely exposed to the mighty Southern Ocean. Here there are good surfing beaches, long expanses of sand, sheltered bays and harbours and stark, weathered cliffs. The western side of the peninsula is more sheltered. There are very few commercial developments on the southeast's coastline and it is easy to find quiet, secluded beaches for swimming, surfing, fishing or walking. Just off South Australia's mainland, Kangaroo Island boasts both pristine swimming beaches and ruggedly beautiful windswept cliffs.

★ Cape Jervis ②

🏄 🌊 🛟 🚻 ⛺

Visitors to the tiny hamlet of Cape Jervis can see Kangaroo Island *(see p346)*, 16 km (10 miles) away across Backstairs Passage. The cape has good boating and fishing and is a hang-gliding centre.

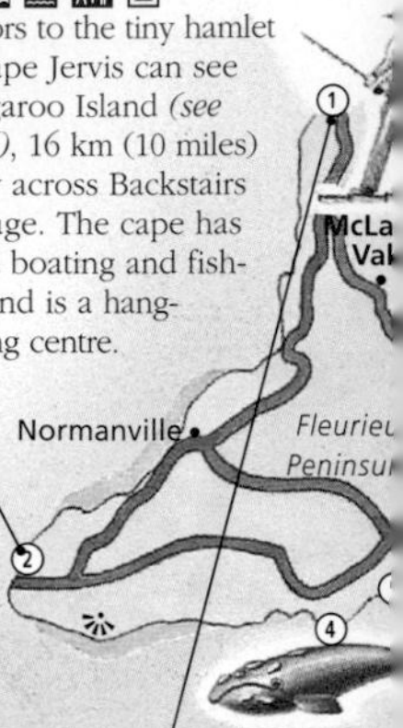

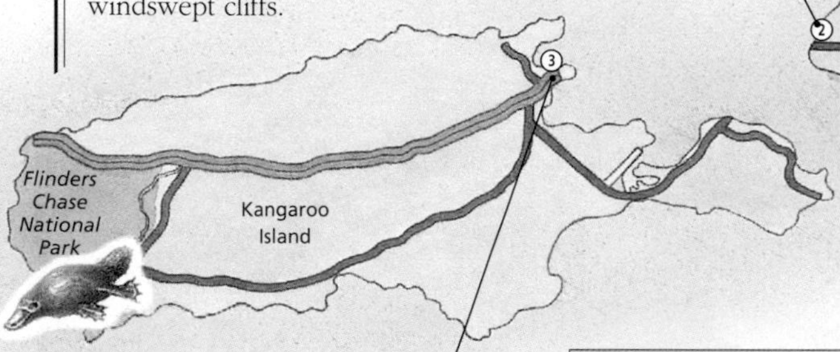

★ Kingscote, Kangaroo Island ③

🏄 🌊 🧍 🛟 ♿ 🚻 ⛺

Kingscote, the island's largest town has a small sandy beach with a tidal pool. There is rich birdlife in swampland south of the town.

★ Port Noarlunga ①

🏄 🌊 🛟 🚻 ⛺

Port Noarlunga boasts a fantastic beach and a protected reef with marine ecosystems that can be explored by snorkellers and scuba divers on a fully marked 800-m (2,600-ft) underwater trail.

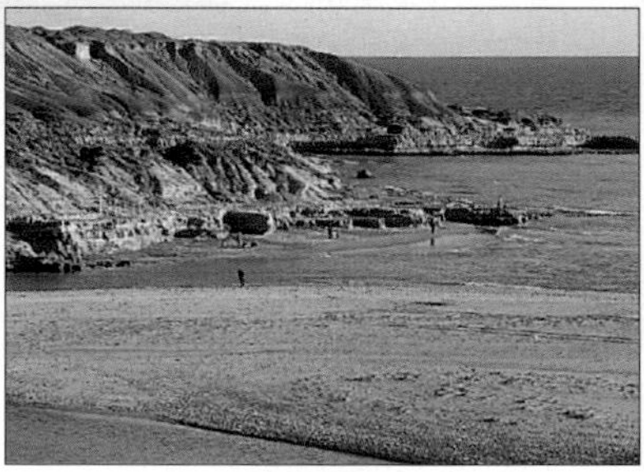

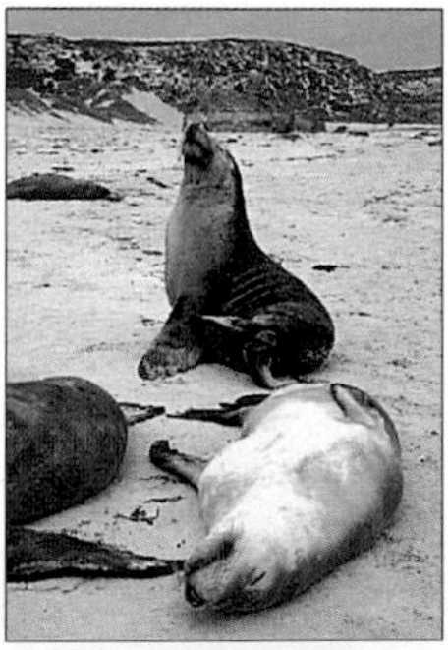

***Flinders Chase National Park** covers the western end of Kangaroo Island with undisturbed eucalypt forests and grassland, and seal-inhabited windswept beaches.*

Waitpinga Beach ④

🏄 🛟 🚻 ⛺

Waitpinga Beach, on the southern coast of the Fleurieu Peninsula, is a spectacular surfing beach with waves rolling in off the Southern Ocean. Strong, unpredictable currents make the beach unsafe for swimming and suitable for experienced surfers only. The long stretch of clean white sand is a favourite for beach walkers.

Victor Harbor ⑤

🏄 🌊 🏊 🛟 ♿ 🚻 ⛺

Holiday homes have been built in Victor Harbor since the 19th century. It later became a whaling station, but today southern right whales can be seen from June to October frolicking offshore.

Port Elliot ⑥

🏄 🌊 🛟 🚻 ⛺

Port Elliot, together with nearby Victor Harbor, has long been a favourite place to escape the summer heat of Adelaide. Established in 1854 as a port for the Murray River trade, the town has a safe swimming beach and a fine cliff-top walk.

Hindmarsh Island ⑦

🏄 🌊 🛟 🚻 ⛺

The quiet escapist destination of Hindmarsh Island can be reached by a free ferry from the town of Goolwa 24 hours a day. On the island there are several good vantage points from which visitors can see the mouth of the Murray River.

LOCATOR MAP

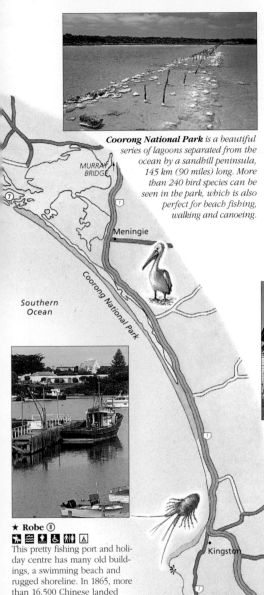

Coorong National Park is a beautiful series of lagoons separated from the ocean by a sandhill peninsula, 145 km (90 miles) long. More than 240 bird species can be seen in the park, which is also perfect for beach fishing, walking and canoeing.

KEY

	Highway
	Major road
	Minor road
	River
✵	Viewpoint

McLaren Vale, just inland from the coast of the Fleurieu Peninsula, is an important wine-producing region in South Australia (see pp330–31). In addition to 50 wineries, most of which are open for tastings, the vale has many excellent restaurants. On the main road is the Visitors' Centre, which is staffed by members of the local Winemakers' Association.

★ Robe ⑧

This pretty fishing port and holiday centre has many old buildings, a swimming beach and rugged shoreline. In 1865, more than 16,500 Chinese landed here and walked to Victoria's gold fields to avoid an immigration tax payable by those landing in Victoria *(see p428).*

★ Beachport ⑨

Historic Beachport was first settled as a whaling station in the 1830s. Today it is a quiet, unspoiled haven with swimming, surfing and fishing from its beaches, and a host of other water sports available.

0 kilometres   20

0 miles   20

Old Government House in Belair National Park

Belair National Park ②

[(08) 8278 5477. 🚍 from Adelaide. ☐ 8am–sunset. ● 25 Dec. 🅿 for cars only. ♿ limited.

ESTABLISHED IN 1891, Belair is the eighth-oldest national park in the world. Only 9 km (5 miles) from Adelaide, it is one of the most popular parks in South Australia. Tennis courts and pavilions are available for hire and there are picnic facilities throughout the park. Visitors can meander through the tall eucalypt forests and cool valleys, and see kangaroos, emus, echidnas and other native wildlife.

In spring, many native plants bloom. The park is closed occasionally in summer on days of extreme fire danger.

Within the park lies **Old Government House**. Built in 1859 as the governor's summer residence, it offers a glimpse of the lifestyle enjoyed by the colonial gentry.

⛪ Old Government House
Belair National Park. [(08) 8278 5477. ☐ Sun, public hols. ● Good Fri, 25 Dec. 🅿

Warrawong Sanctuary ③

[(08) 8370 9197. 🚍 Aldgate. ☐ 6:30am–10pm daily. ● 25 Dec. 🅿 ♿ limited. 🎥 obligatory.

WARRAWONG Sanctuary attempts to reverse the disastrous trends of recent years which have seen the extinction of 32 mammal species from South Australia.

Only 20 km (13 miles) from Adelaide, via the town of Stirling, the 32 ha (80 acres) of privately owned native bushland is surrounded by a vermin-proof fence. Into this environment Warrawong's owners have introduced some 15 mammal species, many of which are endangered. These include bettongs, potoroos and quolls *(see p443)*. Warrawong Sanctuary is also the location of Australia's only successful platypus breeding programme.

Guided walks are conducted throughout the day, but should be booked in advance. Accommodation and meals are also available *(see p483)*.

Hahndorf ④

👥 1,750. 🚍 from Adelaide. ℹ 41 Main St (08) 8388 1185.

HAHNDORF is the oldest surviving German settlement in Australia. The first settlers arrived in 1838 aboard the *Zebra* under the command of Captain Dirk Hahn. Escaping religious persecution in their homeland, they settled in the Adelaide Hills and established Hahndorf (Hahn's Village), a German-style town.

The tree-lined main street has many examples of classic German architecture, such as houses with *fachwerk* timber framing filled in with wattle

Kangaroo roaming through Warrawong Sanctuary in the Adelaide Hills

Nineteenth-century mill in the historic town of Hahndorf

and daub, or brick. Visitors can enjoy the town's historic atmosphere by taking a horse-drawn carriage tour.

Just outside Hahndorf is **The Cedars**, the former home of South Australia's best-known landscape artist, the late Sir Hans Heysen (see p30). Both his home and his studio are open to the public. South of the town is Nixon's Mill, a stone mill built in 1842.

The Cedars
Heysen Rd. (08) 8388 7277.
Sun–Fri. 25 Dec.

Strathalbyn **5**

2,700. Railway Station, South Terrace (08) 8536 3212.

THE DESIGNATED heritage town of Strathalbyn was originally settled by Scottish immigrants in 1839. Links with its Scottish ancestry can still be seen today in much of the town's architecture, which is reminiscent of small highland towns in Scotland.

Situated on the banks of the Angas River, Strathalbyn is dominated by St Andrew's Church with its sturdy tower. A number of original buildings have been preserved. The police station, built in 1858, and the 1865 courthouse together house the National Trust Museum. The prominent two-storey London House, built as a general store in 1867, has, like a number of buildings in or near the High Street, found a new use as an antiques store. As in many country towns in Australia, the hotels and banks are also architectural reminders of the past.

About 16 km (10 miles) south-east of Strathalbyn, on the banks of the Bremer River, is Langhorne Creek, renowned as one of the earliest wine-growing regions in Australia.

St Andrew's Church, Strathalbyn

Mount Lofty **6**

Mount Lofty Summit Rd. Mount Lofty Summit Information Centre (08) 8370 1054.

THE HILLS OF the Mount Lofty Ranges form the backdrop to Adelaide. The highest point, Mount Lofty, reaches 727 m

(2,385 ft) and offers a fine view of the city from the modern lookout at the summit, where there is also an interpretive centre. The hills are dotted with grand summer houses to which Adelaide citizens retreat during the summer heat.

Just below the summit is the **Cleland Wildlife Park** where visitors can stroll among the resident kangaroos and emus, have a photograph taken with a koala or walk through the aviary to observe native birds at close quarters.

About 1.5 km (1 mile) south of here, Mount Lofty Botanic Gardens feature temperate-climate plants such as rhodo-dendrons and magnolias.

Cleland Wildlife Park
Mount Lofty Summit Rd. (08) 8339 2444. daily. 25 Dec.

Birdwood **7**

600. National Motor Museum, Main St (08) 8568 5577.

NESTLED IN THE Adelaide Hills is the quiet little town of Birdwood. In the 1850s, wheat was milled in the town and the old wheat mill now houses Birdwood's most famous asset: the country's largest collection of vintage, veteran and classic motor cars, trucks and motor-bikes. The **National Motor Museum** has more than 300 on display and is considered to be one of the best collections of its kind in the world.

National Motor Museum
Main St. (08) 8568 5006.
daily. 25 Dec.

Hand-feeding kangaroos at Cleland Wildlife Park, Mount Lofty

Kangaroo Island 8

Sea Link ferry connection from Cape Jervis. **i** *The Gateway Information Centre, Howard Drive, Penneshaw (08) 8553 1185.*

Remarkable Rocks at Kirkpatrick Point, Kangaroo Island

KANGAROO ISLAND, Australia's third-largest island, is 155 km (96 miles) long and 55 km (34 miles) wide. Located 16 km (10 miles) off the Fleurieu Peninsula, the island was the site of South Australia's first official colonial settlement, established at Reeves Point in 1836. The settlement was short-lived, however, and within just four years had been virtually abandoned. The island was then settled by degrees during the remainder of the 19th century as communications improved with the new mainland settlements.

There is no public transport on Kangaroo Island and visitors must opt to travel either on a tour or by car. Many of the roads are unsealed and should be driven on with care.

Sparsely populated and geographically isolated, the island has few introduced predators and is a haven for a wide variety of animals and birds, many protected in its 19 conservation and national parks.

At Kingscote and Penneshaw fairy penguins can often be seen in the evenings, and the south coast windswept beach of Seal Bay is home to a large colony of Australian sea lions. In Flinders Chase National Park, kangaroos will sometimes approach visitors, but feeding them is discouraged.

The interior is dry, but does support tracts of mallee scrub, and eucalypts. The coastline, however, is varied. The north coast has sheltered beaches ideal for swimming. The south coast, battered by the Southern Ocean, has more than 40 shipwrecks. At Kirkpatrick Point to the southwest stands a group of large rocks. Aptly named Remarkable Rocks, they have been eroded into weird formations by the winds and sea.

Mount Gambier 9

23,000. ✈ 🚌 🚊 **i** *Jubilee Hwy East (08) 8724 9750.*

MOUNT GAMBIER is a major regional city midway between Adelaide and Melbourne, named after the extinct volcano on the slopes of which the city lies. Established in 1854, it is now surrounded by farming country and large pine plantations. The volcano has four crater lakes which are attractive recreation spots, with walking trails, picnic facilities and a wildlife park. The Blue Lake, up to 85 m (280 ft) deep, is a major draw between November and March when its water mysteriously turns an intense blue. From April to October, it remains a dull grey.

There are also a number of caves to explore within the city. Engelbrecht Cave is popular with cave divers, and the exposed Umpherston Sinkhole has fine terraced gardens.

Strange and vividly coloured water of Mount Gambier's Blue Lake

Sharam's Cottage, the first house built in Penola

Penola ⓾

🏃 *3,400.* 🚌 ❚ *27 Arthur St*
(08) 8737 2855.

ONE OF THE oldest towns in the Southeast, Penola is the commercial centre of the Coonawarra wine region *(see pp330–31).* The region's first winery was built in 1893. There are now some 20 wineries, most of which are open for sales and tastings.

Penola itself is a quiet town which takes great pride in its history. A heritage walk takes visitors past most of its early buildings, including the restored Sharam's Cottage, which was built in 1850 as the first dwelling in Penola.

ENVIRONS: Situated 27 km (17 miles) north of Penola, Bool Lagoon, designated a wetland of international significance by UNESCO, is an important refuge for an assortment of native wildlife including more than 150 species of birds. With boardwalks and hides, the park provides an opportunity to observe at close quarters many of these local and migratory birds *(see p329).*

Naracoorte Caves Conservation Park ⓫

❚ *(08) 8762 2340.* 🚌 *from Adelaide.* ◯ *9am–5pm daily (last tour 3:30pm).* ⬤ *25 Dec.* 🖾 🖊 🖵

LOCATED 12 KM (7 miles) south of Naracoorte is the Naracoorte Caves Conservation Park. Within this 600-ha (1,500-acre) park, there are 60 known caves, most notably Victoria Cave, which has been placed on the World Heritage List as a result of the remarkable fossil deposits discovered here in 1969 *(see pp22–3).* Guided tours of this and three other caves are available. From November to February thousands of bent wing bats come to breed in the Maternity Cave. They can be seen leaving the cave en masse at dusk to feed. Entrance to this cave is forbidden, but visitors can view the inside via infra-red cameras in the park.

Ancient stalactites inside one of the Naracoorte caves

Murray River ⓬

🚌 *from Adelaide.* ❚ *Renmark (08) 8586 6704.*

AUSTRALIA'S LARGEST river is a vital source of water in this, the driest state in Australia. As well as supplying water for Adelaide it supports a vigorous local agricultural industry which produces 40 per cent of all Australian wine *(see pp330–31).* It is also a popular destination for houseboating, water-skiing and fishing.

The town of Renmark, close to the Victoria border, lies at the heart of the Murray River irrigation area and is home to the Riverlands' first winery. At the town's wharf is the restored paddlesteamer *Industry,* now a floating museum and a reminder of days gone by.

Just south of Renmark, Berri is the area's commercial centre and site of the largest combined distillery and winery in the southern hemisphere. The Murray River meanders through Berri and on to the small town of Loxton before winding up towards the citrus centre of Waikerie. Surrounded by more than 5,000 ha (12,000 acres) of orchards, Waikerie is a favourite gliding centre and has hosted the world gliding championships.

Another 40 km (25 miles) downstream, the Murray River reaches the town of Morgan, its northernmost point in South Australia, before it turns south towards the ocean. The **Port of Morgan Museum**, located in the old railway station, aims to recapture the river-trading days, telling the story of what was once the second-busiest port in the state. The *Mayflower,* the oldest surviving paddlesteamer in the state, is moored next to the museum.

🏛 **Port of Morgan Museum**
Morgan Railway Station. ❚ *(08) 8235 9266.* ◯ *2–4pm daily.* ⬤ *25 Dec.* 🖾

An old paddlesteamer cruising along the Murray River

Barossa Valley Tour ⓭

Riesling grapes

The Barossa, comprised of the Barossa and Eden valleys, is one of Australia's most famous wine regions. First settled in 1842 by German Lutheran immigrants, villages were soon established at Bethany, Langmeil (now Tanunda), Lyndoch and Light's Pass. The peasant farmers soon developed a largely self-sufficient agrarian community centred on their churches. Winemaking later became their focus and there are now 50 wineries in the region. Signs of German traditions can be seen in the 19th-century buildings, churches and in the region's food, music and festivals.

Seppeltsfield ⑤
Between Tanunda and Greenoch, this winery was established in 1851 by the pioneering German family Seppelt. A historic complex of splendid stone buildings, it is reached via an avenue of palm trees planted in the 1920s.

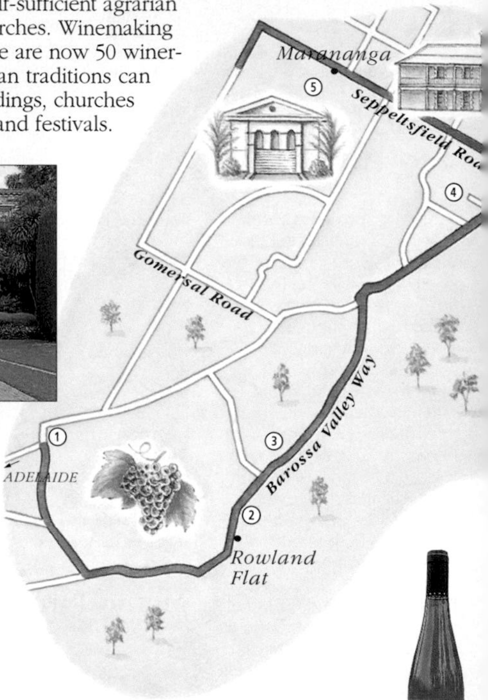

Château Yaldara ①
This impressive stone château surrounded by vineyards near Lyndoch was built by Herman Thumm shortly after he arrived from Europe in 1947. It houses a fine collection of art and antiques, and tours are conducted daily.

Orlando ②
Established in 1847, this is one of the largest wineries in Australia. Famous for its popular Jacob's Creek range, it is the country's top wine exporter and has 20 per cent of the Australian market.

Peter Lehmann ④
A significant producer of quality Barossa wines, this winery is run by Peter Lehmann and his son, Doug, both well-known characters in the valley. Wine-tasting and picnic facilities are available.

Grant Burge ③
Grant and Helen Burge bought a historic winery in Tanunda in 1988 and undertook extensive restoration work. It is now a fully working wine centre which features a beautifully restored tasting room with custom-made chandeliers and ornamental glass.

0 km 2

0 miles 2

Key

Tour route

Other roads

Penfolds ⑥

Established in 1844, Penfolds moved to this a site on the outskirts of Nuriootpa in 1974. This major winery matures its range of red and white table wines and ports in barrels made on the premises. Many wines are available for tasting and buying at the cellar door.

Wolf Blass ⑦

One of the younger wineries in the Barossa, established in 1973, Wolf Blass boasts elaborate tasting rooms and a wine heritage museum. It specializes in premium red and white table wines, and sparkling and fortified wines.

Saltram ⑧

Established in 1859, this historic winery is set in beautiful gardens on a Barossa hillside outside Angaston. Popular with red and fortified wine enthusiasts, Saltram also has an excellent bistro near its cellars, which is open for lunch daily.

Collingrove Homestead, Angaston ⑨

Now owned by the National Trust, Collingrove was built in 1856 as a home for a member of the influential pioneering Angas family. It has original furnishings and is set in an English-style garden. Accommodation is available.

Herbig Family Tree ⑩

The large, hollow red gum tree bears evidence to the hard lives and remarkable ingenuity of the early settlers. It was home to a German settler, Friedrich Herbig, his wife and their first child, who was born in their tree home. As the family increased, eventually to 16 children, Herbig built a pine cottage and later a stone house.

TIPS FOR DRIVERS

Although a tour of the Barossa Valley can be made in a day from Adelaide, the region is best seen and enjoyed by taking advantage of the excellent local accommodation and restaurants. The roads are generally good, although drivers should take special care on those that are unsealed. Visitors planning to visit a number of wineries and sample the produce may prefer to take one of the many tours or hire a chauffer-driven vehicle.

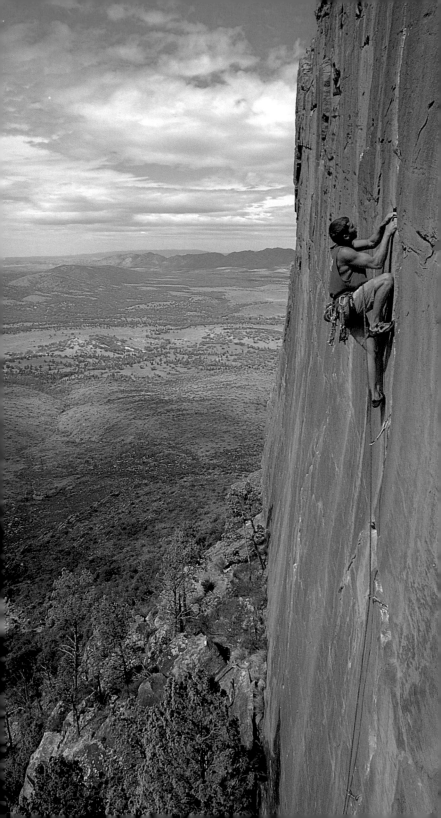

THE YORKE AND EYRE PENINSULAS AND THE FAR NORTH

FROM THE LUSH CLARE VALLEY *and the dunes of the Simpson Desert, to the saltbush of the Nullarbor Plain, the land to the north and west of Adelaide is an area of vast distances and dramatic changes of scenery. With activities ranging from surfing on the coast to bushwalking in the Flinders Ranges, one is never far from awesome natural beauty.*

South Australia was first settled by Europeans in 1836, but suffered early financial problems partly due to economic mismanagement. These were largely remedied by the discovery of copper at Kapunda, north of Adelaide, in 1842, and at Burra, near Clare, in 1845. As these resources were depleted fresh discoveries were made in the north of the Yorke Peninsula, in the area known as Little Cornwall, at the town of Wallaroo in 1859 and at Moonta in 1861. By the 1870s, South Australia was the British Empire's leading copper producer, and copper, silver and uranium mining still boosts the state's economy today.

The Yorke and Eyre Peninsulas are major arable areas, producing more than 10 per cent of Australia's wheat and much of its barley. They also have several important fishing ports, most notably Port Lincoln, the tuna-fishing capital of the country. Both peninsulas have stunning coastal scenery. The Yorke Peninsula, only two hours' drive from Adelaide, is a popular holiday destination with excellent fishing, reef diving and surfing opportunities. The much larger Eyre Peninsula is also renowned for fishing and has many superb beaches. Despite extensive arable use, it still retains about half of its land area as parks, reserves and native bushland.

To the west, the vast Nullarbor Plain stretches far into Western Australia *(see p311)*, with the Great Victoria Desert extending above it. Much of this region is taken up by Aboriginal lands and the Woomera prohibited military area.

North of the Yorke Peninsula lies the rugged majesty of the Flinders Ranges. Rich with sights of deep Aboriginal spiritual and cultural significance, the ranges are also home to abundant flora and fauna, and make for superb bushwalking. Further north, the immense, inhospitable but starkly beautiful desert regions of the South Australian Outback provide a challenging but rewarding destination for adventurous travellers.

Oyster beds in Coffin Bay at the southern tip of the Eyre Peninsula

◁ **Rock climbing at Moonarie in the spectacular Flinders Ranges National Park**

Exploring the Yorke and Eyre Peninsulas

JUST NORTH of Adelaide *(see pp336–41)* lie the green hills of the Clare Valley; then, further inland, as the rainfall diminishes, the countryside changes dramatically. First comes the grandeur of the Flinders Ranges with rugged mountains and tranquil gorges. West of Adelaide are two peninsulas, at the head of which is the industrial triangle of Port Pirie, Port Augusta and Whyalla. The Yorke Peninsula is Australia's richest barley growing district. Eyre Peninsula is also a wheat and barley producing area. From here the barren Nullarbor Plain runs beyond the Western Australian border.

Fishing boats moored in the harbour of Port Lincoln

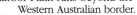

N U L L A R B O R
P L A I N

⑬

Norseman

Great Australian Bight

NUNDROO

CEDUNA

⑫

Southern Ocean

Everε

STREAKY BAY

COFFIN NATIONAL P

GETTING AROUND

Despite the sparse population, there is an extensive road network throughout the region. The Stuart Hwy runs up from Adelaide to Coober Pedy and beyond into the Northern Territory, and the Eyre Hwy wends its way from Adelaide along the tops of the Yorke and Eyre peninsulas, across the Nullarbor Plain and into Western Australia. There is no state railway, but interstate trains running from Sydney to Perth, and Adelaide to Alice Springs and Melbourne, stop at major towns in the region. Scheduled buses serve most towns, and there are air services from Adelaide to regional airports in Port Lincoln, Ceduna, Coober Pedy, Whyalla, Port Augusta and Renmark.

Raging waters of the Great Australian Bight

SIGHTS AT A GLANCE

Ceduna 12
Clare Valley 6
Coffin Bay National Park 11
Little Cornwall 5
Maitland 4
Minlaton 2
Nullarbor Plain 13
Port Augusta 8
Port Lincoln 10
Port Pirie 7
Port Victoria 3
Whyalla 9
Yorketown 1

The Far North
See pp360–61
Coober Pedy 14
Flinders Ranges 18
Lake Eyre National Park 17
Simpson Desert Conservation Park 16
Witjira National Park 15

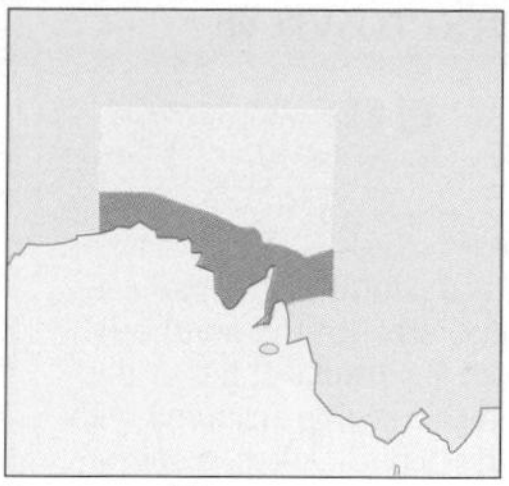

LOCATOR MAP

The Yorke and Eyre Peninsulas

The Far North pp360–61

Saltbush landscape of the Eyre Peninsula

KEY

Highway

Major road

Minor road

Scenic route

River

Viewpoint

SEE ALSO

• ***Where to Stay*** pp483–4

• ***Where to Eat*** pp515–17

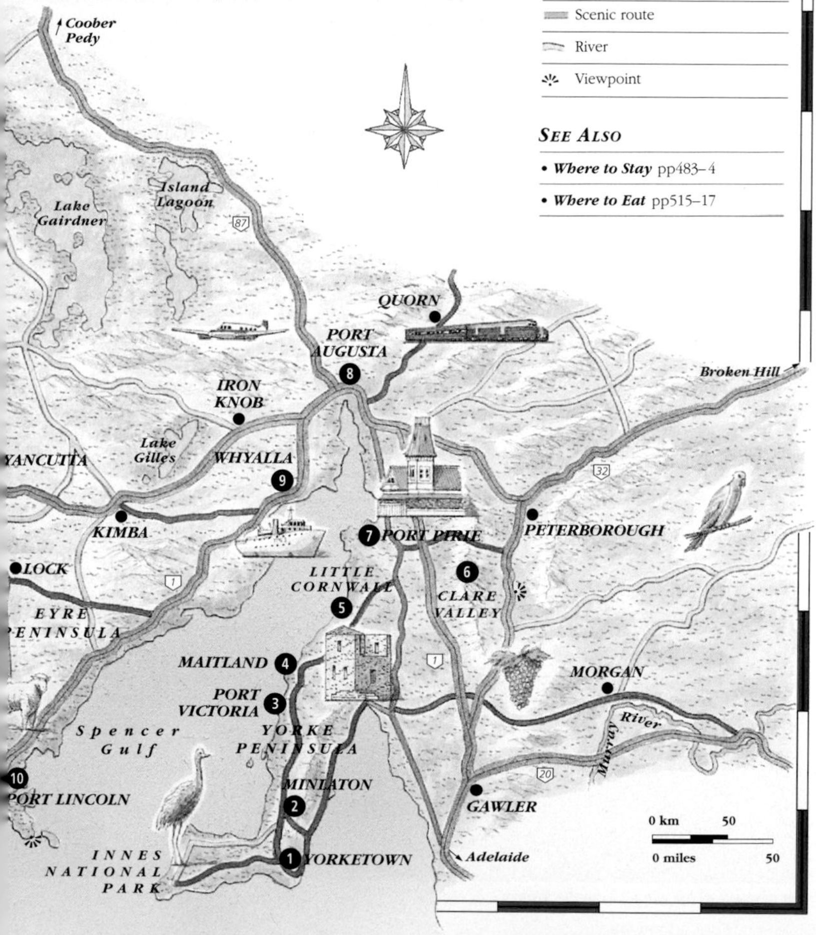

Coober Pedy
Island Lagoon
Lake Gairdner
87
QUORN
PORT AUGUSTA
8
Broken Hill
IRON KNOB
Lake Gilles
YANCUTTA
WHYALLA
9
32
KIMBA
7 PORT PIRIE
PETERBOROUGH
LOCK
1
LITTLE CORNWALL
5
6
CLARE VALLEY
EYRE PENINSULA
MAITLAND 4
1
MORGAN
PORT VICTORIA 3
River
Murray
Spencer Gulf
YORKE PENINSULA
20
10
PORT LINCOLN
MINLATON
2
GAWLER
0 km 50
0 miles 50
INNES NATIONAL PARK
1 YORKETOWN
Adelaide

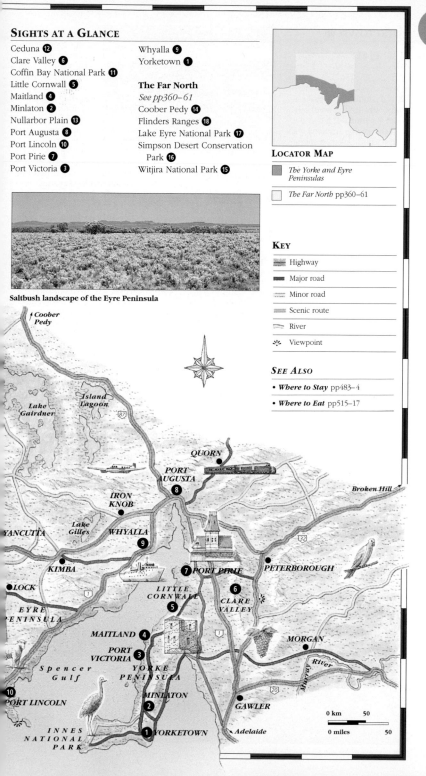

Yorketown ❶

🏛 *750.* 🚌 ℹ️ *50 Moonta Rd, Kadina (08) 8821 2333.*

YORKETOWN is the commercial centre of the earliest settled area on the southern Yorke Peninsula. It lies at the heart of a region scattered with nearly 300 salt lakes, many of which mysteriously turn pink at various times of the year, depending on climatic conditions. From the late 1890s until the 1930s, salt harvesting was a major industry in this part of South Australia.

Approximately 70 km (40 miles) southwest of Yorketown, at the tip of the Yorke Peninsula, is the spectacular Innes National Park. The park's geography changes from salt lakes and low mallee scrub inland to sandy beaches and steep, rugged cliffs along the coast. Kangaroos and emus have become accustomed to the presence of humans and are commonly seen, but other native inhabitants, such as the large mallee fowl, are more difficult to spot.

There is good surfing, reef diving and fishing in the park, especially at Browns Beach, the wild Pondalowie Bay, Chinamans Creek and Salmon Hole. Other beaches are considered unsafe for swimming. Also in the park are the rusting remains of the shipwrecked barque *Ethel*, which ran aground in 1904 and now lies with part of its hull protruding through the sand below the limestone cliffs of Ethel Beach.

"Red Devil" fighter plane in Minlaton

Minlaton ❷

🏛 *800.* 🚌 🚆 ℹ️ *59 Main St (08) 8853 2600.*

CENTRALLY LOCATED, Minlaton is a service town to the surrounding farming community. Minlaton's claim to fame, however, is as the destination of the very first air mail flight across water in the southern hemisphere. Pilot Captain Harry Butler, a World War I fighter ace, set off on this record-breaking mission in August 1919 from Adelaide. Minlaton's Butler Memorial houses his 1916 Bristol fighter plane, "Red Devil", believed to be the only one left in the world, as well as displays detailing Butler's life.

Port Victoria ❸

🏛 *350.* ℹ️ *50 Moonta Rd, Kadina (08) 8821 2333.*

LYING ON the west coast of the Yorke Peninsula, Port Victoria is today a sleepy holiday destination, popular with anglers, swimmers and divers.

In the early part of the 20th century, however, it was a busy sea port with large clippers and windjammers loading grain bound for the northern hemisphere. The last time a square rigger used the port was in 1949. The story of these ships and their epic voyages is told in the **Maritime Museum**, located adjacent to the jetty in a timber goods shed.

About 10 km (6 miles) off the coast lies Wardang Island, around which are eight known shipwrecks dating from 1871. Divers can follow the Wardang Island Maritime Heritage Trail to view the wrecks, each of which has an underwater plaque. Boats to the island can be chartered, but permission to land must be obtained from the Community Council in Point Pearce, the nearby Aboriginal settlement which administers the island.

🏛 **Maritime Museum**
Main St, Foreshore. 📞 *(08) 8834 2057.* ⭘ *Sun.* 📷 ♿

Maitland ❹

🏛 *1,100.* 🚌 🚆 ℹ️ *50 Moonta Rd, Kadina (08) 8821 2333.*

SURROUNDED BY some of the most productive farmland in Australia, Maitland lies in the centre of the Yorke Peninsula, on a ridge

Vast expanse of the salt lakes in the Yorketown region

overlooking the Yorke Valley and Spencer Gulf. Originally proclaimed in 1872, it is now the service centre for the surrounding community.

The pretty town, laid out on a classic grid pattern, retains many fine examples of colonial architecture, including the Maitland Hotel, built in 1874, and the 1875 St Bartholomew's Catholic Church.

The **Maitland Museum** has an agricultural and folk collection housed in three buildings and focuses on the region's history and development.

🏛 **Maitland Museum**
Cnr Gardiner & Kilkerran terraces.
📞 (08) 8832 2220. ⏱ Sun, school hols. ⬤ Good Fri, 25 Dec. 📷 ♿

Miners' cottages in Little Cornwall

Little Cornwall ❺

🚗 Kadina. 🚌 Kadina. ℹ 50 Moonta Rd, Kadina (08) 8821 2333.

THE THREE TOWNS of Moonta, Kadina and Wallaroo were established after copper discoveries on Yorke Peninsula in 1859 and 1861. Collectively the towns are known as the "Copper Triangle" or "Little Cornwall". Many miners from Cornwall, England, came here in the 19th century seeking their fortunes. The biennial festival "Kernewek Lowender" (see p38) celebrates this Cornish heritage. The wealth created by the mines has left the towns with fine architecture.

Wallaroo, the site of the first mine, was also a shipping port for ore. When mining finished, the port remained

Former timber shed now home to the Maritime Museum, Port Victoria

important for agricultural exports. The **Heritage and Nautical Museum** is in the old post office.

Moonta, once home to Australia's richest copper mine, contains a group of sites and museums in the **Moonta Mines State Heritage Area**. The 1870 Miner's Cottage is a restored wattle and daub cottage. The history museum is in the old Victorian school. Also of interest is the Moonta Mines Railway, a restored light-gauge locomotive.

Kadina, the Yorke Peninsula's largest town, is the commercial centre of the area. The **Kadina Heritage Museum** has interesting displays on mining and folk history of the area.

🏛 **Heritage and Nautical Museum**
Owen Terr & Emu St. 📞 (08) 8823 3015. ⏱ Wed, Thu, Sat–Sun, school hols. ⬤ 25 Dec. 📷 ♿
🎃 **Moonta Mines State Heritage Area**
Moonta Rd. 📞 (08) 8825 1892. ⏱ Wed, Fri, Sat–Sun, school hols. ⬤ Good Fri, 25 Dec. 📷 ♿
🏛 **Kadina Heritage Museum**
Matta Rd. 📞 (08) 8821 2721. ⏱ daily. ⬤ 25 Dec. 📷 ♿

FISHING AND DIVING ON THE YORKE PENINSULA

There are fantastic opportunities for on- and offshore fishing and diving in the waters off the Yorke Peninsula. Many of the coastal towns have jetties used by keen amateur fishermen, and around Edithburgh anglers may catch tommy ruff, garfish and snook. Divers can enjoy the southern coast's stunning underwater scenery with brightly coloured corals and fish.

Offshore, the wreck of the *Clan Ranald* near Edithburgh is a popular dive and, off Wardang Island, eight wrecks can be explored on a unique diving trail. Angling from boats can be equally fruitful and local charter boats are available for hire.

A large blue grouper close to a diver in waters off the Yorke Peninsula

Restored 19th-century buildings at Burra Mine near the Clare Valley

Clare Valley ❻

🚉 *Clare.* 🛈 *Town Hall, 229 Main North Rd, Clare (08) 8842 2131.*

FRAMED BY the rolling hills of the northern Mount Lofty Ranges, the Clare Valley is a picturesque and premium wine-producing region. At the head of the valley lies the town of Clare. This pretty, regional centre has many historic buildings, including the National Trust Museum, housed in the old Police Station, and Wolta Wolta, an early pastoralist's home, built in 1864, which has a fine collection of antiques.

Sevenhill Cellars, 7 km (4 miles) south of Clare, is the oldest vineyard in the valley. It was established by Austrian Jesuits in 1851, originally to produce altar wine for the colony. The adjacent St Aloysius Church was completed in 1875. The winery is still run by Jesuits and now produces both altar and table wines.

East of Sevenhill lies the pleasant heritage town of Mintaro, with many buildings making extensive use of the slate quarried in the area for more than 150 years. Also worth visiting is **Martindale Hall**, an elegant 1879 mansion situated just southeast of town.

Twelve km (7 miles) north of Clare lies **Bungaree Station**. This self-contained Merino sheep-farming complex was established in 1841 and is now maintained as a working 19th-century model. From the historic exhibits visitors can learn about life and work at the station.

About 35 km (22 miles) northeast of Clare is the charming town of Burra. Five years after copper was discovered here in 1845, Burra was home to the largest mine in Australia. As such it was the economic saviour of the fledgling state, rescuing it from impending bankruptcy. Once five separate townships, Burra is now a State Heritage Area.

The **Burra Mine** site, with its ruins and restored buildings around the huge open cut, is one of the most exciting industrial archaeological sites in Australia. An interpretive centre at the Bon Accord Mine allows visitors access to the original mine shaft. The miners' dugouts, still seen on the banks of Burra Creek, were once home to more than 1,500 mainly Cornish miners. Paxton Square Cottages, built between 1849 and 1852, are unique in Australian mining history as the first decent accommodation provided for miners and their families. Many old buildings, including the police lockup and stables, the Redruth Gaol and the Unicorn Brewery Cellars, have been carefully restored, as have a number of the 19th-century shops and houses. A museum with various displays chronicling the history of the area is located in Burra's market square.

🏛 **Sevenhill Cellars**
College Rd, Sevenhill. 📞 *(08) 8843 4222.* ◯ *Mon–Sat.* ♿
🏛 **Martindale Hall**
Manoora Rd, Mintaro. 📞 *(08) 8843 9088.* ◯ *daily.* 📷
🏛 **Bungaree Station**
Port Augusta Rd, Clare. 📞 *(08) 8842 2677.* ◯ *tours only.* 📷 ♿
🏛 **Burra Mine**
Market St, Burra. 📞 *(08) 8892 2154.* ◯ *daily.* 📷 ♿ *limited.*

Port Pirie ❼

🚶 *15,000.* 🚉 🚌 🚏 🛈 *Mary Elie St (08) 8633 8700.*

PORT PIRIE was the state's first provincial city. An industrial hub, it is the site of the largest lead smelter in the southern hemisphere.

In the town centre, the **National Trust Museum** comprises three well-preserved buildings: the pavilion-style railway station built in 1902, the former Customs House and the Old Police Building. The Regional Tourism and Arts Centre, located in the former 1967 railway station, features artworks on lead, zinc and copper panels interpreting the city's historic wealth.

Every October, Port Pirie hosts the South Australian Festival of Country Music.

🏛 **National Trust Museum**
Ellen St. 📞 *(08) 8632 2272.* ◯ *daily.* ● *25 Dec.* ♿ *limited.*

Victorian grandeur of Port Pirie's old railway station

Harbour view of Port Augusta, backed by its power stations

Port Augusta **8**

🏛 14,000. ✈ 🚌 🚍 🚆 🛈 41 Flinders Terrace (08) 8641 0793.

SITUATED at the head of Spencer Gulf, Port Augusta is at the crossroads of Australia; here lies the intersection of the Sydney–Perth and Adelaide–Alice Springs railway lines, as well as the major Sydney–Perth and Adelaide–Darwin highways. Once an important port, its power stations now produce 40 per cent of the state's electricity. The coal-fired Northern Power Station, which dominates the city's skyline, offers free conducted tours.

Port Augusta is also the beginning of South Australia's Outback region. The School of the Air and the Royal Flying Doctor Service offices, both of which provide essential services to inhabitants of remote stations, are open to the public (see p249). The **Wadlata Outback Centre** imaginatively tells the story of the Far North from 15 million years ago when rainforests covered the area, through Aboriginal and European history, up to the present day and into the future.

Australia's first **Arid Lands Botanic Garden** was opened nearby in 1996. This 200-ha (500-acre) site is an important research and education facility, as well as a recreational area. It also commands fine panoramic views of the Flinders Ranges to the east (see p361).

🏛 Wadlata Outback Centre
Flinders Terrace. 【 (08) 8642 4511. ⬤ daily. ⬤ 25 Dec. 🏷 🔇
♣ Arid Lands Botanic Garden
Stuart Hwy. 【 (08) 8641 1049. ⬤ daily. ⬤ 25 Dec. 🔇 limited.

Whyalla **9**

🏛 26,000. ✈ 🚌 🛈 Port Augusta Rd, Lincoln Hwy (1 800) 088 589.

AT THE GATEWAY to the Eyre Peninsula, Whyalla is the state's largest provincial city. Originally a shipping port for iron ore mined at nearby Iron Knob, the city was transformed in 1939 when a blast furnace was established, a harbour created and a shipyard constructed. The shipyard closed in 1978; however, the first ship built there, the HMAS Whyalla (1941), is now a major display of the **Whyalla Maritime Museum**.

Although an industrial centre, Whyalla has a number of fine beaches and good fishing. The **Whyalla Wildlife and Reptile Sanctuary** has a collection of native and exotic animals, including koalas, monkeys and a black leopard.

🏛 Whyalla Maritime Museum
Lincoln Hwy. 【 (08) 8645 8900. ⬤ daily. ⬤ Good Fri, 25 Dec. 🔇 🔇 museum only.
🦎 Whyalla Wildlife and Reptile Sanctuary
Lincoln Hwy. 【 (08) 8645 7044. ⬤ daily. ⬤ 25 Dec. 🔇 🔇

HMAS *Whyalla*, docked beside the Whyalla Maritime Museum

Stunning coastline of Whalers Way at the southern end of the Eyre Peninsula near Port Lincoln

Port Lincoln ⑩

🏠 *13,000.* ✈ 🚌 ℹ *3 Adelaide Pl (1 800) 629 911 or (08) 8683 3544.*

AT THE SOUTHERN end of the Eyre Peninsula, Port Lincoln sits on the shore of Boston Bay, one of the world's largest natural harbours. A fishing and seafood processing centre, it is home to Australia's largest tuna fleet.

Locals celebrate the start of the tuna season every January with the Tunarama Festival *(see p37).* This raucous event includes processions, concerts and a tuna-tossing competition.

Fishing and sailing are popular activities. Visitors can take a boat trip to Dangerous Reef, 31 km (20 miles) offshore, to view great white sharks from the relative safety of the boat or submerged cage. In the middle of the bay lies Boston

Island, a working sheep station including an 1842 slab cottage.

The Port Lincoln area has several buildings of note. South of Port Lincoln, **Mikkira Station**, established in 1842, is one of the country's oldest sheep stations. Today it is ideal for picnics or camping, with a restored pioneer cottage and a koala colony. The **Koppio Smithy Museum**, located in the Koppio Hills 40 km (25 miles) north of Port Lincoln, is an agricultural museum with a furnished 1890 log cottage and a 1903 smithy that gives a glimpse into the lives of the pioneers.

Just 20 km (12 km) south of Port Lincoln is Lincoln National Park with its rocky hills, sheltered coves, sandy beaches and high cliffs. The park is also rich in birdlife. Emus and parrots are common and ospreys and sea eagles frequent the coast. Just west of the park, Whalers

Way has some of Australia's most dramatic coastal scenery. This land is private and entry is via a permit available from the visitors' centre.

🚏 **Mikkira Station**
Fishery Bay Rd. 📞 *(08) 8685 6020.* 🈚

🏛 **Koppio Smithy Museum**
Via White Flat Rd. 📞 *(08) 8684 4243.* 🈂 *Tue–Sun.* ● *25 Dec.* 🈚 ♿

The prime surfing spot of Almonta Beach in Coffin Bay National Park

Coffin Bay National Park ⑪

🚌 *Port Lincoln.* ℹ *(08) 8688 3111.* 🈂 *daily.* ● *25 Dec.* 🈚 *per vehicle.* ♿ *limited.*

TO THE WEST of the southern tip of the Eyre Peninsula is Coffin Bay Peninsula, which is part of the Coffin Bay National Park. This unspoilt area of

---

Wedge-tailed eagle

WILDLIFE OF THE EYRE PENINSULA

An enormous variety of wildlife inhabits the Eyre Peninsula. Emus and kangaroos are common, and the hairy-nosed wombat is found in large numbers on the west coast. Wedge-tailed eagles soar over the Gawler Ranges, while sea eagles, ospreys, albatrosses and petrels are all seen over the coast. In the water, dolphins, sea lions and occasional great white sharks feast on an abundance of marine life. The most spectacular sight, however, are the southern right whales which breed at the head of the Great Australian Bight every June to October. They can be seen from the cliffs at the Head of Bight, just east of the Nullarbor National Park.

coastal wilderness has exposed cliffs, sheltered sandy beaches, rich birdlife and fantastic fishing. Wildflowers in the park can be quite spectacular from early spring to early summer.

There are several scenic drives through the park, but some roads are accessible to 4WD vehicles only. A favourite route for conventional vehicles is the Yangie Trail from the small town of Coffin Bay to Yangie and Avoid bays. To the east of Point Avoid is one of Australia's best surfing beaches, Almonta Beach.

Coffin Bay town has long been a popular centre for windsurfing, swimming, sailing and fishing. It now also produces high-quality oysters. The Oyster Walk is a pleasant walking trail along the foreshore through native bushland.

Ceduna ⓬

🏛 3,600. ✈ 🚌 ℹ 58 Poynton St (08) 8625 2780.

A**T THE TOP** of the west side of the Eyre Peninsula, sitting on the shores of Murat Bay, Ceduna is the most westerly significant town in South Australia before the start of the Nullarbor Plain. The town's name comes from the Aboriginal word *chedoona*, meaning "resting place".

Today, Ceduna is the commercial centre of the far west. Within the town is the **Old Schoolhouse National Trust Museum** with its collections of restored farm equipment

An Indian-Pacific train crossing the vast Nullarbor Plain

from early pioneer days. It also has an interesting display on the British atomic weapons tests held at nearby Maralinga in the 1950s, and a small selection of Aboriginal artifacts.

In the 1850s, there was a whaling station on St Peter Island, just off the coast of Ceduna, but now the town is a base for whale-watchers. Southern right whales can be seen close to the shore from June to October from the head of the Bight, 300 km (185 miles) from Ceduna.

The relatively new industry of oyster farming has established itself west and east of Ceduna at Denial and Smoky bays. Between Ceduna and Penong, a tiny hamlet 73 km (45 miles) to the west, there are detours to surfing beaches including the legendary Cactus Beach. Keen surfers are found here all year round trying to catch some of the best waves in Australia, rolling in from the great Southern Ocean.

🏛 Old Schoolhouse National Trust Museum
Park Terrace. 📞 (08) 8625 2780. 🕐 Mon–Sat. ⬤ 25 Dec. 📷 ♿

Nullarbor Plain ⓭

🚌 Port Augusta. 🚌 Ceduna.
ℹ Ceduna (08) 8625 2780.
🕐 9am–5:30pm Mon–Fri, 10am–4pm Sat-Sun. ⬤ Good Fri, 25 Dec.

T**HE HUGE EXPANSE** of the Nullarbor Plain stretches from Nundroo, about 150 km (95 miles) west of Ceduna, towards the distant Western Australia border 330 km (200 miles) away, and beyond into Western Australia *(see p311).*

This dry, dusty plain can be crossed by rail on the Trans-Australian Railway or by road on the Eyre Highway. The train travels further inland than the road, its route giving little relief from the flat landscape. The highway lies nearer the coast, passing a few isolated sights of interest on its way west.

Just south of the small town of Nundroo lies Fowlers Bay. Good for fishing, it is popular with anglers seeking solitude. West of here, the road passes through the Yalata Aboriginal Lands and travellers can stop by the roadside to buy souvenirs from the local people. Bordering Yalata to the west is Nullarbor National Park. This runs from the Nullarbor Roadhouse hamlet, 130 km (80 miles) west of Nundroo, to the border with Western Australia 200 km (125 miles) away. The Eyre Highway passes through the park, close to the coastal cliffs. This stretch of the plain has some spectacular views over the Great Australian Bight.

The world's longest cave system runs beneath the plain, and the border area has many underground caves and caverns. These should only be explored by experienced cavers, however, as many are flooded and dangerous.

Watching southern right whales from Head of Bight, near Ceduna

The Far North

S OUTH AUSTRALIA'S OUTBACK is an enormous area of harsh but often breathtaking scenery. Much of the region is untamed desert, broken in places by steep, ancient mountain ranges, huge salt lakes, gorges and occasional hot springs. Although very hot and dry for most of the year, many places burst into life after heavy winter rains and hundreds of species of wildflowers, animals and birds can be seen. The area's recent history is one of fabled stock routes, now Outback tracks for adventurous travellers. Isolated former mining and railway towns now cater for Outback tourists. Vast areas in the west form extensive Aboriginal lands, accessible by permit only, and the Woomera prohibited military area.

KEY

■ The Far North

□ The Yorke and Eyre Peninsulas see pp350–59

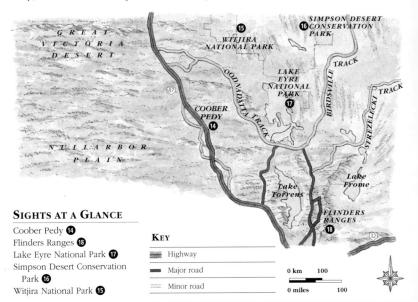

SIGHTS AT A GLANCE

Coober Pedy ⑭
Flinders Ranges ⑱
Lake Eyre National Park ⑰
Simpson Desert Conservation Park ⑯
Witjira National Park ⑮

KEY

▬ Highway

▬ Major road

▭ Minor road

0 km 100
0 miles 100

Coober Pedy ⑭

🚶 3,500. ✈ 🚌 ℹ 773 Hutchinson St, 1800 637 078 .

O NE OF AUSTRALIA'S most famous Outback towns, Coober Pedy, 850 km (530 miles) northwest of Adelaide, is an unusual settlement in the heart of an extremely hostile landscape. Frequent dust-storms and a colourless desert landscape littered with abandoned mines contribute to the town's desolate appearance, familiar from films such as *Mad Max* and *Red Planet*.

Opal was discovered here in 1915, and today Coober Pedy produces 70 per cent of the

world's supply. Mining claims, limited to one per person, can measure no more than 100 m by 50 m (320 ft by 160 ft). For this reason opal mining is the preserve of individuals, not large companies, and this adds to the town's "frontier" quality.

Coober Pedy's name comes

Underground troglodyte home known as a dugout in Coober Pedy

from the Aboriginal *kupa pit*, meaning white man's hole, and is apt indeed. Not only the mines, but also houses, hotels and even churches are built underground. This way, the inhabitants escape the extreme temperatures of up to 50°C (122°F) during the day and 0°C (32°F) at night. Several such homes are open to the public.

The **Underground Art Gallery** displays Aboriginal art. It also has displays relating to opal mining, and visitors can dig for their own opals.

🏛 **Underground Art Gallery**
Hutchinson St. 📞 (08) 8672 5985.
🕐 daily. 🌐 ⚑ 🚻

Witjira National Park ⓖ

🄸 *Pink Roadhouse, Oodnadatta (08) 8670 7822 or (1 800) 802 074.* ⬜ *daily.* **Park Office** *1800 816 078.* ⬜ *Mon–Fri.*

ABOUT 200 KM (125 miles) north of Coober Pedy lies the small town of Oodnadatta, where drivers can check the road and weather conditions before heading further north to Witjira National Park.

Witjira has dunes, saltpans, boulder plains and coolibah woodlands, but it is most famous for its hot artesian springs. Dalhousie Springs has more than 60 active springs with warm water rising from the Great Artesian Basin. These springs supply essential water for Aborigines, pastoralists and wildlife, including water snails, unique to the area.

Simpson Desert Conservation Park ⓖ

🄸 *Pink Roadhouse, Oodnadatta (08) 8670 7822.* ⬜ *daily. Desert Parks pass required.* **Park Office** *1800 816 078.* ⬜ *Mon–Fri.*

THE SIMPSON DESERT Conservation Park is at the very top of South Australia, adjoining both Queensland and the Northern Territory. It is an almost endless series of sand dunes, lakes, spinifex grassland and gidgee woodland.

The landscape is home to some 180 bird, 92 reptile and 44 native mammal species, some of which have developed nocturnal habits as a response to the aridity of the region.

Dunes stretching to the horizon in Simpson Desert Conservation Park

Lake Eyre National Park ⓖ

🄸 *Coober Pedy, (08) 8672 5298.* ⬜ *Mon–Fri.* ⬤ *public hols.* **Park Office** *1800 816 078.* ⬜ *Mon–Fri.*

LAKE EYRE National Park encompasses all of Lake Eyre North and extends eastwards into the Tirari Desert. Lake Eyre is Australia's largest salt lake, 15 m (49 ft) below sea level at its lowest point, with a salt crust said to weigh 400 million tonnes. Vegetation is low, comprising mostly blue bush, samphire and saltbush. On the rare occasions when the lake floods, it alters dramatically: flowers bloom and birds such as pelicans and gulls appear, turning the lake into a breeding ground.

Flinders Ranges ⓖ

🚃 *Hawker, Wilpena.* 🄸 *Wilpena (08) 8648 0048.* ⬜ *daily.* **Park Office** *(08) 8648 0049.*

THE FLINDERS RANGES extend for 400 km (250 miles) from Crystal Brook, just north of the Clare Valley, far into South Australia's Outback. A favourite with bushwalkers, the ranges encompass a great diversity of stunning scenery and wildlife, much of it protected in several national parks.

In the southern part of the Flinders Ranges is Mount Remarkable National Park, renowned for its fine landscape, abundant wildflowers and excellent walking trails.

About 50 km (30 miles) north of here is the town of Quorn, start of the restored Pichi Richi Railway. North of Quorn lie the dramatic Warren, Yarrah Vale and Buckaringa gorges.

Much of the central Flinders Ranges are contained within the Flinders Ranges National Park. This beautiful park's best-known feature is Wilpena Pound, an elevated natural basin covering some 90 sq km (35 sq miles) with sheer outer walls 500 m (1,600 ft) high.

To the north is Gammon Ranges National Park, with mountain bushwalking for the experienced only. Just outside the park is **Arkaroola**, a tourist village and wildlife sanctuary offering guided tours and a useful interpretive centre.

🦘 Arkaroola
Via Wilpena or Leigh Creek. 🄲 *1800 676 042.* ⬜ *daily.* 🎟 *for tours.*

Shimmering expanse of Lake Eyre, the largest salt lake in Australia

VICTORIA

Victoria at a Glance

THE STATE OF VICTORIA can be easily divided into two distinct geographical halves, east and west. Western Victoria is known for its unusual landforms, including the Grampians and the Twelve Apostles. It was also the site of Australia's wealthiest gold rush during the 19th century, the legacy of which can be seen in the ornate buildings in the many surviving gold rush towns *(see pp50–51)*. Eastern Victoria's cooler climate benefits the vineyards that produce world-class wines, while the Alps are Victoria's winter playground. The rugged coastline is known for its lakes, forests and wildlife. Melbourne, the state's capital, is the second most populous city in Australia.

WESTERN VICTORIA
(see pp412–27)

Halls Gap is the only settlement within the Grampians National Park (see p417). *The rest of this beautiful area is filled with dramatic rock formations, spectacular ridges and wildflowers unique to the region.*

Ballarat's Arch of Victory on the Avenue of Honour commemorates the soldiers of World War I. It is also the western entrance to this provincial city, which grew up during the 1850s gold rush (see pp424–5).

The Twelve Apostles *is the evocative name given to these eroded limestone rock formations in Port Campbell National Park, seen from the Great Ocean Road* (see pp418–19). *Sunset is the best time to fully appreciate the view.*

◁ **The Cathedral in Mount Buffalo National Park**

Château Tahbilk is one of the best known of all the northeastern Victorian vineyards, not only for its excellent wines but also for the pagoda-style architecture of its winery. Eastern Victoria's cool climate has led to a range of successful wineries *(see pp438–9)*.

The Victorian Alps come into their own during the winter months as a premier ski area *(see p436)*.

EASTERN VICTORIA
(see pp428–39)

MELBOURNE
(see inset)

0 kilometres   100

0 miles   100

MELBOURNE
(see pp372–411)

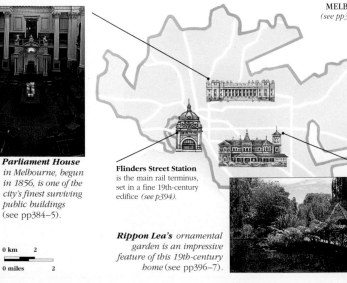

Parliament House in Melbourne, begun in 1856, is one of the city's finest surviving public buildings *(see pp384–5)*.

Flinders Street Station is the main rail terminus, set in a fine 19th-century edifice *(see p394)*.

Rippon Lea's ornamental garden is an impressive feature of this 19th-century home *(see pp396–7)*.

0 km   2

0 miles   2

Melbourne's Best: Parks and Gardens

VISITORS TO MELBOURNE should not miss the city's magnificent public and private gardens. A large proportion of the city's parks and gardens were created in the 19th century and have a gracious quality which has earned Victoria the nickname of Australia's "Garden State". Central Melbourne is ringed by public gardens, including the outstanding Royal Botanic Gardens, visited by more than one million people each year. Melbourne also has a network of public parks which offer a mix of native flora and fauna with recreational activities. The annual Open Garden Scheme *(see p36)* allows visitors into some of the best private gardens in Melbourne and Victoria.

LANDSCAPE GARDENS

MELBOURNE ABOUNDS with carefully planned and formal 19th-century gardens, designed by prominent landscape gardeners.

A variety of trees from all over the world lines the formal avenues of **Carlton Gardens**, designed in 1857 by Edward La Trobe Bateman. The aim of the design was for every path and flowerbed to focus attention on the Exhibition Building, constructed in 1880 *(see p387)*. The main entrance path leads from Victoria Street to the Hochgurtel Fountain, in front of the Exhibition Building, decorated on its upper tier

Statue of Simpson and his donkey in Kings Domain

with stone birds and flowers which are indigenous to the state of Victoria.

The attractive **Fitzroy Gardens** in the heart of the city were also first designed by Bateman in 1848. His original plans were later revised by a Scotsman, James Sinclair, to make them more sympathetic to the area's uneven landscape. The avenues of elms that lead in to the centre of the gardens from the surrounding streets create the shape of the Union Jack flag and are one of the most distinctive features of the gardens *(see pp384–5)*. Fitzroy Gardens' Conservatory is renowned for its five popular annual plant shows.

Statue of Queen Victoria in her eponymous gardens

The **Queen Victoria Gardens** are considered one of the city's most attractive gardens. They were created as a setting for a new statue of the queen, four years after her death, in 1905. Roses now surround the statue. A floral clock near St Kilda Road was given to Melbourne by Swiss watchmakers in 1966. It is embedded with some 7,000 flowering plants.

Kings Domain *(see p390)* was the dream of a German botanist, Baron von Mueller, who designed this impressive garden in 1854. The garden is dominated by elegant statues, including one of Simpson, a stretcher bearer during World War I, with his faithful donkey. There are also fountains, silver birch and the imposing Shrine of Remembrance.

BOTANIC GARDENS

BEGUN IN 1846, the **Royal Botanic Gardens** now cover 36 ha (90 acres). Botanist Baron von Mueller became the director of the gardens in 1857 and began to plant both indigenous and exotic shrubs on the site, intending the gardens to be a scientific aid to fellow biologists. Von Mueller's successor, William Guilfoyle, made his own mark on the

Conservatory of flowers in Fitzroy Gardens

Ornamental lake in the Royal Botanic Gardens

design, by adding wide paths across the gardens and an ornamental lake.

Today, the gardens are home to more than 10,000 plant species *(see pp390–91)*.

RECREATIONAL GARDENS AND PARKS

MELBURNIANS ARE avid sports participants as well as spectators, and many of the city's gardens offer a range of sporting facilities in attractive surroundings.

Flagstaff Gardens take their name from the site's role as a signalling station from 1840, warning of ships arriving in the Port of Melbourne. In the 1860s, with advances in communication, this role was no longer required and gardens were laid out on the land instead. Today the gardens are used for their recreational facilities, which include tennis courts, a children's playground and a barbecue area.

The **Alexandra Gardens** were designed in 1904 as a riverside walk along the Yarra River. Today, as well as the major thoroughfare of Alexandra Avenue, there is an equestrian path, a cycle path, boat sheds and barbecue facilities.

The **Treasury Gardens** were designed in 1867 and are lined along its avenues with Moreton Bay Figs, offering welcome shade in the summer heat. The location in the centre of the city makes these gardens very popular with office workers during their lunch breaks. The gardens also host regular evening concerts and other entertainment gatherings and an outdoor art show.

Established in 1856, **Yarra Park** is today home to the city's most well-known sports grounds, Melbourne Park, home of the Australian Open, and the Melbourne Cricket Ground *(see p389)*. The wood and bark of the indigenous river red gums in

the park were once used for canoes and shields by local Aborigines and many still bear the scars.

Fawkner Park, named after Melbourne's co-founder, John Fawkner *(see pp48–9)*, was laid out in 1862 and became a large sports ground in the 1890s. Despite a temporary role as a camp site for the Armed Services during World War II, the 40 ha (100 acres) of the park are still used for cricket, football, hockey and softball games.

Another popular sporting area with Melburnians is **Princes Park**. Two sports pavilions were constructed in 1938, as were two playing fields. The park now contains a football oval and the unique "Fun and Fitness Centre", a jogging track lined with exercise equipment at stages along its 3-km (1.8-mile) route. A gravel running track was also added in 1991.

Cricket match in progress in Fawkner Park

Melbourne's Best: Architecture

Iₙ 1835, Melbourne was a village of tents and imper-
manent dwellings. Fed by the wealth of the 1850s'
gold rush and the economic boom of the 1880s, it
rapidly acquired many graceful buildings. Today, the
city's architecture is very eclectic, with a strong Victorian element. The range of architectural styles is
impressive, from beautiful restorations to outstanding
contemporary novelties. The city's tallest building is
the 1986 Rialto twin tower complex *(see p379)*.

Early colonial Cook's Cottage

EARLY COLONIAL

In colonial days, it was
quite common for small
edifices, such as La Trobe's
Cottage, to be shipped
from England as skilled
builders were in short
supply. Other imported
structures included timber
cottages and corrugated
iron dwellings.

Wood structure   Wooden shutters   Chimney

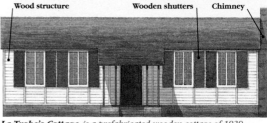

La Trobe's Cottage is a prefabricated wooden cottage of 1839.

HIGH VICTORIAN

During the 19th century, Melbourne erected several grand state
buildings equal to those in the USA and Europe. State Parliament
House, begun in 1856, included a central dome in its original
design which was omitted due to lack of funds *(see p384)*. South
of the city is the 1934 Shrine of Remembrance, which demonstrates the 20th century's yearning for classical roots *(p390)*.

Detail of Parliament House

Doric columns   Balustrade   Arched windows

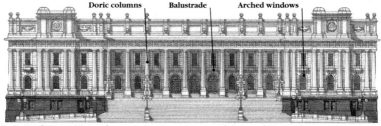

State Parliament House has an impressive entrance with its grand Doric columns.

Cast-iron lacework at Tasma Terrace

TERRACE HOUSING

Terrace houses with cast-iron lace balconies
were popular during the Victorian era. Tasma
Terrace (1868–86) was designed by Charles
Webb and is unusual for its three-storey
houses, double-storey being more typical.

Cast-iron filigree   Arched window
balconies

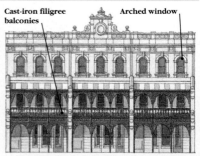

Tasma Terrace is now home to the National Trust.

MODERNISM AND POST-MODERNISM

The latter half of the 20th century has seen a range of post-modern buildings erected in Melbourne. The National Gallery of Victoria was designed by Sir Roy Grounds *(see p394)* and completed in 1968. It was the first time bluestone, unique to Melbourne and widely used in the 19th century, was used in a modern structure. The stained-glass ceiling of the Great Hall was designed by Leonard French.

Unique bluestone walls of the National Gallery of Victoria

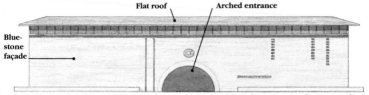

Flat roof   Arched entrance

Bluestone façade

The National Gallery of Victoria has a monumental façade, impressive for its smooth simplicity and lack of ornamental details.

Multicoloured façade   Steel railings   Lighting

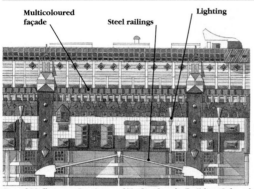

Royal Melbourne Institute of Technology's Building 8 façade is a complex blend of bright colours and diverse shapes.

CONTEMPORARY

Melbourne is known for its vibrant, experimental architecture scene. Some of the most radical Australian buildings of the 1990s can be found here. The Royal Melbourne Institute of Technology's Building 8 was designed by Peter Corrigan in 1994. The building's interior and façade is both gaudy and Gaudían, with its bold use of primary colours. Whatever your judgment, it cannot help but attract the attention of every visitor to the northern end of the city.

SPORTS ARCHITECTURE

Melbourne's modern architecture clearly reflects the importance of sport to its citizens. Melbourne Park, built in 1988, has a retractable roof, a world first, and seats more than 15,000 people at its centre court.

Aerial view of the glass roof and stadium at Melbourne Park

Retractable roof   Glass exterior

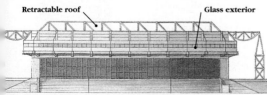

Melbourne Park was designed by Philip Cox and now hosts the annual Australian Open tennis championships.

WHERE TO FIND THE BUILDINGS

La Trobe's Cottage
p391.
National Gallery of Victoria
p394.
Melbourne Park
Map 2 F4.
Royal Melbourne Institute of Technology's Building 8, Swanston Street.
Map 1 C2.
Shrine of Remembrance
p390.
State Parliament House
p384.
Tasma Terrace, Parliament Place.
Map 2 E2.

Wines of Victoria

V ICTORIA IS HOME to approximately 320 wineries located in 19 distinct wine regions, some easily reached in less than an hour by car from the state capital, Melbourne. The northeast is famous for its unique fortified Muscats and Tokays (often described as liquid toffee), while from the cooler south come silky Chardonnays and subtle Pinot Noirs. There is no better way to enjoy Victorian wine than in one of the wealth of restaurants and bistros in cosmopolitan Melbourne *(see pp517–19)*.

***Cabernet Merlot** is the most popular and respected of the Church Hill wine range.*

Cellar stacked with wine at Seppelt's Great Western

***Heathcote Winery** near Bendigo produces fine whites, including a Chardonnay, in a region better known for its reds. Its Shiraz, however, is also of very high quality.*

Wentworth

MILDURA •

Ouyen •

• Sea Lake

Horsham •

Glenelg River

BAL

Hamilton •

Lake
Corang

Co

KEY FACTS

Location and Climate
Warm in the north, cool in the south, Victoria's climate spectrum yields a diversity of wines. Many small, high-quality producers have been in the vanguard of the Australian wine revolution, which began in the 1970s.

Grape Varieties
Victoria's varied climate and soil means it is possible to grow a full range of grape varieties.

Reds include Shiraz, Merlot, Cabernet Sauvignon and Pinot Noir. Whites include Semillon, Gewürztraminer, Riesling, Chardonnay, Marsanne, Frontignac and Pinot Gris. Victoria also produces excellent *Méthode Champenoise* sparkling wine.

Good Producers
Mildara, Mitchelton, Morris, Yarra Burn, Brown Bros, de Bortoli, Chateau Rémy, Water Wheel, Seppelt's Great Western, Trentham Estate, Bailey's.

***Blue Pyrenees Estate** in Avoca is a Cabernet-based wine produced by Chateau Rémy.*

Mick Morris sampling his famous Muscat from barrels

How Victoria's Famous Muscats and Tokays are Made

Brown Muscat and Muscadelle grapes are picked late, when they are at their sweetest, to produce fine Muscats and Tokays respectively. Once the grapes have been crushed, the resulting juice is often fermented in traditional open concrete tanks which have been in use for generations. The wine is then fortified with top-quality grape spirit, which will give it an ultimate alcohol strength of around 18.5 per cent. The solera system, in which young vintages are blended with older ones, gives more depth to the wines and also ensures that they retain a consistent quality. Some wineries, such as Morris, use a base wine combined with vintages going back more than a century. The flavour of wine in the oldest barrel is so intense that one teaspoon can add a new dimension to 200 l (45 gal) of base wine.

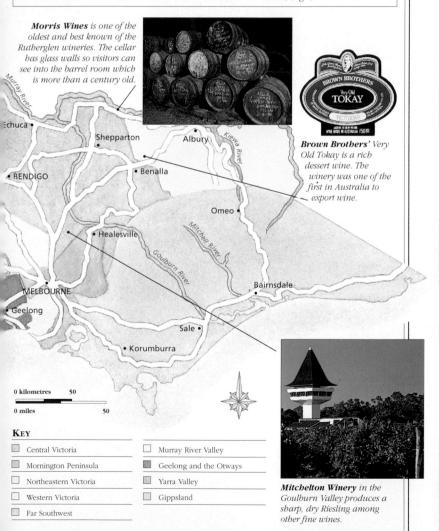

Morris Wines is one of the oldest and best known of the Rutherglen wineries. The cellar has glass walls so visitors can see into the barrel room which is more than a century old.

Brown Brothers' Very Old Tokay is a rich dessert wine. The winery was one of the first in Australia to export wine.

BROWN BROTHERS
Very Old
TOKAY
VICTORIA
WINE MADE IN AUSTRALIA 750 ml

Murray River

Echuca
Shepparton
Albury
Kiewa River
BENDIGO
Benalla
Omeo
Mitchell River
Healesville
Goulburn River
MELBOURNE
Bairnsdale
Geelong
Sale
Korumburra

0 kilometres 50

0 miles 50

KEY

Central Victoria	Murray River Valley
Mornington Peninsula	Geelong and the Otways
Northeastern Victoria	Yarra Valley
Western Victoria	Gippsland
Far Southwest	

Mitchelton Winery in the Goulburn Valley produces a sharp, dry Riesling among other fine wines.

MELBOURNE

J OHN BATMAN, *the son of a Sydney convict, arrived in what is now known as the Port Phillip district in 1835 and met with Aboriginal tribes of the Kulin, from whom he "purchased" the land. In just over two decades Melbourne grew from a small tent encampment to a sprawling metropolis. Today it is thriving as the second-largest city in Australia.*

Melbourne's rapid growth was precipitated in the 1850s by the huge influx of immigrants seeking their fortunes on the rich gold fields of Victoria. This caused a population explosion of unprecedented proportions as prospectors decided to stay in the city. The enormous wealth generated by the gold rush led to the construction of grand public buildings. This development continued throughout the land boom of the 1880s, earning the city the nickname "Marvellous Melbourne". By the end of the 19th century, the city was the industrial and financial capital of Australia. It was also the home of the national parliament until 1927, when it was moved to purpose-built Canberra *(see p183).*

Fortunate enough to escape much damage in World War II, Melbourne hosted the summer Olympics in 1956. Dubbed the "Friendly Games", the event generated great changes in the city's consciousness. The postwar period also witnessed a new wave of immigrants who sought better lives here. Driven by the will to succeed, they introduced Melburnians to a range of cultures, transforming the British traditions of the city. This transformation continues today with the arrival of immigrants from all parts of Asia.

Melbourne holds many surprises: it has the most elaborate Victorian architecture of all Australian cities; it has a celebrated range of restaurant cuisines and its calendar revolves around hugely popular spectator sports and arts events *(see pp36–9).* While the climate is renowned for its unpredictability, Melburnians still enjoy an outdoor lifestyle, and the city possesses a unique charm that quietly bewitches many visitors.

Melbourne's café society relaxing along Brunswick Street

◁ Flinders Street Station and St Paul's Cathedral, seen from Queens Bridge

Exploring Melbourne

MELBOURNE is organized informally into precincts. Collins Street is a business centre and the site of the city's smartest stores. To the east is the parliamentary precinct. Swanston Street contains some fine Victorian architecture. The south bank of the river is arts-orientated, including the Victoria Arts Centre. The city also devotes much land to parks and gardens.

Shrine of Remembrance near the Royal Botanic Gardens

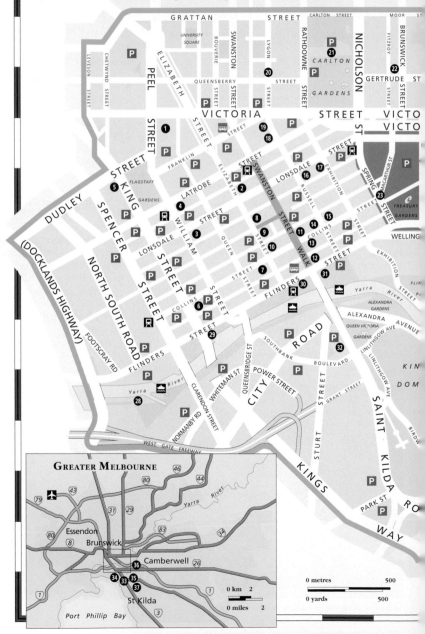

GETTING AROUND

Despite the comprehensive transport system of trams, trains, buses and the Met, many Melburnians use cars for commuting *(see pp402–403)*. This has resulted in a network of major roads and highways that lead in all directions from Melbourne's central grid through inner and outer suburbs. CityLink is a tollway linking several of the city's major access routes; drivers must purchase a pass in advance of travelling on CityLink roads. The city's flat landscape is also well suited to bicycles.

LOCATOR MAP

SIGHTS AT A GLANCE

Historic Streets and Buildings

Brunswick Street & Fitzroy **22**
Chapel Street **35**
Chinatown **16**
Como House **37**
Federation Square **31**
Fitzroy & Acland streets **33**
Flinders Street Station **30**
General Post Office **8**
Lygon Street **20**
Melbourne Town Hall **11**
No. 120 Collins Street **15**
No. 333 Collins Street **7**
Old Magistrate's Court **18**
Old Melbourne Gaol **19**
Regent Theatre **13**
Rippon Lea pp396–7 **36**
Royal Exhibition Building **21**
Royal Mint **4**
Supreme Court **3**

Churches and Cathedrals

St Francis' Church **2**
St James' Old Cathedral **5**
St Paul's Cathedral **12**
Scots' Church **14**

Shops and Markets

Block Arcade **10**
Queen Victoria Market **1**
Royal Arcade **9**

Museums and Galleries

Australian Gallery of Sport and Olympic Museum **24**
Gold Treasury Museum **23**
Melbourne Aquarium **29**
Melbourne Museum **21**
Museum of Chinese Australian History **17**
National Gallery of Victoria **32**
Polly Woodside Maritime Museum **28**

Parks and Gardens

Albert Park **34**
Melbourne Park **26**
Royal Botanic Gardens and Kings Domain pp390–91 **27**

Modern Architecture

Rialto Towers **6**

Sports Ground

Melbourne Cricket Ground **25**

SEE ALSO

- *Street Finder* pp404–11
- *Where to Stay* pp484–6
- *Where to Eat* pp517–19

KEY

	Swanston Street Precinct *see pp376–7*
	Street-by-Street map *see pp384–5*
	The Yarra River *see pp392–3*
	Bus station
	Train station
P	Parking
	River boat stop

Gothic turrets of the Old Magistrate's Court

Swanston Street Precinct

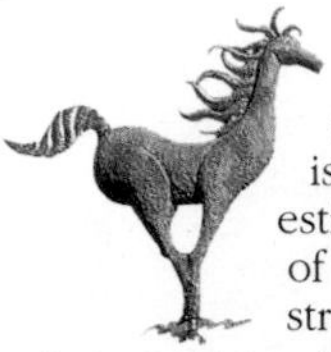

Swanston Street sculpture

Swanston Street, home to Melbourne's town hall and other major civic buildings, has always been a hub of the city. It is also exemplary of one of the most interesting relics of Melbourne: an ordered grid of broad, evenly measured and rectilinear streets, lanes and arcades. The street is also an eclectic illustration of the city's Victorian and 20th-century public architecture. In 1992, the area between Flinders Street and Franklin Street was converted into a pedestrian precinct until 7pm at night.

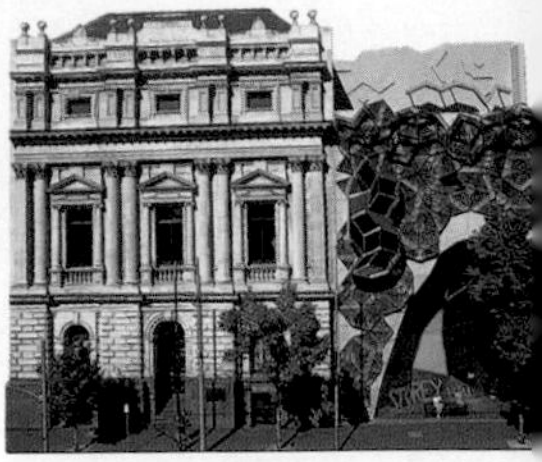

Classically inspired Storey Hall, neighbour of the RMIT Building

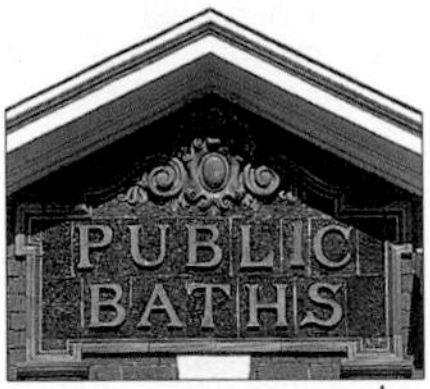
PUBLIC
BATHS

The City Baths are set in a beautiful Edwardian building with twin cupolas as a distinctive feature. They have been carefully restored to their original 1903 condition.

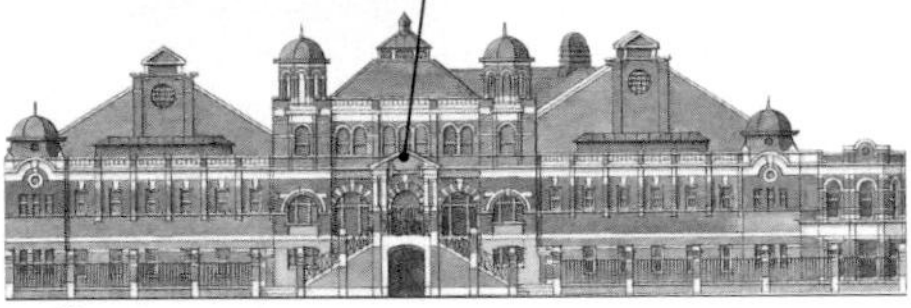

1 **City Baths**

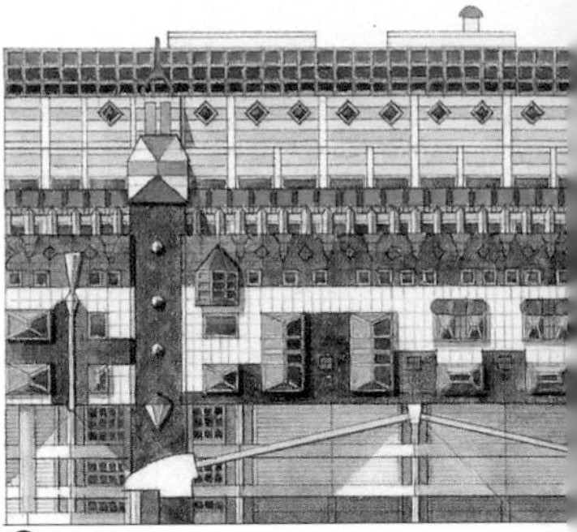

2 **RMIT Building 8**

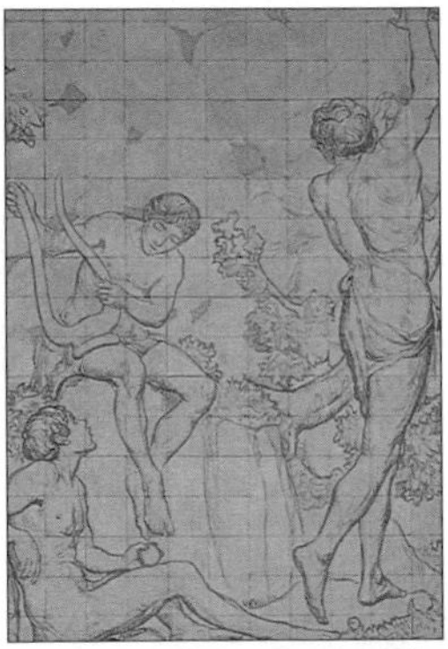

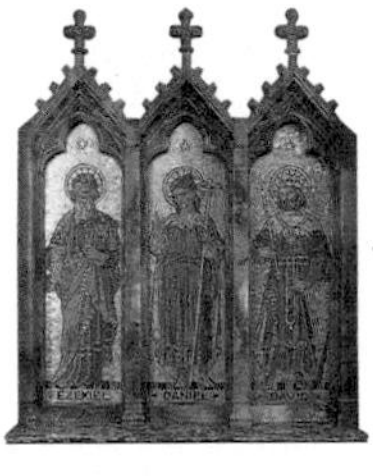

St Paul's Cathedral
Architect William Butterfield designed St Paul's in a Gothic Revival style in the 1880s 12

Melbourne Town Hall
The city's town hall was built in 1867, funded by proceeds of the gold rush (see pp50–51) 11

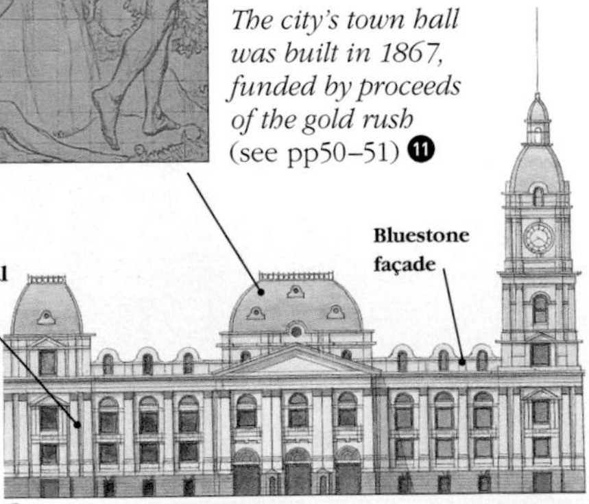
Neo-Classical columns
Bluestone façade

4 **Melbourne Town Hall**

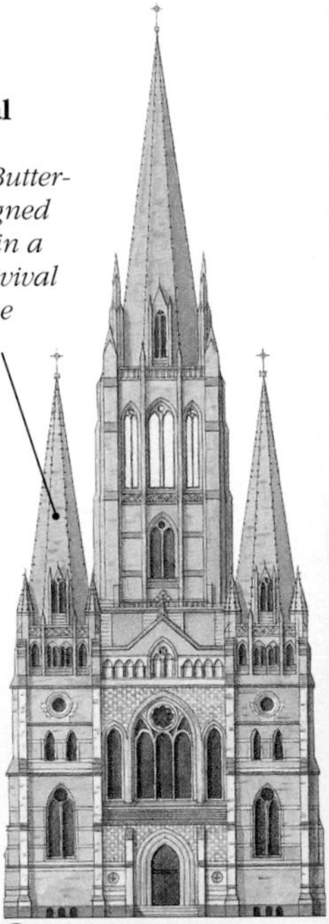

5 **St Paul's Cathedral**

Building 8, RMIT (Royal Melbourne Institute of Technology), is a gaudy, contemporary blend of bold, primary colours utilized within horizontal and vertical lines. It was met with very mixed reviews by Melburnians when it was completed.

LOCATOR MAP
See Melbourne Street Finder, Map 1

The State Library was the first design by noted architect Joseph Reed in 1854. Inside is an attractive octagonal reading room, covered by the central dome which was added in 1913.

Neo-Classical Corinthian columns line the façade.

③ **STATE LIBRARY OF VICTORIA**

Flinders Street Station
Melbourne's busiest rail terminus is one of the most recognizable sights in the city ㉚

Young and Jackson's, a 19th-century hotel known for its nude portrait *Chloe*, is protected by the National Trust.

Melbourne Central is one of the most popular shopping areas in the city centre *(see pp398–9).*

Station clock

Glass dome

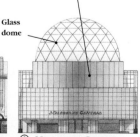

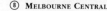

⑥ **FLINDERS STREET STATION**

⑦ **YOUNG AND JACKSON'S**

⑧ **MELBOURNE CENTRAL**

Fruit stall in Queen Victoria Market

Queen Victoria Market ❶

Elizabeth, Therry, Peel & Victoria sts.
Map 1 A2. ☎ (03) 9320 5822.
🚇 Flagstaff & Melbourne Central
(Elizabeth St exit). 🚋 Elizabeth St
routes. ◯ 6am–2pm Tue & Thu;
6am–6pm Fri; 6am–3pm Sat;
9am–4pm Sun. ● Mon, Wed, Good
Fri, 25 Dec. 🚻 ⚹

Melbourne's main fresh produce and general goods market has a strange history, occupying the site of the original Melbourne General Cemetery, which was first used in 1837. In 1877, the idea of converting part of the original cemetery into a market-place for fruit and vegetables was considered a practical one. At the time, it involved the relocation of only three graves. However, the choice created controversy which did not settle down for some time, as the market's popularity made it necessary to acquire further portions of the cemetery. In 1917, an act of Parliament granted the removal of 10,000 remains and the cemetery was razed. Exhumations continued until 1922.

The market began with the construction of the Wholesale Meat Market. In 1884, the Meat Market and Elizabeth Street shop façades were built. Further extensions continued to be built until 1936. Today the complex, occupying 7 ha (17 acres), attracts 130,000 visitors per week. Its decorative high-vaulted ceilings and open sides add to its ornate atmosphere. About 1,000 stalls sell fresh fruit and vegetables, fish, meat, cheese and organic food, that reflects the city's multicultural population. Walking heritage and food tours are also available.

St Francis' Church ❷

326 Lonsdale St. **Map** 1 C2. ☎ (03)
9663 2495. 🚇 Melbourne Central.
🚋 Elizabeth St routes. ◯ 7am–
6:30pm daily. 🚻 ⚹ by arrangement.

St Francis' church today is Australia's busiest Roman Catholic church, with 10,000 visitors each week. Built between 1841 and 1845 on the site of an earlier church, it is also Victoria's oldest.

Renowned for its beauty, the church began as a simple Neo-Gothic building and has undergone many alterations. It was the target of a $2.8 million restoration appeal, and major renovations were completed in the early 1990s.

During the ceiling restoration, treasures from the 1860s, such as a painting of angels, stars and a coat of arms, were discovered and beautifully restored. Vandalized statues have since been replaced by faithful copies.

The church holds regular services, and has one of Australia's most celebrated resident choirs.

Roof detail of St Francis' Church

Supreme Court ❸

210 William St. **Map** 1 B3. ☎ (03)
9603 6111. 🚇 Flagstaff. 🚋 City
Circle & Bourke St routes.
◯ 8am–5pm Mon–Fri; courts sit
10am–4:15pm. 🚻

When the Port Phillip district was still part of the New South Wales colony, criminal and important civil cases were heard in Sydney. To ease the inconvenience, Melbourne's first resident judge arrived in 1841 to set

Domed library in the Supreme Court

up a Supreme Court in the city. Following the Separation Act of 1850, which established the Colony of Victoria, the city set up its own Supreme Court in 1852. The court moved to the present building, with a design inspired by the Four Courts of Dublin in Ireland, in 1884.

The Supreme Court is an imposing building, with street façades on Lonsdale, William and Little Bourke streets. Its style is Classical, with a projecting portico and a double arcade with Doric and Ionic columns. Internally, a labyrinthine plan is centred on a beautiful domed library. The large bronze figure of Justice, defying tradition, is not blindfolded: rumour has it that an early Melbourne judge persuaded the authorities that Justice should be "wide-eyed if not innocently credulous". The Supreme Court is now classified by the National Trust.

Royal Mint ❹

280 William St. **Map** 1 B3. **(** (03) 9670 1219 or 9672 2400. **🚇** Flagstaff. **🚋** 23, 24, 30, 34. **🚌** Lonsdale & Queen sts routes. **⬤** to the public.

THIS FORMER MINT, built between 1871 and 1872, contains two courts which were until recently used to cope with the overflow from the Supreme Court.

The building replaced Melbourne's first Exhibition Building, erected in 1854 and subsequently destroyed by fire. When the mint opened in 1872 it processed finds from the Victoria gold fields and was a branch of the Royal Mint of London. The actual coining processes took place in an area now occupied by the car park. After the Commonwealth of Australia was founded in 1901 *(see p52)*, new silver coinage was designed, which the mint produced from 1916 to the mid-1960s. The Melbourne site ceased production in 1967 when the Royal Mint

Royal Mint crest

was relocated to Canberra. Although the Royal Mint building is now closed to the general public, visitors can still take in its imposing structure from the outside.

St James' Old Cathedral tower

St James' Old Cathedral ❺

Cnr King & Batman sts. **Map** 1 A2. **(** (03) 9329 0903. **🚇** Flagstaff. **🚋** 23, 24, 30, 34, 48, 75. **🚌** 220, 232. **⬤** 10:30am–3:30pm Mon–Wed & Fri; 10am service Sun. **⬤** public hols. **♿ 📷** by appointment.

ST JAMES' was the first Anglican cathedral in the city, used until St Paul's opened in 1891 *(see p381)*. It was first built near the corner of Little Collins and William streets to replace a wooden hut, known as the "Pioneers' Church".

It was relocated to its present site between 1913 and 1914. The stones were numbered to ensure that the original design was replicated. However, a few changes were made, such as a lower ceiling, a shortening of the sanctuary and a reshaping of the bell tower.

St James' was designed in a colonial Georgian style. The foundations are made of bluestone and the main walls were constructed with local sandstone. The cathedral was opened for worship on 2 October 1842, but was not consecrated until 1853. Charles Perry, the city's first bishop,

was enthroned here in 1848. The cathedral is still used for regular services. A small museum contains photographs, historic documents and cathedral mementos.

Rialto Towers ❻

525 Collins St. **Map** 1 B4. **(** (03) 9629 8222. **🚇** Spencer St. **🚋** Collins St routes. **⬤** 10am–10pm Sun–Thu; 10am–11pm Fri & Sat. **♿ ♿**

RIALTO TOWERS is the tallest office building in the southern hemisphere, with 58 floors above street level and 8 below. From street level up, it measures 253 m (830 ft).

The structure was built in 1986 by Australian developer Bruno Grollo, who was also responsible for the city's new casino on the Yarra River *(see p393)*. An observation deck was opened on the 55th floor in 1994 and now draws 1,500 visitors a day to see panoramic views of the city. There is also a half-hourly screening of a 20-minute film introducing visitors to the sights of Melbourne.

The lift travels from the ground floor to the 55th floor in 38 seconds and is one of the fastest in the world.

The mighty Rialto Towers

No. 333 Collins Street ❼

333 Collins St. **Map** 1 C3. ☎ *(03)
9204 3352.* ☐ *Flinders St.* ☷ *Collins
St routes.* ☐ *7:30am–6:30pm
Mon–Fri.* ☖ ☑

COMPLETED IN 1991, No. 333
Collins Street is a modern
office block built around an
existing edifice. It is the
earlier building, however,
that is the most striking.

Originally constructed in
the 1890s, No. 333 was the
headquarters of the Commercial Bank of Australia (CBA).
The bank was founded in
1866, but by the time No. 333
opened in 1893 the bank was
in crisis. Following a crash in
land and stock prices, the
CBA called in its main over-
drafts, which only helped to
accelerate the decline of the
economy. It was only with
the acceptance of a reconstruction plan by shareholders,
as well as 30 years of careful
management of its debts, that
the bank was able to recover.

The original building was
designed by architects Lloyd
Tayler and Alfred Dunn. The
banking chamber and vestibule, with their domed ceiling,
have been restored and are
now used as the foyer of the
modern complex. The CBA
merged with the Bank of
New South Wales in 1981 to
become Westpac, one of
Australia's major banks. Since
1996, No. 333 has been
owned by Wing On, a Hong
Kong company.

General Post Office façade

General Post Office ❽

Cnr Little Bourke St Mall & Elizabeth
St. **Map** 1 C3. ☎ *13 13 18.*
☐ *Flinders St & Melbourne Central.*
☷ *Bourke & Elizabeth sts routes.*
☐ *8:15am–5:30pm Mon–Fri,
10am–3pm Sat.* ● *Sun, public hols.*
☖ *via Little Bourke St.*

MELBOURNE'S FIRST postal
service was operated
from a site near the corner of
Kings Street and Flinders Lane.
Frequent floods, for which
the area became renowned,
forced a move to the current
site, where the post office
opened in 1841.

The present structure was
begun in 1859 and completed
in 1907. The first and second
floors were built between
1859 and 1867, with the third
floor and clocktower added

between 1885 and 1890. These
various stages have resulted
in an unusual combination of
styles, with Doric columns on
the ground floor, Ionic on the
second and Corinthian on the
topmost level.

The building underwent a
number of renovations to
adapt its 19th-century design
to the requirements of a major
postal system. These have
included a post-World War I
redesign of its main hall under
the direction of architect Walter
Burley Griffin *(see p189).*
Further redevelopment is
expected. When this takes
place, all post office oper-
ations will be relocated to
the corner of Elizabeth and
Little Bourke streets.

Royal Arcade entrance

Royal Arcade ❾

Elizabeth, Bourke & Little Collins sts.
Map 1 C3. ☎ *(03) 9670 7777.*
☐ *Flinders St.* ☷ *Bourke, Elizabeth
& Collins sts routes.* ☐ *7am–6pm
Mon–Thu, 7am–8pm Fri, 9am–5pm
Sat, 11am–5pm Sun.*

ROYAL ARCADE is Melbourne's
oldest surviving arcade. It
is part of a network of lanes
and arcades which sprang up
to divide the big blocks of the
city grid into smaller segments.
The network was designed in
1837 by the government surveyor, Robert Hoddle.

The original arcade, built in
1869 and designed by Charles
Webb, runs between Bourke
Street Mall and Little Collins
Street. An annexe, with an
entrance on Elizabeth Street,
was added in 1908. A statue
of Father Time, originally on

Domed ceiling of No. 333 Collins Street

the Bourke Street façade, is now located inside the arcade at the northern end.

The arcade's most famous inhabitants are statues of Gog and Magog, mythical representations of the conflict between the ancient Britons and the Trojans. They are modelled on identical figures in the Guildhall in the City of London. Between them is Gaunt's Clock, crafted by an original tenant of the arcade, Thomas Gaunt.

Block Arcade ⑩

282 Collins St. **Map** 1 C3. 【 (03) 9654 5244. ▯ Flinders St. ▯ Swanston & Collins sts routes. ▯ 10am–5:30pm Mon–Thu, 10am–7pm Fri, 10am–5pm Sat, noon–5pm Sun. ⬤ Good Fri, 25 Dec. ▯ ▯

BUILT BETWEEN 1891 and 1893, with period details including a mosaic floor and a central dome, Melbourne's most opulent arcade was named after the promenade taken by fashionable society in the 1890s. Known as "doing the block", the walk involved strolling down Collins Street between Elizabeth and Swanston streets.

The arcade was restored in 1988. It still includes the Hopetoun Tea-rooms, which have been in place since the structure was opened. Guided tours of the arcade are available.

Block Arcade façade

Chapel of Ascension in St Paul's Cathedral

Melbourne Town Hall ⑪

Swanston St. **Map**1 C3. 【 (03) 9658 9800. ▯ Flinders St. ▯ Swanston & Collins sts routes. ▯ 7:30am–5pm Mon–Fri (ground level foyer only). ⬤ public hols. ▯ ▯ obligatory for areas other than ground level foyer.

MELBOURNE TOWN HALL was completed in 1870, designed by Joseph Reed's company, Reed & Barnes. The portico was added in 1887. From here there are views of Swanston Street (see pp 376–7) and the Shrine of Remembrance in the Botanic Gardens (see p390).

Stained glass in Melbourne Town Hall

An adjacent administration block and the council's second chamber were added in 1908. This chamber combines a Renaissance-style interior with uniquely Australian motifs, such as a ceiling plasterwork of gum nuts.

A fire in 1925 destroyed much of the building's interior, including the main hall which had to be rebuilt. The entrance to the building shows four motifs on the young city's coat of arms: a whale, a ship, a bull and a sheep, signifying the main colonial industries. In 1942, the College of Arms ordered an inversion of the motifs according to heraldic convention. This explains the discrepancy between earlier and later coats of arms.

St Paul's Cathedral ⑫

Cnr Swanston & Flinders sts. **Map** 2 D3. 【 (03) 9650 3791. ▯ Flinders St. ▯ Swanston, Flinders & Collins sts routes. ▯ 7am–6pm daily. ▯ ▯

ST PAUL'S CATHEDRAL was built in 1866 to replace a far smaller church of the same name on the site.

Construction, however, was plagued by difficulties, with dissension between the English architect, William Butterfield, and the Cathedral Erection Board. Butterfield was contemptuous of the board's wish to have the cathedral face Princes Bridge and their choice of stones for the construction, such as Barrabool and Hawkesbury sandstone. Building began in 1880, but Butterfield tendered his resignation in 1884. The final stages of construction were supervised by the architect Joseph Reed, who also designed many of the fittings. The cathedral was eventually consecrated in 1891.

There are many outstanding internal features, including the reredos (altar screen) made in Italy from marble and alabaster inset with glass mosaics. The organ, made by TC Lewis & Co. of London, is the best surviving work of this great organ-builder. The cathedral also has a peal of 13 bells – a rarity outside the British Isles.

Regent Theatre ⓭

191 Collins St. **Map** 2 D3. *(03) 9299 9800.* ☐ *Flinders St.* 🚊 *Swanston & Collins sts routes.* ♿ ✔ *outside performance times.*

Assembly hall adjacent to Scots' Church

W HEN THE Regent Theatre's auditorium was destroyed by fire in April 1945, the Lord Mayor of Melbourne promised the public that it would be rebuilt, despite the scarcity of building materials due to World War II. Such was the popularity and local importance of the theatre.

Known as "Melbourne's Palace of Dreams", it was first constructed and opened by the Hoyts Theatre Company in 1929. Its lavish interiors emulated both the glamour of Hollywood and New York's impressive Capitol Theater.

The building had two main venues. The auditorium upstairs, for live stage and musical entertainment, was known as the Regent Theatre. Downstairs, the Plaza Theatre was originally a ballroom, but, following the success of the "talkies", it was converted into a cinema.

Fortunately, the magnificent decor of the Plaza Theatre was not damaged in the fire of 1945. The renovated auditorium opened to the public again in 1947.

The advent of television soon resulted in dwindling cinema audiences, and the Regent Theatre closed for almost three decades. The complex has now been restored again and was re-opened in 1996.

Scots' Church ⓮

99 Russell St (cnr Collins St). **Map** 2 D3. *(03) 9650 9903.* ☐ *Flinders St & Parliament.* 🚊 *Swanston & Collins sts routes.* ◯ *11am–2pm Mon–Wed.* ✝ *1pm, Wed; 11am & 7pm, Sun.* ♿ ✔ *on request.*

S COTS' CHURCH, completed in 1874, was intended at the time to be "the most beautiful building in Australia". It was designed by Joseph Reed in an "early English" style, with bluestone used in the foundations and local Barrabool stone making up the superstructure.

The site also includes an assembly hall which was completed in 1913.

No. 120 Collins Street ⓯

120 Collins St. **Map** 2 D3. *(03) 9654 4944.* ☐ *Flinders St & Parliament.* 🚊 *Collins St routes.* ◯ *6:45am–6:45pm Mon–Fri.* ♿

B UILT IN 1991, No. 120 Collins Street was designed by Daryl Jackson and Group Hassell. This office block is now a city landmark. Its communications tower is the highest point in the city,

Grandiose foyer of the Regent Theatre, restored to its original glory

standing 262 m (860 ft) tall. Original 1908 Federation-style professional chambers, which were built on the grounds of the 1867 St Michael's Uniting Church, are incorporated into the building.

The major tenant of this 52-storey building is the Australian company BHP Petroleum.

Chambers at No. 120 Collins Street

Chinatown ⑯

Little Bourke St. **Map** 2 D2.
🚉 Parliament. 🚋 Swanston & Bourke sts routes.

WHEN CHINESE immigrants began arriving in Melbourne to seek gold during the 1850s, many European residents were decidedly hostile. Only recent arrivals in the area themselves, they were still insecure about how strongly their own society had been established. This led to racial tension and violence.

The very first Chinese immigrants landed in Australia as early as 1818, but it was during the late 1840s that larger contingents arrived. These newcomers replaced the pool of cheap labour which had dried up with the winding down of convict settlements in the new colonies. This wave of immigration was harmonious until the vast influx of Chinese visitors who came not for labour, but to seek their fortune in the Victorian gold fields in the 1850s. The large numbers of

immigrants and a decline in gold finds made the Chinese targets of vicious and organized riots.

This attitude was sanctioned by government policy. The Chinese were charged a poll tax in most states of £10 each – a huge sum, particularly as many were peasants. Even harsher was a restriction on the number of passengers that boat-owners could carry. This acted as a disincentive for them to bring Chinese immigrants to Australia. What resulted were "Chinese marathons", as new arrivals dodged the tax by landing in "free" South Australia and walking to the gold fields, covering distances of up to 800 km (500 miles) (see pp50–51).

As an immigrant society in Melbourne, the Chinese were highly organized and self-sufficient. A city base was established during the 1850s, utilizing the cheap rental district of the city centre. As with other Chinatowns around the world, traders could live and work in the same premises and act as a support network for other Chinese immigrants. The community largely avoided prejudice by starting up traditional Asian businesses which included market gardening, laundering, green grocers and furniture-making (but work had to be stamped "Made by Chinese labour").

Stone lion in the Museum of Chinese Australian History

Traditional gateway in Little Bourke Street, Chinatown

Today, Chinatown is known for its restaurants and Chinese produce shops, with the community's calendar culminating in its New Year celebrations in February (see p37). Ironically, in view of the early prejudices, this community is now one of Australia's oldest and most successful.

Museum of Chinese Australian History ⑰

22 Cohen Place (off Little Bourke St).
Map 2 D2. 📞 (03) 9662 2888.
🚉 Parliament. 🚋 Swanston & Bourke sts routes. 🕐 10am – 4:30pm daily. ⬤ Good Fri, 25 Dec.
🖼 ♿ 📷

OPENED IN 1985 to preserve the heritage of Australians of Chinese descent, this museum is in the heart of Chinatown. The subjects of its displays range from the influx of Chinese gold-seekers in the 1850s to exhibitions of contemporary Chinese art, thus offering a comprehensive history of the Chinese in Victoria and their cultural background. The second floor holds regular touring exhibitions from China and displays of Chinese art. On the third floor is a permanent exhibition covering many aspects of Chinese-Australian history, including elaborate costumes, furniture and temple regalia.

In the basement, another permanent exhibition traces the experiences of Chinese gold miners – visitors step into a booth which creaks and moves like a transport ship, then view dioramas of gold field life, a Chinese temple and a tent theatre used by Chinese performers to entertain miners. A guided heritage walk through Chinatown is also available.

The museum also houses the beautiful Melbourne Chinese dragon, the head of which is the largest of its kind anywhere in the world.

Street-by-Street: Parliament Area

St Patrick's Cathedral icon

THE PARLIAMENT PRECINCT on Eastern Hill is a gracious area of great historic interest. Early founders of the city noted the favourable aspect of the hill and set it aside for Melbourne's official and ecclesiastical buildings. The streets still retain the elegance of the Victorian era; the buildings, constructed with revenue from the gold rush *(see pp50–51)*, are among the most impressive in the city. The Fitzroy Gardens, on the lower slopes of the hill, date back to the 1850s *(see pp366–7)* and provide a peaceful retreat complete with woodlands, glades, seasonal plantings and magnificent elm tree avenues.

The Windsor Hotel, with its long and ornate façade, was built in 1884 and is the grandest surviving hotel of its era in Australia *(see p486)*.

Stanford Fountain
The beautiful centrepiece of the elegant Gordon Reserve was sculpted by the prisoner William Stanford while he was serving his sentence.

★ Treasury Building
This Renaissance Revival style building was designed by draughtsman John James Clark in 1857. Built as government offices, with vaults to house the treasury's gold, it is now the Museum of Melbourne.

Cook's Cottage
This cottage was the English home of the parents of Captain James Cook (see p46). It was shipped to Australia in 1933 piece by piece and now houses displays about Cook and 18th-century life.

★ Parliament House

The Legislative Council in this 1850s building sits in a lavish, Corinthian chamber. The crimson colour scheme is copied from the UK's House of Lords.

LOCATOR MAP
See Melbourne Street Finder Map 2

Tasma Terrace is a superb example of Melbourne's distinctive terrace houses with ornate cast-iron decoration *(see pp368–9)*. It is now the headquarters of the National Trust.

St Patrick's Cathedral

This is one of the best examples of Gothic Revival church architecture in the world. It was constructed between 1858 and 1897, with its impressive spires completed in 1937.

★ Fitzroy Gardens

Landscape gardener James Sinclair was responsible for the superb features of these formal gardens, including winding paths, a fern gully, flowerbeds and avenues of blue gums, planes and elms.

CATHEDRAL PLACE

ALBERT STREET

| 0 metres | 100 |
| 0 yards | 100 |

KEY

– – – Suggested route

STAR SIGHTS

★ Fitzroy Gardens

★ Parliament House

★ Treasury Building

Old Magistrate's Court ⑱

Cnr La Trobe & Russell sts. **Map** 1 C2. ▢ *Museum.* ▣ *La Trobe & Swanston sts routes.* ● *to public.*

THE MELBOURNE Magistrate's Court, also called City Court, occupied this building until 1995. The area was formerly known as the police precinct – this is because the court lies opposite the former police headquarters, a very striking Art Deco skyscraper completed in the early 1940s, and next door to the Old Melbourne Gaol.

Built in 1911, the court's façades are made of native Moorabool sandstone. The building's intricate, Roman-esque design features gables, turrets and arches. It originally contained three courtrooms and offices, with a two-storey octagonal main vestibule at the centre of its labyrinth of rooms.

The future use of the Old Court is still being decided.

Ornate Romanesque tower of the Old Magistrate's Court

Old Melbourne Gaol ⑲

Russell St. **Map** 1 C2. ▮ *(03) 9663 7228.* ▢ *Melbourne Central.* ▣ *La Trobe & Swanston sts routes.* ○ *daily.* ● *Good Fri, 25 Dec.* ▨ ▮ � *limited (ground floor only).*

VISITING THE Old Melbourne Gaol, Victoria's first extensive gaol complex, is a chilling experience, especially

Corridor of cells in Old Melbourne Gaol

on a night tour. Between 1845 and 1929, it was the site of 135 executions. Today's National Trust penal museum is housed in the Second Cell Block. Behind this was the Female Ward for women prisoners, now demolished. Still in existence, though not part of the museum, is the prison chapel.

Ghosts are often reported at the gaol, which is hardly surprising given the tragic and grisly accounts of prisoners' lives and deaths. Conditions, based on London's Penton-ville Model Prison, were grim: regulated, silent and anony-mous. When first incarcerated, prisoners were held in soli-tary confinement and were not permitted to mix with other prisoners until a later date, set according to their sentence. Exhibits showing these con-ditions include prisoners'

chains and a frame used for flogging. But perhaps the most compelling exhibits are the many accounts of prisoners who were condemned to die at the gaol, accompanied by their death masks. Ned Kelly's death mask is the most famous of those on display.

Many inmates were badly treated. Basilio Bondietto, an Italian immigrant, was con-victed of murder in 1876 on circumstantial evidence. He spoke no English, had no interpreter at his trial and apparently did not understand that he was condemned to death until hours before his execution. Another case is that of Frances Knorr, hanged in 1894 amid much public controversy after being con-victed of murdering three babies in her care. Knorr had been left pregnant and pen-niless when her husband was

---

NED KELLY

The most well-known execution at the Melbourne Gaol was that of Ned Kelly, Australia's most famous bushranger, on 11 November 1880. Edward "Ned" Kelly was the son of Ellen and ex-convict "Red" Kelly. At the time of Ned's final imprisonment and execution, Ellen was serving a sentence in the gaol's Female Ward after hitting a policeman over the head when he visited her house. She was therefore able to visit her son, who

Ned Kelly's death mask

had been captured at Glenrowan on 28 June 1880 *(see p439)*. A crowd of 4,000 waited outside the gaol when Kelly was executed, most of them to lend their support to a man perceived to be rightfully rebelling against the English-based law and police authorities. In one instance, the Kelly Gang burned a bank's records of outstanding loans so they no longer had to be repaid. The controversy over whether Kelly was hero or villain continues to this day.

jailed for selling furniture bought on hire purchase. Her appointed hangman committed suicide days before his execution, after his own wife threatened to leave him if he was the one to execute Knorr.

Italian restaurant in Lygon Street

Lygon Street ⑳

Lygon St, Carlton. **Map** 1 C1.
🚊 1, 22. 🚌 200, 201, 207.

THIS ITALIAN-INFLUENCED street is one of the main café, restaurant and delicatessen areas in central Melbourne (*see pp517–19*).

The strong Italian tradition of Lygon Street began at the time of mass post-World War II immigration. With a general exodus to the suburbs in the 1940s, Carlton became unfashionable and new immigrants were able to buy its 19th-century houses and shops cheaply. More importantly, the immigrants were central in protecting these Victorian and Edwardian houses, which were built with post-gold rush wealth, from government plans to fill the area with low-income Housing Commission homes.

A distinctive architectural trait of Lygon Street's two-storey shops is their street verandas, built to protect both customers and merchandise from the sun. In the mid-1960s, the area became fashionable with university students, many of whom moved in to take advantage of its cheap accommodation, then stayed on after graduating to become the base of the suburb's contemporary middle-class and professional community. The

Coffee grinder in a Lygon Street coffee house

street is only one block from the main University of Melbourne campus and can be reached from the city centre by foot, bus or tram. Its wide street resembles a French boulevard and is well suited to the Lygon Street Festa held here every year (*see p36*).

Melbourne Museum ㉑

Carlton Gardens, Melbourne. **Map** 2 D1. 📞 *(03) 8341 7777.* 🚌 *86, 96.* ⏰ *10am–6pm daily.*

HAVING OPENED IN 2001, the Melbourne Museum is the newest museum in the city. Housed in an ultra-modern facility in verdant Carlton Park, it has exhibits over six levels, half of which are below ground level. Diverse displays offer insights into science, technology, the environment, the human mind and body, Australian society and indigenous cultures.

One of the highlights is Bunjilaka, the Aboriginal Centre. It combines exhibition galleries with a performance space and meeting rooms. *Wurreka*, the 50-m- (150 feet) long zinc wall etching at the entrance is by Aboriginal artist Judy Watson. The Two Laws gallery, which treats the Indigenous Australians' systems of knowledge, law and property, is fascinating.

The Forest Gallery is a living, breathing exhibit, featuring 8,000 plants from 120 different species. It is also home to around 20 different vertebrate species, including snakes, birds, fish and hundreds of insects. This gallery explores the complex ecosystem of Australia's temperate forests, using plants and animals, art and multimedia installations, soundscapes and other activities.

A dedicated children's museum is in a gallery that resembles a tilted, blue cube. The Blue Box houses multisensory displays exploring the theme of growth. There are also Children's Pathways throughout the rest of the museum, providing activities for children in other galleries.

One of the most popular exhibits is in the Australia Gallery. This treats the life of Phar Lap, the champion Australian racehorse of the early 1930s. Exhibits include race memorabilia of the period. Phar Lap himself is seen in an Art-Deco inspired showcase. Other curiosities on show in the museum include the skeleton of a blue whale, a car from Melbourne's first tram, a windmill and the Hertel, the first car to be imported.

Adjacent to the Melbourne Museum is the **Royal Exhibition Building**, offering an interesting 19th-century counterpoint to the Museum's modern architecture. The Exhibition Building was built for the 1880 International Exhibition and is one of the few remaining structures from the 19th-century world fairs. It was designed by Joseph Reed, whose fine work can be found throughout Melbourne.

Elegant Royal Exhibition Building, near the Melbourne Museum

Leisurely café society in Brunswick Street

Brunswick Street and Fitzroy ②

Brunswick St. **Map** 2 E1. 🚇 *11*.

NEXT TO THE university suburb of Carlton, Fitzroy was the natural choice for a post-1960s populace of students and other bohemian characters, who took advantage of the area's cheap postwar Housing Commission properties, unwanted by wealthier Melburnians. Despite some recent gentrification, Fitzroy's main strip, Brunswick Street, maintains an alternative air and a cosmopolitan street life.

Today, Brunswick Street is a mix of cafés, restaurants and trendy shops. The Brunswick Street parade, held for the opening of the city's Fringe Festival each September, is very popular. Nearby Johnston Street is home to Melbourne's Spanish quarter. Both streets are most lively on Saturday nights.

Gold Treasury Museum ②

Old Treasury Building, Spring Street (top of Collins Street). **Map** 2 D2. 📞 *(03) 9651 2233*. 🚋 *109*. 🕐 *9am–5pm Mon–Fri, 10am–4pm Sat, Sun & Public Hols.* ⚫ *Good Fri, 25 & 26 Dec.* 🎦 🎦 *11am & 3pm*.

THE GOLD TREASURY Museum is housed within Melbourne's beautiful, 19th-century Old Treasury Building (see p384). Designed in 1857 by John James Clark, a nine-teen year old architectural prodigy, it provided secure storage for gold that flooded into Melbourne from the wealthy Victorian gold fields. It also served as office accommodation for the Governor of Victoria (a role it still fulfils to this day).

As well as an opportunity to see the building itself, a visit to the museum includes a look at the gold vaults that lie beneath the building. The vaults contain a dynamic multi-media exhibition *Built on Gold*, which tells the story of how Melbourne developed into a city of enormous wealth in a remarkably short period of ten years. In this time it went from a small colonial outpost to a city with grand buildings and boulevards, a dynamic theatre culture, a passion for sport and political activism.

Making Melbourne, a permanent exhibition on the ground floor, explores Melbourne's history from the gold rushes of 1852 up until the present day. This more traditional exhibition, which includes a number of famous paintings of Melbourne from the National Gallery of Victoria, provides visitors with an opportunity to explore the economic, cultural and recreational aspects of the city's contemporary life.

Drawn from galleries and musuems from all over Australia, the temporary exhibition gallery hosts a new exhibition every six weeks. On display are a range of visual arts including sculpture, textiles, photography and architecture.

Australian Gallery of Sport and Olympic Museum ②

Melbourne Cricket Ground, Yarra Park, Jolimont. **Map** 2 F3. 📞 *(03) 9657 8879*. 🚉 *Jolimont*. 🚋 *48, 75*. 🕐 *10am–4pm daily.* ⚫ *Good Fri, 25 Dec.* 🎦 🎦 🎦

LOCATED AT THE Melbourne Cricket Ground (MCG), this museum is a sport buff's delight. The gallery, devoted to the history of 20 selected sports, including cycling, boxing and football, was opened in 1986. It includes exhibitions, such as "Australian Rules", on the history of Australian Football League clubs, and an Australian Cricket Hall of Fame.

The Olympic Museum was added to the gallery in the late 1980s. It documents the history of summer Olympic meets, reincarnated in Athens in 1896. Australia, Greece and the United Kingdom are the only three countries to have competed at all of the modern summer games.

The Australian Cricket Hall of Fame is the most recent addition, opened in 1996, with ten Australian players as initial members. These include Sir Donald Bradman, Victor Trumper and Dennis Lillee. Each player is presented through a comprehensive historical display.

The gallery and museum can also be seen as part of the one-hour MCG tour.

Olympic Cauldron on display in the Olympic Museum

World-famous Melbourne Cricket Ground backed by the city skyline

Melbourne Cricket Ground ㉕

Yarra Park, Jolimont. **Map** 2 F3.
☎ (03) 9657 8879. 🚇 Jolimont.
🚊 48, 75 (special trams run on
sports event days). ◯ for tours or
sports events only. 🎫 ⚒ ⚑
obligatory.

M ELBOURNE Cricket Ground
(MCG) is Australia's
premier sports stadium and
a cultural icon. The land was
granted in 1853 to the Melbourne Cricket Club (MCC),
itself conceived in 1838.

The MCG predominantly
hosts cricket and Australian
Rules football, being the site
for test matches and the first
one-day international match
and for the Australian Football League Grand Final, held
on the last Saturday of September (see p36). There have been
numerous stands and pavilions
over the years, each superseded at different times by
reconstructions of the ground.
An 1876 stand, now demol-
ished, was reversible, with
spectators able to watch cricket
on the ground and football in
the park in winter. The most
recent development was the
Great Southern Stand, completed in 1992; the MCG can
now seat crowds of more
than 100,000. The Olympic
and Members stands are also
under reconstruction.

Guided tours take visitors
through the members' pavilion,
which includes the MCC's
museum and library. Tours
run on all non-event days.
Access is via the Australian
Gallery of Sport and Olympic
Museum. Non-sporting events,
such as pop concerts, are also
held at the venue.

Melbourne Park ㉖

Batman Ave. **Map** 2 F4. ☎ (03)
9286 1234. 🚇 Flinders St & Richmond. 🚊 70. ◯ 9am–5pm Mon–
Fri, or during events. ⚒

M ELBOURNE PARK (formerly
known as the National
Tennis Centre) on the northern bank of the Yarra River, is
Melbourne's sports and large-
scale concerts venue. Events
include the Australian Open

(see p37), one of the four
Grand Slam competitions
of tennis, played under
Melbourne Park's unique
retractable roof (see p369).
There are also 23 outdoor
and five indoor tennis courts
for public use.

Next to Melbourne Park is
the Vodafone Arena, which is
home to the popular Victorian
Titans basketball team. It also
hosts a stadium for tennis,
basketball, cycling and
concerts, all covering an area
of 2.4 ha (6 acres). Opposite
the park is the Sports and
Entertainment Centre, which
was originally built for the
1956 Olympics but is now
being redeveloped.

Nearby Olympic Park is the
location for international and
national athletics meets, as
well as regular soccer and
rugby competitions.

Australian Open tennis championship in Melbourne Park

Royal Botanic Gardens and Kings Domain ㉗

Shrine of Remembrance crypt plaque

Tᴴᴇꜱᴇ ᴀᴅᴊᴏɪɴɪɴɢ ɢᴀʀᴅᴇɴꜱ, established in 1852, form the green heart of Melbourne on what was originally a swamp on the edge of the city. The Botanic Gardens house one of the finest collections of botanic species in the world, as well as being highly regarded for their landscape design. William Guilfoyle, curator of the Gardens between 1873 and 1909, used his knowledge of English garden design to create a horticultural paradise. Kings Domain, once an inner-city wilderness, became instead a gracious parkland. Its civic function grew over the years, with the establishment of its monuments, statues, cultural venues and the hilltop residence of the Governor of Victoria.

Sidney Myer Music Bowl is an architecturally acclaimed music "shell" which can accommodate up to 15,000 people for open-air concerts and ballets. In winter the stage becomes an ice rink.

Pioneer Women's Garden
This sunken, formal garden was built in 1934 to honour the memory of Victoria's founding women. A still, central pool is adorned by a bronze, female statue.

Observatory Gate Precinct

★ **Shrine of Remembrance**
Based on the description of the Mausoleum of Halicarnassus in Asia Minor, now Turkey, this imposing monument honours Australian soldiers who gave their lives in war.

0 metres   200
0 yards   200

VISITORS' CHECKLIST

St Kilda Rd. **Map** 2 F5. ℹ️
Birdwood Ave (03) 9252 2300.
🚃 *3, 5, 6, 8, 15, 16, 64, 67, 72.*
⏰ *7:30am daily, closing times
vary seasonally.* ♿ 📷 *11am &
2pm Sun–Fri.* 🔲 🍴 🔲

★ **Government House**
*This elaborate Italianate building is a landmark of the
gardens. Tours of the state rooms are held each week.*

**The Perennial
Border,** based on
designer Gertrude
Jekyll's traditional
colour scheme, is
planted with pastels,
contrasting with grey
and silver foliage.

**The Temple
of the Winds**

Algerian Oak
*This magnificent mature oak
in the centre of the Oak Lawn
is particularly spectacular
when it flowers in September.*

★ **Ornamental Lake**
*William Guilfoyle's lake
forms the centrepiece of the
Gardens. It reflects his
adherence to 18th-century
English garden design, which
used water as a feature.*

Arid Garden
*Desert region plants from
Australia and around the
world thrive in this special
garden, watered by a small
stream which acts as a
natural oasis.*

STAR FEATURES

★ **Government House**

★ **Ornamental Lake**

★ **Shrine of
Remembrance**

La Trobe's Cottage was shipped from England
in 1839 and was home to Victoria's first governor,
Charles La Trobe. The building is now preserved
by the National Trust.

The Yarra River

THE YARRA RIVER winds for 240 km (150 miles) from its source in Baw Baw National Park to the coast. The river has always been vital to the city, not just as its major natural feature, but also in early settlement days as its gateway to the rest of the world. Today, the Yarra is a symbol of the boundary between north and south Melbourne and many citizens live their whole lives on one side or the other. Since the 1980s, the rejuvenation of the central section of the river has given the south bank an important focus. The river is also used for sport: rowers in training are a daily sight and cycle trails run along much of the river.

LOCATOR MAP
See Melbourne Street Finder, maps 1, 2

★ **National Gallery of Victoria**
Recently redeveloped, the Gallery houses one of the largest collections of international works of art in Australia 32

The Victorian Arts Centre is home to the Australian Ballet and the Melbourne Theatre Company. The 115-m (375-ft) spire is now a Melbourne landmark.

Victoria College of the Arts

St Kilda Road · **Sturt Street** · **Kavanagh Street** · **Southbank Blvd**

Flinders Street Station
Melbourne's main railway terminus backs on to the Yarra River. A pedestrian walkway links the north and south of the city 30

Concert Hall

Southgate footbridge

★ **Polly Woodside Maritime Museum**
The restored 1885 barque is the main feature of this highly respected maritime museum 28

Melbourne Exhibition Centre is home to various annual expositions, covering subjects as diverse as motor cars, DIY and alternative medicine.

The Melbourne Convention Centre is the largest conference centre in the southern hemisphere.

Aquarium

0 metres   100
0 yards   100

The Crown Entertainment Centre cost A$1 billion to construct and includes the country's largest casino. A luxury hotel is part of the complex *(see p486)*.

KEY

– – –   Suggested route

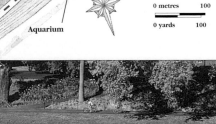

Yarra River Rowers
Professional and amateur rowing teams are a regular sight on the Yarra River, and regattas are a regular event. Rowing boats can be hired at various points along the riverbanks.

STAR SIGHTS

★ **National Gallery of Victoria**

★ **Polly Woodside Maritime Museum**

***Polly Woodside* barque moored on the Yarra River**

Polly Woodside Maritime Museum 🕮

Lorimer St East, Southbank. **Map** 1 A5. 🎫 *(03) 9699 9760.* 🚆 *Spencer St.* 🚊 *12, 96, 109.* ⛴ *Grimes Street Bridge.* ⏲ *10am–4pm daily.* ● *Good Fri, 25 Dec.* 📷 🚻 *except for ship.* 📷 *book in advance.*

WHEN THE *Polly Woodside,* an 1885 barque built in Belfast, was retired from service in the 1960s, she was the only deep-water commercial ship still afloat in Australia.

Even in 1885, the *Polly Woodside* was rare, as only one in four ships were then built with sails. Designed as a cargo ship for the South American trade, she carried coal to Chile, returning to Great Britain loaded with nitrate fertilizer. By 1897, she had rounded Cape Horn 16 times. She continued her extensive world travels until 1904, when she was sold to New Zealand owners for whom she traded around the Tasman Sea until 1924. The last 40 years of her working life were spent as a coal hulk, servicing steamships in the Port of Melbourne. Donated to the National Trust in 1968, she has now been restored by skillful and dedicated volunteers.

Visitors to the *Polly Woodside* can be shown how her crews lived on board and study old boat-building skills and various nautical models, displays and memorabilia.

Melbourne Aquarium 🕮

Cnr Queenswharf Rd & King St. **Map** 1 B4. 🎫 *(03) 9620 0999.* 🚆 *Spencer St, Flinders St.* ⏲ *Jan: 9:30am–9pm daily; Feb–Dec: 9:30am–6pm daily.* 📷 🚻 📷 📷

FEATURING species from the southern oceans, the Melbourne Aquarium puts humans close to some of the exotic inhabitants of the deep. Among the exhibits is the 2.2m-litre Oceanarium, housing sharks and rays as well as vibrantly coloured fish, which is approached through a viewing cylinder that places visitors in the middle of the swarming ocean life. Also worth a view is the coral atoll.

Flinders Street Station 🕮

Cnr Flinders & Swanston sts. **Map** 1 C4. 🎫 *13 16 38.* 🚊 *Swanston St and Flinders St. routes.* 🚻

FLINDERS STREET STATION is the central metropolitan train terminus of Melbourne and one of the city's favourite meeting places. Generations of Melburnians have met each other on the corner steps of the station "Under the Clocks". Although the

Polly Woodside museum exhibit

original clocks are now operated by computer rather than by hand, they remain in working order. The Flinders Street site has been part of the public transport network since the city's early days. The first steam train in Australia left Flinders Street Station, then a small wooden building at the end of Elizabeth Street, in 1854. The present station building, completed in 1910, was designed by Fawcett & Ashworth. The bronze domed building with its bright yellow brickwork was fully restored and refurbished in 1981.

Federation Square 🕮

Cnr Flinders & Swanston sts. **Map** 1 C4. 🎫 *13 16 38.* 🚊 *Swanston St and Flinders St. routes.* 🚻

MELBOURNE'S NEWEST public space, Federation Square commemorates the centenary of the federation of the Australian states and opened in late 2001. It combines open spaces – both outdoor, with Civic Plaza, and indoor, with a 100–metre glass atrium overlooking the Yarra River, which has a performance amphitheatre at one end – with new cultural instititions, and shops, restaurants and cafés. The Ian Potter Centre–NGV: Australian Art, an offshoot of the National Gallery of Victoria, displays works from the museum's extensive collection of Australian art, with space for temporary exhibitions focusing on contemporary art. Nearby, the Australian Centre for the Moving Image celebrates images on multimedia and film.

Flinders Street Station façade at night

View of Albert Park Lake and its wetlands

National Gallery of Victoria ❸❷

180 St Kilda Rd (285 Russell St until 2004). **Map** 2 D4. ▟ *(03) 9208 0222.* ◻ *10am–5pm daily.* ⬤ *Good Fri, 25 Apr, 25 Dec.* ♿ 🖻

THE FIRST PUBLIC art gallery in Australia, the National Gallery of Victoria opened in 1861 and housed the original State Museum *(see p377)*. The gallery moved to St Kilda Rd in 1968 and contains the largest and widest ranging art collection in the country. Its most significant bequest, from Melbourne entrepreneur Alfred Felton in 1904, included works by many great artists, and it is considered to have one of the finest collections of Old Masters in the world. Its collection of contemporary Australian art is also outstanding and the gallery holds major exhibitions all year round.

Major renovations of the building will be completed by 2004, but the vision of the current area as a "cultural centre" was fulfilled with the adjacent Victorian Arts Centre in 1984 *(see p392)*.

Fitzroy and Acland Streets ❸❸

St Kilda. **Map** 5 B5. 🚋 *96.* 🚌 *246, 600, 623, 606.* ⛴ *St Kilda Pier.*

SITUATED 6 km (4 miles) south of the city centre, St Kilda has long been the most popular seaside suburb of Melbourne. Given the built-up, suburban nature of many of the bay's beaches, it is the closest Melbourne comes to possessing a beach resort.

During the boom-time era of the 1880s *(see pp50–51)*, the suburb was inhabited by many wealthy families before it became more fashionable to live in the suburb of Toorak or on the peninsulas. Other well-off Victorians would holiday in St Kilda during the summer. St Kilda Pier, still a magnet for visitors, was erected in 1857.

Today St Kilda is densely populated, with many Art Deco apartment blocks. The neighbourhood's main streets are Fitzroy and Acland. The latter, renowned as a district of Jewish delicatessens and cake shops, is packed with visitors on Sundays. Fitzroy Street is filled with up-market restaurants and shops. Rejuvenated in the 1980s, the beachside esplanade attracts crowds to its busy arts and crafts market each Sunday.

Another popular outing is a ferry trip across the bay, including a visit to the World Trade Centre on the Yarra River *(see pp392–3)* and destinations further afield.

Melbourne tram running along Fitzroy Street

Albert Park ❸❹

Canterbury Rd, Albert St & Lakeside Drive. **Map** 5 B3. 🚋 *96.*

ENCOMPASSING the remains of a former natural swampland, Albert Park Lake is the attractive centrepiece of a 225-ha (555-acre) parkland which includes sporting fields, a public golf course and many other recreational facilities. However, it is now predominantly known as the site of the annual Australian Formula One Grand Prix, which covers a 5,260-m (5,754-yd) circuit around the lake *(see p38)*. Apart from the Grand Prix, the park is used for a variety of purposes. There is a new, popular aquatic and indoor sports centre. Wetlands have also been developed to promote a diverse wildlife. One of the most popular activities at the park is sailing, whether by small yacht, rowing boat or model boat.

A large, ancient river red gum tree standing in the centre of the park is also reputed to have been the site of many Aboriginal *corroborees* (festive night dances).

Chapel Street ❸❺

South Yarra, Prahran and Windsor. **Map** 6 E3. 🚉 *South Yarra, Prahan.* 🚋 *6, 8, 72.*

CHAPEL STREET, Melbourne's most fashionable street, with price-tags to match, is lined with shops selling local and international fashion designs. A youthful clientele swarms the street at weekends. Up-market restaurants and cafés abound and the nearby Prahran Market sells the best in fresh, delicatessen produce.

Crossing Chapel Street is Toorak Road, whose "village" is patronized by Melbourne's wealthiest community. More akin to the bohemian area of Brunswick Street *(see p388)* is Greville Street to the west, with its cafés, bars and chic second-hand shops.

An annual Chapel Street food and fashion festival is held on the last Sunday before the Melbourne Cup *(see p37)*.

Rippon Lea ❸

RIPPON LEA MANSION, designed by Joseph Reed and built in 1868, is now part of a National Trust estate. The house is a much loved fixture of the city's heritage. The first family of Rippon Lea were the Sargoods, who were renowned party hosts during the 1880s and 1890s. The next owner, Premier Sir Thomas Bent, sold off parts of the estate in the early 1900s. The Nathans bought Rippon Lea in 1910 and restored its reputation as a family home. Benjamin Nathan's daughter Louisa added a ballroom and swimming pool to the house, which were the venue for parties in the 1930s and 1940s. The formal gardens are a main highlight.

Façade of the elegant mansion, Rippon Lea

Arched windows are a recurring decorative theme throughout the house, bordered by polychrome bricks.

Victorian Bathroom
The decor of the bathroom has been restored to its original Victorian style as installed by the Sargoods. The earth closets were ingeniously processed into liquid manure and recycled for use in the garden.

The conservatory housed ferns and orchids, beloved flowers of both Frederick Sargood and Benjamin Nathan. Horticultural experts were regularly invited to Rippon Lea.

Main entrance

STAR FEATURES

★ **Dining Room**

★ **Sitting Room**

The main staircase is oak and mahogany like much of the rest of the house. Mirrors, another recurring theme in the house, are fitted into an archway at the foot of the stairs, courtesy of Louisa Jones.

★ **Dining Room**
American walnut blends with an Italian Renaissance style for the dining furniture of Louisa Jones.

VISITORS' CHECKLIST

192 Hotham St, Elsternwick.
Map 6 F4. (03) 9523 6095.
Rippon Lea. 67. 216, 219. 10am–5pm daily.
Good Fri, 25 Dec.
ground floor only.
obligatory.

The Tower was an unusual feature in the design of a domestic house. In this case, it may have been inspired by Sargood, who wanted his home to have the ornateness of a church.

The brickwork was inspired by a trip by Joseph Reed to Lombardy in Italy, where he came across this polychrome design.

Swimming pool and ballroom

★ **Sitting Room**
Louisa Jones looked to the grand mansions of Hollywood film stars in the 1930s for much of her interior design, including the plush sitting room.

Como House and its driveway

Como House ㊲

Cnr Williams Rd & Lechlade Ave, South Yarra. **Map** 4 F4. (03) 9827 2500. South Yarra. 8.
10am–5pm daily. Good Fri, 25 Dec. ground floor and grounds only. obligatory.

BEGUN IN 1847 by Edward Eyre Williams, Como House was occupied by the Armytage family for almost a century (1865–1959).

One of Como's highlights is its vast collection of original furnishings. These include pieces collected by the Armytage matriarch, Caroline, whilst on a Grand Tour of Europe during the 1870s, and include marble and bronze statues. The tour was undertaken as an educational experience for her nine children after the death of her husband, Charles Henry. It was important to this prominent Melbourne family to be seen as well educated. On their return, they held a series of sophisticated parties at the house.

Set in the picturesque remnants of its once extensive gardens, the house overlooks Como Park and the Yarra River. The original facets of the magnificent grounds, designed by William Sangster (who also had an input at Rippon Lea), remain: the fountain terrace, croquet lawn and hard standing area at the front of the house.

Como was managed by the Armytage women from 1876 until it was purchased by the National Trust in 1959.

The house has undergone major restoration work over the decades since its acquisition by the National Trust; the most recent efforts were completed in 2001.

SHOPPING IN MELBOURNE

THE CENTRAL BUSINESS DISTRICT is a magnet for the city's shoppers. Major department stores are supplemented by a network of boutiques and specialist shops, many of which are tucked away in arcades and lanes. There is also a strong network of inner-city and suburban shopping streets: fashionable clothing and retail stores abound in inner-city areas, while large one-stop shopping towns are a feature of Greater

High fashion in Chapel Street

Melbourne. There are areas known for particular products, such as High Street, which runs through Armadale and Malvern, with its proliferation of antiques stores. The city's multicultural society is also reflected in its shopping districts: Victoria Street, Richmond, has a stretch of Vietnamese stores; Sydney Road, Brunswick, is renowned for its shops selling Middle Eastern goods; and Carlisle Street, St Kilda, has many Jewish delicatessens.

Façade of the huge Myer Melbourne department store

SHOPPING HOURS

IN VICTORIA, most traders open seven days a week. Some small businesses close on Sundays but, increasingly, many are open, competing with the long hours of chain stores and supermarkets (some of which are open 24 hours a day). Standard hours are 9am to 5:30pm (10am to 6pm in the CBD), although some retailers have extended hours on Thursdays or Fridays. Hours can also vary at weekends. Christmas Day and Good Friday are the only days when most shops close.

DEPARTMENT STORES

THERE ARE THREE major department stores in central Melbourne: **Myer**, **David Jones** and **Daimaru**, all of which are open for business seven days a week.

Australia's largest department store, Myer Melbourne, encompasses a full two blocks of the city centre, with seven floors in Lonsdale Street and six in Bourke Street. Its main

entrance is in Bourke Street Mall. David Jones, known to Melburnians as DJs, is known for its more up-market stock and high-quality service, both of which are reflected in its elegant interiors. The store has three sites within the city, with a main entrance adjacent to Myer in Bourke Street Mall; opposite is its menswear department. A third section is accessed in Little Bourke Street, again adjacent to Myer.

Daimaru is Melbourne's most recent addition to its department stores and has a distinctive and distinguished air, combining the influence of its Japanese-based owners with an Australian flavour. There are six floors offering a huge range of goods.

ARCADES, MALLS AND SHOPPING CENTRES

MELBOURNE'S BEST arcades and malls are located in the heart of the central business district. Chief among these are Bourke Street Mall (see pp376–7), with shopfronts for the Myer and David Jones

department stores. Occupied mostly by speciality stores and boutiques, other arcades and malls include the **Galleria Shopping Plaza**, with an emphasis on Australiana and Australian-owned stores. The ABC Shop sells merchandise of the national television and radio network, such as books and videos. Australian Geographic is an excellent shop for information on Australian landscape and geology.

Located on Collins Street, renowned for its up-market shops, clothing and shoes, are **Australia on Collins**, Block Arcade (see p381) and the **234 Collins Street**. Australia on Collins comprises 60 shops on five levels, with fashion, homeware and other retail stores. The Sportsgirl Centre is known for its designer fashion shops, located on three levels. Both complexes have food halls. Block Arcade, itself of historic interest, sells

Ornate and elegant interior of the restored Block Arcade

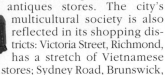

Locally grown fruit on sale at Queen Victoria Market

more classic clothing amid a beautifully restored 1890s interior; it also has an entrance on Elizabeth Street.

Further up on Collins Street, past Russell Street, there are stores located in **Collins Place** (at the foot of the Sofitel Hotel, formerly the Regent) and in the lobby of the Hyatt Hotel *(see p485)*. Another arcade of historic and architectural interest is Royal Arcade, which contains 30 retail outlets *(see p380)*. Running between Bourke Street Mall and Little Collins Street, further east, you will find **The Walk Arcade**, containing a small selection of smart and exclusive boutiques.

Little Bourke Street, above Elizabeth Street, and the intersecting Hardware Lane, are well known for a range of stores specializing in travel and adventure products.

Melbourne Central is the city's most outstanding shopping centre. Running between Lonsdale and La Trobe streets (enter on Swanston st), it has 180 shops spread over a labyrinthine six levels, all arranged around the building's glass-coned tower. Daimaru department store is part of this complex.

Although it is located on the south bank of the Yarra River, away from the city centre, the **Southgate Complex**, with its 40 shops on three levels, should not be missed. Products include up-market fashion and shoes, music, furniture, jewellery and ethnic products. The new casino on the Yarra River also features selected retail outlets *(see pp392–3)*.

MARKETS

MELBOURNE HAS a number of fresh food markets. The most notable is the Queen Victoria Market *(see p378)*.

Other kinds of market are also popular. There is a huge second-hand goods market held each Sunday in the southeastern suburb of Camberwell. An arts and crafts market is also held on Sundays on the Upper St Kilda Esplanade.

Crowds gathering at the Sunday craft market on St Kilda Esplanade

SHOPPING STRIPS

VILLAGE-STYLE shopping centres abound in the many suburbs of Melbourne. Popular spots include High Street in Armadale; Sydney Road in Brunswick; Brunswick Street in Fitzroy; Bridge Road in Richmond; Chapel Street in South Yarra; and Mailing Road in Canterbury.

Another major shopping centre in South Yarra is **The Como Centre**, which has stores selling furniture, homewares and fashion.

ENTERTAINMENT IN MELBOURNE

MELBOURNE COULD be defined as Australia's city of the arts. All year round there is a wealth of cultural events and entertainment on offer. The city's major festivals include the Melbourne Festival and Moomba *(see pp37–8)*. There are also fringe festivals and many other independent events. The Victorian Arts Centre, which includes

Art Deco cinema sign in Chapel Street

the Melbourne Concert Hall *(see p392)*, is home to the state's theatrical companies and hosts both national and international groups. Large concerts are held at Melbourne Park Entertainment Centre or the Melbourne Cricket Ground *(see p389)*. Cinema chains are supplemented by smaller venues devoted to arthouse and revival films.

Evening concert at the Sidney Myer Music Bowl *(see p390)*

INFORMATION

THE BEST GUIDE to the range of events in Melbourne is the entertainment guide in the *Age*, published each Friday. This has comprehensive listings, along with more information on all the upcoming highlights. The tabloid newspaper *Herald Sun* and both newspapers' Sunday editions are also good sources of information and reviews. There is an array of free publications covering arts, entertainment and the nightclub scene. Visitors can obtain these from retailers and cafés in main inner-city precincts such as Fitzroy *(see p395)* and St Kilda. The

Melbourne Visitor Information Centre has a range of publications listing events.

There are also a number of websites that provide good events coverage, as well as other information helpful to visitors: **www.melbourne. citysearch.com.au** and **www.visitvictoria.com** are both worth a look. The **Victorian Arts Centre** *(see p392)* has a bi-monthly diary which it mails out free of charge worldwide, covering all up-to-date events at the complex. Most ticket agencies and some individual venues also provide information of current events taking place in the city.

TICKET BOOKING AGENCIES

BUYING TICKETS in Melbourne is reasonably straightforward. There are two major ticket booking agencies in Victoria, **Ticketmaster 7** (with more than 50 outlets) and **Ticketek** (with more than 30 outlets). One other agency, **Save Time Services**, charges a slightly higher rate for tickets, but customers can

Grand 1930s foyer of the Regent Theatre *(see p382)*

make advance bookings (before tickets are officially released) and are always provided with the best seats available. There are some venues which handle their own bookings independently, but these are rare and tickets for most major events are more easily purchased at these agencies.

Bookings can either be made in person at the various outlets, or with a credit card by phone, fax or post. The agencies also accept bookings from overseas. If not bought directly over the counter, tickets can be mailed out to customers for a small handling fee. If the event is impending, tickets can usually be picked up at the venue half-an-hour before the booked performance starts.

The hours for outlets vary according to their location, but almost all are open Monday through to Saturday, and some are open on Sundays. Neither Ticketmaster BASS nor Ticketek offer refunds or exchanges, unless a show is

Façade of the Princess Theatre, by the Parliamentary Precinct *(see p384)*

Street entertainers, a regular sight throughout Melbourne

cancelled. Remember that a nominal booking fee will be added to all ticket prices bought via a ticket agency.

TICKET DEALS

SOME MAJOR COMPANIES, particularly those playing at the Victorian Arts Centre, offer special "rush hour" ticket deals. These are available for tickets purchased in person after 6pm. The Half Tix booth in Bourke Street Mall *(see pp376–7)* offers half-price deals for many events. Tickets must be bought in person and paid for in cash. They are also generally available only on the day of performance. Shows with tickets available are displayed at the booth.

Half Tix ticket booth sign in Bourke Street Mall

SECURING THE BEST SEATS

IF BOOKING IN PERSON, you can usually consult a floorplan showing the location of available seats. Over the telephone, both Ticketmaster 7 and Ticketek have a "best available" system, with remaining seats arranged in a best-to-last order by

individual venues. It is also possible to request particular seats and the booking agency will check their availability. Some seats are retained for sale at the venue itself and this can be a way of getting good seats at the last minute.

DISABLED VISITORS

THE VAST MAJORITY of venues have access and facilities for disabled visitors. Booking agencies will take this into account, so specify any special requirements when purchasing tickets. You should also enquire at individual venues to check on facilities.

OUTDOOR AND STREET ENTERTAINMENT

DESPITE ITS changeable climate, Melbourne has a strong tradition of outdoor and street entertainment. Every summer there is a broad programme of theatre and music for adults and children in most major parks and gardens. Many performances in summer are held in the evenings at sunset.

Street buskers, many travelling on an international circuit, also frequent a number of areas, the most popular being Fitzroy *(see p395)* and St Kilda, and appear at festivals. The main spot in the city centre for regular street performances is the Bourke Street Mall, outside Myer and David Jones department stores *(see p398)*. Southgate and the Victorian Arts Centre also have regular programmes featuring free weekend street entertainment.

MELBOURNE PRACTICAL INFORMATION

Road sign

MELBOURNE IS WELL SERVED by public transport and is easy to negotiate, given the grid structure of the city centre and the flat layout of its suburbs. The state government has upgraded many public facilities in recent years, aimed at attracting both business and tourists. Driving in the city is also easy and taxis are plentiful. Bureaux de change and automatic cash dispensers are located throughout the city. Melbourne is safe compared with many major cities, but common sense will also keep you out of trouble.

DRIVING AND CYCLING IN MELBOURNE

DRIVING IN Melbourne is straightforward. Cars queue on the left to turn right at some intersections, marked by Safety Zone signs, to accommodate trams. Cars left in No Parking zones will be towed away. The city has a long tollway system known as CityLink, which uses electronic tolling: drivers must purchase a pass before travelling.

Melbourne's flat landscape is well suited to cyclists and there are many cycle tracks. Helmets are compulsory. Information on bicycle hire and good cycle routes can be found at **Bicycle Victoria**.

TRAVELLING BY PUBLIC TRANSPORT

MELBOURNE HAS A comprehensive system of trains, buses and trams, known as The Met. This system also provides access to country and interstate travel, operated by the **CountryLink** network.

The main railway station for suburban services is Flinders Street Station *(see p394)*. Spencer Street Station is the main terminus for country and interstate trains.

The free City Circle Tram circuits the city. Information is available from train stations. The City Explorer is a tourist bus that departs the Town Hall at half-hour intervals.

TRAM ROUTES

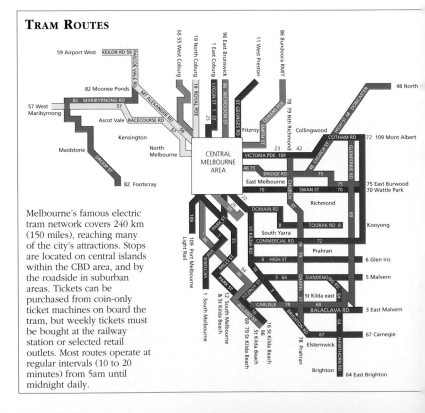

Melbourne's famous electric tram network covers 240 km (150 miles), reaching many of the city's attractions. Stops are located on central islands within the CBD area, and by the roadside in suburban areas. Tickets can be purchased from coin-only ticket machines on board the tram, but weekly tickets must be bought at the railway station or selected retail outlets. Most routes operate at regular intervals (10 to 20 minutes) from 5am until midnight daily.

Flinders Street Station, the city's main suburban rail terminus

Details are available from the **Melbourne Visitor Information Centre**.

Another way to get around the city is via water taxis and cruises along the Yarra River.

TICKETS

METROPOLITAN TICKETS can be bought from railway stations and other retail outlets, or on board trams. There are yearly, monthly, weekly, daily and two-hour tickets for use on all transport. Group tickets are also a good buy.

Central Melbourne area

KEY

■	Swanston Street
□	Elizabeth Street
■	William Street
■	Latrobe Street
■	Bourke Street
■	Collins Street
■	Flinders Street
■	Batman Street
■	City Circle
■	Suburban trams

TOURIST INFORMATION

THE MAIN TOURIST information stop in Melbourne is the Melbourne Visitor Information Centre, which has free maps and guides to all attractions and activities. They will also provide information on accommodation and arrange bookings. Next door, the **City Experience Centre** provides information in six languages, and can arrange free guides.

There is a range of free travel publications available from information centres, covering attractions in Melbourne and Victoria.

DISABLED TRAVELLERS

THE USEFUL "CBD Mobility Map" is available from the Victoria Visitor Information Centre, showing access and facilities available in the city for people with limited mobility. The majority of public facilities in the city have disabled access and toilets. Parking zones are allocated in the city and suburbs for disabled drivers; disabled driver permits are available from Melbourne Town Hall (see p381).

City Wanderer Bus, touring the city's main attractions

DIRECTORY

DRIVING AND CYCLING

Bicycle Victoria
(03) 9328 3000.

CityLink
13 26 29.

Royal Automobile Club of Victoria
13 11 11.

Met Shop
103 Elizabeth St.
13 16 38.

Met Information Line
13 16 38.

PUBLIC TRANSPORT

CountryLink
Spencer Street Station.
13 22 32.

Coach Terminus and Booking Centre
Travel Coach Australia
58 Franklin St.
(03) 9663 3299.

Airport Transfers
(03) 9335 3066.

City Explorer Bus
Melbourne Town Hall,
Swanston St.
(03) 9650 7000.

RIVER CRUISES

Melbourne Water Taxis
Southgate.
(03) 9686 0914.

Williamstown Bay and River Cruises
Southgate, No 7
Exhibition Centre, St Kilda Pier.
(03) 9397 2255 W
www.williamstownferries.com.au

TOURIST INFORMATION

Melbourne Visitor Information Centre
Cnr Swanston & Little Collins sts.
9658 9955.

Melbourne Town Hall,
90–120 Swanston St.
(03) 9658 9955.

Victorian Tourism Information Service
13 28 42.

MELBOURNE STREET FINDER

THE KEY MAP BELOW shows the areas of Melbourne covered in the *Street Finder*. All places of interest in these areas are marked on the maps in addition to useful information, such as railway stations, bus termini and emergency services. The map references given for sights described in the Melbourne chapter refer to the maps on the following pages. Map references are also given for the city's shops and markets *(see pp398–9)*, entertainment venues *(see pp400–401)*, as well as hotels *(see pp484–6)* and restaurants *(see pp517–19)*. The different symbols used for catalogue sights and other major features on the *Street Finder* maps are listed in the key below.

Bourke Street sculpture

KEY

Major sight

Place of interest

Other building

Railway station

Bus terminus

Coach station

Ferry boarding point

Taxi rank

Parking

Tourist information

Hospital with casualty unit

Police station

Church

Synagogue

Mosque

Post office

Golf course

Highway

Railway line

One-way street

Pedestrianized street

0 metres 250

0 yards 250

VICTORIA STREET

SPENCER STREET

FLINDERS STREET

Dennis Halpern sculpture at the city's Southgate complex *(see pp392–3)*

0 kilometres 1

0 miles 1

Red brick façade of the City Baths on Swanston Street *(see pp376–7)*

Ornamental lake at Rippon Lea *(see pp396–7)*

View of the Collins Street area from Princes Bridge on the Yarra River

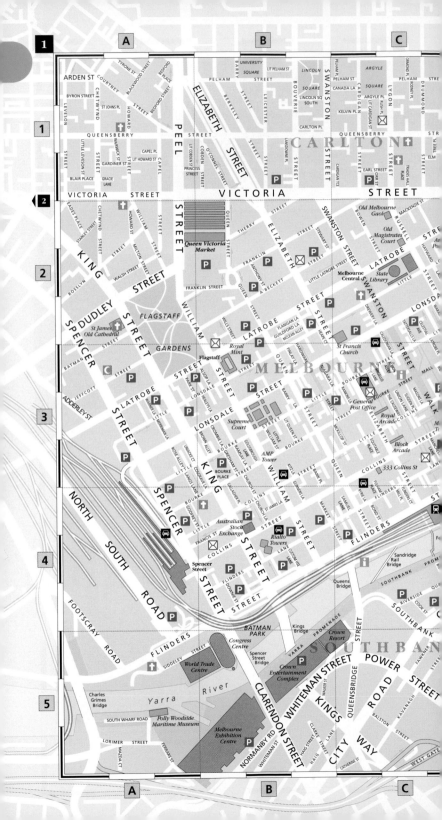

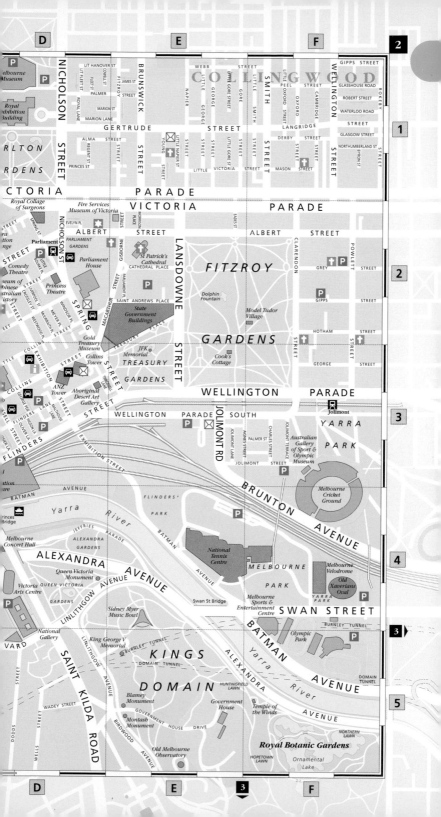

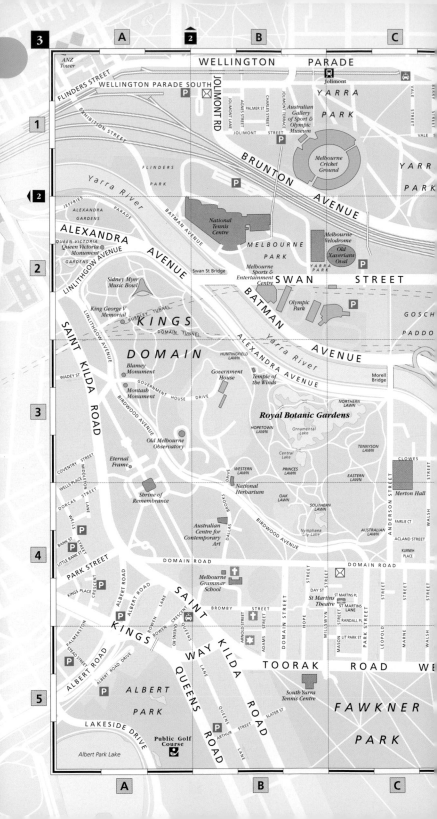

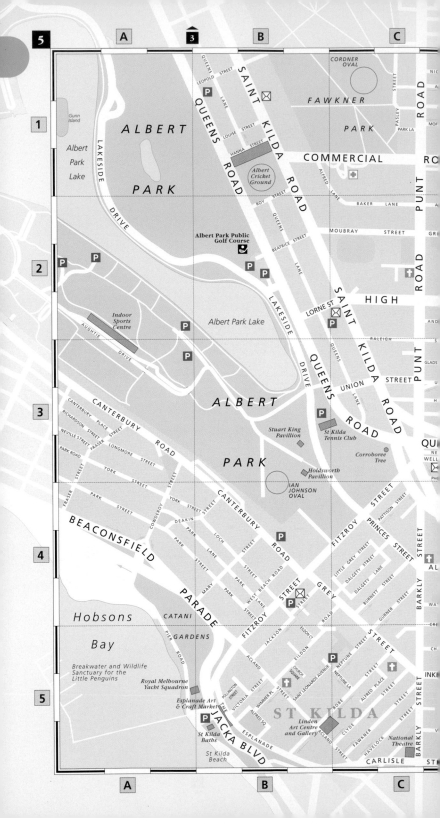

WESTERN VICTORIA

THE THEME OF WESTERN VICTORIA *is diversity. For nature lovers, there is the bare beauty of the mallee deserts of the north or the forested hills and coastal scenery of the south. For a sense of the region's history, 19th-century gold-mining towns lie in the centre, surrounded by beautiful spa towns which have attracted visitors for more than a century. The area's sights are all within easy reach of one another.*

Just as the Aboriginal tribes of Western Victoria had their lives and culture shaped by the region's diverse landscape, so the lives of the early European settlers were inevitably determined by the region's geographical features and immense natural resources.

The discovery of gold was the single most important event in Victoria's economic history, drawing prospectors from all over the world and providing the state with unprecedented wealth. Part of the legacy of this period is seen in the grand 19th-century buildings still standing in a number of central western towns. Also of interest are the spa towns clustered nearby, which draw their therapeutic waters from the same mineral-rich earth.

To the northwest, Victoria's major agricultural region, the Murray River, supports several large townships. The area is blessed with a Mediterranean-type climate, resulting in wineries and fruit-growing areas. In the south, the spectacular Grampian mountain ranges have long been of significance to the Aborigines. Fortunately, the steep cliffs and heavily forested slopes offered little prospect for development by early settlers and this beautiful area is today preserved as a wilderness. Wheat and sheep farmers have settled in parts of the mallee region in the north of Western Victoria but, as in the Grampians, other settlers have been discouraged by its semi-arid conditions, and large areas of this stunning desert vegetation and its native wildlife have been left intact.

The southwestern coast was the site of the first settlement in Victoria. Its towns were developed as ports for the rich farmland beyond and as whaling stations for the now outlawed industry. Besides its history, this coastline is known for its extraordinary natural scenery of sandstone monoliths, sweeping beaches, forests and rugged cliffs.

Pioneer Settlement Museum, a re-created 19th-century port town on the Murray River at Swan Hill

◁ **The spectacular coastal rock formations of the Twelve Apostles in Port Campbell National Park**

Exploring Western Victoria

Western victoria abounds with holiday possibilities. The spa towns close to Melbourne make perfect weekend retreats, with excellent facilities set amid gentle rural scenery. By contrast, the large number of historic sites and architectural splendours of the gold fields region requires an investigative spirit and sightseeing stamina. The Grampians National Park contains trekking opportunities and rugged views, while the mallee region offers wide open spaces and undulating sandhills. The Murray River towns have their fair share of historic sites, as well as many recreational facilities, restaurants and accommodation. The Great Ocean Road is a popular touring destination – set aside several days to explore the historic towns and scenic beauty of the coastline.

Rupertswood mansion in the Macedon Ranges

GETTING AROUND

The roads in Western Victoria are well signed and offer good roadside facilities. The Western Hwy is the route to Ballarat, the Grampians and the mallee region. The Calder Hwy leads to the spa country and beyond to Bendigo, where it connects with highways to Mildura, Swan Hill and Echuca. Take the Princes Hwy to reach Geelong and the Great Ocean Road. All these places can also be reached by rail or a combination of rail and connecting coaches. However, in remoter areas, public transport may be a problem. A good solution is to take one of the many tours offered by Melbourne's private bus companies (see p403).

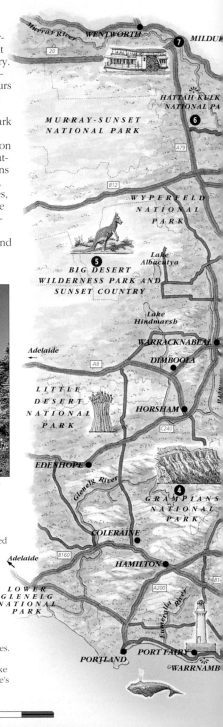

Key

- Highway
- Major road
- Scenic route
- River
- Viewpoint

Sandstone arch at Loch Ard Gorge along the Great Ocean Road

Sights at a Glance

Ballarat pp424–5 13
Bellarine Peninsula 2
Bendigo 10
Big Desert Wilderness Park and Murray-Sunset Country 5
Castlemaine 12
Echuca 9
Geelong 3
Grampians National Park 4
Hattah-Kulkyne National Park 6
Maldon 11
Mildura 7
Sovereign Hill 14
Swan Hill 8
Werribee Park 1

Tour

Macedon Ranges and Spa Country 15

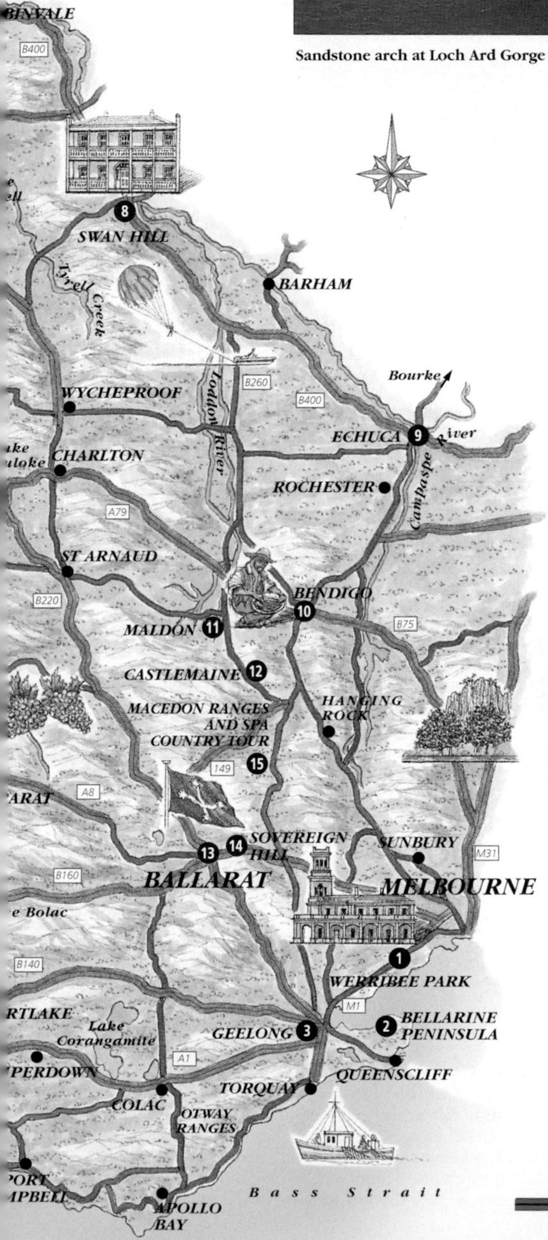

Striking rock formations of Grampians National Park

0 kilometres 50

0 miles 50

See Also

- ***Where to Stay*** pp486–8
- ***Where to Eat*** pp519–21

Flamboyant Italianate façade of Werribee Park Mansion

Werribee Park ❶

Werribee. **(** (03) 9741 2444.
🚇 Werribee. 🅾 daily. ⬤ 25 Dec.
🏛 ♿ ground floor only. 🗝

FROM 1860 UNTIL 1890, the wool boom made million-aires of Australia's sheep farmers, with the Chirnside family of Werribee Park and later of Victoria's Western District among the richest and most powerful. Their former mansion is a striking Italian-ate house, built between 1873 and 1878. It has now been restored to reflect the lifestyle of wealthy pastoral families. Visitors can stroll through the sandstone mansion and see the room where renowned opera singer Dame Nellie Melba once slept. A wing added in the 1930s has been converted into a luxury hotel.

Next to Werribee Park Mansion and its formal gardens with popular picnic areas is the Victoria State Rose Garden, laid out in a symbolic Tudor Rose-shaped design. It contains more than 4,500 beautiful rose bushes of different varieties and colours that are in flower from November to April. Also attached to Werribee Park is **Victoria's Open Range Zoo**, containing a range of exotic animals, including giraffes and hippopotami. The State Equestrian Centre is also part of the estate. This is home to some of Australia's premier show-jumping and polo events. For bird-watchers,

Chaise longue in Werribee Park

the nearby Werribee sewage farm and Point Cook Coastal Park provide magnificent views of some rare species from specially designated hides. Migratory birds such as the eastern curlew and tiny red-necked stint spend the whole summer in these protected wetlands before flying north to Japan and Siberia.

🐾 Victoria's Open Range Zoo
Werribee Park Mansion. **(** (03) 9731 9600. 🅾 daily. 🏛 ♿
🗝 preferred.

Bellarine Peninsula ❷

🚉 Geelong. 🚌 Geelong.
🚢 Ocean Grove, Point Lonsdale, Portarlington, Queenscliff.
⛴ Queenscliff. 🛈 Queenscliff (03) 5258 4843.

THE BELLARINE PENINSULA, at the western entrance to Port Phillip (see p430), is one of Melbourne's many summer resorts. The white sand beaches of Barwon Heads, Point Lonsdale and Ocean Grove mark the start of the Great Ocean Road and its famous surf beaches (see pp418–19).

The little village of **Point Lonsdale** lies at the entrance to the treacherous Heads – the most dangerous entry to any bay in the world due to its churning seas and whirlpools.

It is only 3 km (2 miles) from Point Lonsdale, across the swirling water (known as the Rip) with its hidden rocks, to Point Nepean on the Morn-ington Peninsula in Eastern Victoria (see p432).

The graceful old town of **Queenscliff** faces Port Phillip Bay so its beaches are calm. Its fort was the largest British defence post in the southern hemisphere during the 1880s, when a Russian invasion was feared. At the time Queenscliff was also a fashionable resort for Melburnians – its elegant hotels, such as the Vue Grand, are reminders of that opulent era (see p488). St Leonards and Portarlington are also popular holiday villages.

The peninsula has around 20 wineries, most offering cellar door sales and tastings.

Graceful wrought-iron detail on a Queenscliff façade

Geelong ❸

🏙 180,000. ✈ 🚉 🚌 🚢 🛈 26–32 Moorabool St (03) 5222 2900.

GEELONG is the second largest city in the state and has a rural and industrial past. Positioned on the north-facing and sheltered Corio Bay, the city has started to look once again on its port as a recre-ational front door, so popular in the first years of the 20th century. The wooden 1930s bathing complex at Eastern Beach, with its lawns, sandy beach and shady trees, was restored to its former Art Deco glory in 1994. Steampacket Place and Pier are part of a redevelopment project that has seen the gradual reno-vation of the old warehouses into a thriving waterfront quarter filled with excellent seafood restaurants, cafés, shops and hotels.

Opposite Steampacket Place are the historic wool stores. Wool was auctioned, sold and stored here prior to its being shipped around the globe from the 1880s until the 1970s. This generated Geelong's wealth. Now these buildings are being transformed; the largest houses the award-winning **National Wool Museum**, tracing Australia's wool heritage from the shearing shed to the fashion catwalks.

A short drive from Geelong is the Brisbane Ranges National Park, near Anakie, which has lovely walks and native wildflowers, such as grevilleas, wattles and wild orchids, in bloom between August and November. Nearby is Steiglitz, a ghost town from the 1850s gold rush. Only a few buildings remain of this once thriving town, among them the elegant 1870s courthouse.

🏛 **National Wool Museum**
26–32 Moorabool St. 📞 (03) 5227 0701. ⏲ daily. ⬤ Good Fri, 25 Dec. ♿ ♿

The Grampians National Park ④

📷 Stawell. 🚌 Halls Gap.
ℹ Stawell (03) 5358 2314; Halls Gap (03) 5356 4381; Brambuk Aboriginal Centre (03) 5356 4452. ⏲ daily.

THE MOUNTAINS, cliffs and sheer rock faces of the Grampians rise like a series of

FLORA AND FAUNA OF THE GRAMPIANS

The Grampians are a haven for a wide range of birds, animals, native wildflowers and plants. The park is home to almost one-third of all Victorian plant species, with many, such as the Grampians guinea flower and boronia, found only within its rocky walls. Koalas grunt at night around Halls Gap and the kangaroos at Zumsteins are unusually tame and friendly. The air, trees and scrub teem with beautiful blue wrens, rainbow lorikeets, gang gang cockatoos, scarlet robins and emus. In spring, various wildflowers, orchids and pink heath burst from every crevasse and valley floor, and the creeks and rivers are full of rare brown-tree frogs. Just south of the Grampians in the town of Hamilton, a surviving eastern barred bandicoot, once thought to be extinct, was recently discovered on the town rubbish tip. It was quickly rescued and has now become part of an active breeding and protection programme.

Rainbow lorikeet

waves above the flat western plains. Within this awesome national park, the third largest in Victoria, is a diversity of natural features and wildlife.

There are craggy slopes, cascading waterfalls and sandstone mountain tops, all formed 400 million years ago by an upthrust of the earth's crust. It has been known as *gariwerd* for thousands of years to local Aboriginal tribes, for whom it is a sacred place, and 80 percent of Victoria's indigenous rock art is here. The Brambuk Living Culture Centre near Halls Gap is run by local Aboriginal communities who conduct tours to the many sites.

The Grampians offer many different experiences for tourists. Day trips take in the spectacular MacKenzie Falls and the Balconies rock formation. Longer stays offer bush camping, wildflower studies, exploration of the Victoria Valley over the mountains from Halls Gap and overnight hiking trips in the south of the park. Experienced rock climbers come from around the world to tackle the challenging rock forms in the park and also at the nearby Mount Arapiles.

Excellent maps of the area and guides to the best walks are all available from the park's visitors' centre.

Panoramic view from the rugged crags of the Grampians

The Great Ocean Road Coastline

THE GREAT OCEAN ROAD is one of the world's great scenic drives. Close to Melbourne, pretty holiday towns are linked by curving roads with striking views at every turn. Inland, the road cuts through the Otways, a forested landscape, ecologically rich and visually splendid. Between Port Campbell and Port Fairy is a landscape of rugged cliffs and swirling seas. The giant eroded monoliths, the Twelve Apostles, in Port Campbell National Park, are an awesome spectacle. To the far west, old whaling ports provide an insight into one of Australia's early industries; at Warrnambool, southern right whales can still seen.

Portland, *a deep-water port at the end of the Princes Highway, was the site of the first European settlement in Victoria in 1834. Stunning scenery of craggy cliffs, blowholes and rough waters can be found near the town at Cape Bridgewater.*

A1

Tower Hill Game Reserve

B120

CAMPERDOWN

MOUNT GAMBIER   Portland

A1

Lady Julia Percy Island

①

②

Southern Ocean

B100

★ Port Fairy ①

🚻 ♿ 🏊 ⛵ 🎣 Ⓐ

The tiny cottages of Port Fairy are reminders of the days when the town thrived as a centre for whaling in the 1830s and 1840s. Although the whaling industry has come to an end, the town is now a popular tourist destination.

★ Warrnambool ②

🚻 🚶 🏊 ⛵ 🎣 ♿ Ⓐ

This coastal town is best known for the southern right whales that can often be spotted off Logans Beach between May and October. The town itself has many fine art galleries, museums and old churches.

```
0 kilometres        25

0 miles             25
```

KEY

≈≈	Highway
▬	Major road
┈	Minor road
〰	River
⁑	Viewpoint

Tower Hill Game Reserve, *13 km (8 miles) west of Warrnambool, is set in an extinct volcano crater. Dusk is the best time to visit and spot emus, koalas and kangaroos roaming the forests.*

***Otway National Park** provides an introduction to some of the species of the southern temperate rainforest, including a famed 400-year-old myrtle beech tree.*

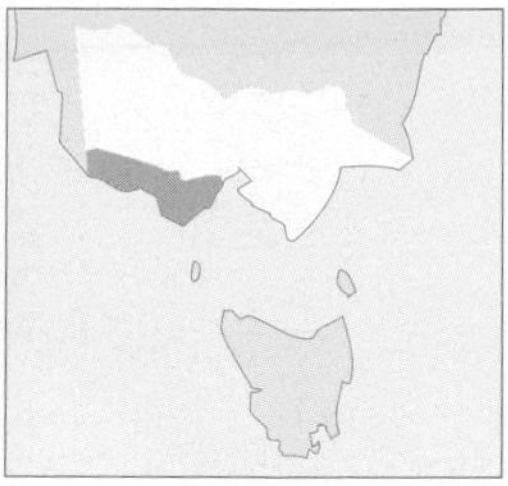

LOCATOR MAP

★ Loch Ard Gorge ⑤
♿
This treacherous area claimed the clipper *Loch Ard* in 1878. Local walks focus on the shipwreck, geology and Aboriginal history of the site.

★ Johanna Beach ⑦
🏄 🌊 🛟 🚻 ⛺
Another of Victoria's renowned surf beaches is backed by rolling green hills. The area is quite remote, but popular with campers in summer.

★ Lorne ⑨
🏄 🌊 🎣 🛟 ♿ ⛺ 🚻
Very crowded in summer, this charming seaside village boasts excellent cafés, restaurants and accommodation. Nearby forests provide a paradise for walkers.

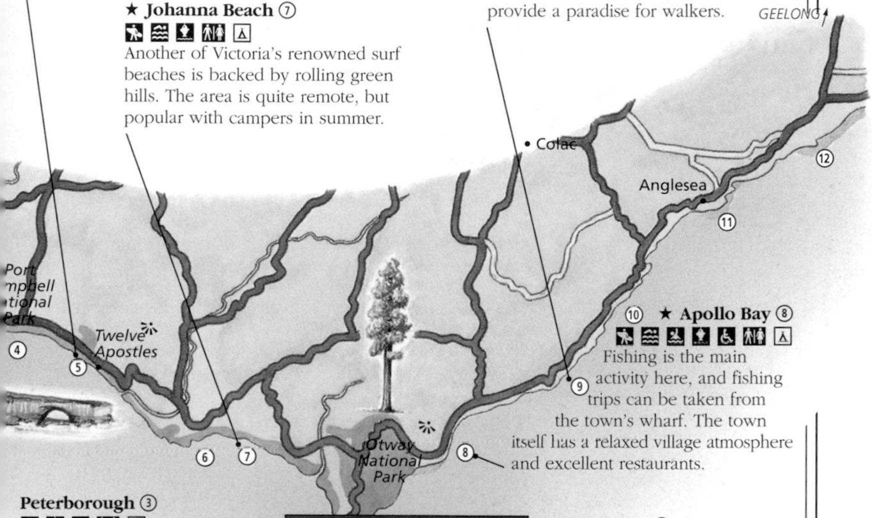
GEELONG
Colac
Anglesea
Twelve Apostles
Otway National Park

★ Apollo Bay ⑧
🏄 🌊 🎣 🛟 ♿ 🚻 ⛺
Fishing is the main activity here, and fishing trips can be taken from the town's wharf. The town itself has a relaxed village atmosphere and excellent restaurants.

Peterborough ③
🏄 🛟 🌊 🚻 ⛺
Victoria's dairy industry is based on this stretch of coastline. A popular rock pool beneath the cliff is known as the Grotto.

Port Campbell ④
🏄 🛟 ♿ 🌊 🚻 ⛺
Port Campbell beach is a sandy bay, safe for swimming. The town, set on a hill, has great views of the ocean.

Moonlight Head ⑥
🛟
Massive cliffs give way to rock platforms here in the heart of Otway National Park. Embedded anchors are reminders of the many ships lost along this perilous coastline.

Aireys Inlet ⑩
🏄 🌊 🎣 🛟 ♿ ⛺ 🚻
The red and white lighthouse is a landmark of this tiny coastal town with its beautiful ocean views.

Point Addis ⑪
🏄 🛟
The Great Ocean Road leads right to the headland with spectacular views from the car park of waves beating the rocks. There are also steps leading down the cliff for a more exhilarating experience of the rolling surf.

Bells Beach ⑫
🏄 🛟 🚻
An underwater rock platform is one of the natural features which contribute to the excellent surfing conditions at Bells. An international surfing competition is held here at Easter, bringing thousands of tourists to the area *(see p38)*.

Murrayville track in the Big Desert Wilderness Park

Big Desert Wilderness Park and Murray-Sunset Country ❺

🚌 Hopetoun. 🚍 Hopetoun. ℹ️ 75 Lascelles St, Hopetoun (03) 5083 3001; Parks Victoria Information Line 131963.

VICTORIA IS SO OFTEN seen as the state of mountains, green hills, river valleys and beaches that many visitors don't realize a large part of the west of the state is arid desert and mallee scrubland.

These are areas of beauty and solitude, with sand hills, dwarf she-oaks, lizards, snakes and dry creek systems. Big Desert Wilderness Park and Murray-Sunset Country are true deserts, with hot days and freezing nights. Murray-Sunset Country is also home to Australia's rarest bird, the black-eared minor.

To the south, Wyperfeld and Little Desert national parks are not true deserts, as they contain lake systems that support diverse flora and fauna.

Hattah-Kulkyne National Park ❻

🚌 Mildura. 🚍 Mildura. ℹ️ Mildura (03) 5021 4424; Parks Victoria Information Line 13 19 63.

UNLIKE ITS DRIER mallee region counterparts, Hattah-Kulkyne National Park is a haven of creeks and lakes that are linked to the mighty Murray River through a complex billabong (natural waterhole) overflow system.

Its perimeters are typical dry mallee country of low scrub, mallee trees and native pine woodland, but the large lakes, including Lake Hattah, Mournpoul and Lockie, are alive with bird and animal life. Ringed by massive red gums, the surrounding habitat is home to an abundance of emus, goanna lizards and kangaroos. The freshwater lakes teem with fish, while pelicans, ibis, black swans and other water birds flock on the surface.

The lakes are ideal for canoeing, and the twisting wetlands and billabongs along the Murray and in Murray-Kulkyne Park make for fine fishing, picnics, camping and bird-watching. The region is also home to Victoria's largest flower, the Murray lily.

Mildura ❼

🏠 25,000. ✈️ 🚌 🚍 ℹ️ 180–190 Deakin Ave (03) 5021 4424.

IN 1887, Mildura was little more than a village on the banks of the Murray River, situated in the middle of a red sandy desert. That year, two Canadian brothers, William and George Chaffey, came to town direct from their successful irrigation project in California and began Australia's first large-scale irrigation scheme. Since then, the red soil, fed by the Murray and Darling rivers, has become a vast plain of farms stretching for nearly 100 km (60 miles).

Today, Mildura is a modern city with a thriving tourist trade. The former home of William Chaffey, the magnificent **Rio Vista**, is worth a visit. Built in 1890, it has now been restored with its original furnishings. Grapes, olives, avocados and citrus fruit are grown successfully in the region and the area is rapidly

---

THE MURRAY RIVER PADDLESTEAMERS

Old paddlesteamer on the Murray River

Between the 1860s and 1880s, Australia's economy "rode on the sheep's back" – from the Western District of Victoria to the Diamantina Plains in central Queensland, wool was king. But the only way to transport it from the remote sheep stations to coastal ports and then on to its thriving English market was by river. There were no roads other than a few dirt tracks, so the paddlesteamers that plied the Murray, Murrumbidgee and Darling river systems were the long-distance lorries of the day. Towing barges loaded with wool, they reached the Port of Echuca after sailing for days from inland Australia. Then, stocked up with supplies for the sheep stations and distant river settlements, they returned upriver. However, by the 1890s railway lines had crept into the interior and the era of the paddlesteamer was gone. Now the Port of Echuca is once again home to beautifully restored, working paddlesteamers, such as the PS *Emmylou*, PS *Pride of the Murray* and PS *Adelaide*.

Rio Vista, the elaborate home of irrigation expert William Chaffey, in Mildura

expanding its vineyards and wineries *(see pp370–71)*.

The stark desert of Mungo National Park is only 100 km (60 miles) to the east of town.

🏛 Rio Vista
199 Cureton Ave. 📞 *(03) 5023 3733.* ⬜ *daily.* ⬤ *Good Fri, 25 Dec.* 📷 ♿ *ground floor only.*

Swan Hill ❽

🏚 *10,000.* 🚉 🚌 📾 ℹ *306 Campbell St (03) 5032 3033.*

BLACK SWANS are noisy birds, as the early explorer Major Thomas Mitchell discovered in 1836 when his sleep was disturbed by their early morning calls on the banks of the Murray River. That's how the vibrant river town of Swan Hill got its name, and the black swans are still a prominent feature.

One of the most popular attractions of Swan Hill is the **Pioneer Settlement Museum**, a 3-ha (7-acre) living and working re-creation of a river town at the turn of the 20th century. The settlement buzzes with the sound of printing presses, the blacksmith's hammer, the smell of the bakery and general daily life. "Residents" dress in period clothes and produce old-fashioned goods to sell to tourists. Some of the log

buildings are made of Murray pine, a hardwood tree impenetrable to termites. The sound and light show at night is particularly evocative.

A large paddlesteamer, the PS *Pyap*, plies the Murray River, taking visitors on leisurely one-hour cruises. It runs twice daily from the pioneer settlement, past the spot where Major Mitchell spent his famous sleepless night.

🏛 Pioneer Settlement Museum
Horseshoe Bend, Swan Hill. 📞 *(03) 5032 1093.* ⬜ *daily.* ⬤ *25 Dec.* 📷 🖥 ♿

Echuca ❾

🏚 *11,000.* 🚉 🚌 📾 ℹ *2 Heygarth St (03) 5480 7555.*

EX-CONVICT and entrepreneur Henry Hopwood travelled to the Murray River region in 1853, at the end of his prison sentence. He seized upon the need for a river punt at the Echuca crossing by setting up a ferry service, as well as the Bridge Hotel. However, Echuca really came into its own in 1864 when the railway from Melbourne reached the port. Suddenly the town, with its paddlesteamers on the Murray River, became the largest inland port in Australia.

Today the port area features horse-drawn carriages, working steam engines and old-fashioned timber mills. Tours of the area are available, along with regular river trips on a paddlesteamer. Visit the Star Hotel and discover the secret tunnel that let patrons leave after hours. There is also a paddlesteamer display opposite the hotel.

Approximately 30 km (19 miles) upstream from Echuca is Barmah Forest, the largest red gum forest in the world. A drive in the forest, with its 300-year-old river red gums and important Aboriginal sites, is highly recommended, as is the wetlands ecocruise that operates out of Barmah.

Gum trees on the road to Barmah Forest, outside Echuca

Bendigo ❿

🚶 *85,000.* ✈ 🚉 🚌 🚊
ℹ *51–67 Pall Mall (03) 5444 4445.*

BENDIGO celebrated the gold rush like no other city, and with good reason – the finds here were legendary. In 1851, the first year of gold mining, 23 kg (50 lbs) of gold were extracted from only one bucketful of dirt. When the surface gold began to disappear, the discovery of a gold-rich quartz reef in the 1870s reignited the boom.

Reflecting the city's wealth, Bendigo's buildings are vast and extravagant, often combining several architectural styles within one construction. Government architect GW Watson completed two buildings, the Law Courts and Post Office, in the French and Italian Renaissance styles. The tree-lined boulevard Pall Mall is reminiscent of a French provincial city. The elegant Shamrock Hotel opened to great fanfare in 1897 and is still in operation *(see p487)*. The European-style building is given a distinctly Australian feel with its front veranda. Self-guided heritage walk brochures are available from Bendigo's information centre, and the Vintage Talking Tram provides an excellent commentary on the town's history.

A major part of Bendigo's gold rush history was made by its Chinese population. The **Joss House**, dating from the 1860s, is a restored Chinese temple. It is a reminder of the

Entrance to the Chinese Joss House in Bendigo

Typical 19th-century building in Maldon

important role played by the Chinese in the history of Bendigo and continues to be used as a place of worship. The **Golden Dragon Museum** also has displays that chart the history of the Chinese in the city. A ceremonial archway links the museum with the **Garden of Joy**, built in 1996. Based on a traditional Asian design, the garden resembles the Chinese landscape in miniature, with valleys, mountains, trees and streams.

The **Bendigo Art Gallery** has a splendid collection of Australian painting, including works depicting life on the gold fields. Nearby are shops selling pieces from Australia's oldest working pottery, established in 1858.

Bendigo's local pottery

The **Central Deborah Gold-mine** holds tours, taking visitors down 86 m (260 ft) into the last deep reef mine in town. There are also displays on mining techniques.

🛕 **Joss House**
Finn St, North Bendigo. 📞 *(03) 5442 1685.* ⬤ *daily.* ⬤ *25 Dec.* 🎫
🏛 **Golden Dragon Museum and Garden of Joy**
5–11 Bridge St. 📞 *(03) 5441 5044.* ⬤ *daily.* ⬤ *25 Dec.* 🎫 ♿
🏛 **Bendigo Art Gallery**
42 View St. 📞 *(03) 5443 4991.* ⬤ *daily.* ⬤ *25 Dec.* 🎫 ♿ *by arrangement.*
🛕 **Central Deborah Goldmine**
76 Violet St. 📞 *(03) 5443 8322.* ⬤ *daily.* ⬤ *25 Dec.* 🎫 ♿

Maldon ⓫

🚶 *1,200.* 🚉 🚌 ℹ *High St (03) 5475 2569.*

THE PERFECTLY preserved town of Maldon offers an outstanding experience of an early gold-mining settlement. This tiny town is set within one of the loveliest landscapes of the region. The hills, forests and exotic trees are an attractive setting for the narrow streets and 19th-century buildings. Maldon was declared Australia's "First Notable Town" by the National Trust in 1966. Cafés, galleries and museums cater to the town's stream of tourists.

Other attractions include a 70-minute round-trip ride aboard a steam train to Muckleford and Carmen's Tunnel, an old gold mine. Visit at Easter to see the glorious golden leaves of the plane, oak and elm trees. There is also an Easter Fair, including an Easter parade and a street carnival *(see p38)*.

Castlemaine ⓬

🚶 *7,000.* 🚉 🚉 🚌 ℹ *Market Building, Mostyn St (03) 5470 6200.*

CASTLEMAINE'S elegance reflects the fact that gold finds here were brief but extremely prosperous. The finest attraction is the Market Hall, built in 1862. Architect William Benyon Downe designed this building in the Palladian style, with a portico and a large arched entrance leading into the building's restrained interior. The building is now the Visitors' Information Centre. **Buda Historic Home and Garden** was occupied from 1863 to 1981 by Hungarian silversmith, Ernest Leviny, and his family. The house displays an extensive collection of arts and crafts works. The property is also noted for its largely intact 19th-century garden, a unique survivor of its period.

Castlemaine is also home to many writers and artists from Melbourne and has a lively collection of museums, cafés and restaurants.

🏛 Buda Historic Home and Garden

42 Hunter St. 📞 *(03) 5472 1032.* ◯ *Wed–Sun.* ● *Good Fri, 25 Dec.* 📝 ♿ *teahouse and upper garden area.*

Ballarat ⓭

See pp424–5.

Sovereign Hill ⓮

Bradshaw St, Ballarat. 📞 *(03) 5331 1944.* ◯ *daily.* ● *25 Dec.* 📝 📷 ♿

SOVEREIGN HILL is the gold fields' living museum. Located on the outskirts of Ballarat *(see pp424–5)*, it offers visitors the chance to

---

THE CHINESE ON THE GOLD FIELDS

The first Chinese gold-seekers landed in Melbourne in 1853. Their numbers peaked at around 40,000 in 1859. They worked hard in large groups to recover the tiniest particles of gold, but the Europeans became hostile, claiming that the new arrivals were draining the colony's wealth. In 1857, several Chinese were murdered. The state government tried to quell hostility by introducing an entry tax on Chinese who arrived by boat – the Chinese then landed in neighbouring states and walked overland to Victoria. At the end of the gold rush many stayed on to work as gardeners, cooks and factory hands. There is still a large Chinese community in the state.

Chinese working on the gold fields

---

explore a unique period of Australia's history. Blacksmiths, hoteliers, bakers and grocers in full period dress ply their trades on the main streets, amid the diggers' huts, tents, old meeting places and the Chinese Village. Among the most absorbing displays are those that reproduce gold mining methods. The town's fields produced an estimated 640,000 kg (630 tonnes) of gold before being exhausted in the 1920s.

The nearby Gold Museum is part of the Sovereign Hill complex. Its changing exhibits focus on the uses of gold throughout history and its appeal as a decorative metal.

Sovereign Hill opens in the evenings for an impressive sound and light show, which re-enacts the events of the Eureka Stockade *(see p424)*.

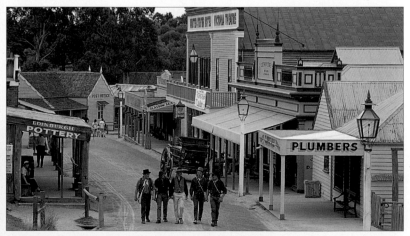

Actors in period costume walking along the main street in Sovereign Hill

Ballarat

Ballarat gold nugget

I<small>N</small> 1851, the cry of "Gold!" shattered the tranquillity of this pleasant, pastoral district. Within months, tent cities covered the hills and thousands of people were pouring in from around the world, eager to make their fortune. While there were spectacular finds, the sustainable prosperity was accrued to traders, farmers and other modest industries, and Ballarat grew in proportion to their growing wealth. The gold rush petered out in the late 1870s. However, the two decades of wealth can still be seen in the lavish buildings, broad streets, ornate statuary and grand gardens. Today, Ballarat is Victoria's largest inland city.

Ornate façade of Her Majesty's Theatre on Lydiard Street

🏛 Ballarat Fine Art Galley
40 Lydiard St North. ☎ (03) 5320 5858. ◻ daily. ● Good Fri, 25 Dec. 🖼 ♿

Ballarat has always enjoyed the spirit of benefaction. Huge fortunes were made overnight and much of these found their way into the town's institutions. Ballarat Fine Art Gallery has been a major recipient of such goodwill, enabling it to establish an impressive reputation as Australia's largest and arguably best provincial art institution.

More than 6,000 works chart the course of Australian art from colonial to contemporary times. Gold field artists include Eugene von Guerard, whose work *Old Ballarat as it was in the summer of 1853–54* is an extraordinary evocation of the town's early tent cities. The gallery's star exhibit is the original Eureka Flag, which has since come to symbolize the basic democratic ideals which are so much a part of modern Australian society.

🏚 Montrose Cottage
111 Eureka St. ☎ (03) 5332 2554. ◻ daily. ● 25 Dec. 🖼 ♿

This tiny but beautifully proportioned cottage, built around 1856, was the home of John Alexander, an ex-miner and stonemason, and is the last surviving original miner's cottage in the city. It is furnished with pieces from the era, including a 19th-century

🏚 Lydiard Street
The wealth of the gold fields attracted a range of people, among them the educated and well travelled. Lydiard Street reflects their influence as a well-proportioned streetscape, boasting buildings of exemplary quality and design.

At the northern end lies the railway station. Built in 1862, it features an arched train entrance and Tuscan pilasters. A neat row of four banks was designed by prominent architect Leonard Terry, whose concern for a balanced streetscape is clearly expressed in their elegant façades. Her Majesty's Theatre is an elaborate 19th-century structure and Australia's oldest surviving purpose-built theatre.

Opposite the theatre is Craig's Royal Hotel, begun in 1852. The hotel was extensively renovated in 1867 for a visit by Prince Alfred, Duke of Edinburgh, including the construction of a special Prince's Room and a further

22 bedrooms. In 1881, royal lanterns were constructed outside to honour a visit by the Duke of Clarence and the Duke of York (later King George V). This historic hotel is still in operation *(see p487)*.

THE EUREKA STOCKADE

An insurrection at Eureka in 1854, which arose as a result of gold diggers' dissatisfaction with high licensing fees on the gold fields, heralded the move towards egalitarianism in Australia. When hotel-owner Peter Bentley was acquitted of murdering a young digger, James Scobie, after a row about his entry into the Eureka Hotel, it incited anger among the miners. Led by the charismatic Peter Lalor, the diggers built a stockade, burned their licences and raised the blue flag of the Southern Cross, which became known as the Eureka Flag. On Sunday, 3 December 1854, 282 soldiers and police made a surprise attack on the stockade, killing around 30 diggers. After a public outcry over the brutality, however, the diggers were acquitted of treason and the licence system was abolished.

Rebel leader Peter Lalor

Lily pond in Ballarat's beautiful Botanical Gardens

sewing machine and baby's cradle, and provides a window into the life of a middle-class family on the fields.

On the same site is the Eureka Museum, which features a fascinating exhibition on the women of the gold fields. This often overlooked subject is movingly recounted here with a display of photographs, written accounts and domestic implements.

🌿 Botanical Gardens

Wendouree Drive. ((03) 5320 7444. ○ daily. ● 25 Dec. ♿ 🚻 📷

The Botanical Gardens, in the northwest of the city, are a telling symbol of Ballarat's desire for Victorian gentility. The rough and ready atmosphere of the gold fields could be easily overlooked here among the statues, lush green lawns and exotic plants.

The focus of the gardens has always been aesthetic rather than botanical, although four different displays are exhibited each year in the Robert Clark Conservatory. The most famous of these is the lovely begonia display, part of the Begonia Festival held here each March (*see p38*).

There is a Statuary Pavilion featuring female biblical figures in provocative poses, as well as a splendid centrepiece, *Flight from Pompeii.* The Avenue of Prime Ministers is a double row of staggered busts of every Australian prime minister to date, stretching off into the distance. The gardens run along the shores of the expansive Lake Wendouree.

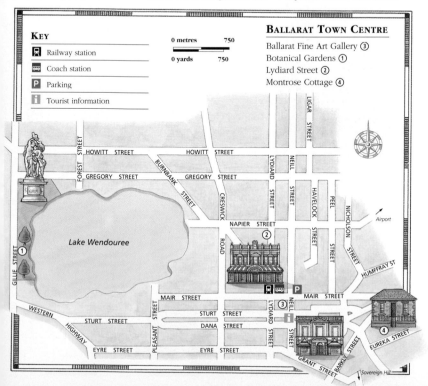

KEY

🚆 Railway station

🚌 Coach station

🅿 Parking

ℹ Tourist information

0 metres 750

0 yards 750

BALLARAT TOWN CENTRE

Ballarat Fine Art Gallery ③
Botanical Gardens ①
Lydiard Street ②
Montrose Cottage ④

Lake Wendouree

Tour of the Macedon Ranges and Spa Country ⑮

Victoria's Macedon Ranges and Spa Country lie to the northwest of Melbourne. The landscape is dotted with vineyards, small townships, craft markets and bed-and-breakfasts *(see pp487–8)*. The tour follows the Calder Highway, once taken by gold prospectors to the alluvial fields of Castlemaine and Bendigo *(see pp422–3)* before heading west into the spa country around Daylesford. The region's wealthy past is reflected in the 19th-century bluestone buildings, including wool stores and stately homes.

Malmsbury ⑧
During the gold rush, this peaceful hamlet was a busy stop for prospectors on their way to the gold fields.

Hepburn Springs ⑨
The Mineral Reserve is a large area of native bushland. It is an idyllic place for walkers and those who want to "take the waters" from the old-fashioned pumps.

Trentham Falls ⑩
Victoria's largest single-drop falls, 33 m (108 ft) high, are a few minutes' walk from Falls Road.

BENDIGO

Malmsbury Reservoir

Lauriston Reservoir

Upper Coliban Reservoir

Daylesford

WOMBAT STATE FOREST

Lerderderg River

BALLARAT

C316
C317
C318

RUPERTSWOOD AND THE ASHES

During the Christmas of 1882, eight members of the touring English cricket team were house guests of Sir William John Clarke at Rupertswood. The English won a social game between them and their hosts. Lady Clarke burnt a bail, placed the ashes in an urn and presented them to the English captain, Ivo Bligh. The urn was later presented to Marylebone Cricket Club by Bligh's widow, and thus the cricketing tradition of contesting for The Ashes began.

The original 1882 Ashes urn

| 0 kilometres | 5 |
| 0 miles | 5 |

KEY

▬▬ Tour route

═══ Other roads

☀ Viewpoint

Kyneton [7]
Historic Kyneton was once a supply town for diggers during the gold rush. It still has part of its 19th-century streetscape intact. The town is hidden from the road by trees.

Woodend [6]
Named for its location at the edge of the Black Forest, Woodend has long been a haven for travellers. It has many restaurants, hotels and speciality shops.

Hanging Rock [5]
This rock was formed 6 million years ago when lava rose up from the earth's surface and solidified. Erosion has caused the fissures through which you can now walk. Scene of the film *Picnic at Hanging Rock*, the area is steeped in Aboriginal history.

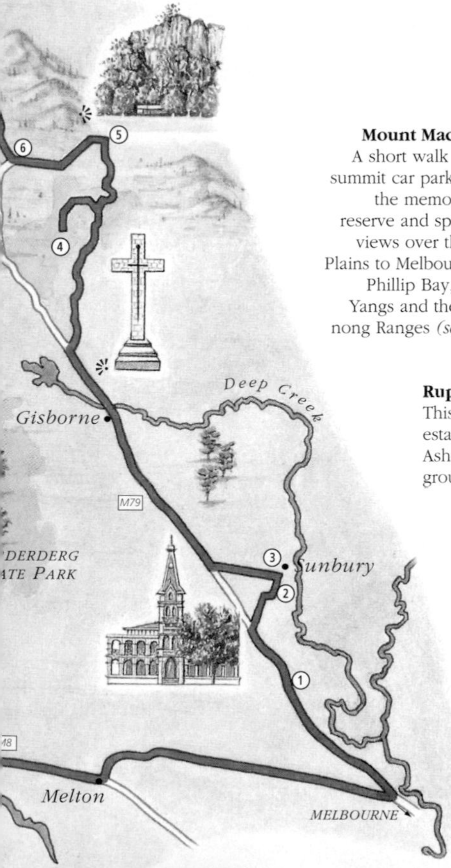
6
5
4
Gisborne
Deep Creek
M79
3
Sunbury
2
1
Melton
MELBOURNE

Mount Macedon [4]
A short walk from the summit car park leads to the memorial cross reserve and spectacular views over the Keilor Plains to Melbourne, Port Phillip Bay, the You Yangs and the Dandenong Ranges *(see p433)*.

Rupertswood [3]
This Italianate mansion was built in 1874. The estate includes the cricket field on which The Ashes were created. The once magnificent grounds are now used by a boys' school.

Goona Warra [2]
The original vineyards of this 1863 bluestone winery were replanted during the 1980s. They now produce highly respected cool-climate wines, available for tasting and sales daily from the cellar door *(see pp370–71)*.

Organ Pipes [1]
These 20-m (65-ft) basalt columns were formed by lava flows a million years ago. The Pipes can be seen from a viewing area near the car park or via a trail down to the creek bed.

Tips for Drivers

Tour length: *215 km (133 miles).*
Stopping off points: *There are numerous places to stay and eat along the route, particularly at Woodend and Daylesford. Daylesford is also ideal for a romantic dinner or weekend lunch* (see p520).

EASTERN VICTORIA

ASTERN VICTORIA *is a region of immense natural beauty with snow-topped mountains, eucalypt forests, fertile inland valleys, wild national parks and long sandy beaches. Some of the state's finest wine-growing areas are here, set around historic towns of golden sandstone. Fast rivers popular with rafters flow through the region and ski resorts resembling Swiss villages are found in the Victoria Alps.*

Eastern Victoria has a range of attractions for the visitor. The fertile plains of the north-east, crossed by the Goulburn, Ovens, King and Murray rivers, offer a feast for the tastebuds: Rutherglen red wines; Milawa mustards; local cheeses; and luscious peaches, pears and apricots from Shepparton. Historic 19th-century towns such as Beechworth and Chiltern are beautifully preserved from their gold-mining days. Glenrowan is the site where Australia's most famous bushranger, Ned Kelly, was captured. An old-fashioned paddlesteamer rides regularly on the broad Murray River near Wodonga.

But towards the Victoria Alps and the towns of Bright and Mansfield another landscape emerges. This one is wild and very beautiful. In winter there is exciting downhill skiing among the snow gums and peaks at village resorts such as Mount Buller and Falls Creek. In summer, walk among the wild flowers in Alpine National Park, hike to the summit of Mount Feathertop, or try a rafting expedition down rivers such as the mighty Snowy.

To the east of Melbourne are the magnificent beaches of the Gippsland region. Favourite attractions here include Phillip Island with its fairy penguins, and Wilsons Promontory National Park with its wildlife, granite coves and pristine waters. Near the regional centres of Sale and Bairnsdale lie the Gippsland Lakes, Australia's largest inland waterway and an angler's paradise. Beyond, stretching to the New South Wales border, is Croajingolong National Park and 200 km (125 miles) of deserted coastline.

Canoeing down the Kiewa River near Beechworth in Eastern Victoria

◁ **Mount Buller Alpine Village ski resort high in the Victorian Alps**

Exploring Eastern Victoria

Excellent highways give access to the most popular tourist attractions and towns of Eastern Victoria. The Dandenong Ranges, Yarra Valley and Phillip Island are within an easy day trip from Melbourne; the region's coastline, which includes Gippsland Lakes, around Lakes Entrance, Wilsons Promontory and Croajingolong National Park, is further to the south and east. The mountains, ski resorts and inland farm valleys are better accessed from the northeast of the state. While most of the major sights can be reached by road, some areas of the Gippsland forests and the Victorian Alps must be explored in 4WD vehicles.

0 kilometres 25

0 miles 25

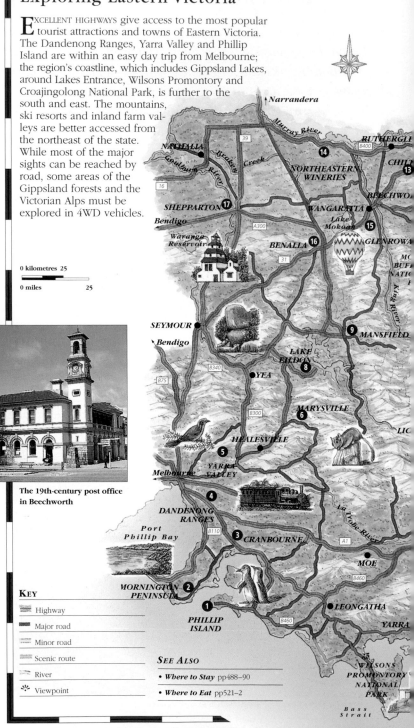

The 19th-century post office in Beechworth

KEY

~~~ Highway

▬▬ Major road

··· Minor road

═══ Scenic route

～ River

☼ Viewpoint

SEE ALSO

• **Where to Stay** pp488–90

• **Where to Eat** pp521–2

SIGHTS AT A GLANCE

Beechworth 12
Benalla 16
Bright 11
Chiltern 13
Cranbourne 3
Dandenong Ranges 4
Glenrowan 15
Lake Eildon 8
Licola 7
Mansfield 9
Marysville 6
Mornington Peninsula 2
Mount Beauty 10
Northeastern Wineries 14
Phillip Island 1
Shepparton 17
Yarra Valley 5

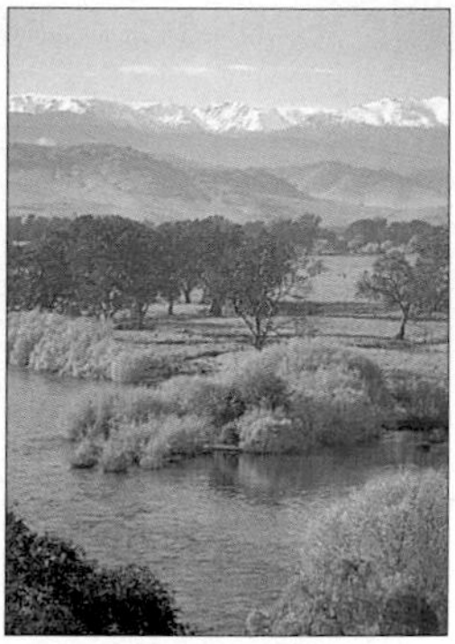

Upper Murray Valley in the heart of northeastern Victoria

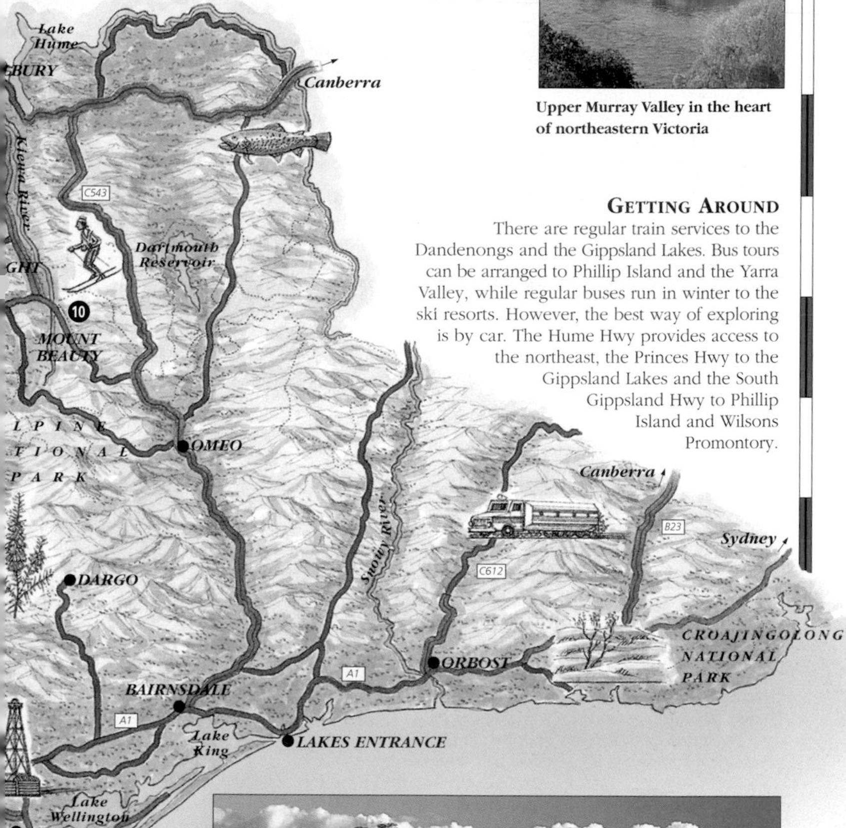

GETTING AROUND

There are regular train services to the Dandenongs and the Gippsland Lakes. Bus tours can be arranged to Phillip Island and the Yarra Valley, while regular buses run in winter to the ski resorts. However, the best way of exploring is by car. The Hume Hwy provides access to the northeast, the Princes Hwy to the Gippsland Lakes and the South Gippsland Hwy to Phillip Island and Wilsons Promontory.

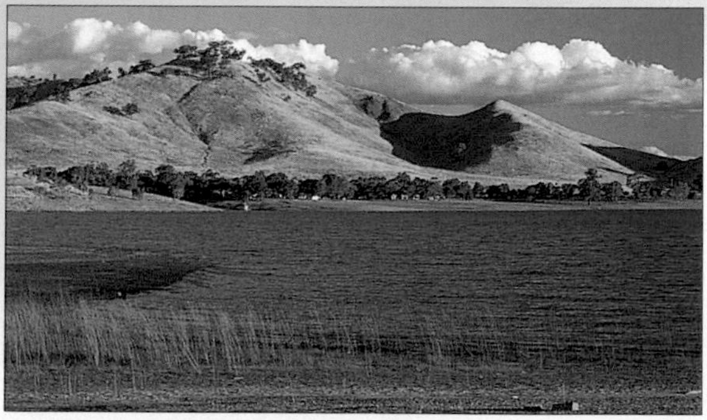

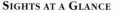

Lake Eildon at the gateway to the Victorian Alps

Phillip Island ❶

🏠 Cowes. 🚌 Cowes. 🛈 Newhaven
(03) 5956 7447. ☐ 9am– 5pm daily;
summer hols: 9am–6pm daily.

Rock pools at Sorrento on the Mornington Peninsula

THE PENGUIN PARADE on Phillip Island is an extraordinary natural spectacle and one of Eastern Victoria's most popular tourist attractions. Every evening at sunset at all times of the year, hundreds of little penguins come ashore at Summerland Beach and waddle across the sand to their burrows in the spinifex tussocks (spiky clumps of grass), just as their ancestors have been doing for generations. Once ashore, the small penguins spend their time in the dunes preening themselves and, in summer, feeding their hungry chicks, seemingly oblivious to visitors watching from raised boardwalks.

At Seal Rocks, off the rugged cliffs at the western end of the island, is Australia's largest colony of fur seals. Some 7,000 of these seals can be seen playing in the surf or feeding their pups on the rocks. Tourists can watch them from the cliff top or on an organized boat trip. Live film footage of the seals is transmitted to the Seal Rocks Sealife Centre, an interpretive centre at The Nobbies. There is also a large koala colony on Phillip Island.

Cape Woolamai, with its red cliffs and wild ocean seas, has good walking trails, birdwatching opportunities and surfing. The peaceful town of Cowes is ideal for swimming, relaxing and dining out on the island's fine seafood (see p522).

Fairy penguins making their way up the sand dunes of Phillip Island

Mornington Peninsula ❷

🚇 Frankston. 🚌 to most peninsula towns. 🚢 Stony Point, Sorrento. 🛈 Dromana (03) 5987 3078.

ONLY AN HOUR'S drive from Melbourne, on the east side of Port Phillip Bay, the Mornington Peninsula is the city's summer and weekend getaway. From Frankston down to Portsea near its tip, the area is ideal for relaxing beach holidays. The sandy beaches facing the bay are sheltered and calm, perfect for windsurfing, sailing or paddling, while the rugged coast fronting the Bass Strait has rocky reefs, rock pools and surf beaches.

Arthur's Seat, a high, bush ridge, has a spectacular chairlift ride offering views of the peninsula. The surrounding Red Hill wineries are fast gaining a reputation for their fine Chardonnays and Pinot Noirs. Sip a glass of one of these wines in the historic village of Sorrento or take a ferry trip across the narrow and treacherous Rip to the beautiful 19th-century town of Queenscliff (see p416).

Running the length of the peninsula, the Mornington Peninsula National Park has lovely walking tracks. Point Nepean, formerly a quarantine station and defence post, is now part of the national park. The beach at the tip of The Heads and Cheviot Beach, where Prime Minister Harold Holt disappeared while surfing in 1967, are both beautiful spots.

ENVIRONS: The village of Flinders is a peaceful, chic seaside resort, while Portsea is the summer playground of Melbourne's rich and famous. The atmosphere at the remote French Island, a short ferry trip from Crib Point, is unique, with no electricity or telephones. The island also teems with wildlife, including wallabies and the rare potoroo.

Royal Botanic Gardens, Cranbourne ❸

Off South Gippsland Hwy, 1000 Ballarto Rd. 🚗 (03) 5990 2200. 🚇 Cranbourne. 🚌 Cranbourne. ☐ 9am–5pm daily. ● Good Fri, 25 Dec, days of total fire ban. ♿

THE ROYAL BOTANIC GARDENS in Melbourne are the city's pride and joy (see pp390–91), but they have not concentrated exclusively on native flora. The Cranbourne Botanic Gardens fill that niche. Amid the lakes, hills and dunes of this bushland park, banksias, wattles, grevilleas, casuarinas, eucalypts and pink heath bloom, while wrens, honeyeaters, galahs, rosellas, cockatoos and parrots nestle among the gardens' trees.

The Dandenong Ranges ❹

📷 *Ferntree Gully & Belgrave.* 🚌 *to most towns.* ℹ️ *Upper Ferntree Gully (03) 9758 7522.* 🕐 *9am–5pm daily.*

Since the mid-19th century, the Dandenong Ranges, to the east of Melbourne, have been a popular weekend retreat for city residents. The cool of the mountain ash forests, lush fern gullies and bubbling creeks provide a welcome relief from the bayside heat. The area abounds with plant nurseries, bed-and-breakfasts and tearooms, reached via twisting mountain roads that offer striking views over Melbourne and the bay.

The great gardens of the Dandenongs, many of which once belonged to the mansions of wealthy families, are magnificent for walks and picnics. Particularly popular is the Alfred Nicholas Memorial Garden at Sherbrooke with its oaks, elms, silver birches and Japanese maples around a boating lake. Flowers are the obvious attraction of the National Rhododendron Gardens at Olinda and Tesselaar's Tulip Farm at Silvan. A steam train, Puffing Billy, runs several times daily from Belgrave through 24 km (15 miles) of gullies and forests to Emerald Lake and on to Gembrook.

The superb lyrebird makes its home in the Dandenongs, particularly in Sherbrooke

Domaine Chandon vineyard in the Yarra Valley

Forest. The 7-km (4-mile) Eastern Sherbrooke Lyrebird Circuit Walk through mountain ash offers a chance to glimpse these beautiful but shy birds. Another tranquil walk is the 11-km (6-mile) path from Sassafras to Emerald.

Healesville Sanctuary, with its 30 ha (75 acres) of natural bushland, remains the best place to see indigenous Australian animals in relatively relaxed captivity. Highlights of any visit are the sightings of rare species such as platypuses, marsupials and birds of prey. This is a popular place to bring children who want to learn about Australian wildlife.

Sparkling wine of the Yarra Valley

🍴 **Healesville Sanctuary**
Badger Creek Rd, Healesville. 📞 *(03) 5962 4022.* 🕐 *9am–5pm daily.*
📷 ♿

The Yarra Valley ❺

📷 *Lilydale.* 🚌 *Healesville service.* ℹ️ *Healesville (03) 5962 2600.*

The beautiful Yarra Valley, at the foot of the Dandenong Ranges, is home to some of Australia's best cool-climate wineries *(see pp370–71).* They are known for their *Méthode Champenoise* sparkling wines, Chardonnays and Pinot Noirs. Most of the wineries are open daily for wine tastings. Several also have restaurants, serving food to accompany their fine wines.

Just past the bush town of Yarra Glen with its old hotel, the Yarra Glen Grand *(see p490),* is the historic Gulf Station. Owned by the National Trust, it provides an authentic glimpse of farming life at the end of the 19th century.

Famous Puffing Billy steam train, making its way through the Dandenong Ranges

Eastern Victoria's Coastline

THE BEAUTIFUL COASTLINE of Gippsland is equal to any natural wonder of the world. Approximately 400 km (250 miles) of deserted beaches, inlets and coves are largely protected by national park status. There is the largest inland lake system in Australia, Gippsland Lakes, the pristine sands of Ninety Mile Beach and rare natural features such as the Mitchell River silt jetties. Birds, fish, seals and penguins abound in the area. With little commercial development, the coastline is a popular location with anglers, sailors, divers, swimmers and campers.

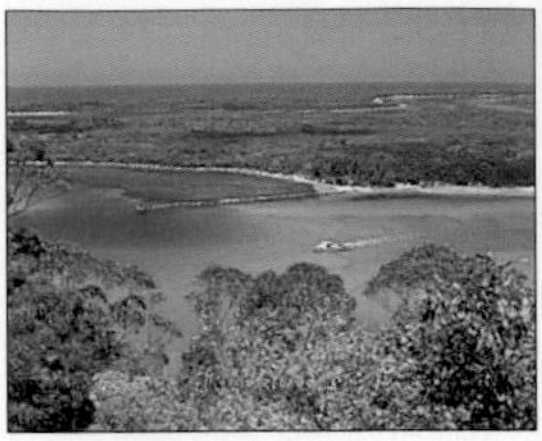

★ Lakes Entrance ⑨

🏊 🌊 ⛺ 🏖 ♿ 🚻

Lakes Entrance is the only entrance from the Gippsland Lakes to the sea, through the treacherous Bar. This major fishing port is also well equipped with motels, museums and theme parks for children.

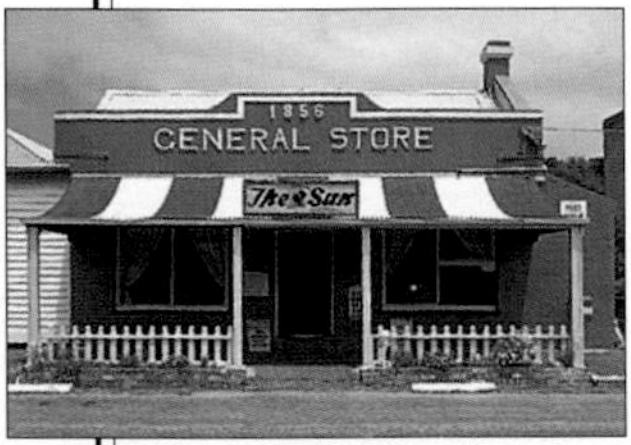
1856
GENERAL STORE
The Sun

Port Albert, *the oldest port in Gippsland, was used by thousands of gold diggers heading for the Omeo and Walhalla gold fields in the 1850s. Quaint buildings with shady verandas line its streets, and it is home to the oldest pub in the state.*

★ Letts Beach (90 Mile Beach) ⑤

🏊 🌊 🏖 🚻

This sandy beach benefits from the ocean on one side and beautiful lakes on the other. Part of the Lakes National Park, the beach is home to the endangered fairy tern.

Corner Inlet ②

🌊 🚻

This small inlet protects some of the world's most southerly mangroves and seagrass beds, as well as rare birds such as the red-necked stint.

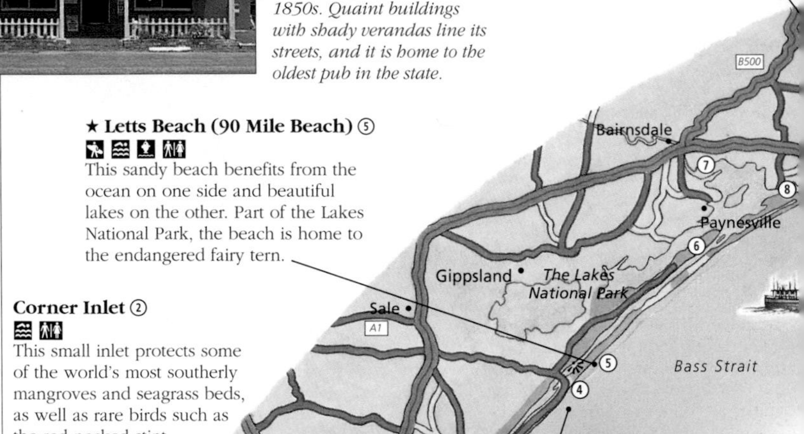
B500
Bairnsdale
7
8
Paynesville
6
Gippsland
The Lakes National Park
Sale
A1
5
Bass Strait
4
Seaspray

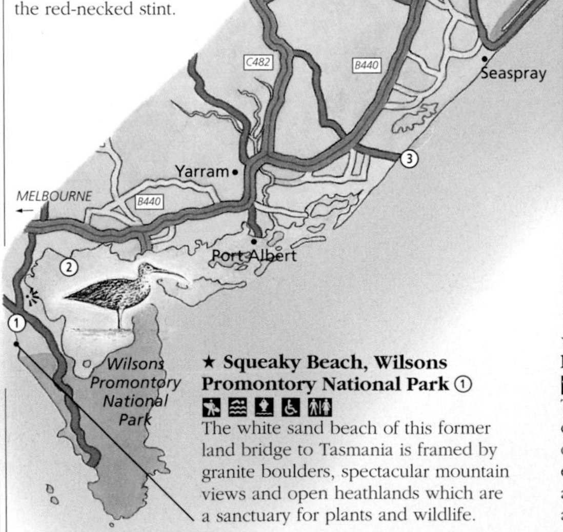
C482
B440
3
Yarram
MELBOURNE
B440
Port Albert
2
1
Wilsons Promontory National Park

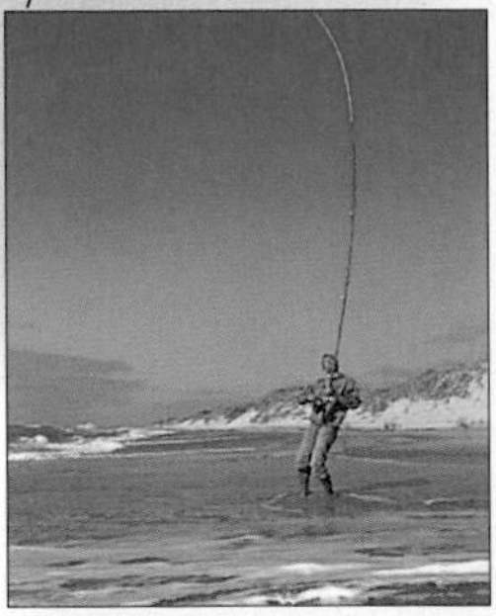

★ Golden Beach (90 Mile Beach) ④

🏊 🌊 🏖 🚻

The calm waters of this stretch of ocean make it a popular destination for water sports enthusiasts. Fishing and sailing are two of the regular activities available in the area.

★ Squeaky Beach, Wilsons Promontory National Park ①

🏊 🌊 🏖 ♿ 🚻

The white sand beach of this former land bridge to Tasmania is framed by granite boulders, spectacular mountain views and open heathlands which are a sanctuary for plants and wildlife.

Bairnsdale is one of the major towns of the Gippsland region, together with its neighbour, Sale. St Mary's Church, in the centre of the town, has unusual Italianate-style painted walls and ceilings, as well as beautiful carved statuary set in its exterior walls.

★ Gipsy Point, Mallacoota Inlet ⑫

This idyllic spot within a pleasant holiday region is ideal for summer picnics. Bird-watching and bushwalking are popular local activities.

LOCATOR MAP

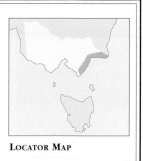

BEGA

⑫

⑪

Croajingolong National Park

Orbost

⑩

⑨

A1

Woodside Beach ③

This easily accessible white sandy beach is popular with families, sunbathers and surfers. The area behind the beach benefits from many well-signposted bushwalks.

Gippsland Lakes ⑥

The lagoons, backwaters, islands and lakes of this region make up Australia's biggest inland waterway. Lakeside settlements are home to large sailing and fishing fleets.

Eagle Point ⑦

Silt banks from the Mitchell River stretch 8 km (5 miles) out into Lake King from Eagle Point. The silt banks are second only in length to those of the Mississippi River.

Metung ⑧

This pretty boating and holiday region, popular with campers, benefits from hot mineral pools.

Marlo ⑩

Located at the mouth of the great Snowy River, Marlo is a popular holiday destination, particularly with avid local anglers. Nearby is the large town of Orbost, the centre of East Gippsland's extensive timber industry.

Mallacoota ⑪

This remote fishing village is extremely popular with both Victorian and overseas tourists. It is set on an inland estuary of the Bass Strait, ideal for canoeing, fishing and sailing.

Croajingolong National Park is a magnificent stretch of rugged and coastal wilderness, classified as a World Biosphere Reserve. Captain Cook caught his first sight of Australia in 1770 at Point Hicks.

0 kilometres	25
0 miles	25

KEY

▨	Freeway
▬	Major road
═	Minor road
～	River
☆	Viewpoint

Beech trees of the Yarra Ranges near Marysville

Marysville **6**

🏃 670. 🚌 ℹ️ *Marysville Visitors' Information Centre, Murchison St (03) 5963 4567.*

W ITHIN A TWO-HOUR drive of Melbourne, through the tall trees of the Black Spur and the Dom Dom Saddle in the Upper Yarra Ranges, is the 19th-century resort town of Marysville. Gracious old guesthouses provide a picturesque base from which to follow Lady Talbot Drive along the snow-fed Taggerty River or take walks in the "Beeches" temperate rainforest, home to the rare Leadbeater's possum.

Just outside town are the Steavenson Falls, which are floodlit at night. Nearby are the mountains of the Cathedral Ranges and the snow fields of Lake Mountain, which have 42 km (26 miles) of cross-country trails.

Licola **7**

🏃 20. 🚍 *Heyfield.* ℹ️ *Maffra Visitor Information Centre, 8 Johnson St (03) 5141 1811.*

L ICOLA IS A TINY mountain village perched on the edge of Victoria's mountain wilderness. North of Heyfield and Glenmaggie, follow the Macalister River Valley north to Licola. The 147-km (90-mile) journey from Licola to Jamieson, along unsealed roads, takes in the magnificent scenery of Victoria's highest peaks. Only 20 km (12 miles) from Licola is

SKI RESORTS OF VICTORIA

Victoria's world-class ski resorts open for business from June to September. Mount Buller, Falls Creek and Mount Hotham are the main resort villages nestling in the Alpine National Park. Mount Buller is closest to Melbourne and is the most fashionable; Falls Creek and Mount Hotham are better for a longer stay. Dinner Plain and Mount Stirling are both cross-country skiing areas. Pistes are not as long as in Europe or the USA, but the views of the High Plains are an unmissable experience. Off-piste skiing is inadvisable as the mountains are wild and the weather is unpredictable.

Snow-clad Mount Buller

Mount Tamboritha and the start of the popular Lake Tarli Karng bushwalk in the Alpine National Park.

Lake Eildon **8**

🚗 *Eildon.* ℹ️ *Eildon Visitors' Information Centre, Main St, Eildon (03) 5774 2909.*

L AKE EILDON, the catchment for five major rivers, including the Goulburn River, is a vast irrigation reserve that turns into a recreational haven in summer. Surrounded by the Great Dividing Range and Fraser and Eildon national parks, the lake is a good location for water-skiing, houseboat holidays, horse-riding, fishing and hiking. Kangaroos, koalas and rosellas abound around the lake, and trout and Murray cod are common in the Upper Goulburn River and in

the lake. Canoeing on the Goulburn River is also a popular activity.

A variety of accommodation is available, from rustic cabins and camp sites in Fraser National Park to luxurious five-star lodges and guesthouses *(see pp488–90).*

Mansfield **9**

🏃 2,500. 🚗 ℹ️ *Visitors' Information Centre, Historic Mansfield Railway Station (03) 5775 1464.*

M ANSFIELD, a country town surrounded by mountains, is the southwest entry point to Victoria's alpine country. A memorial in the main street of Mansfield, near the 1920s cinema, commemorates the death of three troopers shot by the infamous Ned Kelly and his gang at nearby Stringybark Creek in

Blue waters of Lake Eildon, backed by the Howqua Mountain Ranges

Classic 19th-century architecture in the rural town of Mansfield

1878 – the crime for which he was hung in Melbourne in 1880 (see p386).

The scenery of Mansfield became well known as the location for the 1981 film *The Man from Snowy River*, which was based on the poet "Banjo" Paterson's legendary ballad of the same name (see p31). Many local horsemen rode in the film and they still contest Crack's Cup each November (see p37). Riders traverse a mountainous track through tall mountain ash, cross rivers and descend steep hills, demonstrating traditional bush skills of both horse and rider.

ENVIRONS: The excellent downhill slopes of the Mount Buller ski resort is less than one hour's drive from Mansfield. The Mount Stirling Alpine Resort offers year-round activities, such as mountain bike riding (see p527).

Mount Beauty ⑩

🏠 2,300. 🚌 ℹ️ Kiewa Valley Hwy (03) 5754 1962.

THE TOWN OF Mount Beauty was first built to house workers on the Kiewa hydro-electricity scheme in the 1940s. It has since developed into a good base for exploring the beauty of the Kiewa Valley, with its tumbling river and dairy farms. Also nearby is the wilderness of the Bogong High Plains and the Alpine National Park, with their walks, wildflowers and snow gums.

Within the national park, Mount Bogong, Victoria's highest mountain, rises an impressive 1,986 m (6,516 ft)

above the town. The sealed mountain road to Falls Creek is one of the main access routes to Victoria's ski slopes in winter. In summer, Rocky Valley Dam near Falls Creek is a popular rowing and high-altitude athletics training camp. There are beautiful bush walks, and at the top of the High Plains in summer, there are opportunities for fishing, mountain biking, horse-riding and hang-gliding.

Bright ⑪

🏠 2,500. 🚌 ℹ️ 119 Gavan St (03) 5755 2275.

BRIGHT IS a picturesque mountain town near the head of the Ovens River Valley, with the towering rocky cliffs of Mount Buffalo to the west and the peak of the state's

second highest mountain, Mount Feathertop, to its south. The trees along Bright's main street flame into spectacular colours of red, gold, copper and brown for its Autumn Festival in April and May (see p38). In winter, the town turns into a gateway to the snow fields, with the resorts of Mount Hotham and Falls Creek in the Victorian Alps close by. In summer, swimming and fly-fishing for trout in the Ovens River are popular activities.

The spectacular **Mount Buffalo National Park** is also popular all year round; visitors can camp amid the snow gums by Lake Catani and walk its flower-flecked mountain pastures and peaks, fish for trout, hang-glide off the granite tors over the Ovens Valley or rock-climb the imposing sheer cliffs. The gracious Mount Buffalo Chalet, built by the state government in 1910, retains its old-world charm and regularly hosts summer musical events, such as Opera in the Alps (see p37). In winter, its cosy fires and grand dining room make it a popular hotel for skiers avoiding the jetset life of other resorts (see p489).

🌿 **Mount Buffalo National Park**
Mount Buffalo Rd. 🅲 13 19 63.
📷 ♿ some areas.

Buffalo River meandering through Mount Buffalo National Park

Typical 19th-century honey granite building in Beechworth

Beechworth ⑫

🏃 3,500. 🚉 ℹ️ *Shire Hall, Ford St (03) 5728 3233.*

BEAUTIFULLY sited in the foothills of the Victorian Alps, Beechworth was the centre of the great Ovens gold fields during the 1850s and 1860s *(see pp50–51)*. At the height of its boom, the town had a population of 42,000 and 61 hotels.

Today, visiting Beechworth is like stepping back in time. One of the state's best-preserved gold rush towns, it contains more than 30 19th-century buildings now classified by the National Trust. Its tree-lined streets feature granite banks and a courthouse, hotels with wide verandas and dignified brick buildings on either side. The majority of these are still in daily use, modern life continuing within edifices of a bygone era.

A large majority of the old buildings are now restaurants, and bed-and-breakfasts. Dine in the stately old bank which is now the Bank Restaurant *(see p521)*, stand in the dock of the courthouse where Ned Kelly was finally committed for his trial in Melbourne *(see p386)* and marvel at the old channel blasted through the granite to create a flow of water in which miners panned for gold.

The evocative Chinese cemetery is also worth a visit as a poignant reminder of the hundreds of Chinese who worked and died on the gold fields *(see pp50–51)*.

Chiltern ⑬

🏃 1,500. 🚉 ℹ️ *30 Main St (03) 5726 1611, (03) 5726 1537.*

THIS SLEEPY VILLAGE was once a booming gold mining town with 14 suburbs. Only 1 km (0.6 miles) off the Hume Highway, halfway between the major towns of Wangaratta and Wodonga, today its colonial architecture and quiet atmosphere, as yet unspoiled by large numbers of tourists, make a visit to this pleasant town a worthwhile experience.

Chiltern has three National Trust properties: Dow's Pharmacy; the Federal Standard newspaper office; and Lakeview House. The last is the former home of Henry

Handel Richardson, the pen name of Ethel Robertson, who wrote *The Getting of Wisdom (see p31)*. Chiltern was her childhood home. The house, on Lake Alexander, has been restored with period furniture, and gives an insight into the life of the wealthy at the turn of the 20th century.

An unusual sight is the **Famous Grapevine Attraction** museum. This shows the oldest and largest grapevine in the southern hemisphere – it once covered Chiltern's Star Hotel in its entirety.

For opening hours and other information on these attractions, check with the tourist information office in the town.

Lakeview House in Chiltern

Northeastern Wineries ⑭

🚉 *Wangaratta & Rutherglen.*
🚉 *Wangaratta & Rutherglen.*
ℹ️ *Rutherglen (02) 6032 9166; Wangaratta (03) 5721 5711.* **Campbells Winery** 📞 *(02) 6032 9458.* ◐ *9am–5pm daily.* ● *Good Fri, 25 Dec.* **Chambers Winery** 📞 *(02) 6032 8641.* ◐ *9am–5pm Mon–Sat, 11am–5pm Sun & public hols.* ● *Good Fri, 25 Dec.* **Brown Bros** 📞 *(03) 5720 5500.* ◐ *9am–5pm daily.* ● *Good Fri, 25 Dec.*

THE NORTHEASTERN area of Victoria is famous throughout the world for its vineyards and wineries *(see pp370–71)*. In a region that now spreads south to encompass the King and Ovens valleys around Glenrowan, Milawa, Everton, Rutherglen and Whitfield, the wines produced can vary in style enormously, depending on the elevation and micro-climate of each vineyard.

Rutherglen is best known for its full-bodied "Rutherglen Reds", such as Cabernet Sauvignons from 100-year-old wineries including Campbells

Rows of grapevines in one of northeastern Victoria's many vineyards

Elegant Benalla Art Gallery on the shores of Lake Benalla

and Chambers. The Muscats, Tokays and ports from both Rutherglen and Glenrowan are even more internationally renowned, with Bullers, Morris and Bailey's among the best. Rutherglen itself is a graceful town lined with antiques shops, and an abundance of hotels (see p489) and restaurants (see p522).

The grapes grown in the cool-climate region around Whitfield and Milawa make for crisp whites and lighter, softer reds. One of the more popular wineries in Northeastern Victoria is Brown Brothers at Milawa. The winery is open daily for both wine tasting and sales at the cellar door, and its excellent restaurant specializes in local delicacies from the region, including particularly good trout, cheese, honey and lamb. While at Milawa, visits to the Milawa Cheese Factory and Milawa Mustards to sample these two local products are recommended.

Iron effigy of Ned Kelly

Siege Street near the town's railway station, Kelly was finally captured after more than two years on the run. During this time he had earned almost hero status among Victoria's bush poor, particularly its many Irish Catholic farming families, as a Robin Hood-type character. Kelly knew the country around Glenrowan, especially the lovely Warby Ranges, in great detail and often used Mount Glenrowan, west of town, as a lookout. He was later hanged at Melbourne Gaol.

Today Glenrowan thrives on its Kelly history as a tourist attraction. A giant iron effigy of the bushranger greets visitors at the entrance to the town and there are various displays, museums and re-enactments depicting the full Kelly story, including his last defeat.

Glenrowan ⓯

🚶 1,000. 🚉 🚏 Wangaratta
ℹ️ Kate's Cottage, Gladstone St (03) 5766 2448.

Glenrowan was the site of the last stand by Australia's most notorious bushranger, Ned Kelly, and his gang (see p386). In a shootout with police in 1880, on

Benalla ⓰

🚶 8,500. 🚉 🚌 🚏 ℹ️ The Creators' Gallery, 14 Mair St (03) 5762 1749.

The rural town of Benalla is where Ned Kelly grew up and first appeared in court at the age of 15. Today it is most famous for its art gallery, built over Lake Benalla, which contains a fine collection of contemporary and Australian art. A Rose Festival is held in its magnificent rose gardens each November (see p37).

The town is also known as the Australian "capital" of gliding, with excellent air thermals rising from both the hot plains and nearby mountains.

Shepparton ⓱

🚶 30,000. 🚉 🚌 🚏 🚆
ℹ️ 534 Wyndham St (03) 5831 4400.

The modern city of Shepparton, at the heart of the fertile Goulburn River Valley, is often called the "fruit bowl of Australia". The vast irrigation plains around the town support Victoria's most productive pear, peach, apricot, apple, plum, cherry and kiwi fruit farms. A summer visit of the town's biggest fruit cannery, SPC, when fruit is being harvested, reveals a hive of activity.

The area's sunny climate is also ideal for grape growing. The two well-known wineries of Mitchelton and Château Tahbilk, 50 km (30 miles) south of town, are both open for tours and wine tastings (see pp370–71).

Harvesting fruit in Shepparton's orchards

TASMANIA

Tasmania's Wildlife and Wilderness

Tasmanian blue gum

Tasmania's landscape varies dramatically within its small area. Parts of Tasmania are often compared to the green pastures of England; however, the west of the state is wild and untamed. Inland there are glacial mountains and wild rivers, the habitat of flora and fauna unique to the island. More than 20 per cent of the island is now designated as a World Heritage Area *(see pp22–3).*

Russell Falls at Mount Field National Park

MOUNTAIN WILDERNESS

Inland southwest Tasmania is dominated by its glacial mountain landscape, including the beautiful Cradle Mountain – the natural symbol of the state. To the east of Cradle Mountain is the Walls of Jerusalem National Park, an isolated area of five rocky mountains. To the south is Mount Field National Park, a beautiful alpine area of glacial tarns and eucalypt forests, popular with skiers in the winter months.

Deciduous beech (Nothofagus gunnii) *is the only such native beech in Australia. The spectacular golden colours of its leaves fill the mountain areas during the autumn.*

Cradle Mountain, looking down over a glacial lake

The Bennett's wallaby (Macropus rufogriseus) *is native to Tasmania's mountain regions. A shy animal, it is most likely to be spotted at either dawn or dusk.*

COASTAL WILDERNESS

Tasmania's eastern coastline is often balmy in climate and sustains a strong fishing industry. The western coast, however, bears the full brunt of the Roaring Forties winds, whipped up across the vast expanses of ocean between the island state and the nearest land in South America. As a result, the landscape is lined with rocky beaches and raging waters, the scene of many shipwrecks during Tasmania's history.

The Tasmanian devil (Sarcophilus harrisii) *is noisy, potentially vicious and one of only three marsupial carnivores that inhabit the island.*

Banksia *comes in many varieties in Tasmania, including* Banksia serrata *and* Banksia marginata. *It is distinctive for its seed pods.*

Rugged coastline of the Tasman Peninsula

◁ **Autumn in Pine Valley, Cradle Mountain Lake St Clair National Park**

Calm area of Franklin Lower Gordon Wild River

RIVER WILDERNESS

The southwest of Tasmania is well known for its wild rivers, particularly among avid white-water rafters. The greatest wild river is the 120-km (75-mile) Franklin River, protected within Franklin-Gordon Wild Rivers National Park by its World Heritage status. This is the only undammed wild river left in Australia, and despite its some-times calm moments it often rages fiercely through gorges, rainforests and heathland.

Huon pine (Lagaro-strobus franklinii) *is found in the south-west and in the south along the Franklin-Gordon River. It is prized for its ability to withstand rot. Some examples are more than 2,000 years old.*

Brown trout (Salmo trutta), *an intro-duced species, is abundant in the wild rivers and lakes of Tasmania, and a popular catch with fly-fishers.*

The eastern quoll (Dasyurus viverrinus) *thrives in Tasmania, where there are no predatory foxes and forests are in abundance.*

PRESERVING TASMANIA'S WILDERNESS

An inhospitable climate, rugged landforms and the impenetrable scrub are among the factors that have preserved such a large proportion of Tasmania as wilderness. Although there is a long history of human habitation in what is now the World Heritage Area (Aboriginal sites date back 35,000 years), the population has always been small. The first real human threat occurred in the late 1960s when the Tasmanian government's hydro-electricity programme drowned Lake Pedder despite conservationists' protests. A proposal two decades later to dam a section of the Franklin River was defeated when the federal government intervened. The latest threat to the landscape is tourism. While many places of beauty are able to withstand visitors, others are not and people are discouraged from visiting these areas.

Protest badges

Dam protests were common occurrences in Tasmania during the 1980s, when conservationists protested against the damming of the Franklin River. The No Dams *sticker became a national symbol of protest.*

TASMANIA

HUMAN HABITATION *of Tasmania dates back 35,000 years, when Aborigines first reached the area. At this time it was linked to continental Australia, but waters rose to form the Bass Strait at the end of the Ice Age, 12,000 years ago. Dutch explorer Abel Tasman set foot on the island in 1642 and inspired its modern name. He originally called it Van Diemen's Land, after the governor of the Dutch East Indies.*

Belying its small size, Tasmania has a remarkably diverse landscape that contains glacial mountains, dense forests and rolling green hills. Its wilderness is one of only three large temperate forests in the southern hemisphere; it is also home to many plants and animals unique to the island, including a ferocious marsupial, the Tasmanian devil. Tasmanians are fiercely proud of their landscape and the island saw the rise of the world's first Green political party, the "Tasmanian Greens". One-fifth of Tasmania is protected as a World Heritage Area *(see pp22–3)*.

The Tasmanian Aboriginal population was almost wiped out with the arrival of Europeans in the 19th century, however more than 4,000 people claim Aboriginality in Tasmania today. Evidence of their link with the landscape has survived in numerous cave paintings. Many Aboriginal sites remain sacred and closed to visitors, but a few, such as the cliffs around Woolnorth, display this indigenous art for all to see.

The island's early European history has also been well preserved in its many 19th-century buildings. The first real settlement was at the waterfront site of Hobart in 1804, now Tasmania's capital and Australia's second-oldest city. From here, European settlement spread throughout the state, with the development of farms and villages, built and worked by convict labour.

Today, Tasmania is a haven for wildlife lovers, hikers and fly-fishermen, who come to experience the island's many national parks and forests. The towns scattered throughout the state, such as Richmond and Launceston, with their rich colonial histories, are well worth a visit, and make excellent bases from which to explore the surrounding wilderness.

The historic port area of Battery Point in Hobart

◁ Breathtaking natural scenery in the Walls of Jerusalem National Park

Exploring Tasmania

Part, and yet not a part, of Australia, Tasmania's distinctive landscape, climate and culture are largely due to its 300-km (185-mile) distance from the mainland. The isolation has left a legacy of unique flora and fauna, fresh air, an abundance of water and a relaxed lifestyle. More than 27 per cent of Tasmania's land surface is given over to agriculture, with the emphasis on wine and fine foods. The state also benefits from vast expanses of open space, since approximately 40 per cent of Tasmanians live in the capital, Hobart. Tasmania, therefore, offers the perfect opportunity for a relaxing holiday in tranquil surroundings.

Nelson Falls in Franklin-Gordon Wild Rivers National Park

Yachts in Constitution Dock, Hobart

STANLEY

17 WOOLNORTH **15**

MARRAWAH SMITHTON

Arthur River

BURNIE

14

DEVONPO

WARATAH

ROSEBERY

ZEEHAN

Southern Ocean

CRADLE MOUNTAIN LAKE ST CLAIR NATIONAL PARK

18

QUEENSTOWN

STRAHAN

20 FRANKLIN-GORDON WILD RIVERS NATIONAL PARK

19 MACQUARIE HARBOUR

MOUNT FI NATIONAL PA

SOUTHW NATION PARK

KING ISLAND

0 km 15

0 miles 15

KING ISLAND

16 KING ISLAND

B25

KING ISLAND

TASMANIA

0 km 25

0 miles 25

SEE ALSO

• *Where to Stay* pp490–91

• *Where to Eat* pp522–3

Getting Around

Within this small, compact island, traffic is rarely a problem, and any visitor can journey across the diverse landscape with little difficulty. While all major cities and towns are linked by fast highways and major roads, some of the most splendid mountain, lake, coastal and rural scenery lies off the key routes, along the many alternative and easily accessible country roads. A car is recommended, but coach services run between most towns and to some of the state's natural attractions.

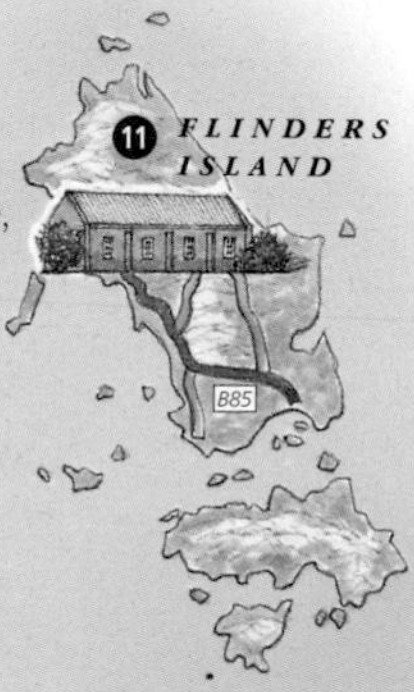

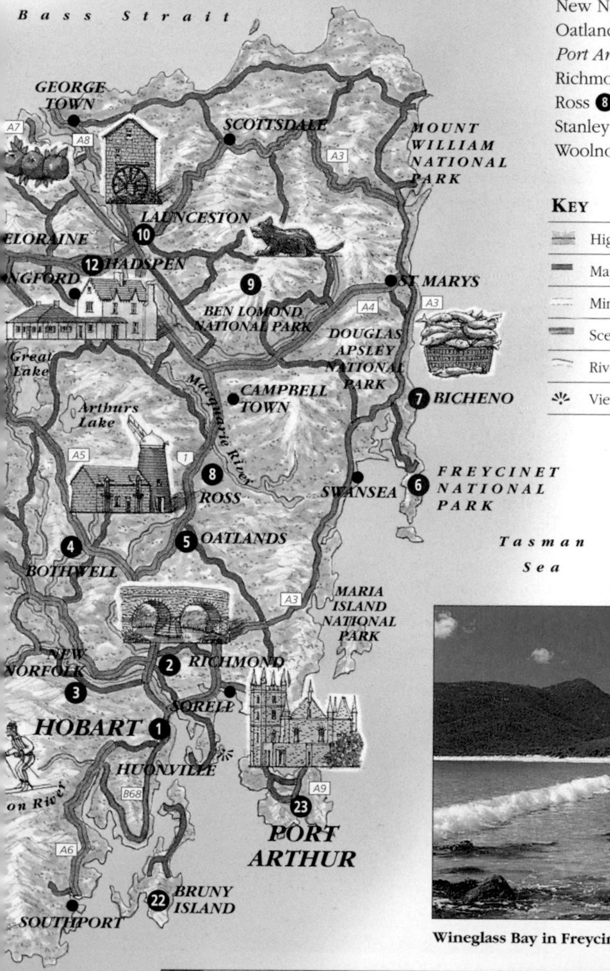

Sights at a Glance

Ben Lomond National Park 9
Bicheno 7
Bothwell 4
Bruny Island 22
Burnie 14
Cradle Mountain Lake St Clair National Park 18
Devonport 13
Flinders Island 11
Franklin-Gordon Wild Rivers National Park 20
Freycinet National Park 6
Hadspen 12
Hobart pp448–9 1
King Island 16
Launceston 10
Macquarie Harbour 19
Mount Field National Park 21
New Norfolk 3
Oatlands 5
Port Arthur pp458–9 23
Richmond 2
Ross 8
Stanley 15
Woolnorth 17

Key

- Highway
- Major road
- Minor road
- Scenic route
- River
- Viewpoint

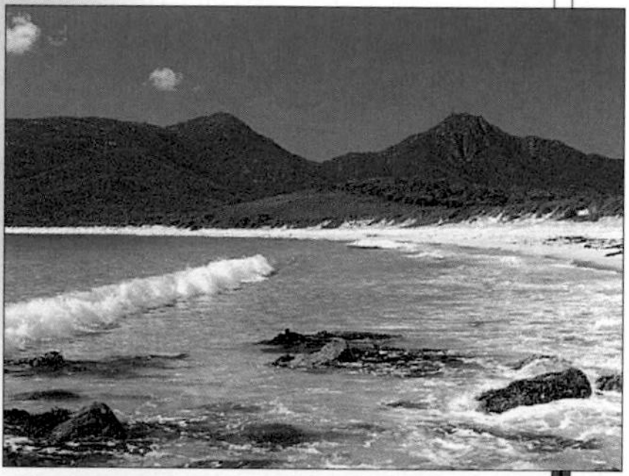

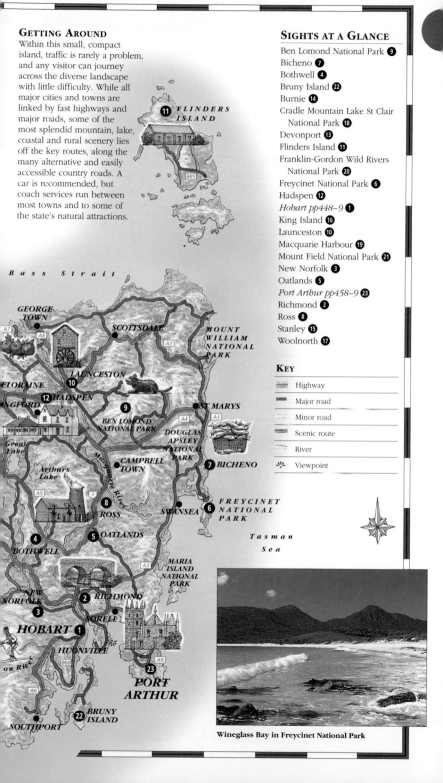

Wineglass Bay in Freycinet National Park

Hobart ①

Hobart phone box

SPREAD OVER seven hills between the banks of the Derwent River and the summit of Mount Wellington, Australia's second oldest city has an incredible waterfront location, similar to that of her "big sister", Sydney. Hobart began life on the waterfront and the maritime atmosphere is still an important aspect of the city. From Old Wharf, where the first arrivals settled, round to the fishing village of Battery Point, the area known as Sullivans Cove is still the hub of this cosmopolitan city. Like the rest of the state, the capital city makes the most of its natural surroundings.

General view of Hobart and its docks on the Derwent River

🚇 Constitution Dock
Davey St.
The main anchorage for fishing boats and yachts also serves as the finish line of the annual Sydney to Hobart Yacht Race. This famous race attracts an international field of competitors. After a Boxing Day start, most sailors dock here in time for New Year celebrations *(see p37).*

Constitution Dock borders the city and the old slum district of Wapping, which has now been redeveloped. Many of the old warehouses have also been restored to include restaurants and cafés. One such warehouse houses the state's most idiosyncratic seafaring restaurant, The Drunken Admiral, with its bizarre collection of maritime paraphernalia.

🚇 Parliament House
Salamanca Place. 【 (03) 6233 2200.
☐ Mon–Fri. ● public hols. 🚻 🛗
non-sitting days.
One of the oldest civic buildings in Hobart, Parliament House was designed by the colonial architect John Lee Archer and built by convicts between 1835 and 1841. The House of Assembly and cellars of the building are now open for public tours.

🏛 Tasmanian Museum and Art Gallery
40 Macquarie St. 【 (03) 6211 4177.
☐ daily. ● Good Fri, 25 April, 25 Dec. 🚻 🛗
This 1863 building, designed by the city's best-known colonial architect, Henry Hunter, is now home to a fine collection of early prints and paintings of Tasmania, Aboriginal artifacts, as well as botanical displays of native flora.

🚇 Theatre Royal
29 Campbell St. 【 (03) 6233 2299.
Auditorium ☐ Mon–Sat. ● public hols. 🎭 for shows only. 🚻 🛗
Built in 1837, this is the oldest theatre in Australia. Almost gutted by fire in the 1960s, the ornate decor has since been meticulously restored. Many notable actors rate this one of the most charming theatres in the world.

🚇 Criminal Courts and Penitentiary Chapel
6 Brisbane St. 【 (03) 6231 0911.
☐ daily. ● Good Fri, 25 Dec. 🎭 🛗 obligatory.
In colonial days, courts and prison chapels were often set next to each other, making the dispensing of swift judgment convenient. The complex also exhibits underground passages, solitary confinement cells and an execution yard.

🚇 Salamanca Place
Once the site of early colonial industries, from jam-making to metal foundry and flour milling, this graceful row of sandstone warehouses at Salamanca Place is now the heart of Hobart's lively atmosphere and creative spirit.

Mount Wellington towers above the buildings lining the waterfront, which have been converted into art and craft galleries, antique furniture stores and antiquarian book shops. The Salamanca Arts Centre includes contemporary artists' studios, theatres and exhibition galleries. The area also has some of the city's best pubs, cafés and restaurants *(see pp522–3).*

Bustling Saturday market in Salamanca Place

The quarter's pulse reaches a peak every Saturday morning, with the famous Salamanca Market. Arts, crafts and fresh food fill the stalls, attracting crowds of people.

🏛 Battery Point

☎ *(03) 6223 7570 for historic tours.*

This maritime village grew up on the hilly promontory adjacent to the early settlement and wharves. The strategic site, with its views down to the Derwent River, was originally home to a gun battery, positioned to ward off potential enemy invasions. The old guardhouse, built in 1818, now lies within a leafy park, just a few minutes' walk from Hampden Road with its range of antiques shops, art galleries, tea-rooms and restaurants.

Battery Point retains a strong sense of history, with its narrow gas-lit streets lined with tiny fishermen's and workers' houses, cottage gardens and colonial mansions and pubs, such as the Shipwright's Arms. The informative Hobart Heritage Walks depart daily at 10am from the Visitors Centre on Davey and Elizabeth streets.

🏛 Maritime Museum

Cnr Davey & Argyle sts. ☎ *(03) 6234 1427.* ○ *daily.* ● *Good Fri, 25 Dec.* 📷 ♿

Steeped in seafaring history, the Maritime Museum is housed in the Carnegie Building, the former Hobart Public Library It contains a fascinating collection of old relics, manuscripts and voyage documents, as well as an important photographic collection which records Tasmania's maritime history.

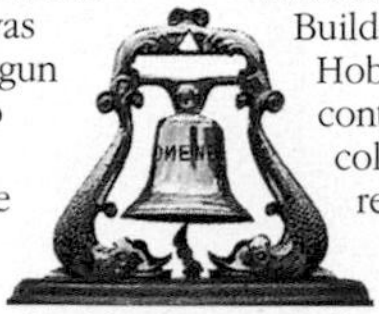

Maritime Museum bell

🏛 Castray Esplanade

Castray Esplanade was originally planned in the 19th century as a riverside walking track and it still provides the most pleasurable short stroll within the city.

> **Visitors' Checklist**
>
> Hobart. 👥 *195,000.* ✈ *20 km (12 miles) NE of the city.* 🚌 *Tasmanian Red Line Coaches, Transit Centre, 199 Collins St.* ℹ *20 Davey St (03) 6230 8233.* 🎉 *Sydney–Hobart Yacht Race (26–29 Dec).*

En route are the old colonial Commissariat Stores. These have now been beautifully renovated for inner-city living, architects' offices and art galleries, focussing on Tasmanian arts and crafts.

🏛 Narryna Heritage Museum

103 Hampden Rd, Battery Point.

☎ *(03) 6234 2791.* ○ *10:30am–5pm Tue-Fri, 2–5pm Sat & Sun.*

Located in an elegant 1836 Georgian house, called Narryna, in Battery Point, this is the oldest folk museum in Australia. The beautiful grounds make a fine backdrop for an impressive collection of early Tasmanian pioneering relics.

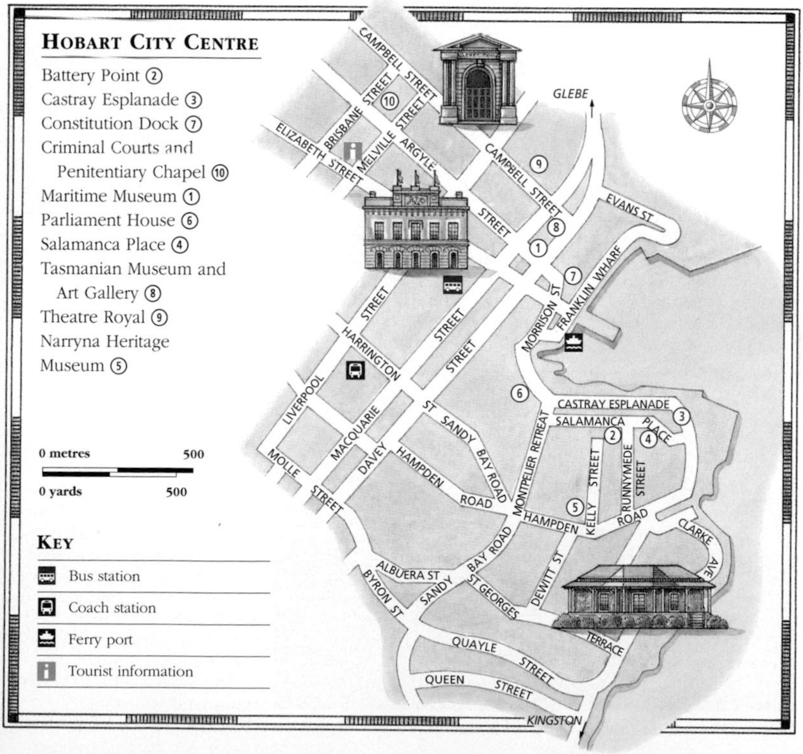
HOBART CITY CENTRE
Battery Point 2
Castray Esplanade 3
Constitution Dock 7
Criminal Courts and Penitentiary Chapel 10
Maritime Museum 1
Parliament House 6
Salamanca Place 4
Tasmanian Museum and Art Gallery 8
Theatre Royal 9
Narryna Heritage Museum 5
0 metres 500
0 yards 500
KEY
Bus station
Coach station
Ferry port
Tourist information
CAMPBELL STREET
BRISBANE STREET
MELVILLE STREET
ELIZABETH STREET
ARGYLE STREET
GLEBE
EVANS ST
FRANKLIN WHARF
MORRISON ST
HARRINGTON STREET
LIVERPOOL STREET
MACQUARIE STREET
DAVEY STREET
MOLLE STREET
SANDY BAY ROAD
HAMPDEN ROAD
CASTRAY ESPLANADE
SALAMANCA PLACE
MONTPELIER RETREAT
KELLY STREET
RUNNYMEDE STREET
CLARKE AVE
DEWITT ST
ALBUERA ST
BYRON ST
ST GEORGES TERRACE
QUAYLE STREET
QUEEN STREET
KINGSTON

Hop farm on the Derwent River in New Norfolk

Richmond ❷

🏚 800. 🚌 ℹ️ *Old Hobart Town, Bridge St (03) 6260 2502.*

IN THE HEART of the countryside, 26 km (16 miles) from Hobart, lies the quaint village of Richmond. This was the first area granted to free settlers from England for farming, and at its centre they established a township reminiscent of their homeland. Richmond now includes some of Australia's oldest colonial architecture. Most of the buildings were constructed by convicts, including the sandstone bridge built in 1823, the gaol of 1825 and the Roman Catholic Church of 1834.

Today, Richmond is a lively centre for rural artists and artisans. On the main street, between the old general store and post office, they occupy many of the historic homes and cottages.

New Norfolk ❸

🏚 5,900. 🚌 ℹ️ *Circle St (03) 6261 0700.*

FROM HOBART, the Derwent River heads north, then veers west through the Derwent River Valley. The hop farms and oast houses along the willow-lined river are testimony to the area's history of brewing.

At the centre of the valley, 38 km (24 miles) from Hobart, is the town of New Norfolk. Many of the first settlers in the region abandoned the colonial settlement of Norfolk Island to come here, hence the name. One of Tasmania's classified historic towns, it contains many interesting buildings, such as the Bush Inn of 1815, which claims to be one of Australia's oldest licensed pubs.

Typical 19th-century building in Bothwell

Bothwell ❹

🏚 400. 🚌 ℹ️ *Australasian Golf Museum, Market Place (03) 6259 4033.*

NESTLED IN THE Clyde River Valley, Bothwell's wide streets are set along a river of the same name, formerly known as the "Fat Doe" river after a town in Scotland. The area's names were assigned by early Scottish settlers, who arrived from Hobart Town in 1817 with their families and 18-l (5-gal) kegs of rum loaded on bullock wagons.

The town's heritage is now preserved with some 50 National Trust buildings dating

Richmond Bridge, constructed with local sandstone

from the 1820s, including the Castle Hotel, the Masonic Hall (now an art gallery), Bothwell Grange Guest House and the Old Schoolhouse, now home to the Australasian Golf Museum. The stone heads above the door of the Presbyterian St Luke's Church depict a Celtic god and goddess. Even the town's golf course has a claim on history as the oldest in Australia, as it was laid out in the 1820s.

The town lies at the centre of the historic sheep-farming district of Bothwell, stretching along Lakes Hwy from the southern midlands to the famous trout fishing area of the Great Lakes. It is also the gateway to the ruggedly beautiful Central Plateau Conservation Area – a tableland which rises abruptly from the surrounding flat countryside to an average height of 600 m (nearly 2,000 ft).

Oatlands ❺

🏃 550. 🚗 ℹ️ *Central Tasmanian Tourism Centre, 85 High St (03) 6254 1212.*

Oᴀᴛʟᴀɴᴅs was one of a string of military stations established in 1813 during the construction of the old Midlands Hwy by convict chain gangs. Colonial Governor Lachlan Macquarie ordered the building of the road in 1811, to connect the southern settlement of Hobart *(see pp448–9)* with the northern settlement of Launceston *(see p453)*. During a later trip, he chose locations for the townships en route, naming them after places in the British Isles. The road ran through the area of Tasmania corresponding in name and geography to that of the British Midlands region, giving it its original name, but since the 1990s it has been dubbed the Heritage Hwy.

Oatlands soon became one of the colonial coaching stops for early travellers. Today, it has the richest endowment of Georgian buildings in the country, mostly made of local sandstone, including the 1829 courthouse and St Peter's Church (1838). As a result,

Coles Bay, backed by the Hazards Mountains, Freycinet Peninsula

the township is classified by the National Trust. Its most distinctive building, the Oatlands Flour Mill, was in operation until 1890.

Distinctive façade of the Oatlands Flour Mill

Freycinet National Park ❻

🚗 *from Bicheno.* **Parks and wildlife station** 📞 *(03) 6257 0107.* ⏰ *9am–5pm daily.* ⚫ *25 Dec.*

Tʜᴇ ғʀᴇʏᴄɪɴᴇᴛ ᴘᴇɴɪɴsᴜʟᴀ on the east coast of Tasmania is a long, narrow neck of land jutting south, dominated by the granite peaks of the Hazards Mountain Range. Named after an early French maritime explorer, the peninsula consists of ocean beaches on its eastern rim and secluded coves and inlets to the west. The fishing village of Coles Bay lies in the largest cove, backed by the Hazards.

Freycinet National Park on the tip of the peninsula is criss-crossed with walking tracks along beaches, over mountains, around headlands

and across lagoons. The most popular walk is Wineglass Bay – a short, steep trip up and over the saddle of the mountains. The blue waters of the bay are cupped against a crescent of golden sand, which inspired the name.

The drive up the east coast is a highlight of Tasmania. There are ocean views, cliffs, sandy coves and marshlands inhabited by black swans. There are many small towns en route such as Orford and Swansea for overnight stays.

Bicheno ❼

🏃 750. 🚗 ℹ️ *Bicheno Penguin Tours, Tasman Hwy (03) 6375 1333.*

Tᴏɢᴇᴛʜᴇʀ ᴡɪᴛʜ Coles Bay, Bicheno is the holiday centre of Tasmania's east coast. In summer, the bay is is very popular due to its sheltered location, which means temperatures are always a few degrees warmer than elsewhere in the state.

The area also includes Tasmania's smallest national park, the 16,080 ha (39,700 acre) Douglas Apsley National Park. It contains the state's largest dry sclerophyll forest, patches of rainforest, river gorges, waterfalls and spectacular views along the coast. This varied landscape can be taken in along a three-day north to south walking track through the park. The north of the park is only accessible by 4WD. Other attractions in the area include the Apsley Gorge Winery and a 3-km long penguin breeding colony.

Man-O-Ross Hotel at the Four Corners of Ross crossroads

Ross ❽

🏛 *300.* 🚌 ℹ️ *Tasmanian Wool Centre, Church St (03) 6381 5466.*

SET ON THE BANKS of the Macquarie River, Ross, like Oatlands (*see p451*), was once a military station and coaching stop along the Midlands Hwy. It lies at the heart of the richest sheep farming district in Tasmania, internationally recognized for its fine merino wool. Some of the large rural homesteads in the area have remained within the same families since the 1820s when the village was settled.

The town's most famous sight is Ross Bridge, built by convict labour and opened in 1836. It features 186 unique carvings by convict sculptor Daniel Herbert, who was given a Queen's Pardon for his intricate work. The town centres on its historic crossroads, the Four Corners of Ross: "Temptation,

Man O'Ross hotel sign

Damnation, Salvation and Recreation". These are represented respectively on each corner by the Man-O-Ross Hotel, the jail, the church and the town hall.

Ben Lomond National Park ❾

🚠 *when ski slopes are open.* ℹ️ *Gateway Tasmania Travel Centre, cnr St John & Paterson sts, Launceston (03) 6336 3133.* 📷

IN THE HINTERLANDS between the Midlands and the east coast, 50 km (30 miles) southeast of Launceston, Ben Lomond is the highest mountain in northern Tasmania and home to one of the state's two main ski slopes. The 16,000-ha (40,000-acre) national park surrounding the mountain covers an alpine plateau of barren and dramatic scenery, with views stretching over the northeast of the

state. The vegetation includes alpine daisies and carnivorous sundew plants. The park is also home to wallabies, wombats and possums. From Conara Junction on the Heritage Hwy, take the Esk Main Road east before turning off towards Ben Lomond National Park.

The mountain's foothills have been devastated by decades of mining and forestry, and many of the townships, such as Rossarden and Avoca, have since suffered an economic decline. The road through the South Esk Valley along the Esk River loops back to the valley's main centre of Fingal. From here, you can continue through the small township of St Marys before joining the Tasman Hwy and travelling up the east coast.

Launceston ❿

🏛 *67,000.* ✈ 🚌 🚏 *Georgetown* ⛴ *summer only.* ℹ️ *Gateway Tasmania Travel Centre, cnr St John & Paterson sts (03) 6336 3133.*

IN COLONIAL DAYS, the coach ride between Tasmania's capital, Hobart, and the township of Launceston took a full day, but today the 200-km (125-mile) route is flat and direct. Nestling in the Tamar River Valley, Launceston was settled in 1804 and is Australia's third-oldest city. It has a charming ambience of old buildings, parks, gardens, riverside walks, craft galleries and hilly streets lined with

Alpine plateau in Ben Lomond National Park, backed by Ben Lomond Mountain

Riverside view of Penny Royal World in Launceston

weatherboard houses. The **Queen Victoria Museum and Art Gallery** has the country's largest provincial display of colonial art, along with an impressive modern collection. It also shows Aboriginal and convict relics, and has displays on minerals, flora and fauna of the region.

Penny Royal World in Paterson Street is a complex of historic windmills, corn mills and gunpowder mills, moved from their original locations stone by stone. The working replica of a 19th-century gunpowder mill has 14 barges that take visitors underground to observe the production process. All the mills are linked with museums, restaurants and accommodation via a restored tram.

Cataract Gorge Reserve is alive with birds, wallabies, pademelons, potoroos and bandicoots, only a 15-minute walk from the city centre. A chairlift, believed to have the longest central span in the world, provides a striking aerial overview.

🏛 **Penny Royal World**
147 Paterson St, Launceston.
☎ (03) 6331 6699. ◷ Jan–Apr:
9am–4:30pm daily. ● May–Dec.
◪ & limited.

🏛 **Queen Victoria Museum and Art Gallery**
2 Wellington St, Launceston.
☎ (03) 6323 3777. ◷ 10am–5pm
daily. ● Good Fri, 25 Dec. &

ENVIRONS: In the 1830s, the Norfolk Plains was a farmland district owned mainly by wealthy settlers who had been enticed to the area by land grants. The small town of **Longford**, with its historic inns and churches, is still the centre of a rich agricultural district renowned for stock farming. It also has the greatest concentration of colonial mansions in the state. Many, such as Woolmers and Brickendon, are open for public tours.

Cape Barren geese in the Patriarch Sanctuary on Cape Barren Island

Flinders Island ⓫

✕ from Launceston, Melbourne
⛴ from Launceston, Bridport.
ℹ Gateway Tasmania Travel Centre,
cnr St John & Paterson sts,
Launceston (03) 6336 3133.

ON THE NORTHEASTERN tip of Tasmania, in the waters of the Bass Strait, Flinders Island is the largest within the Furneaux Island Group. These 50 or so dots in the ocean are

all that remains of the land bridge which once spanned the strait to the continental mainland *(see pp18–19)*.

Flinders Island was also the destination for the last surviving 133 Tasmanian Aborigines. With the consent of the British administration, the Reverend George Augustus Robinson brought all 133 of them here in the 1830s. His aim was to "save" them from extinction by civilizing them according to European traditions and converting them to Christianity. In 1847, however, greatly diminished by disease and despair, the 47 survivors were transferred to Oyster Cove, a sacred Aboriginal site south of Hobart, and the plan was deemed a failure. Within a few years, all full-blooded Tasmanian Aborigines had died.

Much of Flinders is now preserved as a natural reserve, including Strezelecki National Park, which is particularly popular with hikers. Off the island's south coast is Cape Barren Island, home to the Patriarch Sanctuary, a protected geese reserve.

Flinders Island is reached by air from Launceston and Melbourne. There is also a leisurely ferry trip aboard the *Matthew Flinders* from Launceston and the small coastal town of Bridport.

Entally House in Hadspen

Hadspen **⑫**

🏘 1,700. 🚍 ℹ️ *Gateway Tasmania Travel Centre, cnr St John & Paterson sts, Launceston (03) 6336 3133.*

H EADING WEST along the Bass Highway, a string of historic towns pepper the countryside from Longford through to Deloraine, surrounded by the Great Western Tiers Mountains. The tiny town of Hadspen is a picturesque strip of Georgian cottages and buildings which include an old 1845 coaching house.

The town is also home to one of Tasmania's most famous historic homes open to the public. Built in 1819 on the bank of the South Esk River, the beautiful **Entally House**, with its gracious veranda, has its own chapel, stables, horse-drawn carriages and lavish 19th-century furnishings.

Period furniture in Entally House

🏛 **Entally House**
Old Bass Hwy, via Hadspen. 📞 (03) 6393 6201. ◯ *daily.* ● *Good Fri, 25 Dec.* 🎦 ♿

Devonport **⑬**

🏘 23,000. ✈ 🚍 🚌 ⛴
ℹ️ *Devonport Visitor Centre, 92 Formby Rd (03) 6424 4466.*

N AMED AFTER the county of Devon in England, the state's third-largest city is strategically sited as a river and sea port. It lies at the junction of the Mersey River and the Bass Strait, on the north coast. The dramatic

rocky headland of Mersey Bluff is 1 km (0.6 miles) from the city centre, linked by a coastal reserve and parklands. Here Aboriginal rock paintings mark the entrance of **Tiagarra**, the Tasmanian Aboriginal art and culture centre, with its collection of more than 2,000 ancient artifacts.

From Devonport, the overnight car and passenger ferry *Spirit of Tasmania* sails to the Port of Melbourne on the mainland several times each week. With a local airport, Devonport is also an excellent starting point for touring northern Tasmania. Heading northwest, the old coast road offers unsurpassed views of the Bass Strait.

🏛 **Tiagarra**
Mersey Bluff, Devonport. 📞 (03) 6424 8250. ◯ *9am–5pm daily.* ● *Good Fri, 25 Dec.* 🎦 ♿

Burnie **⑭**

🏘 16,000. ✈ 🚍 🚌 ℹ️ *Civic Square Precinct (03) 6434 6111.*

F URTHER ALONG the northern coast from Devonport is Tasmania's fourth-largest city, founded in 1829. Along its main streets are many attractive 19th-century buildings decorated with wrought ironwork. Until recently, Burnie's prosperity centred on a thriving wood-pulping industry. One of the state's main enterprises, Associated Pulp and Paper Mills, established in 1938, was sited here. The city in recent times

has shed its industrial character, although some industry survives, notably the Lactos company, which has won many awards for its French- and Swiss-style cheeses. The factory is open for tours and cheese tastings.

Burnie also has a number of gardens, including Fern Glade, where platypuses are often seen. Situated on Emu Bay, the area's natural attractions include forest reserves, fossil cliffs, waterfalls and canyons and panoramic ocean views from nearby Round Hill.

"The Nut" chairlift in Stanley

Stanley **⑮**

🏘 470. 🚍 ℹ️ *Stanley Visitors Centre, 45 Main Rd (03) 6458 1330.*

T HE ROCKY promontory of Circular Head, known locally as "the Nut", rises 152 m (500 ft) above sea level and looms over the fishing village of Stanley. A chairlift up the rock face offers striking views of the area.

Stanley's quiet main street runs towards the wharf, lined with fishermen's cottages and many bluestone buildings dating from the 1840s. Stanley also contains numerous top-quality bed-and-breakfasts and cafés serving fresh, local seafood *(see p523).*

Nearby, **Highfield House** was the original headquarters of the Van Diemen's Land

Company, a London-based agricultural holding set up in 1825. The home and grounds of its colonial overseer are now open for public tours.

⊞ Highfield House
Greenhills Rd, via Stanley. **(** (03) 6458 1100. **○** Oct–Apr: 10am–4pm daily. **●** May–Sep. **◙**

King Island ⑯

⊠ **ℹ** Tasmanian Travel and Information Centre, cnr Davey & Elizabeth sts, Hobart (03) 6230 8233.

LYING OFF THE northwestern coast of Tasmania in the Bass Strait, King Island is a popular location for wildlife lovers. Muttonbirds and sea elephants are among the unusual attractions.

Divers also frequent the island, fascinated by the ship-wrecks that lie nearby. The island is also noted for its cheese, beef and seafood.

Woolnorth ⑰

Via Smithton. **ℹ** Woolnorth Rd (03) 6452 1493. **◙** obligatory.

THE HUGE sheep, cattle and dairy farming property on the outskirts of Smithton is the only remaining land holding of the Van Diemen's Land Company. The last four Tasmanian tigers held in captivity were caught in the bush backing on to Wool-

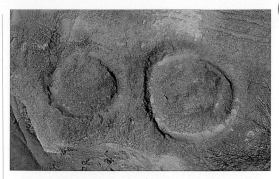

Aboriginal rock carvings in Woolnorth

north in 1908. Day-long tours of the property, booked in advance, include a lunch of local beef fillet and a trip to Cape Grim, known for the cleanest air in the world.

Cradle Mountain Lake St Clair National Park ⑱

▣ Cradle Mountain, Lake St Clair. **ℹ** Cradle Mountain (03) 6492 1110 (pre-book shuttle from gate to visitor area); Lake St Clair (03) 6289 1172. **◙ ♿**

THE DISTINCTIVE jagged peaks of Cradle Mountain are now recognized as an international symbol of the state's natural environment. The second-highest mountain in Tasmania reaches 1,560 m (5,100 ft) at the northern end of the 161,000-ha (400,000-acre) this national park. The

park then stretches 80 km (50 miles) south to the shores of Lake St Clair, the deepest freshwater lake in Australia.

In 1922, the area became a national park, founded by Austrian nature enthusiast Gustav Weindorfer. His memory lives on in his forest home Waldheim Chalet, now a heritage lodge in Weindorfer's Forest. Nearby at Ronny Creek is the registration point for the celebrated Overland Track, which traverses the park through scenery ranging from rainforest, alpine moors, buttongrass plains and water-fall valleys. Walking the track takes an average of five days, stopping overnight in tents or huts. At the halfway mark is Mount Ossa, the state's highest peak at 1,617 m (5,300 ft). In May, the park is ablaze with the autumn colours of Tasmania's deciduous beech *Nothofagus gunnii*, commonly known as "Fagus" *(see p442)*.

Lake St Clair backed by the jagged peaks of Cradle Mountain

Boats sailing on the deceptively calm waters of Macquarie Harbour

Macquarie Harbour ⑲

🚌 Strahan. 🛈 Strahan (03) 6471 7622.

OFF THE WILD, western coast of Tasmania there is nothing but vast stretches of ocean until the southern tip of Argentina, on the other side of the globe. The region bears the full brunt of the "Roaring Forties" – the name given to the tremendous winds that whip southwesterly off the Southern Ocean.

In this hostile environment, Tasmania's Aborigines survived for thousands of years before European convicts were sent here in the 1820s and took over the land. Their harsh and isolated settlement was a penal station on Sarah Island, situated in the middle of Macquarie Harbour.

The name of the harbour's mouth, "Hell's Gates", reflects conditions endured by both seamen and convicts – shipwrecks, drownings, suicides and murders all occurred here. Abandoned in 1833 for the "model prison" of Port Arthur *(see pp458–9)*, Sarah Island and its penal settlement ruins can be viewed on a guided boat tour available from the fishing port of Strahan.

Strahan grew up around an early timber industry supported by convict labour. It became well-known in the early 1980s when protesters from across Australia came to Strahan to fight government plans to flood the wild and beautiful Franklin River for a hydroelectric scheme. A fascinating exhibition at the visitor centre in Strahan charts the drama of Australia's most famous environmental protest.

Strahan today is one of Tasmania's loveliest towns, with its old timber buildings, scenic port and natural backdrop of fretted mountains and dense bushland. The town's newest attraction is a restored 1896 railway, which travels 35 km (22 miles) across rivers and mountains to the old mining settlement at Queenstown.

Franklin-Gordon Wild Rivers National Park ⑪

🚌 Strahan. 🛈 Strahan (03) 6471 7622.

ONE OF AUSTRALIA'S great wild river systems flows through southwest Tasmania. This spectacular region consists of high ranges and deep gorges. The Franklin-Gordon Wild Rivers National Park extends southeast from Macquarie Harbour and is one of four national parks in the western part of Tasmania that make up the Tasmanian Wilderness World Heritage Area *(see pp22–3)*. The park takes its name from the Franklin and Gordon rivers, both of which were saved by conservationists in 1983.

Within the park's 442,000 ha (1,090,000 acres) are vast tracts of cool temperate rainforest, as well as waterfalls and dolerite- and quartzite-capped mountains. The flora within the park is as varied as the landscape, with impenetrable horizontal scrub, lichen-coated trees, pandani plants and the endemic conifers, King William, celery top and Huon pines. The easiest way into this largely trackless wilderness is via a boat cruise from Strahan. Visitors can disembark and take a short walk to see a 2,000-year-old Huon pine. The park also contains the rugged peak of

Imposing Frenchmans Cap looming over the Franklin-Gordon Wild Rivers National Park

Idyllic, deserted beach on the rugged Bruny Island

Frenchmans Cap, accessible to experienced bushwalkers. The Franklin River is also renowned for its rapids, which challenge whitewater rafters.

The Wild Way, linking Hobart with the west coast, runs through the park. Sections of the river and forest can be reached from the main road along short tracks. Longer walks into the heart of the park require a higher level of survival skills and equipment.

Russell Falls in Mount Field National Park

Mount Field National Park ㉑

📷 🏨 (03) 6288 1149. 🏞

LITTLE MORE THAN 70 km (45 miles) from Hobart along the Maydena Road, Mount Field National Park's proximity and beauty make it a popular location with nature-loving tourists. As a day trip from the state capital, it offers easy access and a diversity of Tasmanian vegetation and wildlife along well-maintained walking tracks.

The most popular walk is also the shortest: the 10-minute trail to Russell Falls starts out from just within the park's entrance through a temperate rainforest environment. Lake Dobson car park is 15 km (9.5 miles) from the park's entrance up a steep gravel path. This is the beginning of several other short walks and some more strenuous day walks.

Truganini, the Bruny Island Aborigine

The 10-km (6-mile) walk to Tarn Shelf is a bushwalker's paradise, especially in autumn, when the glacial lakes, mountains and valleys are spectacularly highlighted by the red-orange hues of the deciduous beech trees. Longer trails lead up to the higher peaks of Mount Field West and Mount Mawson, southern Tasmania's premier ski slope.

Bruny Island ㉒

📷 to Kettering, Mon–Fri only.
⛴ from Kettering. 🏨 Bruny D'Entrecasteaux Visitors' Centre, ferry terminal, Kettering (03) 6267 4494.

ON HOBART'S back doorstep, yet a world away in landscape and atmosphere, the Huon Valley and D'Entrecasteaux Channel can be enjoyed over several hours or days. In total, the trip south from Hobart, through the town of Huonville, the Hartz Mountains and Southport, the southernmost town in the country, is only 100 km (60 miles). On the other side of the channel are the orchards, craft outlets and vineyards around Cygnet.

The attractive marina of Kettering, just 40 minutes' drive from Hobart, is the departure point for a regular ferry service to Bruny Island.

The name Bruny Island actually applies to two islands joined by a narrow neck. The south island townships of Adventure Bay and Alonnah are only a half-hour drive from the ferry terminal in the north. Once home to a thriving colonial whaling industry, Bruny Island is now a haven for bird-watchers, boaters, swimmers and camel riders along its sheltered bays, beaches and lagoons.

Unfortunately, Bruny Island also has a sadder side to its history. Truganini, of the Wuenonne people of Bruny Island, is said to have been one of Tasmania's last full-blooded Aborigines. It was also from the aptly named Missionary Bay on the island that Reverend Robinson began his ill-fated campaign to round up the indigenous inhabitants of Tasmania for incarceration (see p453).

Port Arthur ㉓

Handcuffs from Port Arthur museum

PORT ARTHUR was established in 1830 as a timber station and a prison settlement for repeat offenders. While transportation to the island colony from the mainland ceased in 1853, the prison remained in operation until 1877, by which time some 12,000 men had passed through what was commonly regarded as the harshest institution of its kind in the British Empire. Punishments included incarceration in the Model Prison, a separate building from the main penitentiary, where inmates were subjected to sensory deprivation and extreme isolation in the belief that such methods promoted "moral reform". Between 1979 and 1986, a conservation project was undertaken to restore the prison ruins. The 40-ha (100-acre) site is now Tasmania's most popular tourist attraction.

Commandant's House
One of the first houses at Port Arthur, this cottage has now been restored and furnished in early 19th-century style.

The Semaphore was a series of flat, mounted planks that could be arranged in different configurations, in order to send messages to Hobart and across the peninsula.

The Guard Tower was constructed in 1835 in order to prevent escapes from the prison and pilfering from the Commissariat Store, which the tower overlooked.

To Isle of the Dead cemetery

JETTY ROAD

0 metres   50
0 yards   50

★ **Penitentiary**
This building was thought to be the largest in Australia at the time of its construction in 1844. Originally a flour mill, it was converted into a penitentiary in the 1850s and housed almost 500 prisoners in dormitories and cells.

STAR FEATURES

★ **Model Prison**

★ **Penitentiary**

Hospital
This sandstone building was completed in 1842 with four wards of 18 beds each. The basement housed the kitchen with its own oven, and a morgue, known as the "dead room".

The Paupers' Mess was the dining area for poor prisoners.

Museum and café

Asylum
By 1872, Port Arthur's asylum housed more than 100 mentally ill or senile convicts. When the settlement closed, it became the town hall, but now serves as a museum and café.

CAMP STREET

ON STREET

Trenthan Cottage

★ Model Prison
Influenced by Pentonville Prison in London, this 1840s design was thought to provide "humane" punishment. Convicts lived in 50 separate cells in silence and anonymity, referred to by number not by name.

CHURCH STREET

Government Cottage
was built in 1853 and was used by visiting dignitaries and government officials.

Church
Built in 1836, Port Arthur's church was never consecrated because it was used by all denominations. The building was gutted by fire in 1884, but the ruins are now fully preserved.

TRAVELLERS' NEEDS

WHERE TO STAY

THE WIDE RANGE of places to stay in Australia is a reflection of the country's size, diversity and emergence as a major tourist destination. There are tropical island resorts, luxury and "boutique" city hotels, ski lodges, converted shearers' quarters on vast sheep stations, colonial cottage bed-and-breakfasts, self-catering apartments,

Sydney hotel doorman

youth hostels, houseboats and, of course, all the usual international chain hotels. Whether you simply want a bed for the night or an all-inclusive holiday resort, the appropriate accommodation can always be found. The listings on pages 466–91 give full descriptions of places to stay to suit all budgets throughout the country.

Art Deco façade of the Criterion Hotel in Perth *(see p480)*

GRADINGS AND FACILITIES

AUSTRALIA HAS no formal national grading system. Terms such as four- and five-star are often used, but have no official imprimatur. State motoring organizations and some state and regional tourism bodies do, however, produce their own rankings and they are a useful indicator of standards and facilities.

In hotels and motels, air-conditioning in summer and heating in winter are almost always provided. Other standard features generally include coffee- and tea-making facilities, televisions, radios and refrigerators. En suite bathrooms are the norm, but specify if you want a bathtub: shower cubicles are more common. For double rooms, you will need to stipulate whether you require a double bed or twin beds. Luxury accommodation often features on-site swimming pools, exercise facilities and a hotel bar or restaurant.

PRICES

PRICES FOR accommodation vary according to location and the facilities on offer. At the top end of the scale, the presidential, or similar, suite in a luxury hotel may have a four-figure daily rate, while a bed in a backpacker hotel will generally cost less than A$20. Budget motels and the majority of bed-and-breakfasts operate within the A$50–A$100 range. Prices may be increased slightly during peak seasons, but equally many hotels offer discount rates during the low season.

BOOKINGS

PRESSURE ON room availability is increasing, especially in the capital cities and the Queensland coastal destinations. This becomes particularly acute during any major cultural and sporting events *(see pp36–9)*. It is therefore advisable to book as far in advance as possible and also to specify if any special needs or requests are required.

State tourist offices can help with or make bookings. Major airlines serving Australia also often have discounted packages on offer to cater to all price ranges *(see pp542–5)*.

CHILDREN

TRAVELLING WITH children is relatively easy throughout Australia. Almost all accommodation will provide a small bed or cot in family rooms, often at no extra charge – enquire about any special rates in advance. Many major

Hyatt Hotel near the Parliamentary Triangle in Canberra *(see p472)*

Ornate Victorian architecture of the Vue Grand Hotel in Queenscliff *(see p488)*

hotels also offer baby-sitting services, while smaller establishments will be happy to check on a sleeping child while the parents are dining.

However, some of the country house hotels are strictly child-free zones.

Conrad International luxury hotel in Brisbane *(see p473)*

DISABLED TRAVELLERS

AUSTRALIAN BUILDING codes now stipulate that any new buildings or renovations must provide facilities for the disabled. It is always advisable, however, to check on the facilities in advance.

LUXURY HOTELS AND RESORTS

THE CAPITAL CITIES of each state are well endowed with luxury hotels. Well-known, international names such as **Hyatt**, **Hilton**, **Regent**, **Sheraton** and **Inter-**

Continental stand side by side with such local institutions as The Windsor in Melbourne *(see p485)*.

Major tourist destinations abound with both luxury and budget beach resorts.

CHAIN HOTELS

THERE ARE various chain hotels and motels throughout Australia, which offer reliable and comfortable, if occasionally bland and indistinctive, accommodation. They vary in style and price, from the luxury **Parkroyal** group to cheaper but also reliable and well-known motel chains such as **Flag**, **Metro Inns**, **Best Western**, **Country Comfort** and **Travelodge**. These hotels are particularly popular with business travellers and often have facilities such as fax and electronic communications available.

Stained glass at Simpsons in Sydney *(see p467)*

COUNTRY HOUSE HOTELS

COUNTRY HOUSE hotels, ranging from elegant mansions to simple bed-and-breakfast cottages, now exist throughout Australia. These offer personalized accommodation and an insight into the Australian way of life, in contrast to chain hotels. Many of these hotels have only one or two rooms so that stays are extremely peaceful, with many of the comforts of home.

Among the best country houses are those found in the wine regions *(see pp32–3)*, around the old gold fields *(see pp50–51)* and in Tasmania *(see pp440–59)*. The **Australian Tourist Commission** and state tourist offices will be able to supply full, up-to-date listings of bed-and-breakfast accommodation available in each area of the country.

Indoor pool at the Observatory Hotel in Sydney *(see p468)*

"The Grand" function room in the Windsor Hotel, Melbourne *(see p486)*

BOUTIQUE HOTELS

MANY OF THE "boutique" hotels in Australia offer high-quality accommodation, often with luxury facilities, within an intimate atmosphere and few rooms.

Most boutique hotels do not advertise in brochures, but operate through recommendations. However, the Australian Tourist Commission and other state tourist offices will provide information. Some of the best are also listed on the following pages.

Australian bed and breakfasts (B&Bs), many in heritage-listed premises, also tend to be of a high standard. They range from farmstays to glamorous country house hotels.

Backpackers' resort sign

BACKPACKER HOTELS AND YOUTH HOSTELS

ONE OF THE fastest growing areas of Australia's accommodation industry is hotels for the increasing number of young backpackers. Despite their budget prices and basic facilities, the majority are clean and comfortable, although standards can vary widely in different areas.

The internationally renowned **Youth Hostel Association** also has its own chain of hostels across the country, in all the major cities, ski resorts and many of the national parks. These offer clean and comfortable accommodation, particularly for those travellers on a tight budget.

While it is necessary to book in advance at some hostels, others do not take bookings and beds are on a first come, first served basis. Apartments, rooms and dormitories are all available, but dormitories are often mixed sex; check, if necessary, before arriving.

The backpacker scene changes quickly, so it is often worth asking other travellers for the latest developments and for their recommendations, as well as gathering up-to-date information from the state tourist offices.

It is also worth remembering that, despite its name, the Youth Hostel Association also caters for senior citizens.

PUB ACCOMMODATION

AUSTRALIAN PUBS are generally also referred to as hotels because historically they accommodated travellers. Many pubs still offer bed-and-breakfast accommodation. The quality can vary, but they are usually good value for money.

SELF-CATERING APARTMENTS

SELF-CATERING apartments are the latest accommodation trend in Australia. Full kitchen and laundry facilities are usually provided. Within cities, some apartments also cater for business travellers, complete with fax and other communications amenities.

Ornate Victorian Lenna of Hobart Hotel in Tasmania's capital *(see p491)*

Classic Australian pub accommodation at the Bellbird Hotel in the Hunter Valley *(see p469)*

Prices can vary, but they are generally on a par with the major chain motels.

FARM STAYS AND HOUSEBOATS

MANY LARGE sheep and cattle stations have now opened their doors to the public, and welcome visitors for farm stays. These offer a unique insight into rural Australian life. Many are situated near major cities, while others are located in the vast Outback *(see pp24–5)*. Accommodation may be in traditional shearers' or cattle herders' quarters, or within the homestead itself. A stay usually includes the opportunity to become involved in the daily working life of the station. State tourist offices will supply all necessary details.

Another interesting and very relaxing holiday can be had on a houseboat along the vast Murray River which crosses from New South Wales and Victoria to South Australia. An international driving licence is the only requirement to be your own riverboat captain.

CAMPING AND CARAVAN PARKS

CAMP SITES for both tents and caravans are found throughout the country, with the majority dotted along the vast coastline and in the many inland national parks. This form of accommodation offers a cheap and idyllic way of enjoying the natural beauty and wildlife of Australia.

Many camp sites allow "walk in" camping without the need for booking, provided space is available. However, some areas may require a camping permit, so it is always advisable to check with state or local tourist offices in advance.

The majority of caravan parks have on-site vans for rent at relatively low prices. Facilities usually include adequate laundry and shower blocks and often a small general store for basic food and drink supplies.

DIRECTORY

TOURIST OFFICES

Australian Tourist Commission
UK
10–18 Putney Hill,
London SW15 6AA.
[(020) 8780 2229.
United States
Suite 1920,
2049 Century Park East,
Los Angeles, CA 90067.
[(310) 229 4870.

Tourism NSW
106 George St,
Sydney, NSW 2000.
[13 20 77.

Queensland Travel Centre
243 Edward St,
Brisbane, QLD 4001.
[13 18 01.

Darwin Region Tourism Association
38 Mitchell St,
Darwin NT 0801.
[(08) 8981 4300.

Western Australia Tourist Centre
469 Wellington St,
Perth, WA 6000.
[1300 361 351.

South Australian Travel Centre
18 King William St,
Adelaide, SA 5000.
[1300 655 276.

Victoria Visitor Information Centre
55 Collins St,
Melbourne, VIC 3000.
[(03) 9653 9777.

Tasmanian Travel & Information Centre
22 Elizabeth St,
Hobart, Tasmania 7000.
[(03) 6230 8235.

LUXURY HOTELS

Hilton
[(02) 9209 5209.

Hyatt
[13 12 34.

Inter-Continental
[(02) 9253 9000.

Regent
[1800 142 163.

Sheraton
[1800 656 535.

CHAIN HOTELS

Best Western
[13 17 79.

Centra Hotels
[1300 363 300.

Country Comfort
[1800 065 064.

Flag
[13 24 00.

Metro Inns
[1800 004 321.

Travelodge
[1300 728 628.

BACKPACKER HOTELS AND YOUTH HOSTELS

YHA Australia
422 Kent St,
Sydney,
NSW 2000.
[(02) 9261 1111.

Choosing a Hotel

THE HOTELS in this guide have been selected for their good value, excellent facilities and location. This chart lists the hotels by region, starting with Sydney. The colour codes of each region are shown on the thumb tabs. This list also highlights the various facilities on offer at each establishment. For restaurant listings see pages 498–523.

	NUMBER OF ROOMS	RESTAURANT	CHILDREN'S FACILITIES	GARDEN/TERRACE	SWIMMING POOL

SYDNEY

BONDI BEACH: *Ravesi's on Bondi Beach* $$
Cnr Campbell Parade & Hall St, NSW 2026. (*(02) 9365 4422.* FAX *(02) 9365 1481.* The relaxed style of Bondi is reflected here. Some of the suites have private balconies overlooking the ocean. ☎ TV ▤ ✉

| 16 | ● | ■ | | |

BOTANIC GARDENS AND THE DOMAIN: *Inter-Continental Sydney* $$$$
117 Macquarie St, NSW 2000. **Map 1 C3.** (*(02) 9253 9000.* FAX *(02) 9240 1240.* The old 1851 Treasury Building blends with a modern lobby constructed beneath vaulted arches three storeys high in this architecturally impressive hotel. ☎ 24 TV ▤ & P ✉

| 503 | ● | ■ | | ■ |

BOTANIC GARDENS AND THE DOMAIN: *Sir Stamford* $$$$
93 Macquarie St, NSW 2000. **Map 1 C3.** (*(02) 9252 4600.* FAX *(02) 9252 4286.* Open fireplaces and antique furniture create a quiet ambience, while the rooftop pool has wonderful views. ☎ 24 TV ▤ & P ✉

| 105 | ● | ■ | | ■ |

CITY CENTRE: *Castlereagh Inn* $$
169–171 Castlereagh St, NSW 2000. **Map 1 B5.** (*(02) 9284 1000.* FAX *(02) 9284 1999.* The restored dining room, with its chandeliers and crisp white linen, is a feature of this old-world hotel. ☎ TV ▤ ✉

| 82 | ● | ■ | | |

CITY CENTRE: *All Seasons Premier Menzies* $$$
14 Carrington St, NSW 2000. **Map 1 A4.** (*(02) 9299 1000.* FAX *(02) 9290 3819.* The award-winning "Menzies" boasts an indoor Roman bath amongst its facilities. The Sporters Bar and Bistro with its 15 monitors continuously relays sporting events. ☎ 24 TV ▤ & P ✉

| 446 | ● | ■ | | ■ |

CITY CENTRE: *Sydney Marriott* $$$
36 College St, NSW 2000. **Map 4 F3.** (*(02) 9361 8400.* FAX *(02) 9361 8599.* Ideal for the business traveller with its conference rooms, business centre and an executive lounge. ☎ 24 TV ▤ & P ✉

| 241 | ● | ■ | | ■ |

CITY CENTRE: *The York* $$$$
5 York St, NSW 2000. **Map 1 A3.** (*(02) 9210 5000.* FAX *(02) 9290 1487.* Distinguished by its individually designed apartments, this hotel offers pretty furnishings and spacious balconies. ☎ TV ▤ & limited. P ✉

| 130 | ● | ■ | ● | ■ |

CITY CENTRE: *Hilton Sydney* $$$$
259 Pitt St, NSW 2000. **Map 1 B5.** (*(02) 9266 2000.* FAX *(02) 9265 6062.* A well-established five-star hotel with a wide range of services. Don't miss the ornate and historic Marble Bar. ☎ 24 ▤ & P ✉

| 585 | ● | ■ | | ■ |

CITY CENTRE: *Sheraton on the Park* $$$$
161 Elizabeth St, NSW 2000. **Map 1 B5.** (*(02) 9286 6000.* FAX *(02) 9286 6686.* This stylish refurbished hotel is convenient for business, shopping and the oasis-like Hyde Park *(see p89).* ☎ 24 TV ▤ & P ✉

| 557 | ● | ■ | | ■ |

CITY CENTRE: *Westin* $$$$
1 Martin Pl, NSW 2000. **Map 1 B4.** (*(02) 8223 1111.* FAX *(02) 8223 1222.* Located in the heart of Sydney and part of the redeveloped General Post Office. Rooms are spacious. ☎ TV ▤ ❯ ▦ ❚❚ ≋ & P ✉

| 417 | ● | ■ | | |

DARLING HARBOUR: *Furama Hotel* $$
68 Harbour St, NSW 2000. **Map 4 D3.** (*(02) 9281 0400.* FAX *(02) 9281 1212.* With Darling Harbour on its doorstep the heritage-listed Furama is ideal for business and leisure travellers alike. ☎ TV ▤ P ✉

| 304 | ● | | | |

DARLING HARBOUR: *Carlton Crest* $$$
169–179 Thomas St, Haymarket NSW 2000. **Map 4 D5.** (*(02) 9281 6888.* FAX *(02) 9281 6688.* Built within an old hospital, the hotel has large rooms, a rooftop pool, barbecue area and putting green. ☎ TV ▤ & P ✉

| 251 | ● | ■ | ● | ■ |

		Price categories description	NUMBER OF ROOMS	RESTAURANT	CHILDREN'S FACILITIES	GARDEN/TERRACE	SWIMMING POOL

Price categories for a standard double room per night, inclusive of service charges and any additional taxes.
$ under A$100
$$ A$100–A$150
$$$ A$150–A$200
$$$$ A$200–A$250
$$$$$ over A$250

RESTAURANT
Hotel restaurant or dining room usually open to non-residents unless otherwise stated.

CHILDREN'S FACILITIES
Indicates child cots and/or a baby-sitting service available. A few hotels also provide children's portions and high chairs in the restaurant.

GARDEN/TERRACE
Hotel with a garden, courtyard or terrace, often providing tables for eating outside.

SWIMMING POOL
Hotel with an indoor or outdoor swimming pool, or with hot spas for use by residents.

Hotel		NUMBER OF ROOMS	RESTAURANT	CHILDREN'S FACILITIES	GARDEN/TERRACE	SWIMMING POOL
DARLING HARBOUR: *Four Points Sheraton* — 161 Sussex St, NSW 2000. Map 4 D2. (02) 9299 1231. FAX (02) 9299 3340. Sleek design includes 19th-century buildings with an antique pub as the hotel's bar. All rooms have a harbour view.	$$$	645	●	■	●	
DARLING HARBOUR: *Novotel Sydney on Darling Harbour* — 100 Murray St, Pyrmont, NSW 2009. Map 3 C2. (02) 9934 0000. FAX (02) 9934 0099. This hotel offers panoramic views from comfortable rooms, as well as a gym, tennis court and sauna.	$$$	527	●	■		■
DARLING HARBOUR: *Waldorf Apartment Hotel* — 57 Liverpool St, NSW 2000. Map 4 E3. (02) 9261 5355. FAX (02) 9261 3753. With more than 50 restaurants nearby, the well-equipped kitchens in these spacious one- and two-bedroom apartments may not get used often. The balcony bar overlooks the city.	$$$	48	●	■		
KINGS CROSS AND DARLINGHURST: *Macleay Serviced Apartments* — 28 Macleay St, Potts Point NSW 2011. Map 2 E5. (02) 9357 7755. FAX (02) 9357 7233. These apartments are minutes away from the city's busiest tourist spots. Some have views of the Harbour Bridge.	$$	80				
KINGS CROSS AND DARLINGHURST: *Kirketon* — 229 Darlinghurst Rd, Darlinghurst, NSW 2011. Map 5 A2. (02) 9332 2011. FAX (02) 9332 2499. A fashionable boutique hotel, also home to Salt, one of Sydney's best restaurants.	$$$	140	●	■	●	■
KINGS CROSS AND DARLINGHURST: *Medusa* — 267 Darlinghurst Rd, Darlinghurst NSW 2010. Map 5 B1. (02) 9331 1000. FAX (02) 9380 6901. Situated in the heart of Sydney's café culture. Rooms are decorated with wonderful colours and rich textures.	$$$	18			●	
KINGS CROSS AND DARLINGHURST: *Simpsons of Potts Point* — 8 Challis Ave, Potts Point NSW 2011. Map 2 E4. (02) 9356 2199. FAX (02) 9356 4476. Built in 1892 as a family residence, this hotel has been restored, with splendid stained-glass windows.	$$$	14		■		
KINGS CROSS AND DARLINGHURST: *W Hotel* — 6 Cowper Wharf Rd, Woolloomooloo NSW 2011. Map 2 D5. (02) 9331 9000. FAX (02) 9331 9031. Engaging and stylish hotel in the heart of a luxury marina and entertainment complex.	$$$$$	140	●	■		■
MANLY: *Manly Pacific Parkroyal* — 55 North Steyne, NSW 2095. (02) 9977 7666. FAX (02) 9977 7822. Situated on Manly's beach, the hotel has unbeatable views, as well as light, airy rooms. There are bars, restaurants and a nightclub, and plenty of local pubs and cafés nearby.	$$$	170	●	■		■
PADDINGTON: *Paddington Grand National* — 161 Underwood St, NSW 2021. Map 6 D4. (02) 9363 3096. FAX (02) 9363 3542. Once a pub, this 100-year-old building has been done up with flair, making it a fashionable hang-out with the trend-setting locals.	$	20	●			
PADDINGTON: *The Hughenden Boutique Hotel* — 14 Queen St, Woollahra NSW 2025. Map 6 E4. (02) 9363 4863. FAX (02) 9362 0398. This rambling old building, built in 1876, has been restored with beautifully carved staircases and marble fireplaces.	$$	35	●	■		
THE ROCKS AND CIRCULAR QUAY: *Lord Nelson Brewery Hotel* — 19 Kent St, NSW 2000. Map 1 A2. (02) 9251 4044. FAX (02) 9251 1532. For 150 years, bar-room banter has praised this pub's famous home brews. Upstairs, rustic stone walls are a feature of the cosy bedrooms. This is a great place to meet the locals.	$$	10	●	■		

Price categories for a standard double room per night, inclusive of service charges and any additional taxes.
$ under A$100
$$ A$100–A$150
$$$ A$150–A$200
$$$$ A$200–A$250
$$$$$ over A$250

RESTAURANT
Hotel restaurant or dining room usually open to non-residents unless otherwise stated.
CHILDREN'S FACILITIES
Indicates child cots and/or a baby-sitting service available. A few hotels also provide children's portions and high chairs in the restaurant.
GARDEN/TERRACE
Hotel with a garden, courtyard or terrace, often providing tables for eating outside.
SWIMMING POOL
Hotel with an indoor or outdoor swimming pool, or with hot spas for use by residents.

Hotel	Number of Rooms	Restaurant	Children's Facilities	Garden/Terrace	Swimming Pool
THE ROCKS AND CIRCULAR QUAY: *Russell* $$$ 143a George St, NSW 2000. **Map** 1 B2. ☎ *(02) 9241 3543.* [FAX] *(02) 9252 1652.* A welcoming and intimate hotel, with a rooftop garden perfect for a quiet drink after a hectic day in the city. 🛁 💳	29	●	■	●	
THE ROCKS AND CIRCULAR QUAY: *ANA Hotel Sydney* $$$$ 176 Cumberland St, NSW 2000. **Map** 1 A3. ☎ *(02) 9250 6000.* [FAX] *(02) 9250 6250.* A modern but plush hotel. Look out at the lights of the harbour at night as you sip drinks in the Horizon Bar. 🛁 [24] [TV] ▤ ♿ [P] 💳	570	●	■		■
THE ROCKS AND CIRCULAR QUAY: *Regent Sydney* $$$$ 199 George St, NSW 2000. **Map** 1 B3. ☎ *(02) 9238 0000.* [FAX] *(02) 9251 2851.* Modern and imposing, the hotel has a view of the harbour that's hard to beat. Inside, work up an appetite in the Health Club before eating at one of the two first-class restaurants. 🛁 [24] [TV] ▤ ♿ [P] 🍸 💳	531	●	■		■
THE ROCKS AND CIRCULAR QUAY: *Renaissance Sydney* $$$$ 30 Pitt St, NSW 2000. **Map** 1 B3. ☎ *(02) 9259 7000.* [FAX] *(02) 9251 1122.* Friendly hotel with a magnificent three-tiered lobby, Italian mosaic centrepiece and a top floor executive suite. 🛁 [24] [TV] ▤ ♿ [P] 💳	579	●	■		■
THE ROCKS AND CIRCULAR QUAY: *Observatory* $$$$$ 89–113 Kent St, Millers Point, NSW 2000. **Map** 1 A2. ☎ *(02) 9256 2222.* [FAX] *(02) 9256 2233.* A smart, award-winning hotel which lies at the centre of this historic, 19th-century district. 🛁 [24] [TV] ▤ ♿ [P] 💳	100	●	■		■
THE ROCKS AND CIRCULAR QUAY: *Park Hyatt Sydney* $$$$$ 7 Hickson Rd, The Rocks NSW 2000. **Map** 1 B1. ☎ *(02) 9241 1234.* [FAX] *(02) 9256 1555.* This de luxe hotel on the harbour foreshore is within the shadow of the Harbour Bridge *(see pp76–7).* 🛁 [24] [TV] ▤ ♿ [P] 💳	158	●	■		■
THE BLUE MOUNTAINS AND BEYOND					
ARMIDALE: *Best Western Abbotsleigh* $ 76 Barney St, NSW 2350. ☎ *(02) 6772 9488.* [FAX] *(02) 6772 7066.* A basic travellers' motel which, although centrally located close to Armidale's museums, shops and cafés, remains quiet. 🛁 [TV] ♿ [P] 💳	32	●	■		
BARRINGTON TOPS: *Eaglereach Wilderness Resort* $$$$ Summer Hill Rd, Vacy via Paterson, NSW 2421. ☎ *(02) 4938 8233.* [FAX] *(02) 4938 8234.* With sweeping views over the Barrington Tops, these self-contained lodges can sleep families of eight. 🛁 [TV] ♿ [P] 💳	34	●	■	●	■
BARRINGTON TOPS: *Barrington Guest House* $$$$ Salisbury, via Dungog, NSW 2420. ☎ *(02) 4995 3212.* [FAX] *(02) 4995 3248.* An original 1930s guesthouse surrounded by rainforest and adjacent to the Barrington Tops National Park *(see p167).* ♿ [P] 💳	40	●		●	
BLUE MOUNTAINS: *Crystal Lodge* $$ 19 Abbotsford Rd, Katoomba, NSW 2780. ☎ *(02) 4782 5122.* [FAX] *(02) 4782 3742.* This Art Deco health resort offers a range of "alternative" therapies. All meals are vegetarian and no alcohol is allowed. [P] 💳	18	●		●	
BLUE MOUNTAINS: *Hydro Majestic Hotel* $$$ Great Western Hwy, Medlow Bath, NSW 2780. ☎ *(02) 4788 1002.* [FAX] *(02) 4788 1063.* A romantic hotel high above the cliffs at Medlow Bath, with stunning views across the Megalong Valley. 🛁 [TV] [P] 💳	84	●		●	■
BLUE MOUNTAINS: *Lilianfels* $$$$$ Lilianfels Ave, Katoomba, NSW 2780. ☎ *(02) 4780 1200.* [FAX] *(02) 4780 1300.* A popular conference venue for top managers and politicians, this resort offers first-class service. 🛁 [TV] ▤ ♿ [P] 🍸 💳	86	●	■	●	■

BOURKE: *Bourke Riverside Motel* 3 Mitchell St, NSW 2840. ☎ *(02) 6872 2539.* [FAX] *(02) 6872 1471.* A historic 1875 building on the banks of the mighty Darling River. The motel is quiet, but close to the centre of town. 🚗 [TV] ≡ [P] 💳	$	10			●	■
BROKEN HILL: *The Lodge Motel* Cnr Mica & Chloride sts, NSW 2880. ☎ *(08) 8088 2722.* [FAX] *(08) 8088 2636.* A comfortable and friendly motel in an Edwardian building with a self contained cottage for families or groups. 🚗 [TV] ≡ [P] 💳	$	21		■	●	■
BYRON BAY: *Byron Bay Beach Club* Bayshore Drive, NSW 2481. ☎ *(02) 6685 8000.* [FAX] *(02) 6685 6916.* Private resort set on 93 ha (230 acres) of natural parkland with its own secluded white-sand beach frontage. 🚗 [TV] ♿ [P] 💳	$$	78	●	■	●	■
COFFS HARBOUR: *Pelican Beach Australis* Pacific Hwy, NSW 2450. ☎ *(02) 6653 7000.* [FAX] *(02) 6653 7066.* This family resort, set by the Coffs Harbour ocean beach, features a Kids' Club during holidays and weekends. 🚗 [24] [TV] ≡ ♿ [P] 🍸 💳	$$$	112	●	■	●	■
DUBBO: *Country Comfort Inn* Newell Hwy, NSW 2830. ☎ *(02) 6882 4777.* [FAX] *(02) 6881 8370.* Ten minutes' drive from town, the inn is the closest hotel to the magnificent Western Plains Zoo *(see p172).* 🚗 [TV] ≡ ♿ [P] 💳	$$	60	●	■	●	■
HUNTER VALLEY: *The Bellbird Hotel* 388 Wollombi Rd, Bellbird, NSW 2325. ☎ *(02) 4990 1094.* [FAX] *(02) 4991 5475.* Within minutes of the valley's famous wineries *(see p166)* and golf courses, this historic pub offers bed-and-breakfast. [P] 💳	$	15	●	■	●	
HUNTER VALLEY: *The Olives Country House* Campbell's Lane, Pokolbin, NSW 2320. ☎ *(02) 4998 7838.* [FAX] *(02) 4998 7456.* Relax in the setting of a Tuscan-style country home surrounded by olive trees, vineyards and pleasant gardens. Includes breakfast. 🚗 ♿ [P] 💳	$$$$$	5			●	■
HUNTER VALLEY: *Pepper's Convent* Halls Rd, Pokolbin, NSW 2320. ☎ *(02) 4998 7764.* [FAX] *(02) 4998 7323.* A weekend package in this Gothic-style building provides champagne, canapés and full breakfasts. 🚗 ♿ [P] 💳	$$$$$	17	●	■	●	■
MUDGEE: *Lauralla Historic Guesthouse* [W] www.lauralla.com.au Cnr Lewis & Mortimer sts, NSW 2850. ☎ *(02) 6372 4480.* [FAX] *(02) 6372 3320.* One of Mudgee's finest Victorian mansions close to the town's historic buildings. Lauralla also provides chauffeured wine tours. 🚗 ♿ [P] 💳	$$$	6	●		●	
MUNGO NATIONAL PARK: *Mungo Lodge* [W] www.mungolodge.com.au Arumpo Rd, NSW 3500. ☎ *(03) 5029 7297.* [FAX] *(03) 5029 7296.* Stay right at the gate of Mungo National Park in wooden cabins. 🚗 [TV] ≡ [P] 💳	$	18	●			
NEWCASTLE: *Holiday Inn Esplanade Newcastle* Shortland Esplanade, NSW2300. ☎ *(02) 4929 5576.* [FAX] *(02) 4926 5467.* This de luxe hotel has stunning views from every room of the sweeping Pacific coastline. 🚗 [TV] ≡ ♿ *limited.* [P] 🍸 💳	$$$$	72	●	■		■
TOOWOON BAY: *Kim's Beachside Retreat* Charlton St, NSW 2261. ☎ *(02) 4332 1566.* [FAX] *(02) 4333 1544.* Kim's is expensive, but renowned for its privacy, gourmet food and relaxation. All meals are included in the price. 🚗 [24] [TV] [P] 💳	$$$$$	34	●		●	■
WAGGA WAGGA: *Country Comfort* Cnr Tarcutta & Morgan sts, NSW 2650. ☎ *(02) 6921 6444.* [FAX] *(02) 6921 2922.* Noted for its excellent restaurant, this large motel is only five minutes' walk from the city centre. 🚗 [TV] ≡ ♿ *limited.* [P] 💳	$$	88	●	■		■

THE SOUTH COAST AND SNOWY MOUNTAINS

ADAMINABY: *Reynella Rides and Country Farmstay* Kingston Rd, NSW 2630. ☎ *(02) 6454 2386.* [FAX] *(02) 6454 2530.* A working sheep and cattle farm best known for offering pony treks with bush camping through the Kosciuszko National Park. [P] 💳	$$$$$	20	●		●	
BATEMANS BAY: *The Reef Motor Inn* 27 Clyde St, NSW 2536. ☎ *(02) 4472 6000.* [FAX] *(02) 4472 6059.* Beaches and parks close by; boating and fishing trips available. 🚗 [TV] ≡ [P] 💳	$	34	●	■		■

For key to symbols see back flap

	Price categories for a standard double room per night, inclusive of service charges and any additional taxes. ⓢ under A$100 / ⓢⓢ A$100–A$150 / ⓢⓢⓢ A$150–A$200 / ⓢⓢⓢⓢ A$200–A$250 / ⓢⓢⓢⓢⓢ over A$250	**RESTAURANT** Hotel restaurant or dining room usually open to non-residents unless otherwise stated. **CHILDREN'S FACILITIES** Indicates child cots and/or a baby-sitting service available. A few hotels also provide children's portions and high chairs in the restaurant. **GARDEN/TERRACE** Hotel with a garden, courtyard or terrace, often providing tables for eating outside. **SWIMMING POOL** Hotel with an indoor or outdoor swimming pool, or with hot spas for use by residents.	NUMBER OF ROOMS	RESTAURANT	CHILDREN'S FACILITIES	GARDEN/TERRACE	SWIMMING POOL

	Rooms	Restaurant	Children's Facilities	Garden/Terrace	Swimming Pool
BATEMANS BAY: *Lincoln Downs* ⓢⓢ Princes Hwy, NSW 2536. ((02) 4478 9200. FAX (02) 4478 9299. Lincoln Downs is a luxury country resort by the sea, with an emphasis on relaxation, fine wine and food. ⚑ ▤ P ✑	33	●	■	●	■
BERRY: *Bunyip Inn Guesthouse* ⓢⓢ 122 Queen St, NSW 2535. ((02) 4464 2064. FAX (02) 4464 2324. Housed in an 1889 bank building, this cosy family-run guesthouse is a perfect base from which to explore the region. TV P ✑	13		■	●	
CHARLOTTE PASS: *Mount Kosciuszko Chalet* ⓢⓢⓢ Kosciuszko Rd, NSW 2624. ((02) 6457 5245. FAX 1800 802 687. This chalet, the highest in Australia, offers package deals for two, five and seven nights. Only open in winter for the ski season. ⚑ ✑	35	●	■		
EDEN: *Wonboyn Lake Resort* ⓢⓢ 1 Oyster Lane, Wonboyn Lake, NSW 2551. ((02) 6496 9162. FAX (02) 6496 9100. These self-contained cottages are ideal for a family fishing and beach holiday. Whale-watching is also on offer. ⚑ TV P	14	●			
GOULBURN: *Pelican Sheep Station* ⓢ Braidwood Rd, NSW 2580. ((02) 4821 4668. FAX (02) 4822 1179. This working family farm has groups as large as 60 living, either in their budget bunk-houses suitable for backpackers or in self-contained units. Farm tours and bushwalking are available. P ✑	14	●		●	
GOULBURN: *Loaded Dog Hotel* ⓢⓢ Wallace St, Tarago, NSW 2580. ((02) 4849 4499. FAX (02) 4849 4603. Built in 1848, this working pub retains its wide double-storey veranda and historic feel. An authentic Australian bush experience. P ✑	10	●	■	●	
KIAMA: *The Pines Flag Inn* ⓢⓢ 10 Bong Bong St, NSW 2533. ((02) 4232 1000. FAX (02) 4233 1272. A modern hotel with all mod cons located right in the centre of Kiama. Family rooms available. ⚑ ▤ 24 TV & ✑	29	●			■
MERIMBULA: *Albacore Apartments* ⓢⓢⓢⓢ Market St, NSW 2548. ((02) 6495 3187. FAX (02) 6495 3439. Luxury apartments with beach views from every balcony. Nearby are golf courses, game fishing and surf beaches. ⚑ TV & P ✑	20		■	●	■
NAROOMA: *Mystery Bay Cottages* ⓢ 121 Mystery Bay Rd, Mystery Bay, NSW 2546. (FAX (02) 4473 7431. The Mystery Bay cottages are self-contained and surrounded by open farmland. Each has wood fires, barbecue facilities and two bedrooms overlooking the beach. ⚑ TV P	6		■	●	
THE SOUTHERN HIGHLANDS: *Tree Tops Guesthouse* ⓢⓢⓢ 101 Railway Ave, Bundanoon, NSW 2578. ((02) 4883 6372. FAX (02) 4883 6176. See the spectacular autumn colours from this quiet country retreat furnished with four-poster beds and log fires. ⚑ P ✑	16	●		●	
THE SOUTHERN HIGHLANDS: *Craigieburn* ⓢⓢⓢⓢⓢ Centennial Rd, Bowral, NSW 2576. ((02) 4861 1277. FAX (02) 4862 1690. Less than two hours' drive from Sydney, Craigieburn is a 2-ha (5-acre) garden estate, boasting its own private nine-hole golf course, cricket pitch and tennis courts. All meals are included. ⚑ P ✑	68	●	■	●	■
THE SOUTHERN HIGHLANDS: *Milton Park Country House* ⓢⓢⓢⓢⓢ Horderns Rd, Bowral, NSW 2576. ((02) 4861 1522. FAX (02) 4861 4716. A graceful old mansion set in parkland, providing golf courses, art classes, horse-riding, bush picnics and tennis courts. ⚑ TV & P ✑	40	●	■	●	■

THREDBO: *Novotel Lake Crackenback Resort* Lake Crackenback, Alpine Way, via Jindabyne, NSW 2627. ☎ *(02) 6456 2960.* [FAX] *(02) 6456 1008.* Open during both summer and winter, these luxury self-contained units are ideally located for skiers. 🚗 [TV] ♿ [P] 🍸 💳	$$$$$	46	●	■	●	■
THREDBO: *Thredbo Alpine Hotel* Friday Drive, Thredbo, NSW 2625. ☎ *(02) 6459 4200.* [FAX] *(02) 6459 4201.* A large entertainment and conference complex busy with skiers in the winter months. It is far cheaper during the summer. 🚗 [TV] [P] 💳	$$$$$	64	●	■	●	■
TILBA TILBA: *The Two-Storey Bed & Breakfast* Bate St, Central Tilba, NSW 2546. ☎ *(02) 4473 7290.* [FAX] *(02) 4473 7290.* Located in Central Tilba, the building is over 100 years old and was once the post office and telephone exchange. Close to the beach. [P] 💳	$	3	●	■	●	
WOLLONGONG: *Novotel Northbeach Wollongong* 2–14 Cliff Rd, NSW 2500. ☎ *(02) 4226 3555.* [FAX] *(02) 4229 1705.* Just an hour's drive from Sydney, the hotel nestles between mountains and sea, some rooms have a balcony overlooking the ocean. Peaceful walking and cycle tracks are nearby. 🚗 [24] [TV] [≡] ♿ [P] 🍸 💳	$$$$	204	●	■	●	■

CANBERRA AND ACT

BRINDABELLA: *Brindabella Station* Brindabella Valley, ACT 2611. ☎ *(02) 6236 2121.* [FAX] *(02) 6236 2128.* Bushwalking, bird-watching, horse-riding, 4WD tours and trout fishing are among the activities on offer at this luxury farm resort. [P] 💳	$$$$	6			●	
BUNGENDORE: *Carrington at Bungendore* 21 Malbon St, NSW 2621. ☎ *(02) 6238 1044.* [FAX] *(02) 6238 1036.* A popular weekend retreat for Canberrans, who love to browse among the antiques shops in this early bush town. 🚗 [24] [TV] [P] 💳	$$$	26	●	■	●	
CANBERRA: *Blue and White Lodge* 524 Northbourne Ave, Downer, ACT 2602. ☎ *(02) 6248 0498.* [FAX] *(02) 6248 8277.* Reputedly Canberra's first and most friendly bed-and-breakfast, providing a range of budget and family accommodation. [TV] [≡] [P] 💳	$	19		■		
CANBERRA: *Capital Tower* 2 Marcus Clarke St, ACT 2600. ☎ *(02) 6273 2325.* [FAX] *(02) 6273 4241.* One, two and three bedroom apartments and a quite location make this ideal for families. Tennis and squash available. 🚗 [TV] [≡] [P] 🍸 💳	$	159		■		■
CANBERRA: *City Walk Hotel* 2 Mort St, Canberra City, ACT 2601. ☎ *(02) 6257 0124.* [FAX] *(02) 6257 0116.* In the heart of the city, this budget hotel has backpacker dormitories, as well as comfortable rooms with en-suite facilities. [TV] 💳	$	60	●			
CANBERRA: *Kingston Hotel* Canberra Ave, Kingston, ACT 2602. ☎ *(02) 6295 0123.* [FAX] *(02) 6295 7871.* Low prices make this lively pub popular with backpackers. Cooking facilities are available and the pub itself serves good-value counter meals. 💳	$	36	●			
CANBERRA: *Parkview Lodge* 526 Northbourne Ave, Downer, ACT 2602. ☎ *(02) 6248 0655.* [FAX] *(02) 6247 6166.* This pleasant bed-and-breakfast just north of the city centre, is recommended. All rooms are non-smoking. 🚗 [TV] 🚭 [P] 💳	$	10				
CANBERRA: *Brassey Hotel* Belmore Gardens, Barton, ACT 2600. ☎ *(02) 6273 3766.* [FAX] *(02) 6273 2791.* Set amid flower gardens and peaceful lawns, this hotel is a heritage listed building. Located off a quiet street, near the press club and the National Gallery. 🚗 [TV] [P] 💳	$$	95	●	■	●	
CANBERRA: *Budget International Hotel* 242 Northbourne Ave, Dickson, ACT 2602. ☎ *(02) 6247 6966.* [FAX] *(02) 6248 7823.* Close to the city centre, this hotel is popular with corporate and conference guests for its reasonable rates. 🚗 [TV] [≡] ♿ [P] 💳	$$	156	●		●	■
CANBERRA: *Canberra Rex Hotel* 150 Northbourne Ave, ACT 2601. ☎ *(02) 6248 5311.* [FAX] *(02) 6248 8357.* A friendly up-market hotel, near the university and the city centre. 🚗 [24] [TV] [≡] [P] 🍸 💳	$$	156	●	■		■

For key to symbols see back flap

Price categories for a standard double room per night, inclusive of service charges and any additional taxes. $ under A\$100; $$ A\$100–A\$150; $$$ A\$150–A\$200; $$$$ A\$200–A\$250; $$$$$ over A\$250	**RESTAURANT** Hotel restaurant or dining room usually open to non-residents unless otherwise stated. **CHILDREN'S FACILITIES** Indicates child cots and/or a baby-sitting service available. A few hotels also provide children's portions and high chairs in the restaurant. **GARDEN/TERRACE** Hotel with a garden, courtyard or terrace, often providing tables for eating outside. **SWIMMING POOL** Hotel with an indoor or outdoor swimming pool, or with hot spas for use by residents.	NUMBER OF ROOMS	RESTAURANT	CHILDREN'S FACILITIES	GARDEN/TERRACE	SWIMMING POOL
CANBERRA: *Last Stop Ambledown Brook* $$ Ambledown Brook, 198 Brooklands Rd, via Hall, ACT 2618. *(02) 6230 2280.* FAX *(02) 6230 2280.* Sleep in a converted 1929 Melbourne tram or a 1935 Sydney train carriage at this rustic bed-and-breakfast, just 20 minutes' drive from Canberra. Tennis court available, too.		3		■		■
CANBERRA: *Olims Canberra Hotel* $$ Cnr Ainslie and Limestone aves, Braddon, ACT 2612. *(02) 6248 5511.* FAX *(02) 6247 0864.* Close to the War Memorial and the city centre, this traditional hotel has lovely quiet grounds.		125	●	■	●	
CANBERRA: *University House* $$ Cnr Balmain & Liversidge sts, Acton, ACT 2601. *(02) 6249 5211.* FAX *(02) 6249 5252.* Situated in the gardens of the Australian National University with spacious rooms and an academic ambience.		100	●	■	●	
CANBERRA: *Hotel Kurrajong* $$$ 8 National Circuit, Barton, ACT 2600. *(02) 6234 4444.* FAX *(02) 6234 4466.* A delightful tranquil hotel built in 1926 that has accommodated many of Australia's prime ministers.		26	●			
CANBERRA: *Crown Plaza Canberra* $$$ 1 Binara St, ACT 2601. *(02) 6247 8999.* FAX *(02) 6257 4903.* This four-and-a-half-star hotel in the civic centre of the city is well equipped with a range of facilities and is particularly popular with visiting business people.		293	●	■		■
CANBERRA: *Rydges Lakeside* $$$ London Circuit, Canberra City, ACT 2600. *(02) 6247 6244.* FAX *(02) 6257 3071.* Wonderful views over Lake Burley Griffin distinguish this substantially modernized hotel.		205	●	■		■
CANBERRA: *Hyatt Hotel* $$$$$ Commonwealth Ave, Yarralumla, ACT 2600. *(02) 6270 1234.* FAX *(02) 6281 5998.* One of Canberra's showpiece hotels – a charming country estate, right in the heart of the capital.		249	●	■	●	■
BRISBANE						
CITY CENTRE: *Annies Shandon Inn* $ 405 Upper Edward Street, QLD 4000. *(07) 3831 8684.* FAX *(07) 3831 3073.* A small, privately run bed-and-breakfast situated just off Wickham Terrace on the outer edge of the Central Business District.		19				
CITY CENTRE: *Astor Motel* $ 193 Wickham Terrace, Spring Hill, QLD 4000. *(07) 3831 9522.* FAX *(07) 3831 7360.* One of several budget motels along Wickham Terrace, most of which overlook Albert or Wickham parks. limited.		240	●	■		
CITY CENTRE: *Cosmo on Park Road* $$ 60 Park Road, Milton QLD 4064. *(07) 3858 5999.* FAX *(07) 3858 5988.* Well-appointed apartments for business or pleasure. Centrally located at the river end of the fashionable Park Road precinct.		74		■		
CITY CENTRE: *Holiday Inn* $$ Roma Street, QLD 4003. *(07) 3238 2222.* FAX *(07) 3238 2288.* Reliable and competitively priced, with pleasant service, and no skimping on the room space.		191	●	■		
CITY CENTRE: *Chifley on George* $$$ 103 George St, QLD 4000. *(07) 3221 6044.* FAX *(07) 3221 7474.* Across the road from the Treasury Casino, this refurbished hotel has fairly small but pleasantly furnished rooms.		99	●	■	●	■

CITY CENTRE: *Brisbane Hilton* $$$ 320
190 Elizabeth St, QLD 4000. (07) 3234 2000. FAX (07) 3231 3199.
The Hilton is a by-word for good service and comfort. Its stylish
Atrium Lobby is a favourite meeting place.

CITY CENTRE: *Country Comfort Lennons Hotel* $$$ 154
66 Queen St, QLD 4000. (07) 3222 3222. FAX (07) 3221 9389.
Perfectly situated for shopaholics, the hotel is in Brisbane's main
shopping precinct, Queen Street Mall.

CITY CENTRE: *Novotel Brisbane* $$$ 293
200 Creek St, QLD 4000. (07) 3309 3309. FAX (07) 3309 3308.
In the heart of Brisbane's Central Business District, this is a typical,
well-run Novotel establishment.

CITY CENTRE: *Royal on the Park* $$$ 153
Cnr Alice & Albert sts, QLD 4000. (07) 3221 3411. FAX (07) 3229 9817.
The Royal manages to maintain a certain small-hotel intimacy in the
context of large-hotel convenience.

CITY CENTRE: *Carlton Crest* $$$$ 438
Cnr Ann & Roma sts, QLD 4000. (07) 3229 9111. FAX (07) 3229 9618.
Looking over King George Square and opposite City Hall, the Carlton
Crest is close to all Brisbane's main attractions.

CITY CENTRE: *Mercure Hotel Brisbane* $$$$ 190
85 North Quay, QLD 4000. (07) 3236 3300. FAX (07) 3236 1035.
The Mercure is a good-value modern hotel close to and with views
of the Brisbane River, the Cultural Centre precinct and the South Bank
Parklands.

CITY CENTRE: *Sheraton Brisbane Hotel & Towers* $$$$ 410
249 Turbot St, QLD 4000. (07) 3835 3535. FAX (07) 3835 4960.
Despite being part of a chain, there is an especially friendly atmosphere
as well as the usual quality at this hotel.

CITY CENTRE: *The Stamford Plaza Brisbane* $$$$ 252
Cnr Margaret & Edward sts, QLD 4001. (07) 3221 1999. FAX (07) 3221
6895. This elegant hotel, opposite the Botanic Gardens, boasts one of
the city's best Japanese restaurants.

CITY CENTRE: *Conrad International* $$$$$ 130
130 William St, QLD 4000. (07) 3306 8888. FAX (07) 3306 8880.
A historic building incorporated into the Treasury Casino complex,
this 5-star luxury hotel is situated across the park from the casino
itself.

CITY CENTRE: *Quay West Suites Brisbane* $$$$$ 81
132 Alice St, QLD 4000. (07) 3853 6000. FAX (07) 3853 6060.
Just a short stroll from the city centre, this all-suite hotel provides
well-priced 5-star luxury with wonderful views over the Botanic
Gardens and river.

KANGAROO POINT: *Ryan's on the River* $$$ 23
269 Main Street, QLD 4169. (07) 3391 1011. FAX (07) 3391 1824.
Small comfortably furnished rooms with a lovely gardens as well as
spectacular city and river views.

SPRING HILL: *Metro Inn Tower Mill* $ 78
239 Wickham Terrace, QLD 4000. (07) 3832 1421. FAX (07) 3835 1013.
Built in a circular design to reflect the historic Old Mill opposite, this
is the best of several motels along Wickham Terrace.

SPRING HILL: *Thornbury House B&B* $ 6
1 Thornbury St, QLD 4000. (07) 3832 5985. FAX (07) 3832 7256.
A well-run bed-and-breakfast, in a lovingly restored two-storey
timber "Queenslander" built in 1886. All rooms have private
facilities.

SPRING HILL: *Hotel Grand Chancellor* $$$ 180
Cnr Leichhardt St & Wickham Terrace, QLD 4000. (07) 3831 4055.
FAX (07) 3831 5031. Overlooking the city, the Grand Chancellor
has great views at a reasonable price.

Price categories for a standard double room per night, inclusive of service charges and any additional taxes.

$ under A$100
$$ A$100–A$150
$$$ A$150–A$200
$$$$ A$200–A$250
$$$$$ over A$250

RESTAURANT
Hotel restaurant or dining room usually open to non-residents unless otherwise stated.
CHILDREN'S FACILITIES
Indicates child cots and/or a baby-sitting service available. A few hotels also provide children's portions and high chairs in the restaurant.
GARDEN/TERRACE
Hotel with a garden, courtyard or terrace, often providing tables for eating outside.
SWIMMING POOL
Hotel with an indoor or outdoor swimming pool, or with hot spas for use by residents.

	NUMBER OF ROOMS	RESTAURANT	CHILDREN'S FACILITIES	GARDEN/TERRACE	SWIMMING POOL
WOOLLOONGABBA: *Diana Plaza Hotel* $$ 12 Annerley Rd, QLD 4102. ((07) 3391 2911. FAX (07) 3391 2944. This four-star hotel has a friendly atmosphere and provides standard accommodation, as well as self-catering suites. 🛏 TV 🍽 P 🗖	67	●	▥		

SOUTH OF TOWNSVILLE

	NUMBER OF ROOMS	RESTAURANT	CHILDREN'S FACILITIES	GARDEN/TERRACE	SWIMMING POOL
AIRLIE BEACH: *Coral Sea Resort* $$$ 25 Ocean View Av, Airlie Beach, QLD 4802. ((07) 4946 6458. FAX (07) 4946 6516 Central four-star acommodation with absolute waterfront. Some suites have a spa on the balcony. 🛏 TV 🍽 🍴 P 🗖	78	●	▥	●	▥
CARNARVON GORGE: *Oasis Wilderness Lodge* $$$ Carnarvon National Park, via Rolleston, QLD 4702. ((07) 4984 4503. FAX (07) 4984 4500. Here you can combine comfort and intimacy with the natural world, in canvas "cabins" set among the trees. 🛏 P 🗖	30	●			
EUMUNDI: *Taylor's Damn Fine B&B* $$ 15 Eumundi-Noosa Rd, Eumundi QLD 4562. ((07) 5442 8685. FAX (07) 5442 8168. Delightful 100-year-old Queenslander home with a restored 1946 railway carriage. In walking distance of Eumundi markets. 🛏 🗖	5		▥	●	▥
FRASER ISLAND: *Fraser Island Retreat* $$$ Happy Valley, QLD 4655. ((07) 4127 9144. FAX (07) 4127 9131. Pleasant and unpretentious, this resort has self-contained, timber lodges with views over Seventy-Five Mile Beach. 🛏 TV P 🗖	9	●	▥	●	▥
FRASER ISLAND: *Kingfisher Bay Resort* $$$$ QLD 4650. ((07) 4120 3333. FAX (07) 4127 9333. On the bay side of Fraser Island, this fashionable resort offers a unique nature tourism experience. 🛏 TV ♿ P 🗖	258	●	▥	●	▥
GOLD COAST: *Royal Pines Resort* $$$$ Ross St, Ashmore, QLD 4214. ((07) 5597 1111. FAX (07) 5597 2277. A sporty resort with a 27-hole golf course, outdoor and indoor tennis courts, a health centre and jogging track. 🛏 24 TV 🍽 ♿ P 🍴 🗖	329	●	▥	●	▥
GOLD COAST: *Sheraton Mirage Gold Coast* $$$$$ Sea World Drive, Main Beach, QLD 4217. ((07) 5591 1488. FAX (07) 5591 2299. Elegantly furnished with antiques and tapestries, the hotel overlooks the ocean. 🛏 24 TV 🍽 ♿ P 🍴 🗖	300	●	▥	●	▥
GOLD COAST HINTERLAND: *Binna Burra Mountain Lodge* $$ Binna Burra Rd, Beechmont, QLD 4211. ((07) 5533 3622. FAX (07) 5533 3658. High in the mountains of Lamington National Park (*see p232*), this is a popular spot with bushwalkers. 🛏 P 🗖	42	●	▥	●	
GOLD COAST HINTERLAND: *O'Reilly's Rainforest Guesthouse* $$$$ Lamington National Park Rd, via Canungra, Green Mountain, QLD 4275. ((07) 5544 0644. FAX (07) 5544 0638. This comfortable guesthouse, run by the third generation of O'Reillys, has a tree walk offering a unique view of the rainforest. Also on offer is a spa and sauna. 🛏 P 🗖	70	●	▥	●	▥
HERVEY BAY: *Hervey Bay Resort Motel* $ 249 The Esplanade, Pialba, QLD 4655. ((07) 4128 1555. FAX (07) 4128 4688. Views over the bay to Fraser Island make this a pleasant stopover for whale-watching. 🛏 TV 🍽 ♿ P 🗖	27	●	▥		▥
HERVEY BAY: *Susan River Homestead Ranch Resort* $$$ Maryborough Rd, QLD 4650. ((07) 4121 6846. FAX (07) 4122 2675. Located only 20 minutes from Fraser island, this is an excellent place for children. Many leisure activities are available. 🛏 P 🗖	16	●	▥	●	▥

MACKAY: *Ocean Resort Village Beachfront* $ 34
5 Bridge Rd, Mackay, QLD 4740. (07) 4951 3200. FAX (07) 4951 3246.
This is a good budget-priced beachfront resort with a barbecue area,
tennis courts and fishing, as well as a pool. 🚐 TV 🍽 P 🐾

MACKAY: *Ocean International Hotel* $$ 46
1 Bridge Rd, Illawong Beach, QLD 4740. (07) 4957 2044. FAX (07) 4957
2636. Mackay's most prestigious hotel, only 3 km (2 miles) from the
town centre, overlooks Sandringham Bay. 🚐 24 TV 🍽 P 🐾

MAGNETIC ISLAND: *Arcadia Hotel Resort* $ 27
Marine Parade, Arcadia, QLD 4819. (07) 4778 5177. FAX (07) 4778 5939.
Budget accomodation set in an attractive mix of gardens and bushland.
At dusk, listen to a magnificent chorus of bird calls. 🚐 TV 🍽 ♿ 🐾

NOOSA VALLEY: *Villa Alba* $$$$ 4
191 Duke Rd, Doonan, Noosa Valley, QLD 4562. (07) 5449 1900. FAX (07) 5449
1300. This newly renovated complex has secluded villas and an ele-
gant dining room. Mediterranean-style pool and gardens. 🚐 TV 🍽 🐾

ROCKHAMPTON: *Country Comfort Inn* $$ 72
86 Victoria Parade, QLD 4700. (07) 4927 9933. FAX (07) 4927 1615.
A high-rise motel on the river front, rated four-and-a-half stars and part
of the Country Comfort chain. Rooms have balconies. 🚐 TV 🍽 P 🐾

SUNSHINE COAST: *French Quarter Resort* $$$ 119
62 Hastings St, Noosa Heads, QLD 4567. (07) 5474 5300. FAX (07) 5474
8122. A resort rated four-and-a-half stars with first class service and a
magnificent lagoon-style pool and spa. Located opposite Main Beach
near the national park. 🚐 TV 🍽 ♿ P 🐾

SUNSHINE COAST: *Sheraton Noosa Resort* $$$$ 169
Hastings St, Noosa Heads, QLD 4567. (07) 5449 4888. FAX (07) 5449 2230.
This five-star resort has a walkway to the beach across the road, and
views of both the ocean and the river. 🚐 TV 🍽 ♿ P 🍴 🐾

TOWNSVILLE: *Seagulls Resort* $$ 70
74 The Esplanade, Belgian Gardens, QLD 4810. (07) 4721 3111. FAX (07)
4721 3133. Close to the city centre, on the seafront, this affordable
resort has low-rise accommodation set among tropical gardens. A
courtesy bus to the city saves on taxi fares. 🚐 TV 🍽 ♿ P 🐾

TOWNSVILLE: *Jupiters* $$$$ 192
Sir Leslie Thiess Drive, QLD 4810. (07) 4722 2333. FAX (07) 4772 4741.
Townsville's only five-star hotel is perched on the breakwater, with
beautiful views of Magnetic Island. 🚐 24 TV 🍽 ♿ P 🍴 🐾

NORTHERN QUEENSLAND

ALEXANDRA BAY: *Daintree Wilderness Lodge* $$$ 10
83 Cape Tribulation Rd, QLD 4873. (07) 4098 9105. FAX (07) 4098 9021.
An environmental award winner, the lodge is set among fan palms.
See the forest canopy from the roof of each villa. 🚐 ♿ P 🐾

BURKETOWN: *Escott Lodge* $ 14
Escott Lodge, QLD 4830. (07) 4748 5577. FAX (07) 4748 5551.
This is a working cattle station in the remote Gulf Savannah, north-
west of Burketown. Amid the sheer vastness of the Outback, 4WD
safaris and croc-spotting trips are also on offer. 🍽 P 🐾

CAIRNS: *Cairns Colonial Club Resort* $$ 346
18 Cannon St, Manunda, QLD 4870. (07) 4053 5111. FAX (07) 4053 7072.
These 80 self-contained units are popular with families. Organized
leisure activities include bushwalking. 🚐 TV 🍽 ♿ P 🍴 🐾

CAIRNS: *Mercure Harbourside* $$ 173
209 The Esplanade, QLD 4870. (07) 4051 8999. FAX (07) 4051 0317.
Well located on the waterfront; every room here has a view of either
Trinity Bay or the rainforest-clad mountains. 🚐 24 TV 🍽 ♿ P 🐾

CAIRNS: *Cairns International* $$$$ 321
17 Abbott Street, QLD 4870. (07) 4031 1300. FAX (07) 4031 1465.
An established, luxury hotel in downtown Cairns popular with film
stars during the marlin fishing season. 🚐 24 TV 🍽 ♿ P 🐾

Price categories for a standard double room per night, inclusive of service charges and any additional taxes.
$ under A$100
$$ A$100–A$150
$$$ A$150–A$200
$$$$ A$200–A$250
$$$$$ over A$250

Restaurant
Hotel restaurant or dining room usually open to non-residents unless otherwise stated.
Children's Facilities
Indicates child cots and/or a baby-sitting service available. A few hotels also provide children's portions and high chairs in the restaurant.
Garden/Terrace
Hotel with a garden, courtyard or terrace, often providing tables for eating outside.
Swimming Pool
Hotel with an indoor or outdoor swimming pool, or with hot spas for use by residents.

	Number of Rooms	Restaurant	Children's Facilities	Garden/Terrace	Swimming Pool
Cairns: *Radisson Plaza at the Pier* $$$$$ Pierpoint Rd, QLD 4870. ☎ *(07) 4031 1411.* [FAX] *(07) 4031 3226.* Close to the shops and restaurants of Pier Marketplace, and handy for Trinity Wharf for boat trips and other tours. ❄ [24] [TV] ≣ ♿ [P] 🍸 💳	220	●	■		■
Cape Tribulation: *Coconut Beach Rainforest Resort* $$$$ Cape Tribulation Rd, QLD 4873. ☎ *(07) 4098 0033.* [FAX] *(07) 4098 0047.* This appealing resort has 40 freestanding villas in the rainforest, while the dining *bure* (island hut) looks out to sea. ❄ [P] 💳	67	●	■	●	■
Daintree: *Daintree Eco Lodge and Spa* $$$$$ 20 Daintree Rd, QLD 4873. ☎ *(07) 4098 6100.* [FAX] *(07) 4098 6200.* Stay inside the forest canopy in raised timber cabins, where marble floors and ceiling fans add to the tropical atmosphere. ❄ [TV] ≣ [P] 💳	15	●	■		■
Longreach: *Albert Park Motor Inn* $ Sir Hudson Fysh Drive, QLD 4730. ☎ *(07) 4658 2411.* [FAX] *(07) 4658 3181.* The closest accommodation to the Stockman's Hall of Fame *(see p249)*, this motel has an award-winning garden. ❄ [TV] ≣ ♿ [P] 💳	56	●	■	●	■
Malanda: *Honeyflow Country Homestead* $$ Heidke Rd, QLD 4885. ☎ *(07) 4096 8173.* [FAX] *(07) 4096 8099.* A delightful bed-and-breakfast in a colonial homestead. Good for exploring the Atherton Tablelands. ❄ [TV] ♿ [P] 💳	4		■	●	
Mossman: *Silky Oaks Lodge and Healing Waters Spa* $$$$$ Finlayvale Rd, Mossman River Gorge, QLD 4873. ☎ *(07) 4098 1666.* [FAX] *(07) 4098 1983.* Twenty minutes' drive from Port Douglas, this is one of the most popular wilderness lodges of the Far North. ❄ ≣ [P] 💳	50	●		●	■
Mount Isa: *Mercure Inn Burke and Wills* $$ Cnr Grace & Camooweal sts, QLD 4825. ☎ *(07) 4743 8000.* [FAX] *(07) 4743 8424.* Centrally located in the centre of Mount Isa, this is a modern motel with a pool and spas. ❄ [TV] ≣ [P] ≋ 💳	56	●	■		■
Port Douglas: *Coconut Grove Motel* $ 58 Macrossan St, QLD 4871. ☎ *(07) 4099 5124.* [FAX] *(07) 4099 5144.* These motel apartment units are good value and there is a popular on-site restaurant. ❄ ♿ [P] 💳	24	●	■	●	■
Port Douglas: *Radisson Treetops Resort* $$$$ 316 Port Douglas Rd, QLD 4871. ☎ *(07) 4030 4333.* [FAX] *(07) 4030 4323.* Dine among the trees in one of five treehouses in this resort on the corner of Wharf and Macrossan streets. ❄ [24] [TV] ≣ ♿ [P] 🍸 💳	303	●	■	●	■
Port Douglas: *Sheraton Mirage* $$$$$ Port Douglas Rd, QLD 4871. ☎ *(07) 4099 5888.* [FAX] *(07) 4099 5398.* Built behind the casuarina trees lining Four Mile Beach, the hotel is surrounded by lagoons and lush gardens. ❄ [24] [TV] ≣ ♿ [P] 🍸 💳	294	●	■	●	■
DARWIN AND THE TOP END					
Cobourg Peninsula: *Seven Spirit Bay Wilderness Lodge* $$$$$ Gurig National Park, Arnhem Land, NT 0886. ☎ *(08) 8979 0277.* [FAX] *(08) 8979 0282.* This award-winning lodge on the remote Cobourg Peninsula is only accessible by aircraft. Explore pristine wilderness, with tropical forest walks and crocodile spotting. ❄ 🍸 💳	24	●		●	■
Darwin: *Frogshollow Backpackers* $ 27 Lindsay St, NT 0800. ☎ *(08) 8941 2600.* [FAX] *(08) 8941 0758.* This spacious, popular hostel is close to the city centre, with two spas, communal kitchen and an airport pick-up service. ♿ [P] ≋ 💳	25		■	●	■

DARWIN: *Alatai Holiday Apartments* ⓢⓢ 71
Cnr McMinn & Finniss sts, NT 0800. **(** (08) 8981 5188. **FAX** (08) 8981 8887.
These modern self-contained apartments are set around a swimming
pool. The restaurant serves fine Malaysian food. 🖼 TV 🗐 🕭 P 🗷

DARWIN: *Metro Inn* ⓢⓢ 60
38 Gardens Rd, NT 0800. **(** (08) 8981 1544. **FAX** (08) 8941 2541. This basic but
friendly motel has rooms and self-contained units. 🖼 TV 🗐 P 🗷

DARWIN: *Mirrambeena Tourist Resort* ⓢⓢ 224
64 Cavenagh St, NT 0800. **(** (08) 8946 0111. **FAX** (08) 8981 5116.
The hotel complex has picturesque gardens with waterfalls, pools
and spas. 🖼 TV 🗐 🕭 P 🗾 🗷

DARWIN: *Top End Hotel* ⓢⓢ 40
Cnr Mitchell & Daly sts, NT 0800. **(** (08) 8981 6511. **FAX** (08) 8941 1253.
A modern hotel on the central city fringe, with an award-winning bar
and grill. 🖼 TV 🗐 P 🗷

DARWIN: *Carlton Hotel* ⓢⓢⓢ 197
The Esplanade, NT 0800. **(** (08) 8980 0800. **FAX** (08) 8980 0888.
Darwin's finest de luxe hotel faces the Esplanade Gardens and has
superb views across the harbour. 🖼 24 TV 🗐 🕭 P 🗾 🗷

DARWIN: *Marrakai Luxury All-Suites* ⓢⓢⓢ 26
93 Smith St, NT 0800. **(** (08) 8982 3711. **FAX** (08) 8981 9283.
For a luxury long-term stay, these self-contained apartments are
equipped to the highest standard. 🖼 TV 🗐 P 🗷

DARWIN: *MGM Grand Darwin* ⓢⓢⓢ 96
Gilruth Ave, The Gardens, NT 0800. **(** (08) 8943 8888. **FAX** (08) 8943 8999.
The casino hotel offers executive suites and large, well-equipped
rooms, some with views over the bay. 🖼 24 TV 🗐 🕭 P 🗾 🗷

DARWIN: *Rydges Plaza Darwin* ⓢⓢⓢ 233
32 Mitchell St, NT 0800. **(** (08) 8982 0000. **FAX** (08) 8981 1765.
Rooms with views of the harbour are available at this four-star
modern hotel in the centre of town. 🖼 24 TV 🗐 🕭 P 🗾 🗷

DARWIN: *Novotel Atrium Darwin* ⓢⓢⓢⓢ 138
100 The Esplanade, NT 0800. **(** (08) 8941 0755. **FAX** (08) 8981 9025.
Built around a glass atrium with an indoor rainforest and creek, the
hotel is noted for its cocktail bar. 🖼 24 TV 🗐 🕭 P 🗷

HOWARD SPRINGS: *Melaleuca Homestead* ⓢⓢ 4
163 Melaleuca Rd, NT 0835. **(** (08) 8983 2736. **FAX** (08) 8983 3314
This low-level homestead surrounded by bush lies near the lovely
Howard Springs nature reserve. 🖼 🗐 P

KAKADU NATIONAL PARK: *Kakadu Lodge and Caravan Park* ⓢⓢ 42
Jabiru Drive, Jabiru, NT 0886. **(** (08) 8979 2422. **FAX** (08) 8979 2254.
Budget dormitory accommodation with cheap bunks. Families will
usually be given a four-bunk room to themselves. 🗐 P 🗷

KAKADU NATIONAL PARK: *Gagadju Crocodile Hotel* ⓢⓢⓢⓢ 110
Flinders St, Jabiru, NT 0886. **(** (08) 8979 2800. **FAX** (08) 8979 2707.
A hotel built in the shape of a crocodile, with its entrance through the
jaws! It has all the luxuries of any major hotel. 🖼 TV 🗐 🕭 P 🗷

KATHERINE: *Springvale Homestead Tourist Park* ⓢ 60
Shadforth Rd, NT 0850. **(** (08) 8972 1355. **FAX** (08) 8972 3201.
Motel-style accommodation situated on the beautiful Katherine River.
Canoe and swim with local Aborigines in the cool river. 🖼 🗐 P 🗷

KATHERINE: *Knotts Crossing Resort* ⓢⓢ 125
Cnr Giles & Cameron sts, NT 0850. **(** (08) 8972 2511. **FAX** (08) 8972 2628.
A well-equipped tourist resort offering basic budget rooms with some
cooking facilities, set in pleasant surroundings. 🖼 TV 🗐 🕭 P 🗷

THE RED CENTRE

ALICE SPRINGS: *Desert Rose Inn* ⓢ 75
15 Railway Terrace, NT 0870. **(** (08) 8952 1411. **FAX** (08) 8952 3232. This central
motel has rooms overlooking the MacDonnell Ranges. 🖼 TV 🗐 🕭 P 🗷

For key to symbols see back flap

<table>
<tr><td colspan="2">

Price categories for a standard double room per night, inclusive of service charges and any additional taxes.
ⓢ under A$100
ⓢⓢ A$100–A$150
ⓢⓢⓢ A$150–A$200
ⓢⓢⓢⓢ A$200–A$250
ⓢⓢⓢⓢⓢ over A$250

</td><td colspan="5">

RESTAURANT
Hotel restaurant or dining room usually open to non-residents unless otherwise stated.
CHILDREN'S FACILITIES
Indicates child cots and/or a baby-sitting service available. A few hotels also provide children's portions and high chairs in the restaurant.
GARDEN/TERRACE
Hotel with a garden, courtyard or terrace, often providing tables for eating outside.
SWIMMING POOL
Hotel with an indoor or outdoor swimming pool, or with hot spas for use by residents.

</td></tr>
</table>

	Price	Number of Rooms	Restaurant	Children's Facilities	Garden/Terrace	Swimming Pool
ALICE SPRINGS: *Melanka Motel* 94 Todd St, NT 0870. **(** *(08) 8952 2233.* **FAX** *(08) 8952 2890.* Patronized by backpackers from all over the world, this budget accommodation provides a clean, comfortable, no-frills environment. 🗐 **P** 🏖	ⓢ	68	●	■	●	■
ALICE SPRINGS: *The Territory Inn* Leichhardt Terrace, NT 0870. **(** *(08) 8952 2066.* **FAX** *(08) 8952 7829.* Distinguished by its casual and friendly atmosphere, the motel has six rooms equipped for disabled travellers. 🔼 TV 🗐 ♿ **P** 🏖	ⓢⓢ	108	●	■	●	■
ALICE SPRINGS: *The Outback Inn Resort* Stephens Rd, NT 0870. **(** *(08) 8952 6100.* **FAX** *(08) 8952 1988.* Lying at the foot of the East MacDonnell Ranges, many of the rooms have spectacular views. 🔼 TV 🗐 ♿ **P** 🍴 🏖	ⓢⓢ	140	●	■	●	■
ALICE SPRINGS: *Alice Springs Resort* 34 Stott Terrace, NT 0870. **(** *1 300 139 889.* **FAX** *(08) 8953 0995.* This central hotel on the banks of the dry Todd River is well equipped with facilities, including a heated pool. 🔼 TV 🗐 **P** 🏖	ⓢⓢⓢ	144	●	■	●	■
ALICE SPRINGS: *Mercure Inn Diplomat* Cnr Gregory Terrace & Hartley St, NT 0870. **(** *(08) 8952 8977.* **FAX** *(08) 8953 0225.* In the centre of town, the rooms in this hotel all open onto a balcony or the garden. 🔼 TV 🗐 ♿ **P** 🏖	ⓢⓢⓢ	81	●	■	●	■
ALICE SPRINGS: *Rydges Plaza Hotel* Barrett Drive, NT 0870. **(** *(08) 8950 8000.* **FAX** *(08) 8952 3822.* This is Alice Springs' premier hotel, lying on the eastern bank of the Todd River only 1.5 km (1 mile) from town. 🔼 24 TV 🗐 ♿ **P** 🍴 🏖	ⓢⓢⓢ	235	●	■	●	■
ROSS RIVER: *Ross River Homestead* Ross Hwy, NT 0871. **(** *(08) 8956 9711.* **FAX** *(08) 8956 9823.* A major stop for visitors travelling to sites in the East MacDonnell Ranges, this rural homestead is close to Trephina Gorge. It offers activities such as boomerang throwing and whip cracking. 🔼 🗐 **P** 🏖	ⓢⓢ	78	●	■	●	■
TENNANT CREEK: *Eldorado Motor Inn* Paterson St, Stuart Hwy, NT 0860. **(** *(08) 8962 2402.* **FAX** *(08) 8962 3034.* A crossroads for travellers driving all over Australia, this friendly motel has a number of family suites. 🔼 TV 🗐 ♿ **P** 🏖	ⓢ	78	●	■	●	■
WATARRKA NATIONAL PARK: *Kings Canyon Resort* Luritja Rd, NT 0872. **(** *(08) 8956 7442.* **FAX** *(08) 8956 7410.* As this is the only accommodation at Kings Canyon, there are a variety of options, including backpacker dormitories and caravan and camp sites, all in a stunning wilderness location. 🔼 TV 🗐 ♿ **P** 🏖	ⓢⓢⓢⓢ	128	●	■	●	■
YULARA: *Desert Gardens Hotel* Yulara Drive, NT 0872. **(** *1300 139 889.* **FAX** *(02) 9332 4555.* This luxurious four-star hotel has deluxe rooms with views of Uluṟu. It is conveniently located for trips to the national park *(see pp278–81).* 🔼 TV 🗐 **P** 🏖	ⓢⓢⓢⓢⓢ	160	●	■	●	■
YULARA: *Outback Pioneer Hotel* Yulara Drive, NT 0872. **(** *1300 139 889.* **FAX** *(02) 9332 4555.* A relaxed country-style hotel catering for families, with 12 charmingly rustic cabins on offer. 🔼 TV 🗐 ♿ **P** 🏖	ⓢⓢⓢⓢⓢ	137	●	■	●	■
YULARA: *Sails in the Desert Hotel* Yulara Drive, NT 0872. **(** *1300 139 889.* **FAX** *(02) 9332 4555.* An award-winning native garden plus rooms with views of Uluṟu make this a sought-out luxury hotel. 🔼 TV 🗐 ♿ **P** 🏖	ⓢⓢⓢⓢⓢ	224	●	■	●	■

Perth and the Southwest

Albany: *Flinders Park Lodge* Cnr Lower King & Harbour rds, WA 6330. ☎ *(08) 9844 7062.* [FAX] *(08) 9844 8044.* This pretty guesthouse is set in landscaped grounds with excellent views towards Oyster Harbour. 🚭 [P] 💳	$	8			●	
Bunbury: *The Rose Hotel* Victoria St, WA 6230. ☎ *(08) 9721 4533.* [FAX] *(08) 9721 8285* One of the best-preserved historic buildings in the city centre, this Victorian hotel retains the opulence and extravagant details of the glory days of the 19th century. ≡ ♿ [P] 💳	$	25	●			
Busselton: *Prospect Villa* 1 Pries Ave, WA 6280. ☎ *0417 099 307.* [FAX] *(08) 9752 2273.* Within walking distance of Geographe Bay, this 1844 bed-and-breakfast has an elegant country-style decor. [TV] [P] 💳	$	4			●	
Denmark: *The Peppermints* Happy Valley Rd, WA 6333. ☎ *(08) 9840 9305.* [FAX] *(08) 9840 9305.* A good base for exploring the local country. The farm has one bed-and-breakfast room and two cottages in the grounds. 🚭 [P] 💳	$	3			●	
Fremantle: *Fremantle Hotel* Cnr High & Cliff sts, WA 6160. ☎ *(08) 9430 4300.* [FAX] *(08) 9335 2636.* This well-known hotel in one of the port's many Victorian buildings combines modern comfort with antique features. [TV] [P] 💳	$	35			●	
Fremantle: *"Fothergills" of Fremantle* 20 Ord St, WA 6160. ☎ *(08) 9335 6784.* [FAX] *(08) 9430 7789.* An elegant 1892 limestone townhouse, with ocean views and a pretty garden. The rooms are furnished with antiques. 🚭 ≡ [P] 💳	$$	2		■	●	
Fremantle: *Esplanade Hotel* Cnr Marine Terrace & Essex St, WA 6160. ☎ *(08) 9432 4000.* [FAX] *(08) 9430 4539.* This luxury hotel in the heart of Fremantle provides a range of facilities including a sauna, three outdoor spas and bicycle hire. 🚭 [24] [TV] ≡ ♿ [P] 🍸 💳	$$$	259	●	■	●	■
Hyden: *Hyden Wave Rock Hotel* 2 Lynch St, WA 6359. ☎ *(08) 9880 5052.* [FAX] *(08) 9880 5041.* This attractiveRAC three-star hotel near the famous Wave Rock *(see p310)* is furnished with natural jarrah and darkwoods. 🚭 [TV] ≡ ♿ [P] 💳	$$	58	●		●	■
Kalgoorlie: *York Hotel* 259 Hannan St, WA 6430. ☎ *(08) 9021 2337.* [FAX] *(08) 9021 2337.* Built during the region's gold rush era *(see p310)*, the hotel's 19th-century interior has been carefully preserved. [P] 💳	$	20	●			
Margaret River: *The Grange on Farrelly* Farrelly St, WA 6285. ☎ *(08) 9757 3177.* [FAX] *(08) 9757 3076.* Accommodation here is in motel-style rooms in the grounds of the former Davies Homestead, built in 1885. Some rooms have canopy beds with antique and wooden furnishings. 🚭 ≡ [TV] ♿ [P] 💳	$$	29	●	■	●	■
Margaret River: *Gilgara Homestead* 300 Caves Rd, WA 6285. ☎ *(08) 9757 2705.* [FAX] *(08) 9757 3259.* In the heart of Margaret River's wine country, this replica 1870 homestead offers award-winning accommodation. 🚭 [P] 💳	$$$$	6			●	
Norseman: *Norseman Hotel* Cnr Robert & Talbot sts, WA 6443. ☎ *(08) 9039 1023.* [FAX] *(08) 9039 1503.* This basic two-storey colonial-style hotel is situated in the centre of Norseman. Breakfast is included. [P] 💳	$	25	●		●	
Northam: *Shamrock Hotel* 112 Fitzgerald St, WA 6401. ☎ *(08) 9622 1092.* [FAX] *(08) 9622 5707.* This historic hotel has 14 suites with spa baths and is ideally located in the heart of town. Breakfast is included. 🚭 [TV] ≡ [P] 💳	$	14	●		●	
Pemberton: *Karri Valley Resort* Vasse Hwy, WA 6260. ☎ *(08) 9776 2020.* [FAX] *(08) 9776 2012.* Set amid Pemberton's karri forests, this resort offers attractive accommodation in motel units or chalets. 🚭 ♿ [P] 💳	$$$	68	●	■	●	

For key to symbols see back flap

Price categories for a standard double room per night, inclusive of service charges and any additional taxes.
Ⓢ under A$100
ⓈⓈ A$100–A$150
ⓈⓈⓈ A$150–A$200
ⓈⓈⓈⓈ A$200–A$250
ⓈⓈⓈⓈⓈ over A$250

RESTAURANT
Hotel restaurant or dining room usually open to non-residents unless otherwise stated.
CHILDREN'S FACILITIES
Indicates child cots and/or a baby-sitting service available. A few hotels also provide children's portions and high chairs in the restaurant.
GARDEN/TERRACE
Hotel with a garden, courtyard or terrace, often providing tables for eating outside.
SWIMMING POOL
Hotel with an indoor or outdoor swimming pool, or with hot spas for use by residents.

		NUMBER OF ROOMS	RESTAURANT	CHILDREN'S FACILITIES	GARDEN/TERRACE	SWIMMING POOL
PERTH: *Rose & Crown Hotel* @ rcrown@iinet.net.au	Ⓢ	32	●	■	●	■
105 Swan St, Guildford, WA 6055. **(** (08) 9299 6717. **FAX** (08) 9377 1628. The oldest hotel trading in Western Australia, accommodation is in motel units next to the colonial Georgian building. 🛏 TV 🗐 ♿ P ✒						
PERTH: *Criterion Hotel*	ⓈⓈ	69	●			
560 Hay St, WA 6000. **(** (08) 9325 5155. **FAX** (08) 9325 4176. This unique Art Deco building in the centre of town was completely renovated in 1996. The price includes breakfast. 🛏 TV 🗐 ♿ P ✒						
PERTH: *Miss Maud Swedish Hotel*	ⓈⓈ	52	●			
97 Murray St, WA 6000. **(** (08) 9325 3900. **FAX** (08) 9221 3225. A traditional smorgasbord breakfast is included at this stylish boutique hotel, with murals and pine furniture in all rooms. 🛏 24 TV 🗐 ✒						
PERTH: *Sullivan's Hotel*	ⓈⓈ	71	●	■	●	■
166 Mounts Bay Rd, WA 6000. **(** (08) 9321 8022. **FAX** (08) 9481 6762. This small family-owned hotel next to Perth's beautiful Kings Park *(see p298)* has a friendly and homely atmosphere. 🛏 TV 🗐 ♿ P ✒						
PERTH: *Rendezvous Observation City Hotel*	ⓈⓈⓈⓈ	333	●	■		■
The Esplanade, Scarborough Beach, WA 6019. **(** (08) 9340 5555. **FAX** (08) 9245 1345. This modern hotel is a landmark on Scarborough Beach. Many rooms have ocean views. 🛏 24 TV 🗐 ♿ P 🍽 ✒						
PERTH: *Burswood International Resort Casino*	ⓈⓈⓈⓈⓈ	414	●	■	●	■
Great Eastern Hwy, Burswood, WA 6100. **(** (08) 9362 7777. **FAX** (08) 9470 2553. This up-market hotel resort lies on the Swan River, within a landscaped park and with great city views. 🛏 24 TV 🗐 ♿ P 🍽 ✒						
ROTTNEST ISLAND: *Rottnest Lodge Resort*	ⓈⓈⓈ	80	●	■	●	■
Rottnest Island, WA 6161. **(** (08) 9292 5161. **FAX** (08) 9292 5158. A rare opportunity to stay in the cells of this 19th-century prison, known as the Quod, for Aboriginal convicts *(see p300)*. 🛏 TV ♿ ✒						
YORK: *Imperial Hotel*	Ⓢ	18	●		●	
83 Avon Terrace, WA 6302. **(** (08) 9641 1010. **FAX** (08) 9641 2201. Old-world charm and a pretty garden make this Victorian hotel in historic York an attractive place to stay. P ✒						

NORTH OF PERTH

		NUMBER OF ROOMS	RESTAURANT	CHILDREN'S FACILITIES	GARDEN/TERRACE	SWIMMING POOL
BROOME: *Mangrove Hotel*	ⓈⓈ	69	●	■	●	■
Carnarvon St, WA 6725. **(** (08) 9192 1303. **FAX** (08) 9193 5169. Set among beautiful gardens, this friendly hotel has views across Roebuck Bay and is close to Broome's Chinatown. 🛏 TV 🗐 P ✒						
BROOME: *Cable Beach Intercontinental Resort*	ⓈⓈⓈⓈ	267	●	■	●	■
Cable Beach Rd, WA 6725. **(** (08) 9192 0400. **FAX** (08) 9192 2249. Overlooking Broome's celebrated Cable Beach, this luxury resort has studio rooms, bungalows and suites. 🛏 TV 🗐 ♿ P ✒						
CARNARVON: *Fascine Lodge*	ⓈⓈ	61	●	■	●	■
34 David Brand Drive, WA 6701. **(** (08) 9941 2411. **FAX** (08) 9941 2491. A variety of comfortable units set around a patio and pool. Wheelchair access is to the ground floor only. 🛏 TV 🗐 ♿ limited. P ✒						
DAMPIER: *Mercure Dampier*	ⓈⓈ	63	●	■	●	■
The Esplanade, WA 6713. **(** (08) 9183 1222. **FAX** (08) 9183 1028. Only 50 m (55 yards) from the beach, the Mercure Dampier offers three self-contained family suites, ideal for those visiting the region with children. 🛏 TV 🗐 P ✒						

DENHAM: *Heritage Resort Hotel* $$$
Cnr Knight Terrace & Durlacher St, WA 6537. ((08) 9948 1133. FAX (08) 9948 1134. An affordable family hotel on the ocean front. The hotel is well placed for tours to Shark Bay *(see pp318–19)*. 🖥 TV 🍽 ᕋ P 🌐
27

EXMOUTH: *Exmouth Cape Tourist Village* $
Truscott Crescent, WA 6707. ((08) 9949 1101. FAX (08) 9949 1402. Reasonably priced chalets, as well as camping and a caravan park. Services include free bicycles, vehicle hire and dive shop. 🖥 🍽 P 🌐
65

FITZROY CROSSING: *Fitzroy River Lodge* $$$
Great Northern Hwy, WA 6765. ((08) 9191 5141. FAX (08) 9191 5142. Set in 20 ha (50 acres) of Kimberley country, this Outback station offers rooms, cottages and caravans. 🖥 TV 🍽 ᕋ P 🌐
40

GERALDTON: *Best Western Hospitality Inn* $$
Cathedral Ave, WA 6530. ((08) 9921 1422. FAX (08) 9921 1239. Close to the centre of Geraldton, accommodation at this chain hotel includes a small number of apartments. 🖥 TV 🍽 ᕋ P 🌐
55

KALBARRI: *Kalbarri Beach Resort* $$
Clotworthy St, WA 6536. ((08) 9937 1061. FAX (08) 9937 1323. A good base for exploring Kalbarri National Park, with modern self-catering two-bedroom apartments. 🖥 TV 🍽 P 🌐
114

MONKEY MIA: *Monkey Mia Dolphin Resort* $$$
Monkey Mia Rd, Shark Bay, WA 6537. ((08) 9948 1320. FAX (08) 9948 1034. Right on the beach next to the dolphin feeding area, this resort is perfect for dolphin-watching. 🖥 🍽 ᕋ P 🍴 🌐
44

MOUNT HART: *Mount Hart Homestead* $$$$
Via Gibb River Rd, WA 6728. ((08) 9191 4645. FAX (08) 9191 7836. In the King Leopold Mountain Range, at the heart of the Kimberley, this tranquil hotel includes breakfast and dinner in the price. P 🍴 🌐
13

NEW NORCIA: *Monastery Guesthouse* $
WA 6509. ((08) 9654 8002. FAX (08) 9654 8097. Rooms and meals are free at this quiet Benedictine monastery, although a donation of around $45 per person per night is suggested to help towards maintenance. 🖥 ᕋ P 🌐
15

NEW NORCIA: *New Norcia Hotel* $
Great Northern Hwy, WA 6509. ((08) 9654 8034. FAX (08) 9654 8011. Built in 1927, the New Norcia has a majestic central staircase and antique furnishings. Sports facilities include a golf course and excellent tennis courts. P 🌐
17

ADELAIDE AND THE SOUTHEAST

ADELAIDE: *Tiffins on the Park* $$
176 Greenhill Rd, Parkside, SA 5063. ((08) 8271 0444. FAX (08) 8272 8675. Just outside Adelaide city square, this hotel is located amid tree-lined streets, a short drive from the city centre. 🖥 24 TV 🍽 P 🌐
54

ADELAIDE: *Adelaide Terrace Apartments* $$$
80 Sturt St, SA 5000. ((08) 8294 5004. FAX (08) 8294 5004. Two-storey two-bedroom units are available here, right in the centre of Adelaide. All mod cons – even a laundry. 🖥 TV 🍽 P 🌐
3

ADELAIDE: *Chifley on South Terrace* $$$
226 South Terrace, SA 5000. ((08) 8223 4355. FAX (08) 8232 5997. Right in the city square, all rooms overlook either the beautiful South Parklands or the hotel's pool and gardens. 🖥 TV 🍽 P 🍴 🌐
96

ADELAIDE: *Hilton Adelaide* $$$
233 Victoria Square, SA 5000. ((08) 8217 2000. FAX (08) 8211 7035. Everything you would expect from a Hilton hotel, centrally located, next to the vibrant Central Market and the surrounding restaurant area *(see pp514–15)*. 🖥 24 TV 🍽 ᕋ P 🍴 🌐
380

ADELAIDE: *North Adelaide Heritage Accommodation* $$$
109 Glen Osmond Rd, Eastwood, SA 5063. ((08) 8272 1355. FAX (08) 8272 1355. Choose from 17 suites and restored cottages dotted all over North Adelaide. 🖥 24 TV 🍽 ᕋ *limited.* P 🌐
12

<table>
<tr><td colspan="2">

Price categories for a standard double room per night, inclusive of service charges and any additional taxes.

$ under A$100
$$ A$100–A$150
$$$ A$150–A$200
$$$$ A$200–A$250
$$$$$ over A$250

</td>
<td colspan="5">

RESTAURANT
Hotel restaurant or dining room usually open to non-residents unless otherwise stated.
CHILDREN'S FACILITIES
Indicates child cots and/or a baby-sitting service available. A few hotels also provide children's portions and high chairs in the restaurant.
GARDEN/TERRACE
Hotels with a garden, courtyard or terrace, often providing tables for eating outside.
SWIMMING POOL
Hotel with an indoor or outdoor swimming pool, or with hot spas for use by residents.

</td></tr>
</table>

	NUMBER OF ROOMS	RESTAURANT	CHILDREN'S FACILITIES	GARDEN/TERRACE	SWIMMING POOL
ADELAIDE: *Novotel on Hindley, Adelaide* $$$$ 65 Hindley St, SA 5000. (08) 8231 5552. FAX (08) 8237 3800. A quiet oasis within one of the busiest sections of the city. Hindley Street is the hub of Adelaide nightlife.	181	●	●		●
ADELAIDE: *Hyatt Regency* $$$$$ North Terrace, SA 5000. (08) 8231 1234. FAX (08) 8238 2392. Next to the Adelaide Casino, this luxury hotel is typical of the Hyatt hotel chain. Most of the rooms have spectacular views of the city.	367	●	●		●
ADELAIDE: *Stamford Plaza Hotel* $$$$$ 150 North Terrace, SA 5000. (08) 8461 1111. FAX (08) 8231 7572. Well-appointed rooms have views either over the city or the parklands towards North Adelaide.	335	●	●	●	●
ANGASTON: *Collingrove Homestead* $$$ Eden Valley Rd, SA 5353. (08) 8564 2061. FAX (08) 8564 3600. Stay in refurbished servants' quarters in this 1850s country house owned by the National Trust.	6			●	
COONAWARRA: *Chardonnay Lodge* $$ Riddoch Hwy, SA 5263. (08) 8736 3309. FAX (08) 8736 3383. In the midst of the Coonawarra vineyards, this family-run lodge has large rooms and a good restaurant.	38	●	●	●	●
GLENELG: *Stamford Grand Hotel* $$$$$ Moseley Square, SA 5045. (08) 8376 1222. FAX (08) 8376 1111. Close to all the excellent amenities in Adelaide's premier beach suburb, all rooms have views of either the sea or the Adelaide Hills.	241	●	●		●
HAHNDORF: *The Hahndorf Old Mill* $ 98 Main Rd, SA 5245. (08) 8388 7888. FAX (08) 8388 7242. Part of an 1854 flour mill has been incorporated into this complex in Australia's oldest German town (*see p344*).	23	●	●	●	
KANGAROO ISLAND: *Ozone Seafront Hotel* $$ The Foreshore, Kingscote, SA 5223. (08) 8553 2011. FAX (08) 8553 2249. This friendly, comfortable hotel is located on the rocks where penguins nest every night.	37	●	●	●	●
KANGAROO ISLAND: *Wisteria Lodge Motel* $$$ 7 Cygnet Rd, Kingscote, SA 5223. (08) 8553 2707. FAX (08) 8553 2200. All rooms have views over the sea from either a balcony or patio. The landscaped foreshore is ideal for walking.	20	●	●	●	●
KANGAROO ISLAND: *Wanderer's Rest* $$$ Bayview Rd, American River, SA 5221. (08) 8553 7140. FAX (08) 8553 7282. With panoramic views over American River, this is a great spot to enjoy bushland pleasures in peace and comfort.	9	●		●	●
LYNDOCH: *Barossa Park Motel* $ Barossa Valley Hwy, SA 5351. (08) 8524 4268. FAX (08) 8524 4725. This motel, with its garden of 25,000 roses, is situated at the gateway to the Barossa Valley (*see pp348–9*). There are daily tours of the château and its art collection, as well as wine tasting.	34	●	●	●	●
MARANANGA: *The Hermitage of Marananga* $$$$ Cnr Seppeltsfield & Stonewell rds, SA 5355. (08) 8562 2722. FAX (08) 8562 3133. High on a hill top in the heart of Barossa Valley wine country, with luxury suites, each with a private patio area.	11	●	●	●	●

MOUNT GAMBIER: *Lakes Resort* 17 Lakes Terrace West, SA 5290. ☎ *(08) 8725 5755.* [FAX] *(08) 8723 2710.* On the slopes of the extinct volcano. There is a variety of options on offer, from budget rooms to executive suites. 🛁 [TV] ▤ [P] 🍸 💳	$$	40	●	■	●	■
MYLOR: *Warrawong Sanctuary* Cnr Stock & William rds, SA 5152. ☎ *(08) 8370 9197.* [FAX] *(08) 8370 8332.* Stay in luxurious tents in the middle of this wildlife sanctuary *(see p344)*. The tariff includes a three-course evening meal in the restaurant, guided walks and a cooked breakfast. 🛁 ▤ [P] 💳	$$$	15	●	■	●	
PADTHAWAY: *Padthaway Estate Homestead* Riddoch Hwy, SA 5271. ☎ *(08) 8765 5039.* [FAX] *(08) 8765 5097.* A luxury guesthouse in an 1882 two-storey mansion. Out of the way, it is ideal for those who value the peace and quiet of the country. [P] 💳	$$$$	6	●		●	
ROBE: *Robe House* Hagen St, SA 5276. ☎ *(08) 8768 2770.* [FAX] *(08) 8768 2770.* The oldest house in town, built in 1847, now contains three comfortable, self-contained apartments. 🛁 [TV] [P] 💳	$	3			●	
STIRLING: *Thorngrove Manor Hotel* 2 Glenside Lane, SA 5152. ☎ *(08) 8339 6748.* [FAX] *(08) 8370 9950.* A multi-towered, castle-like folly in the peaceful Adelaide Hills, where the emphasis is on privacy and indulgence. 🛁 [24] [TV] ♿ [P] 💳	$$$$$	6	●	■	●	
TANUNDA: *Barossa Weintal Resort* Murray St, SA 5352. ☎ *(08) 8563 2303.* [FAX] *(08) 8563 2279.* Centrally located at Tanunda, the largest of the Barossa Valley towns *(see pp348–9)*. Great for access to all the wineries. 🛁 [TV] ▤ ♿ [P] 💳	$$	40	●	■	●	■
VICTOR HARBOR: *Whaler's Inn* The Bluff, Encounter Bay, SA 5211. ☎ *(08) 8552 4400.* [FAX] *(08) 8552 4240.* Each of the two-storey, three-bedroom apartments has a fully equipped kitchen and a double spa bath overlooking a private courtyard. The view takes in Encounter Bay. 🛁 [TV] ▤ ♿ [P] 💳	$$	14	●	■	●	■

THE YORKE AND EYRE PENINSULAS

ARKAROOLA: *Arkaroola Resort* Arkaroola Wildlife Sanctury, SA 5700. ☎ *(08) 8648 4848.* [FAX] *(08) 8648 4846* The largest resort in the Flinders Ranges offers a wide range of accommodation. Scenic flights and 4WD tours are available. 🛁 ▤ [P] 💳	$	62	●	■	●	■
AUBURN: *Rising Sun Hotel* Main North Rd, SA 5451. ☎ *(08) 8849 2015.* [FAX] *(08) 8849 2266.* Rooms and Victorian mews suites are on offer at this family-owned hotel at the gateway to the Clare Valley. 🛁 [TV] ♿ [P] 💳	$	10	●		●	
BLINMAN: *Blinman Hotel* Main St, SA 5730. ☎ *(08) 8648 4867.* [FAX] *(08) 8648 4621.* In the centre of the Flinders Ranges, so it's an easy drive to all the major attractions. Join the locals for a drink in the front bar. 🛁 ▤ ♿ [P] 💳	$	17	●		●	■
BURRA: *Burra Heritage Cottages* Tivers Row, 8–18 Truro St, SA 5417. ☎ *(08) 8892 2461.* [FAX] *(08) 8892 2948.* Spacious 1856 bluestone cottages with woodfires and old-style radios. TVs are available upon request. 🛁 ♿ [P] 💳	$$	6		■	●	
CLARE: *Clare Valley Motel* 74a Main North Rd, SA 5453. ☎ *(08) 8842 2799.* [FAX] *(08) 8842 3121.* A peaceful but central base from which to explore the wineries and other attractions of the region. 🛁 [TV] ▤ [P] 💳	$	33	●	■	●	■
COOBER PEDY: *The Underground Motel* Catacomb Rd, SA 5723. ☎ *(08) 8672 5324.* [FAX] *(08) 8672 5911.* Cool underground rooms are essential in the fierce summer heat of this Outback town *(see p360)*. Watch the spectacular sunsets over the desert from the veranda. 🛁 [TV] [P] 💳	$	8		■	●	
COOBER PEDY: *Desert Cave Hotel* Hutchinson St, SA 5723. ☎ *(08) 8672 5688.* [FAX] *(08) 8672 5198.* A luxury underground troglodyte hotel *(see p360)*, with shops, bars and restaurants dug out of the ground. 🛁 [TV] ▤ ♿ [P] 🍸 💳	$$$	50	●	■		■

For key to symbols see back flap

Price categories for a standard double room per night, inclusive of service charges and any additional taxes.

$ under A$100
$$ A$100–A$150
$$$ A$150–A$200
$$$$ A$200–A$250
$$$$$ over A$250

RESTAURANT
Hotel restaurant or dining room usually open to non-residents unless otherwise stated.

CHILDREN'S FACILITIES
Indicates child cots and/or a baby-sitting service available. A few hotels also provide children's portions and high chairs in the restaurant.

GARDEN/TERRACE
Hotel with a garden, courtyard or terrace, often providing tables for eating outside.

SWIMMING POOL
Hotel with an indoor or outdoor swimming pool, or with hot spas for use by residents.

	Price	Number of Rooms	Restaurant	Children's Facilities	Garden/Terrace	Swimming Pool
EDITHBURGH: *The Anchorage Motel* 25 O'Halloran Parade, SA 5583. (08) 8852 6262. FAX (08) 8852 6147. One- and two-bedroom units on the foreshore near the jetty. Fish-cleaning tables and boat-washing facilities are provided for avid anglers and sailors *(see p355)*. 🛏 TV P 🌿	$	11		■	●	
MINTARO: *Martindale Hall* Manoora Rd, Mintaro, SA 5415. (08) 8843 9088. FAX (08) 8843 9082. Have the run of South Australia's finest mansion, and enjoy formal dinners served by a butler and maid. P 🌿	$	9				
PORT LINCOLN: *Blue Seas Motel* 7 Gloucester Terrace, SA 5606. (08) 8682 3022. FAX (08) 8682 6932. In the heart of Port Lincoln, this motel overlooks Boston Bay and is close to all amenities and tourist attractions. 🛏 TV 🍽 P 🌿	$	15		■	●	
PORT LINCOLN: *Lincoln Cove Apartments* Bridge Crescent, SA 5606. (08) 8683 0495. FAX (08) 8683 0495. Three-bedroom apartments provided with spas, dishwashers and laundry facilities. Minimum bookings of two nights. 🛏 TV P 🌿	$$	5			●	
RAWNSLEY PARK: *Rawnsley Park Cabins* Hawker-Wilpena Rd, SA 5434. (08) 8648 0030. FAX (08) 8648 0013. Set in beautiful country at the base of Rawnsley Bluff. Horse-riding and bushwalking are available on the doorstep. 🛏 🍽 P 🌿	$	28		■		
WHYALLA: *Alexander Motor Inn* 99 Playford Ave, SA 5600. (08) 8645 9488. FAX (08) 8645 2211. Single rooms and two-bedroom suites are available here. The restaurant has a special house-guest menu *(see p517)*. 🛏 TV 🍽 P 🌿	$	40	●	■	●	■
WILPENA: *Wilpena Pound Resort* Wilpena, SA 5434. (08) 8648 0004. FAX (08) 8648 0028. Landscaped grounds offer a contrast to the often harsh surroundings. An ideal base for walking, 4WD tours and scenic flights. 🛏 TV 🍽 ♿ P 🌿	$$	60	●	■	●	■
MELBOURNE						
ALBERT PARK: *Hotel Victoria* 123 Beaconsfield Parade, VIC 3004. Map 2 D5. (03) 9690 3666. FAX (03) 9699 9570. This boutique hotel, built in 1888, has spectacular views across Port Phillip Bay, especially from the corner rooms. 🛏 TV P 🌿	$$	27	●			
ALBERT PARK: *Carlton Crest Hotel* 65 Queens Rd, VIC 3004. Map 3 B5. (03) 9529 4300. FAX (03) 9521 3111. Generous-sized rooms, some with views of Albert Park Lake. The hotel is convenient for city transport. 🛏 24 TV 🍽 ♿ P 🛎 🌿	$$$	374	●	■		■
ALBERT PARK: *Park Royal on St Kilda Road* 562 St Kilda Rd, VIC 3004. Map 2 D5. (03) 9529 8888. FAX (03) 9525 1242. St Kilda Road is a grand tree-lined boulevard which links the city with the beach. Rooms have city or park views. 🛏 24 TV 🍽 ♿ P 🛎 🌿	$$$$$	220	●	■	●	■
CARLTON: *Downtowner on Lygon* 66 Lygon St, VIC 3053. Map 1 C1. (03) 9663 5555. FAX (03) 9662 3308. Quality motel accommodation conveniently located in bustling Lygon Street's restaurant strip *(see p387)*. 🛏 TV 🍽 ♿ P 🛎 🌿 ♨	$$$	98	●	■	●	■
CITY CENTRE: *Holiday Inn Melbourne* Cnr Flinders & Spencer sts, VIC 3005. Map 1 C4. (03) 9648 2777. FAX (03) 9629 5624. On the bank of the Yarra River, close to Southgate, the Arts Centre complex and other attractions. 🛏 24 TV 🍽 ♿ P 🛎 ♨ 🌿	$$$	385	●	■		■

CITY CENTRE: *Rydges Melbourne* 186 Exhibition St, VIC 3000. **Map 2 D2.** ☎ *(03) 9662 0511.* FAX *(03) 9663 6988.* A stylish hotel in the heart of the theatre district, with luxury suites for those who wish to be pampered. 👪 [24] [TV] ≣ ♿ [P] 🏊 💳	$$$	363	●	■		■
CITY CENTRE: *Victoria Hotel* 215 Little Collins St, VIC 3000. **Map 2 D3.** ☎ *(03) 9653 0441.* FAX *(03) 9650 9678.* Built in 1880, the hotel is centrally located, close to theatres, restaurants and shops. ♿ ≣ 👪 [TV] [P] 🚭 💳	$$$	468	●	■		
CITY CENTRE: *All Seasons Crossley* 51 Little Bourke St, VIC 3000. **Map 1 B2.** ☎ *(03) 9639 1639.* FAX *(03) 9639 0566.* Exceptional service for business travellers and tourists alike, with large rooms, some with great views of the city. 👪 [TV] ≣ [P] 🍸 💳	$$$$	89	●	■		
CITY CENTRE: *Novotel Melbourne On Collins* 270 Collins St, VIC 3000. **Map 1 C3.** ☎ *(03) 9667 5800.* FAX *(03) 9667 5805.* Melbourne's most centrally located hotel has spacious rooms overlooking the retail precinct of Collins Street. 👪 [24] [TV] ≣ ♿ [P] 🍸 💳	$$$$	323	●	■		■
CITY CENTRE: *Melbourne Marriott Hotel* Cnr Exhibition & Lonsdale sts, VIC 3000. **Map 2 D2.** ☎ *(03) 9662 3900.* FAX *(03) 9663 4297.* A favourite haunt of Melbourne's theatre crowd, with elegantly appointed rooms and suites. 👪 [24] [TV] ≣ ♿ [P] 🍸 🚭 💳	$$$$	185	●	■	●	■
CITY CENTRE: *Adelphi* 187 Flinders Lane, VIC 3000. **Map 2 D3.** ☎ *(03) 9650 7555.* FAX *(03) 9650 2710.* A small luxury hotel known for both its innovative design and its restaurant in the hotel basement *(see p517)*. 👪 [24] [TV] ≣ [P] 🍸 🚭 💳	$$$$$	34	●	■		■
CITY CENTRE: *Grand Hyatt* 123 Collins St, VIC 3000. **Map 2 D3.** ☎ *(03) 9657 1234.* FAX *(03) 9650 3491.* A member of the Hyatt hotel chain, this luxury hotel is within walking distance of many of the city's chic shops. 👪 [24] [TV] ≣ ♿ [P] 🍸 🚭 💳	$$$$$	550	●	■		■
CITY CENTRE: *Grand Mercure* 321 Flinders Lane, VIC 3000. **Map 2 D3.** ☎ *(03) 9629 4088.* FAX *(03) 9629 4066.* Every suite has an intimate, luxurious atmosphere. Executive suites overlook a courtyard garden. 👪 [24] [TV] ≣ ♿ [P] 🍸 🚭 💳	$$$$$	58	●	■	●	
CITY CENTRE: *Hotel Lindrum* 26 Flinders St, VIC 3000. **Map 2 D3.** ☎ *(03) 9668 1111.* FAX *(03) 9668 1199.* A chic hotel, offering sophisticated contemporary accommodation. Minimalist décor with home comforts. 👪 [TV] ≣ 🚭 💳	$$$$$	59	●	■		
CITY CENTRE: *Le Meridien at Rialto* 495 Collins St, VIC 3000. **Map 1 B4.** ☎ *(03) 9620 9111.* FAX *(03) 9614 1219.* Cleverly constructed behind a historic façade with modern interior decor. Some rooms overlook the stylish atrium. 👪 [24] [TV] ≣ ♿ [P] 🍸 🚭 💳	$$$$$	244	●	■		■
CITY CENTRE: *Oakford Gordon Place* 24 Little Bourke St, VIC 3000. **Map 1 B2.** ☎ *(03) 9663 2888.* FAX *(03) 9639 1537.* This historic boutique hotel offers de luxe studios and apartments built around an attractive courtyard. 👪 [TV] ≣ [P] 🍸 💳	$$$$$	82	●	■	●	■
CITY CENTRE: *Seville Park Suites* 333 Exhibition St, VIC 3000. **Map 2 D2.** ☎ *(03) 9668 2500.* FAX *(03) 9668 2599.* One- and two-bedroom suites are available in this modern hotel close to the theatre district and Chinatown. 👪 [TV] ≣ ♿ [P] 🚭 💳	$$$$$	144	●	■	●	■
CITY CENTRE: *Hotel Sofitel Melbourne* 25 Collins St, VIC 3000. **Map 2 D3.** ☎ *(03) 9653 0000.* FAX *(03) 9650 4261.* The hotel occupies the top floors of an old building, with all rooms benefitting from stunning views. 👪 [24] [TV] ≣ ♿ [P] 🍸 🚭 💳	$$$$$	363	●	■		
CITY CENTRE: *Stamford Plaza Melbourne* 111 Little Collins St, VIC 3000. **Map 2 D3.** ☎ *(03) 9659 1000.* FAX *(03) 9659 0999.* An elegant foyer, with twin towers and an atrium. The stylish suites have fully equipped kitchens. 👪 [24] [TV] ≣ ♿ [P] 🍸 🚭 💳	$$$$$	283	●	■		■
CITY CENTRE: *The Windsor* 103 Spring St, VIC 3000. **Map 2 D2.** ☎ *(03) 9633 6000.* FAX *(03) 9633 6001.* This grand Victorian hotel is a Melbourne institution. Rooms provide charm and five-star luxury. 👪 [24] [TV] ≣ ♿ [P] 🍸 🚭 💳	$$$$$	180	●	■		

For key to symbols see back flap

Price categories for a standard double room per night, inclusive of service charges and any additional taxes.
$ under A$100
$$ A$100–A$150
$$$ A$150–A$200
$$$$ A$200–A$250
$$$$$ over A$250

RESTAURANT
Hotel restaurant or dining room usually open to non-residents unless otherwise stated.
CHILDREN'S FACILITIES
Indicates child cots and/or a baby-sitting service available. A few hotels also provide children's portions and high chairs in the restaurant.
GARDEN/TERRACE
Hotel with a garden, courtyard or terrace, often providing tables for eating outside.
SWIMMING POOL
Hotel with an indoor or outdoor swimming pool, or with hot spas for use by residents.

	NUMBER OF ROOMS	RESTAURANT	CHILDREN'S FACILITIES	GARDEN/TERRACE	SWIMMING POOL
EAST MELBOURNE: *Georgian Court* $$ 21–25 George St, VIC 3002. (03) 9419 6353. FAX (03) 9416 0895. Traditional bed-and-breakfast style is found in this large Georgian house in historic East Melbourne. TV P ▤ ✉	31		■		
EAST MELBOURNE: *Magnolia Court Boutique Hotel* $$$ 101 Powlett St, VIC 3002. (03) 9419 4222. FAX (03) 9416 0841. This family-owned hotel in a leafy inner suburb is located in an historical setting. Several rooms have their own balconies. ⌨ TV ▤ P ✉	26		■	●	
EAST MELBOURNE: *Hilton on the Park* $$$$$ 192 Wellington Parade, VIC 3002. (03) 9419 2000. FAX (03) 9419 2001. An established five-star hotel overlooking the Fitzroy Gardens, a short walk from the city centre. ⌨ 24 TV ▤ & P ⛏ ✈ ✉	405	●	■		■
FITZROY: *Royal Gardens Quest Inn* $$$$ 8 Royal Lane, VIC 3065. **Map** 2 D1. (03) 9419 9888. FAX (03) 9416 0451. Set in one of Melbourne's cosmopolitan northern suburbs, next to Carlton Gardens. A range of apartments is available. ⌨ TV P ✉	70		■	●	■
RICHMOND: *Rydges Riverwalk* $$$ 649 Bridge Rd, VIC 3121. **Map** 4 D3. (03) 9246 1200. FAX (03) 9246 1222. With views over the Yarra River, this is a pleasant spot for those who want something quieter than the city centre. ⌨ 24 TV ▤ & P ✉	94	●	■	●	
ST KILDA: *Boutique Hotel Tolarno* $$ 42 Fitzroy St, VIC 3182. **Map** 5 B4. (03) 9537 0200. FAX (03) 9534 7800. In the heart of St Kilda's café scene, this restored art deco and retro hotel caters particularly for the arts community. ⌨ TV ▤ ✉	31	●	■	●	
ST KILDA: *Novotel St Kilda* $$$ 16 The Esplanade, VIC 3182. **Map** 5 B5. (03) 9525 5522. FAX (03) 9525 5678. Close to the city, but with the relaxed atmosphere of a seaside resort. Some rooms have views of the bay. ⌨ 24 TV ▤ & P ⛏ ✉	202	●	■		■
ST KILDA: *Robinsons by the Sea* $$$ 335 Beaconsfield Pde, VIC 3182. **Map** 5 B5. (03) 9534 2683. FAX (03) 9534 2683. Melbourne's premier B&B in a charmingly restored Victorian terrace, opposite the beach and close to the cafés and restaurants of Fitzroy Street. TV ✈ ✉	5	●	■	●	■
SOUTHBANK: *Crown Towers* $$$$$ 8 Whiteman St, VIC 3006. **Map** 1 B5. (03) 9292 6666. FAX (03) 9292 6600. Spacious, luxurious rooms are furnished in rich silks and warm timbers. All rooms feature city or bay views. ⌨ 24 TV ▤ & P ⛏ ✈ ✉	480	●	■	●	■
SOUTHBANK: *Sheraton Towers Southgate* $$$$$ 1 Southgate Ave, VIC 3006. **Map** 1 C4. (03) 9696 3100. FAX (03) 9690 6581. Modern but with a Victorian elegance, the hotel is on the south bank of the Yarra River, close to local attractions. ⌨ 24 TV ▤ & P ⛏ ✈ ✉	387	●	■		■
SOUTH YARRA: *The Tilba* $$$ 30 West Toorak Rd, VIC 3141. **Map** 4 D5. (03) 9867 8844. FAX (03) 9867 6567. Charming Victorian mansion, with period furniture and antiques. Within easy reach of the city centre. ⌨ TV ▤ P ✈ ✉	18		■	●	
SOUTH YARRA: *The Como Melbourne* $$$$$ 630 Chapel St, VIC 3141. **Map** 4 E5. (03) 9824 2222. FAX (03) 9824 1263. Set on South Yarra's stylish café street, this hotel is a favourite with entertainers and sports people. Expect top personal service and a free daily limousine to the city centre. ⌨ 24 TV ▤ & P ⛏ ✉	107	●	■	●	■

WESTERN VICTORIA

APOLLO BAY: *Greenacres Country House by the Sea* — $$ — 26
Great Ocean Rd, VIC 3233. ((03) 5237 6309. FAX (03) 5237 6891.
This hotel offers old-world charm combined with modern facilities.
The hotel is within walking distance of Apollo Bay's seaside
attractions. Spa available.

APOLLO BAY: *Claerwen Retreat* — $$$ — 8
Tuxion Rd, VIC 3233. ((03) 5237 7064. FAX (03) 5237 7054.
A luxury retreat overlooking the coast with stunning views from all
rooms. The retreat is entirely non-smoking.

APOLLO BAY: *Whitecrest Holiday Retreat* — $$$ — 11
5230 Great Ocean Rd, VIC 3221. ((03) 5237 0228. FAX (03) 5237 0245.
This family-owned retreat specializes in romantic weekend stays. All
the rooms have fireplaces and fantastic ocean views.

APOLLO BAY: *Chris's Beacon Point Restaurant & Villas* — $$$$$ — 6
280 Skenes Creek Rd, VIC 3233. ((03) 5237 6411. FAX (03) 5237 6930.
This perfect weekend getaway is situated in an elevated bush-
land setting, with ocean views and an excellent restaurant *(see p519)*.
All rooms have a spa bath.

BALLARAT: *Craig's Royal Hotel* — $ — 43
10 Lydiard St South, VIC 3350. ((03) 5331 1377. FAX (03) 5331 7103.
This grand gold rush hotel in the heart of Ballarat is close to all the
sights of historic Lydiard Street *(see p424)*.

BALLARAT: *Ansonia* — $$ — 20
32 Lydiard St South, VIC 3350. ((03) 5332 4678. FAX (03) 5332 4698.
A family-owned hotel in a renovated 1870s building. The facilities on
offer include a library, guest lounge and café.

BALLARAT: *Ballarat Heritage Homestay* — $$$ — 5
PO Box 1360, VIC 3354. ((03) 5332 8296. FAX (03) 5331 3358.
All the comforts of modern life, plus a historic experience in five
Victorian and Edwardian cottages in the Ballarat area.

BENDIGO: *Greystanes Manor* — $$ — 7
57 Queen St, VIC 3550. ((03) 5442 2466. FAX (03) 5442 244/.
Near the major sights, this small Victorian boutique hotel has rooms
decorated with antiques.

BENDIGO: *Shamrock Hotel* — $$ — 30
Cnr Pall Mall & Williamson sts, VIC 3552. ((03) 5443 0333. FAX (03) 5442 4494.
This central Heritage Hotel built in 1897 has rooms overlooking the
main street and adjacent parklands.

DAYLESFORD: *Central Springs Inn* — $$ — 26
Cnr Camp & Howe Sts, VIC 3460. ((03) 5348 3134. FAX (03) 5348 3967.
Located in the heart of Daylesford, the Inn offers spa, open-fire and
family rooms and suites, and a restaurant.

DAYLESFORD: *Lake House* — $$$$ — 33
3 King St, VIC 3460. ((03) 5348 3329. FAX (03) 5348 3995.
Ideal for an indulgent weekend away. Stylish rooms overlook
picturesque Lake Daylesford.

DUNKELD: *Southern Grampians Cottages* — $$ — 9
Victoria Valley Rd, VIC 3294. ((03) 5577 2457. FAX (03) 5577 2489.
Rustic log cabins surrounded by spectacular mountain scenery. This is
an ideal base for bushwalking and wildlife observation.

ECHUCA: *Echuca Gardens* — $$ — 3
103 Mitchell St, VIC 3564. ((03) 5480 6522.
Only ten minutes' walk from the town centre, this bed-and-breakfast has
views of the water gardens and the state forest.

ECHUCA: *Echuca's River Gallery Inn* — $$$ — 8
578 High St, VIC 3564. ((03) 5480 6902. FAX (03) 5480 6902.
Right in the port area beside the Murray River, this restored 1860s
building has log fires and spas in most rooms.

For key to symbols see back flap

	Price categories for a standard double room per night, inclusive of service charges and any additional taxes. $ under A$100 $$ A$100–A$150 $$$ A$150–A$200 $$$$ A$200–A$250 $$$$$ over A$250	**RESTAURANT** Hotel restaurant or dining room usually open to non-residents unless otherwise stated. **CHILDREN'S FACILITIES** Indicates child cots and/or a baby-sitting service available. A few hotels also provide children's portions and high chairs in the restaurant. **GARDEN/TERRACE** Hotel with a garden, courtyard or terrace, often providing tables for eating outside. **SWIMMING POOL** Hotel with an indoor or outdoor swimming pool, or with hot spas for use by residents.	NUMBER OF ROOMS	RESTAURANT	CHILDREN'S FACILITIES	GARDEN/TERRACE	SWIMMING POOL

		Rooms	Rest	Child	Gard	Swim
GEELONG: *Lilydale House Home Hosting* $$ 100 Dog Rocks Rd, VIC 3221. 【 (03) 5276 1302. FAX (03) 5276 1026. Close to the Great Ocean Road (*see pp418–19*), this homestead, set in 80 ha (200 acres) of bush, is noted for its warm welcome. 🚌 P ⚡ 🌳		3		■	●	■
KYNETON: *Kyneton Country House* $$ 66 Jennings St, VIC 3444. 【 (03) 5422 3556. FAX (03) 5422 3556. A restored 1862 homestead with romantic rooms and hillside views. Mount Macedon, Hanging Rock and gold fields are nearby. 🚌 P ⚡ 🌳		4		■	●	
LORNE: *Stanmorr Bed & Breakfast* $$$ 64 Otway St, VIC 3232. 【 (03) 5289 1530. FAX (03) 5289 2805. Popular with weekenders from Melbourne, this Victorian house has period rooms, some with views of the bush and water. 🚌 TV P 🌳		6			●	
LORNE: *Cumberland Lorne Resort* $$$$ 150–178 Mountjoy Parade, VIC 3232. 【 (03) 5289 2400. FAX (03) 5289 2256. Apartments, each with separate living room, kitchen, spa and balcony, look out over the ocean. 🚌 TV P 🍴 🌳		99	●	■	●	■
MALDON: *Heritage Cottages of Maldon* $$ 41 High St, VIC 3463. 【 (03) 5475 1094. FAX (03) 5475 1880. Eight restored 1850s cottages, with wood fires in winter and pretty gardens, are located in and around Maldon. 🚌 TV P ⚡ 🌳		8		■	●	
MILDURA: *Grand Hotel* $$ Cnr Deakin Ave & Seventh St, VIC 3502. 【 (03) 5023 0511. FAX (03) 5022 1801. Set in the heart of Mildura, this popular hotel has a range of rooms and suites, some with river views. 🚌 24 TV 🍴 ♿ P ⚡ 🌳		102	●	■	●	■
OCEAN GROVE: *Ti-Tree Village* $$$ 34 Orton St, VIC 3226. 【 (03) 5255 4433. FAX (03) 5255 5700. Sixteen self-contained cottages within attractive gardens, close to the beach and fifteen minutes from the Great Ocean Road. 🚌 TV P 🌳		16		■	●	
PORT FAIRY: *Seacombe House Motor Inn* $$$ 22 Sackville St, VIC 3284. 【 (03) 5568 1082. FAX (03) 5566 2323. Modern motel and cottages dating from 1847 in the centre of a heritage fishing and holiday town. 🚌 TV 🍴 ⚡ 🌳		18	●		●	
PORTLAND: *Victoria House* $$ 5–7 Tyers St, VIC 3305. 【 (03) 5521 7577. FAX (03) 5523 6300. This 1853 building is set within a picturesque cottage garden. The house is conveniently located close to the beach, shops and wineries. 🚌 TV P ⚡ 🌳		8		■	●	
QUEENSCLIFF: *Mietta's Queenscliff Hotel* $$$$ 16 Gellibrand St, VIC 3225. 【 (03) 5258 1066. FAX (03) 5258 1899. Some of the rooms look out over Port Phillip Bay at this Victorian hotel, which is also noted for its restaurant's cuisine (*see p521*). 24 ⚡ 🌳		21	●		●	
QUEENSCLIFF: *Vue Grand* $$$$ 46 Hesse St, VIC 3225. 【 (03) 5258 1544. FAX (03) 5258 3471. Magnificently restored to its original Victorian splendour, this grand, ornately decorated hotel is located at the centre of old Queenscliff. 🚌 TV ♿ P ⚡ 🌳		32	●	■	●	■
WARRNAMBOOL: *Manor Gums* $$$ Shady's Lane, Mailors Flat, VIC 3275. 【 (03) 5565 4410. FAX (03) 5565 4409. A family-owned bed-and-breakfast close to the town centre and to the whale-watching facilities at Logans Beach (*see p418*). 🚌 TV P 🌳		4			●	

EASTERN VICTORIA

BAIRNSDALE: *Riversleigh Country Hotel* $$ 20
1 Nicholson St, VIC 3875. **(** *(03) 5152 6966.* **FAX** *(03) 5152 4413.*
Two restored Victorian mansions have been converted to offer 20
luxurious rooms in the Gippsland's regional centre of Bairnsdale *(see
pp434–5)*, overlooking the Mitchell River.

BEECHWORTH: *Finches of Beechworth* $$$ 6
3 Finch St, VIC 3747. **(** *(03) 5728 2655.* **FAX** *(03) 5728 2656.*
Beautiful 1880 home with a secluded English-style garden at the
centre of a historic town.

DANDENONG RANGES: *Penrith Country House and Cottages* $$$ 6
1411–1413 Mt Dandenong Tourist Rd, Mt Dandenong, VIC 3767. **(** *(03) 9751
2391.* **FAX** *(03) 9751 2391.* This is the place to go for old English gardens,
relaxation, romance, log fires and luxury.

DINNER PLAIN: *Crystal Creek Resort* $$$ 13
Big Muster Drive, VIC 3898. **(** *(03) 5159 6422.* **FAX** *(03) 5159 6500.*
Suites are available in this spectacular summer and winter resort.
Good for skiing or mountain walks and rides.

EILDON: *Parkview Motor Inn* $ 12
Skyline Rd, VIC 3713. **(** *(03) 5774 2165.* **FAX** *(03) 5774 2155.*
Located in the heart of Eildon, some of the units have cooking
facilities. Family rooms are also available.

FALLS CREEK: *The Falls Creek Hotel* $$$$ 24
Ski Bowl, VIC 3699. **(** *(03) 5758 3282.* **FAX** *(03) 5758 3296.*
Excellent ski runs pass right in front of the hotel. Ski hire is available
in winter. *summer only.*

GIPPSLAND LAKES: *Wattle Point Holiday Retreat* $ 10
200 Wattle Point Rd, Wattle Point, VIC 3875. **(** *(03) 5157 7517.* **FAX** *(03) 5157
7517.* Stay in small timber lodges, surrounded by nature, on the shores
of the lakes. Enjoy the outdoor mineral water spa.

LAKES ENTRANCE: *Emmanuel Holiday Apartments* $$ 8
90 Marine Parade, VIC 3909. **(** *(03) 5155 2600.* **FAX** *(03) 5155 2401.*
The apartments are suitable for both backpackers and families, being
close to the beach and with views over the lake.

MANSFIELD: *Mansfield Valley Motor Inn* $ 22
Maroondah Hwy, VIC 3722. **(** *(03) 5775 1300.* **FAX** *(03) 5775 1693.*
Close to local ski resorts, the motel is near the historic town centre
and makes a good base for country exploring.

MANSFIELD: *Howqua Dale Gourmet Retreat* $$$$ 6
Howqua River Rd, VIC 3722. **(** *(03) 5777 3503.* **FAX** *(03) 5777 3896.*
Run by two well-known chefs, Howqua Dale is an award-winning
country-house hotel by the Howqua River.

MORNINGTON PENINSULA: *Carmel's Bed and Breakfast* $$ 6
142 Ocean Beach Rd, Sorrento, VIC 3943. **(** *(03) 5984 3512.* **FAX** *(03) 5984
0146.* A relaxed but historic guesthouse by the sea, with self-contained
units. Perfect for both summer and winter holidays.

MORNINGTON PENINSULA: *Peppers Delgany* $$$$ 34
Point Nepean Rd, Portsea, VIC 3944. **(** *(03) 5984 4000.* **FAX** *(03) 5984 4022.*
A cross between a castle and a classic folly, this National Trust
classified mansion has luxury rooms and elegant restaurants.

MOUNT BUFFALO: *Mount Buffalo Chalet* $$$$ 97
Mount Buffalo National Park, VIC 3745. **(** *(03) 5755 1500.* **FAX** *(03) 5755
1892.* High above the Ovens Valley, with magnificent views and great
for both winter skiing and summer sports. Full board.

MOUNT BULLER: *Mount Buller Chalet Hotel* $$$$ 65
Mount Buller Village, VIC 3723. **(** *(03) 5777 6566.* **FAX** *(03) 5777 6455.*
Each room in this ski resort has majestic views over the
Victorian Alps. In summer, go mountain-bike riding. *summer only.*

Price categories for a standard double room per night, inclusive of service charges and any additional taxes. $ under A$100 $$ A$100–A$150 $$$ A$150–A$200 $$$$ A$200–A$250 $$$$$ over A$250	**RESTAURANT** Hotel restaurant or dining room usually open to non-residents unless otherwise stated. **CHILDREN'S FACILITIES** Indicates child cots and/or a baby-sitting service available. A few hotels also provide children's portions and high chairs in the restaurant. **GARDEN/TERRACE** Hotel with a garden, courtyard or terrace, often providing tables for eating outside. **SWIMMING POOL** Hotel with an indoor or outdoor swimming pool, or with hot spas for use by residents.		

	No. of Rooms	Restaurant	Children's Facilities	Garden/Terrace	Swimming Pool
PHILLIP ISLAND: *Narrabeen Gourmet Retreat* $$ 16 Steele St, Cowes, VIC 3922. ((03) 5952 2062. FAX (03) 5952 3670. Specializing in romantic and gourmet "getaway" weekends; all rooms are cosy. No children allowed. ■ P ≥ ✎	5	●		●	
PHILLIP ISLAND: *Rothsaye on Lovers Walk Bed-and-Breakfast* $$$ 2 Roy Court, Cowes, VIC 3922. ((03) 5952 2057. FAX (03) 5952 2691. Facing a swimming beach and close to the main town of Cowes, Rothsaye has three cottages. No children allowed. ■ TV ▤ & P ≥ ✎	5			●	
RUTHERGLEN: *Ophir Estate* $$$ Stillards Lane, VIC 3685. ((02) 6032 8920. FAX (02) 6032 9911. In Victoria's wine-growing area, this emu and elk organic farm has bed and breakfast rooms or two cottages for couples or groups. ■ ≥ & P ✎	14	●	■	●	
SOUTH GIPPSLAND: *Waratah Park Country House* $$$ Thomson Rd (off Walkerville Fish Creek Rd), Waratah Bay, VIC 3959. ((03) 5683 2575. FAX (03) 5683 2275. Surrounded by farmland, this country retreat overlooks the coastline. Dinner is included in the weekend luxury package. ■ TV P ≥ ✎	6	●		●	
WILSONS PROMONTORY: *Tidal River Cottages* $$ National Parks Service, Tidal River, VIC 3690. ((03) 5680 9500. FAX (03) 5680 9516. The only accommodation other than bush camping in the Wilsons Promontory National Park. & P ✎	30		■	●	
YARRA VALLEY: *Sanctuary House Motel* $ Badger Creek Rd, Healesville, VIC 3777. ((03) 5962 5148. FAX (03) 5962 5392. This bush retreat is close to the Healesville Sanctuary (*see p433*). With sauna, spa, barbeque area and children's playground. ■ TV ▤ P ✎	13	●	■	●	■
YARRA VALLEY: *The Yarra Glen Grand Hotel* $$ 19 Bell St, Yarra Glen, VIC 3775. ((03) 9730 1230. FAX (03) 9730 1124. The imposing hotel looms over the town and its vineyards. Visits to wineries (*see pp370–71*) are available from the hotel. ■ TV ▤ P ≥ ✎	10	●	■		

TASMANIA

	No. of Rooms	Restaurant	Children's Facilities	Garden/Terrace	Swimming Pool
BICHENO: *Bicheno Gaol Cottages* $$ Cnr James & Burgess sts, TAS 7215. ((03) 6375 1430. FAX (03) 6375 1866. The Gaol House is the oldest building in this seaside holiday town and is within walking distance of all the main sights. TV & P ≥ ✎	3	●		●	
BRUNY ISLAND: *Morella Island Retreats* $$$ 46 Adventure Bay Rd, TAS 7150. ((03) 6293 1131. FAX (03) 6293 1137. Five themed cottages in a garden setting on the "neck" of Bruny Island, with incredible views. TV ■ P ✎	5	●	■	●	
BURNIE: *The Duck House* $$ 26 Queen St, TAS 7320. ((03) 6431 1712. FAX (03) 6431 1712. An early 20th-century cottage with a pleasant veranda, lounge, kitchen and homemade breakfast provisions. TV ≥ P	2		■	●	
COLES BAY: *Freycinet Lodge* $$$ Freycinet National Park, TAS 7215. ((03) 6257 0101. FAX (03) 6257 0278. Award-winning, ecologically friendly lodge overlooking Giant Oyster Bay, backed by the Hazards Mountain Range. ■ & P ≥ ✎	60	●	■	●	
CRADLE MOUNTAIN: *Cradle Mountain Lodge* $$$$ Cradle Mountain Rd, TAS 7306. ((03) 6492 1303. FAX (03) 6492 1309. This comfortable sanctuary has basic alpine accommodation in log cabins, some with spas. ■ & P ✎	98	●	■	●	

DEVONPORT: *Birchmore Bed and Breakfast* $$ 7
8–10 Oldaker St, TAS 7310. ((03) 6423 1336. FAX (03) 6423 1338.
De luxe guesthouse with classically furnished double and single
suites. Breakfast is served in the conservatory. ▮ TV ▮ P ▮ ▮

HOBART: *Colonial Battery Point Manor* $$ 10
13 Cromwell St, Battery Point, TAS 7004. ((03) 6224 0888. FAX (03) 6224
2254. This four-and-a-half-star bed and breakfast, furnished in a classic
European style, has glorious views of the marina. ▮ TV ▮ P ▮ ▮

HOBART: *Avon Court Apartments* $$$ 8
4 Colville St, Battery Point, TAS 7004. ((03) 6223 4837. FAX (03) 6223 7207.
One- and two-bedroom fully self-contained apartments in historic
Battery Point. ▮ TV P ▮ ▮

HOBART: *Corinda's Cottage* $$$ 3
17 Glebe St, Glebe, TAS 7000. ((03) 6234 1590. FAX (03) 6234 2744.
This stone cottage, in the gardens of a Victorian mansion, was once
the servants' quarters. TV P ▮ ▮

HOBART: *Lenna of Hobart* $$$ 50
20 Runnymede St, Battery Point, TAS 7004. ((03) 6232 3900. FAX (03) 6224
0112. A boutique, heritage-listed hotel just around the corner from
Salamanca Place. ▮ 24 TV P ▮ ▮

LAUNCESTON: *Alice's Cottages and Spa Hideaway* $$$ 11
129 Balfour St, TAS 7250. ((03) 6334 2231. FAX (03) 6334 2696.
Whimsically furnished in an *Alice in Wonderland* theme, these
1840s cottages are stocked with breakfast provisions. ▮ TV P ▮ ▮

LAUNCESTON: *Country Club Resort* $$$$ 104
Country Club Ave, Prospect Vale, TAS 7140. ((03) 6335 5777. FAX (03) 6335
5706. This luxurious hotel, 5 km (3 miles) south of the town, is ideal
for a relaxing stay, including on-site gaming tables. ▮ TV ▮ P ▮ ▮

LONGFORD: *The Racecourse Inn* $$$ 5
114 Marlborough St, TAS 7301. ((03) 6391 2352. FAX (03) 6391 2430.
This restored Georgian inn on the outskirts of this historic town is a
great base for exploring the northern countryside. ▮ TV ▮ P ▮ ▮

NEW NORFOLK: *Glen Dhu Country Retreat* $$ 2
Glen Dhu Rd, Molesworth, TAS 7140. ((03) 6261 4443. FAX (03) 6261 4443.
These restored hop pickers' cottages, "Platypus" and "Wombat", are
close to Derwent Valley and Mount Field National Park. ▮ TV ▮ P

NEW NORFOLK: *Tynwald Willow Bend Estate* $$ 8
Hobart Rd, TAS 7140. ((03) 6261 2667. FAX (03) 6261 2040.
Overlooking the Lachlan and Derwent rivers, this establishment is part
of an old flour mill. Pool and tennis courts available. ▮ TV P ▮

RICHMOND: *Hatcher's Manor* $$$ 8
73 Prossers Rd, TAS 7025. ((03) 6260 2622. FAX (03) 6260 2744.
A luxury rural getaway for couples and families, Hatcher's Manor is set
among gardens, orchards and a private lake. ▮ TV ▮ ▮ P ▮ ▮

ROSS: *Colonial Cottages of Ross* $$ 4
Church St, TAS 7209. ((03) 6381 5354. FAX (03) 6331 1895.
Furnished with pine and locally restored antiques, these cottages have
been part of the historic town of Ross since the 1840s. ▮ P ▮

STANLEY: *Gateforth Cottages* $$ 14
Black River, TAS 7321. ((03) 6458 3230. FAX (03) 6458 3237.
These farm cottages are part of the Cottages of the Colony group.
They overlook the Bass Strait and its quiet beaches. ▮ TV P ▮ ▮

STRAHAN: *Franklin Manor* $$$ 18
The Esplanade, TAS 7468. ((03) 6471 7311. FAX (03) 6471 7267.
This old harbour master's home is now a welcoming manor
overlooking Macquarie Harbour. ▮ TV P ▮ ▮

TASMAN PENINSULA: *Norfolk Bay Convict Station* $$ 5
5862 Arthur Hwy, Taranna, TAS 7180. ((03) 6250 3487. FAX (03) 6250 3487.
Built with convict labour, the Commissariat Store for colonial supplies
is now a haven of comfort with log fires and bay views. ▮ TV P ▮

For key to symbols see back flap

WHERE TO EAT

AUSTRALIA HAS DEVELOPED its own culinary identity in the past 20 years or so and modern Australian food, often with a Mediterranean or Asian twist, is now widely available. Reflecting the country's multicultural population, there is also a wealth of ethnic restaurants. Every cuisine, from Algerian to Zambian, is on a menu somewhere in Australia, particularly in the major cities. Australian restaurants

Fresh seafood, Chinese style

make good use of the variety of homegrown produce, especially seafood and beef. No Australian meal is complete without a glass of one of the many local wines or beers *(see pp496–7)*. For a cheaper eating-out option, try one of the many BYO (Bring Your Own) unlicensed restaurants, where customers take their own wine, but may be charged a minimal corkage fee.

Marco Polo Restaurant at the Conrad in Brisbane *(see p505)*

TYPES OF RESTAURANTS

ALL MAJOR Australian cities offer a wide choice of restaurants. Formal dining establishments, bistros, stylish cafés and pubs are all readily available to suit any budget. Food on offer ranges from haute cuisine to informal snacks. Outside the main cities, some of the best restaurants can be found in the many wine regions and often in the wineries themselves *(see pp32–3)*.

Prices, however, vary widely. They tend to be highest in Sydney, Melbourne and other major tourist resorts, although prices are usually lower than in comparable places in Europe and the United States. As a general guideline, the bill at a showcase Melbourne or Sydney restaurant featuring a celebrity chef will be about A$100 per head, including a shared bottle of wine. At a

Bring Your Own (BYO) or an unpretentious Asian restaurant it may only be A$30 per head or less. A counter meal at a pub or in a snack bar should generally cost no more than A$10 per head.

A welcome new trend in Australia is the increasing emphasis on courtyard, garden, boulevard and other outdoor eating facilities, making the most of the country's benevolent climate.

EATING HOURS AND RESERVATIONS

MOST RESTAURANTS serve lunch between 12:30pm and 3pm; dinner is served from 6:30 to 10:30pm. Many establishments, however, particularly the big city bistros and cafés, have become more flexible, opening for breakfast and closing late. Most budget and ethnic restaurants often close a little earlier, at around 9:30pm, depending on the

demand. Most establishments are also open seven days a week, 365 days a year. However, it is advisable to check in advance with individual restaurants, particularly those outside the capital cities. To avoid disappointment, advance telephone bookings are generally recommended.

PAYING AND TIPPING

MAJOR CREDIT CARDS are accepted in the majority of Australian restaurants, although it is a good idea to confirm this in advance or on arrival. A General Service Tax (GST) is added to restaurant bills in Australia, but tipping is not compulsory. In recognition of outstanding service or a particularly fine meal, a small gratuity is always appreciated. How much to leave is the prerogative of the customer, but 10 per cent of the total bill would generally be regarded

Skillogalee Winery and Restaurant in the Clare Valley *(see p516)*

The popular Fez Café in Darlinghurst, Sydney *(see p499)*

or district *(see pp32–3)*. Wine is sold by the bottle, carafe or glass. There is usually a good choice of beers, ales, ciders and spirits as well.

BYO restaurants, which are not licensed to sell alcohol, are extremely popular in Australia and offer diners the opportunity to bring the wines they wish to drink with their meal, although beer is not usually permitted. For non-alcohol drinkers, tap water is entirely safe, but many people prefer to drink bottled still or sparkling water. Fresh fruit juices are also very popular *(see pp496–7)*.

as generous. This can be left either as a cash tip on the table when you are ready to leave or by adding it to the total if paying your bill by cheque or credit card.

Façade of the Café Capri brasserie in Darwin *(see p509)*

CHILDREN

FEW RESTAURATEURS will refuse admission to children as long as they are well behaved. Many restaurants also provide high chairs and a children's menu. The best budget options for families are hamburger chains or Italian or Asian eateries.

WHEELCHAIR ACCESS

SPURRED BY legislation in the various states, most restaurants now provide special wheelchair access and toilet facilities for the disabled.

However, it is still advisable to check in advance on the facilities available.

VEGETARIANS

IT IS RARE for a restaurant not to feature at least one dish for vegetarians, and a variety of choices is the norm, particularly in regions where there is an abundance of home-grown produce. There are also specialist vegetarian restaurants and cafés in the major cities. For further information, check the vegetarian specialities column on pages 498–523.

ALCOHOL AND OTHER DRINKS

IF A RESTAURANT is described as licensed, it refers to its licence to sell alcohol. Australian wine lists are outstanding and generally highlight the wines of the particular state

DRESS

DRESS CODES are virtually non-existent in Australian restaurants, although a handful of the more up-market establishments may ask men to wear a tie in the evenings. Most establishments, however, including beachside cafés, frown on scant beachwear and flip flops or sandals.

For most situations, the phrase "smart casual" sums up the Australian approach to eating out.

SMOKING

SMOKING is now banned inside restaurants and cafés, although smoking is permitted at outside tables. Fines may be levied if these regulations are disregarded. Smoking restrictions, however, are rarely applied in traditional pubs.

Café Provincial in the heart of Fitzroy in Melbourne *(see p518)*

What to Eat in Australia

Steak pie with tomato sauce

Aa USTRALIA BEGAN TO DEVELOP its own cuisine in the 1970s. Creative chefs use local ingredients, blended with the flavours of Europe, Asia and the Middle East, to make dishes with a truly Australian identity. Each area of Australia produces its own speciality: you can sample rock oysters, honey and lamb from New South Wales, olive oil from South Australia, salmon from Tasmania, dairy produce from Victoria, exotic fruit from Queensland and cheese from Western Australia. And, of course, Australians still love their traditional barbecues!

Eucalypt Honey
Imported bees seem to love the eucalypts. Leatherwood, light in colour, has the strongest flavour.

Potato Wedges
Coated with a spicy seasoning then fried in a two-step process, these chunky variations on the humble chip are usually served with sour cream and chilli sauce.

Yum Cha
Literally "drinking tea", this Chinese feast includes dim sum, or steamed dumplings stuffed with meat, fish or vegetables.

Focaccia
This Italian-style sandwich has gourmet antipasto, salad and meat slices between toasted slabs of crusty flat bread.

Lebanese Mezes
Expect an array of appetizers including pulse and vegetable dips, marinated and grilled vegetables and filled pastries.

Crab
Scallops
Balmain bug
Lobster
Rock oysters
King prawns
Mussels

Seafood Platter
Coming from comparatively clean waters, Australian seafood is both abundant and of extremely high quality.

Mixed Leaf Salad
Garden-fresh salad features on most menus. It is served here with feta cheese and grilled vegetables.

Char-grilled Kangaroo Fillet
A relatively recent addition to butchers' shelves, low-fat kangaroo fillet is usually served rare.

Thai Green Curry
Chicken is the favourite variety, but a tasty vegetarian version is also commonly served.

Kebabs

Chicken wings

Baby octopus

Seared Beef Fillet
Australian beef, here wrapped in paperbark, is usually served with the season's vegetables.

Barbecue
Meat, poultry and fresh seafood such as baby octopus are char-grilled on a barbecue and usually accompanied by bread and green salad.

Freshwater Crayfish
Also known as "yabbies", this main dish is usually served simply on a bed of greens with a dipping sauce such as aïoli.

Blue-eyed Cod
Although known as cod, it is in fact trevalla, a deep sea fish of meaty texture and mild flavour. It is often served in thick steaks.

Lamb Loin Fillet
Thick slices of tender seared lamb served on a salad of rocket and fresh snow peas are ideal summer eating.

Baked Ricotta Cake
Indigenous Australian ingredients such as rosella buds may appear in a range of desserts.

Pavlova
This meringue dessert is topped with fresh cream and summer fruit such as passion fruit.

Mixed Berry Ice Cream
Home-made ice creams, such as raspberry or honey, are often served with seasonal fruit.

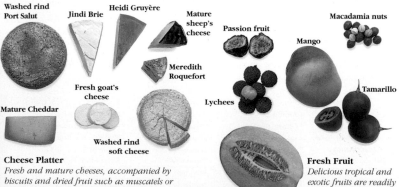

Washed rind
Port Salut

Jindi Brie

Heidi Gruyère

Mature sheep's cheese

Passion fruit

Mango

Macadamia nuts

Meredith Roquefort

Fresh goat's cheese

Lychees

Tamarillo

Mature Cheddar

Washed rind
soft cheese

Cheese Platter
Fresh and mature cheeses, accompanied by biscuits and dried fruit such as muscatels or figs, are the perfect way to finish a meal.

Rockmelon

Fresh Fruit
Delicious tropical and exotic fruits are readily available year round.

What to Drink in Australia

Semillon Chardonnay

A SEVEN-COURSE Australian meal, the old joke goes, is a meat pie and a six-pack of beer. Australians do love their beer, but today they also relish some of the best good-value wine in the world *(see pp32–3)*. It is estimated that there are 10,000 different Australian wines on the market at any one time. While the health-conscious can choose from dozens of bottled waters and fresh fruit juices, this is also the country that makes alcoholic lemonade from its lemon crop and another alcoholic drink from rhubarb. Imported wines, beers and spirits are also readily available.

SPARKLING WINE

Pinot Noir Chardonnay

AUSTRALIAN WINEMAKERS make fine use of the three classic Champagne grapes, Chardonnay, Pinot Noir and Pinot Meunier, to make internationally respected sparkling wines, some selling for only a few dollars. Red Shiraz grapes are also uniquely used to make an unusual and popular sparkling burgundy.

MAJOR WINE REGIONS

1. Hunter Valley
2. Mudgee
3. Riverina
4. Yarra Valley
5. Geelong
6. Northeastern Victoria
7. Clare Valley
8. Barossa Valley & Adelaide Hills
9. Coonawarra & Padthaway
10. Margaret River
11. Tasmania

South Australia is the country's largest producer of wine.

Grange Hermitage

WHITE WINE

Rhine Riesling

Botrytis Semillon

WHEN AUSTRALIANS first adopted table wines in the 1960s and 1970s, their preference was for a sweet, Moselle-type wine – Riesling and Gewürtztraminer. Later, they embraced drier styles of wine, such as Semillon, Sauvignon Blanc and Chardonnay, the world's leading white wine grape. They also began to show a passion for wood-matured wines. Today other varieties, such as Marsanne, have been successfully planted. Australian winemakers also use *botrytis cinera*, or noble rot, to make luscious dessert wines. Victoria's Muscats and Tokays are also of an international standard *(see p371)*.

Grape picking by hand in the Hunter Valley north of Sydney

The Chardonnay grape *lends its honey-rich tones to many of Australia's premium wines.*

GRAPE TYPE	BEST REGIONS	BEST PRODUCERS
Chardonnay	Barossa Valley	Penfold's, Peter Lehmann
	Hunter Valley	Rosemount Estate, Tyrrell's
	Yarra Valley	Coldstream Hills, St Hubert's
Riesling	Barossa Valley	Leo Buring, Orlando
(Rhine Riesling)	Clare Valley	Petaluma, Grosset
Semillon	Hunter Valley	McWilliam's, Rothbury Estate
	Margaret River	Leeuwin, Evans & Tate
Semillon Chardonnay	Hunter Valley	Rosemount Estate
Semillon (dessert)	Riverina	De Bortoli
Muscat/Tokay	Northeastern Victoria	Bailey's, Campbell's, Morris

Vineyards of Leeuwin Estate, Margaret River

RED WINE

AUSTRALIA'S BENCHMARK red is Grange Hermitage, the creation of the late vintner Max Schubert in the 1950s. He preferred wines that required at least a decade's cellaring. In contrast, Wolf Blass, a winemaker of the current style, championed the "drink-now" approach with quickly maturing wines. Winemakers frequently blend wines from different districts and states. Lighter reds, which may be served slightly chilled, have recently been introduced.

Shiraz   **Pinot Noir**

GRAPE TYPE	BEST REGIONS	BEST PRODUCERS
Cabernet Sauvignon	Barossa Valley	Henschke, Penfold's, Wolf Blass
	Coonawarra	Bowen Estate, Lindeman's, Rouge Homme, Wynn's
	Margaret River	Leeuwin Estate, Vasse Felix
Shiraz (Hermitage)	Barossa Valley	Henschke, Penfold's, Wolf Blass
	Hunter Valley	Brokenwood, Lindeman's
	Margaret River	Cape Mentelle
Pinot Noir	Geelong	Bannockburn, Scotchman's Hill
	Hunter Valley	Rothbury Estate
	Yarra Valley	Coldstream Hills, Diamond Valley
Cabernet Shiraz	Barossa Valley	Penfold's, Wolf Blass
	Coonawarra	Leconfield, Lindeman's, Mildara
	Margaret River	Cape Mentelle

Cabernet Sauvignon *from the Coonawarra district is one example of this popular quality red grape.*

BEER

MOST AUSTRALIAN BEER is vat fermented real ale or lager, both consumed chilled. Full-strength beer has an alcohol content of around 4.8 per cent, mid-strength beers have around 3.5 per cent, while "light" beers have less than 3 per cent. Traditionally heat sterilized, cold filtration is now becoming increasingly popular.

Among the hundreds of fine lagers and stouts are James Boag and Cascade from Tasmania, Castlemaine XXXX from Queensland, Fosters and Melbourne Bitter from Victoria, Toohey's red and blue labels from New South Wales and Cooper's Sparkling Ale, known locally as lunatic soup, from South Australia. Aficionados of real ale should seek out one of the pub breweries throughout Australia. Beer in Australia is ordered by the glass size and brand name.

Tooheys Red Bitter   **Cascade Premium Lager**

SPIRITS

AUSTRALIAN DISTILLERS produce fine dark and white rums from Queensland's sugar cane plantations *(see p238)*. The more notable labels include Bundaberg, from the town of that name, and Beenleigh. Australia's grape vintage is also the basis of good-value domestic brandies. Popular labels are St Agnes and Hardy's.

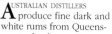

Bundaberg rum

OTHER DRINKS

WITH A CLIMATE ranging from tropical to alpine, Australia has year-round fresh fruit for juicing. Its apples are also used to make cider. Scores of still and sparkling mineral and other bottled waters now supply an annual market of nearly 200 million litres. Hepburn Spa, Deep Spring and Mount Franklin have national distribution. Coffee, prepared in a wide variety of ways, is another popular drink with Australians.

White coffee

Pear and kiwi frappé

Banana smoothie

Strawberry juice

Caffe latte

Choosing a Restaurant

THE RESTAURANTS in this guide have been selected across a wide range of price categories for their exceptional food, good value and interesting location. They are listed here by region, starting with Sydney. The thumb tabs on the pages use the same colour-coding as the corresponding regional chapters in the main section of this guide.

	OUTDOOR EATING	VEGETARIAN SPECIALITIES	BAR AREA	FIXED-PRICE MENU	CHILDREN'S FACILITIES
SYDNEY					
BONDI BEACH: *Ravesi's on Bondi Beach* $$$$ Cnr Campbell Parade & Hall St, NSW 2026. ((02) 9365 4422. Sit on the oceanfront balcony and enjoy fish and chips with aïoli followed by mango brûlée. Popular for breakfast. 🍴 👶 📧	■	●			■
BOTANIC GARDENS AND THE DOMAIN: *Botanic Gardens Restaurant* $$$$ Mrs Macquarie's Rd, NSW 2000. **Map 2 D4.** ((02) 9241 2419. The lovely balcony looks out over the Royal Botanic Gardens *(see pp102–103)* in this lunchtime venue. The food has a definite French accent with an emphasis on seafood. ● *D.* 👶 📧	■	●			■
CITY CENTRE: *Grand Taverna* $$ Sir John Young Hotel, 557 George St, NSW 2000. **Map 4 E3.** ((02) 9267 3608. This popular pub bistro serves traditional Spanish dishes, including prawns, octopus and paella. ● *Sun.* 👶 📧	■		■		
CITY CENTRE: *Casa Asturiana* $$$ 77 Liverpool St, NSW 2000. **Map 4 E3.** ((02) 9264 1010. Tapas are the main attraction in this family-run restaurant, including favourites such as squid and sardines. ● *Sat & Mon L.* 👶 *limited.* 📧		●			
CITY CENTRE: *Criterion Brasserie* $$$$ Lobby Level, MLC Centre, Martin Pl, NSW 2000. **Map 1 B4.** ((02) 9233 1234. Chic decor and old-fashioned family service make this a popular venue. The house special is a meze platter. 👶 📧 ● *Sun.*	■	●			
CITY CENTRE: *Edna's Table* $$$$ 204 Clarence St, NSW 2000. **Map 1 B4.** ((02) 9231 1400. The unusual Outback menu includes dishes such as trout wrapped in *bok choy* and paperbark, served with local bush tomato aïoli, and grilled emu fillet with fennel and *nashi*. ● *Mon D, Sat L, Sun.* 🍴 👶 📧	■	●		●	
CITY CENTRE: *Banc* $$$$$ 53 Martin Place, NSW 2000. **Map 1 B4.** ((02) 9233 5300. Grandly housed in the lobby of a former bank, Banc's unashamedly French-influenced food is served in stylish surroundings. ● *Sat L, Sun, Mon.* 🍴 📧			■		
CITY CENTRE: *Forty One* $$$$$ Level 41, Chifley Tower, Chifley Square, NSW 2000. **Map 1 B4.** ((02) 9221 2500. Impressive vistas of the city and Sydney Harbour match a fine European-based menu with Asian influences. ● *Sat L, Sun D.* 🍴 👶 📧		●		●	
DARLING HARBOUR: *Golden Century* $$ 393–399 Sussex St, NSW 2000. **Map 4 E4.** ((02) 9212 3901. Customers can select their (Cantonese) dinner here from one of the live seafood tanks, then discuss with the waiter how it should be prepared. 🍴 📧		●			
DARLING HARBOUR: *Golden Harbour* $$ 31–33 Dixon St, NSW 2000. **Map 4 D3.** ((02) 9212 5987. The queues for *yum cha* here can wind out into the street, but it is worth the wait for the splendid dumplings with snow-pea leaves. 📧		●		●	
DARLING HARBOUR: *Silver Spring* $$ Sydney Central, cnr Hay & Pitt sts, NSW 2000. **Map 4 E4.** ((02) 9211 2232. Waiters communicate by walkie-talkie as they seat diners in this hectic restaurant, serving *yum cha* and Cantonese specialities. 🍴 👶 📧		●			
DARLING HARBOUR: *Kamogawa* $$$$ 1st Floor, 177 Sussex St, NSW 2000. **Map 1 A5.** ((02) 9299 5533. A largely Japanese clientele comes here to enjoy *kaiseki* menus (7 to 12 courses) and *tatami* rooms, where you sit on the floor. ● *L Sat–Mon.* 📧		●			

	Outdoor Eating	Vegetarian Specialities	Bar Area	Fixed-Price Menu	Children's Facilities

Price categories for a three-course meal for one, including half a bottle of house wine and service charges.

$ under A\$25
$$ A\$25–A\$35
$$$ A\$35–A\$50
$$$$ A\$50–A\$70
$$$$$ over A\$70

OUTDOOR EATING
Some tables on a patio or terrace.
VEGETARIAN SPECIALITIES
One menu always includes a varied selection of vegetarian dishes.
BAR AREA/COCKTAIL BAR
There is a bar area or cocktail bar within the restaurant, available for drinks and/or bar snacks.
FIXED-PRICE MENU
A fixed-price menu available at a good rate, at lunch, dinner or both, usually with three courses.
CHILDREN'S FACILITIES
Small portions and/or highchairs available on request.

Entry	$	Outdoor Eating	Vegetarian Specialities	Bar Area	Fixed-Price Menu	Children's Facilities
KINGS CROSS AND DARLINGHURST: *No Names* 1st Floor, 81 Stanley St, NSW 2010. **Map** 5 A1. *(02) 9360 4711.* Despite there being no sign, you will have little trouble finding this excellent spaghetti canteen. Just look for the queue.	$		●		●	■
KINGS CROSS AND DARLINGHURST: *Fishface* 132 Darlinghurst Rd, NSW 2010. **Map** 5 B1. *(02) 9332 4803.* The menu changes daily in this tiny café, but always includes some of the best-value seafood on offer in Sydney. ● *L.*	$$	■	●			
KINGS CROSS AND DARLINGHURST: *JuJu's* 320 Kingsgate Shopping Centre, NSW 2011. *(02) 9357 7100.* Popular with Japanese students, excellent Japanese food is served in a traditionally decorated dining room. ● *L, Mon.*	$$		●			
KINGS CROSS AND DARLINGHURST: *Oh! Calcutta!* 251 Victoria St, NSW 2010. **Map** 5 B2. *(02) 9360 3650.* The menu at this award-winning restaurant spans the entire Middle East and Indian subcontinent – try the Afghani *mantu* (steamed dumplings) filled with ground lamb and celery. ● *Sat–Thu L.*	$$		●			
KINGS CROSS AND DARLINGHURST: *The Edge* 60 Riley St, NSW 2010. **Map** 5 A1. *(02) 9360 1372.* This re-creation of a 1930s French brasserie includes wooden floors and marble bars. The wood-fired pizzas are delicious. ● *Mon.*	$$$	■	●	■		
KINGS CROSS AND DARLINGHURST: *Fez Café* 247 Victoria St, NSW 2010. **Map** 5 B1. *(02) 9360 9581.* Fez's Middle-Eastern menu begins with a Turkish platter of dips and pickled vegetables followed by Moroccan *tagines* (stews).	$$$	■	●			
KINGS CROSS AND DARLINGHURST: *Macleay Street Bistro* 73a Macleay St, NSW 2011. **Map** 2 E5. *(02) 9358 4891.* The French menu sits comfortably with the once bohemian life of Kings Cross. Arrive early at weekends to get a table. ● *L.*	$$$	■	●			
KINGS CROSS AND DARLINGHURST: *Mezzaluna* 123 Victoria St, NSW 2011. **Map** 2 E5. *(02) 9357 1988.* The fine northern Italian cuisine, excellent wines and wonderful views of the city skyline here are not to be missed. ● *Sat L, Sun.*	$$$$	■	●			
KINGS CROSS AND DARLINGHURST: *Otto* The Wharf, 6 Cowper Wharf Rd, Woolloomooloo, NSW 2011. **Map** 2 D5. *(02) 9368 7488.* This trendy spot in the Finger Wharf complex boasts alto-trattoria food that is full of flavour. Its bar is one of the smartest waterside drinking spots. ● *Mon.*	$$$$	■	●	■		
KINGS CROSS AND DARLINGHURST: *Beppi's* Cnr Stanley & Yurong sts, NSW 2010. **Map** 4 F3. *(02) 9360 4558.* Beppi's has been in existence since 1956, and is still a shrine for the finest Italian food, wine and service. ● *Sat L, Sun.*	$$$$$		●			
KINGS CROSS AND DARLINGHURST: *Tetsuya's* 529 Kent St, NSW 2011. **Map** 1 A2. *(02) 9267 2900.* At one of Sydney's best restaurants, the Franco-Japanese food is prepared by renowned chef Tetsuya Wakada. The 12-course set menu for dinner changes daily. ● *Sun, Mon; L Tue–Thu.*	$$$$$		●		●	
MANLY: *Armstrong's Manly* Manly Wharf, NSW 2095. *(02) 9976 3835.* The harbour views, a relaxed atmosphere and superb seafood make this a quintessential Sydney dining experience.	$$$	■	●			■

Price categories for a three-course meal for one, including half a bottle of house wine and service charges.
$ under A$25
$$ A$25–A$35
$$$ A$35–A$50
$$$$ A$50–A$70
$$$$$ over A$70

Outdoor Eating
Some tables on a patio or terrace.
Vegetarian Specialities
One menu always includes a varied selection of vegetarian dishes.
Bar Area/Cocktail Bar
There is a bar area or cocktail bar within the restaurant, available for drinks and/or bar snacks.
Fixed-Price Menu
A fixed-price menu available at a good rate, at lunch, dinner or both, usually with three courses.
Children's Facilities
Small portions and/or highchairs available on request.

Manly: *Le Kiosk* $$$$$
1 Marine Parade, Shelly Beach, NSW 2095. ☎ *(02) 9977 4122.*
This sandstone cottage, set in a subtropical garden, offers excellent seafood platters and crisp Australian white wine. 🚭 ♿ 🍷 💳

Paddington: *Bistro Lulu* $$$
257 Oxford St, NSW 2025. ☎ *(02) 9380 6888.*
Luke Mangan cooks in this intimate, woody, neo-bistro. The French-influenced menu includes rabbit *rillettes.* ● *L Mon–Thu* 🚭 💳

Paddington: *Lucio's* $$$$
47 Windsor St, NSW 2021. **Map 6 D3.** ☎ *(02) 9380 5996.*
Phone a day ahead and order the house speciality, *pesce al sale* (fish baked in a rock salt mould), at this institution famed for its up-market northern Italian menu. ● *Sun.* 🚭 ♿ *limited.* 🍷 💳

Paddington: *Claude's* $$$$$
10 Oxford St, Woollahra, NSW 2025. **Map 6 D4.** ☎ *(02) 9331 2325.*
Discretion and fine service are the bywords at Claude's, which is renowned for the skills of its chef. ● *Sun, Mon.* 🚭 💳

Parramatta: *Barnaby's Riverside* $$
66 Phillip St, NSW 2150. ☎ *(02) 9633 3777.*
Barnarby's menu combines European and Asian cuisine. Try the mixed grill of fresh seafood or the prime beef rib. ● *Sun D.* 🚭 ♿ 💳

Parramatta: *Courtney's Brasserie* $$$$
2 Horwood Place, NSW 2150. ☎ *(02) 9635 3288.*
This convict-built building began as a soldiers' mess in 1830. The menu includes Szechuan king prawns and fresh fish. ● *Sun, Sat L.* 🚭 ♿ 💳

The Rocks and Circular Quay: *ECQ* $$$
Quay Grand Hotel, East Circular Quay, NSW 2000. **Map 1 B3.** ☎ *(02) 9256 4022.*
Regardless of the great food – champagne and oysters or a simple caesar salad – the harbour view will grab your attention. ♿ 🍷 💳

The Rocks and Circular Quay: *The Wharf Restaurant* $$$
Pier 4, Hickson Rd, Millers Point, NSW 2000. **Map 1 A1.** ☎ *(02) 9250 1761.*
Set at the end of the wharf, there are fine views of the harbour here and good simple fare, such as pasta, risotto and seafood. ● *Sun.* ♿ 💳

The Rocks and Circular Quay: *Aria* $$$$$
19/2 Circular Quay East, NSW 2000. **Map 1 C3.** ☎ *(02) 9252 2555.*
Matthew Moran serves fine modern Australian cuisine, in a delightful dining room with views over the harbour. The pan-fried snapper with prawn colcannon is recommended. ● *L, Sun.* 🚭 ♿ ✺ 🍷 💳

The Rocks and Circular Quay: *Bel Mondo* $$$$$
Level 3, Argyle Dept Store, 18–24 Argyle St, NSW 2000. **Map 1 B2.**
☎ *(02) 9241 3700.* The northern Italian menu, combined with the views of the Sydney Opera House *(see pp80–81)*, provides one of the best dining experiences in the city. 🚭 ♿ *limited.* 🍷 💳

The Rocks and Circular Quay: *Guillaume at Bennelong* $$$$$
Sydney Opera House, Bennelong Point, NSW 2000. **Map 1 C2.**
☎ *(02) 9250 7578.* Located in one of the Opera House's shells, with stunning views to match the menu. ● *L, Sun.* 🚭 ♿ *on request.* 🍷 💳

The Rocks and Circular Quay: *Rockpool* $$$$$
107 George St, NSW 2000. **Map 1 B3.** ☎ *(02) 9252 1888.*
The modish lounge bar at the front of the restaurant sets the scene for fine seafood by one of Sydney's leading chefs. ● *Sat L, Sun.* 🚭 🍷 💳

Restaurant	Outdoor Eating	Vegetarian Specialities	Bar Area	Fixed-Price Menu	Children's Facilities
Manly: Le Kiosk	■	●			
Paddington: Bistro Lulu		●		●	
Paddington: Lucio's					
Paddington: Claude's				●	
Parramatta: Barnaby's Riverside	■	●		●	■
Parramatta: Courtney's Brasserie	■	●			■
The Rocks and Circular Quay: ECQ		●			
The Rocks and Circular Quay: The Wharf Restaurant	■	●			
The Rocks and Circular Quay: Aria		●			
The Rocks and Circular Quay: Bel Mondo	■	●		●	
The Rocks and Circular Quay: Guillaume at Bennelong	●	■			
The Rocks and Circular Quay: Rockpool			■		

THE BLUE MOUNTAINS AND BEYOND

ARMIDALE: *Jitterbug Mood* $$$
115 Rusden St, NSW 2350. ((02) 6772 3022.
Bookings are advised at this popular eatery. The atmosphere is intimate, while the food is genuinely multicultural. ● L, Sun & Mon D. ⚡ 📧

BALLINA: *Shelley's on the Beach* $$
Shelley Beach Rd, NSW 2478. ((02) 6686 9844.
This beach café is true Australia: superb seafood, reasonable prices, a casual atmosphere and ocean views. ● D. ⚡ 📧

BLACKHEATH: *Glenella Guesthouse* $$$
56 Govetts Leap Rd, NSW 2785. ((02) 4787 8352.
This established guesthouse offers modern Australian food set amongst beautiful surroundings. 🍷 📧

BLACKHEATH: *Vulcans Café* $$$
33 Govetts Leap Rd, NSW 2785. ((02) 4787 6899.
Sydney chef Phillip Searle runs Vulcan's in the old Blackheath Bakery. Try beef followed by checkerboard ice cream. ● Mon–Thu. ⚡ 🦽 📧

BLACKHEATH: *Cleopatra Guesthouse and Restaurant* $$$$$
118 Cleopatra St, NSW 2785. ((02) 4787 8456.
This restaurant has won numerous awards for its French-Australian cuisine, including fish soups and sensational desserts. The chocolate pudding oozes with chocolate sauce. ● Mon–Sat L. 🍷 📧

BROKEN HILL: *Alfresco* $$
397 Argent St, NSW 2880. ((08) 8087 5599.
This bustling café is great for travellers with its long opening hours and affordable menu of pizzas, pancakes, pasta and steaks. ⚡ 🦽 📧

BYRON BAY: *Raving Prawn Restaurant* $$$
Feros Arcade, Johnson St, NSW 2481. ((02) 6685 6737.
Despite its unprepossessing setting, this restaurant has an excellent, constantly changing seafood menu. ● Sun & Mon, Tue–Sat L. ⚡ 🦽 📧

BYRON BAY: *Dish* $$$$
Cnr Jonson & Marvel sts, NSW 2481. ((02) 6685 7320.
This stylish café/restaurant offers sensational modern Mediterranean cuisine, sometimes with an Asian twist. 🦽 🍷 📧

BYRON BAY: *Fins* $$$$
Beach Hotel, cnr Jonson & Bay sts, NSW 2450. ((02) 6685 5029.
Sophisticated modern seafood with an emphasis on freshness and flavour is on the menu here. Don't miss the desserts. 🦽 🍷 📧

COFFS HARBOUR: *Star Anise Restaurant* $$$$
93 Grafton St, NSW 2450. ((02) 6651 1033.
There is usually a daily seafood special at this restaurant. The delicious desserts are hard to pass up. ● Sun–Tue, Sat L. 🍽 ⚡ 📧

KATOOMBA: *Darleys* $$$$$
Lillianfels, Lillianfels Ave, Katoomba, NSW 2780. ((02) 4780 1200.
Set in an elegant 19th-century house, Darleys makes use of local produce such as trout and wild mushrooms. ● Mon & Tue. 🍷 📧

LEURA: *Silk's Brasserie* $$$$
128 The Mall, NSW 2780. ((02) 4784 2534.
Chefs Thomas Dottard and David Waddington prepare modern mountain fare in their highly respected restaurant. Silk's has won the American Express best restaurant award in the western region. 🦽 🍷 📧

NEWCASTLE: *Scratchley's on the Wharf Restaurant* $$$
200 Wharf Rd, NSW 2300. ((02) 4929 1111.
This bright and breezy waterfront restaurant with great views also claims to have the best seafood, steak and chicken in town. 🍷 🍽 📧

NEWCASTLE: *Seaspray Restaurant* $$$
Noah's on the Beach, cnr Shortland Esplanade & Zaara St, NSW 2300.
((02) 4929 5181. Located right on the waterfront, Seaspray offers a special whale-watching menu during May and June, when migrating whales may be seen from the restaurant's windows. 🦽 🎵 📧

For key to symbols see back flap

<table>
<tr><td colspan="2">

Price categories for a three-course meal for one, including half a bottle of house wine and service charges.
$ under A$25
$$ A$25–A$35
$$$ A$35–A$50
$$$$ A$50–A$70
$$$$$ over A$70

</td><td colspan="6">

OUTDOOR EATING
Some tables on a patio or terrace.
VEGETARIAN SPECIALITIES
One menu always includes a varied selection of vegetarian dishes.
BAR AREA/COCKTAIL BAR
There is a bar area or cocktail bar within the restaurant, available for drinks and/or bar snacks.
FIXED-PRICE MENU
A fixed-price menu available at a good rate, at lunch, dinner or both, usually with three courses.
CHILDREN'S FACILITIES
Small portions and/or highchairs available on request.

</td></tr>
</table>

		OUTDOOR EATING	VEGETARIAN SPECIALITIES	BAR AREA	FIXED-PRICE MENU	CHILDREN'S FACILITIES
NEWCASTLE: *View Factory Arts-Café* Cnr Scott & Telford sts, NSW 2300. (02) 4929 4580. This chic waterfront brasserie makes excellent use of the local seafood in its innovative dishes. ● *Mon, Tue–Sun L.*	$$$		●	■		
NEWCASTLE: *The Scott Street Café Restaurant* 19 Scott St Newcastle East, NSW. (02) 4927 0107. The menu here is predominantly Mediterranean. Generous servings of dishes such as prawn ravioli or duck with celeriac mash. ● *Sun, Mon.*	$$$$		●			
NEWCASTLE: *Tongue 'n Groove* 196 Union St, The Junction, NSW 2300. (02) 4940 8133. Popular with the locals, this eatery serves modern Australian food. The atmosphere is friendly and there is great music.	$$$$	■	●			■
POKOLBIN: *Casuarina Restaurant* Hermitage Rd, NSW 2320. (02) 4998 7888. This long-established restaurant, surrounded by vineyards, offers Mediterranean cuisine. Flambés are a speciality. ● *Mon–Fri L.*	$$$$	■	●	■	●	■
POKOLBIN: *Robert's at Pepper Tree* Halls Rd, NSW 2320. (02) 4998 7330. Set in a listed 1876 ironbark cottage, this delightful restaurant provides regional food with a French influence.	$$$$	■	●		●	■
POKOLBIN: *Chez Pok at Peppers* Peppers Guesthouse, Ekerts Rd, NSW 2320. (02) 4998 7596. Multi-award-winning Chez Pok offers Australian fare with European and Asian influences, and views of the distant vineyards.	$$$$$	■	●	■		■
PORT MACQUARIE: *Harpo's* 4 Flynn St, Flynn's Beach, NSW 2444. (02) 6583 1401. Marx Brothers memorabilia adorns this eatery which serves classic fare such as steak and prawns. ● *L, Sun & Mon.*	$$	■	●	■	●	■
PORT STEPHENS: *Merretts at the Anchorage* Corlette Point Rd, NSW 2315. (02) 4984 2555. Set right on the water, there is no better place to sample the local seafood prepared with Asian influences.	$$$	■	●		●	
WAGGA WAGGA: *Indian Tavern Tandoori Restaurant* 176 Baylis St, NSW 2650. (02) 6921 3121. This Indian restaurant rates well for its meticulous preparation. Try the butter chicken flavoured with cashew nut butter. ● *L.*	$$		●			■
**THE SOUTH COAST AND SNOWY MOUNTAINS**						
BATEMANS BAY: *Starfish Deli* Shop 1–2, Promenade Plaza, Clyde St, NSW 2536. (02) 4472 4880. This up-market bistro overlooking the inky Clyde River serves excellent wood-fired pizza, seafood and Clyde River oysters.	$$$	■	●	■	●	■
BERRIMA: *The White Horse Inn* Market Place, NSW 2577. (02) 4877 1204. Built as a wayside inn in 1832, the White Horse now serves hearty but sophisticated meals. Accommodation is also available.	$$$$	■	●			■
BRAIDWOOD: *Doncaster Inn Guesthouse* Wilson St, NSW 2622. (02) 4842 2356. This converted convent serves excellent French food prepared with local Australian produce. ● *L, Mon–Thu & Sun D.* limited.	$$$		●		●	

EDEN: *Eden Fishermen's Club* $$$
Imlay St, NSW 2551. ((02) 6496 1577.
The emphasis at the cavernous Fishermen's Club is on quantity,
but the local tuna, crayfish and prawns are hard to beat. 🎵 🍴

GOULBURN: *The Rimbolin* $$$
380 Auburn St, NSW 2580. ((02) 4821 7633.
By day the Rimbolin is a gourmet café; at night, it is an intimate
restaurant serving more refined meals. ● *Mon & Tue D.* 🍴 🎵 🍴

GOULBURN: *Willow Vale Mill Restaurant and Guesthouse* $$$
Willowvale Mill, Laggan via Crookwell, NSW 2583. ((02) 4837 3319.
Slightly off the beaten track, potato farmer-cum-chef Graham Liney
serves up hearty meals to suit the season using local produce,
including game and fish, and vegetables from the garden. Guest
rooms are also available. 🍷 🦽 *limited.* 🍴

NOWRA: *The Boatshed Restaurant* $$$$
Wharf Rd, NSW 2541. ((02) 4421 2419.
Perched by the Shoalhaven River, this is a lovely place to sample the
local seafood. Booking is essential at weekends. ● *Sun, Mon L.* 🦽 🍴

SNOWY MOUNTAINS: *Duffers Ridge Restaurant* $$$
Novotel Lake Crackenback Resort, Alpine Way via Jindabyne, NSW 2627.
((02) 6456 2960. Duffers Ridge restaurant looks out over the silver
lake to the mountains all around. The international and modern
Australian menu features fondues, kangaroo and trout. 🦽 🍷 🍴

SOUTHERN HIGHLANDS: *Blue Cockerel Bistro* $$
95 Hume Hwy, Mittagong, NSW 2575. ((02) 4872 1677.
French-born chef Martial Cosyn features seasonal, local produce here,
especially berrries, asparagus and meat dishes. ● *L, Sun, Mon.* 🍴

SOUTHERN HIGHLANDS: *Horderns* $$$$
Horderns Rd, Bowral, NSW 2576. ((02) 4861 1522.
Modern Australian food with European and Asian influences is served
in this elegant country restaurant with two dining rooms. Bookings are
advised and accommodation is also available *(see p471).* 🦽 🍷 🍴

TILBA TILBA: *Valley Country Home* $$$$
Guluga Track, NSW 2546. ((02) 4473 7405.
The Swiss-trained chef in this coastal establishment serves dishes such
as seafood chowder, veal loin and fresh ratatouille. 🍴 🦽 🍷 🍴

ULLADULLA: *Cookaburra's* $$$
Shop 2, 10 Wason St, NSW 2539. ((02) 4454 1443.
This little restaurant features local seafood caught by the fishing fleet at
Ulladulla. The menu swings between East and West – dishes include
prawn and coriander ravioli with lime soy. 🍴 🍴

WOLLONGONG: *Due Mezzi* $$$
233 Princes Hwy, Bulli, NSW 2516. ((02) 4229 5633.
Due Mezzi is an eclectic restaurant where chef Lorenzo Pagnan
produces anything from Egyptian chicken salad, to grilled
cuttlefish and North African duck salad. ● *Mon–Wed, Thu–Sat L.*
Sun D. 🍴 🦽 *limited.* 🍴

CANBERRA AND ACT

CANBERRA: *Taj Mahal* $
39 Northbourne Ave, Canberra City, ACT 2601. ((02) 6247 6528.
The bustling Taj Mahal serves good, cheap Indian food. The Tandoori
chicken is particularly recommended. ● *Sat L, Sun, Mon L, Tue L.* 🍴

CANBERRA: *Timmy's Kitchen* $
Manuka Village Centre, Furneaux St, Manuka, ACT 2603.
((02) 6295 6537. This tiny Chinese/Malaysian restaurant is a true
Canberra experience and very popular with locals. The Southeast
Asian food is good and cheap. 🍴 🍴

CANBERRA: *The High Court Café* $$
High Court of Australia, Parkes Place, Parkes, ACT 2600. ((02) 6270 6828.
Situated in the glass edifice of the High Court, this restaurant offers an
elegant lunch while overlooking the lake. ● *D, Sat, Sun.* 🦽

For key to symbols see back flap

Price categories for a three-course meal for one, including half a bottle of house wine and service charges.
$ under A$25
$$ A$25–A$35
$$$ A$35–A$50
$$$$ A$50–A$70
$$$$$ over A$70

OUTDOOR EATING
Some tables on a patio or terrace.
VEGETARIAN SPECIALITIES
One menu always includes a varied selection of vegetarian dishes.
BAR AREA/COCKTAIL BAR
There is a bar area or cocktail bar within the restaurant, available for drinks and/or bar snacks.
FIXED-PRICE MENU
A fixed-price menu available at a good rate, at lunch, dinner or both, usually with three courses.
CHILDREN'S FACILITIES
Small portions and/or highchairs available on request.

	Outdoor Eating	Vegetarian Specialities	Bar Area	Fixed-Price Menu	Children's Facilities
CANBERRA: *Ruby Chinese Restaurant* ($$) 18–20 Woolley St, Dickson, ACT 2602. (02) 6249 8849. Ruby's has a fascinating reputation as being the place where spies of all nationalities rendezvous. Specializing in live seafood, it is in the heart of Canberra's only "Chinatown" street.		●	■	●	
CANBERRA: *The Chairman and Yip* ($$$) 108 Bunda St, Canberra City, ACT 2601. (02) 6248 7109. This is a Chinese restaurant that has the local food critics raving. The menu is light, fresh and inventive. ● Sat L.	■	●	■		
CANBERRA: *Republic* ($$$) 20 Allara St, Canberra City, ACT 2600. (02) 6247 1717. The atmosphere here is noisy and colourful, and the modern Australian menu is light, elegant and interesting. ● Sat, Sun, D.	■	●	■		
CANBERRA: *Rosso Restaurant* ($$$) Palmerston Lane, Manuka, ACT 2603. (02) 6295 6703. This small restaurant has both Japanese- and European-influenced dishes on the menu, served in an intimate atmosphere. ● Sun.			■		
CANBERRA: *Tosolini's* ($$$) Bailey's Corner, cnr London Circuit & East Row, Canberra City, ACT 2600. (02) 6247 4317. Tosolini's is the place to be seen among the hip youth scene. Its food is inexpensive and cosmopolitan, and the coffee is arguably the best in the city. There is a another Tosolini's in Manuka and Woden with equally good coffe and Italian food.	■	●		●	
CANBERRA: *Tu Tu Tango* ($$$) 124 Bunda St, Canberra City, ACT 2600. (02) 6257 7100. A mix of Deep South and Californian cuisine results in the award-winning menu at Tu Tu Tango.	■	●	■		■
CANBERRA: *The Boat House by the Lake* ($$$$) Grevillea Park, Menindee Drive, Barton, ACT 2600. (02) 6273 5500. Situated on the northern edge of Lake Burley Griffin, the Boat House offers stunning views of Canberra's prominent landmarks. The menu is modern Australian. ● Sun, Sat L.	■	●		●	■
CANBERRA: *Cavalier Carousel Restaurant* ($$$$) Red Hill Lookout, Red Hill, ACT 2603. (02) 6273 1808. The Cavalier is something of an institution in Canberra, serving international food and contemporary Australian cuisine. The views are stunning. ● Sun.		●	■		■
CANBERRA: *Fringe Benefits* ($$$$) 54 Marcus Clarke St, Canberra City, ACT 2601. (02) 6247 4042. Named after the 1980s Bill that meant work lunches were no longer tax deductible, this remains a magnificent restaurant serving regional French food and classical cuisine. ● Sat L., Sun.	■		■		
CANBERRA: *Hill Station Restaurant* ($$$$) 51 Sheppard St, Hume, ACT 2620. (02) 6260 1393. Hill Station was once an isolated sheep farm which has been converted into a lovely restaurant, serving sophisticated country-style cooking. Book ahead. Sat L, Sun L, D Fri, D Sat.	■	●	■	●	■
CANBERRA: *The Lobby Restaurant* ($$$$) King George Terrace, Parkes, ACT 2600. (02) 6273 1563. In the shadow of Parliament House, The Lobby is a favourite with politicians. Its food is modern Australian. L Mon–Fri, D Tue–Sat.	■	●			

Restaurant	Price					
CANBERRA: *Axis* National Musuem of Australia, Acton Peninsula Acton, ACT 2601. ☎ *(02) 6208 5176.* One of three cafés and restaurants in the museum, Axis is the flagship, with glorious views and food with flair. ♿ 🍷 💳	$$$$$	■	●			
QUEANBEYAN: *Byrne's Mill* 55 Collett St, Queanbeyan, ACT 2620. ☎ *(02) 6297 8283.* This restaurant set in a century-old, heritage-listed mill wins culinary awards for its adventurous new cuisine and great desserts. ● *L Tue–Fri, D Tue–Sat.* 🍷 💳	$$$$$	■	●			■
BRISBANE						
ALBION: *Breakfast Creek Hotel* 2 Kingsford Smith Drive, QLD 4010. ☎ *(07) 3262 5988.* An institution since its construction in 1889, this is the place for a typical Australian barbecue – and you can choose your own steak. 💳	$$	■	●	■	●	■
CITY CENTRE: *Pancakes at the Manor* 18 Charlotte St, QLD 4000. ☎ *(07) 3221 6433.* This casual eatery is set in a renovated old church. Drop in day or night for a steak, salad, burger or a gourmet pancake. 💳	$$		●		●	■
CITY CENTRE: *Augello's* 695 Brunswick St, QLD 4005. ☎ (07) 3254 0275. With able staff in the kitchen, the food here is simple modern Australian and big on flavour. Try the wasabi king prawns in won ton wraps. ♿ 🍷 💳	$$$	■	●	■	●	■
CITY CENTRE: *Shingle Inn* 254 Edward St, QLD 4000. ☎ (07) 3221 9039. Opened in the 1930s, Shingle Inn serves many Australian favourites: pavlova, lemon meringue pie and waffles. ● *Sun.* ♿	$$$		●			
CITY CENTRE: *Customs House Brasserie* 399 Queen Street, QLD 4000. ☎ *(07) 3365 8999.* Situated in a heritage building overlooking the river which also contains a gallery and a cultural centre, this stylish café serves fresh and imaginative Australian food. ● *Sun & Mon D.* ♿ 🍷 💳	$$$$	■	●	■		■
CITY CENTRE: *Il Centro* Eagle St Pier, QLD 4000. ☎ *(07) 3221 6090.* Set in the Eagle Pier district, Il Centro is an up-market modern Italian restaurant with river views and a stylish dining area set around a large open kitchen. Be sure to sample the extensive wine list. ♿ 🍷 💳	$$$$	■	●	■		■
CITY CENTRE: *Marco Polo* Level 2, Conrad International Treasury Casino, William St, QLD 4000. ☎ *(07) 3306 8888.* This up-market restaurant serves "East meets West" cuisine. As a unique gimmick, its menu is influenced by Marco Polo's travels through Asia. ● *L.* ♿ 🍷 💳	$$$$		●	■	●	
CITY CENTRE: *Parklands* Rydges South Bank, Glenelg St,QLD 4101. ☎ *(07) 3364 0844.* The restaurant in Rydges South Bank Hotel boasts a casual atmosphere, with an emphasis on steak and seafood. There is a seafood buffet on Friday and Saturday nights. ● *Sun.* ♿ 🍷 💳	$$$$	■	●	■		■
CITY CENTRE: *Philip Johnson at Victoria's* Level 6 Hilton Hotel, 190 Elizabeth St, QLD 4000. ☎ *(07) 3231 3195.* This fine restaurant is now under the expert guidance of local culinary maestro Philip Johnson of E'cco fame. ♿ 💳	$$$$					
CITY CENTRE: *Tables at Toowong* 85 Miskin St, QLD 4066. ☎ (07) 3371 4558. Winner of a Best Restaurant Award, Tables at Toowong serves outstanding food popular with celebrities. ● *Tue– Sat L.* 💳	$$$$	■	●		●	
CITY CENTRE: *E'cco* Cnr Adelaide and Boundary sts, QLD 4000. ☎ *(07) 3831 8344.* Set in a former tea warehouse, the award-winning E'cco's emphasis is on quality produce and mouthwatering flavours at very good value. ● *Sun & Mon, Sat L.* ⛱ 💳	$$$$$		●	■	●	■

For key to symbols see back flap

Price categories for a three-course meal for one, including half a bottle of house wine and service charges.
$ under A$25
$$ A$25–A$35
$$$ A$35–A$50
$$$$ A$50–A$70
$$$$$ over A$70

Outdoor Eating
Some tables on a patio or terrace.
Vegetarian Specialities
One menu always includes a varied selection of vegetarian dishes.
Bar Area/Cocktail Bar
There is a bar area or cocktail bar within the restaurant, available for drinks and/or bar snacks.
Fixed-Price Menu
A fixed-price menu available at a good rate, at lunch, dinner or both, usually with three courses.
Children's Facilities
Small portions and/or highchairs available on request.

Restaurant	Outdoor Eating	Vegetarian Specialities	Bar Area	Fixed-Price Menu	Children's Facilities
City Centre: *Michael's Riverside Restaurant* $$$$$ Riverside Centre, 123 Eagle St, QLD 4000. ☎ (07) 3832 5522. Run by top restaurateur Michael Platsis, this signature restaurant offers wonderful food and superb views. ● *L Sat, L Sun.* ♿ 🍷 💳	■	●	■	●	■
City Centre: *Pier Nine* $$$$$ 1 Eagle Street, QLD 4000. ☎ *(07) 3229 2194.* Three-time winner of the American Express Best Restaurant award, this seafood restaurant is one of Brisbane's finest eateries. ♿ 🍷 💳		●	■		■
City Centre: *Siggi's at the Port Office* $$$$$ Cnr Edward & Margaret sts, QLD 4000. ☎ (07) 3221 4555. One of Brisbane's most elegant restaurants. French cuisine is served with a contemporary Australian flavour. ● *Sat, Sun, L.* ♿ 🍷 💳	■	●	■	●	■
Fortitude Valley: *Giardinetto* $$$ 366 Brunswick St, QLD 4006. ☎ *(07) 3252 4750.* This cosy, café-style restaurant features the work of local artists on the walls. The *spagetti marinara* is delicious. ● *Sat L, Sun L, Mon L.* ♿ 🍾 💳	■	●	■		■
Hamilton: *Bretts Wharf Seafood Restaurant* $$$ 449 Kingsford Smith Drive, QLD 4007. ☎ (07) 3868 1717. Take in the city skyline from across the river while sampling some of Queensland's best seafood. ♿ 🍷 🍾 💳	■	●	■		■
Milton: *La Dolce Vita Café and Restaurant* $$$$ 20 Park Rd, QLD 4064. ☎ (07) 3368 3805. This family-owned restaurant serves risotto and pasta, as well as some delicious *gelati* and Italian cakes. ♿ ♫ 🍾 💳	■	●			■
Milton: *Ryans's Riverfront Seafood Restaurant* $$$$ Cnr Coronation Drive and Park Rd, QLD 4064. ☎ (07) 3368 1200. Situated in a heritage-listed building overlooking the river, this restaurants serves the freshest seafood possible. 🍾 🍷 💳		●	■	●	■
Mount Coot-tha: *Kuta Cafe* $ Sir Samuel Griffith Drive, QLD 4066. ☎ (07) 3369 9922. The casual eating option at the Mt Coot-tha Lookout *(see p222)* – come here for breakfast, lunch, dinner or a Devonshire tea. ♿ 💳	■	●			■
Mount Coot-tha: *Mount Coot-tha Summit Restaurant & Bar* $$$$ Sir Samuel Griffith Drive, QLD 4066. ☎ (07) 3369 9922. This à la carte restaurant offers breathtaking views from Brisbane to Moreton Bay day or night. ♿ 🍷 💳	■	●	■	●	■
Newstead: *Breakfast Creek Wharf Seafood Restaurant* $$$ 192 Breakfast Creek Rd, QLD 4006. ☎ (07) 3252 2451. Explorer John Oxley breakfasted at this spot, and a replica of his ship is the focus of the decor in this smart but casual restaurant, famed for its excellent seafood. ♿ 🍷 💳	■	●	■	●	■

South of Townsville

Restaurant	Outdoor Eating	Vegetarian Specialities	Bar Area	Fixed-Price Menu	Children's Facilities
Boreen Point: *The Jetty* $$$$ 1 Boreen Pole, QLD 4680. ☎ *(07) 5485 3167.* Located on the water's edge, this is famous for its fresh local produce. The wonderful setting makes it an unmissable lunch venue. ♿ 💳		●		●	■
Gladstone: *Swaggies Australian Restaurant* $$$ 56 Goondoon St, QLD 4680. ☎ *(07) 4972 1653.* Swaggies specializes in native Australian cuisine, such as kangaroo, emu or crocodile. ● *Sat & Sun L.* ♿ 🍷 💳	■	●	■		■

GLADSTONE: *Flinders Seafood Restaurant* $$$$ ⬛ ● ⬛   ⬛
Cnr Oaka Lane & Flinders Parade, QLD 4680. *(07) 4972 8322.*
Winner of the Central Queensland best restaurant award for five years,
Flinders is famous for its chilli and its steamed mudcrab. 🅱 🍷 🐾 🎫

MACKAY: *Fratini on the Waterfront* $$$$ ⬛ ● ⬛   ⬛
8 River St, QLD 4740. *(07) 4957 8131.*
The deck overlooking the river provides an idyllic setting. The
menu ranges from light meals to baked whole barramundi.
● *Sat L, Sun.* 🅱 🍷 🎫

NOOSA HEADS: *Berardo's* $$$$ ● ⬛
Hastings St, QLD 4567. *(07) 5447 5666.*
One of Noosa Head's most popular eateries, the menu features mostly
organic, biodynamic and free range produce. ● *L.* 🅱 🍷 🎫

NOOSA HEADS: *Riva* $$$$ ⬛ ●   ⬛
The Wharf, Quamby Pl, Noosa Sound, QLD 4567. *(07) 5449 2440.*
Situated on the Noosa River, this restaurant specializes in seafood
prepared in a crisp, Mediterranean style. ● *Sun D.* 🎫

NOOSA HEADS: *Season* $$$$ ⬛ ● ⬛ ● ⬛
25 Hastings St, QLD 4567. *(07) 5447 3747.*
The atmosphere in this bistro is relaxed, with an emphasis on modern
Australian food. The food ranges from seafood and pasta to poultry
and game, and the fresh-made lemonade is a treat. Children are
welcome. 🍴 🐾 🅱 🎫

NOOSA HEADS: *Saltwater* $$$$$ ⬛ ●   ⬛
8 Hastings St, QLD 4567. *(07) 5447 2234.*
This stylish establishment is one of Noosa's top restaurants and its
owners and chef are enthusiastic supporters of local produce,
including Noosa prawns and ginger from Buderim. The menu is
almost all seafood and the upstairs dining area is set on the roof. 🍷 🎫

NOOSAVILLE: *The Boathouse Café* $$$ ⬛ ●   ⬛
142 Gympie Terrace, QLD 4700. *(07) 5474 4444.*
This riverfront café offers wood-roasted dishes, including pizza topped
with moretan bay bugs or lamb and onion jam. ● *Mon, Tue.* 🐾 🎫

NORTHERN QUEENSLAND

CAIRNS: *Barnacle Bill's Seafood Inn* $$$$ ⬛ ● ⬛   ⬛
65 The Esplanade, QLD 4870. *(07) 4051 2241.*
Barnacle Bill's is a seafood restaurant known for its good food and
service. Try the hot jambalaya or the blackened fish. ● *L.* 🅱 🎫

CAIRNS: *Kani's* $$$$ ⬛ ● ⬛ ● ⬛
59 The Esplanade, QLD 4870. *(07) 4051 1550.*
Kani's main emphasis is seafood, but the excellent menu is aimed
at all tastes and includes prime steaks as well. ● *L.* 🎫

CAIRNS: *Red Ochre Grill* $$$$ ⬛ ● ⬛   ⬛
Cnr Shields & Sheridan sts, QLD 4870. *(07) 4051 0100.*
If you want Australian "bush tucker" with a modern flavour, this is
where to find it. The mallee-fired char-grill imparts a unique flavour to
the meat, particularly kangaroo. ● *Sun L.* 🍴 🍷 🅱 🎫

CAIRNS: *Tawny's* $$$$ ⬛   ⬛   ⬛
Marlin Parade, QLD 4870. *(07) 4051 1722.*
This is Cairns' best seafood restaurant. Tawny's floor-to-ceiling
windows make the most of its waterfront setting. ● *L.* 🅱 🎫

CHARLEVILLE: *Outback Restaurant* $$$ ⬛ ● ⬛   ⬛
Mulga Country Motor Inn, Cunnamulla Rd, QLD 4470. *(07) 4654 3255.*
A pleasant eatery in a garden setting overlooking a pool, the
Outback offers both international and Australian cuisine.
● *Sun, Mon–Sat L.* 🅱 🍷 🎫

CLONCURRY: *Gidgee Bar and Grill* $$$ ⬛   ⬛   ⬛
Matilda Hwy, QLD 4824. *(07) 4742 1599.*
Specialities at this Outback establishment include local beef
and seafood flown in fresh from the Gulf of Carpentaria.
● *L, Sun.* 🅱 🎫

Price categories for a three-course meal for one, including half a bottle of house wine and service charges.
$ under A$25
$$ A$25–A$35
$$$ A$35–A$50
$$$$ A$50–A$70
$$$$$ over A$70

Outdoor Eating
Some tables on a patio or terrace.
Vegetarian Specialities
One menu always includes a varied selection of vegetarian dishes.
Bar Area/Cocktail Bar
There is a bar area or cocktail bar within the restaurant, available for drinks and/or bar snacks.
Fixed-Price Menu
A fixed-price menu available at a good rate, at lunch, dinner or both, usually with three courses.
Children's Facilities
Small portions and/or highchairs available on request.

Cunnamulla: *Warrego Hotel/Motel* $$
9 Louise St, QLD 4490. ☎ *(07) 4655 1737.*
Part of a typical country pub, the pleasant dining room is where the locals go for a night out, but it also welcomes travellers with its friendly service. ♿ 💳

Daintree: *Jacanas Restaurant* $$
Daintree Village, QLD 4873. ☎ *(07) 4098 6146.*
Overlooking the Daintree River, this friendly restaurant makes the most of the barramundi prevalent in the area. ♿ 💳

Longreach: *Jolly Jumbuck Restaurant* $$$
Jumbuck Motel, Sir Hudson Fysh Drive, QLD 4730. ☎ *(07) 4658 1799.*
This better than average motel restaurant serves a range of dishes, especially local beef and seafood. ● *Sun, Mon–Sat L.* ♿ 💳

McKinlay: *Walkabout Creek Hotel* $$
Matilda Hwy, QLD 4823. ☎ *(07) 4746 8424.*
Famous as a location for the film *Crocodile Dundee*. Host Paul Collins offers good home-style meals with traditional Australian hospitality. ♿ 💳

Mount Isa: *The Carpenteria Buffalo Club* $$$
102 Camooweal St, QLD 4825. ☎ *(07) 4743 2365.*
With a restaurant, a café and three bars, the Club is known for its great atmosphere, top food, including char-grilled steaks and barramundi, and friendly service. ♿ 💳

Mount Isa: *The Verona* $$$$
The Mercure Hotel, Marian St, QLD 4825. ☎ *(07) 4743 3024.*
Very up-market for an Outback restaurant, the food ranges from steak to seafood. ● *Sun–Mon L.* ♿ 🍸 💳

Port Douglas: *On the Inlet* $$$
3 Inlet St, QLD 4871. ☎ *(07) 4099 5255.*
Specializing in superb fish and chips, and seafood fresh from the trawlers, this is ideal for a casual lunch or a sunset dinner. ♿ 💳

Port Douglas: *La Marina Ristorante Italiano* $$$$
Marina Mirage, Wharf Rd, QLD 4871. ☎ *(07) 4099 5548.*
Renowned for homemade pasta and sumptuous desserts, La Marina has won the Queensland Tourism and Travel Corporation Restaurant of the Year award. ♿ 💳

Port Douglas: *Lime Restaurant & Bar* $$$$
38 Macrossan St, QLD 4871. ☎ *(07) 4099 6536.*
Mudcrabs are a favourite in this restaurant that specializes in local produce with an Asian influence. ♿ 🍸 💳

Port Douglas: *Salsa Bar and Grill* $$$$
Wharf St, QLD 4871. ☎ *(07) 4099 4922.*
Offering Australasian style cuisine with a Tex-Mex influence, this restaurant is popular both with tourists and locals. ♿ 💳

Port Douglas: *Catalina* $$$$$
22 Wharf St, QLD 4871. ☎ *(07) 4099 5287.*
A meal in the garden here under the stars is unforgettable. Feast on whole mud crabs, crayfish or fresh oysters. ● *L, Mon.* ♿ 🍸 💳

Winton: *The Winton Club* $
Vindex St, QLD 4735. ☎ *(07) 4657 1488.*
The Winton Club operates a good-value Chinese restaurant with some Australian dishes included on the menu. 💳

	Outdoor Eating	Vegetarian Specialities	Bar Area	Fixed-Price Menu	Children's Facilities
Cunnamulla: Warrego Hotel/Motel	■	●	■		■
Daintree: Jacanas Restaurant	■	●	■		■
Longreach: Jolly Jumbuck Restaurant	■	●	■		■
McKinlay: Walkabout Creek Hotel	■	●	■		●
Mount Isa: The Carpenteria Buffalo Club		●	■		■
Mount Isa: The Verona		●	■	●	■
Port Douglas: On the Inlet	■	●	■		■
Port Douglas: La Marina Ristorante Italiano	■	●		●	■
Port Douglas: Lime Restaurant & Bar	■	●	■		■
Port Douglas: Salsa Bar and Grill	■	●	■		■
Port Douglas: Catalina	■	●	■		■
Winton: The Winton Club		●	■		■

DARWIN AND THE TOP END

DARWIN: *Rumpoles* $
Supreme Court Complex, State Square, Bennett St, NT 0800. (08) 8941
1513. If imposing surroundings are to your taste, Rumpoles café
provides a cool escape from the tropics outside. ● Sat & Sun L, D. ♿

DARWIN: *Speakers Corner Café* $
Ground Floor, Parliament House, NT 0800. (08) 8981 4833.
Lunch alongside the Northern Territory's politicians and bureaucrats
in a casual setting within the parliament building, and enjoy the views
over Darwin Harbour. ● Sat & Sun L, D. ♿

DARWIN: *Escape@Nightcliff* $$
40 Progress Drive, Nightcliff, NT 0810. (08) 8948 2773.
Relax in a tropical shady setting in this informal, outdoor café,
ideal for a quick coffee or for a late evening light meal. ♿

DARWIN: *The Magic Wok* $$
48 Cavanagh St (in GPO Building), NT 0810. (08) 8981 3332.
Choose your own selection from a huge range of fresh vegetables,
meats and sauces to be stir-fried by chefs on a turbo-wok.
● Sat & Sun L.

DARWIN: *Café Capri* $$$
37 Knuckey St, NT 0800. (08) 8981 0010.
This is a modern brasserie-style restaurant with a stylish decor and a
relaxed ambience. The Australian-Mediterranean fare is excellent. ♿

DARWIN: *Charlie's Restaurant* $$$
Cnr Knuckey St & Austin Lane, NT 0800. (08) 8981 3298.
Charlie's is a Darwin institution, where every Friday people gather for a
long lunch. The menu includes good homemade pasta. ● Sun L.

DARWIN: *Cornucopia Museum Café* $$$
Museum & Art Gallery of the NT, Conacher St, Fanny Bay, NT 0820.
(08) 8981 1002. A favourite place for Sunday brunch, this café offers
good food, including barramundi and kangaroo. The shaded outdoor
terrace looks out over Fannie Bay. ● Fri & Sat L. ♿

DARWIN: *Crustaceans on the Wharf* $$$
Stokes Hill Wharf, NT 0800. (08) 8981 8658.
Excellent seafood is served, and the outdoor tables take advantage of
the sea breeze in the dry season. ● L, Sun.

DARWIN: *Dragon Court* $$$
MGM Grand Darwin, Gilruth Ave, Mindil Beach, NT 0810. (08) 8943 8888.
This award-winning South-East Asian style restaurant specializes in
Cantonese cuisine and banquets. ● Mon & Tue. ♿

DARWIN: *Twilight on Lindsay* $$$
2 Lindsay St, NT 0800. (08) 8981 8631.
In the gardens of a historic house, this cool and comfortable restaurant
serves modern Australian cuisine. ● Sun, Sat–Tue L. ♿

DARWIN: *La Chaumiere* $$$$$
13 Shepherd St, NT 0800. (08) 8981 2879.
This stylish, family-run restaurant is set in an old home and offers
traditional French food and excellent service. ● Sun.

KAKADU: *Aurora Kakadu Lodge Poolside Bistro* $$
Kakadu Frontier Lodge, Jabiru, NT 0886. (08) 8979 2422.
Eat beside the swimming pool at this lodge (see p477). The food is quite
basic, but the barramundi and steak are excellent. ● L (seasonal). ♿

KAKADU: *Escarpment Restaurant* $$$$
Gagadju Crocodile Holiday Inn, Flinders St, Jabiru, NT 0886. (08) 8979 2800.
The restaurant of this crocodile-shaped hotel (see p477) offers modern
Australian food. Crocodile and barramundi are specialities. ♿

KATHERINE: *Aussie's Bistro* $
Katherine Hotel, Cnr Katherine Tce & Giles St, NT 0850. (08) 8972 1622.
Come here for a typical Australian pub meal. Main courses include
steak, barramundi and buffalo accompanied by a local beer. ♿

For key to symbols see back flap

Price categories for a three-course meal for one, including half a bottle of house wine and service charges.	Outdoor Eating / Vegetarian Specialities / Bar Area / Fixed-Price Menu / Children's Facilities
$ under A$25	
$$ A$25–A$35	
$$$ A$35–A$50	
$$$$ A$50–A$70	
$$$$$ over A$70	

OUTDOOR EATING Some tables on a patio or terrace.
VEGETARIAN SPECIALITIES One menu always includes a varied selection of vegetarian dishes.
BAR AREA/COCKTAIL BAR There is a bar area or cocktail bar within the restaurant, available for drinks and/or bar snacks.
FIXED-PRICE MENU A fixed-price menu available at a good rate, at lunch, dinner or both, usually with three courses.
CHILDREN'S FACILITIES Small portions and/or highchairs available on request.

Restaurant	Price	Outdoor Eating	Vegetarian Specialities	Bar Area	Fixed-Price Menu	Children's Facilities
KATHERINE: *Nitmiluk Bistro* — Nitmiluk National Park, NT 0850. (08) 8972 1253. This bistro is perched on a wide terrace and serves light, modern meals. Watch the sunset after a day exploring. ● Dec–Mar.	$$	■	●			■

THE RED CENTRE

Restaurant	Price	Outdoor Eating	Vegetarian Specialities	Bar Area	Fixed-Price Menu	Children's Facilities
ALICE SPRINGS: *Bar Doppio* — Shop 2, Fan Arcade, Todd Mall, NT 0870. (08) 8952 6525. The food at this lunch spot is inspired by the Mediterranean and Middle East. ● D.	$	■	●			
ALICE SPRINGS: *International Travellers Café* — Annies Place, 4 Traeger Ave, NT 0870. (08) 8952 1588. A broad menu, with dishes ranging from Mediterranean fare to barramundi and kangaroo steaks and vegetable curries.	$	■	●	■	●	
ALICE SPRINGS: *Kings Bistro* — Lasseters Casino, 93 Barrett Drive, NT 0870. (08) 8950 7777. Kings' main feature is its three-course fixed-price buffet, although à la carte meals are on offer. The cuisine is international.	$$	■	●	■	●	■
ALICE SPRINGS: *Bojangles Saloon and Restaurant* — 80 Todd St, NT 0870. (08) 8952 2873. Bojangles serves Northern Territory meats, including crocodile, emu, camel and kangaroo.	$$$		●	●		■
ALICE SPRINGS: *Keller's Swiss & Indian Restaurant* — 20 Gregory Terrace, NT 0870. (08) 8952 3188. An odd combination but both Swiss and Indian dishes are excellent. Desserts are Swiss and quite rich. ● L, Sun.	$$$	■	●			■
ALICE SPRINGS: *Oscar's Café Restaurant* — Cinema Complex, Todd Mall, NT 0870. (08) 8953 0930. Oscar's menu is European with dishes from Italy, Portugal and Spain, and an emphasis on seafood. Bookings are recommended.	$$$		●	■		■
ALICE SPRINGS: *The Overlanders Steakhouse* — 72 Hartley St, NT 0870. (08) 8952 2159. Overlanders is renowned for its huge "Drovers Blowout", featuring crocodile, barramundi, camel, kangaroo and emu.	$$$		●		●	■
ALICE SPRINGS: *The Sport Bistro* — Ansett Building, Todd Mall, NT 0870. (08) 8953 0935. The menu here offers classic bistro food – good steak, seafood and pasta. ● Sun, Mon, Sat L.	$$$$	■	●	■		■
ROSS RIVER: *Ross River Resort* — Ross Hwy, NT 0871. (08) 8956 9711. Hearty Australian meals in large portions are served at the homestead. Accommodation is also available (see p478).	$$	■	●	■		■
WATARRKA: *Carmichael's* — Kings Canyon Resort, Luritja Rd, Watarrka National Park, NT 0872. (08) 8956 7442. The resort restaurant, with outstanding views towards the canyon and over the desert wilderness, has an appealing buffet.	$$$$		●	●	●	■
YULARA: *Bough House Restaurant* — Outback Pioneer Hotel, Yulara Drive, NT 0872. (08) 8957 7888. The restaurant of the Outback Pioneer Hotel (see p478) is known for its carvery and buffet. Children under the age of 15 eat for free.	$$$	■	●	■	●	■

YULARA: *Rockpool Restaurant* $$$
Sails in the Desert Hotel, Yulara Drive, NT 0872. (*(08) 8956 2200.*
Overlooking the hotel pool *(see p479)*, the Rockpool has an emphasis
on Thai dishes. ● *L.* & ♟ 🖺

YULARA: *Kuniya Room* $$$$
Sails in the Desert Hotel, Yulara Drive, NT 0872. (*(08) 8956 2200.*
The most up-market of dining options in Yulara, the cuisine is
modern Australian with an international influence. ● *L.* ♟ 🖺

PERTH AND THE SOUTHWEST

ALBANY: *Kooka's Restaurant* $$$
204 Stirling Terrace, WA 6330. (*(08) 9841 5889.*
This fine restaurant serves modern Australian food with both
French and Indian influences. ● *Sun & Mon, Sat L.* 🌂 🖺

BUNBURY: *Alexander's Bistro* $$$
Lord Forrest Hotel, Symmons St, WA 6230. (*(08) 9721 9966.*
This restaurant is stylish and relaxed, attracting a mixed crowd. Light
meals have a Mediterranean influence. & ♫ ♟ 🖺

BUSSELTON: *Newtown House* $$$$
Bussell Hwy, Vasse, WA 6280. (*(08) 9755 4485.*
The Newtown House menu uses fresh local produce. Among the
specialities are pan-fried quail with risotto cakes and lavender ice
cream with hot caramel souffle. ● *Sun–Mon.* 🌂 & 🖺

COWARAMUP: *Cullen's Restaurant* $$$
Cullen Winery, Caves Rd, WA 6284. (*(08) 9755 5656.*
This winery restaurant, set beneath peppermint trees, serves modern
Australian cuisine. Excellent wine list, of course. ● *D.* & ♟ 🖺

FREMANTLE: *The Bamboo Café* $
73 George Street, WA 6160. (*(08) 9339 6352.*
This friendly café offers excellent vegetarian food, including
delicious desserts. 🌂

FREMANTLE: *Benny's Bar and Café* $$$
10 South Terrace, WA 6160. (*(08) 9433 1333.*
Mediterranean style dining, from light snacks to full dinners. Features
live entertainment Wedesday to Saturday nights. & ♟ ♫ 🖺

FREMANTLE: *Sicilian Café and Restaurant* $$$
480 Hay St, Subiaco, WA 6160. (*(08) 9380 4554*
This Italian restaurant, with ocean views, is renowned for its family
atmosphere and generous servings of pizza and seafood. ♟ 🖺

KALGOORLIE: *Basil's on Hannan* $$
268 Hannan St, WA 6430. (*(08) 9021 7832.*
Basil's serves good Mediterranean food, but is best known for its desserts,
particularly the chocolate Kalgoorlie Mud Cake. 🌂 & 🖺

KALGOORLIE: *Star Bistro* $$$
The Star and Garter Hotel, 497 Hannan St, WA 6430. (*(08) 9026 3399.*
Meals are a la carte with a salad and vegetable buffet. Try their
showcase of native dishes, including camel, wallaby and
rainbow trout. & P 🖺

MARGARET RIVER: *Marron Farm Café* $$
Wickham Rd, Witchcliffe, WA 6286. (*(08) 9757 6279.*
This café is set on one of the southwest's marron farms. Many dishes
on the menu feature this crayfish-like delicacy. ● *Fri.* 🖺

MARGARET RIVER: *The 1885 at The Grange on Farrelly* $$$
Farrelly St, WA 6285. (*(08) 9757 3177.*
One of Western Australia's finest restaurants, The 1885 uses fresh
regional produce to create innovative, beautifully presented dishes.
Accommodation is also available *(see p479)*. ● *L, Sun.* & ♫ ♟ 🖺

MARGARET RIVER: *Leeuwin Estate Winery Restaurant* $$$$
Leeuwin Estate Winery, Stevens Rd, WA 6825. (*(08) 9759 0000.*
Beside the Leeuwin Estate winery *(see p32)*, this restaurant offers a dis-
tinguished menu. Winery tour and tastings are also available. & ♟ 🖺

Price categories for a three-course meal for one, including half a bottle of house wine and service charges.	OUTDOOR EATING Some tables on a patio or terrace. VEGETARIAN SPECIALITIES One menu always includes a varied selection of vegetarian dishes. BAR AREA/COCKTAIL BAR There is a bar area or cocktail bar within the restaurant, available for drinks and/or bar snacks. FIXED-PRICE MENU A fixed-price menu available at a good rate, at lunch, dinner or both, usually with three courses. CHILDREN'S FACILITIES Small portions and/or highchairs available on request.
$ under A$25 $$ A$25–A$35 $$$ A$35–A$50 $$$$ A$50–A$70 $$$$$ over A$70	

	Price	OUTDOOR EATING	VEGETARIAN SPECIALITIES	BAR AREA	FIXED-PRICE MENU	CHILDREN'S FACILITIES
MUNDARING: *The Loose Box* 6825 Great Eastern Hwy, WA 6073. (*(08) 9295 1787.* This multi–award-winning restaurant has a seasonal menu utilising the best local produce, including that from its own gardens.	$$$$	■	●	■	●	■
PEMBERTON: *Gloucester Ridge Café* Gloucester Ridge Vineyard, Burma Rd, WA 6260. (*(08) 9776 1035.* This elegant restaurant offers quality Australian cuisine accompanied by the vineyard's own wines.	$$$	■	●	■	●	■
PERTH: *Canton Restaurant* 532 Hay St, WA 6000. (*(08) 9325 8865.* One of Perth's oldest Chinese restaurants, the Canton has been open since 1965. Banquets are a speciality.	$$		●	■	●	
PERTH: *The Moon* 323 William St, Northbridge, WA 6000. (*(08) 9328 7474.* This trendy late-night café serves light meals and snacks, including delicious pasta dishes and a particularly good Caesar salad.	$$	■	●		●	
PERTH: *Jetty's Restaurant & Café* Sorrento Quay, Hillary's Boat Harbour, WA 6000. (*(08) 9448 9066.* Built out over the water with magnificent views, this restaurant offers family dining, with a smorgasbord for breakfast, lunch and dinner.	$$$	■	●	■	●	■
PERTH: *Romany* 188 William St, WA 6000. (*(08) 9328 8042.* This Italian restaurant claims to be the oldest in Perth. It offers generous servings at reasonable prices.	$$$		●			■
PERTH: *Valentino's Restaurant* 27 Lake St, Northbridge, WA 6000. (*(08) 9328 2177.* Serving Italian and Asian-influenced food. The chef's speciality is the exceptional seafood platter.	$$$	■	●			■
PERTH: *C-Lounge Restaurant* 33rd Floor, 44 St George's Terrace, Perth WA 6000. (*(08) 9325 4844.* Perched 180 m (590 ft) above ground level, this restaurant offers unpretentious Australian cuisine, accompanied by spectacular views. *Sat & Sun L.*	$$$$			●	■	●
PERTH: *Level 1 Bar and Grill* 778 Hay St, WA 6000. (*(08) 9321 9141.* Located near His Majesty's Theatre, customers are invited to begin their meal before the performance and return for dessert after the show. *limited.*	$$$$			●	■	■
PERTH: *The Moorings Café on the Jetty* Old Perth Port, Barrack St Jetty, WA 6000. (*(08) 9325 4575.* Perched on the jetty, with fabulous views across the Swan River, this airy restaurant serves Australian specialities, such as kangaroo loin served with redcurrant and black pepper sauce.	$$$$	■	●			■
ROTTNEST ISLAND: *Vlamingh's* Rottnest Hotel, Bedford Ave, WA 6161. (*(08) 9292 5011.* With views of the Thomson Bay, Vlamingh's serves international cuisine, including a delicious Thai curry and local fish dishes.	$$$	■	●	■	●	■
WILLYABRUP: *Flutes* Brookland Valley Vineyard, Caves Rd, WA 6284. (*(08) 9755 6250.* This award-winning restaurant, set amid a vineyard overlooking a lake, offers modern Australian food.	$$$$	■	●			■

WILLYABRUP: *Vasse Felix* Caves Rd, Willyabrup, WA 6284. ☎ *(08) 9756 5000.* Part of the oldest winery in the region, the food matches the quality of the wines. Mediterranean and Asian flavours on the menu. ● *D.* 🍷 💳	$$$$	■	●			■
YORK: *Craig's 1853 Bistro* Castle Hotel, 97 Avon Terrace, WA 6302. ☎ *(08) 9641 1007.* This bistro, part of the 19th-century Castle Hotel, offers good-value meals. ♿ 💳	$$$	■	●	■		■

NORTH OF PERTH

BROOME: *Chin's Restaurant* 7 Hammersley St, WA 6725. ☎ *(08) 9192 1466.* In the centre of Broome's historic Chinatown *(see p322)*, Chin's is the pick of the area's Chinese restaurants. ● *L.* 🌳 💳	$$		●			■
BROOME: *Lord Mac's* Cable Beach Club Resort, Cable Beach Rd, WA 6725. ☎ *(08) 9192 0400.* The resort's main restaurant offers a fixed-price buffet or à la carte meals in beautiful sub-tropical surroundings. ♿ ♫ 🍷 💳	$$$	■	●	■	●	■
BROOME: *The Tides Garden Restaurant* Mangrove Hotel, 120 Carnarvon St, WA 6725. ☎ *(08) 9192 1303.* This pleasant restaurant offers outdoor eating overlooking the bay. The steak and seafood are recommended. ♿ 💳	$$$	■	●	■		■
CARNARVON: *Dragon Pearl Chinese Restaurant* 17 Francis St, WA 6701. ☎ *(08) 9941 1941.* Carnavon's only independent restaurant, the Dragon Pearl offers standard Chinese dishes to eat in or take away. ● *Mon.* ♿ 💳	$$		●	■	●	■
DENHAM: *The Old Pearler Restaurant* 71 Knight Terrace, WA 6537. ☎ *(08) 9948 1373.* On the Denham seafront, this homely little restaurant, made out of shells, offers local seafood such as grilled snapper and crayfish. 🌳 ♿ 💳	$$$	■	●			■
EXMOUTH: *The Whaler's Restaurant* 5 Kennedy St, WA 6707. ☎ *(08) 9949 2416.* This alfresco restaurant offers light meals and snacks, as well as an evening dinner menu of fresh local seafood and fish dishes. ♿ 💳	$$$	■	●			■
GERALDTON: *Beach Break Seafood and Steakhouse* 166 Chapman Rd, WA 6530. ☎ *(08) 9964 3382.* This informal restaurant specializes in seafood and steaks, in particular the delicious lobster. ● *L.* ♿ 💳	$$$	■	●			■
KALBARRI: *Zuytdorp Restaurant* Cnr Grey & Clotworthy sts, WA 6536. ☎ *(08) 9937 2222.* Zuytdorp's is popular for its fixed-price smorgasbord and for pricing its children's meals according to the age of the child. ● *L.* ♿ 🍷 💳	$$		●	■	●	■
MONKEY MIA: *The Bough Shed Restaurant* Shark Bay, WA 6537. ☎ *(08) 9948 1171.* This pretty beach restaurant is located close to the dolphin feeding area *(see p319)*. Meals are served throughout the day. ♿ 💳	$$$	■	●	■		■
NEW NORCIA: *Salvado's Restaurant* Monastery Roadhouse, Great Northern Hwy, WA 6509. ☎ *(08) 9654 8020.* This basic roadhouse serves budget meals. The menu includes the famous New Norcia breads, which are baked in the monastery bakehouse and now sold all over Western Australia. ♿ 💳	$		●			■

ADELAIDE AND THE SOUTHEAST

ADELAIDE: *Café Paesano* 100 O'Connell St, North Adelaide, SA 5006. ☎ *(08) 8239 0655.* This bustling café with its streetside tables could be in the owner's native Italy. The food is unpretentious, robust family fare. ♿ 💳	$	■	●			■
ADELAIDE: *Stanley's Great Aussie Fish Café* 76 Gouger St, SA 5000. ☎ *(08) 8410 0909.* This bustling restaurant specializes in fresh seafood, simply prepared. The grilled octopus and Moreton Bay Bugs are superb. ♿ 💳	$	■		■	●	■

	Outdoor Eating	Vegetarian Specialities	Bar Area	Fixed-Price Menu	Children's Facilities
Price categories for a three-course meal for one, including half a bottle of house wine and service charges. $ under A$25 $$ A$25–A$35 $$$ A$35–A$50 $$$$ A$50–A$70 $$$$$ over A$70 **OUTDOOR EATING** Some tables on a patio or terrace. **VEGETARIAN SPECIALITIES** One menu always includes a varied selection of vegetarian dishes. **BAR AREA/COCKTAIL BAR** There is a bar area or cocktail bar within the restaurant, available for drinks and/or bar snacks. **FIXED-PRICE MENU** A fixed-price menu available at a good rate, at lunch, dinner or both, usually with three courses. **CHILDREN'S FACILITIES** Small portions and/or highchairs available on request.					
ADELAIDE: *Jasmin Restaurant* ($)($) 31 Hindmarsh Square, SA 5000. (08) 8223 7837. Authentic Indian dishes make interesting use of local produce such as barramundi, goat and kangaroo. ● Sun, Mon, Sat L.	■	●	■	●	
ADELAIDE: *Jolleys Boathouse* ($)($)($) Jolleys Lane, SA 5000. (08) 8223 2891. Set in a converted boathouse on the River Torrens, Jolleys' menu is contemporary with a hint of Mediterranean and Asian. ● Sun D.	■	●	■		■
ADELAIDE: *Le Zinc* ($)($)($) 41 Gouger St, SA 5000. (08) 8212 2345. Excellent French bistro-style food served simply but well is available in this wine bar cum restaurant. ● Sat L, Sun, Mon.	■		■		
ADELAIDE: *The Oxford* ($)($)($) 101 O'Connell St, North Adelaide, SA 5006. (08) 8267 2652. The Oxford has a minimalist feel. The food is similarly contemporary and served with great style.	■		■	●	■
ADELAIDE: *Universal Wine Bar* ($)($)($) 285 Rundle St, SA 5000. (08) 8232 5000. This modern bistro serves Australian cuisine and has an excellent wine list. Duck risotto with rabbit sausage is a typical dish. ● Sun.	■	●	■		■
ADELAIDE: *Alphutte* ($)($)($)($) 242 Pulteney St, SA 5000. (08) 8223 4717. This is a contemporary version of a traditional Swiss alpine hut. The food is also Swiss, with fondues a speciality. ● Sat & Sun.		●	■	●	■
ADELAIDE: *Nediz Restaurant* ($)($)($)($) 170 Hutt St, SA 5000. (08) 8223 2618. This restaurant has a well-deserved reputation for blending influences from Europe and Asia with fresh local produce. ● Sun & Mon.	■	●		●	
ADELAIDE: *Shiki Restaurant* ($)($)($)($) Hyatt Regency Hotel, North Terrace, SA 5000. (08) 8231 1234. This Japanese *teppanyaki* restaurant has five teppan counters and one tempura counter. Sushi is also available. ● L, Sun, Mon.		●		●	■
ADELAIDE: *The Grange Restaurant* ($)($)($)($)($) Hilton International Hotel, 233 Victoria Square, SA 5000. (08) 8217 2000. Cheong Liew, one of Australia's most influential chefs, blends Asian flavours with classic cooking techniques. ● L, Sun, Mon D.		●	■	●	
BARMERA: *Bonneyview Winery Restaurant* ($)($) Sturt Hwy, SA 5345. (08) 8588 2279. Like many restaurants attached to wineries, this is a family-owned establishment set in attractive surroundings. ● Sun–Thu D.	■	●	■	●	■
BRIDGEWATER: *Bridgewater Mill* ($)($)($)($) Mount Barker Rd, SA 5155. (08) 8339 3422. Set in a renovated 1860s flour mill, this restaurant blends European and Asian techniques with fresh local ingredients. ● Tue, Wed, D.	■		■		■
COONAWARRA: *Chardonnay Lodge Restaurant* ($)($) Riddoch Hwy, SA 5263. (08) 8736 3309. This restaurant, with adjacent accommodation *(see p482)*, serves regional fare prepared with sophisticated style.		●	■		■

COONAWARRA: *The Hermitage* $$$$
Riddoch Hwy, SA 5263. ((08) 8737 2122.
Set amid the Coonawarra vineyards, the Hermitage serves an
ever-changing selection of adventurous regional dishes. 🚻 🍷 🥗

CRAFERS: *The Summit* $$$
Mount Lofty Summit Rd, SA 5152. ((08) 8339 2600.
This restaurant is situated on the top of Adelaide's highest mountain.
The decor is modern and stylish, as is the menu. 🚻 🍷 🥗

CRAFERS: *Hardy's* $$$$
74 Summit Rd, SA 5152. ((08) 8339 5656.
The menu here has a strong regional and seasonal emphasis featuring
dishes of local smoked salmon, venison and veal. The wine list
features many wines from award-winning local wineries. 🚻 🥗

KANGAROO ISLAND: *The Old Post Office Restaurant* $$$
Penneshaw, SA 5222. ((08) 8553 1063.
The menu takes advantage of seasonal ingredients, with a distinct
Mediterranean style and an emphasis on seafood. ● *L, Tue & Wed D.* 🚻 🥗

MARANANGA: *The Hermitage of Marananga* $$$$
Cnr Seppeltsfield & Stonewell rds, SA 5355. ((08) 8562 2722.
Choose between silver service dining by candlelight or alfresco eating
amid the vines. In either case, the food is outstanding. 🚻 🍷 🥗

PADTHAWAY: *Padthaway Estate Homestead* $$$$$
Riddoch Hwy, SA 5271. ((08) 8765 5039.
Elegant dining can be had in this 1882 two-storey Victorian mansion.
Accommodation is also available *(see p483)*. ● *L, Tue–Wed D.* 🍷 🥗

THE YORKE AND EYRE PENINSULAS

ARKAROOLA: *Native Pine Restaurant* $$
Arkaroola Village, SA 5732.
Located in the Arkaroola Wildlife Sanctuary *(see p361)*, this restaurant
provides a small but appetizing menu, including kangaroo with
quandong sauce. Barbecues are held adjacent to the restaurant. 🥗

AUBURN: *Rising Sun Hotel Restaurant* $$$
Main North Rd, SA 5451. ((08) 8849 2015.
The Rising Sun Hotel *(see p483)* has an extensive menu and meals are
served in either the saloon or the dining room. 🍷 🚻 🥗

AUBURN: *Tatehams* $$$$
Main North Rd, SA 5451. ((08) 8849 2030.
The sophisticated menu features local produce such as saltbush lamb.
A five-course *dégustation* menu is available. ● *Mon, Tue.* 🚻 🍷 🥗

BLINMAN: *Blinman Hotel Restaurant* $$
Main St, SA 5730. ((08) 8648 4867.
The choice at this remote country pub is wide and the food is
excellent. Accommodation is also available *(see p483)*. 🚻 🥗

CLARE: *Brice Hill Vineyard Restaurant* $$
Main North Rd, SA 5453. ((08) 8842 1796.
This hillside restaurant offers good views over the valley,
an extensive dinner menu and light lunches. ● *Mon & Tue.* 🥗

CLARE: *Clarevale Restaurant* $$
15 Lennon St, SA 5453. ((08) 8842 1222.
This 1878 building, originally a coach house, now houses a friendly,
casual restaurant. A constant favourite is the char-grilled steak. There
is also a children's video and play area. ● *Mon–Thu.* 🚻 🍷 🥗

COOBER PEDY: *Umberto's* $$$
Desert Cave Hotel, Hutchinson St, SA 5723. ((08) 8672 5688.
The elegant menu is varied and interesting. Try the basil crêpe with
smoked emu and *crème fraîche* as a start to your meal. ● *L.* 🚻 🍷 🥗

EDITHBURGH: *Sails Seafood and Steak Restaurant* $
Troubridge Hotel, Blanche St, SA 5583. ((08) 8852 6013.
The name says it all – simple food, fresh and substantial.
The fish is regularly caught within sight of the hotel. 🚻 🥗

For key to symbols see back flap

	OUTDOOR EATING	VEGETARIAN SPECIALITIES	BAR AREA	FIXED-PRICE MENU	CHILDREN'S FACILITIES
Price categories for a three-course meal for one, including half a bottle of house wine and service charges. ⑤ under A$25 ⑤⑤ A$25–A$35 ⑤⑤⑤ A$35–A$50 ⑤⑤⑤⑤ A$50–A$70 ⑤⑤⑤⑤⑤ over A$70	**OUTDOOR EATING** Some tables on a patio or terrace. **VEGETARIAN SPECIALITIES** One menu always includes a varied selection of vegetarian dishes. **BAR AREA/COCKTAIL BAR** There is a bar area or cocktail bar within the restaurant, available for drinks and/or bar snacks. **FIXED-PRICE MENU** A fixed-price menu available at a good rate, at lunch, dinner or both, usually with three courses. **CHILDREN'S FACILITIES** Small portions and/or highchairs available on request.				
HAWKER: *Old Ghan Restaurant* ⑤⑤ Old Railway Station, Leigh Creek Rd, SA 5434. 〖 (08) 8648 4176. Located in the former railway station of the Old Ghan *(see p361)*, the restaurant caters particularly well for children. ● Mon & Tue. 🍷 🍴	■	●	■	●	■
MINTARO: *Mintaro Mews* ⑤⑤⑤ Burra St, SA 5415. 〖 (08) 8843 9001. Specialities of this hotel restaurant are grilled minted sheep's cheese and duck with a port and pepperberry glaze. ● L, Wed, Thu. 🍷 🍴	■	●	■	●	
PORT LINCOLN: *Bugs Restaurant* ⑤ Harwill Court, SA 5606. 〖 (08) 8682 6244. Bugs is a bistro-style restaurant offering excellent-value pasta dishes, steak, veal and seafood, with warming soups in winter. 🍴	■	●			■
PORT LINCOLN: *Mortons on the Bay* ⑤⑤ 12 Tasman Terrace, SA 5606. 〖 (08) 8682 1197. This popular restaurant serves good-quality well-prepared seafood, caught locally, as well as steaks. ● L, Sun D. ♿ 🍴		●	■		■
PORT VINCENT: *Gerimia's* ⑤⑤ Marine Parade, SA 5581. 〖 (08) 8853 7021. A surprisingly good restaurant in this fishing town, Gerimia's offers local fish and excellent roasted duck. ● L, Mon & Tue D (Nov–Jun). 🍴			■		■
QUORN: *Old Willows Brewery Restaurant* ⑤⑤ Port Augusta Rd, Pichi Richi Pass, SA 5433. 〖 (08) 8648 6391. In the beautifully restored 1880 Willows Brewery, the restaurant serves innovative Australian cuisine including a crocodile starter and quandong pie for dessert. ● Mon–Wed. ♿ 🍷 🍴	■	●	■	●	■
SEVENHILL: *Skillogalee Winery and Restaurant* ⑤⑤ Trevarrick Rd, Via Clare, SA 5453. 〖 (08) 8843 4311. Open fires in winter and the veranda in spring make this an idyllic dining setting. The food is simple yet superb. ● D 🍴	■				■
WHYALLA: *Alexander Motor Inn Restaurant* ⑤⑤ 99 Playford Ave, SA 5600. 〖 (08) 8645 9488. The eclectic menu includes *escargots*, Indian prawns and Mongolian lamb, as well as local oysters and kangaroo fillet. ● L. 🍷 🍴		●	■	●	■
MELBOURNE					
ALBERT PARK: *The Point* ⑤⑤⑤⑤ Aquatic Drive, VIC 3206. **Map 5 A2.** 〖 (03) 9682 5544. This elegant restaurant at the edge of Albert Park Lake specializes in modern Australian food and has great views across to the city. 🍴	■	●	■		
CARLTON: *Abla's* ⑤⑤ 109 Elgin St, VIC 3053. **Map 1 C1.** 〖 (03) 9347 0006. Melbourne's best Lebanese eatery. Fixed menus for tables of two or more on Friday and Saturday nights. ● Sat–Wed L, Sun D. 🍴 🍴		●		●	
CARLTON: *Jimmy Watson's* ⑤⑤⑤⑤ 333 Lygon St, VIC 3053. **Map 1 C1.** 〖 (03) 9347 3985. The food at this acclaimed restaurant is inventive yet casual while the long-established wine bar is legendary. ● Sun, Mon D. 🍷 🍴	■	●	■	●	
CARLTON: *Toofey's Seafood Restaurant* ⑤⑤⑤⑤⑤ 162 Elgin St, VIC 3123. **Map 1 C1.** 〖 (03) 9347 9838. This is considered by many to be Melbourne's best seafood restaurant. It also serves great homemade ice cream. ● Mon, Sat L, Sun. 🍷 🍴					

CENTRAL MELBOURNE: *Café K* $$
35 Little Bourke St, VIC 3000. **Map 1 C3.** ☎ *(03) 9639 0414.*
This popular café serves good Australian-Mediterranean food in a stylish setting and at an affordable price. ● *Sat L, Sun L.* 🍷 💳

CENTRAL MELBOURNE: *Nudel Bar* $$
76 Bourke St, VIC 3000. **Map 1 C3.** ☎ *(03) 9662 9100.*
Noodles of all shapes and sizes are served here – hot, cold, thick, thin, sweet and savoury. All cuisines are covered. 💳

CENTRAL MELBOURNE: *Il Solito Posto* $$$
The Basement, 113 Collins St, VIC 3000. **Map 2 D3.** ☎ *(03) 9654 4466.*
This stylish place has a hectic and popular ground floor bar area serving light meals, while the rustic cellar restaurant downstairs offers more substantial northern Italian dishes. ● *L, Sun.* 💳

CENTRAL MELBOURNE: *Kuni's* $$$
56 Little Bourke St, VIC 3000. **Map 1 C3.** ☎ *(03) 9663 7243.*
An excellent value-for-money Japanese restaurant serving delicious food at the sushi bar or in the dining area. ● *Sun.* 💳

CENTRAL MELBOURNE: *Madam Fang* $$$
27–29 Crossley St, VIC 3000. **Map 1 C3.** ☎ *(03) 9663 3199.*
Modern Asian cuisine is served here, such as spicy croquettes with sour-plum chilli sauce. ● *Sat L, Sun.* 🍷 💳

CENTRAL MELBOURNE: *Becco* $$$$
11–25 Crossley St, VIC 3000. ☎ *(03) 9663 3000.*
This three-in-one establishment includes a shop, restaurant and bar. The innovative Italian menu includes fresh pasta, pappardelle with oxtail ragu and homemade torrone. All day snack menu. ● *Sun.* 🍷 💳

CENTRAL MELBOURNE: *The European* $$$$
161 Spring St, VIC 3000. ☎ *(03) 9654 0811.*
This chic café/restaurant is a great place for coffee, a pre-theatre drink or a sit-down dinner. The upstairs bar is one of Melbourne's best. 💳

CENTRAL MELBOURNE: *ezard at adelphi* $$$$$
187 Flinders Lane, VIC 3000. **Map 2 D3.** ☎ *(03) 9639 6811.*
In the ultra-modern basement of the Adelphi Hotel *(see p485)*, inventive dishes, combining various styles, are served. 🍷 💳

CENTRAL MELBOURNE: *Flower Drum* $$$$$
17 Market Lane, VIC 3000. **Map 1 C2.** ☎ *(03) 9662 3655.*
Melbourne's top Chinese restaurant serves complex and subtle dishes, such as their peerless Peking duck. ● *Sun L.* 🍷 💳

CENTRAL MELBOURNE: *Grossi Florentino* $$$$$
80 Bourke St, VIC 3000. **Map 1 B3.** ☎ *(03) 9662 1811.*
An old-world elegance of wood panelling and painted murals is complemented by very good traditional Italian food. There is more casual dining in the bistro and cellar bar downstairs. ● *Sun.* 🍷 💳

CENTRAL MELBOURNE: *Langton's Restaurant and Wine Bar* $$$$$
61 Flinders Lane, VIC 3000. ☎ *(03) 9663 0222.*
A sophisticated establishment and popular gathering spot for city professionals and local celebrities who enjoy the excellent modern European food on offer. ● *Sat L, Sun.* 🍷 💳

CENTRAL MELBOURNE: *Mask of China* $$$$$
115–117 Little Bourke St, VIC 3000. **Map 1 C3.** ☎ *(03) 9662 2116.*
An up-market and elegant Chinese restaurant featuring the exquisite dishes of the Chiu Chow cuisine. ● *Sat L.* 🍷 💳

COLLINGWOOD: *Jim's Greek Tavern* $$
32 Johnston St, VIC 3066. ☎ *(03) 9419 3827.*
The village atmosphere of this warm and lively restaurant has attracted Melburnians for more than 25 years. Diners are offered a range of classic dishes, including dips, seafood and grilled meats. 🍾 💳

FITZROY: *The Vegie Bar* $
380 Brunswick St, VIC 3065. **Map 2 E1.** ☎ *(03) 9417 6935.*
Fresh juices, organic wines and vegetarian dishes from around the world are features of this colourful, bustling café. ♿ 💳

Café K		●	■	●	
Nudel Bar	■	●			
Il Solito Posto		●	■		
Kuni's		●	■	●	
Madam Fang		●	■		
Becco		●	■		
The European	■	●	■		
ezard at adelphi		●	■		
Flower Drum				●	
Grossi Florentino	■	●	■		
Langton's Restaurant and Wine Bar	■		■	●	
Mask of China		●		●	■
Jim's Greek Tavern	■	●			
The Vegie Bar	■	●			■

For key to symbols see back flap

Price categories for a three-course meal for one, including half a bottle of house wine and service charges.
$ under A$25
$$ A$25–A$35
$$$ A$35–A$50
$$$$ A$50–A$70
$$$$$ over A$70

OUTDOOR EATING
Some tables on a patio or terrace.
VEGETARIAN SPECIALITIES
One menu always includes a varied selection of vegetarian dishes.
BAR AREA/COCKTAIL BAR
There is a bar area or cocktail bar within the restaurant, available for drinks and/or bar snacks.
FIXED-PRICE MENU
A fixed-price menu available at a good rate, at lunch, dinner or both, usually with three courses.
CHILDREN'S FACILITIES
Small portions and/or highchairs available on request.

	OUTDOOR EATING	VEGETARIAN SPECIALITIES	BAR AREA	FIXED-PRICE MENU	CHILDREN'S FACILITIES
FITZROY: *Mario's Café* $$ 303 Brunswick St, VIC 3065. **Map** 2 E1. (03) 9417 3343. Good café food is complemented here by white tablecloths, good service and excellent coffee.	■	●			
FITZROY: *Café Provincial* $$$ 299 Brunswick St, VIC 3065. **Map** 2 E1. (03) 9417 2228. A bustling, bohemian café set in a refurbished pub and serving inexpensive French and Italian fare.	■	●	■		
FITZROY: *Guernica* $$$$ 257 Brunswick St, VIC 3065. **Map** 2 E1. (03) 9416 0969. Guernica's exceptional food is modern Australian in style with Asian and Middle Eastern influences. Check the daily specials. ● *Sun.*		●			
KEW: *Beate's Restaurant* $$$$ Studley Park Boathouse, Boathouse Rd, VIC 3101. (03) 9853 1828. Upstairs in an 1863 boathouse with views of the Yarra River, the emphasis is on local produce. ● *Sun–Tue, Sat L. Open daily in summer.*		●			■
RICHMOND: *Vlado's* $$$$ 61 Bridge Rd, VIC 3121. **Map** 4 D1. (03) 9428 5833. This long-established steakhouse is a place for meat-eaters who like their steaks large and full of flavour. ● *Sat L, Sun.*				●	
ST KILDA: *Café di Stasio* $$$$ 31 Fitzroy St, VIC 3182. **Map** 5 B4. (03) 9525 3999. This sophisticated and lively restaurant serves contemporary Italian food. Try their famous crayfish omelette, roast duck or any of their fresh truffle dishes.	■	●			
ST KILDA: *The Stokehouse* $$$$ 30 Jacka Boulevard, VIC 3182. **Map** 5 B5. (03) 9525 5555. Situated on the beachfront, the restaurant upstairs serves excellent seafood, while downstairs, the bistro serves casual fare.	■	●	■		■
SOUTHBANK: *Blakes* $$$$$ Ground level, Southgate, VIC 3006. (03) 9699 4100. This popular restaurant serves modern Australian food with Asian and European influences, overlooking the Yarra River and the city skyline.		●		●	■
SOUTHBANK: *Walter's Wine Bar* $$$$$ Level 3 Southgate, VIC 3006. **Map** 1 C4. (03) 9690 9211. Overlooking the Yarra River, this is a fantastic spot for a leisurely alfresco lunch, dinner or late-night snack.	■	●	■		
SOUTH MELBOURNE: *Colonial Tramcar Restaurant* $$$$ Tramstop 125, Normanby Rd, VIC 3025. (03) 9696 4000. The world's only travelling tramcar restaurant provides a unique Melbourne experience. Booking is essential.		●		●	
SOUTH MELBOURNE: *The Isthmus of Kra* $$$$ 50 Park St, VIC 3205. (03) 9690 3688. Modern Thai cuisine, with Chinese and Malay influences, is a feature of this award-winning restaurant. Popular dishes include the red duck curry and the romantically named oysters of passion. ● *Sat & Sun L.*	■	●		●	
SOUTH MELBOURNE: *O'Connell's* $$$$ Cnr Montague & Coventry sts, VIC 3205. (03) 9699 9600. This one-time pub incorporates a stylish restaurant serving a modern Middle Eastern and North African menu. ● *Sat L, Sun, Mon D.*	■	●	■		■

SOUTH YARRA: *Caffè e Cucina* $$$$
581 Chapel St, VIC 3141. **Map 4 E5.** (*(03) 9827 4139.*
This bustling Italian café, reminiscent of Rome and Milan, is a perennial favourite with Melbourne's young celebrities. ● *Sun.* ♟ 🍴

SOUTH YARRA: *France-Soir* $$$$
11 Toorak Rd, VIC 3141. **Map 4 E5.** (*(03) 9866 8569.*
A long-established French restaurant, France-Soir serves traditional fare such as filet Béarnaise and crème brûlée. ♟ 🍴

SOUTH YARRA: *Lynch's* $$$$$
133 Domain Rd, VIC 3141. **Map 3 C4.** (*(03) 9866 5627.*
This charming restaurant is beautifully furbished and romantically lit. The food is international with a French influence. ● *Sat L, Sun L.* 🕭 ♟ 🍴

WINDSOR: *Jacques Reymond Restaurant* $$$$$
78 Williams Rd, VIC 3181. **Map 6 F3.** (*(03) 9525 2178.*
In an elegant 19th-century villa, outstanding modern Australian dishes with a French influence are served. The game and seafood are superb. ● *Sat L, Sun & Mon.* 🕭 ♟ 🍴

WESTERN VICTORIA

APOLLO BAY: *Buff's Bistro* $$
51–53 Great Ocean Rd, VIC 3233. (*(03) 5237 6403.*
Buffs' tavern-style bistro is lively and modern, and serves Mediterranean fare, with the emphasis on seafood. 🕭 🍴

APOLLO BAY: *Chris's Beacon Point Restaurant & Villas* $$$$
280 Skenes Creek Rd, VIC 3233. (*(03) 5237 6411.*
Chef Chris Talihmanidis blends Mediterranean flavours with local produce. Specialities include *kakavia* (Greek seafood soup). ♟ 🍴

APOLLO BAY: *Whitecrest Oceanside Resort* $$$$
5230 Great Ocean Rd, Wongarra, VIC 3221. (*(03) 5237 0228.*
A romantic restaurant with ocean views, offering contemporary Australian cuisine. ● *L, Tue & Wed D.* 🕭 ♟ 🍴

BALLARAT: *Ansonia* $$$
32 Lydiard St South, VIC 3350. (*(03) 5332 4678.*
This contemporary restaurant is in the historic heart of Ballarat *(see pp424–5).* The menu is Australian with a Mediterranean influence. 🍴

BALLARAT: *Europa Café* $$$
411 Sturt St, VIC 3350. (*(03) 5331 2486.*
Europa is a smart bistro and café bar serving modern Italian and Australian food, including kangaroo dishes. ● *Sun–Wed D.* 🕭 ♟ 🍴

BALLARAT: *L'espresso* $$$
417 Sturt St, VIC 3350. (*(03) 5333 1789.*
This popular restaurant serves modern Australian food with an Italian influence, such as risotto and pasta dishes. ● *Sun–Wed D.* 🍴

BENDIGO: *Bazzani* $$$$
Howard Place, VIC 3550. (*(03) 5441 3777.*
This smart restaurant, housed in an 1880s listed building, serves both Australian and Italian food, with some Asian influences. 🕭 🎵 ♟ 🍴

BENDIGO: *Whirrakee* $$$$
17 View Point, VIC 3550. (*(03) 5441 5557.*
At this warm and inviting restaurant, local wines are served with a menu that draws inspiration from the world's major cuisines. ● *Sat–Tue L, Sun & Mon D.* ♟ 🍴

CASTLEMAINE: *Globe Garden Restaurant* $$$$$
81 Forest St, VIC 3450. (*(03) 5470 5055.*
Housed in a converted 1850s pub, the Globe has an elegant dining room overlooking a courtyard garden. The food is modern and highly acclaimed. ● *Mon & Tue, Wed–Sat L.* 🕭 🍴

DAYLESFORD: *Frangos & Frangos* $$$$
82 Vincent St, VIC 3460. (*(03) 5348 2363.*
Greek-influenced country cooking is served at this old country pub. Choose between the casual café and the formal restaurant area. 🍴

For key to symbols see back flap

Price categories for a three-course meal for one, including half a bottle of house wine and service charges.
$ under A$25
$$ A$25–A$35
$$$ A$35–A$50
$$$$ A$50–A$70
$$$$$ over A$70

OUTDOOR EATING
Some tables on a patio or terrace.
VEGETARIAN SPECIALITIES
One menu always includes a varied selection of vegetarian dishes.
BAR AREA/COCKTAIL BAR
There is a bar area or cocktail bar within the restaurant, available for drinks and/or bar snacks.
FIXED-PRICE MENU
A fixed-price menu available at a good rate, at lunch, dinner or both, usually with three courses.
CHILDREN'S FACILITIES
Small portions and/or highchairs available on request.

	OUTDOOR EATING	VEGETARIAN SPECIALITIES	BAR AREA	FIXED-PRICE MENU	CHILDREN'S FACILITIES
DAYLESFORD: *Lake House* $$$$$ King St, VIC 3460. (*(03) 5348 3329.* Everything on the menu at Victoria's premier gourmet retreat, from the pastries to the charcuterie, preserves and chocolates, is made in the kitchen. The wine list is one of Australia's best. & 🍷 🌿	■	●	■	●	■
ECHUCA: *Echuca Cock 'n' Bull Restaurant* $$$ 17–21 Warren St, VIC 3564. (*(03) 5480 6988.* Located in a restored 1869 hotel, the restaurant serves high-quality, well-presented international cuisine. ● *Sun, Mon.* & 🌿	■	●	■		
GEELONG: *Café Botticelli* $$ Shop 9, 111 Pakington St, VIC 3218. (*(03) 5229 8292.* This friendly place with an eclectic decor serves simple Mediterranean fare such as spagetti marinara, a tapas platter and a platter of different meze. ● *Sun.* & 🌿	■	●	■		
GEELONG: *Le Parisien* $$$$ 15 Eastern Beach Rd, VIC 3218. (*(03) 5229 3110.* Popular dishes at this appealing French restaurant include chicken with King Island brie and a sweet chilli sauce and roasted duck glazed with honey and cointreau. 🌿		●	■		■
LORNE: *Kosta's Taverna* $$$$ 48 Mountjoy Parade, VIC 3232. (*(03) 5289 1883.* This colourful and lively restaurant serves modern Australian food with a distinctly Greek flavour. ● *Tue (May–Nov).* 🎵 🌿	■	●	■		■
MILDURA: *Ziggy's Café* $$ 145 Eighth St, VIC 3500. (*(03) 5023 2626.* This popular café offers fare more up-market than its prices suggest. The food is both Mediterranean and Australian. ● *Mon.* & 🌿	■	●			
MILDURA: *Stefano's Restaurant* $$$$$ Mildura Grand Hotel Resort, Seventh St, VIC 3500. (*(03) 5023 0511.* Set in the cellars of the late–19th-century Grand Hotel, Stefano's offers fabulous Italian food made with local produce. ● *L, Sun D.* 🍷 🌿		●	■	●	■
MOONAMBEL: *Warrenmang Vineyard Resort* $$$$$ Mountain Creek Rd, VIC 3478. (*(03) 5467 2233.* At this outstanding resort, set in the heart of Victoria's Pyrenees winegrowing district, the modern, regional menu relies heavily on top-quality locally grown produce. Dinner is a fixed-price, five-course banquet. 🍷 🌿	■	●	■	●	■
PORT FAIRY: *Merrijig Inn* $$$$ 1 Campbell St, VIC 3284. (*(03) 5568 2324.* Located in an 1841 Georgian inn, Merrijig serves a combination of Australian bush food, Mediterranean dishes and local seafood. ● *L, Mon, Tue.* & 🌿		●	■		
QUEENSCLIFF: *Mietta's Queenscliff Hotel* $$$$$ 16 Gellibrand St, VIC 3225. (*(03) 5258 1066.* Dinner is unforgettable in the grand, candlelit dining room of this restored Victorian hotel. The food on the menu is mainly classical French cuisine. ● *Sun–Tue L.* 🍷 🌿	■	●	■	●	
QUEENSCLIFF: *Vue Grand* $$$$ 46 Hesse St, VIC 3225. (*(03) 5258 1544.* A resident French chef prepares innovative dishes using fresh and local produce. & 🌿	■	●	■	●	■

WARRNAMBOOL: *Freshwater Café* 78 Liebig St, VIC 3280. ☎ *(03) 5561 3188.* Fresh seafood, such as Tasmanian oysters and blue swimmer crab, is the focus of this contemporary restaurant. ● *Mon–Thu L, Sun.* ▤	$$$		●	■		
EASTERN VICTORIA						
BAIRNSDALE: *Riversleigh Country Hotel* I Nicholson St, VIC 3747. ☎ *(03) 5152 6966.* Mediterranean and Italian flavours dominate the menu at this well-regarded Gippsland restaurant, housed in a restored Victorian guesthouse. ● *Sun, Sat–Tue L.* ♿ ▤	$$$$	■	●	■		■
BEECHWORTH: *The Bank* 86 Ford St, VIC 3747. ☎ *(03) 5728 2223.* This old Bank of Australasia, which once stored gold from the Victorian gold rush *(see pp50–51)*, is now a venue for candlelit dinners. Local beef and fish are specialities. ● *Mon–Sat L winter; Mon–Thu L summer.* ♿ 🍷 ▤	$$$$	■	●			
BRIGHT: *Caffe Bacco* 24 Anderson St, VIC 3741. ☎ *(03) 5750 1711.* This relaxed café/wine bar serves light, well-prepared Italian-style food using the best of the locally grown produce. The cakes and coffee are particularly good. ● *Mon–Wed L, Mon & Tue D.* ▤	$$	■	●	■		
BRIGHT: *Simone's* Ovens Valley Motor Inn, Cnr Great Alpine Way Rd & Ashwood Ave, VIC 3741. ☎ *(03) 5755 2022.* Simone's serves superlative modern Italian food made with local produce. Signature dishes include homemade pasta and braised Buckland Valley kid with wild spinach. ● *L.* 🍷 ▤	$$$		●	■		■
DANDENONG RANGES: *Wild Oak Café* 232 Ridge Rd, Mount Dandenong, VIC 3767. ☎ *(03) 9751 2033.* The Wild Oak Café has an open, relaxed layout where diners can see their bread, main courses and desserts being freshly prepared. Eat under the shade of an oak tree on sunny days. ◩ ▤	$$$	■	●			■
DANDENONG RANGES: *Sacrebleu!* 1526 Mount Dandenong Tourist Rd, Olinda, VIC. ☎ *(03) 9751 2520.* This bistro on Melbourne's outer fringe serves metropolitan standards, such as onion soup and steak frites, together with some enticing dishes derived from the former French colonies in Indochina and North Africa. 🍷 ◩ ▤	$$$$		●			
MILAWA: *The Epicurean Centre* Brown Bros Winery, Bobinawarrah Rd, off Snow Rd, VIC 3678. ☎ *(03) 5720 5540.* This large pavilion attached to the Brown Bros winery *(see p371)* provides lunches using the region's best produce. A glass of matched wine is included in the price of each dish. ● *D.* ♿ 🍷 ▤	$$$	■	●	■	●	■
MORNINGTON PENINSULA: *Arthurs* Arthurs Seat Scenic Rd, Arthurs Seat, Dromana, VIC 3936. ☎ *(03) 5981 4444.* Magnificently positioned overlooking Port Phillip Bay, Arthurs has a formal dining room serving magnificent modern European dishes on weekends. Downstairs, the Vineyard Bar and Café offers more casual fare every day of the week. ● *Mon–Thu, Fri L, Sun D.* ♿ 🍷 ▤	$$$$	■		■		●
MORNINGTON PENINSULA: *Castle at Delgany* Peppers Delgany, Point Nepean Rd, Portsea, VIC 3944. ☎ *(03) 5984 4000.* Seafood, such as sand crabs, scallops, snapper and whiting, as well as local lamb and veal, are all served in the grand Delgany mansion *(see p489)*. ♿ ▤	$$$$$	■	●	■	●	■
MOUNT BULLER: *Pension Grimus* 149 Breathtaker Rd, VIC 3723. ☎ *(03) 5777 6396.* A European-style alpine chalet with wood carvings and big fires offering Austrian fare and a range of schnapps. ● *seasonal.* 🍷 ▤	$$$$			■		■
NAGAMBIE: *Michelton Restaurant* Mitchellstown Rd, off Goulburn Valley Hwy, VIC 3608. ☎ *(03) 5794 2388.* This spacious, modern restaurant in a vineyard overlooking the Goulburn River offers robust regional cuisine, with a list of estate grown wines to match every dish. ● *D.* 🍷 ▤	$$$	■	●	■	●	■

	Price categories / Legend	OUTDOOR EATING	VEGETARIAN SPECIALITIES	BAR AREA	FIXED-PRICE MENU	CHILDREN'S FACILITIES

Price categories for a three-course meal for one, including half a bottle of house wine and service charges.
$ under A$25
$$ A$25–A$35
$$$ A$35–A$50
$$$$ A$50–A$70
$$$$$ over A$70

OUTDOOR EATING
Some tables on a patio or terrace.
VEGETARIAN SPECIALITIES
One menu always includes a varied selection of vegetarian dishes.
BAR AREA/COCKTAIL BAR
There is a bar area or cocktail bar within the restaurant, available for drinks and/or bar snacks.
FIXED-PRICE MENU
A fixed-price menu available at a good rate, at lunch, dinner or both, usually with three courses.
CHILDREN'S FACILITIES
Small portions and/or highchairs available on request.

Restaurant	Price	Outdoor Eating	Vegetarian Specialities	Bar Area	Fixed-Price Menu	Children's Facilities
PHILLIP ISLAND: *The Jetty Restaurant* — 11–13 The Esplanade, Cowes, VIC 3922. (03) 5952 2060. The island's main seafood restaurant, The Jetty Restaurant serves fresh lobster and other local fish. ● Mon–Fri L off-season.	$$$	■	●	■		■
WANGARATTA: *The Vine Hotel* — Detour Rd, VIC 3677. (03) 5721 2605. Chef Carolyn Green serves bistro-style Australian contemporary cuisine featuring local produce such as lamb and fish. ● Sun D, Mon, Tue.	$$$	■	●	■		■
YARRA VALLEY: *Eleonore's at Chateau Yering* — Melba Hwy, Yering, VIC 3777. (03) 9237 3333. Eleonore's offers spacious, formal dining in a grand Victorian mansion in the Yarra Valley wine region, just an hour from Melbourne. The influences are modern European. A café opens daily. ● Mon–Fri L.	$$$$		●	■		■
YARRA VALLEY: *Fergusson of Yarra Glen* — Wills Rd, Yarra Glen, VIC 3775. (03) 5965 2237. This popular restaurant attached to the Fergusson winery combines rustic surroundings with fine food and an atmosphere of wine, song and friendliness. ● D, except by appointment.	$$$$			■	●	
YARRA VALLEY: *De Bortoli Winery and Restaurant* — Pinnacle Lane, Dixons Creek, VIC 3775. (03) 5965 2271. Excellent Italian food, made with gourmet produce from the region, is served among the vines at this vineyard estate. ● Sun–Fri D.	$$$$	■	●		●	■

TASMANIA

Restaurant	Price	Outdoor Eating	Vegetarian Specialities	Bar Area	Fixed-Price Menu	Children's Facilities
COLES BAY: *Freycinet Lodge* — Freycinet National Park, TAS 7215. (03) 6257 0101. Set against this stunning coastline is this low-key but luxurious holiday lodge. Richardsons Bistro opens for breakfast and lunch while the more formal Bay Restaurant serves dinner.	$$$$	■	●	■		■
CRADLE MOUNTAIN: *Highland Restaurant* — Cradle Mountain Lodge, Cradle Mountain, TAS 7306. (03) 6492 1303. Excellent Tasmanian wines and modern Australian cuisine are the specialities of this sophisticated restaurant located on the edge of Tasmania's World Heritage wilderness area.	$$$$		●	■		■
CRADLE VALLEY: *Lemonthyme Lodge* — Dolcoah Rd, off Cradle Mountain Rd, Moina, TAS 7306. (03) 6492 1112. Dine in the largest "log cabin" in the southern hemisphere and enjoy fine Tasmanian country cuisine.	$$$$		●	■	●	■
HOBART: *The Fish Bar* — 50 King St, Sandy Bay, TAS 7005. (03) 6234 5961. Taste the best of Tasmania's seafood, cooked simply, marinated or grilled, in a relaxed and fun atmosphere.	$$				●	■
HOBART: *Blue Skies* — Ground Floor, Murray Street Pier, TAS 7000. (03) 6224 3747. The Blue Skies' waterfront location has inspired its seaside decor. The menu offers some of the most imaginative fish dishes in the city.	$$$	■	●	■		■
HOBART: *Da Angelo Ristorante* — 47 Hampden Rd, Battery Point, TAS 7004. (03) 6223 7011. This little piece of Italy located in the gas-lit area of Battery Point serves homemade pasta, pizza and ice cream. Book well ahead. ● L.	$$$		●			■

HOBART: *Drunken Admiral* $$$
17–19 Hunter Street, Old Wharf, TAS 7000. ((03) 6234 1903.
Tasmania's most distinctive seafarers' restaurant serves fresh
fish in both traditional and international styles. ● L. 🖼

HOBART: *Kelleys* $$$
5 Knopwood St, Battery Point, TAS 7004. ((03) 6224 7225.
An Australian Gold Plate award-winner, Kelleys serves fresh seafood
and Tasmanian wines. ● L Sat & Sun. 🖼 🖼

HOBART: *Mit Zitrone* $$$
333 Elizabeth Street, TAS 7000. ((03) 6234 8113.
A warm and lively atmosphere has made this eatery one of
the city's perennial favourites. Pop in for great coffee and
cakes, or enjoy a meal off the creative menu including saffron soup
and tea-smoked quail. ● Sun & Mon. 🖼 🖼

HOBART: *The Point* $$$$
Wrest Point, 410 Sandy Bay Rd, TAS 7000. ((03) 6221 1719.
Superb views are a feature of this revolving restaurant in Australia's
longest-running casino. An international/modern Australian menu
caters to a broad clientele. ● Sat L, Sun. 🖼 🖼

HOBART: *Prossers On The Beach* $$$$
Beach Road, Long Point, Sandy Bay, TAS 7005. ((03) 6225 2276.
Set in The Sandy Bay Regatta Pavilion overlooking Hobart's most
popular beach, it is not surprising that Prossers' speciality is seafood.
● Sat–Tue L, Sun. 🖼 🖼

HOBART: *Rockerfellers* $$$$
11 Morrison St, TAS 7000. ((03) 6234 3490.
Spanish tapas and other popular international dishes are on offer at this
lively eatery, popular with a younger crowd. ● L Sat & Sun. 🖼 🖼

LAUDERDALE: *Eating on the Edge* $$$
13 North Terrace, TAS 7021. ((03) 6248 7707.
Eating on the Edge is a casual beachside restaurant with stunning
views, serving fine Italian food including seafood. ● Mon, Tue–Sat L. 🖼

LAUNCESTON: *Pepper Berry Café* $$
91 George Street, TAS 7250. ((03) 6334 4589.
A Tasmanian native bush berry, which inspired the name, is incorpor-
ated in much of the food, from muffins to ice cream and fish dishes.
● Sun, Mon–Wed D. 🖼 🖼

LAUNCESTON: *Stillwater* $$$$
Ritchies Mill, 2 Bridge Rd, TAS 7250. ((03) 6331 4153.
Situated on the banks of the Tamar River, this sophisticated eatery
offers everything from early breakfasts to casual lunches, pre-dinner
drinks and formal dining by night. 🖼 🖼

LAUNCESTON: *Fee and Mee* $$$$
190 Charles St, TAS 7250. ((03) 6331 3195.
Tasmania's finest restaurant is housed in an elegant Georgian house
and offers exquisite, innovative food along with carefully chosen local
wines. ● L, D Sun. 🖼 🖼 🖼

RICHMOND: *Prospect House* $$$
1384 Richmond Rd, TAS, 7025. ((03) 6260 2207.
Fine food is served in the elegant atmosphere of this Georgian
country mansion. Accommodation is also available. ● Mon & Tue L.
🖼 🖼

SHEFFIELD: *Weindorfers* $$$
Gowrie Park, TAS 7306. ((03) 6491 1385.
In memory of Gustav and Kate Weindorfer (see p455), Weindorfer's
serves hearty portions of home-cooked Swedish-Tasmanian food.
● Aug & Sep. 🖼 🖼

STRAHAN: *Franklin Manor* $$$$
The Esplanade, TAS 7468. ((03) 6471 7311.
An award-winning wine list is just one of the attractions of this elegant
restaurant. Tasmanian produce features extensively on the modern
Australian menu. ● L. 🖼 🖼 🖼

For key to symbols see back flap

SHOPPING IN AUSTRALIA

AUSTRALIA HAS MUCH to offer the visiting shopper beyond the standard tourist fare of koala bear purses and plastic boomerangs. The tourist shops can be worth exploring, some stock being of a high standard and including goods not available in other countries. In each state capital, especially Sydney *(see pp128–31)* and Melbourne *(see pp398–9)*, there are precincts and open-air markets with a range of shops, stalls and cafés to

Colourful craft shop sign in Margaret River

explore. Wine and gourmet food products are a major attraction, and a wide range of reasonably priced world-class goods is available. Australian contemporary design has a refreshing irreverence for convention – look out for homewares and fashion in the inner-city precincts. In country areas, unusual items made by local craftspeople make good buys. Australia recently introduced a goods and services tax (GST), adding 10 per cent to the cost of most items.

Browsers at a stall in Mindil Beach Sunset Markets, Darwin *(see p264)*

SHOPPING HOURS

STANDARD WEEKDAY opening times are 9am–5:30pm, Monday to Friday. Late night shopping is usually available on Thursdays or Fridays, when stores stay open until 9pm. Weekend hours vary greatly. Deregulation has meant that many stores, particularly in city locations, open on both Saturday and Sunday. In most country areas, however, stores will open only until 1pm on Saturday. Many supermarkets in city and suburban areas now operate 24 hours. Bookshops and other specialist shops stay open late – until around 10pm – in downtown areas.

HOW TO PAY

MAJOR CREDIT cards are accepted by most stores, generally with a minimum purchase limit. Identification, such as a valid passport or

driver's licence, is required when using traveller's cheques. Personal cheques are also accepted at the majority of larger stores, with identification, but a telephone check on your account may be made. Payment by cash is the preferred method for traders and can be used to negotiate a lower price for your goods in some instances.

RIGHTS AND REFUNDS

THE LAWS on consumer rights in Australia vary slightly from state to state. If you have a complaint or query, look under "Consumer" in the government section at the front of the White Pages telephone directory. If the goods purchased are defective in any way, customers are entitled to a full refund. If you decide you don't like an item, try to get a refund, but you will probably have to

settle for a credit note or exchange. As a general rule, the larger the store, the more protected you are – you can always ask to speak to a manager or customer relations officer if you are unhappy with the service you receive.

ESSENTIALLY AUSTRALIAN

ABORIGINAL ART is available for purchase from community-owned or managed galleries in the Northern Territory and good specialist galleries in the cities. Take the time to discuss the work with the painter or gallery staff: spiritual and cultural meanings are inextricably linked with aesthetic properties, and the painting or artifact that you choose will be all the more valuable with a little knowledge. These

Shoppers in London Court, Perth's Tudor-style street *(see p296)*

Arts and crafts stall at Kingston Bus Depot Sunday market, Canberra

artworks are by their nature expensive, so do not be beguiled by cheaper imitations.

Australia produces 95 per cent of the world's opals. Their quality varies greatly, so when considering a purchase a little research will go a long way. Opals are widely available at duty-free stores. Many other places will deduct the luxury excise tax from the price if you produce your passport.

Outback clothing is a specialist industry in Australia. Most items available are very durable and some have considerable fashion value. Look for Akubra hats, boots by RM Williams and Driza-bone overcoats in camping and army stores; they will be cheaper here than in the stores which specifically aim for the tourist market.

Fresh fish on display at Wollongong Fish Market (see p178)

MARKETS

MOST AUSTRALIAN cities have a large central produce market and a range of small community markets that operate at the weekend. The bustling city food markets are as sensational for their vibrant multicultural atmosphere as they are for the extraordinary range of fresh, cheap produce available. Look out for local specialities such as cheeses, olives and unusual fruits. Melbourne's Queen Victoria Market (see p378) and the Adelaide Central Market (see p338) are particularly good and well worth visiting. Community markets, such as those in Paddington, Sydney (see p121), and Salamanca Place, Hobart (see p448), offer an interesting and eclectic range of locally designed clothing and crafts. In a class of their own, the Mindil Beach Sunset Markets in Darwin combine eating, shopping and entertainment in a spectacular tropical setting (see p264).

DEPARTMENT STORES

DEPARTMENT stores occupy the up-market end of the chain-store scale and sell quality merchandise. They include names such as Myer, David Jones and Grace Brothers (see p398) and some of the top stores are sumptuously decorated. Local and overseas designer fashions, top-brand cosmetics and all manner of household goods and furnishings can be purchased. These stores are competitive and will often match prices on identical items found at more downmarket stores. Their shopper facilities and standards for customer service are excellent.

SHOPPING PRECINCTS

BECAUSE THE city centres have been colonized by the retail giants in Australia, many small and interesting shops have moved out to the lively precincts that lie somewhere between the city centre and suburbia. These precincts represent some of the best and most interesting shopping in the country. Young designer outlets, specialist book stores, craft studios and galleries sit next to food stores, cafés, restaurants and bars. Some of these precincts are decidedly up-market, while others relish their bohemian roots. There is nearly always a strong mix of cultural influences – Jewish, Italian, Lebanese, Vietnamese, for example – depending on the area and the city. Ask at tourist information centres for the best precincts in each city.

Herbal infusions on sale in Brisbane's Chinatown (see p218)

OUT OF TOWN

SHOPPING IN Australian country areas can be a mixed experience. In some areas the range of standard items is limited and prices can be much higher than you would expect to pay in the city. However, there are always unexpected surprises such as dusty second-hand shops with rare knick-knacks at absurdly low prices and small craft outlets and galleries with unusual items that make great gifts.

The attractive tiled interior of a shopping arcade in Adelaide

SPECIALIST HOLIDAYS AND OUTDOOR ACTIVITIES

To make the most of a trip to a country as vast and geographically diverse as Australia, a specialist holiday is an excellent idea. Whether you're pursuing an interest, acquiring a new skill or learning about the environment, such holidays can be very rewarding experiences. There is a wide range of specialist operators to choose

Sign for glass-bottom boat tour in Western Australia

from. If travelling to Australia from abroad, the best starting points are the local Australian Tourism Commission offices or your local travel agent. Once in the country, the state tourism associations *(see p535)* can offer expert advice, make bookings with reputable companies and contact local activity associations for information.

Bushwalking in Namadgi National Park in the ACT *(see p199)*

BUSHWALKING

National parks are without doubt the best places for bushwalking in Australia. Not only do they preserve the best of the country's natural heritage, but they also offer expert advice and well-marked trails for bushwalkers. These parks are state-managed and each state has a central information service. Look under "National Parks" in the government listings at the front of the telephone directory.

Equipment, including backpacks, boots and tents, is available for hire from camping stores in city and country areas. Joining up with a tour is a good alternative for those planning long bushwalking trips, as tour members will benefit from a guide's expertise on local flora and fauna, and access to remote wilderness areas. Exceptional bushwalking regions in Australia include Cradle Mountain in Tasmania

(see p455), the MacDonnell Ranges in the Northern Territory *(see p276)* and the Blue Mountains in New South Wales *(see pp162–5)*.

CYCLING

With its vast stretches of near-empty roads, many of them without a hill in sight, it is no wonder that Australia is becoming increasingly popular as a long-distance cycling destination. Visitors can bring their own bicycles, but are advised to check first whether this is acceptable with the airlines. Trains and buses will usually carry bikes provided they are dismantled. To hire a bike in Australia, look under "Bicycles" in the Yellow Pages. Bike helmets are a legal

requirement throughout Australia and can be bought cheaply or hired.

Many cyclists spend several days on the road camping along the way, while others will arrange an itinerary that allows them to stop for the comfort of a bed and meal in a town. The wine-growing areas of South Australia *(see pp330–31)*, the Great Ocean Road in Victoria *(see pp418–19)* and almost anywhere in Tasmania *(see pp444–59)* are terrific cycling destinations.

Bicycling associations in Australia also arrange regular cycling tours that anyone can join. These include accommodation, food and vehicle back-up; most of the organizations are non–profit-making, so the costs are generally low. Contact **Bicycle New South Wales** for a catalogue specializing in Australian cycling publications. They will also provide information on their sister associations in other states.

Cycling around Canberra's lake *(see pp186–7)*

ADVENTURE SPORTS

APPROPRIATE TRAINING is a component of adventure sports in Australia, so novices are always welcome alongside more expert adventurers. Contact specialist tour operators or national associations *(see p529)* for information about anything from a one-day class to a two-week tour.

Abseiling, canyoning, rock climbing and caving are all popular in Australia, which has some fantastic natural landscapes ideally suited to these pursuits. The Blue Mountains are something of a mecca for enthusiasts of all the above. Naracoorte in South Australia *(see p347)* is a great location for caving, while the Grampians National Park in Victoria *(see p417)* attracts a large share of abseilers and climbers.

Climbing on Wilsons Promontory in Victoria *(see p434)*

GOLF

THERE ARE 1,450 golf courses in Australia and 1,580 golf clubs. Many clubs have affiliations with clubs overseas and offer reciprocal membership rights, so members should check with their own club before leaving home. There are also public municipal golf courses in many towns.

Australian courses are of a high standard, and Melbourne is home to two of the top 30 courses in the world, the Royal Melbourne and Kingston Heath. A round of golf will cost anything from A$20–$250. Contact the **Australian Golf Union** for further information.

Camel trekking along Cable Beach, Broome *(see p322)*

ABORIGINAL HERITAGE TOURS

ABORIGINAL HERITAGE TOURS can range from a visit to an Aboriginal art gallery to days spent with an Aboriginal guide touring Arnhem Land or Kakadu National Park in the Northern Territory *(see pp268–9)*. With the highest percentage of Aboriginal land and people in the country, the Northern Territory has the greatest number of activities, but there are sights and operators all over Australia. The focus of activities varies and may encompass a number of themes, including traditional bush food, hunting, rock art and Aboriginal culture.

Perhaps the best aspect of many of these tours is the chance to see the remarkable Australian landscape from a different perspective; Aboriginal spirituality is closely linked with the land. In addition, some tours will journey to Australia's most remote areas and travel through Aboriginal lands that are usually closed to all but members of the local Aboriginal communities.

CAMEL TREKKING

CAMELS HAVE been an invaluable form of transport in Australia's Outback since Afghan-run camel trains were used to carry goods across the Australian desert from the 1840s until the coming of the railway. Joining a camel trek today is still an adventure, and activities range from a one-hour jaunt to a two-week trek. Food and accommodation (usually camping) are provided by tour operators. Alice Springs *(see pp274–5)* is the most popular starting point, but tours are available country-wide.

AERIAL TOURS

AERIAL TOURS can provide an exhilarating overview of an area and are a good option for time-restricted travellers who want to see some of the more far-flung attractions. Aerial safaris, stopping at major sights, are popular in the Outback. For charter flights to Australia's furthest flung territory, Antarctica, contact **Croydon Travel**.

Seaplane moored at Rose Bay in Sydney, ready for a scenic flight

FISHING

AUSTRALIA has around four million fishing enthusiasts and, given the country's natural advantages, it's not difficult to see why. Vast oceans, a 12,000-km (7,500-mile) shoreline and a large inland river system, all combined with a terrific climate, make Australia a haven for local and visiting anglers alike.

Fishing for barramundi in the remote inland waters of the Northern Territory and game fishing off Australia's tropical coastline for species such as black marlin and yellowfin tuna are among the world's best fishing experiences. You will need to join a charter as these activities require a great deal of local expertise. Most operators will provide equipment.

The inland waters of Tasmania are famed for their excellent trout fishing prospects. The estuaries and beaches in the southern states, such as the Fleurieu Peninsula in South Australia (see pp342–3), are full of species such as bream, salmon and flathead.

Mural advertising the services of a boat charter company

Small boats are readily available for hire and fishing tackle can be purchased and occasionally hired at most of the popular fishing destinations around the country. Each state has a government department with a special fisheries section. Staff provide excellent information on locations, restrictions and safety issues. Check the weather forecast and heed warnings about dangerous spots, particularly rock platforms.

ECOTOURISM

THIS RELATIVELY new tourism concept has its roots in activities as old as bird watching and wildflower identification. It incorporates many of the activities mentioned in this section, but is generally distinguished by its emphasis on issues concerning the appreciation and

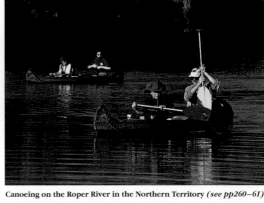

Canoeing on the Roper River in the Northern Territory (see pp260–61)

conservation of the natural heritage. Given Australia's enormous natural bounty, it is hardly surprising that the market is now flooded with operators offering an astonishing range of nature-based activities. These encompass wildlife watching (including whales, birds and dolphins), nature walks, and trekking and rafting expeditions to remote wilderness areas. Visitors can also stay at resorts which are operated along strictly "green" guidelines. These are eco-friendly and are usually located within some of the most environmentally valuable regions in the country. The **Ecotourism Association of Australia** can provide information on tour operators and publications.

WATER SPORTS

AUSTRALIA IS ONE of the world's great diving destinations, and the Great Barrier Reef is the centre of most of the diving activity (see pp204–209). Visitors can combine a holiday on the reef with a few days of diving instruction from one of the many excellent schools in the area. There are opportunities for diving all around Australia, however, and other popular locations include Rottnest Island (see pp300–301) and Esperance (see p311) in Western Australia and the beautiful World Heritage Area of Lord Howe Island off the coast of New South Wales.

Canoeing in Australia can mean a quiet paddle in a hireboat on a city lake, or an exciting adventure in a kayak on the high seas. It is a reasonably priced sport and is widely available throughout the country. Popular spots include the Murray River (see p347), Sydney Harbour (see pp136–7) and the rivers of national parks nationwide.

Whitewater rafting is another favourite sport in this land of outdoor enthusiasts and there are many opportunities for people of all abilities to have a go. The inexperienced can try a day with an instructor on an easy run; the confident can tackle a two-week tour on the rafter's mecca, the Franklin-Gordon River system in Tasmania (see p456).

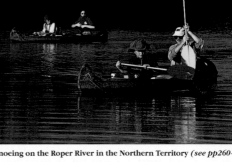

Sailing in Gippsland Lakes Coastal Park, Eastern Victoria (see p434)

Long stretches of unspoilt coastline, remote bays and harbours, tropical reefs and uninhabited islands make Australia an excellent destination for sailing enthusiasts. Skippered cruises are the most usual kind of holiday, but some visitors will want to hire a vessel and set off for themselves – a practice known as bareboating. To do this you will need to prove to the operator that you are an experienced sailor. It is difficult to beat the tropical splendours of the Whitsunday Islands in Queensland *(see p208)* as a location. Other popular sailing areas include Pittwater in New South Wales and Queensland's Gold Coast *(see pp230–31).*

Australia is also world-renowned for its abundance of outstanding surfing beaches. For more information about the country's best places to surf, see pages 34–5.

SKIING

THE SKI SEASON in Australia extends from June to September. Downhill skiing is restricted to the Victoria Alps *(see p436)*, the New South Wales mountains and two small resorts in Tasmania *(see p457)*. The ski villages have excellent facilities, but the fields can get crowded during school holidays and long weekends, and prices for ski-lifts and equipment hire can be high.

Upland areas around these resorts are superb for cross-country skiing. Traversing gentle slopes and rounded

Skiing Eagle Ridge on Mount Hotham in the Victoria Alps

peaks, skiers will be treated to glimpses of Australia's rare alpine flora and fauna, and spectacular sweeping scenery.

SPECTATOR SPORTS

MOST SPORTS ENTHUSIASTS will enjoy taking in a fixture during their trip, while a few visitors come to Australia especially for a sporting event, such as yacht races, cricket or tennis events. Early booking is advisable as competition for tickets can be fierce. Regular highlights include the Australian Tennis Open, Melbourne Cup and the Grand Prix, all Melbourne events, and international Test cricket and the Australian Open golf that moves from state to state each year *(see pp36–9)*. Rugby League and Australian Rules football are the most popular spectator sports. The finals are the main event, but excitement is high at almost any match.

AFL Australian Rules football grand final in Melbourne

SURVIVAL GUIDE

PRACTICAL INFORMATION

AUSTRALIA HAS surged ahead as a major tourist destination in recent years, and the facilities for travellers have kept pace with this rapid development. Visitors should encounter few problems in this safe and friendly destination. Accommodation and restaurants *(see pp462–523)* are of international standard, public transport is readily available *(see pp544–51)* and

Aquarium sign in Queensland

tourist information centres are everywhere. The following pages contain useful information for all visitors. Personal Security and Health *(see pp536–7)* details a number of recommended precautions, while Banking and Currency *(see pp538–9)* answers all the essential financial queries. There is also a section detailing the Australian telephone and postal systems *(see pp540–41)*.

Skiers enjoying the slopes at Falls Creek in Eastern Victoria

WHEN TO GO

THE NORTHERN HALF of the country lies in a tropical zone and is subject to "wet" and "dry" seasons *(see pp40–41)*. The dry season falls between May and October, and is regarded as the best time to visit this area. During the wet season, conditions are hot and humid, and many areas are inaccessible because of flooding. For those with an interest in wildlife, however, there are areas such as Kakadu National Park *(see pp268–9)* which are particularly spectacular at this time of year.

The southern half of the continent is temperate and the seasons are the exact opposite to those in Europe and North America. Victoria and Tasmania can be a little cloudy and wet in winter, but they are very colourful and quite balmy in autumn. The vast southern coastline is a popular touring destination during the summer months – the climate is warm, with a gentle breeze. Avoid the

Outback areas during the summer, however, as the temperatures can be extreme. The popular ski season in the Victoria Alps takes place between June and September *(see p436)*. In the states of South Australia and Western Australia, there are spectacular wildflower displays between September and December.

International tourist information sign

ENTRY REQUIREMENTS

VISITORS TO Australia must have a passport valid for longer than the intended period of stay. All visitors other than New Zealand passport holders must also have a visa issued in their own country. Apply either through some travel agents or airlines, at the Australian Embassy or by post – allow at least four weeks for postal applications. Visitors will be asked for proof of a return ticket and of sufficient funds for the duration of their stay. Once in Australia, you

can extend your visa by applying to the **Department of Immigration**, but tourist visas are rarely extended beyond a year.

TOURIST INFORMATION

THE **Australian Tourist Commission** is the central tourism body, but each state and territory has its own tourism authority. Travel centres in the capital cities provide abundant information and these are often the best places to seek advice on specialist tours and to make bookings. Information booths can also be found at airports, tourist sites and in shopping centres. Smaller towns often have tourist offices located in general stores, galleries or petrol stations – look for the blue and white information symbol. In remoter areas, national park visitors' centres will provide useful information on bushwalks and the local terrain.

Visitor information kiosk inside Central Railway Station in Sydney

Corkscrew roller coaster at Seaworld Theme Park on Queensland's Gold Coast *(see p231)*

OPENING HOURS AND ADMISSION PRICES

MOST MAJOR TOURIST SITES are open seven days a week, but it is always advisable to check first. In smaller centres, galleries and other sites are often closed during the early part of the week. Compared to Europe, admission prices are generally moderate and, in some cases, admission is free. Exceptions are major touring exhibitions at art galleries, zoos, theme parks and specialist attractions such as Sovereign Hill in Ballarat *(see p423).* Make the most of weekdays – locals will be competing for viewing space at weekends.

ETIQUETTE

WHILE AUSTRALIAN society is generally laid-back, there are a few unwritten rules which visitors should follow. Eating and drinking is frowned upon while travelling on public transport, in taxis and also in many shops and galleries. Dress codes are casual, particularly in summer when the weather is hot, but some bars and restaurants may require men to wear shirts and have a ban on jeans and sports shoes. Topless bathing is accepted on many beaches, but it is advisable to see what the locals are doing.

Tipping is optional in Australia; however, 10 per cent of the final bill for good service in a restaurant is customary, as is a couple of dollars for taxi drivers, hotel porters and bar tenders.

Smoking is prohibited in all public buildings, on public transport, in taxis, in cafés and restaurants, and in most stores. Ask about smoking policies when booking hotels.

DISABLED TRAVELLERS

DISABLED TRAVELLERS can generally expect the best in Australia in terms of facilities. Many hotels, restaurants, tourist sites, cinemas, theatres, airports and shopping centres have wheelchair facilities, and guide dogs for the blind are always welcomed.

Traditionally, public transport is a problem for wheelchair users, although most states are now making their systems more accessible to disabled travellers. Contact the transport authority state by state for more detailed information. Tourist information centres and council offices can provide maps that show sites with wheelchair access.

One of the most useful organizations for disabled travellers is the **National Information Communication Awareness Network (NICAN)** in Canberra. This nationwide database provides information on disabled facilities in different parts of the country and, if they don't have the appropriate information at hand, they will do their best to seek it out. They also have details of many publications specifically written for disabled travellers in Australia.

Circular Quay Station, Sydney, accessible to disabled travellers

AUSTRALIAN TIME ZONES

Australia is divided into three separate time zones: Western Standard Time, Central Standard Time and Eastern Standard Time. Eastern Australia is two hours ahead of Western Australia; Central Australia is one-and-a-half hours ahead. Daylight saving is observed in New South Wales, the ACT, Victoria and South Australia, from October to March, which adds an hour to the time differences.

City and State	Hours + GMT
Adelaide (SA)	+9.5
Brisbane (QLD)	+10
Canberra (ACT)	+10
Darwin (NT)	+9.5
Hobart (TAS)	+10
Melbourne (VIC)	+10
Perth (WA)	+9
Sydney (NSW)	+10

+9   +9.5   +10

Student travellers exploring Australia's landscape

TRAVELLING WITH CHILDREN

AUSTRALIA, with its beautiful sandy beaches, abundant wildlife and open spaces and opportunity for adventure, is an ideal destination for children. Most hotels welcome children as guests and can usually provide all the necessary facilities, such as cots, highchairs and, in some cases, babysitting services. However, some of the smaller bed-and-breakfasts advertise themselves as child-free zones.

Restaurants are also generally welcoming to children and offer children's portions, although it is advisable to check first with the more up-market establishments. City department stores and most major tourist sites have feeding and nappy-changing rooms as standard features.

Parents travelling with young children are also encouraged through the range of discounts on air, coach, train and boat travel to which children are entitled *(see pp542–51).*

Children less than four years of age travelling in cars must be restrained in infant seats according to Australian guidelines. As many cars do not have these restraints as standard fixtures, it is essential that prior arrangements are made. **Hire for Babe** leases restraints, as well as pushchairs and baby carriers; deliveries can be made to airports and hotels. Car hire firms in the larger cities will generally make arrangements to supply restraints on behalf of clients for a small extra charge.

International student ISIC card

STUDENT TRAVELLERS

THE INTERNATIONAL Student Identity Card (ISIC) is available to all students worldwide in full-time study. The ISIC card should be purchased in the student's own country at a Student Travel Association (STA) office. The card can be purchased in Australia only by students enrolled at an Australian educational institution.

Card-holders are entitled to substantial discounts on overseas air travel and a 25 per cent reduction on domestic flights within Australia *(see pp542–5).* There is also a 15 per cent reduction on private coach travel *(see p547)* and discounts on admission prices to cinemas, galleries, museums and the majority of other tourist sites.

GUIDED TOURS AND EXCURSIONS

TOURS AND EXCURSIONS offer the visitor different ways of exploring cities and their surroundings – from bus tours, jaunts on a Harley Davidson, guided nature walks, harbour cruises and river runs, to aerial adventures by hot-air balloon, seaplane or helicopter. As well as an easy way to take in sights, it helps you get a feel for new surroundings.

Mother and child feeding some of Australia's famous marsupials

NEWSPAPERS, TELEVISION AND RADIO

AUSTRALIA HAS two national newspapers, *The Australian*, a well-respected broadsheet with excellent national and overseas news coverage, and the *Australian Financial Review*, which largely reports on international monetary matters. The *Bulletin* and *Time* are Australia's leading weekly international news magazines; the *Bulletin* is also known for its excellent arts and media coverage. All major foreign newspapers and magazines are readily available in the state capitals and in some of the larger towns. Each state capital also has its own broadsheet and usually a tabloid newspaper as well.

The Australian Broadcasting Corporation (ABC) is a nationwide television station which provides excellent news and current affairs coverage, children's programmes and high-quality local and international drama. In addition, the corporation has its own AM and FM radio stations which offer a wide range of services, including news, rural information for farmers, arts commentary,

Logo for the ABC television network

modern and classical music, magazine-style women's programmes and an acclaimed nationwide channel for the under thirties called Triple J. SBS (Special Broadcasting Service) is Australia's other state-run television network and caters to Australia's many cultures with foreign language programmes for both television and radio. There are also three commercial television stations in Australia, Channels 7, 9 and 10, all of which offer a range of soap operas, news, sports, game shows and other light entertainment.

In all state capitals there is an enormous variety of local FM and AM radio stations. Details of current programming are available in local newspapers. Of interest also are the community radio stations which cater to local cultural and social interests.

The standard of all Australian broadcasting is generally considered to be high.

ELECTRICAL APPLIANCES

AUSTRALIA'S electrical current is 240–250 volts AC. Electrical plugs have either two or three pins. Most good hotels will provide 110-volt shaver sockets and hair dryers, but a flat, two- or three-pin adaptor will be necessary for other appliances. Buy these from electrical stores.

Standard Australian three-pin plug

CONVERSION CHART

Imperial to Metric
1 inch = 2.54 centimetres
1 foot = 30 centimetres
1 mile = 1.6 kilometres
1 ounce = 28 grams
1 pound = 454 grams
1 pint = 0.6 litres
1 gallon = 4.6 litres

Metric to Imperial
1 centimetre = 0.4 inches
1 metre = 3 feet, 3 inches
1 kilometre = 0.6 miles
1 gram = 0.04 ounces
1 kilogram = 2.2 pounds
1 litre = 1.8 pints

DIRECTORY

IMMIGRATION

Department of Immigration
Chan St, Belconnen,
ACT 2617.
☎ (02) 6264 1111.

DISABLED TRAVELLERS

NICAN
PO Box 407, Curtin,
ACT 2605.
☎ 1800 806 769.

CHILDREN'S FACILITIES

Hire for Babe
4 Larken Ave,
Baulkham Hills,
NSW 2153.
☎ (02) 9838 4789.

TOURIST COMMISSION OFFICES

United Kingdom
Gemini House,
10–18 Putney Hill,
London SW15 6AA.
☎ (020) 8780 2229.

USA and Canada
Suite 1920,
2049 Century Park East,
Los Angeles,
CA 90067.
☎ (310) 229 4870.

STATE TOURIST OFFICES

ACT
330 Northbourne Ave,
Dickson, ACT 2602.
☎ (02) 6205 0666.
w *www.canberra tourism.com.au*

New South Wales
106 George St,
Sydney, NSW 2000.
☎ 13 20 77.
w *www.tourism.nsw. gov.au*

Northern Territory
38 Mitchell St,
Darwin, NT 0800.
☎ (08) 8981 4300.
w *www.nttc.com.au*
Gregory Terrace,
Alice Springs,
NT 0870.
☎ (08) 8952 5800.

Queensland
30 Makerston St,
Brisbane, QLD 4001.
☎ (07) 3874 2800.
w *www.queensland-holidays.com.au*
51 The Esplanade,
Cairns, QLD 4870.
☎ (07) 4051 3588.

South Australia
18 King William St,
Adelaide, SA 5000.
☎ 1300 655 276.
w *www.southaustralia. com*

Tasmania
22 Elizabeth St,
Hobart, TAS 7000.
☎ (03) 6230 8235.
w *www.discover tasmania.com*

Western Australia
469 Wellington St,
Perth, WA 6000.
☎ 1300 361 351.
w *www.western australia.net*

Victoria
Town Hall, cnr Swanston
& Little Collins sts,
Melbourne, VIC 3000.
☎ 13 28 42

Personal Security and Health

National park sign

AUSTRALIA HAS a low crime rate and is generally regarded as a safe tourist destination. There is a strong police presence in all the state capitals, and even small towns will have at least one officer. In terms of climate and environment, however, Australia is a tough country, and visitors must observe safety procedures whether travelling to remote areas or merely planning a day at the beach. If you get into trouble, contact one of the national emergency numbers in the telephone directory.

Police vehicle

Fire engine

Intensive care ambulance

LOOKING AFTER YOUR PROPERTY

LEAVE VALUABLES and important documents in your hotel safe, and don't carry large sums of cash with you. Traveller's cheques are generally regarded as the safest way to carry large sums of money. It is also worth photocopying vital documents in case of loss or theft.

Be on guard against pickpockets in places where big crowds gather. Prime areas for petty theft are popular tourist attractions, beaches, markets, sporting venues and on peak-hour public transport.

Never carry your wallet in an outside pocket where it is an easy target for a thief. Wear shoulder bags and cameras with the strap across your body and with any clasps fastened. If you have a car, always try to park in well-lit, reasonably busy streets. Lock the vehicle securely and don't leave any valuables or property visible that might attract a thief.

PERSONAL SAFETY

THERE ARE FEW, if any, off-limit areas in Australian cities. Red-light districts may be a little seedy, but the fact that they are often busy and well policed probably makes them safer than the average suburban street at night. Avoid poorly lit areas and parks at night. Buses (and trams in Melbourne) are regarded as a safe means of travel at night. However, when travelling by train it is worth remembering that many

Ambulance paramedic

stations are not staffed after hours, particularly in suburban areas. Travel in the train carriage nearest the driver or those marked as being safe for night travel. Taxis are a safe and efficient way of getting around late at night. Hitch-hiking is not an advisable option for any visitor to Australia, and for women it can be particularly dangerous.

Country towns can shut down fairly early in Australia, which is often a surprise to many visitors. It is advisable to reach a destination before nightfall and avoid wandering around looking for accommodation or a meal after dark. The majority of places are extremely friendly to travellers. However, in remote areas, visitors do stand out and as such are potential targets if a threat exists.

MEDICAL MATTERS

AUSTRALIA'S MEDICAL services are among the best in the world. Under reciprocal arrangements visitors from the UK, New Zealand, Malta, Italy, Finland, Sweden and Holland are entitled to free hospital and medical treatment provided by Australia's national insurance scheme, Medicare. Medicare does not, however, cover dental work, so dental insurance is worth considering. Visitors from countries other than those mentioned will face prohibitive medical bills if uninsured.

Park ranger   **Policeman**   **Fire officer**

Arrangements for adequate medical cover should be made before leaving home.

Dial 000 in any part of the country for ambulance assistance. Most public hospitals have a casualty department. For less urgent treatment, however, queues can be very long. There are 24-hour medical centres in the major cities and doctors in or nearby most country towns. Look in the local Yellow Pages under "Medical Practitioners".

There are dental hospitals in the state capitals that provide emergency treatment. Call the **Australian Dental Association** for emergency advice on treatment and a list of appropriate dentists practising in your area.

Chemist shop in Sydney

PHARMACIES

PHARMACIES (or chemist shops as they are known in Australia) are liberally scattered throughout cities and suburbs, but can be thin on the ground in remote areas, so it is advisable to stock up before heading off. Unrestricted drugs such as painkillers and other goods such as cosmetics, toiletries, suncreams and baby products are standard stock items available in all chemist

shops. Most pharmacies will provide free advice on minor ailments, but foreign prescriptions can only be met if they are endorsed by a local medical practitioner.

Hotel staff and hospitals will direct you to after-hours pharmacies in major cities.

ENVIRONMENTAL HAZARDS

TAKE CARE when going out in the sun – the ultraviolet rays are very intense in Australia, even on cloudy days. Wear an SPF 15+ sunblock at all times if your skin is exposed to direct and sustained sunlight. Sunglasses and hats are recommended, and stay out of the sun between 10am and 2pm.

Tasmania parks logo

Lifesavers patrol many beaches in populated areas, and red and yellow flags indicate safe swimming areas. However, it is vital to remember that there are vast stretches of unpatrolled beaches in Australia and many of these are subject to dangerous rips. Certain rips can be so strong that even wading can pose a threat, especially for elderly people and children. Follow local advice and, if in any doubt, do not swim.

Never underestimate the Australian bush. Even in well-trodden areas, hikers can lose their way. Always ask advice and inform someone of your route. Staff at national parks can offer expert advice along with maps, and will keep a note of your intended trip.

Take a basic first aid kit, food and water, and extra clothing. In many regions, temperatures plummet when the sun sets.

Australia shelters some of the most venomous creatures on earth. While it is highly unlikely that you will be bitten, basic precautions such as good boots and a wary eye are necessary. Snake-bite victims should be kept calm while emergency help is sought. Try to identify the creature by size and colour so that the appropriate antivenom can be administered.

Crocodiles are fascinating but dangerous creatures. In the northern regions of the continent, heed the warning signs and make enquiries if you intend to swim in remote, unpatrolled areas. Box jellyfish patrol tropical waters between October and May. They are hard to see and their sting is extremely dangerous. Again, observe the signs.

Bush fires are a fact of life in Australia. When planning a camping trip, ring the **Rural Fire Service** to check on restrictions. Total fire bans are not uncommon during warm, dry seasons. Avoid high-risk areas and dial 000 if in immediate danger from fire.

Surf lifesaving sign indicating a dangerous undertow or "rip"

Banking and Local Currency

BRANCHES OF NATIONAL, state and some foreign banks can be found in the central business districts of Australia's state capitals. Suburban shopping centres and country towns will often have at least one branch of a major Australian bank. If travelling to remote areas, find out what banking facilities are available in advance. Banks generally offer the best exchange rates; money can also be changed at bureaux de change, large department stores and hotels. There is no limit to the amount of personal funds that can be taken in or out of Australia, although cash amounts of A$10,000 or more must be declared to customs on arrival or prior to departure.

High street bank logos

BANKING

BANK TRADING HOURS are generally from 9:30am to 4pm Monday to Thursday and 9:30am to 5pm on Fridays. Outside banking hours, many transactions can be handled through automatic teller machines. All the current exchange rates are displayed either in the windows or foyers of most of the major banks.

Automatic cash dispenser

TRAVELLER'S CHEQUES

AUSTRALIAN DOLLAR traveller's cheques issued by major names such as Thomas Cook and American Express are usually accepted (with a passport) in large shops. You may have problems, however, cashing these in smaller outlets. Foreign currency cheques can be cashed at all major banks, bureaux de change and established hotels in the main cities.

Banks are generally the best places to go to cash traveller's cheques as their fees are lower.

Westpac Bank will cash traveller's cheques in Australian dollars without charge. ANZ, the National and Commonwealth banks charge a small fee for this service. A passport or another form of photo ID is usually needed to cash traveller's cheques at a bank.

CREDIT CARDS

ALL WELL-KNOWN international credit cards are widely accepted in Australia. Major credit cards such as VISA, MasterCard, Diners Club and American Express can be used to book and pay for hotel rooms, airline tickets, car hire, tours and concert and theatre tickets. Credit cards are accepted in most restaurants and shops, where the logos of all recognized cards are usually shown on doors and counter tops. You can also use credit cards in automatic teller machines at most banks to withdraw cash.

Credit cards are also a very convenient way to make telephone bookings and avoid the need to carry large sums of cash. They can be particularly useful in emergencies or if you need to return home at short notice.

You should always carry an emergency cash amount, however, if travelling to remote areas, particularly the Outback. Credit cards may not be accepted at small stores and cafés, and alternatives may not always be available.

AUTOMATIC TELLER MACHINES AND ELECTRONIC TRANSFER

AUTOMATIC TELLER machines can be found in most banks, as well as in shopping and tourist areas. In most cases it is possible to access foreign accounts from ATMs by using a linked credit card. Ask your bank about making your card valid for this kind of use.

Linking credit and other bank accounts in this way will also give you access to EFTPOS (Electronic Funds Transfer at Point Of Sale). Pay for goods using a card, and funds are automatically debited from your chosen bank account. In many stores customers will also be allowed to withdraw cash, providing a purchase has been made. This is a useful facility if the town you are in doesn't have an appropriate ATM. It is also a good alternative to using credit in every instance.

BUREAUX DE CHANGE

AUSTRALIAN CITIES and larger towns, particularly those popular with tourists, have many bureaux de change. These are usually open Monday to Saturday from 9am to 5:30pm. Some branches also operate on Sundays.

While the opening hours of bureaux de change make them a convenient alternative to a bank, their commissions and fees are generally higher.

DIRECTORY

FOREIGN CURRENCY EXCHANGE

American Express
📞 1300 139 060 .

Commonwealth Bank
📞 (02) 9312 0944

Thomas Cook
📞 1800 801 002.

Westpac
📞 13 20 32 or 1800 632 308.

LOCAL CURRENCY

THE AUSTRALIAN currency is the Australian dollar (A$), which breaks down into 100 cents (c). The decimal currency system now in place has been in operation since 1966.

Single cents may still be used for some prices, but as the Australian 1c and 2c coins are no longer in circulation, the total amount to be paid will be rounded up or down to the nearest five cents.

It can be difficult to change A$50 and A$100 notes, so avoid using them in smaller shops and cafés and, more particularly, when paying for taxi fares. If you do not have change, it is always wise to tell the taxi driver before you start your journey to avoid any misunderstandings. Otherwise, when you arrive at your destination, you may have to find change at the nearest shop or ATM.

To improve security, as well as increase their lifespan, all Australian bank notes have now been plasticized.

Bank Notes
Australian bank notes are produced in denominations of A$5, A$10, A$20, A$50 and A$100. Plastic bank notes and the old paper notes are both in circulation: paper notes are still legal tender but are being phased out.

A$100 note

A$50 note

A$20 note

A$10 note

A$5 note

5 cents (5c)   10 cents (10c)   20 cents (20c)   50 cents (50c)

1 dollar (A$1)   2 dollars (A$2)

Coins

Coins currently in use in Australia are 5c, 10c, 20c, 50c, A$1 and A$2. There are several different 50c coins in circulation; all are the same size and shape, but have different commemorative images on the face. The 10c and 20c coins are useful for local telephone calls (see pp540–41).

Using Australia's Telephones

Australia's public payphones are generally maintained in good working order. They are widely available on streets throughout cities and in country towns, as well as in cafés, shops, post offices, public buildings, railway and service stations. It is wise to invest in a phonecard to avoid the annoyance of looking for change. Also avoid making calls from hotel rooms as hotels set their own rates. Use the hotel foyer payphone instead.

Using a mobile phone at Bondi

Telstra Corporation logo

PUBLIC TELEPHONES

Most payphones accept both coins and phonecards, although some operate solely on phonecards and major credit cards. Phonecards can be bought from selected newsagents and news kiosks, as well as from the many other outlets displaying the blue and orange Telstra sign.

Although slightly varied in shape and colour, all public telephones have a hand-held receiver and a 12-button key pad, as well as clear instructions (in English only), a list of useful phone numbers and telephone directories.

Telstra payphones

PAYPHONE CHARGES

Local calls are untimed and cost 40 cents. Depending on where you are, "local" means the city and its suburbs, or outside the city, a defined country region. **Telstra** can provide information on exact costs. Dial the free-phone number 1800 113 011 for an estimate of the cost of long-distance and international calls. Phonecard and credit card phones all have a A$1.20 minimum fee. Long-distance calls are less expensive if you dial without the help of an operator. You can also save money on all calls by phoning during off-peak periods. Peak and discount calling times fall into three periods. Peak times are between 7am–7pm Monday to Friday. There are capped call rates between 7pm and midnight Sunday to Friday and between 4pm and midnight on Saturday. All other times are economy rate.

MOBILE TELEPHONES

Mobile telephones are used widely in Australia. Short-term rentals are available to visitors, but mobile calls are costly – even local calls are billed at an STD rate.

Making calls while driving is illegal and carries a stiff fine. Many places in remote Australia are not on the mobile net.

FAX SERVICES

Many Australian post offices offer a fax service. There are also many copy shops that will send or receive faxes on your behalf. Look under the heading "Facsimile and Telex Communication Services" in the Yellow Pages.

Post offices charge per-page fees to send a fax within Australia. The cost per page is reduced if you are sending more than one page. If you are not sure of a correct fax number, you can fax a document to the nearest post office, who will then deliver it to the right address by mail. There is an additional small delivery fee for this service.

TELEPHONE DIRECTORIES

Each city and region in Australia has two telephone directories: the White Pages and the Yellow Pages. The White Pages list private and business numbers in

USING A COIN/PHONECARD OPERATED PHONE

1 Lift the receiver and wait for the dialling tone.

2 Insert the coins required or a Telstra phonecard.

3 Dial the number and wait to be connected.

4 The display shows you how much value is left on your phonecard or coins. When your money runs out you will hear a warning beep. Insert more coins or a new phonecard.

5 Replace the receiver at the end of the call and withdraw your card or collect any unused coins.

6 When you finish your call, the phonecard is returned to you with a hole punched in it showing the approximate remaining value.

Phonecards
These are available in A$5, A$10, A$20 and A$50 denominations.

alphabetical order. They also have a guide to emergency services and government departments. The Yellow Pages list businesses under relevant headings such as Dentists, Car Hire and so on.

USEFUL INFORMATION

**Telstra Mobile
Sales**
▌ *13 18 00* .

REACHING THE RIGHT NUMBER

• To ring Australia from the UK dial 0061, then the area code, then the local number.
• To ring Australia from the USA or Canada dial 011 61, then the area code, then the local number.
• For long-distance direct-dial calls outside your local area code, but within Australia (STD calls), dial the appropriate area code, then the number.
• For international direct-dial calls (IDD calls): dial **0011**, followed by the country code (USA and Canada: 1; UK: 44; New Zealand: 64), then the city or area code (omit initial 0) and then the local number.
• Directory information with automatic connection to local and national destinations: dial **12455**.
• Local and national directory enquiries: dial **12455**.
• Reverse charge or third party charge calls: dial **12550**.
• National and international operator assisted calls: dial **1234** or **12550**.
• National and international call-cost enquiries: dial **1800 113 011**.
• Numbers beginning with **1 800** are usually toll-free numbers, but not always.
• Numbers beginning with **13** are charged at a rate that is slightly higher than the local call rate.
• Numbers with the prefix **014**, **015**, **018**, **019**, **040**, **041** or **042** are mobile or car phones.
• See also Emergency Numbers, *p537*.

Postal Services

POST OFFICES are open 9am–5pm weekdays, and some branches are open on Saturday mornings. Telephone **Australia Post Customer Service** for details of opening times. Many post offices offer a wide range of services, including poste restante and electronic post. In country towns, the local general store is often also a post office. Look for the red and white postal sign.

Australian Post logo

Australian postman

DOMESTIC AND INTERNATIONAL MAIL

ALL DOMESTIC MAIL is first class and usually arrives within one to five days, depending on distance. Be sure to include postcodes on mailing addresses to avoid delays in delivery.

Express Post, for which you need to buy the special yellow and white envelopes sold in post offices, guarantees next-day delivery in certain areas of Australia. Air mail

Labels used for overseas mail

Typical stamps used for local mail

Stamp from a scenic series issue

will take from five to ten days to reach most countries. There are two types of international express mail. EMS International Courier will reach nearly all overseas destinations within two to three days, whereas Express Post International takes four to five days.

Standard and express postboxes

POSTBOXES

AUSTRALIA HAS both red and yellow postboxes. The red boxes are for normal postal service; yellow boxes are used exclusively for Express Post. Both types of postbox can be found on most street corners as well as outside post offices. If a yellow postbox is not to be seen, go to a post office and deliver your express mail over the counter.

POSTE RESTANTE

POSTE RESTANTE can be sent to any post office in Australia. Mail should be addressed clearly and marked "poste restante". Visitors picking up mail will need to produce a passport or other proof of identity.

USEFUL INFORMATION

Australia Post Customer Service Centre
▌ *13 13 18*.

TRAVEL INFORMATION

WHILE SOME VISITORS to Australia may choose to arrive by sea ship, the vast majority arrive by air. Once here, flying between locations is also the most popular form of long-distance travel, but there are some other choices, all of which offer the chance to see something of the country along the way. The national rail network links all major

Airport Express bus into central Sydney

cities, while coach routes provide regular services to most provincial and country areas. If you have the time, driving in Australia is an excellent option. Boat travel is best for those wanting to visit Australia's islands, principally Tasmania, but regular services run to other island destinations such as Rottnest Island off the coast of Western Australia (see pp300–301).

International Qantas flight arriving in Sydney

ARRIVING BY AIR

A USTRALIA is served by around 50 international airlines. The Australian airline **Qantas** has a worldwide network and offers the most flights in and out of Australia every week. Qantas is also the main domestic carrier in Australia (see p544). **Air New Zealand**, Qantas and **United Airlines** have regular flights from the USA, with a range of stopovers available. The large Asian and European carriers, **British Airways**, **Singapore Airlines**, **Cathay Pacific** and **Japan Airlines**, offer many routes and stopovers on the Europe-Asia-Australia run. Canadian travellers can fly **Canadian Airlines**, which connects with Qantas flights in Hawai'i.

INTERNATIONAL FLIGHTS

F LIGHTS BETWEEN Australia and Europe take upwards of 22 hours, and with delays you may be in transit for more than 30 hours. A stopover in Asia is worth considering for

the sake of comfort, especially if travelling with children, as is one in Hawai'i or the Pacific islands for visitors from the USA. Also, consider arranging flights so that they account for international time differences. Arriving in the afternoon, spending the rest of the day

awake, then going to sleep in accordance with local time will help to counteract jet lag.

Australia has several international air terminals, so visitors can choose different arrival and departure points. Sydney and Melbourne have major airports servicing flights from all over the world. Sydney, the busiest, can be congested. Melbourne is consistently voted one of the world's best airports by travellers. Hobart has flights from New Zealand in the summer months, while Adelaide has direct flights to Singapore and flights to Europe via Sydney or Melbourne. Visitors to the west coast can arrive in Perth, which serves flights from Africa and Asia and direct flights from the UK. Darwin, Brisbane and Cairns mostly service Asia, but there are a few possibilities for connections from Europe.

AIRPORT	INFORMATION
Sydney	((02) 9667 9111
Melbourne	((03) 9297 1600
Brisbane	((07) 3406 3190
Cairns	((07) 4052 9703
Perth	((08) 9478 8888
Adelaide	((08) 8308 9211
Darwin	((08) 8920 1805
Hobart	((03) 6216 1600

Singapore Airlines 747 taking off at Perth Airport

AIR FARES

FLIGHTS TO AUSTRALIA can be expensive, especially during December, the peak season. January to April is slightly cheaper. During the off-peak season, airlines offer Apex fares that are often 30–40 per cent below economy fares (see p544). Many stipulate arrival and departure times and carry cancellation penalties. Round-the-world fares are good value and increasingly popular.

Check with discount travel agents if you can fly at short notice, as they regularly receive unsold tickets from the airlines. In these cases, flexibility isn't usually a feature.

ON ARRIVAL

JUST BEFORE setting down in Australia you will be given custom documents to fill in. On arrival you will be asked to present your documents, including passport, at the Entry Control Point (see p532). You will also be asked to throw away any food items. You can then collect your baggage and, if you have nothing to declare, proceed straight into the main area of the airport.

Larger airports have better services, but most have good shopping, postal and medical facilities. You can hire cars and change money at all airports. Taxis and buses are available for transport into city centres.

Arrangements for domestic flight connections are usually made when purchasing your

Check-in information board at Sydney Airport

original ticket. Airline staff will advise you how to proceed. In Melbourne, the domestic and international services are in the same terminal. In many places the terminals are separate and distances can be long – 10 km (6 miles) in the the case of Perth. Free shuttle buses transfer passengers between terminals.

DIRECTORY

AIRLINE CARRIERS

Air New Zealand
13 24 76.

British Airways
Sydney (02) 8904 8800.
Melbourne (03) 9656 8133.
Perth (08) 9425 7711.

Canadian Airlines
1300 655 767.

Cathay Pacific
13 17 47.

Japan Airlines
Sydney (02) 9272 1111.
Brisbane (07) 3229 9916.

Qantas
13 13 13.

Singapore Airlines
13 10 11.

United Airlines
13 17 77.

DISTANCE FROM CITY	TAXI FARE TO CITY	BUS TRANSFER TO CITY
9 km (6 miles)	A$25	30 mins
22 km (14 miles)	A$30	30 mins
15 km (9 miles)	A$25	30 mins
6 km (4 miles)	A$10	10 mins
15 km (9 miles)	A$26	25 mins
6 km (4 miles)	A$17	15 mins
6 km (4 miles)	A$15	15 mins
22 km (14 miles)	A$25	20–30 mins

Domestic Air Travel

AIR TRAVEL accounts for a large proportion of long-distance journeys in Australia and is by far the most practical way of taking in a country of this size, particularly for those with time constraints. The main domestic air carriers in Australia, **Qantas** and **Virgin Blue**, concentrate on the high-volume interstate routes, while a host of small operators handle air travel within states and to remote locations. Fares can be expensive, but with the range of discounts available in this deregulated and aggressively competitive industry, it is unlikely that you will ever have to pay the full fare, providing you plan your air trips in advance. Spectacular speciality aerial tours of distant or hard-to-reach landmarks are also available *(see p527)*.

Domestic plane at Yulara airport, near Uluru *(see p281)*

Tiny domestic terminal in Birdsville, Queensland

AIR ROUTES AND AIRLINES

AUSTRALIA'S air network is vast, but reasonably streamlined, so arranging flights to even the most remote spots should never be a problem. It is possible to fly direct between most major destinations such as Sydney–Darwin or Melbourne–Perth. However, for smaller centres, you will invariably have to fly first to the capital city in the state, and then on to your destination. The small airlines that cover out-of-the-way routes are, in most cases, affiliated with either Qantas or Ansett, which means bookings can be made through the large carriers' centralized booking services.

DISCOUNTS FOR OVERSEAS VISITORS

DISCOUNTED domestic air travel is often offered as part of an international package, so check with your travel agent about booking domestic trips before leaving home.

Once in Australia, both Ansett and Qantas offer immediate discounts to overseas travellers, which range from 25–40 per cent; proof of overseas residence is required when booking these tickets. Various air passes are available from the airlines which allow you to make a number of single flights for a set price. You can then move from leg to leg around the country rather than having to make return flights, which are normally expensive. When buying these passes abroad, you are sometimes required to pay half the cost before leaving home and half when booking the flights. In these cases, avoid buying too many flights in case your plans change. The passes are flexible, but restrictions do apply.

APEX FARES

ADVANCE Purchase Excursion fares (Apex) are widely available for round-trip travel in Australia, and offer as much as 55 per cent off the full economy fare. There is usually no refund on these tickets, but flight times can often be altered. The general rule is that the further in advance you book your ticket, the better the discount. A 14-day advance booking will give you the best discount, then seven days, five days and so on. In most cases, you will be required to stay a Saturday night. Keep an eye out for very cheap, one-off fares advertised during quiet

Plane on the harbourside runway, Hamilton Island *(see p208)*

periods of the year, usually on popular routes such as Melbourne to Sydney. There is very little flight flexibility on these tickets and passengers are strictly required to fly within a set period of time.

It is always worth ringing both Qantas and Ansett to compare current deals. Discounted travel for children is standard on domestic flights.

Fly-Drive Deals

A GREAT WAY to see Australia is to fly to a destination and then continue on by car. Arrangements can be made for different pick-up and drop-off points for hire vehicles. For example, you could pick up a car in Sydney, drive to Brisbane, fly to Alice Springs and then pick up a car there. Ansett and Qantas have deals with Avis and Hertz respectively, and the car hire companies offer discounts to passengers who are travelling on those airlines (see p548).

Queueing for taxis at Sydney Airport domestic terminal.

Baggage Restrictions

P ASSENGERS travelling economy on domestic flights may check in one piece of baggage weighing no more than 32 kg (70 lbs). For children under three who are travelling free, Ansett allows one piece of baggage. Qantas has a policy of charging A$10 per item; however, in many instances if there is no excess baggage on the flight, the charge is not applied. The cabin baggage allowance is strictly enforced. Personal

QANTAS

Qantas logo

items such as walking sticks, cameras, handbags, briefcases and overcoats are all classified and weighed as part of the hand luggage allowance.

Checking In

A IRLINES request that you check in at least 30 minutes before your flight time. While it is not necessary to confirm flights, it is a good idea to call the airline to ensure that the flight is on time. Make sure you alight at the right terminal as many domestic and international terminals are at separate locations.

DIRECTORY

DOMESTIC AIRLINES

Qantas Airways
Domestic Reservations
☎ 13 13 13.

Virgin Blue
Domestic Reservations
☎ 13 67 89.

PRINCIPAL DOMESTIC AIR ROUTES

Domestic flights cover vast distances. Sydney to Perth, for example, is 3,400 km (2,225 miles) and a flight of 5 hours; the 2,600-km (1,615-mile) flight from Adelaide to Darwin is 3.5 hours.

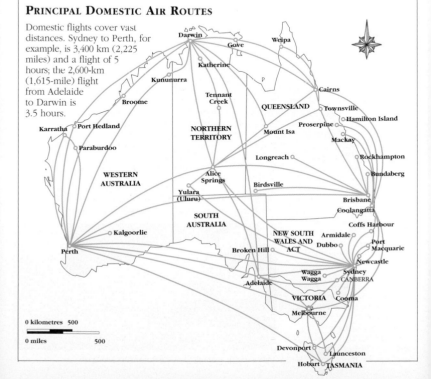

Travelling by Train and Coach

THE AUSTRALIAN continent does not have a comprehensive rail network. With its small population, the country has never been able to support an extensive system of railways and, in fact, services have declined in number over recent decades. However, there are several opportunities for rail enthusiasts: Australia still offers some of the world's great train trips, as well as regular services linking the cities of the east coast. Train journeys should also be considered for quick trips away from the city centres. Coach trips fill any gaps in overland travel in Australia, servicing major centres and remote outposts alike.

The fabled Ghan railway runs between Adelaide and Alice Springs where there is a museum recounting its history *(see p275)*. The 1,559-km (970-mile) trip offers amazing desert scenery and takes two days.

Three different lines run the 1,681 km (1,045 miles) between Brisbane and Cairns: the Queenslander, the Sunlander and the Spirit of the Tropics. Another Queensland journey is aboard the Gulflander, a 152-km (95-mile) trip through some of Australia's most remote country.

The Overland (Melbourne–Adelaide) and the fast XPT trains (Brisbane–Sydney–Melbourne) have a more utilitarian approach to train travel.

Mass Transit Railway Station in Perth

THE AUSTRALIAN RAIL NETWORK

RAILWAYS IN Australia are state-operated. **Countrylink**, the federal body, oversees the various services. A staff change at state borders is the only indication most passengers get of a state-by-state system at work.

Train travel is cheaper than flying, but journey times are long. The Sydney–Brisbane trip takes 13.5 hours and Sydney–Melbourne takes 10.5 hours.

The prospects for rail travel within state boundaries vary. An increasingly common way of coping with the expense of maintaining rail systems is to substitute state-run coach services on under-used lines.

State governments accept responsibility for providing access to most areas, so where there is no rail network, such as in Tasmania, there will be an efficient, cheap coach network instead. Queensland, however, has increased its rail services, most of which are aimed at the tourist market.

SPECIALITY TRIPS

THE CHANCE to take in some of the country's extraordinary landscapes are what makes rail journeys in Australia so special. Standards are high, often with a level of luxury reminiscent of the grand old days of rail travel.

The Indian Pacific route takes three days to cover the 4,352 km (2,700 miles) from Sydney to Perth. The 478-km (300-mile) crossing of the Nullarbor Plain *(see p311)* is on the world's longest length of straight railway track.

TRAVEL CLASSES

THERE ARE three types of travel available on most interstate trains. Overnight services, such as Melbourne–Adelaide, offer first-class sleeper, first-class sit-up and economy sit-up. In addition, the Indian Pacific, the Ghan and various Queensland trains offer economy sleepers. All long-distance trains have dining facilities. First-class travel includes meals in the price of your ticket.

Motorail means you can travel with your car. The service is expensive, however, and you are better off hiring a car at your destination.

TICKETS AND BOOKINGS

BOOKINGS for rail travel can be made with travel agents, at railway stations or by telephoning Rail Australia's central free-phone number.

Indian Pacific Railway, running from Sydney to Perth

Greyhound coach station in Sydney

There are a number of passes available to overseas visitors. The Austrail Pass allows travel anywhere in Australia, including metropolitan services, over consecutive days – there are 14-, 21- and 30-day passes available. The Austrail Flexipass offers between 8 and 29 days of travel which can be taken any time over a six-month period.

Standard rail fares are high in Australia. However, there is a good range of rail fare discounts with up to 40 per cent off advance bookings.

COACH TRAVEL

COACH TRAVEL in Australia is cheap, efficient and generally safe. The two main operators are **Greyhound Pioneer** and **McCafferty's**. They both have a range of passes that greatly reduce the cost of any extended travel. The Greyhound Aussie Explorer Pass is available on 12 pre-set routes, while the Aussie Kilometre pass offers greater flexibility; McCafferty's Coast and Centre pass will take you from Cairns, down the east coast of Australia and then up to Uluru and Alice Springs. However, it is worth remembering that this kind of travel can mean day after day on the road and nights spent sleeping upright.

There are a range of other companies operating at a local level. These are good for trips to particular sights or national parks. Tourist information bodies in each state will give you advice on which company services which route (see p535).

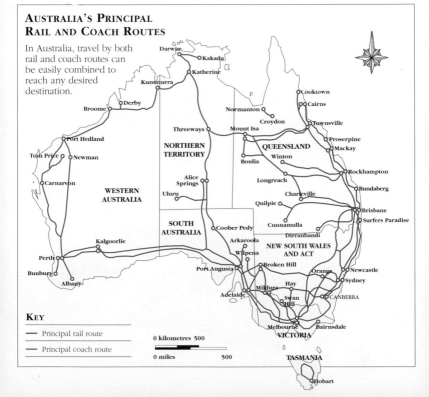

AUSTRALIA'S PRINCIPAL RAIL AND COACH ROUTES

In Australia, travel by both rail and coach routes can be easily combined to reach any desired destination.

KEY

— Principal rail route

— Principal coach route

0 kilometres 500

0 miles 500

Travelling by Car and Four-Wheel Drive

Great Ocean Road sign

IT IS WELL WORTH CONSIDERING hiring a car when visiting Australia. Other modes of transport will get you around the cities and from one country town to another, but, once you arrive in a rural area or a small town, you may find it impossible to explore the area other than on foot or with a tour. Australia offers the motorist the chance to meander through areas such as the vineyard regions of South Australia *(see pp330–31)*, the Southern Highlands of New South Wales *(see pp178–9)* and the Great Ocean Road of Victoria *(see pp434–5)*, as well as the experience of Outback travel on near-empty roads.

Driving through the Pinnacles in Nambung National Park *(see p316)*

DRIVING LICENCES

PROVIDING your driving licence is in English and you have proof that you are a tourist, there is no need for an additional permit when driving in Australia. If the licence is not in English, you must carry a translation. It is a legal requirement that you have your licence with you at all times when driving.

CAR HIRE

RENTAL CARS are available just about anywhere in Australia. They can be picked up at the airport on arrival, or arrangements can be made for delivery to your hotel. The big car rental firms **Avis**, **Budget**, **Hertz** and **Thrifty** have nationwide networks – an advantage if you are considering making several different trips across the continent. Check with your travel agent before leaving home about discounts or special fly-drive offers.

Rates vary from around A$55 a day for a small car to A$100 a day for larger vehicles. It is invariably more expensive to hire a 4WD vehicle; rates average out at around A$120 and are more costly in remote areas where the demand is high. You can reduce daily rates by hiring over longer periods (usually three days and over), or if you accept a limited kilometre/mileage deal. These deals usually give you the first 100 km (60 miles) a day as part of the daily charge, and a per kilometre rate after that. This is well worth considering for inner-city driving, but not good value beyond the city limits where distances can add up very quickly. The smaller local operators offer very competitive rates, sometimes as low as A$25 a day, but read the small print carefully. Often the quote does not include the extras that the larger companies consider standard. If travelling with children, make sure the car is equipped with restraints according to Australian guidelines *(see p534)*.

Credit cards are the preferred method of payment when hiring a car. If paying with cash you will usually be required to pay the full cost of the rental, plus a deposit, when you pick up the car.

INSURANCE

FOR PEACE OF MIND it is a good idea to have comprehensive insurance when hiring a car. "Third party fire and theft" insurance is standard and included in the cost of the hire, as is insurance against accidental damage to the hire car. However, you will have to pay extra to reduce the excess payment. From upwards of A$7 a day, you can bring the excess down from around A$2,000 to a more comfortable A$100. This option is usually only offered by the larger car hire companies. Personal accident plans are also available, but they may not be necessary, depending on the cover

Car and van rental company in Sydney

offered with your own travel insurance. Four-wheel drive vehicles attract an excess rate of around A\$4,000. For A\$20 a day this can be reduced to a A\$1,000, but never lower than this figure. Car hire companies will not offer insurance on any off-road driving, regardless of the vehicle type. Higher rates of insurance apply to drivers under the age of 25. Car hire in Australia is often not available to drivers under the age of 21.

Petrol station in Sydney

PETROL

PETROL IS CHEAP in urban areas of Australia, about half the price of petrol in Europe, but in remote regions of the country prices rise considerably. It is dispensed by the litre and can be purchased in leaded, regular unleaded, premium unleaded and diesel grades. Many petrol stations are self-service and most accept major credit cards and have an EFTPOS facility *(see pp538–9)*.

RULES OF THE ROAD

AUSTRALIANS drive on the left-hand side of the road and give way to the right in all circumstances unless otherwise indicated. Drivers must also give way to emergency vehicles – if possible, pull over to the side of the road when you hear a siren. The speed limit is 60 km/h (37 mph) in cities, towns and suburban areas and 100–110 km/h (62–68 mph) on major highways. The wearing of seat belts is compulsory for drivers and passengers.

Drink-driving laws are strictly enforced in Australia. The legal blood alcohol level is 0.05 per cent maximum. Should you be involved in an accident while over the alcohol limit, your vehicle insurance may be invalidated. Police in country areas are just as vigilant as their counterparts in the city, and it is not unusual to see a random breath-test taking place on an otherwise deserted road.

Beware of kangaroos sign

Any accident involving injury in Australia must be reported to the police within 24 hours. In Western Australia all accidents must be reported and in other states it is advisable to do so if there is considerable property damage. Always get insurance details from the other motorist. Do not admit fault – it is better to tell the police your version of events and let them decide.

The city of Melbourne has two road laws worth noting. First, motorists must stop behind a stationary tram to allow passengers to alight. Second, at certain city intersections, motorists who intend to turn right must pull over to the left of the intersection *(see pp402–403)*. Called hook turns, they are clearly indicated and are designed to prevent traffic queuing across tram tracks.

ROAD CONDITIONS

AUSTRALIA'S road network is quite remarkable considering the distances it has to cover. Stretches of multi-lane highways are to be found on most of the major routes. The majority of other routes are covered by two-lane highways, which are generally well sealed and signposted. Unsealed dirt roads can always be found in country regions, but are rarely the only means of getting to a destination unless you are travelling through particularly remote country. Tollways are restricted to areas in the immediate vicinity of the large

cities, such as the Western Motorway that covers part of the Sydney–Blue Mountains route. Melbourne has an intricate tollway system which is currently under construction. Service stations are plentiful along all the well-travelled routes, but they can be few and far between in the Outback. A particularly Australian and very dangerous road hazard is the prevalence of wildlife crossing country highways. This danger increases greatly at dusk and after dark when the nocturnal mammals, such as kangaroos and wallabies, surface to feed, but are often hard to see by the motorist.

ROADSIDE ASSISTANCE

CAR HIRE COMPANIES will look after breakdowns of their rental cars and, if necessary, arrange for vehicle replacements. State-based motoring organizations provide roadside assistance for members around the country. The organizations also sell maps and guides in their central branches, and are a great source of information on road rules, road conditions and Outback driving. Members of motoring organizations in Great Britain, Canada and the United States usually have reciprocal membership rights with Australian organizations.

Royal Automobile Association vehicle in Adelaide

South approach to the Harbour Bridge in Sydney

INNER CITY DRIVING

IF YOU ARE planning to drive within any city, a good street directory will be essential. If possible, avoid peak-hour traffic (7:30–9:30am and 4:30–7:30pm). Traffic reports are broadcast on radio stations.

The larger the city, the more difficult it will be to park in the city centre. Parking restrictions are clearly signposted and usually specify an hour or two of metered parking during business hours. Make sure you carry coins for the meters. Many cities have clearway zones that apply at certain times of the day and vehicles will be towed away if they are found parked here during these times. If this happens, telephone the local traffic authority or the police to find out where your vehicle has been impounded. Car parks are also to be found in and around city centres. Make sure you are clear about the cost before you park.

OUTBACK DRIVING

FOR ANY Outback travel, it is important to first check your route to see if a 4WD is required. Although some Outback areas now have roads of a high enough standard to carry conventional cars, a 4WD will be essential to travel to some wild and remote areas. Motoring organizations and tourist information centres can provide information that will enable you to assess your journey properly.

There are a number of basic points of safety that should be observed on any trip of this kind. Plan your route and carry up-to-date maps. If you are travelling between remote destinations, inform the local police of your departure and expected arrival times. Check road conditions before you start and carry plenty of food and water. Make sure you know where you can get petrol and carry extra supplies if necessary. If you run out of petrol or break down, remain with your vehicle. It offers some protection from the elements and, if you fail to arrive at the expected time, a search party will be sent out to look for you.

The **Australian Council of the Royal Flying Doctor Service (RFDS)** can offer safety advice to Outback tourists. You can also hire radio sets that have an emergency call button to the RFDS from **McKays Communication**. You should also observe important guidelines to protect the land. Native flora and fauna should not be removed or damaged. Stick to vehicle tracks, carry a stove and fuel to avoid lighting fires, and take all rubbish with you. Be aware of Aboriginal land boundaries and national parks and leave gates as you find them: either open or shut.

DIRECTORY

CAR HIRE COMPANIES

Avis
📞 13 63 33.

Budget
📞 13 27 27.

Hertz
📞 13 30 39.

Thrifty
📞 1300 367 227.

MOTORING ORGANIZATIONS

New South Wales and ACT
National Road and Motorist's Association (NRMA).
📞 13 11 11.

Northern Territory
Automobile Association of NT Inc (AANT).
📞 (08) 8981 3837.

Queensland
Royal Automobile Club of Queensland (RACQ).
📞 13 19 05.

South Australia
Royal Automobile Association of SA Inc (RAA).
📞 (08) 8202 4600.

Tasmania
Royal Automobile Club of Tasmania (RACT).
📞 (03) 6232 6300.

Victoria
Royal Automobile Club of Victoria (RACV).
📞 13 19 55.

Western Australia
Royal Automobile Club of WA Inc (RAC).
📞 (08) 9421 4444.

OUTBACK DRIVING

Australian Council of the Royal Flying Doctor Service
📞 (02) 9299 5766.

McKays Communication
📞 (02) 6884 5237.

Driving a 4WD along the Gibb River Road in the Kimberley

Travelling by Ferry and Cruise Boat

F OR AN ISLAND CONTINENT, Australia has surprisingly few tourist cruises on offer. The most important route is that between Melbourne and Tasmania. Elsewhere ferries run between the mainland and island destinations such as Rottnest Island, Western Australia *(see pp300–301)*, and Fraser Island, off the Queensland coast *(see p234)*. There are, however, plenty of cruises of local waterways. Large cruise ships concentrate on the local Pacific area and in most cases sail in and out of Sydney.

The *QEII* passenger ship berthed at Circular Quay, Sydney

ARRIVING BY BOAT

T HERE IS PROBABLY no better way of arriving in Australia than to sail into Sydney Harbour aboard a cruise ship. Cruising is expensive, however, and the services to Australia are very limited. In terms of getting to Australia from the USA or Europe, you may have to wait for the next world cruise on **P&O** or **Cunard Line** vessels. Another option is to fly to an Asian city such as Hong Kong and join up with **Princess Cruises**. Sydney is the main port of call for most cruise ships, and its two passenger terminals have excellent facilities.

FERRIES TO TASMANIA

T HE *Spirit of Tasmania* takes just over 14 hours to cross the Bass Strait from Melbourne to the island state of Tasmania. It runs at 6pm, Monday to Saturday, departing alternately from Port Melbourne and Devonport. The ship has every level of accommodation ranging from reclining cruise seats and backpacker berths to fully equipped suites. There are several restaurants, shops, and entertainment for children. The fares are reasonable considering the experience – a double cabin will cost around A$450 return for a couple in off-peak season, less if you book during a special offer period.

ISLAND CRUISES AND FERRIES

A SEALINK ferry departs from Cape Jervis, south of Adelaide, for Kangaroo Island *(see p346)*. In Western Australia, regular ferries run to Rottnest Island from Perth. There are many services between the mainland and the Barrier Reef islands *(see p208)*. A boat also runs between Seisia, Cape York, and Thursday Island, *(see p244)*. Contact the **Queensland Government Travel Centre** for more information.

RIVERS AND HARBOURS

H IRING A HOUSEBOAT is an excellent way of seeing some of Australia's spectacular river scenery. Popular spots include the Hawkesbury River, New South Wales, and the Murray River which runs through New South Wales, Victoria and South Australia. There are tours of Darwin and Sydney harbours, cruises of the Swan River in Perth and the Yarra River in Melbourne. State tourist authorities can provide details *(see p535)*.

Taking the ferry to Rottnest Island

DIRECTORY

SHIPPING COMPANIES

P & O
Sydney.
[13 24 69.
Southampton,
UK.
[(01703) 534 200.

Princess Cruises
San Francisco, USA.
[(001 415) 781 1169.

Cunard Line
New York, USA.
[(1 800) 221 4770.
Southampton,
UK.
[(023) 8063 4166.

Sealink
Kangaroo Island.
[13 13 01.

Spirit of Tasmania
Hobart.
[13 20 10.

TOURIST INFORMATION

Queensland Travel Centre
243 Edward St, Brisbane.
[13 18 01.

General Index

Acknowledgments

DORLING KINDERSLEY would like to thank the following people whose contributions and assistance have made the preparation of this book possible.

CONSULTANT
Helen Duffy is an editor and writer. Since 1992 she has managed and contributed to a range of tourist publications on Australia.

MAIN CONTRIBUTORS
Louise Bostock Lang is a writer and editor who has worked on a number of Dorling Kindersley Travel Guides and published four other books.
Jan Bowen is a travel broadcaster and writer. Her travel books include *The Queensland Experience*.
Paul Kloeden lives in Adelaide. A freelance writer and historian, his work ranges from travel articles to government-sponsored heritage surveys.
Jacinta le Plaistrier is a Melbourne-based journalist, poet and librettist. She has contributed travel articles to numerous Australian publications.
Sue Neales is a multi-award winning Australian journalist. Her travel articles have appeared in major Australian newspapers and magazines.
Ingrid Ohlsson is a Melbourne-based writer who has contributed to a number of Australian travel publications.
Tamara Thiessen is a Tasmanian freelance travel writer and photographer.

ADDITIONAL CONTRIBUTORS
Tony Baker, Libby Lester.

ADDITIONAL PHOTOGRAPHY
Simon Blackall, DK Studio, Geoff Dunn, Jean-Paul Ferrero, Jean-Marc La Roque, Michael Nicholson, Alan Williams.

CARTOGRAPHY
Lovell Johns Ltd, Oxford, UK; ERA-Maptec Ltd, Dublin, Ireland.

PROOF READER
Sam Merrell.

INDEXER
Hilary Bird.

DESIGN AND EDITORIAL
Duncan Baird Limited
PICTURE RESEARCH Victoria Peel
DTP DESIGNER Rhona Green
Dorling Kindersley Limited
SENIOR MANAGING EDITOR Vivien Crump
MANAGING EDITOR Helen Partington
PROJECT EDITOR Rosalyn Thiro
DEPUTY ART DIRECTOR Gillian Allan
ART EDITOR Stephen Bere
MAP CO-ORDINATORS Emily Green, David Pugh
PRODUCTION David Proffit
Rosemary Bailey, Hanna Bolus, Sue Callister, Wendy Canning, Lucinda Cooke, Bronwen

Davies, Stephanie Driver, Jonathan Elphick, Fay Franklin, Gail Jones, Christine Keilty, Esther Labi, Maite Lantaron, Ciaran McIntyre, Claudine Meissner, John Miles, Tania Monkton, Gloria Nykl, Michael Palmer, Manisha Patel, Luise Roberts, Mark Sayers, Adrian Tristram, Lynda Tyson.

SPECIAL ASSISTANCE
Sue Bickers, Perth; Craig Ebbett, Perth; Peter Edge, Met. Office, London; Chrissie Goldrick, The Image Library, State Library of NSW; Cathy Goodwin, Queensland Art Gallery; Megan Howat, International Media & Trade Visits Coordinator, WA Tourist Commission; John Hunter and Fiona Marr, CALM, Perth; Vere Kenny, Auscape International; Selena MacLaren, SOCOG; Greg Miles, Kakadu National Park; Ian Miller, Auslig; Gary Newton, Perth; Murray Robbins, Perth; Ron Ryan, Coo-ee Historical Picture Library; Craig Sambell and Jill Jones, GBRMPA; Norma Scott, Australian Picture Library; Andrew Watts, QASCO; and all state tourist authorities and national park services.

PHOTOGRAPHY PERMISSIONS
Dorling Kindersley would like to thank the following for their kind assistance and permission to photograph at their establishments: Art Gallery of WA; Australian Museum; National Gallery of Australia; Australian War Memorial; Ayers House; Department of Conservation and Land Management (WA); Department of Environment and Natural Resources (Adelaide); Department of Environment (Queensland); Government House (Melbourne); Hermannsburg Historic Precinct; Jondaryan Woolshed Historical Museum; Museum and Art Gallery of NT; Museum of WA; National Gallery of Victoria; National Maritime Museum; National Museum of Australia; National Parks and Wildlife Services (all states); National Trust of Australia (all states); Parliament House (Melbourne); Port Arthur Historic Site; Powerhouse Museum; Rottnest Island Authority; Royal Flying Doctor Service of NT; Shrine of Remembrance Trustees (Victoria); South Australian Museum; *Spirit of Tasmania*; Supreme Court (Melbourne); Tandanya National Aboriginal Cultural Institute Inc; Victoria Arts Centre Trust; WA Maritime Museum; and all the other sights too numerous to thank individually.

PICTURE CREDITS
t = top; tl = top left; tlc = top left centre; tc = top centre; trc = top right centre; tr = top right; cla = centre left above; ca = centre above; cra = centre right above; cl = centre left; c = centre; cr = centre right; clb = centre left below; crb = centre right below; cb = centre below; bl = bottom left; br = bottom right; b = bottom; bc = bottom centre; bcl = bottom centre left; bcr = bottom centre right; (d) detail.

Works of art have been reproduced with the

permission of the following copyright holders: *Goanna Dreaming*, 1996 © Michael Tommy Jabanardi 339l; *Ngalyod and Ngalkunburriyaymi*, Namerredje Guymala, c.1975, Natural pigments on bark, The National Museum (Canberra) ©1978 Aboriginal Artists Agency Limited 13c,

The publisher would like to thank the following individuals, companies and picture libraries for their kind permission to reproduce their photographs: ALLSPORT: 529b, 38t; ARDEA LONDON LTD: © D Parer & E Parer Cook 208tr; © Ron and Valerie Taylor 208cla; ART GALLERY OF NSW: © Ms Stephenson-Meere 1996, *Australian Beach Pattern* 1940, Charles Meere (1890–1961) oil on canvas, 91.5 x 122cm, 61tl; © The Cazneau Family 1996, *Bridge Pattern*, Harold Cazneaux (1878–1953), gelatin silver photography, 29.6 x 21.4cm, gift of the Cazneaux family, 1975, 68bc(d); © Lady Drysdale 1996 *Sofala* 1947 Russell Drysdale (1912-81), oil on canvas on hardboard, 71.7 x 93.1cm 106tr; *Sunbaker* 1937, Max Dupain, gelatin silver photograph, 38.3 x 43.7cm 106ca; *Madonna and Child With Infant St John The Baptist* c. 1541, Domenico Beccafumi, oil on wooden panel 92 x 69cm 106clb; © Tiwi Design Executive 1996, *Pukumnai Grave Posts, Melville Island* 1958, various artists, natural pigments on wood, 165.1 x 29.2cm, gift of Dr Stuart Scougall 1959, 107t; © DACS 1996, *Nude in a Rocking Chair* 1956, Pablo Picasso (1881–1973), oil on canvas, 195 x 130cm, 107ca; Art Gallery of NSW Foundation purchase 1990, *A Pair of Tomb Guardian Figures*, late 6th century AD Early, Unknown (China), sculpture earthenware with traces of red and orange pigment, 93 x 82cm 107crb; *The Golden Fleece – Shearing at Newstead* 1894, Tom Roberts, oil on canvas 104 x 158.7cm 107b; © Estate of Francis Bacon, *Study for Self Portrait* 1976, Francis Bacon (1901–92), oil and pastel on canvas, 198 x 147.5cm, 108tr; *Interior With Wardrobe Mirror* 1955, oil on canvas on paperboard 91.4 x 73.7cm 108cla; © Wendy and Arkie Whitely 1996, *The Balcony 2* 1975, Brett Whitely (1939–92), oil on canvas, 203.5 x 364.5cm 108b; © ASSOCIATED PRESS, LONDON: 55t; AUSCAPE INTERNATIONAL: 35cr; © Kathie Atkinson 22clb; © Nicholas Birks 336bl; © Donna Browning 260br; © John Cancalosi 21clb, 237bl; © Kevin Deacon 21cr; © Jean-Paul Ferrero 2–3, 19b, 20t, 22cla, 151crb, 153trb, ba, 229, 234cl, 250–251, 252cb, 255t, 280cl, 443t, bra, 460–461; © Jeff & Sandra Foott 21br; © Brett Gregory 162b, 442bl; © Dennis Harding 23b, 440–441, 444; © Andrew Henley 36ra; © Matt Jones 269cra, b; © Mike Langford 23crb; © Wayne Lawler 153cr; © Geoffrey Lea 445b; © Darren Leal 20br, 235t, 236t, 237cr; © Reg Morrison 20bca, 234cr, 442tr, 443cl; © Jean-Marc La Roque 14t, 20cr, 23cr, 24-25c, 173t, 230cla, 231cb, 253br, 272l, 362-363, 368t, 369t, cb, 377cla, 416cr, 418t, cl, 420t, 532cl; ©

Jamie Plaza Van Roon 20bl, 21cl, 153t, cb, 226; © Becca Saunders 21cb; © Gary Steer 24tl; AUSTRALIAN BROADCASTING CORPORATION: 535t; AUSTRALIAN MUSEUM www.austmus.gov.au: 26cl, 90cla, 90clb, 91crb; AUSTRALIAN PICTURE LIBRARY: 14c, 150clb, 544cl, 546b, 547t; Adelaide Freelance 359b; Douglas Baglin 43ca; John Baker 16b, 17tr, 165t, 170ba, 241t, 405b, 421tr; JP & ES Baker 152b, 174, 459cra; John Carnemolla 11t, 25crb, 34l, 35cra, 36clb, 37t, l, 39cr, 138b, 150cl, 176t, 202cla, 254tr, 256cl, 326cb, 343t, 357t, 358bl, 364cl, 543c, 544b; Sean Davey 34–35c; R. Eastwood 458tr; Flying Photos 534b; Evan Gillis 359t; Owen Hughes 245b; S & B Kendrick 327b, 346t; Ian Kenins 389t; Craig La Motte 203b; Michael Lees 417b; Gary Lewis 36t; Lightstorm 180b, 352b, 353c, 453cb; Johnathan Marks 177cr, 418crb; Aureo Martelli 163cra; David May 203t; Leo Meier 23t, 242cl, 244t, 255clb; Photo-Index 249b; Fritz Prenzel 418b, 432b; Dereck Roff 36b; Stephen Sanders 344b; Peter Solness 34tr; Oliver Strewe 28cl, 29tr; Neale Winter 360b; Gerry Withom 163t; AUSTRALIAN WAR MEMORIAL: 193c.

© MERVYN BISHOP: 55cb; GREG BARRETT, THE AUSTRALIAN CHAMBER ORCHESTRA: 129b; BARTEL PHOTO LIBRARY: 165b; BILL BACHMAN: 22t, 24cl, 27c, 29tl, 39t, b, 157b, 159t, 202clb, 237br, 248b, 266t, 267c, b, 268bl, 279b, 288b, 319crb, 327bra, 428, 436tr; BRIDGEMAN ART LIBRARY London/ New York: *Kangaroo Dreaming with Rainbow Serpent*, 1992 (acrylic) Michael Nelson Tjakamarra (b.c.1949), Corbally Stourton Contemporary Art, London © Aboriginal Artists Agency Ltd 8–9; *Bush Plum Dreaming* 1991 (acrylic) by Clifford Possum Tjapaltjarri (b.c.1932), Corbally Stourton Contemporary Art, London © Aboriginal Artists Agency Ltd 29cr; *Men's Dreaming* 1990 (acrylic) by Clifford Possum Tjapaltjarri (b.c.1932), Corbally Stourton Contemporary Art, London © Aboriginal Artists Agency Ltd 26c; *Kelly in Spring*, 1956 (ripolin on board) by Sidney Nolan (1917–92), Arts Council, London © Lady Mary Nolan 30bl; National Maritime Museum, London 45bla(d); British Museum 47cra; Mitchell Library, State Library of NSW 50tr, bl, 51tl; National Library of Australia 46tr(d), 49tl, cb, 50–51c; *Bush Tucker Dreaming*, 1991 (acrylic) by Gladys Napanangka (b.c.1920) Corbally Stourton Contemporary Art, London, © Aboriginal Artists Agency Ltd 255cr; *The Ashes*, 1883 (The Urn) Marylebone Cricket Club, London, 426b; BRITSTOCK-IFA/ GOTTSCHALK: 252ca; GRANT BURGE WINES PTY LTD: 348b.

CANBERRA TOURISM: 183b, 526c; CENTREPOINT MANAGEMENT: 87br; CEPHAS PICTURE LIBRARY: Andy Christodolo 155t, 324-325, 330bla, 331c, 370cla; Chris Davis 326cl; Mick Rock 15t, 32cl, 154tl, cl, 155cr, 166tr, cla, 33br, 331c, 333b, 348clb, 349tr, 371t, ca, b; BRUCE COLEMAN LTD: John Cancalosi

65b; Alain Compost 329tl; Francisco Futil 64tr; Hans Reinhard 328bcl; Rod Williams 329bl; COLORIFIC: 27t; Bill Angove 255b, 285c; Bill Bachman 249t, 258, 351, 389b; Penny Tweedie 257t, 259b; Patrick Ward 227b; COO-EE HISTORICAL PICTURE LIBRARY: 9c, 28-29c, 29b, 30tl, 31cr, 45t, 46b, 47ba, 48bra, 52cr, 53clb, 149c, 201c, 251c, 283c, 325c, 423cr, 424b, 441c, 443bl, 457c, 461c, 531c; SYLVIA CORDAIY PHOTO LIBRARY LTD: © John Farmer 326bl; Nick Rains 288c, 361t.

DIXON GALLERIES, STATE LIBRARY OF NSW: 76tr; © DOMAINE CHANDON, AUSTRALIA: 433c; © KEN DONE: © DW STOCK PICTURE LIBRARY: 180tr; P Brunotte 549b; M French 548b.

MARY EVANS PICTURE LIBRARY: 57ca.

FAIRFAX PHOTO LIBRARY: 54clb, bcb, 77bra, 138 cla, 161br(d), 264br; Ken James: 129tr; McNeil 116b

RONALD GRANT ARCHIVE: Buena Vista 17b; Universal 31b; © GREAT BARRIER REEF MARINE PARK AUTHORITY: 207t, 209t, cr; Photo: S Browne 207bl; Photo: W Craik 204b; Photo: N Collins 204cla; Photo: L Zell 205b, 206ca

ROBERT HARDING PICTURE LIBRARY: 282-283, 367t, 543t; © Rolf Richardson 290; © Nick Servian 332, 550t; C Moore Hardy: 128br; HOOD COLLECTION, STATE LIBRARY OF NSW: 77bl; HORIZON: © Andris Apse 271b; HUTCHISON LIBRARY: © R. Ian Lloyd 12, 530-531; © Sarah Murray 546c

IMAGES COLOUR LIBRARY: 22b, 203ca, 279t, 281b; THE IMAGE LIBRARY, STATE LIBRARY OF NSW: 30tr, 32b, 44tl, cb, 45c, 48bla, 51crb, 54t, 341br

Ali Kayn: 384cla; © DR RUTH KERR (Commissariat Stores, Brisbane) 214bl

FRANK LANE PICTURE LIBRARY – Images of Nature: 20clb, 207br, 328tl; © Tom & Pam Gardner 21bc, 329bcr; © David Hosking 21tr, 329tr, cb; © E & D Hosking 329crb, 443cra, cb; © M Hollings 328crb; © Gerard Lacz 153br; © Silvestris 208tl, 442tl; © Martin Withers 162cl, 328clb; LEISURE RAIL, RAIL AUSTRALIA: 546tl; LOCHMAN TRANSPARENCIES: © Bill Belson 315r; © Wade Hughes 288t; © Jiri Lochman 299t, 300cl; © Marie Lochman 285tc, 301 t; © Dennis Sarson 295cr; © Len Stewart 295b.

© GREG MILES (ENVIRONMENTAL MEDIA): 268br; © MIRROR AUSTRALIAN TELEGRAPH PUBLICATIONS: 54cr; MITCHELL LIBRARY, STATE LIBRARY OF NSW: 44blb; 46-47c, 48b, 64tl, 77cra, 104c, 105t; MUSEUM OF CONTEMPORARY ART, SYDNEY: Tony Dhanyula, Nyoka (Mud Crabs) circa 1984, ochres and synthetic polymer on bark, JW Power Bequest, purchased 1984, Ramingining Collection, 60cl; COLLECTION OF THE NATIONAL GALLERY OF AUSTRALIA,

CANBERRA: Tom Roberts, In a corner in a Macintyre 1895, oil on canvas, 73.4 x 88.0cm, 194cl; Margaret Preston, The Native Fuscia 1925, woodblock print on paper, 44.8 x 28.2cm, 194cb; Aristide Maillol, The Mountain (La Montagne) 1937, lead, 167,4 (h) x 193.0 (w) x 82.3 (d)cm 194b; Artist Unknown Kamakura period, Japan, Prince Shotoku praying to the Buddha c. 1300, wood, gesso and lacquer, height 48.2cm, 195tl; © ARS, NY and DACS, London 1997, Jackson Pollock, Blue Poles 1952, oil enamel and aluminium paint on canvas, 212.0 x 489.0cm, 195cra; © Bula'bula Arts, Ramingining Artists, Raminginging, Central Arnhem Land, NT, The Aboriginal Memorial 1998, natural pigments on wood: an installation of 200 hollow log coffins, height 40.0 to 327.0cm, purchased with the assistance of funds from gallery admission charges and commissioned in 1987, 195cr; NATIONAL LIBRARY OF AUSTRALIA: 31t, 42, 45bra (original in possession of the WA Museum), 48ca, 49cra 51cra, 52tl, 189br; Rex nan Kivell Collection 45crb, b, 47crb; ES Theodore, Campaign Director, ALP State of NSW, Trades Hall 52clb; NATIONAL MARITIME MUSEUM, SYDNEY: 47tl, 93cra, 96tl, clb, 97cra, 97tl, bc; NATURE FOCUS: H & J Bestel 442cl; Rob Blakers 442br; John Fields 64b; Dave Watts 442cr; Babs & Bert Wells 279cra, 328br; © Australian Museum 26tl, 28tr, Carl Bento 60cla; NATIONAL MUSEUM OF AUSTRALIA: © Australia-China Friendship Society, The Harvest of Endurance Scroll. The scroll is of 18 segments, ink and colour on paper, mounted on silk and paper 197t, Untitled by Charlie Alyungurra, 1970 pigment on composite board 197c, The Mermaid Coffin by Gaynor Peaty, 197b; NATIONAL TRUST OF AUSTRALIA: © Christopher Groenhout 396cl, 397tl, b; NATURAL HISTORY PHOTOGRAPHIC AGENCY: © A.N.T 20cl, 153ca, 205t, 287bl, br, 328tr, cr, 442cra, cb, 446t; © Patrick Faggot 240; © Pavel German 278tl; © Martin Harvey 21ca; © Ralph & Daphne Keller 286bca; © Norbert Wu 206tl; PETER NEWARK'S HISTORICAL PICTURES: 25cr, 46clb, 363ca; TOURISM NSW: 170cl, cb; NORTHERN TERRITORY LIBRARY: 256-257c, 257crb; Percy Brown Collection 256br; N Gleeson Collection 256tr; NUCOLORVUE PRODUCTIONS PTY LTD: 49b

Photography courtesy of the Olympic Co-ordination Authority: 139 cla; Photo: Karl Carlstrom 139 clb; © OPEN SPACES PHOTOGRAPHY: Photo: Andrew Barnes 429b; Photo: Glen Tempest 350, 527cl, 529t; © OUTBACK PHOTOGRAPHICS, NT: Steve Strike 1994 280tr; Steve Strike 1995 281c; OXFORD SCIENTIFIC FILMS: © Mantis Wildlife Films 286cl; © Babs & Bert Wells 286clb.

PARLIAMENT HOUSE: The Hon Max Willis, RFD, ED, LLB, MLC, President, Legislative Council, Parliament of NSW. The Hon J Murray, MP, Speaker, Legislative Assembly, Parliament of NSW. Artist's original sketch of the historical painting in oils by Algernon Talmage, RA, *The Founding of Australia*. Kindly loaned to the Parliament of NSW by Mr Arthur Chard of Adelaide, 78t; PHOTO INDEX: 55 b, 284clb, 285tr, b, 286t, bl, br, 286-287c, 294bla, 299b, 300tr, 302b, 305cr, 311t, c, b; © PHOTOTONE COLONIAL LIBRARY: 51b; PICTOR INTERNATIONAL. 210, 346b; PLANET EARTH PICTURES: © Gary Bell 200–201, 204tl, 206tr, b, 207c; © Daryl Torkler 137b; © Norbert Wu 355b; © POLYGRAM/PICTORIAL PRESS 25t; POWERHOUSE MUSEUM Reproduced courtesy of the Trustees of the Museum of Applied Arts and Sciences, Sydney: 46tl, 50tl, 53blb, 60tl, Marinco Kojdanovski 60br, 98tr, 98clb; Sue Stafford 98tl; © SUSANNA PRICE 417tr

QANTAS: 52brb, 545ca; COLLECTION OF THE QUEENS-LAND ART GALLERY: R Godfrey Rivers, *Under the Jacaranda,* 1903, oil on canvas, 220t; Russell Drysdale, *Bushfire* 1944, oil and ink on canvas on composition board, 62 x 77cm, Gift of Capt Neil McEacharn through CL Harden 1954, 220c; © Succession Picasso/DACS 1997, Pablo Picasso, *La Belle Hollandaise* 1905, gouache on cardboard mounted on wood, 77 x 66.3cm, purchased 1959 with funds donated by Major Harold de Vahl Rubin, 220clb; Rupert Bunny, *Bathers* 1906, oil on canvas, 229.2 x 250cm, purchased 1988, 221t; William Robinson, *William and Shirley, flora and fauna*, 1985, oil on canvas, Gallery Foundation, 221b; © QUEENSLAND BALLET: 220b; JOHN OXLEY LIBRARY, STATE LIBRARY OF QUEENSLAND: 234br; QUEENSLAND TRAVEL AND TOURIST CORPORATION: 33t, 202b, 230bl

SAND HILLS VINEYARD: 154cra; SCIENCE CENTRE (BRISBANE): 214clb; © SKYSCANS/Photographer: David Hancock 257cr, b; SOUTHLIGHT PHOTO AGENCY: © Milton Wordley 327c, 330t, crb, 331br; SPECTRUM COLOUR LIBRARY: 24b, 26b, 37crb, 231cr, 254tl, 278-279c, 327tl, 361b, 544t; © TONY STONE IMAGES: 310; Doug Armand 270; Gary John Norman 35t; Fritz Prenzel 13b, 18–19c, 223t; Robin Smith 38b, 159b, 175b; Oliver Strewe 20crb; Penny Tweedie 27b; Ken Wilson 54 br; CHARLES STURT UNIVERSITY WINERY: 154b; SYDNEY FILM FESTIVAL: 130c; SYDNEY HARBOUR FORESHORE AUTHORITY: 69tl, 73ca, 92bc, 93cra, 93bl; SYDNEY JEWISH MUSEUM: 61br; SYDNEY OPERA HOUSE TRUST: 80tr, cla, clb, b, 81t, crb, bl; Photography courtesy of the Sydney Organizing Committee for the Olympic Games (SOCOG): 139t

STATE LIBRARY OF TASMANIA: 47trb; TENTERFIELD DISTRICT & VISITORS' INFORMATION: 151tl; TOURISM TASMANIA: 459cr; TRIP & ARTDIRECTORS PHOTOGRAPHIC LIBRARY: Eric Smith 25bl, 198b, 437b; D Silvestris 342b

NATIONAL GALLERY OF VICTORIA: © Ann M Mills 1996, *The Bridge in Curve*, Grace Cossington Smith 1930, 77tl; TOURISM VICTORIA: 397tr

COURTESY OF WATERMARK PRESS (SYDNEY): 53t; © WILDLIGHT PHOTO AGENCY: Ellen Camm 151tr; Greg Hard 34tl; Carolyn Jones 211b, 365cra; Tom Keating 289cr, crb; 313b; Mark Lang 148–149, 168t; Philip Quirk 15b, 17cl, 35b, 173b, 162tl, Sean Santos 172b; Grenville Turner 171cr, 289t, br; WORLD PICTURES: 18t, 19t, 56-57, 192c, 209b, 242b, 243t, 293r, 430l

ZEFA: 18cl, 459t

Front Endpaper: All special photography except: AUSCAPE INTERNATIONAL: © Dennis Harding Rbc; © Jamie Plaza Van Roon Rtcr; AUSTRALIAN PICTURE LIBRARY: JP & ES Baker Rcrb; © Bill Bachman Lbr; COLORIFIC/BILL BACHMAN: Rtl; ROBERT HARDING PICTURE LIBRARY: © Rolf Richardson Ltl; © Nick Servian Lclb; NHPA: © Patrick Faggot Rtcl; © OPEN SPACES PHOTOGRAPHY: Glen Tempest Lcl; © PICTOR INTERNATIONAL: Rtr; TONY STONE IMAGES: Doug Armand Ltr

JACKET:

All special photography except AUSTRALIAN PICTURE LIBRARY: Sean Davey front bottom left; FLPA T & P Gardener spine top; IMAGES COLOUR LIBRARY: front top; NHPA © ANT front bottom centre; WILDLIGHT PHOTO AGENCY: Philip Quirk back top left.

All other images © Dorling Kindersley.
For further information see: www.dkimages.com

Sydney Transport Map

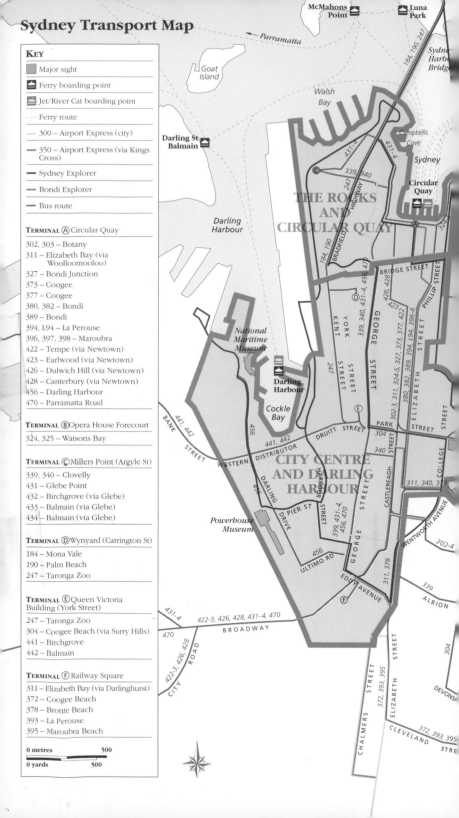

KEY

- ▨ Major sight
- ⛴ Ferry boarding point
- ⛴ Jet/River Cat boarding point
- ---- Ferry route
- —— 300 – Airport Express (city)
- —— 350 – Airport Express (via Kings Cross)
- —— Sydney Explorer
- —— Bondi Explorer
- —— Bus route

TERMINAL Ⓐ Circular Quay

302, 303 – Botany
311 – Elizabeth Bay (via Woolloomooloo)
327 – Bondi Junction
373 – Coogee
377 – Coogee
380, 382 – Bondi
389 – Bondi
394, L94 – La Perouse
396, 397, 398 – Maroubra
422 – Tempe (via Newtown)
423 – Earlwood (via Newtown)
426 – Dulwich Hill (via Newtown)
428 – Canterbury (via Newtown)
456 – Darling Harbour
470 – Parramatta Road

TERMINAL Ⓑ Opera House Forecourt

324, 325 – Watsons Bay

TERMINAL Ⓒ Millers Point (Argyle St)

339, 340 – Clovelly
431 – Glebe Point
432 – Birchgrove (via Glebe)
433 – Balmain (via Glebe)
434 – Balmain (via Glebe)

TERMINAL Ⓓ Wynyard (Carrington St)

184 – Mona Vale
190 – Palm Beach
247 – Taronga Zoo

TERMINAL Ⓔ Queen Victoria Building (York Street)

247 – Taronga Zoo
304 – Coogee Beach (via Surry Hills)
441 – Birchgrove
442 – Balmain

TERMINAL Ⓕ Railway Square

311 – Elizabeth Bay (via Darlinghurst)
372 – Coogee Beach
378 – Bronte Beach
393 – La Perouse
395 – Maroubra Beach

0 metres   500
0 yards   500